Handbook of Contemporary European Social Theory

This innovative publication maps out the broad and interdisciplinary field of contemporary European social theory. It covers sociological theory, the wider theoretical traditions in the social sciences including cultural and political theory, anthropological theory, social philosophy and social thought in the broadest sense of the term.

The volume surveys the classical heritage, the major national traditions and the fate of social theory in a post-national and post-disciplinary era. It also identifies what is distinctive about European social theory in terms of themes and traditions. It is divided into five parts: disciplinary traditions, national traditions, major schools, key themes, and the reception of European social theory in America and Asia.

Thirty-five contributors from nineteen countries, drawn from Europe, Russia, the Americas and Asian Pacific countries have been commissioned to utilise the most up-to-date research available to provide a critical, international analysis and assessment of their area of expertise.

It is an indispensable book for students, teachers and researchers in sociology, cultural studies, politics, philosophy and human geography but will set the tone for future research in the social sciences.

Gerard Delanty is Professor of Sociology at the University of Liverpool, UK. He is Editor of the *European Journal of Social Theory* and author of ten books including *Inventing Europe: Idea, Identity, Reality* (Macmillan, 1995), *Social Theory in a Changing World* (Polity Press, 1999), *Modernity and Postmodernity* (Sage, 2000), *Community* (Routledge, 2003) and (with Chris Rumford) *Rethinking Europe: Social Theory and the Implications of Europeanization* (Routledge, 2005).

Handbook of Contemporary European Social Theory

Edited by
Gerard Delanty

LONDON AND NEW YORK

First published 2006
by Routledge
2 Park Square, Milton Park, Abingdon, Oxon OX14 4RN

Simultaneously published in the USA and Canada
by Routledge
270 Madison Ave, New York, NY 10016

Routledge is an imprint of the Taylor & Francis Group

© 2006 Gerard Delanty for editorial matter and selection; individual chapters, the contributors

Typeset in Times by Taylor & Francis Books
Printed and bound in Great Britain by MPG Books Ltd, Bodmin

British Library Cataloguing in Publication Data
A catalogue record for this book is available from the British Library

Library of Congress Cataloging in Publication Data
A catalog record for this book has been requested

ISBN10: 0-415-35518-4 ISBN13: 978-0-415-35518-6

T&F informa

Taylor & Francis Group is the Academic Division of T&F Informa plc.

Contents

Part 3: Intellectual traditions

Part 4: Themes and Narratives

Part 5: Global perspectives

List of Illustrations

Tables

Figure

Notes on Contributors

Ben Agger works in Critical Theory and Cultural Studies at the University of Texas at Arlington. His most recent books include: *Public Sociology* (Rowman and Littlefield 2000); *Postponing the Postmodern* (Rowman and Littlefield 2002); *The Virtual Self: A Contemporary Sociology* (Blackwell 2004); and *Speeding Up Fast Capitalism* (Paradigm Publishers 2004). He is currently working on *Fast Families: Virtual Children* with Beth Anne Shelton, and he is also working on a book on the 1960s entitled *Hey, Hey, LBJ: Generation and Identity among Sixties People*. He edits the new electronic journal, *Fast Capitalism*, which is posted at www.fastcapitalism.com.

Johann P. Arnason is Emeritus Professor of Sociology at La Trobe University in Melbourne, Australia. He has been Visiting Professor at the Ecole des Hautes Études en Sciences Sociales, Paris, and at the University of Leipzig. In 1999–2000 he was a fellow of the Swedish Collegium for Advanced Studies in the Social Sciences, Uppsala. Until recently he was an editor of the journal *Thesis Eleven*. His publications include: *The Future that Failed: Origins and Destinies of the Soviet Model* (Routledge 1993); *Social Theory and Japanese Experience: The Dual Civilization* (Kegan Paul International 1997); and *Civilizations in Dispute: Historical Questions and Theoretical Traditions* (Brill 2003).

Patrick Baert is Fellow of Selwyn College and University Senior Lecturer in Sociology at the University of Cambridge. He studied at the Universities of Brussels and Oxford, and has held visiting positions in various places, such as Conception, Berlin, Paris, Rome and Vancouver. Amongst his publications are: *Social Theory in the Twentieth Century* (Polity 1998) and *Philosophy of the Social Sciences: Towards Pragmatism* (Polity 2005).

Hauke Brunkhorst is Professor of Sociology at Flensburg University. His publications include: *Der Intellektuelle im Land der Mandarine* (Suhrkamp 1987); *Marcuse zur Einführung*, together with G. Koch (Junius 1988); *Theodor W. Adorno: Dialektik der Moderne* (Piper 1990); *Der entzauberte Intellektuelle* (Junius 1990); *Demokratie und Differenz: Vom klassischen zum modernen Begriff des Politischen* (Fischer 1994); *Solidarität unter Fremden* (Fischer 1997); *Adorno and Critical Theory* (University of Wales Press 1999); *Hannah Arendt* (Beck 1999); *Einführung in die Geschichte politischer Ideen* (Fink UTB 2000); and *Solidarität: Von der Bürgerfreundschaft zur globalen*

Rechtsgenossenschaft (Suhrkamp 2002; English translation, *Solidarity: From Civic Friendship to a Global Legal Community* (MIT Press 2005)).

Fred Dallmayr is Packey J. Dee Professor in the departments of Political Science and Philosophy at the University of Notre Dame (USA). He holds a doctorate from Munich University and a PhD from Duke University (USA). Among his recent publications are: *Beyond Orientalism* (SUNY Press 1996); *Alternative Visions* (Rowman & Littlefield 1998); *Achieving our World: Toward a Global and Plural Democracy* (Rowman & Littlefield 2001); *Dialogue Among Civilizations* (Palgrave/Macmillan 2002); and *Peace Talks: Who Will Listen?* (University of Notre Dame Press 2004).

Gerard Delanty is Professor of Sociology, University of Liverpool, UK and has written on various issues in social theory and general sociology. He is editor of the *European Journal of Social Theory*. His publications include: *Inventing Europe* (Macmillan 1995); *Social Science* (1997; new edition, 2005); *Social Theory in a Changing World* (Polity Press 1998); *Modernity and Postmodernity* (Sage 2000); *Citizenship in a Global Age* (Open University Press 2000); *Challenging Knowledge: The University in the Knowledge Society* (Open University Press 2001); (with Patrick O' Mahony) *Nationalism and Social Theory* (Sage 2002); *Community* (Routledge 2003); (edited) *Adorno: Modern Masters* 4 vols (Sage 2004); (edited with Piet Strydom) *Philosophies of Social Science* (Open University Press 2003); (with Chris Rumford) *Rethinking Europe: Social Theory and the Implications of Europeanization* (Routledge 2005) and (edited with Krishan Kumar) *Handbook of Nations and Nationalism* (Sage 2006).

Alexander Dmitriev is theory editor, Novoe Literaturnoe Obozrenie [*New Literary Review*] (Moscow), and scientific researcher, St Petersburg branch of the Institute for the History of Science and Technique (Russian Academy of Sciences). He is author of the monograph *Marxism without Proletariat: Georg Lukács and Early Frankfurt School in 1920–1930's* (Letnij Sad 2004; in Russian). His articles about Russian Formalism, history of Russian-European intellectual links before and after the First World War were published in: *Cahiers du Monde Russe* (2002, no. 2 and 3); *Sovietique et Post-Sovietique* (2002, no. 4; in French); *New Literary Review* (no. 50, 54, 60 and 66); and *Ab Imperio* (2003, no. 2).

José Maurício Domingues gained his PhD in Sociology at the London School of Economics and Political Science. He is Assistant Professor at Rio de Janeiro Research Institute (IUPERJ) and his publications include: *Modernity Reconstructed* (University of Wales Press 2005); *Social Creativity, Collective Subjectivity and Contemporary Modernity* (Palgrave/Macmillan 2000); and *Sociological Theory and Collective Subjectivity* (Palgrave/Macmillan 1995); and, as co-editor with Leonardo Avritzer, *Modernidade e teoria social no Brasil* (UFMG 2000).

Klaus Eder took his doctorate at the University of Konstanz, and was research fellow from 1971 until 1983 at the Max-Planck-Institut für Sozialwissenschaften at Starnberg/Munich. From 1983 until 1989 he continued researching at the Münchner Projektgruppe für Sozialforschung e.V. The Habilitation at the University of Düsseldorf followed in 1985. In 1986 he received a Heisenberg Grant from the German Science Foundation. From 1989 until 1994 was Professor of Sociology at the European University Institute in Florence. Since 1994 he has been Professor of Sociology at the Humboldt-Universität zu Berlin, where he teaches comparative macrosociology with particular emphasis on the sociology of culture and communication as well as the sociology of collective action. His books include *Geschichte as*

Lernprozess? (Surkamp 1985); *The New Politics of Class* (Sage 1996); and *The Social Construction of Nature* (Sage 1996).

Robert Fine is Professor of Sociology at the University of Warwick. He is currently doing research into the impact of cosmopolitan ideas on the social sciences and on more political and legal debates about humanitarian military intervention. Among his relatively recent publications are: *Democracy and the Rule of Law: Marx's Critique of the Legal Form* (The Blackburn Press 2002); *Political Investigations: Hegel, Marx, Arendt* (Routledge 2001); 'Kantian Cosmopolitanism today: John Rawls and Jurgen Habermas on Immanuel Kant's *Foedus Pacificum*', with Will Smith (*King's College Law Journal*, 15(1) 5–22); 'Habermas's theory of cosmopolitanism', with Will Smith (*Constellations: an International Journal of Critical and Democratic Theory*, 10(4) 467–487); 'Taking the "ism" out of cosmopolitanism; an essay in reconstruction' (in *European Journal of Social Theory*, 6(4) 2003 pp. 451–470); and 'Kant's theory of cosmopolitanism and Hegel's critique' (in *Philosophy and Social Criticism*, 29(6) 609–630).

Heidrun Friese is a researcher at the Ecole des Hautes Études en Sciences Sociales, Paris, and teaches at the Johann Wolfgang Goethe University, Frankfurt am Main. She is currently working on a project on *Modernity and Contingency*. Recent publications include the following edited collections: *Europa: Costituzione e Movimenti Sociali*, co-edited with Giuseppe Bronzini, Antonio Negri and Peter Wagner (Manifestolibri 2003); *Identities: Time, Boundaries and Difference* (Berghahn 2002); *Europa Politica: Ragioni di Una Necessità*, co-edited with Antonio Negri and Peter Wagner (Manifestolibri 2002); and *The Moment: Time and Rupture in Modern Thought* (Liverpool University Press 2001).

Salvador Giner is Emeritus Professor of Sociology, University of Barcelona. He has taught at various British universities, namely King's College Cambridge, Reading, Lancaster and Brunel, and holds visiting appointments at the Universities of Rome, Buenos Aires, and Mexico, amongst others. He is co-founder and president of the Spanish Sociological Association, and editor of *Revista Internacional de Sociología*, as well as a member of the editorial board of several others (*Sociology* [BSA] and *European Journal of Social Theory*). He is Founder and first Director of the Instituto de Estudios Sociales Avanzados, Spain; and President of Academy of Sciences and Humanities of Catalonia, Barcelona. He is author of several works on the history of social thought and sociology, on European social structures, comparative macrosociological studies of Mediterranean Europe, and the sociology of culture and religion.

Austin Harrington is lecturer in Sociology at the University of Leeds, UK, and Research Fellow at the Max Weber Kolleg für kultur- und sozialwissenschaftliche Studien at the University of Erfurt, Germany. He is the author of *Hermeneutic Dialogue and Social Science: A Critique of Gadamer and Habermas* (Routledge 2001); *Art and Social Theory: Sociological Arguments in Aesthetics* (Polity Press 2004); and *Concepts of Europe in Classical Sociology* (Routledge, forthcoming). He is co-author of *The Protestant Ethic Debate: Max Weber's Replies to his Critics, 1907–1910* (Liverpool University Press 2001); editor of *Modern Social Theory: An Introduction* (Oxford University Press 2005); and co-editor of the *Routledge Encyclopedia of Social Theory* (Routledge 2006).

Ulf Hedetoft is Professor of International Studies, Institute for History, International and Social Studies, Aalborg University, and Director of the Academy for Migration Studies in Denmark (AMID). His special interests are: cultural and political issues in international relations, specifically in Europe; nationalism, migration and globalization; transatlantic relations and US foreign policy; and British, German and Danish history, politics and identity. Publications over the last decade include: *Signs of Nations: Studies in the Political Semiotics of Self and Other in Contemporary European Nationalism* (Dartmouth 1995); *Political Symbols, Symbolic Politics: European Identities in Transformation* (Ashgate 1998, editor); *The Postnational Self: Belonging and Identity* (University of Minnesota Press 2002, co-editor); *The Global Turn: Nationalist Encounters with the World* (Aalborg University Press 2003); and *The Politics of Multiple Belonging: Ethnicity and Nationalism in Europe and East Asia* (Ashgate 2004, co-editor).

Agnes Heller is Hannah Arendt Professor of Philosophy, New School University, New York, and author of numerous books, including: *A Theory of History* (Routledge 1982); *Everyday Life* (Routledge 1984); *Beyond Justice* (Blackwell 1988); *An Ethics of Personality* (Blackwell 1996); and *Theory of Modernity* (Blackwell 1999).

David Inglis is Senior Lecturer in Sociology at the University of Aberdeen. He writes in the areas of social theory and the sociology of culture. He has particular interests in the history of modes of consciousness, with reference both to modernity and ancient civilizations. Among his publications are *Confronting Culture: Sociological Vistas* (Polity 2003); *The Uses of Sport* (Routledge 2004); *Culture and Everyday Life* (Routledge 2005); and (with Roland Robertson) *Globalization and Social Theory: Redefining the Social Sciences* (Open University Press, 2005).

Engin F. Isin is Professor and Canada Research Chair in the Division of Social Science at York University. His research has focused on the origins and transformations of 'occidental citizenship' as a political and legal institution that enables various ways of being political. He is the author of *Cities Without Citizens: Modernity of the City as a Corporation* (Black Rose Books 1992); (with Patricia K. Wood) *Citizenship and Identity* (Sage 1999); *Democracy, Citizenship and the Global City* (Routledge 2000; editor); and *Being Political: Genealogies of Citizenship* (University of Minnesota Press 2002). He has also written numerous journal articles, book chapters, technical reports and public lectures and editorials. His most recent books are co-edited (with Bryan S. Turner), *Handbook of Citizenship Studies* (Sage 2002), and (with Gerard Delanty) *Handbook of Historical Sociology* (Sage 2003). His more recent research is on 'oriental citizenship and justice' with a focus on Islamic and Ottoman institution, *waqf*.

Thomas M. Kemple teaches social and cultural theory at the Department of Anthropology and Sociology, University of British Columbia. He is the author of *Reading Marx Writing: Melodrama, the Market, and the 'Grundrisse'* (Stanford 1995) and editor of *The Vocation of Reason: Studies in Critical Theory and Social Science in the Age of Max Weber*, by H. T. Wilson (Brill 2004). Currently he is working on a book-length study of the literary, aesthetic and rhetorical construction of Max Weber's later speeches and essays.

Hans-Herbert Kögler is Associate Professor of Philosophy and Graduate Studies Coordinator at the University of North Florida, Jacksonville, where is also directs the Faculty Seminar 'Social Science and Theory'. His books include: *The Power of Dialogue* (MIT Press 1999); *Michel Foucault* (Metzler 2004); and *Empathy and Agency* (Westview Press 2000; co-editor).

Daniel Levy is Assistant Professor in the Department of Sociology at the State University of New York – Stony Brook. Among his recent publications are: *Old Europe, New Europe, Core Europe: Transatlantic Relations after the Iraq War*, co-edited with Max Pensky and John Torpey (Verso 2005); (with Natan Sznaider) *Memory and the Holocaust in the Global Age* (Temple

University Press 2005); and *Challenging Ethnic Citizenship: German and Israeli Perspectives on Immigration*, co-edited with Yfaat Weiss (Berghahn Books 2002).

Phil Macnaghten is Senior Lecturer and Director of Research at the Institute for Environment, Philosophy and Public Policy (IEPPP), at Lancaster University. He has published widely on the sociology of the environment and is author, with John Urry, of *Contested Natures* (Sage 1998) and *Bodies of Nature* (guest editor of a special issue of *Body and Society*). His research interests centre on the embodied dimensions of people's experience in, and of, technology, the future and the natural world. He is currently directing a major new ESRC funded research project entitled *Nanotechnology, Risk and Sustainability: Moving Public Engagement Upstream*.

Lars Mjøset is Professor of Sociology and Director of the Oslo Summer School for Comparative Social Science Studies at the Social Science Faculty, University of Oslo, Norway. His main areas of research are political economy, comparative historical sociology, and more specifically studies of small open Western European economies, European integration and the modern welfare state. He has also published works on the history of Norwegian sociology and on the philosophy of the social sciences. His books are *The Irish Economy in a Comparative Institutional Perspective* (NESC 1992); *Kontroverser i norsk sosiologi* (Norwegian University Press 1991); and *Norden dagen derpå. De nordiske økonomisk-politiske modellene og deres problemer på 1970- og 1980-tallet* (Norwegian University Press 1986).

Stefan Müller-Doohm is Professor of Sociology at the Carl von Ossietzky University of Oldenburg. His recent publications include an edited work, *Das Interesse der Vernunft: Rückblick auf das Werk von Jürgen Habermas* (Suhrkamp 2000); *Die Soziologie Theodor W. Adornos* (Campus 2001); *Adorno: A Biography* (Polity Press 2005); and *Adorno: Portraits* (Suhrkamp 2005). His current research includes work on critical theory, theories of the public sphere and culture, and analysis on the role of the intellectual.

William Outhwaite studied at the Universities of Oxford and Sussex, and is Professor of Sociology at Sussex. He is the author of *Understanding Social Life: The Method Called Verstehen* (Allen & Unwin 1975; second edition: Jean Stroud 1986); *Concept Formation in Social Science* (Routledge 1983); *New Philosophies of Social Science: Realism, Hermeneutics and Critical Theory* (Macmillan 1987); *Habermas. A Critical Introduction* (Polity Press 1994); and (with Larry Ray) *Social Theory and Postcommunism* (Blackwell 2004). He has also edited *The Habermas Reader* (Polity Press 1996); (with Tom Bottomore) *The Blackwell Dictionary of Twentieth-Century Social Thought* (Blackwell 1993); *The Blackwell Dictionary of Modern Social Thought* (Blackwell 1993); (with Luke Martell) *The Sociology of Politics* (Edward Elgar 1998); and (with Margaret Archer) *Defending Objectivity* (Routledge 2004). He is currently working on a book on society and culture in Europe.

Monica Sassatelli holds a PhD in Sociology from the University of Parma. She has taught sociology at the Universities of Ferrara, Teramo and Urbino and is currently Jean Monnet Fellow at the European University Institute in Florence. She has recently published *Identità, cultura, Europa. Le 'Città europee della cultura'* [*Identity, culture, Europe. The 'European cities of culture'*] (FrancoAngeli 2005).

Piet Strydom an Apartheid émigré, is Senior Lecturer in Sociology at University College Cork, Ireland, and is currently directing research in the environmental area. He has published particularly on social theory and the history and philosophy of the social sciences. His publications include papers in such journals as *Political Studies, Theory, Culture & Society, Philosophy and Social Criticism, European Journal of Social Theory, Current Sociology, Sociological Theory* and *Social Epistemology*, and books entitled *Discourse and Knowledge* (Liverpool University Press 2000); *Risk, Environment and Society* (Open University Press 2002); and *Philosophies of Social Science*, edited and introduced with Gerard Delanty (Open University Press 2003).

Arpad Szakolczai studied at the University of Budapest and has a PhD from the University of Texas at Austin. His recent and major publications include: (with Agnes Horvath) *The Dissolution of Communist Power* (Routledge 1992); *Max Weber and Michel Foucault: Parallel Life-Works* (Routledge 1998); *Reflexive Historical Sociology* (Routledge 2000); (with Giovanna Procacci) *La scoperta della società* (Carocci 2003); and *The Genesis of Modernity* (Routledge 2003), as well as articles and essays in, amongst others: *Social Research*; *American Journal of Sociology*; *Theory, Culture and Society*; *Theoria*; *The European Journal of Social Theory*; and *The European Sociological Review*. He is Professor of Sociology at University College, Cork, Ireland. He is currently working on two book projects: one on the sociology of the Renaissance, with focus on various aspects of 'grace'; and another provisionally entitled 'Overcoming Nihilism', in which he aims to contrast Nietzsche's illuminating but often erratic insights with anthropological findings.

Natan Sznaider is Associate Professor of Sociology at the Academic College of Tel-Aviv-Yaffo in Israel. Recent publications include: (with Daniel Levy) *The Holocaust and Memory in the Global Age* (Temple University Press 2005); 'Money and Honor: About the Impossibility of Honorable Restitution' (chapter in D. Diner (ed.) *Restitution as New World Politics*, Berghahn 2005); (with Daniel Levy) 'Forgive and not Forget: Reconciliation Between Forgiveness and Resentment' (chapter in E. Barkan and A. Karn (eds) *Taking Wrongs Seriously: Apologies and Reconciliation*, Stanford University Press 2005); *Global America: The Cultural Consequences of Globalization*, co-edited with Ulrich Beck and Rainer Winter (Liverpool University Press 2003); and (with Daniel Levy) 'The Institutionalization of Cosmopolitan Morality: The Holocaust and Human Rights' (in *Journal of Human Rights*, 3(2) 143–157).

Göran Therborn is Director of the Swedish Collegium for Advanced Study in the Social Sciences, Uppsala, Sweden. His recent books include: *European Modernity and Beyond: The Trajectory of European Societies, 1945–1995* (Sage 1995); *Between Sex and Power: The Family in the World, 1900–2000* (Routledge 2004); and two edited volumes, *Asia and Europe in Globalization* (Brill 2005) and *Inequalities of the World* (Verso 2006).

Bryan S. Turner was Professor of Sociology at the University of Cambridge (1998–2005), and is currently Professor of Sociology in the Asia Research Institute, National University of Singapore. He is the research leader of the cluster on globalisation and religion, and is currently writing a three volume study of the sociology of religion and editing the Dictionary of Sociology for Cambridge University Press. A book on human rights and vulnerability is to be published in 2006 by Penn State University Press. Recent publications include: *Classical Sociology* (Sage 1999); *The New Medical Sociology* (W. W. Norton 2004); (with Chris Rojek) *Society & Culture: Principles of Scarcity and Solidarity* (Sage 2001); (with June Edmunds) *Generations, culture and society* (Open University Press 2002); and (with Engin Isin) he edited the *Handbook of Citizenship Studies* (Sage 2002).

Frédéric Vandenberghe is senior researcher at the University for Humanist Studies in Utrecht, the Netherlands, and Visiting Fellow of the Ethics/Politics/Economics program at Yale University. He is the author of a two volume book on theories of alienation and reification, *Une histoire critique de la sociologie allemande* (La Découverte 1997/98, English translation forthcoming in the Critical Realism Series, Routledge); a booklet on Georg Simmel, *La sociologie de Georg Simmel* (La Découverte 2001); and a book on biotechnologies, *Complexités du posthumanisme: Critique de l'économie biopolitique* (L'Harmattan 2005).

Peter Wagner is Professor of Social and Political Theory, European University Institute, Florence, and has published widely on social theory and political philosophy. His books include: *Sociology of Modernity* (Routledge 1994); *A History and Philosophy of the Social Sciences* (Sage 2001); and *Theorizing Modernity: Inescapability and Attainability in Social Theory* (Sage 2001).

Harald Wydra teaches Politics at the University of Cambridge, where he is also a Fellow of St Catharine's College. After a PhD in the Social and Political Sciences at the European University Institute in Florence, he taught Political Science at the University of Regensburg. From 2001 to 2002 he was a Research Fellow at the EHESS in Paris. He is the author of *Continuities in Poland's Permanent Transition* (Macmillan 2001) and *Communism and the Emergence of Democracy* (Cambridge University Press, forthcoming). His research interests include politics and societies in Eastern Europe and Russia, political anthropology, cultural politics, and the theorization of uncertainty in politics.

Manuel Pérez Yruela is Research Professor at the Spanish Scientific Research Council (CSIC) and, from 1992, Director of the Institute for Advanced Social Studies (IESA), located in Córdoba, Andalusía. He studied Sociology at the Complutense University of Madrid (Spain, 1972–1975), Lancaster University (United Kingdom, 1976–1977) and Brunel West London University (United Kingdom, 1978–1979). He has published on Rural Sociology, Corporatist Trends in Modern Democracies, and Poverty and Social Exclusion. From 1991 to 2000 he was Director and from 2001 is Editor of *Revista Internacional de Sociología*, one of the best known Spanish sociological journals.

Introduction

Social theory in Europe today

Gerard Delanty

This volume aims to offer the reader a critical overview of current social theory in Europe. It is in this limited sense that the adjective European is used in the title. An appraisal of European social theory is timely for several reasons. First, there is the obvious redefinition in the identity of Europe as a result of the demise of communism, which has led to new political challenges for Europe as well as for the wider world. Related to this there is the increasing importance of postnational developments, such as those relating to the expansion and growing significance of the European Union, and wider processes of globalization. This means that the nature of Europe today is very different from the era of the national state when classical European social theory arose (Delanty and Rumford 2005). It is inevitable that this change in the nature of Europe will have implications for social theory.

Second, there is the increasing significance of post-national developments within European social science, leading to an enhanced consciousness of the European as well as the wider international context as opposed to national traditions. At the moment this is largely expressed in an interest in the cross-fertilization of national traditions in Europe. Thus we find in this volume chapters on European social theory in the widest possible sense of the term, including not just the well known German, French and British national traditions, but also Russian social theory, East Central European, Nordic, Spanish and Italian social theory traditions. All of these traditions constitute the diversity of European social theory, which must be viewed in wider terms than is conventionally the case. The claim is not made that there is a European social theory as such, although there are certain tendencies indicative of such a movement.

Third, there is the wider question of the identity of social theory in the context of disciplinary transformation within the social sciences, new interpretations of the classics, the decline of philosophy as an overarching interpretation of the social sciences (see Turner 1996). Aside from these factors there is of course the obvious fact that there are now many different kinds of social theory in Europe today. While there are several overviews of national and international social theory (see Turner 2000; Ritzer and Smart 2001; Harrington 2005), a study of the broad field of contemporary European social theory has not yet been undertaken. One of the features of contemporary social theory is a diversity of approaches and the demise of the grand theory that Quentin Skinner saw on the rise in 1985 (Skinner 1985). European social theory is not united by any one major school or indeed by any one major theorist. For this reason the approach adopted by most contributors to this volume emphasizes the diversity and cross-fertilization of national and intellectual traditions and schools of thought rather than concentrating on key theorists. For some this amounts to a fragmentation of social theory, but a case could also be made to see the current situation as one of cosmopolitanism as argued by several contributors to this volume (see the contributions by Delanty, Outhwaite, Fine and Turner). While contemporary European social theory cannot escape the shadow of classical social theory, there are significant differences from the classical heritage.

Social theory means different things to different people, but the term is Anglo-American and is not easily translated into European traditions. The English term is often used except in those traditions, such as the German one, where there is a distinct heritage of social theory, although one that is largely confined to sociology. In North America it is partly another term for a more specifically defined sociological theory but is also in competition with it. This is not specific to North America of course, for there is generally a certain association of social theory with sociological theory, that is with a specific sociological mode of theorizing concerned with, for example, middle-range theorizing about social change and sophisticated causal models relating to macro-societal processes. The current appeal of the term social theory as opposed to sociological theory is because it expresses an interdisciplinary kind of sociology and possibly one that is post-disciplinary (see Lemert 1998; Seidman and Alexander 2001). But there is a tension between the more grounded sociological theory, which is linked to empirical research and evidenced based theorizing, on the one side, and on the other a more speculative and culturally oriented social theory which derives, in part, from the humanities.

It is possible to speculate that the turn to social theory in the Anglo-American world is a reaction to the heavily empirical nature of American sociology where theory has generally been understood in neo-positivist terms as hypothesis testing and possibly more broadly a concern with macro-theorizing. Contemporary social theory might thus be seen as an attempt to strike up a new relation between the social and the human sciences. As Ben Agger argues in his chapter, sociology in North America has been resistant to anything like grand theory and as a consequence social theory mostly occurs outside sociology in comparative literature, history, and cultural studies, for example. Thus critical theory was relatively marginalized and not integrated into the discipline. In fact its North American reception was possibly greater in literature and contemporary history than in sociology. This is a contrast with Europe where social theory has been on the whole more integrated into sociology and other social sciences. One only has to consider the reception of Foucault within European sociology to find a marked contrast with American sociology, where he has a much lesser role (although one matched by the tremendous reception of his work in the humanities). In a similar way the American reception of the Frankfurt School has been wider in the humanities than in the social sciences, as evidenced by such critics as Martin Jay.

However, stark contrasts cannot be made with Europe where there are major differences between the national traditions. In Germany the tradition of *Gesellschafttheorie* has always been central to the self-understanding of the discipline of sociology and where it stood for a more systematic theory of modernity. This may explain the dominance of Habermas and Luhmann in contemporary German social theory. Hauke Brunkhorst points out that modern German social theory was rooted deeply in the tradition of philosophical anthropology. Spanish social theory, as noted by Salvador Giner and Manuel Pérez Yruela, also had strong philosophical foundations, concerned as it has been with moral issues, ranging from the earlier 'crisis of our time' literature to the crisis of modernity writings of today. In France, in contrast, as Frédéric Vandenberghe in this volume shows, social theory in this sense of grand theory is an unfamiliar term, but this is because sociology is already theoretical and much of what is called social theory elsewhere would be simply associated with epistemology (see also Gane 2003). Wary of scholastic abstractions, French sociology, which broke more decisively with philosophy than in Germany, has remained largely Durkhemian in this respect. Both Elias and Bourdieu were extremely hostile to philosophy. In the UK today social theory has become a major part of a post-disciplinary kind of sociology, but one that has an unclear relation to the qualitative and quantitative traditions. Today in the UK there are practically three kinds of sociology, quantitative sociology, qualitative sociology, and an interdisciplinary social theory. Much of British social theory, as David Inglis notes, of course also occurs outside sociology, for example in cultural studies, but unlike in North America a good deal of British sociology contains a strong link with social theory, which often simply includes general sociology. In the Scandinavian countries, on the other hand, where sociology is more empirical, social theory has a relatively marginal role within sociology, although, as Lars Mjøset documents in his chapter on Nordic social theory, it is becoming more important as a result of growing interdisciplinarity and the reception of other European and North American approaches. However, the preference is clearly for a grounded social theory. Italian social theory, as Monica Sassatelli shows, occurs as much in political theory as in sociological theory and it is almost impossible to separate social and political theory.

Is it possible to speak of European social theory in a different and stronger sense than simply post-disciplinary sociology? There is a tradition of European social theory that, while heavily on Nordic social theory influenced by sociology, is more than sociology and has its roots in the humanities and especially in philosophy. Fred Dallmayr claims this is based on opposition to a purely spectatorial theorizing aiming at objective knowledge. His notion of social theory is defined in the terms of European thought as a critique of the cult of pure science. Hans-Herbert Kögler discusses this around the hermeneutical tradition and philosophical anthropology. In Germany since the Frankfurt School a philosophical kind of sociology has generally provided the basis for much of what we today call social theory and one associated with grand theory. This tradition, the subject of chapters by Hauke Brunkhorst and Stefan Müller-Doohm, which was part of an attempt to re-orient sociology from positivism, has been very much connected to Western Marxism and philosophical anthropology and a view of the sociologist as a critical intellectual in the public sphere. This is a tradition that was absent in American sociology and which only today is becoming more to the fore. But these authors do have quite different views on social theory: for Brunkhorst it concerns systematic sociological theory, of which Habermas and Luhmann remain the dominant influences; for Müller-Doohm, in his chapter on critical theory, social theory refers to a wider philosophical sociology, albeit one that has lost its orientation today. In any case it must not be forgotten that this conception of a critical social theory was connected with a major methodological drive to re-orient the social sciences in an anti-positivistic direction.

We are not in this situation today. The current situation is characterized by post-disciplinary developments and a related plurality of theoretical and methodological approaches (see Levine 1995; Delanty and Strydom 2003). These tendencies tend to undermine the venture of grand theory that was part of the classical social theory. It is of course true that in the 1980s there were several attempts by European social theorists – Habermas, Luhmann, Giddens – to resurrect grand social theory with a new systematic theory of modernity (Delanty 1999). But these projects – the theory of communicative action, system theory, structuration theory – have not led to a new systematic social theory that has gained general acceptance. Habermas himself has moved into political philosophy and Giddens into a politics of a more partisan nature. Despite Axel Honneth's attempt to re-launch critical theory by returning to sociological questions under the general concept of recognition, a specific future for critical theory to re-orient social science seems doubtful. Although he made important methodological innovations, Bourdieu's own critical sociology never aimed at grand theory or a comprehensive theory of modernity (see Vandenberghe's chapter in this volume). Only in his later writings did he concern himself with explicitly political issues.

Now while it is true that in Europe the older philosophical sociology became marginalized or was directed into cultural critique – one only need to consider the fate of Adorno's efforts to use philosophy to re-launch sociology – it continued to have an important influence, despite its methodological impotence. It preserved a link with a concern with the moral foundation of society and, in many traditions, with a vision of an alternative society. Social theory is one of the main products of this classical European tradition and became the basis of an interdisciplinary social theory that is not at all exclusively part of the sociological tradition. This understanding of the term social theory as a form of critical intellectual engagement pertains to the theoretical dimensions in all the social sciences. This can be simply be called a critical social philosophy of the present. The understanding of theory indicated in this term is closer to the notion of reflection and thus entails an unavoidable degree of philosophy and interdisciplinarity. Such a conception of social theory does not reduce it to sociological theory without severing the connection with social science in favour of a return to the humanities. In this volume, Hans-Herbert Kögler represents such a position with respect to hermeneutics, which he sees of continued relevance in order to mediate macro-theory of global processes and societal structures with a culturally sensitive approach to the contextual modes of human agency.

The rise of social theory in the formerly communist societies is particularly interesting and an example of social theory as an active engagement with the present. The chapters in this volume on Russian social theory and Central European social theory show, in different ways, both an appropriation of the established and largely western approaches, on the one side, and on the other the existence of distinctive national traditions which have been overshadowed by Marxism. While central and Eastern Europe produced well known literary and artistic figures, social and political thinkers outside the Marxist tradition are relatively unknown, with the exception of the polish émigré Zygmunt Bauman and the Hungarian émigré Agnes Heller, the latter being a contributor to the present volume. In their chapter in this volume, Arpad Szakolczai and Harald Wydra have written a corrective to this in their account of theorists such as Jan Patočka, Károly Kerényi, István Bibó and Béla Hamvas. As Alexander Dmitriev argues, Russian social theory contains its own distinctive tradition in addition to the émigré tradition that has been a central feature of much of European social theory in the twentieth century. The chapter offers a rare insight into contemporary Russian social theory, a subject that has received little coverage since Isaiah Berlin's survey (Berlin 1978).

It is undeniably the case that this particular genre of an inter-disciplinary social theory is heavily dominated by sociologists even though it includes a broader field and has a strongly philosophical aspect to it. As David Inglis argues, in Britain, where the term social theory should be extended to include cultural theory, it would include historians such as Peter Burke, social policy theory going back to T. H. Marshall, in anthropology it would include the iconoclastic thinker Ernst Gellner, and political theorists such as Quentin Skinner, sociologists such as Anthony Giddens and Bryan Turner, a social psychologist such as Rom Harré, and a geographer such as Nigel Thrift. However, it must be reiterated that European social theory does not exist in the sense of a social theory that is specifically European as opposed to American. Nevertheless the diffuse field of social theory in Europe is certainly enjoying considerable revival today, not least due to the proliferation of the social sciences in central and Eastern Europe and the need for continued reflection on the ever-changing nature of modernity. In this context William Outhwaite emphasizes the importance of European transformations and the question as to the identity of Europe for contemporary European social theory. In this specific sense, European self-understanding can be seen as an important context for social theory in Europe. The cosmopolitan aspects of this have been noted by Robert Fine and have also been commented on by myself in my chapter on modernity viewed from a cosmopolitan perspective.

The preference for social theory over sociological theory within sociology, in Europe as well as in the wider world, is undoubtedly indicative of a concern with new sociological concerns, in particular those related to issues of culture, identity and globalization. Current theorizing about the social world is very much concerned with the transformation of subjectivity and cognition. In this volume some examples of these concerns are to be found. Daniel Levy and Natan Sznaider discuss the presence of trauma in European self-understanding, arguing that the memory of the holocaust has become one of the defining aspects of a more cosmopolitan kind of European consciousness. The question of the Other in identity is the focus of Heidrun Friese's chapter on cultural identities, a theme that is taken up by Ulf Hedetoft with respect to the wider notion of the nation as a reference point for belonging. It is possible to see these chapters in terms of an attempt to theorize the social field as a conflictual and ambivalent space that is productive of new realities. This perspective is reflected too in the chapters on the city by Engin Isin and the public sphere by Klaus Eder. Here a conception of the social is present that allows for a strong resistance to closure. For Isin the city is the site of historical possibility and one of the central themes in social thought in Europe. In his analysis as a social reality, the city must be understood in terms of the processes of autonomy, accumulation, difference and security. Klaus Eder's chapter on the public sphere follows in this key with an analysis of the post-Habermasian public sphere in light of new processes of democratization and social transformation. The notion of public sphere has increasingly come to be seen as a core concept in modernity and one with a particular relevance in European transformation. These chapters, including the chapter by Phil Macnaghten on nature and embodiment, are all examples of the concern within European social theory with social transformation. It is a feature of current theorizing on Europe that such transformation have a strongly discursive dimension. While a concern with such issues is not specific to social theory in Europe, these themes have become more and more to the fore in recent European social theory in its response to the tremendous social transformations of time and space that have taken place in these countries since the late 1980s.

The caesura of the events of 1989/1990 must be seen in terms of a wider concern with modernity and with the reinterpretation of the social and political (see also Outhwaite and Ray 2005). As argued in different ways by Gerard Delanty, Agnes Heller, Göran Therborn and Peter Wagner in their contributions, modernity has been one of the dominant leitmotifs in European social theory (see also Wagner 1994, 2001; Delanty 2001). For Heller, it is possible to speak of European master narratives, of which she singles out freedom as one of the most pervasive master narratives of European culture. A master narrative is something that transcends particular cultures, but does not become set apart from particular narratives, and master narratives can even be in a relation of tension with each other. It is this creative tension that has been one of the characteristic features of modernity. For this reason the master narrative of freedom is, as Heller argues, fragile. As I have tried to show in my chapter on modernity and the problem of Eurocentrism, modernity must be seen in terms of an interaction of the universal and the particular; it is an on-going process of transformation.

The conception of social theory presented in this volume is one that attempts to avoid a focus on key thinkers. In this respect the aim has been to resist a peculiar kind of Anglo-American social theory, often associated with the undergraduate teaching programmes, whereby social theory is simply the history of sociology. Although certainly a common understanding of social theory, social theory is more than the history of the classical or formative period of a discipline such as sociology. This is a point that Ben Agger makes with particular force in his chapter on American and European traditions. Related to this, and again a peculiarity of the Anglo-American imagination, social theory is often reduced to a critical commentary on European theorists who are often only the sociologists of the past. It would be unfortunate if social theory was to be merely the interpretation of classic authors. Although the history of a discipline and the constant reinterpretation of the classics is important, as Thomas Kemple argues in the opening chapter, social theory is more than this: it is a dynamic interaction with history. The classical figures or founders of social theory were all connected with major events in history, of which he distinguishes three, the Age of Revolution (1789–1871), the Rise of the Social (1872–1919) and the End of History (1920–1945). Without a relation to such major transformations in modernity, social theory is meaningless.

Social theory thus occupies an uncertain ground between, on the one hand, the domain of a post-disciplinary sociology and on the other an interdisciplinary mode of theorizing that is connected to political (what kind of society?) and philosophical questions in epistemology (the nature of truth, questions of method and knowledge) and ontology (the nature of social reality). In this sense it has a less clear-cut identity than the more disciplinary specific endeavours of political theory and sociological theory. As a critical social philosophy, social theory concerns reflection on the social world in the broadest possible sense of the term (Osborne 1998). It is then probably best distinguished from sociological theory in the narrow sense and from the history of sociology. It is unavoidably bound up with critical and normative questions. Several contributors have noted how social theory has always been connected with moral issues. Sociology cannot avoid social theory in so far as sociology concerns normative issues. Austin Harrington makes the point that social theory also concerns questions that are common to theology. It is possible to characterize some of the concerns in terms of the central challenge of transcendence (see also Mellor 2004). In this respect social theory is also connected to political philosophy, as Peter Wagner argues in his contribution to the volume. His argument can be related to Agnes Heller's discussion of European master narratives of freedom, but with a difference. Political philosophy developed around a particular kind of political philosophy, largely individualist liberalism, while social science tended to be positivistic. This dichotomy, which has separated social theory and political philosophy, is now breaking down and new opportunities for the reengagement of social and political theory emerging.

The connection with the political is especially evident in the case of Italian social theory. Monica Sassatelli draws attention to the role of political intellectuals in Italian social theory and to its broadly based interdisciplinary nature. This is a territory that goes back to Vico and Machiavelli and includes Eco, Pareto, Gramsci, Bobbio, Melucci, Pizzorno, Poggi, Agamben and Negri, almost all impossible to place under a particular disciplinary tradition. Wagner's argument is not to be interpreted as a return to the political. In fact this is precisely his criticism of certain current tendencies; rather, the social and the political must be connected, with the normative structures of political discourse being found in social life in modes of reasoning and where even justifications have to be found. There can be little doubt that one of the weaknesses of European social theory is the role of the political. With the single and notable exception of Habermas on the left and Schmidt on the right, European social theorists have not given the political the same degree of attention that American theorists have. Perhaps this accounts for the relative strength of American political theory against social theory. One of the challenges for the future is for European theorists to link social and political theory in new ways.

The question must be asked how adequate the existing approaches and schools of thought are to the tasks facing social theory in light of such current issues as the transformation of the political and wider processes of societal transformation. The critical theory tradition offers an uncertain view to the future; yet, it has established some of the main perspectives on the social world. It is possible to speculate that the future of European social theory will continue to draw from critical theory but it will inevitably take a very different form. As Stefan Müller-Doohm argues, it is possible to speak of critical theory only in the plural since there are varieties of critique today, not all of which can be understood in terms of the original project of Adorno and Horkeheimer. Critical theory was originally conceived of in terms of an immanent understanding of critique as resting upon a normative counter-factual. This was also the position held by Habermas, and mostly a position that he retained when he replaced the theory of cognitive interests with the theory of universal pragmatics, which is now the basis of his discourse ethics. It has been widely recognized by a wide range of positions that the normative assumptions behind this model of critique are no longer credible.

The crisis of normative-critique is reflected in an uncertainty regarding the Marxist heritage. As previously remarked, much of Central and Eastern as well as Russian social theory has repudiated this tradition. For Göran Therborn, in his assessment of the Marxist heritage, one of the key issues is the turn to cultural theory, for which Marxism was never quite equipped. However, he makes the important point that Western Marxist scholarship has been very centrally about the nature of modernity and our present post-Marxist context which has seen the demise of postmodernism does not quite make obsolete some of the central Marxist accounts of modernity. In this respect it is possible to agree with Therborn's claim that social theory is caught between two poles, between providing a comprehensive explanation for social phenomena and also having the task to make sense of the social world. To do this it must be able to interpret the social world. In this context the hermeneutical tradition represents one of the enduring features of European social theory. As an interpretation of the social world, social theory cannot avoid a hermeneutical component. This is one of the key points Hans-Herbert Kögler makes. In his view hermeneutics is essential in a theoretical framework capable of mediating between the macro level of analysis and the culturally grounded dimensions of human agency. The cultural dimension of this is also reflected in what Piet Strydom calls cognitive social theory, which while having its origins in metabiology, includes constructivism and pragmatic sociology. This stresses the constructivist theory of social classifications and definitions of the world. This chapter contains the strongest claim of a common methodological concern in contemporary social theory with identifying cognitive processes, although the argument stops short of a thesis of methodological convergence.

Two other examples of cultural themes in contemporary European social theory are the chapters by Johann Arnason and Robert Fine. Arnason argues the revival of civilizational analysis in recent years was part of the 'historical turn' in the human science and, in his approach, is the basis of a theory of modernity as a multiple condition. Following Benjamin Nelson, the key question for Arnason concerns inter-civilizational encounters within the broad field of modernity. With modernity civilization become more and more embroiled in each other with the result that there can be no clash of intact civilizations. The hermeneutic understanding of modernity as a multiple condition in which civilizational factors continue to play a role contains an implicit cosmopolitan thesis. This thesis – which returns in José Maurício Domingues's chapter on Latin American perspectives on European social theory – is explicitly the theme of Robert Fine's chapter on cosmopolitanism, which he sees as more a research agenda informed by various conceptual, historical and normative considerations than a body of fixed ideas. The cosmopolitan turn is above all about the critique of, what Ulrich

Beck has called, methodological nationalism, that is taking for granted the presuppositions of the nation-state both for the present as well as for the past (Beck 2000, 2002). Although these chapters are by no means comprehensive, they draw attention to some of the central themes in contemporary social theory in Europe. There is a clear move beyond a specific disciplinary restriction on social theory and a growing acknowledgement that social theory as an inter-disciplinarity mode of theorizing the present is also inextricably a post-national endeavour. Cosmopolitanism might be one way of understanding, but cognitive social theory may be another. These approaches and others – critical theory, hermeneutics, the western Marxist heritage, civilizational analysis – reveal a common understanding of social theory as a critical philosophy of the present.

The worst kind of social theory is an obscurantist mode of theorizing, in which theory becomes its own referent and where any connection with substantive issues is lost. The cultural turn in social theory, which brought social theory beyond philosophical sociology, tended towards philosophical abstraction. Many of the claims made by theorists are unsubstantiated by evidence. Social theory as a self-consciously defined critical philosophy of the present has a stronger chance of resisting this tendency if it retains a strong link with empirical research and evidence based arguments. The sociological tradition offers such a safeguard against the tendency which arises out of the confluence of cultural theory with philosophy, for theory to become divorced from substantive issues. The sociological foundations of social theory provide an important corrective to many over-theorized arguments about a wide range of topics. For this reason social theory must be grounded in the social sciences, not necessarily sociology. Rather than retreating into the philosophical abstractions of cultural theory, social theory must situate itself within the social sciences. But this does not mean it must be a slave of the social sciences or become reduced to a formal sociological theorizing. French sociology is an example of the limits of a particular kind of social theory associated with Bourdieu who in vehemently opposing philosophical theory, such as that associated with the post-structuralists, established a theoretical sociology that has reached its limits (see Bourdieu 2004). The result is that post-Bourdiusian sociology is now in search of a new social theory. The main contours of this are outlined by Frédéric Vandenberghe for whom European social theory has entered the 'age of epigones': British social theory has moved beyond Giddens, who has retreated into political philosophy and in France Latour, Boltanski and others have opened up new paths. Although if we are to believe Hauke Brunkhorst, German social theory has not yet entirely advanced beyond Habermas and Luhmann.

Patrick Baert criticizes one of the main developments within the philosophy of social science today to reorient social theory away from, on the one side, the nomological-deductive conception of theory as hypothesis testing, and on the other, grand social theory. This is, what he terms, representational theory, which is very popular in recent British social theory. This is a view of theory as a mapping of the social world, whereby social theory provides to an intellectually impoverished social science the basic ontological building blocks for empirical research. In this approach, which is very strongly present in critical realism, social research reveals the truths of theory. Baert criticizes the relevance of this model of social theory, arguing it leads to outcomes of questionable significance and is premised on discredited philosophical assumptions about the nature of science and research as a mirroring of the social world and thus does not offer an adequate alternative to either positive or to grand theory (see Kemp 2005).

In short it would appear to be the case that social theory needs to move beyond social science in order to be able to influence it, but the danger is that in approaching philosophy it will lose any connection with social science. In this respect Lars Mjøset is right to demand a stronger sense of grounded theory, which can be substantive or formal. But this grounded theory will have to strike a new relation with social theory as social-philosophical reflection. In this respect the salience of critical reflection cannot be neglected. As Patrick Baert argues, social theory is the main vehicle through which intellectual debates in the social and human sciences occur. It is in social theory that some of the most important agendas have been set for the social sciences, as is witnessed by issues such as the public sphere, risk, globalization and networks. Even apparently sociologically specific issues such as the structure and agency debate or Latour's Actor Network Theory are not at all confined to sociologists but have a wider influence. In a recent study of sociology's most influential books over the past twenty-five years, it is notable that most are not in fact written by sociologists (Clawson 1998). For this reason it is difficult to disagree with Baert's preference for social theory over sociological theory.

What is needed is a cosmopolitan kind of social theory that is capable of making sense of major social transformations, which are global as opposed to national or even western (Delanty 2006). Philosophy, in alliance with Marxism, once offered the animus for an older European social theory. With the demise of this tradition, and the absence of a methodological alternative to the neo-positivism that provides a workable feature of much of current social science, social theory is in danger of falling into a kind of solipsism characterized by an obsessive concern with classical sociology. Social theory must recover the social, and articulate some of the key commonalities of the social sciences, if it is to offer a critical interpretation of the present. Surely one of the most important challenges is to link the interdisciplinary field of social theory to the middle range models of sociological theory as well as to empirical social research. But social theory will always be more than sociological theory. It is in this context that there can be fruitful dialogue between European social theory and American sociological theory. But this is not enough. It will also be necessary to go beyond what José Maurício Domingues has referred to the false opposition of a vaguely defined grand theory and a Mertonian verifiable middle range, empirically based theory. This dichotomy developed largely within a European social theory that never had to confront anything fundamentally challenging. Postmodernism fitted into much of European grand theory and the largely American led middle-range sociological theorizing had itself a foundation in European social theory. It may be suggested that it is the current global context that offers a new point of departure for social theory today. It is inevitable that this will demand a very different kind of social theory.

As William Outhwaite argues in his chapter, social theory arose in the context of issues that were specific to Europe and as a result the self-understanding of social theory was defined in terms of the European heritage. Inevitably this entailed a degree of Eurocentrism. There can be little doubt that the social theory of the twentieth-first century will have to address quite different concerns than the project of modernity that emerged in eighteenth-century Europe. While Outhwaite and myself in my own contribution to the volume argue that the categories of European social theory are still relevant to much of the world, this is a view that will not necessarily be widely shared. However, it appears to be the position taken by Alexander Dmitriev with regard to Russian social theory, which in his position must abandon the search for a distinctive Russian social theory. But in this case it may be argued that due to the émigré tradition, Russian social theory has already been part of the European tradition. This is also the basic argument of José Maurício Domingues in his chapter on the Latin American relation to European social theory. Fred Dallmayr also finds common themes in European and Asian social theory. Operating with a wider notion of social theory as a critical philosophy, he draws attention to the rise of subaltern studies in India in the 1980s and to the role of humanist Marxism and especially Gramsci in its inception. Whether in India or in East Asia, there are resonances of western thought – critical theory, hermeneutics, phenomenology – in wide-ranging approaches developed by Buddhist and Confucian thinkers. The central point in his analysis is not that there has been a simple adoption of western thought, but rather a dialogical exchange or interaction. Reflecting Robert Fine's argument that cosmopolitanism has become a new critical agenda, he argues that something like a global network of critical thinking is ultimately what defines social theory in the world.

European social theory no longer exists in an exclusively European or even western world. While many of the central concerns of European social theory have been specific to Europe and the wider western world, social theory in Europe will have to address the global context. Domingues stresses the 'global modern condition' as the location for social theory. On this note Bryan Turner discusses the Asian context and the future of European social theory in a post-European world.

References

Beck, U. (2000) 'The Cosmopolitan Perspective: Sociology of the Second Age of Modernity', *British Journal of Sociology* 51(1) 79–105.

Beck, U. (2002) 'The Cosmopolitan Society and its Enemies', *Theory, Culture and Society* 19(1–2) 17–44.

Berlin, I. (1978) *Russian Thinkers*, Harmondsworth: Penguin Books.

Bourdieu, P. (2004) *Science of Science and Reflexivity*, Cambridge: Polity Press.

Clawson, D. (ed.) (1998) *Required Reading: Sociology's Most Influential Books*, Amherst: University Massachusetts Press.

Delanty, G. (1999) *Social Theory in a Changing World*, Cambridge: Polity Press.

Delanty, G. (2001) *Modernity and Postmodernity*, London: Sage.

Delanty, G. (2005) *Social Science: Philosophical and Methodological Foundations*, (2nd edn/1st edn 1997), Buckingham: Open University Press.

Delanty, G. (2006) 'The Cosmopolitan Imagination: Critical Cosmopolitanism and Social Theory', *British Journal of Social Theory*, 57(1) (forthcoming).

Delanty, G. and Strydom, P. (eds) (2003) *Philosophies of Social Science: The Classic and Contemporary Readings*, Buckingham: Open University Press.

Delanty, G. and Rumford, C. (2005) *Rethinking Europe: Social Theory and the Implications of Globalization*, London: Routledge.

Gane, M. (2003) *French Social Theory*, London: Sage.

Harrington, A. (ed.) (2005) *Modern Social Theory*, Oxford: Oxford University Press.

Kemp, S. (2005) 'Critical Realism and the Limits of Philosophy', *European Journal of Social Theory* 8(2) 171–191.

Lemert, C. (ed.) (1998) *Social Theory: The Multicultural and Classic Readings*, Boulder: Westview.

Levine, D. (1995) *Visions of the Sociological Tradition*, Chicago: University of Chicago Press.

Mellor, P. (2004) *Religion, Realism and Social Theory: Making Sense of Society*, London: Sage.

Osborne, T. (1998) *Aspects of Enlightenment: Social Theory and the Ethics of Truth*, London: UCL Press.

Outhwaite, W. and Ray, L. (2005) *Social Theory and Postcommunism*, Oxford: Blackwell.

Ritzer, G. and Smart, B. (eds) (2001) *Handbook of Social Theory*, London: Sage.

Seidman, S. and Alexander, J. (eds) (2001) *The New Social Theory Reader*, London: Routledge.

Skinner, Q. (ed.) (1985) *The Return of Grand Theory*, Cambridge: Cambridge University Press.

Turner, B. S. (ed.) (2000) *The Blackwell Companion to Social Theory* (2nd edn), Oxford: Blackwell.

Turner, S. (ed.) (1996) *Social Theory and Sociology*, Oxford: Blackwell.

Wagner, P. (1994) *Sociology of Modernity: Liberty and Discipline*, London: Routledge.

Wagner, P. (2001) *Theorizing Modernity*, London: Sage.

Part 1

Disciplinary traditions

Founders, classics, and canons in the formation of social theory

Thomas M. Kemple

At the same time as social theorists today are attempting to contain or promote the spread of their craft, they are also increasingly preoccupied with tracing its genesis and structure by appraising its so-called 'foundational authors,' its 'classical works,' and its 'canonical statements.' Although it may be argued that 'the functional necessity for classics develops because of the need for integrating the field of theoretical discourse' (Alexander 1989: 27), perennial returns to the sources of social thought are not always prompted by professional self-interest or a need for scientific legitimation. Since theorists do not necessarily agree on which authors have been the most influential and which works the most important to their respective disciplines, or which concepts or statements the most widely read, ritually revered, or routinely referred to, the definition and limits of the tradition continue to be matters of considerable dispute. As Peter Baehr (2002) has shown, it is not enough to identify and explicate the key figures and concepts that have contributed to the formation of social theory without at the same time addressing the intellectual networks, modes of textual transmission, and processes of inclusion and exclusion that have made theory a recognizable and definable discipline. Where the event of 'founding' usually implies the constitutive acts of *authors* (often esteemed as scientific heroes or creative geniuses), the emergence of 'classics' often suggests the classification and evaluation of *texts* (often treated as objects of prestige and resources of analysis). Discussions of 'foundational' authors normally employ a repertoire of architectural and genealogical metaphors – the terminology of conceptual 'structures' or 'blueprints,' for example, or the 'conception' and 'birth' of scientific ideas by founding fathers and (occasionally) mothers. By contrast, the notion of a 'classic' work tends to connote a certain timeless quality, sometimes through comparisons with the great European musical compositions of the late eighteenth century or the philosophical treatises of Greek and Roman antiquity, or it suggests a certain 'textual suppleness' that gives a work its cultural resonance for a general reading public or a community of scientific peers. Finally, the idea of an authoritative 'canon' of concepts and phrases is often expressed through analogies to the spheres of aesthetics, literature and religion, as in ceremonial citations of the liturgical trinity of Durkheim/Weber/ Marx, even when they are defiled as social theory's Dead/White/Males. In any case, however it is approached, the history of theory is not only a subject of fascination or fixation, but also a site of ongoing conflict and contestation.

Even when the heritage of social theory is framed in terms of 'founders', classics', or 'canons', its *cycles*, *generations*, and *phases* must also be differentiated and explained. For the most part, modern European social theory may be loosely characterized as an intellectual response to political disputes in Europe – especially revolutionary events and military conflicts involving France and Germany – which then travel or migrate to the English-speaking world and beyond, sometimes eventually returning to their place of origin or occasionally finding a home in non-Western contexts. In particular, these conceptual exchanges and intellectual cycles may be identified by the dominant patterns of cultural change and social stability that distinguish the major periods of modern western history, as they are framed by the French Revolution in the eighteenth century, the Franco-Prussian War in the nineteenth century, and the two World Wars in the twentieth century:

- 1789–1871: The Age of Revolution;
- 1872–1919: The Rise of the Social;
- 1920–1945: The End of History.

Here I can provide only a selective overview of some of the key figures and most interesting ideas from each of these phases, while emphasizing how they contrast with or complement one another and highlighting their importance for social theory today. In order to reveal their influence on or independence from one another, I shall consider these thinkers in sequential pairs, focusing not just on the most familiar authors, established works, or revered concepts, but also on *lost classics* of social theory whose value is only now being appreciated, on *inaugural texts* which continue to open new discursive fields, and on *non-canonical* ways of conceiving the social world that have previously been ignored or disqualified. The life of social theory cannot be captured in skeletal summaries of dead ideas but only as a dynamic process of innovation and struggle, institutionalization and renewal.

1789–1871: The Age of Revolution

Although modern social theory was conceived in the notion of individuality expressed by the Cartesian *cogito*, in the idea of civil society formulated as the Hobbesian problem of order, and in the ideals of reason and freedom articulated in the Kantian definition of enlightenment, its birth-date is marked by a political *event* of world historical importance: the French Revolution of 1789. In effect, theory follows history inasmuch as the beheading of the king, the storming of the Bastille, the 'Declaration of the Rights of Man and Citizen,' as well as their aftermath in Thermidor, Empire, and Restoration all have their conceptual counterparts in subsequent intellectual movements. Nevertheless, as a recent commentator has noted, 'modern social theory, influenced by a German reading of French historical events, the Empire, the Commune, does not now remember the French reading of these events, or understand how the German and the French readings are related' (Gane 2003: 4). German idealism has often been characterized as the theory of the French Revolution, or at least as a reading of French readings of the event, not because it provided prior philosophical inspiration or an illuminating interpretation after the fact, but because of its character as a response to the challenges posed by this epochal moment (Marcuse 1941). Hegel's *Phenomenology of Spirit* of 1806 in particular announces the moment when theory does not just try to resolve intramural disputes between philosophy and science but rather strives to bridge the historical gap between social practice and the political ideals of freedom, equality and fraternity (O'Neill

1996). In *The Communist Manifesto*, Karl Marx and Frederick Engels were therefore not only concerned to promote the next phase of the revolution in 1848, but also to criticize the forgetfulness of their left Hegelian comrades for 'emasculating' the French revolutionary writings by turning them into a palimpsest for the inscription of their own scholastic slogans and pedantic abstractions (Marx and Engels 1998). A deeper appreciation for the epic Hegelian dialectic of lordship and bondage, desire and recognition emerges from the 'unknown Marx' of the posthumous manuscripts and notebooks which only came to light in the twentieth century – especially the *Economic and Philosophical Manuscripts of 1844*, *The German Ideology* drafted with Engels in 1845–1847, and the *Grundrisse*, the notebooks he kept from 1857 to 1858 – and which synthesize the positive insights of the English political economists, particularly their (surplus-) value theory of labour, with a critical and utopian understanding of their determinate negation by the revolutionary agents of history (Kemple 1995). Finally, Marx's *Capital* (first published 1867, with revisions on commodity fetishism included in the 1872 edition) completes this critical conception of *the normality of change* and *the desirability of progress* with a comprehensive theory of the economic as well as social, political, and cultural dimensions of capitalist alienation and exploitation (Wallerstein 1991), thereby setting the stage for theoreticians of revolution in the following century, from Lenin and Gramsci to Althusser and Lefebvre.

In one form or another these are also the themes that underlie the even grander conceptual systems of Auguste Comte and Herbert Spencer during this early phase in the formation of social theory, the reception of which has tended to be reduced to a scrapheap of abstract slogans or glossed as a series of trivial utopian fictions. In the first instance, Comte's famous 'law of the three stages' is an attempt to discern order in progress by providing a theoretical anchor for the drifting moral convictions of the counter-revolutionary era. From the *Cours de philosophie positive* of 1830–1842 to the *Système de politique positive* of 1851–1854, he posits human history first as a unilinear development and then as a cyclical process in which primitivist *theology* (the animistic and fetishistic imagination expressed in myths and legends) is succeeded by modernist *metaphysics* (abstract speculation and critical discussion exemplified in astronomy and physics) before settling into the certainties of *positivism* (empirical demonstration and scientific proof epitomized by biology and 'sociology,' the latter a hybrid Greek and Roman term that Comte himself coined). The resurrection and recycling of these stages is expressed in Comte's later ecstatic vision of a 'Religion of Humanity' (partly inspired by St Simon, his estranged mentor), and in the positivist motto 'Love, Order and Progress,' which articulates the three-dimensional communicative community of women, workers and intellectuals in their respective organization as the heart, hands and head of the body social (Wernick 2001). Comte shares an understanding of how social life is rooted in biological and sociological *evolution* with Spencer, who also speculated on a unitary trajectory of universal progress in all fields 'from incoherent homogeneity to coherent heterogeneity' (Spencer 1972: 71). From the perspective of this longer view of social and cosmic change, Comte and Spencer imagine the social theorist not just as an interpreter and diagnostician of social life, but above all as its legislator and prophet. Even in failure, however, their systems embody a valuable collection of critical insights and contradictory inspirations that were arguably later absorbed or neutralized by their twentieth-century namesakes and nemeses in socio-biology and logical positivism.

Where Comte and Hegel were able to work out their ideas in the protected setting of the university, Spencer and Marx were for the most part left out of established academic institutions: the latter studied in the British Museum while writing articles for the *New York Daily Tribune*; the former achieved notoriety in popular magazines and from well-attended lecture tours in Britain and the US. Although the writings of other independent scholars in the nineteenth century, such as Harriett Martineau in England and Alexis de Tocqueville in France, have drawn increasing attention in recent years, they have not attained the same status as classical, foundational, or canonical. Rather than providing a grand theory to cover broad patterns of historical change, Martineau and de Tocqueville were more concerned with conducting detailed comparative studies of the intimate and often overlooked morals, manners and customs of everyday life. De Tocqueville's celebrated *Democracy in America* is presented in the anecdotal style of a private journal, a travel log and an ethnographer's report on his nine-month trip in 1831 through the eastern and southern United States, initially to study its penal institutions. His aim was to explain to a European readership how the norms, networks and institutions of American civil society foster a distinctive love for liberty and change combined with a fear of radical transformation, expressed in its tendency toward litigiousness and its propensity for submitting to the tyranny of the majority: 'In America, there exist democratic ideas and passions; in Europe we still have revolutionary ones' (de Toqueville 1966: 639). As his later writings make clear, especially *The Old Régime and the French Revolution* published in 1856, one of his principal aims was to warn his fellow Frenchmen about the consequences of relinquishing the aristocratic codes of propriety and prestige in favour of an egalitarian ideology of possessive individualism, having earlier predicted that the illiberal treatment of negroes, women, and natives in America would produce the conditions for social unrest and cultural disorder. By contrast, Martineau's *Society in America*, based on her own trip to the US from 1834–1836, adopts the more critical tone of a liberal social reformer who is guided by scientific knowledge and whose moral scruples call for state intervention to correct the personal ills and political injustices of modern society. Rather than writing for a small circle of gentlemen scholars, Martineau's intellectual aims were primarily didactic and populist, with her best-selling *Illustrations of Political Economy* (serialized from 1832) restaging the ideas of Mill, Malthus and Bentham as moral melodramas, and her free translation of Comte's *Positivist Philosophy* in 1855 simplifying and condensing these difficult ideas for a wider audience. The writings of de Tocqueville and Martineau do not just exemplify the encounter of the early ideas of European social theory with the practicalities of an emerging new social order; their contemporary relevance also consists in demonstrating the importance of theoretically addressing the mundane conventions of ordinary experience and the particularities of everyday life in the modern world, not only in spite of but especially in times of cataclysmic upheaval.

1872–1919: the Rise of the Social

In the wake of the conceptual flights of the age of revolution – which by 1872 had drawn to a close with the emergence of the German Empire after the Franco-Prussian War and of the French Third Republic from the ruins of the Paris Commune – the field of social theory had yet to be methodologically systematized and professionally institutionalized. Rather than redrafting Comte's positivist catechism or extending Spencer's evolutionary doctrine, Emile Durkheim aimed to advance an empirical science of personal morality and social solidarity that would assist in fostering a kind of secular civil religion of responsible individualism protected by a responsive liberal state. Drawing on lessons he learned from Rousseau and Montesquieu, and from his study of German moral philosophers after Kant, but rejecting the theories of collective violence and social imitation proposed by Sorel and Tarde, Durkheim ultimately grounded his notion of *discipline* in an appreciation of the simultaneously secular and sacred character of the social bond. In doing so, he hypothesized a shift from a mythical worldview of traditional community to the organic solidarity of modern society, reformulating Toennies's concepts of *Gemeinschaft* and *Gesellschaft* in the process. The innovative bookends of Durkheim's career – *The Division of Labour in Society* (first published in 1893) and *The Elementary Forms of Religious Life* (which appeared in 1912) – explain how social order is not simply given (*donné*) or made (*fait*) once and for all, but rather achieved through a 'religious' process (*re-ligio*) which involves binding (*lier*) individuals from within by satisfying their needs and desires, and then connecting them again (*relier*) from without through the cultivation of common sympathies, 'at times by regulating each personal existence, at others by rallying these diverse individualities,' as Comte had already argued (quoted in Wernick 2001: 101–102). By contrast, *The Rules of Sociological Method* of 1895 along with its experimental test two years later in *Suicide: A Study in Sociology* offer a more focused account of the modern social sphere conceived as both a *factual order* that may be scientifically observed and a *moral order* that can be politically transformed. As Durkheim (1982: 45) writes in *The Rules*, 'our fundamental principle is the objective reality of social facts,' an aphorism that inspired an array of subsequent strands in social theory from structural-functionalism to ethnomethodology (Garfinkel 2002: 65–66). These methodological and theoretical issues were later taken up in the concept of the 'total social fact' formulated by Marcel Mauss, Durkhem's nephew, research assistant (in compiling the complex statistical tables for *Suicide*), collaborator (in the pathbreaking essay on knowledge categories and collective representations in *Primitive Classification*), and successor (as editor of the influential *Année sociologique*). Above all in his masterful essay on *The Gift* (1925), which examines processes of symbolic exchange in historical and cross-cultural perspective with a view to their contemporary moral and political significance, Mauss also independently influenced several generations of social and cultural theorists, from Levi-Strauss and Derrida to Baudrillard and Bourdieu (Schrift 1997). The legacy of Durkheim and Mauss is not reducible to 'the invention of the social' as an object of scientific knowledge separate from nature, or to 'the discovery of society' as an explanatory variable substituting for due political process; rather, the importance of their contribution consists in posing the question of how society is *made* possible, and thereby in explicating how social things, relations, and associations are assembled and constructed, arranged and maintained through alternating phases of order and disorder (Donzelot 1994; Collins and Makowsky 1998).

Working for the most part in isolation from and ignorance of their French counterparts, Max Weber and his friend Georg Simmel had a more troubled and complex relationship to the concept of 'the social,' and thus to the theories and sciences that attempted to define it. In the nineteenth and early twentieth centuries, the discourse of the social sphere came to address a kind of hybrid realm involving struggles within civil society on the one hand, and conflicts at the heart of political democracy on the other. The adjective 'social' (along with its shorthand nominal expression, 'the social') thus qualified a set of supposedly discrete activities issuing from these birth pangs of the modern era: in attempts to resolve the 'social question' with the aid of professional and philanthropic social services, to observe social problems through the scientific lens of social statistics, to regulate the division of social labour and to pacify social conflicts, and even to renew the social order through the movement of socialism. For Weber, the integrity of theory and the autonomy of knowledge must be assured in the midst of these disputes by enforcing a principle of 'value-freedom' (*Wertfreiheit*) for clarifying the relationship between the vocations of science and politics, and thus between scholarly work in general and the moral or aesthetic values it assumes or analyses (Wilson 2004). From the first edition of *The Protestant Ethic and the Spirit of Capitalism* in 1905 to the monumental and unfinished *Economy and Society* (both of which he was still revising in 1920, the year he died) Weber invoked this principle not just as a *methodological postulate* for liberating pedagogy from the constraints of political ideologies or for eliminating cultural value-judgements from research, but also as a *rule of order* for the proper conduct of scholarly discussion and argument at conferences, in journals, and in the lecture hall (Schluchter 1996; Weber 2004). Rather than advocating the ethical neutrality of social scientific inquiry, or succumbing to intellectual fashions (as he had accused his colleague and rival Sombart of doing), Weber argued that scholars must remain relatively free *from* ideological pressures, cultural prejudices, and political influences at the same time as they free themselves *for* independent scrutiny of inconvenient facts or conflicting viewpoints. For Simmel, whose professional status with respect to the university and the scientific field was never secure, social theory had yet to establish a recognized position in the system of the sciences, with the result that this new way of thinking was still closer to common sense than to disciplinary knowledge. In his innovative *Philosophy of Money* of 1900, the pathbreaking studies collected under the title *Soziologie* in 1908, and the brilliant Nietzsche-inspired pieces on 'the tragedy of culture' of his later writings (Simmel 1997), Simmel's theoretical originality and prescience consist in articulating a distinctive style for envisioning the shifting totality of social life (the process of 'sociation': *Vergesellschaftung*) out of the inimitable uniqueness of the objects of experience, from the ordinary (bridges and doors) to the sublime (alpine adventures and ancient ruins). Besides defining the 'dialectic of enlightenment thought and practice' a problematic that has been revived in recent years by Habermas and others, Simmel and Weber have also helped to reinvigorate a concern for the interpretive and literary dimensions of social and cultural theory not as a substitute for or alternative to its explanatory function, but as its necessary supplement and presupposition (Green 1988).

In some ways, the work of W. E. B. Du Bois and of Charlotte Perkins Gilman during this period in the United States can be understood as a direct challenge to their European contemporaries, or alternatively as extending the 'travelling ideas' of de Tocqueville and Martineau by planting them on American soil. Du Bois's remarkable *Souls of Black Folk*, which first appeared in 1903, is an eclectic collection of sketches and essays that draws as much on the social science conventions (statistics, fieldwork, and historiography) as on artistic inspiration (folk music, poetry and storytelling). Its theoretical underpinnings can be read as an attempt to specify Hegel's grand philosophy of resistance and transcendence (which he studied with his teachers at Harvard and at Humboldt University in Berlin) and as an illustration of Weber's interpretive method of subjective meaning and empathetic understanding (whom he met in Atlanta in the course of Weber's own Tocquevillian voyage through the US in 1904) (Zamir 1995). Du Bois's (2000 [1905]: 40) ambivalent faith in the sciences is eloquently expressed in his appreciation for the 'hesitation' that Comte and Spencer displayed when confronting the incalculable aporias of individual experience, and in the scepticism he expressed towards the use of anthropometric classification and sociological objectification in his famous figure of race relations: 'It is a peculiar sensation, this double-consciousness, this sense of always looking at one's self through the eyes of others, of *measuring one's soul by the tape* of the world that looks on in amused contempt and pity' (Du Bois 1999 [1903]: 11; my emphasis). In contrast to Du Bois (and to Mead and Cooley who were also writing at this time), Gilman did not reach for Goethe or Hegel to articulate her own experience of a twin soul or the bifurcated experience of an estranged self and its other, but rather for the more homely artefacts of the mass media and popular culture, especially those that were produced by or for women. Occasionally employing suspect notions of racial hygiene, mother-right and social selection that had recently been imported from Europe, her most developed work in the social theory of matriarchal feminism, *The Man-Made World: Our Androcentric Culture* published in 1911, was inspired as much by socialist doctrines of the day (especially Engels's) as by social evolutionary theories in circulation at the time (especially those of Ward at the Chicago School): 'Because of her mother-power, [woman] became the first inventor and labourer; being in truth the mother of all industry as well as of all people' (Gilman 1989: 212). Like Martineau and de Tocqueville, Gilman and Du Bois were less likely to find a voice and an echo for their ideas in the halls of the academy or in the stacks of the library than on the pages of a political journal or at the lectern of a public meeting. If Du Bois and Gilman have until recently been denied a place in the canon of social theory, their relative exclusion may be due as much to their sometimes 'unscientific' or 'atheoretical' advocacy for the realization of the ideals of economic equality and political justice as to the uneasiness that later readers experience in confronting the problem of cultural difference and social conflict in terms of the troublesome *bio-social* categories of 'race' and 'sex' that are the focus of their work.

1920–1945: the End of History

One of the lessons for social theory emerging from the era that ended with the Russian Revolution and World War I was that conflicts between and within nations do not just take on global or local significance, but also deeply affect the inner mechanisms of the human psyche, both consciously and unconsciously. The intellectual spread and cultural influence of the psychoanalytic movement between the World Wars can partly be understood as an effect of its attempts to rethink the roots of neurology and clinical psychiatry by integrating concepts from social psychology, sociology, anthropology, and political science. From 'Mass Psychology and the Analysis of the "I"' (published in 1921) to 'Civilization and its Discontents' (written in 1930), Sigmund Freud radicalized and expanded upon his scientific project for psychoanalysis as the rebellious and wounded child of enlightenment social thought. In these later works, his concepts of the death drive and repression are not simply reducible to neuro-biological, intra-psychic or intra-familial dynamics, but are shown to be broadly articulated with the civilizational processes of war and work, and with the social structures of authority and disobedience. In reshaping minds and bodies, the natural environment and the social world, human being has transformed itself through its technologies into a kind of 'prosthetic god': 'He is quite impressive when he dons all his auxiliary organs, but they have not become a part of him and still give him a good deal of trouble on occasion' (Freud 2002 [1930]: 28). Melanie Klein's work during this period revises Freud's evolutionary hypothesis concerning the ontogenetic shift from a natural plenitude (exemplified by the child's symbiosis with the mother) to cultural incorporation and differentiation (imposed by the symbolic law of the father) as *a political, social and technological process*. Klein's focus on the child's pre-Oedipal experience of the reality of phantasy, the creative and transformative potential of the imagination, and the importance of tools and toys as well as language and symbols in the formation of culture and identity, is likewise advanced in part as a civilizational analysis of the paranoid-schizoid and manic-depressive states of modernity (Klein 1983). Her corrective to Freudian androcentrism in reconsidering the mediation of object-relations in the dynamics of subject formation has provided a key source for psychoanalytically-inspired feminist social theory in recent years (Mitchell 1975).

The recent resurgence of interest in the work of thinkers active during the interwar years has been provoked by the redefinition and rediscovery of this relatively neglected period of social theory. Renewed interest in the early work of Schutz, Marcuse and the first generation of the Frankfurt School, for example, has been sustained by waves of academic conferences,

critical commentaries in scholarly journals and anthologies, and the availability of new translations and editions of their work. The writings of other theorists, such as Bakhtin in Russia,
or Mauss, Bataille and the members of the Collège de Sociologie in France, are also being
revived and republished, both because of their remarkable originality and because of their
influence on later thinkers. The case of Norbert Elias's masterpiece, *The Civilizing Process*, a
magisterial sketch of the socio- and psycho-genesis of the disciplinary society since the middle
ages, offers an especially instructive example of how the historical contingencies of publication and translation can delay the reception and distort the appreciation of a great work:
having first appeared in a limited edition while Elias was in exile in England from the Nazis in
1939, it was only translated into English almost 40 years later in two volumes with different
titles and has only recently been published in its entirety (Elias 2000). In spite of his influence
on later thinkers such as Foucault, Bourdieu and Goffman, a clear picture of Elias has yet to
be fully recognized also because, like others of his generation, he developed a unique and
debatable synthesis of his predecessors (especially Weber and Freud) while at the same time
broadly criticizing or remaining aloof from his contemporaries (van Krieken 1998). His teacher and mentor in Frankfurt, Karl Mannheim (who worked in the same building that
housed Adorno and his colleagues at the Institute for Social Research) was also concerned to
mark off a new direction for social theory while being more directly engaged in the ideological and academic disputes of his time. His *Ideology and Utopia* (the 1929 German edition was
expanded for the 1936 English edition) and *Man and Society in an Age of Reconstruction* (again
the 1935 German edition was revised for the 1940 English version) each took a pragmatic
stand against the radical orthodoxy and idealist aspirations of Marxism on the one hand
(exemplified in *History and Class Consciousness* by Lukács, his fellow Hungarian expatriate) and
the conservative and 'reprimitivizing' project of fascism on the other (exemplified in the argument of *Political Theology* by Schmitt, a rival whose intellect he nevertheless admired). In place
of these utopian ideologies, Mannheim advanced his own liberal conception of a free-floating
intelligentsia with both a moral vision for the political vocation of responsible scholarship and
a rational plan for conducting politics itself as a scientific enterprise (Loader and Kettler 2003).
For both Elias and Mannheim, the *reflexive habitus* is not only rooted in the life experience
and social location of the social theorist; as the social studies of science would show later,
these thought collectives and presupposed habits of mind are also produced and problematized
by the disciplined distance that intellectuals try to maintain from their subject of study.

An interesting feature of the twentieth century intellectual migration of German into
Anglo-American social theory (occasionally via a French detour) emerges from the fact that
so many of these thinkers were exiles (Klein, Freud, Mannheim, and Elias all immigrated to
England during this period), and that the renaissance of their ideas has often originated in the
English-speaking world. This phase in the formation of social theory has at times exhibited a
process of 'obliteration through incorporation,' as Merton (1949:4–5) once put it, or of 'neglect
through ignorance,' in which the diversity and critical promise of predecessors are forgotten
or neutralized through conceptual synthesis or methodological standardization. In this regard,
Talcott Parsons's *Structure of Social Action*, first published in 1937, is the paradigmatic 'classic on
classics' in attempting to separate what is vital from what is dead in the heritage of European
social theory by revisiting the graves of the founders, including Marshall and Pareto, but
especially Durkheim and Weber (Alexander 1989: 40). The irony in Parsons's famous opening
question – 'Who now reads Spencer?' – lies not only in suggesting that contemporary readers
may not have evolved beyond Spencer's crude social Darwinism, but also in the fact that
Parsons's own work is now just as unlikely to be read or remembered, having supposedly
been surpassed by later generations of Marxist critical theorists, middle-range empirical

sociologists, systems theorists and social phenomenologists. A parallel case that focuses on figures that Parsons forgot or ignored is exemplified by the very different branch in the genealogy of social theory that passes through the figure of Alexandre Kojève, a Russian born immigrant to Paris who was educated in Berlin, and whose Marx-inspired and Heidegger-inflected lectures on Hegel's *Phenomenology of Spirit* from 1933–1939 were attended by a cohort of influential thinkers (including Sartre, Aron, Merleau-Ponty, Bataille, Lacan, and Hippolyte) who set the stage for post-structuralist, neo-Marxian, and feminist theory in the post-war years. Though less driven by Parsons's ambition for synthesis and systematization, Kojève's vision also entailed returning to the very origin of European social theory while anticipating its end. Where Parsons would prefigure the thesis of the 'end of ideology' as an evolutionary tendency in modern societies that reaches beyond the historical alternatives of capitalism, fascism and socialism (a theme later taken up by Bell and Fukuyama, among others), Kojève (1969: 158–162) would go so far as to speculate on 'the disappearance of Man at the end of History', or more precisely, to announce the dissolution of Occidental Man as an agent of work and warfare who negates the immediacy and facticity of European History (as later writers from Fanon to Said would point out). If classical social theory began as a response to revolution and by acknowledging the imperative of historical change, it appears to end with the prospect of human annihilation in warfare and by radically rethinking the very possibility of historical meaning.

Conclusion

With the identity of 'social theory' in question today, and with its dissemination in so many formats and forums, it is easy to forget that the field has had to undergo a long struggle to secure its institutional place in the university, to find professional legitimacy in international academic societies, scholarly journals and interdisciplinary conferences, and to distinguish itself intellectually from political ideologies and mere 'cultural worldviews.' Social theory has traditionally employed a remarkably wide range of genres and media, and its methods of communication and intended audiences continue to be at least as diverse and multifaceted as its topics and methods of study. In the past, theorists of social life were as likely to publish a political manifesto to stir up the masses, or to comment in a popular periodical on the new spirit of the age, as they were to offer practical advice on public policy in a government report or on personal problems to the masses in the pages of a popular magazine. As a more strictly academic undertaking, social theorizing has become more likely to find expression in the seminar rooms of the university, the libraries of endowed academies, or the private gatherings and correspondence of rivals and colleagues. As new theories continue to diversify, spread and mature, the risk is that the older ones will be strip-mined into slogans, channelled into 'schools' or entrenched into 'paradigms,' thereby inhibiting the adventure of conceptual innovation that may be inspired by returning to the classics, rethinking the founders, and defamiliarizing the canon (Turner 1999).

We have become accustomed in recent years to treating the fragmentation of social theory as itself a symptom of our current world crisis and cultural malaise. The supposed collapse of the grand theories of system and structure and of the classic metanarratives of reason and revolution appear to have left only mini-concepts of identity and personality and minor stories of difference and resistance with a claim to credibility (Lyotard 1984). This latest challenge to the classical heritage has led a chorus of critics to call for the reconstruction of social theory from the ruins, if not through the standardization of terms and the professionalization of methods then through the reconstruction of new conceptual syntheses and abstract comprehensive schemes (Habermas 1984, 1987). As Wolf Lepenies (1988: 7) has argued however, reconsidering the multiplicity or even eccentricity of the classics, canons and founders of social theory may instead require us to refocus attention on the historical phase when it occupied a critical place between the arts and the sciences, and thus before the inter-disciplinary purification of the 'two cultures'. From here, we might begin to unthink the tradition as a resource for problematizing our present and for posing questions to ourselves: to what extent does it make sense to read our own age theoretically and empirically as a time of Durkheimian anomie and cultural chaos, of Marxian class struggle and world alienation, or of Weberian de-enchantment and technological rationalization? And can these grand narratives be sustained or undermined by reinventing the fictional illustrations (Martineau), literary experiments (Gilman), and stylistic innovations (Du Bois) that also characterize our theore-tical heritage? Approaching the other side of contemporary social theory in this way may require us to consider its 'allegorical' dimension as the classical art of thinking and seeing (*theasthai*) – and thus of writing and speaking (*agoruein*) – otherwise (*allo*) than we do.

References

Alexander, J. (1989) *Structure and Meaning: Rethinking Classical Theory*, New York: Columbia University Press.

Baehr, P. (2002) *Founders, Classics, Canons: Modern Disputes over the Origins and Appraisal of Sociology's Heritage*, New Brunswick, NJ: Transaction Publishers.

Collins, R. and M. Makowsky (1998) *The Discovery of Society*, Boston: McGraw Hill.

Donzelot, J. (1994) *L'invention du social: Essai sur le déclin des passions politiques*, Paris: Editions du Seuil.

Du Bois, W. E. B. (1999 [1903]) *The Souls of Black Folk: A Norton Critical Edition*, H. L. Gates, Jr. and T. H. Oliver (eds), New York: W. W. Norton & Co.

Du Bois, W. E. B. (2000 [1905]) 'Sociology Hesitant', in *Boundary 2* 27 (3): 37–44.

Durkheim, E. (1982) *The Rules of Sociological Method and Selected Texts on Sociology and its Method*, S. Lukes (ed.), W. D. Hall (trans.), New York: The Free Press.

Elias, N. (2000) *The Civilizing Process: Sociogenetic and Psychogenetic Investigations* (Revised Edition), Edumud Jephcott (trans.), E. Dunning, J. Goudsblom and S. Mennell (eds), Oxford: Blackwell Publishers.

Freud, S. (2002 [1930]) *Civilization and its Discontents*, D. McLintock (trans.), Introduction by L. Bersani, London: Penguin Books.

Gane, M. (2003) *French Social Theory*, London: Sage Publications.

Garfinkel, H. (2002) *Ethnomethodology's Program: Working Out Durkheim's Aphorism*, Anne Warfield Rawls (ed., intro.), Lanham, MD: Rowman & Littlefield.

Gilman, C. P. (1989) *The Yellow Wallpaper and Other Writings*, Lynn Sharon Schwartz (ed.), New York: Bantam Books.

Green, B. S. (1988) *Literary Methods and Sociological Theory: Case Studies of Simmel and Weber*, Chicago: University of Chicago Press.

Habermas, J. (1984, 1987) *The Theory of Communicative Action, Volumes 1, 2*, Thomas McCarthy (trans.), Boston: Beacon Press.

Kemple, T. M. (1995) *Reading Marx Writing: Melodrama, the Market, and the 'Grundrisse'*, Stanford, CA: Stanford University Press.

Klein, M. (1983) *The Selected Works of Melanie Klein*, Juliet Mitchell (ed., intro.), London: Penguin Books.

Kojève, A. (1969) *Introduction to the Reading of Hegel: Lectures on the 'Phenomenology of Spirit'*, Assembled by Raymond Queneau. Allan Bloom (ed.), James H. Nichols, Jr. (trans.), Ithaca, NY: Cornell University Press.

Lepenies, W. (1988) *Between Science and Literature: The Rise of Sociology*, R. J. Hollingdale (trans.), Cambridge, UK: Cambridge University Press.

Loader, C. and D. Kettler (2003) *Karl Mannheim's Sociology as Political Education*, New Brunswick, NJ: Transaction Publishers.

Lyotard, J.-F. (1984) *The Postmodern Condition: A Report on Knowledge*, Geoff Bennington and Brian Massumi (trans.). Fredric Jameson (foreword), Minneapolis: University of Minnesota Press.

Marcuse, H. (1941) *Reason and Revolution: Hegel and the Rise of Social Theory*, Boston: Beacon Press.

Marx, K. and F. Engels (1998) *The Communist Manifesto: A Modern Edition*, Eric Hobsbawm (intro.), London: Verso.

Merton, Robert K. (1949) *Social Theory and Social Structure*, Glencoe, IL: The Free Press.

Mitchell, J. (1975) *Psychoanalysis and Feminism*, London: Vintage Books.

O'Neill, J. (ed.) (1996) *Hegel's Dialectic of Desire and Recognition: Texts and Commentary*, Albany, NY: State University of New York Press.

Schluchter, W. (1996) *Paradoxes of Modernity: Culture and Conduct in the Theory of Max Weber*, Neil Solomon (trans.), Stanford, CA: Stanford University Press.

Schrift, A. D. (ed.) (1997) *The Logic of the Gift: Toward an Ethic of Generosity*, London: Routlege.

Simmel, G. (1997) *Simmel on Culture: Selected Writings*, D. Frisby and M. Featherstone (eds), London: SAGE Publications.

Spencer, H. (1972) *Herbert Spencer on Social Evolution*, J. D. Y. Peel (ed. intro.), Chicago: University of Chicago Press.

Tocqueville, A. de (1966) *Democracy in America*, J. P. Mayer (ed.), G. Lawrence (trans.), Garden City, NY: Doubleday & Company, Inc.

Turner, B. (1999) *Classical Sociology*, London: Sage Publications.

Van Krieken, R. (1998) *Norbert Elias*, London: Routledge.

Wallerstein, I. (1991) *Unthinking Social Science: The Limits of Nineteenth-Century Paradigms*, Cambridge, UK: Polity Press.

Weber, M. (2004) *The Essential Weber: A Reader*, S. Whimster (ed.), London: Routledge.

Wernick, A. (2001) *Auguste Comte and the Religion of Humanity: The Post-Theistic Program of French Social Theory*, Cambridge, UK: Cambridge University Press.

Wilson, H. T. (2004) *The Vocation of Reason: Studies in Critical Theory and Social Science in the Age of Max Weber*. T. M. Kemple (ed., foreword), Leiden, the Netherlands: Brill Academic Publishers.

Zamir, S. (1995) *Dark Voices: W. E. B. Du Bois and American Thought, 1888–1903*, Chicago: University of Chicago Press.

2

Social theory and the social sciences

Patrick Baert

My argument starts with the observation that whilst social theory has become a central intellectual endeavour in the social sciences, its precise status *vis-à-vis* the social sciences has become increasingly uncertain and needs to be reassessed. On the one hand, social theory has played a central role in the development of the social sciences in the last twenty to thirty years. Initially mainly confined to sociology, debates within social theory have spilled over into the various branches of the social sciences: many social scientists now engage with theoretical issues to a far greater extent than was previously the case. On the other hand, the precise role of theory in empirical research has become increasingly uncertain. Until recently the deductive-nomological model and its realist alternative were dominant ways of thinking about the relationship between theory and empirical research, but both have now been shown to be problematic. It is therefore important to reconsider the precise status of theory and to reassess what theory can achieve and what it is for. One way forward, I will argue, is to conceive of knowledge in terms of cognitive interests and to recognise the importance of self-knowledge as a cognitive interest.

Social theory as facilitator and catalyst

Since the late 1970s, researchers in the social sciences and humanities have shown a growing interest in social theory. Social theory has managed to occupy the position of intellectual facilitator and catalyst in the humanities and the social sciences. By this, I mean that it occupies the space in which cross-disciplinary debates are encouraged, channelled and coordinated, similar to the way in which, in the course of the twentieth century, mathematics has become the language through which insights from one branch of the natural sciences reach other branches. Previously, other academic disciplines (notably philosophy and history) have fulfilled these roles in the social sciences, and there is no reason to assume that social theory will occupy this dominant position forever. For now, however, social theory is the main vehicle through which intellectual debates occur.

Often, social theory acts like a central nervous system: intellectual developments within social theory precede and set the agenda for debates in the social sciences. For example, the issue of the public sphere was initially introduced within social theory (Habermas 1989 [1962]), but has been applied across several disciplines, from media studies (e.g. Dahlgren 1995; Price 1995) and gender studies (e.g. Siltanen and Stanworth 1984) to history (e.g. Landes 1988; Solkin 1993). Another example is the debate around structure and agency, which, again, was initially a mainly theoretical dispute, the fruits of which subsequently became incorporated in a number of social sciences, ranging from political science (e.g. Marsh *et al.* 1999) to economics (e.g. Lawson 1997, 2003). Sometimes, however, developments in social theory are sparked by empirical research, though social theory remains the intellectual clearing-house – the medium through which these new ideas travel. For example, the posthumanist turn in science studies led to theoretical reflection on the nature of the social (see Latour 1993; Law and Hassard 1999), which in turn inspired new research in social anthropology (e.g. Gell 1998). Likewise, the field of gender studies has initiated new theoretical reflections on gender, inequality and identity formation, some of which have influenced diverse disciplines from geography (e.g. McDowell 1999; McDowell and Sharp 1999) to international relations (e.g. Tickner 1992; Hooper 2000).

Initially, the allocation of a central role to theory coincided with the coming of age of the golden generation of European social theory. I am referring to a generation of intellectuals and academics, born in the inter-bellum, including, for instance, Pierre Bourdieu, Niklas Luhmann, Jürgen Habermas, Michel Foucault and Anthony Giddens. The conditions in which they worked partly account for the central role their work came to play. First, they wrote during a period of expansion of higher education, a period also in which the social sciences in particular flourished. New social sciences, such as gender and media studies, came on the scene, and those that already existed became stronger. Second, this generation of social theorists benefited from their association with sociology, which by the 1960s had become a major player in the academic field. It is not a coincidence that of the five social theorists mentioned, four occupied positions in sociology, Foucault being the exception. Third, the political orientations of these authors, and the way in which they incorporated those views in their work, fitted nicely in the progressive intellectual climate in academia at the time. With exceptions like Luhmann (who might be less easily classifiable in this respect), most social theorists regarded themselves as *critical* social theorists, who saw theory and social research as contributing to critical reflection on contemporary society. They differed greatly as to what ought to be criticised, what critique meant and how it could be achieved, but most subscribed to the view that theory or theory-driven research would tie in with a left or left-of-centre political agenda, whether it be a straightforward emancipatory or a deconstructionist one. Fourth, most of these theorists were trained in philosophy or certainly knowledgeable of its recent developments, and they were able to translate 'the social turn' in philosophy into a coherent theoretical programme. By social turn, I refer to the way in which, in the course of the twentieth century, philosophers drew attention to the social nature of entities, which some had assumed to be self-evident, self-sufficient or fixed: for instance, the self, knowledge, rationality or aesthetics. This social turn provided fertile ground for the increasing authority of social theory.

Whereas this generation was initially linked to sociology, their writings quickly found resonance in other fields, such as social anthropology, geography and history. The opening up to other fields is probably even more striking now: it is rare nowadays to find European theorists who write exclusively for a sociological audience. It would be misleading, for instance, to portray Bruno Latour's actor-network theory or Alex Honneth's critical theory as primarily addressing sociologists. This is why it makes more sense to talk about *social* theory rather than *sociological* theory. Sociological theory suggests a discipline-bound form of

15

theorising – theory for sociological research. Sociological theory never existed in its pure form anyway. For instance, during the heyday of structural-functionalism, the application of this theoretical framework was not limited to sociology; social anthropologists were as committed to it as sociologists were. But at least the disciplinary boundaries were clearer then, whereas theorising now affects the social sciences in general – not just sociology. Some American sociologists still use the term 'sociological theory': sociology in the United States is more professionalised, and therefore more preoccupied with guarding its borders with neighbouring disciplines. For most Europeans, the term 'sociological theory' has become an anachronism, a relic from a bygone era when boundaries were clear-cut and movements across borders were prohibited.

Why social theory?

Given the current importance of social theory, one would expect clarity as to its precise role *vis-à-vis* the social sciences. But quite the opposite is the case. There is growing uncertainty as to what social theory can or should achieve, especially in relationship to the various social sciences it is supposed to serve. Ironically, there was more of a consensus on these matters during the period preceding the prominence of social theory. The problem for social theory today is that these earlier views about the relationship between theory and research have been shown to be problematic. Two views, in particular, were widespread until two decades ago, but are no longer tenable. The first view conceives of theory in deductive-nomological terms: as a set of laws and initial conditions, from which empirical hypotheses can be derived. The second view sees theory in representational terms: as providing the conceptual building blocks for capturing or picturing the empirical world. The two views, the deductive and the representational one, are not necessarily mutually exclusive, and some authors subscribed to both. They are, however, analytically distinct.

1. The deductive-nomological view conceives of scientific theories as an explanatory endeavour, accounting for and predicting empirical phenomena (Hempel 1965; Popper 1959 [1934]; 1991a [1963]). Empirical research is a testing device, like a judicial decision, informing the academic community about how valid the theory has proven to be. Philosophers who subscribe to this view are preoccupied with demarcation questions: what is science, and how is it different from, say, pseudo-science or ideology. They would argue that a theory is scientific if it complies with this deductive model, and if it is possible to infer testable hypotheses from the theory. Within this tradition, a consensus has grown that testability comes down to falsifiability: hypotheses are scientific if and only if they are formulated so that they *can* be refuted (Popper 1959 [1934]; 1991a [1963]). From the middle of the twentieth century, social scientists embraced this perspective, thereby celebrating the scientific nature of their intellectual enterprises. This culminated in a distrust of grand theory, notably its historicist and holistic version, in favour of middle range theory, which facilitated focused, empirical research (Merton 1968; see also Popper 1991b [1957]). What type of middle range theory is most appropriate was, of course, open to discussion, with different candidates presenting themselves: for instance, functionalists, rational choice theorists and exchange theorists. But all versions complied with the deductive-nomological structure and employed empirical research as adjudicator.

Proponents of the deductive-nomological view argued that this distinctive method had been widely used in the natural sciences and, more importantly, that it accounted for the obvious success of the natural sciences over the centuries. The first blow to this view came with the publication of compelling work on the history of the natural sciences that showed that this method was not nearly as widespread as Hempel or Popper made us believe, and that it was limited to particular periods in scientific history (e.g. Kuhn 1970). It was also successfully argued that if scientists had proceeded in this deductive-nomological fashion, they would, most likely, not have made the progress they had made (Feyerabend 1975). For instance, scientists often disregard falsifications when they initially create their own theories, but this is not irrational: although early theoretical constructions often have some flaws, they might prove later, after some tweaking, to be highly valuable. The second problem arises once the notion of falsification comes under close scrutiny. The precise status of empirical refutations is unclear given the theory-laden nature of observational statements. Any observation draws on theoretical presuppositions and is fallible; hence it is not fruitful to conceive of testing as a straightforward adjudicating device. Even Lakatos' sophisticated falsifactionism does not solve this dilemma because it is still treats empirical data as adjudicators (see, for instance, Lakatos 1970). The third problem questions the validity of the inductive process by which empirical research results are used to infer statements regarding the truth or falsehood of the hypotheses. This inductive inference is problematic because empirical research provides information about a finite number of observations in very specific circumstances, and a hypothesis refers to an infinite number of cases in any circumstance.

2. In the latter part of the twentieth century, the deductive-nomological view came under intense scrutiny, and gave way gradually to the representational model. According to the representational model, theory provides the ontological building blocks for empirical research. Theorists search for the unchanging foundations of an all-embracing theoretical framework or science of the social. They act with the precision of mathematicians or logicians, defining the precise meaning of central concepts (for example, social structure, culture and agency) and elaborating on the exact link between them. For example, Giddens' duality of structure, Bhaskar's transformational model of social action, or Archer's morphogenic approach all attempt to conceptualise the precise relationship between society and agency (Giddens 1984; Archer 1995, 1996; Bhaskar 1998). Research is then conceived as a mapping device, capturing the various dimensions of social life (see, for example, Layder 1993). Because of its realist undertones, the representational model assumes that scientific research is a revelatory exercise, uncovering hitherto hidden mechanisms or powers. Research is particularly successful if it manages to give a comprehensive account of the social, taking into account both macro- and micro-phenomena and showing the link between them (see Layder 1993). No longer adjudicators of theory, empirical cases are instantiations of the theory. Social research can never help to establish the refutation of theories, but it can show their degree of applicability to empirical cases, and theories gain credence if they can be used to account for a wide variety of social phenomena. The theory is applicable to a particular case if the empirical phenomena can be rephrased in terms of the theory.

This representational model is problematic for a variety of reasons. First, it remains unclear what is to be gained from trying to capture the various dimensions of social reality, as if there would be some virtue in comprehensiveness. Theoretical attempts at linking the different aspects of social life (the macro- and the micro-, structure and agency, etc.) have led to general propositions, the theoretical (or empirical) value of which are questionable. As for the empirical payoff, this type of social research lacks focus and is insufficiently question-driven to be insightful in any way (Baert 1998a: 108–111). Second, recent developments in philosophy have shed serious doubt over the assumption that research is about uncovering previously hidden mechanisms or powers. John Dewey called this assumption the 'spectator theory of knowledge' – 'spectator' because it sees knowledge as reflecting the inner essence of the external world (Dewey 1930: 233ff.). However, researchers do not have some mysterious capacity to 'step outside history' – to assume what Quine called a 'God's eye view' – and capture the world as it *really* is. Recent philosophical developments rightly substitute agency for the metaphor of vision: knowledge is a form of action, bringing about change. Knowledge is about *coping* with the world – not *copying* it (Rorty 1980; 1982). Third, the view of research as exemplifying theory is problematic. It is responsible for the repetitive nature of a great deal of research carried out under a representational banner. Researchers use a theoretical frame of reference to illuminate or rephrase a piece of research, inevitably reinforcing the very same theory. What is to be gained from learning that a certain theory has been applied successfully to a particular setting, if by 'successful' is meant that the setting has been described in terms of the vocabulary of this theory? The answer is very little, especially given that any situation lends itself to an infinite number of descriptions and that very few vocabularies would not lend themselves to applications of this kind.

Old Europe and new pragmatism

The solution, I think, lies in abandoning these two diametrically opposed positions about the relationship between theory and research. The deductive-nomological model sees empirical research as a grand inquisitor, informing the research community about which theories are best and which are to be abandoned. The representational model denigrates empirical research, belittling it as a mere illustration or application of theories, simply a vehicle through which theories are articulated, reproduced and celebrated. This position easily leads to theoretical ossification because empirical research is employed to confirm – not challenge – the theoretical framework that is being adopted. However, the deductive-nomological model does not fare better. It only encourages theoretical change if we are confronted with a vast array of empirical refutations, and given the uncertainty as to what amounts to a valid empirical refutation and given the entrenched nature of research programmes, conceptual change is, in practice, limited. Whilst the two positions are clearly different, both fail to realise how a confrontation with empirical phenomena can encourage us to adopt a new vocabulary, to take a new theoretical perspective on things. To appreciate how research and conceptual innovation can be linked, we need to adopt a very different philosophical outlook, which I will call a 'hermeneutics-inspired pragmatism'. This philosophical position merges old Europe and new pragmatism: it incorporates insights from Continental hermeneutics, in particular Hans-Georg Gadamer, and insights from American neo-pragmatism, notably Richard Bernstein and Richard Rorty. I will first explain to what extent this outlook is pragmatist; I will subsequently clarify the hermeneutic component.

There is little doubt that American pragmatism has had a significant impact on the history of the social sciences, both in North America and elsewhere. Take, for instance, Dewey's effect on educational science, Mead's impact on social psychology and sociology, James' on psychology, and the pragmatist leanings of the Chicago School. These influences are clear and well documented; there is a growing body of historical literature that testifies to this (see, for example, Petras 1968; Lewis 1976; Rock 1979: 24–101; Denzin 1992: 1–20; Joas 1993). Nevertheless, social researchers and theoreticians have neglected American pragmatism in two ways. First, in contrast with the influence of pragmatism on empirical research, its impact on the philosophy of social science is limited, especially in English-speaking circles. Second, whilst social scientists often acknowledge a debt to the classics of American pragmatism, they engage very little with the *current* strands of pragmatism. Indeed, a growing industry of publications on the history of pragmatism (especially in relationship to the social sciences) is accompanied by a glaring ignorance of recent developments in pragmatism. I want to pay attention precisely to these two neglected aspects of pragmatism. I will argue that an inquiry into contemporary pragmatism will help to find a solution to the methodological impasse created by both the deductive-nomological and the representational model.

1. Pragmatists are sceptical of any transcendental form of inquiry. Transcendental forms of inquiry assume that philosophy can provide a-temporal foundations that supposedly ground aesthetic, ethical or cognitive claims (see Rorty 1980: 315–322; Bernstein 1991: 326–327). They might differ in *how* to arrive at the foundations – some might appeal to self-inquiry, some to intuition, some to reason, and so on – but they all assume that we can step outside history. Pragmatists reject this style of reasoning, firstly because they believe transcendental forms of inquiry have never worked, and second because recent developments in analytical philosophy (Quine, Goodman, Sellars) have compromised them (Rorty 1980: 315ff.; 1991: 64–68). Pragmatists prefer to talk about the 'agent's point of view', referring to the impossibility of escaping a conceptual system. This does not mean, however, that knowledge is subjective, if by 'subjective' is meant that knowledge fails to correspond to reality. For pragmatists, knowledge can never correspond to or mirror an external reality, and therefore it does not make sense to say that it fails to correspond to reality. Mirroring is simply the wrong metaphor.

Transcendental forms of inquiry are particularly widespread in the philosophy of social science. Naturalist programmes, such as Popper's, often search for the essence of the scientific method – the key that distinguishes science from and makes it superior to pseudo-science, religion or ideology. For naturalists, natural scientists regularly employ this scientific method, which explains their empirical success; the social sciences might be able to obtain similar success if they adopt the same method. However, detailed research on the natural sciences has shown little methodological unity: the neat deductive-nomological model only applies to certain fields of inquiry. John Dupré and others have demonstrated that biology, for instance, often operates very differently from most chemistry and physics. In contrast to these other natural sciences, biology is not strictly law-governed, nor deterministic. Biologists do not assume that the world is entirely comprehensible, and they work within an instrumental – not a realist – framework (Dupré 1993). The notion of *a* scientific method, applicable across a wide variety of natural sciences, appears fictitious. Even within one discipline, the history of science has taught us that a winning strategy can suddenly become a losing one, and *vice versa*, and that with the arrival of a new paradigm, methodological rules can be altered substantially. Furthermore, transcendental forms of inquiry rest on a selective view of the natural sciences as a neatly demarcated and selective activity. The sociology of sciences has taught us that the closer we look at the practice of science, the less clear the boundaries between science and non-science become. For instance, 'findings' are often contentious as they rely on other equally contentious references that themselves rely on other references, and so on (see, for instance, Latour 1987; Barnes *et al.* 1996).

2. Pragmatists reject the 'spectator theory of knowledge'. As mentioned earlier, John Dewey coined this term to refer to any view of knowledge as a representation of the inner nature of the external world. According to this view, knowledge represents the world as accurately and completely as possible. The spectator theory of knowledge relies on the metaphor of vision: knowledge is supposed to map or mirror the world. Pragmatists wish to break with the metaphor of vision (Rorty 1980). They argue that evolutionary theory shows that knowledge is active – a way of coping with life's pressures. Evolutionary theory teaches us that individuals develop language and knowledge as tools to cope with the external world

(Rorty 1982). However, it would be absurd to argue that they manage to represent the world as it really is. Rather than seeing reality as ready made, complete and waiting to be discovered, knowledge is always in the making. It is about coping with, not copying, the world.

Representational views are widespread in the social sciences, and they manifest themselves in two ways. First, some, such as the anthropologist Claude Lévi-Strauss, assume that social research deals with the mapping of the social – with the uncovering of hitherto latent structures, which exist independently of people's perceptions or accounts. Social researchers are like social cartographers, drawing the social world as it really is, uncovering hidden mechanisms possibly unacknowledged by the people involved. For instance, Lévi-Strauss' research aims at uncovering the binary oppositions underneath the multitude of empirical phenomena (Lévi-Strauss 1972 [1958], 1978 [1973]). Second, some presuppose that social research aims at presenting as complete a picture of the social as possible. Hence the desire to transcend oppositions: between structure and agency, society and the individual, the macro- and micro, and so on. For instance, influenced by Giddens and Roy Bhaskar, Derek Layder suggests we should draw a complete map of the social, taking into account all dimensions of the social: for instance, the various temporal spans and structural as well as agency-related dimensions (Layder 1993).

These exponents of the spectator theory of knowledge are not tenable. First, to view social research as an exercise in social cartography is to assume mistakenly that research passively records external data. The cartography model ignores the way in which researchers draw on interpretative procedures in order to account for the phenomena under investigation. It is misleading to talk about the 'uncovering' of structures 'as they really are'. Just as Stanley Fish has pointed out that it is absurd to assume that we can step outside our interpretative community and go 'back-to-the-text', is equally problematic to hold that the right interpretative method would allow us to gain access to 'reality-out-there'. Research is not a discovery as such, but an active process in which researchers make sense of things. It is not surprising, then, that is perfectly possible to take on board Lévi-Strauss' perspective and to arrive at very different binary oppositions than the ones he claimed to detect (Baert 1998a: 27–29). Second, neither social theory nor social research has gained much from the numerous efforts to transcend the different dimensions of the social. For instance, the preoccupation with linking structure and agency has often led to unfocused empirical research, lacking in empirical relevance and clarity. This type of research is diametrically opposed to question-driven research, which aims to solve specific empirical puzzles. The urge to obtain comprehensiveness often amounts to a lack of intellectual direction (Baert 1998a: 201–202).

3. For pragmatists, research is active – it is always about accomplishing things. This explains their interest in the notion of cognitive interest, referring to the particular aims of research. Naturalist philosophies of social science take for granted that research is about explanation and prediction. This approach has led to sophisticated research programmes, but the drawback is that other cognitive interests did not come to the foreground. In contrast, the pragmatist perspective draws attention to other cognitive aims: understanding, critique and self-emancipation (see also Habermas 1991 [1976]), and, as I will argue, self-understanding. None of the cognitive interests have *a priori* epistemological priority over the others. Pragmatists insist that methodological questions (how should we do research?) always depend on the cognitive interest we pursue (what do we wish to obtain?). For instance, for Richard Rorty, the *Methodenstreit* was not really a proper debate, because a debate requires a common goal. The different opponents in the debate simply wanted different things: hermeneutically inspired historians aimed at understanding the specificity of historical phenomena, whereas positivists aimed at explaining and generalising. There is nothing intrinsic to the social that necessitates one or the other; it depends on what goals we wish to achieve (Rorty 1982: 195–200).

It is within the spirit of pragmatism, with its celebration of diversity, to conceive of types of research in pursuit of new cognitive interests, and I suggest that we take self-understanding seriously as a cognitive interest (see also Baert 2005). By 'self-understanding', I refer to the process by which we exhibit reflexivity, and reassess ourselves, and our cultural presuppositions. By 'self-referential knowledge acquisition', I refer to a mode of knowledge that sets out to achieve this self-understanding. Self-referential knowledge ties in with Gadamer's notion of understanding (Gadamer 1979 [1965]), and it does so in two ways. First, individuals rely on their cultural presuppositions to gain access to what is being studied. Second, the confrontation with the object of research allows individuals to articulate and re-interpret the very same presuppositions. There is a clear dialogical component to this type of knowledge: no longer simply a one-way process, knowledge has become more like a conversation. Individuals learn as much about themselves and about their own culture as they do about what they are studying.

Note that Gadamer used this notion of understanding in ontological terms, whereas I suggest we should pursue this notion as a *methodological* device. It might well be that understanding always involves this conversational model, but there is a lot to be gained from *actively* pursuing the dialogue. Similar to Rorty's proposal for an 'edifying' philosophy (Rorty 1980), this type of research allows individuals to see themselves, their own culture and their own presuppositions from a different perspective, and to contrast this re-assessment with alternative socio-political scenarios. However, Rorty believes that philosophy paves the way towards this self-referential knowledge acquisition, whereas I think social research can achieve this more forcefully because of the extent to which its empirical ingredient forces us to confront difference. It is precisely this encounter that enables individuals to articulate, conceptualise and question their own culture, and empowers them to increase their imaginative capabilities and to conceptualise what is not present.

This proposal incorporates insights from pragmatism and from hermeneutics. It is not, however, a purely philosophical endeavour. It has repercussions for how we think about the relationship between theory and empirical research. Empirical research does not assume the role of adjudicator, nor is it simply a sounding board for theory. Through empirical research, we have the opportunity to reassess our theoretical preconceptions, not because we realise they have been empirically refuted, but because we are able to take a different perspective on things. Closely related to the notion of *Bildung* or edification, empirical research has enabled us to broaden our horizon – for instance, by realising the cultural specificity of ideals or concerns, which we felt so strongly about. Within this perspective, it is essential that researchers have an open mind and are willing to be surprised, affected and moved by what they study. More than forty years ago, Susan Sontag warned of the dangers of literary criticism – whether psychoanalytic or Marxist – with its tendency to impose a framework or theory on any text, play or film (Sontag 1966 [1964]). Unfortunately, social theory has been employed in a similar fashion, with competing schools looking at empirical phenomena through their particular grid and reiterating the framework they already believe in. In 1946, George Orwell pointed out the dangers of '. . . worn-out metaphors which have lost all evocative power and are merely used because they save people the trouble of inventing phrases for themselves' (Orwell 1950 [1946]: 87). Orwell was writing about language in general, but his remarks are remarkably apt to describe how researchers use theory today: followers of theoretical fashions are unable to articulate for themselves what they encounter and, crucially, are unable to use the encounter with empirical phenomena to take on a new perspective.

Not all theory is used this way, though. Some research in the social sciences is compatible with my pragmatist proposal, and I will give examples from five different social sciences. First, since the 'critical turn' of the 1980s, social and cultural anthropology has moved in the direction of self-referential knowledge acquisition (Clifford and Marcus 1986; Marcus and Fischer 1999). Critical of representational models, the critical turn in anthropology uses empirical research to reflect on our own presuppositions and on the discipline of anthropology itself. The aim is to pursue edifying accounts, in which anthropologists open themselves up to new experiences and engage in conversation.

Second, with the arrival of post-processual archaeology, the discipline of archaeology has developed in a similar fashion to anthropology. In contrast with processual or new archaeology (which drew on Hempel to model archaeology on the natural sciences), post-processual archaeology recognises the extent to which our reconstructions of the past tie in with our present concerns and values (Hodder 1991; Shanks and Hodder 1998; Tilley 1998). This type of archaeology also uses the past *intentionally* to criticise some of the deep-seated assumptions of the discipline and to challenge our broader values and beliefs.

Third, whilst traditionally history seeks to reconstruct and explain the past, the main focus of the genealogical method, used by Nietzsche and Foucault, is to reassess and destabilise the present. Genealogical history employs the confrontation with an unfamiliar past as a way to articulate and illuminate the familiar present (Baert 1998b). For instance, Nietzsche's depiction of pre-Christian morality aims to destabilise categories and dichotomies prevalent in contemporary moral systems, just as Foucault's account of the society of spectacle is meant to highlight the nature of the society of surveillance today (Nietzsche 1967 [1886]; Foucault 1977[1975]).

Fourth, some sociological research enables us to develop this type of self-referential knowledge acquisition. For instance, Zygmunt Baumann's critical analysis of the Holocaust enables us to reassess our modern condition and to ponder the possibility of an intricate relationship between salient features of modernity and acts of barbarism of the twentieth century (Bauman 1989), whilst Richard Sennett's work on the social–psychological implications of neo-liberalism invites us to reconsider the value of the alleged freedoms, fluidity and choice in contemporary society (Sennett 1998).

Consistent with my pragmatist proposal, these examples of research pursue self-referential knowledge acquisition. They no longer aim at social cartography, testing and predicting. Whereas most researchers want to eradicate the subjective, pragmatist-inspired research intentionally confronts us with ourselves, with our preconceptions and values. This type of research helps us explore our blind spot, those issues that are hidden to us. It enables us to develop a critique of society but of a particular kind. It is possible to distinguish between three types of critique – which I call the 'descriptive', 'normative' and 'reflexive' critique – and it is the latter that this pragmatist proposal pursues. A descriptive type of critique aims to establish the cognitive validity of a proposition or set of propositions. Empirical research in both the social and natural sciences can provide a critique of this kind. A normative type of critique aims to present a normative yardstick against which the current constellation is judged. Social and political theory can help us to construct such an algorithm, ranging from Marx's utopian vision to Habermas' ideal speech situation. Reflexive critique seeks neither to establish a falsehood, nor a yardstick. It enables us to reassess ourselves and take a broader perspective so that we become aware of the cultural specificity of our values, beliefs and sentiments.

Unlike descriptive critique (tied to empirical research) and normative critique (linked with theory), reflexive critique does not attribute priority to either empirical research or theory. The boundaries between theory and empirical research have become fluid, with a constant flow of exchange between the two. We acknowledge that our experiences are always mediated by a set of presuppositions, but we see the former as an opportunity to reassess the latter.

Such an inter-play between theory and empirical research would also help to counteract the empire building and conceptual solipsism that accompanies so much of contemporary theory formation. No longer tied to their orthodoxy, researchers would be more willing to listen and learn from the experiences of others. As such, the dialogical model between theory and research would, ironically, facilitate another conversation: that between researchers.

References

Archer, M. (1995) *Realist Social Theory: the Morphogenetic Approch*, Cambridge: Cambridge University Press.

Archer, M. (1996) *Culture and Agency: The Place of Culture in Social Theory*, Cambridge: Cambridge University Press.

Baert, P. (1998a) *Social Theory in the Twentieth Century*, Cambridge: Polity Press.

Baert, P. (1998b) 'Foucault's History of the Present as Self-Referential Knowledge Acquisition', *Philosophy and Social Criticism*, 24(6): 111–126.

Baert, P. (2005) *Philosophy of the Social Sciences: Towards Pragmatism*, Cambridge: Polity Press.

Barnes, B., Bloor, D. and Henry, J. (1996) *Scientific Knowledge: A Sociological Analysis*, London: Athlone.

Bauman, Z. (1989) *Modernity and the Holocaust*, Cambridge: Polity Press.

Bernstein, R. J. (1991) *The New Constellation: The Ethical-Political Horizons of Modernity/Postmodernity*, Cambridge: Polity Press.

Bhaskar, R. (1998) *The Possibility of Naturalism: A Philosophical Critique of the Contemporary Human Sciences*, 3rd edition, London: Routledge.

Clifford, J. and Marcus, G. E. (eds) (1986) *Writing Culture: The Poetics and the Politics of Ethnography*, Berkeley: University of California Press.

Dahlgren, P. (1995) *Television and the Public Sphere: Citizenship, Democracy and the Media*, London: Sage.

Denzin, N. (1992) *Symbolic Interactionism and Cultural Studies: The Politics of Interpretation*, Oxford: Blackwell.

Dewey, J. (1930) *The Quest for Certainty: A Study of the Relation of Knowledge and Action*, New York: Minton, Balch.

Dupré, J. (1993) *The Disorder of Things: Metaphysical Foundations of the Disunity of Science*, Cambridge, MA: Harvard University Press.

Feyerabend, P. (1975) *Against Method: Outline of an Anarchistic Theory of Knowledge*, London: Humanities Press.

Foucault, M. (1977 [1975]) *Discipline and Punish: The Birth of the Prison*, London: Allen Lane.

Gadamer, H. G. (1979 [1965]) *Truth and Method*, 2nd edition, London: Sheed & Ward.

Gell, A. (1998) *Art and Agency: An Anthropological Theory*, Oxford: Oxford University Press.

Giddens, A. (1984) *The Constitution of Society: Outline of the Theory of Structuration*, Cambridge: Polity Press.

Habermas, J. (1989 [1962]) *Structural Transformation of the Public Sphere: An Inquiry into a Category of Bourgeois Society*, Cambridge: Polity Press.

Habermas, J. (1991 [1976]) *Knowledge and Human Interests*, Cambridge: Polity Press.

Hempel, G. (1965) *Aspects of Scientific Explanation, and Other Essays in the Philosophy of Science*, New York: Free Press.

Hodder, I. (1991) *Reading the Past*, 2nd edition, Cambridge: Cambridge University Press.

Hooper, C. (2000) *Manly States: Masculinities, International Relations, and Gender Politics*, New York: Columbia University Press.

Joas, H. (1993) *Pragmatism and Social Theory*, Chicago: University of Chicago Press.

Kuhn, T. (1970) *The Structure of Scientific Revolutions*, 2nd edition, Chicago: University of Chicago Press.

Lakatos, I. (1970) 'Falsification and the Methodology of Scientific Research', in I. Lakatos and A. Musgrave (eds) *Criticism and the Growth of Knowledge*, Cambridge: Cambridge University Press: 91–196.

Landes, J. (1988) *Women and the Public Sphere in the Age of the French Revolution*, Ithaca: Cornell University Press.

Latour, B. (1987) *Science in Action*, Milton Keynes: Open University Press.

Latour, B. (1993) *We Have Never Been Modern*, London: Harvester Wheatsheaf.

Law, J. and Hassard, J. (eds) (1999) *Actor Network Theory, and After*, Oxford: Blackwell.

Lawson, T. (1997) *Economics and Reality*, London: Routledge.

Lawson, T. (2003) *Reorienting Economics*, London: Routledge.

Layder, D. (1993) *New Strategies in Social Research: an Introduction and Guide*, Cambridge: Polity Press.

Lévi-Strauss, C. (1972 [1958]) *Structural Anthropology*, Volume 1, Harmondsworth: Penguin.

Lévi-Strauss, C. (1978 [1973]) *Structural Anthropology*, Volume 2, Harmondsworth: Penguin.

Lewis, J. (1976) 'The Classical American Pragmatists as Forerunners to Symbolic Interactionism', *Sociological Quarterly*, 17 (Summer): 347–359.

Marcus, G. E. and Fischer, M. J. (1999) *Anthropology as a Cultural Critique*, 2nd edition, Chicago: University of Chicago Press.

Marsh, D., Buller, J., Hay, C., Johnston, J., Kerr, P., McAnulla, S. and Watson, M. (1999) *Postwar British Politics in Perspective*, Cambridge: Polity Press.

McDowell, L. (1999) *Gender, Identity and Place: Understanding Feminist Geographies*, Cambridge: Polity.

McDowell, L. and Sharp, J. P. (eds) (1999) *A Feminist Glossary of Human Geography*, London: Arnold.

Merton, R. K. (1968) *Social Theory and Social Structure*, Enlarged edition, New York: Free Press.

Nietzsche, F. (1967 [1886]) *Beyond Good and Evil: Prelude to a Philosophy of the Future*, London: George Allen & Unwin.

Orwell, G. (1950 [1946]) 'Politics and the English Language', in G. Orwell (1950) *Shooting an Elephant, and Other Essays*, London: Secker & Warburg: 84–102.

Petras, J. W. (1968) 'John Dewey and the Rise of Interactionism in American Social Theory', *Journal of the History of the Behavioural Sciences*, 2 (April): 132–142.

Popper, K. (1959 [1934]) *The Logic of Scientific Discovery*, London: Hutchinson & Co.

Popper, K. (1991a [1963]) *Conjectures and Refutations*, London: Routledge.

Popper, K. (1991b [1957]) *The Poverty of Historicism*, London: Routledge.

Price, M. (1995) *Television: The Public Sphere and National Identity*, Oxford: Clarendon Press.

Rock, P. (1979) *The Making of Symbolic Interactionism*, Aldershot: Elgar.

Rorty, R. (1980) *Philosophy and the Mirror of Nature*, Oxford: Blackwell.

Rorty, R. (1982) *Consequences of Pragmatism*, New York: University of Minnesota Press.

Rorty, R. (1991) *Philosophical Papers Volume 1: Objectivity, Relativism, and Truth*, Cambridge: Cambridge University Press.

Sennett, R. (1998) *The Corrosion of Character: The Personal Consequences of Work in the New Capitalism*, New York: Norton.

Shanks, M. and Hodder, I. (1998) 'Processual, Postprocessual and Interpretative Archaeologies', in D. S. Whitley (ed.) *Reader in Archaeological Theory*, London: Routledge: 69–98.

Solkin, D. H. (1993) *Painting for Money: The Visual Arts and the Public Sphere in Eighteenth Century England*, New Haven: Yale University Press.

Sontag, S. (1966 [1964]) 'Against Interpretation', in S. Sontag (1966) *Against Interpretation, and Other Essays*, New York: Farrar, Strauss & Giroux: 3–14.

Siltanen, J. and Stanworth, M. (eds) (1984) *Women and the Public Sphere: A Critique of Sociology and Politics*, London: Hutchinson.

Tickner, A. (1992) *Gender in International Relations: Feminist Perspectives on Achieving Global Security*, New York: Columbia University Press.

Tilley, C. (1998) 'Archaeology as Socio-Political Action in the Present', in D. S. Whitley (ed.) *Reader in Archaeological Theory*, London: Routledge: 315–330.

3

Social theory and political philosophy

Peter Wagner

The social sciences inherited from political philosophy their most basic questions. This observation is the starting-point for Luc Boltanski and Laurent Thévenot in *De la justification* (1991: 39) who show that the most clear-cut theoretical approaches in the social sciences – such as the ontological holism in much of sociology and the individualism in economics – should be read as opposed to social metaphysics that are unable to understand the superior principle that they share. Trying to find theoretical reason for assuming that agreement between human beings is possible, both of these approaches presuppose one ground for such agreement – 'collective identity or the market value' (44) – at the expense, though, of losing the understanding of how one form of agreement rather than another emerges. Boltanski and Thévenot call this operation a 'reduction of political metaphysics in the social sciences' (43) and their book is devoted to the 'unconcealing of the underlying political metaphysics'. This operation, however 'is made very difficult because of the rupture with philosophy through which both economics and sociology constituted themselves as scientific disciplines. . . . Both have been born from political philosophies that have served as their matrices and in which the metaphysics are visible' (44).[1]

The reconstruction of those metaphysics that lie behind social-science reasoning, as performed in *De la justification*, has enabled the shift of perspective that has generated the research programme of the group around Boltanski and Thévenot that is discussed elsewhere (Wagner 1999; Wagner 2004). The repertoires of moral-political evaluation that human beings employ in situations in need of justification are practical political philosophies that are derived from the canonized approaches to political theory. Thus, normative political philosophy is indeed empirically found in social life, and this form of reasoning emerges, as is appropriate for the political, whenever there is a search for 'the ground of an agreement', i.e. when a consensus about the interpretation of a situation is to be reached.

While this programme is one of the most important intellectual events in the social and political sciences over the past two decades (see also the discussion in Chapter 6 by Frédéric Vandenberghe), it does not answer all the questions that it raises. Among the criticism it faced, one major accusation held that the approach ultimately favours a return of the political, even though in a particular way, and the neglect of, or the emptying out of, the social. While not doing justice to the work of the group, such reproach nevertheless points to the persistence of the divide between the political and the social, which opened with the rise of the social sciences and cannot easily be undone. In the light of this observation, it remains important to ask what precisely was the nature of that 'rupture with philosophy' that gave birth to the social sciences, what brought it about, and what are its consequences?

Far from giving exhaustive answers to any of these questions, this essay will merely claim that these are important questions to be raised and, possibly, also indicate some directions in which answers may be found. To fully grasp the issues at stake in contemporary social theory, it will need to proceed through a brief historical reconstruction of the way in which the social was separated from the political, and gradually took over the role of the political. The separation of social theory from political philosophy, as diagnosed by Boltanski and Thévenot, is often seen as coinciding with the decline of political philosophy. If this were so, though, then it would be more appropriate to say that the social sciences are a way of solving political issues by other means than philosophy – since political issues will not go away. At a closer look, indeed what happened was not the disappearance of political philosophy, but the alignment of a certain form of political theory, with individualist liberalism at its core, with a rather technocratic understanding of social science. Such a combination of genres reigned over the socio-political world during much of the second post-war period. If there are signs today that the end of that reign is reached, it is high time to understand its mode of governance.

The emergence of the social from within the political

From its origins in ancient Greece, the term 'political' refers to that which (any collectivity of) human beings deal with in common, or to their activity of dealing with certain matters in common. The term 'social' – and its correlates in other European languages – refers, in turn, to the connectedness of a human being to others. We could say that it enables us to talk about situations in which human beings create relations to one another. Logically, it seems, the social should include the political. Not always when human beings relate to one another do they do so with a view to dealing with common matters. Whenever they deal with common matters, though, they need to relate to one another.[2] Rather than merely marking a difference between forms of human relations, though, the rise of social theory from the late eighteenth-century onwards offered a particular interpretation of that difference. A very specific way of talking about connections between human beings, namely, was introduced with the term 'society'; and as a result the term 'social sciences' emerged in the eighteenth-century ever more strongly to gradually replace, or at least diminish the centrality of, terms such as 'moral and political sciences' or 'state sciences'.

The career of the term 'society' went through several phases. Initially, it had no direct political meaning. A 'society' was a voluntary association of human beings that came together for a purpose (Heilbron 1995: 87). Gradually, however, it came to be used in the moral and political sciences, in particular within French and Scottish debates, and it acquired the place of the denomination for the key object of socio-political life there. In combinations such as 'political society' and 'civil society', it referred to nothing else but the state, but from a point of view of contract theory, namely as the aggregation of human beings that have come together for a purpose, implying now that all human beings on a given territory agreed on the purpose, unlike in the earlier 'private' meaning of 'society'. Thus, it retained its original meaning, but was now employed, by way of analogy or counterfactual hypothesis, to explain the emergence of a polity of human beings under conditions of equal liberty. Clearly, a 'social' term was here used for 'political' matters: the bond between those beings was political;

they only linked up to each other because of a common need or purpose. However, it was also a specific way of thinking the political. In the hypothetical state of nature, i.e. 'before' the formation of the contract, politics does not exist, in this view. Such thinking was alien to ancient political thought, in which the human being was a *zoon politikon*, or in other words, in which the question of handling things in common was a constitutive *problématique* of human life. In contract theory, in contrast, based on modernist individualism, the human being was first thought as a being without political bond. It is only the unpredictable or even outright conflict-prone nature of their social relations that made humans create a political bond.[3]

From such a derivation of the political from the social in individualist theorizing, the next step in conceptual development was a novel form of separating the social from the political, from the late eighteenth-century onwards. 'Society' came now to be seen as a phenomenon that was different from the polity, even though it remained articulated with the polity. The idea of 'society' as a *sui generis* reality between the polity and the individuals (or households) continued to suggest, along the lines of the earlier conceptual innovation, that there were social bonds between human beings that were different from their political bonds. In most versions of nineteenth-century social theory, however, the character and extension of the social bond was conceptualized in such a way that it could sustain the political bond (Wagner 2001). Thus, the social was used to solve the problem of the political, a problem that had become intractable, as I will argue later, under conditions of individual liberty. This kind of thinking continues its grip on our ways of conceptualizing the political. The idea of a 'social substrate' necessarily underlying any viable polity, for instance, is used to analyse the relation between the European democratic nation-states and the emerging European polity (e.g. Offe 1998). True, in some versions, most prominently the Marxian one, it was precisely the tension between the structure of the social bond and the structure of the political bond that provided the moving force for social change. Such thinking, though, rather than providing an alternative, merely inverts the idea that a certain structure of social bonds is required to sustain a polity.

The social bond was conceptually separated from the political one only to be reconnected to it in the next conceptual step.[4] The *separation* was necessary, in the first instance, to underpin an individualist conception of freedom; the *reconnection* was necessary to link freedom to predictability. Even given complete autonomy, so the reasoning of the social sciences goes, human beings would reveal themselves driven by a limited number of intelligible inclinations. And this linkage of freedom and predictability became particularly important at the historical moment when the externally imposed barriers to free deliberation threatened to be removed; the moment of the American and French Revolutions.

The moment of the revolution

These revolutions gave institutional expression to the political aspect of a broader culture of individual autonomy that is a key element of modernity. In this sense, much of this era can be seen as a liberation of human beings from imposed ties, but this liberation was far from unproblematic. As Claude Lefort (1986: 214–215) once described this feature of modernity: 'When he is defined as independent, the individual does not exchange ... one certainty against another one. ... The new mode of existence of the individual within the horizons of democracy does not merely emerge as the promise to control one's own destiny, but also and not less as the dispossession of the assurance as to one's identity – of the assurance which once appeared to be provided by one's place, by one's social condition, or by the possibility of attaching oneself to a legitimate authority.' Liberation is here interpreted as an increase of contingency and uncertainty in the lives of human beings.

If this view were unequivocally valid, one should expect a philosophy of contingency – in Richard Rorty's style (1989), for instance – linked to a liberal-individualist political theory to dominate the intellectual scene forever after the successful revolutions.[5] However, historically this was not at all the case. In contrast, 'the historical moment, about which we speak, emerges in such a way that the real rising of the political instance entails its theoretical abatement' (Manent 1994: 123). Instead, the historical moment of liberty coincided with the rise of social theory. 'Society' as the object of the social sciences has been a 'post-revolutionary discovery'; or, to put it even more succinctly, 'the sociological point of view constitutes itself in the moment when the notion of liberty becomes the principal articulation of the human world' (Manent 1994: 75 and 113).[6] Such apparent paradox reveals the aporia of political thought after liberation. Very generally speaking, social theory was exactly a part of the response human beings gave to their new condition of – self-incurred, one might say – contingency and principled uncertainty. Being unable to rely any longer on externally defined certainties, socio-political thinkers started searching for regularities and continuities which exist without being commanded, or even at all created. Social theory has been a means to decrease contingency.

The problem of post-revolutionary liberty

One can understand such intellectual shift by means of a look at the deep shock the revolutions meant to social and political thought (Wagner 1998). In a first step, somewhat schematically described, the experience demanded the substitution of the republican concept of liberty for a liberal one.[7] In the Hobbes-Lockean lineage, liberals define liberty as non-interference. The state, founded by free contract, dominates over the individuals, but it interferes with their liberties only to the degree required for the maintenance of order. The liberal tradition needs to draw a strong boundary between the public and the private; whatever social bonds exist in the latter, they will not impact on the former, the form of which is determined by reason. Since non-interference of the public into the private is the supreme principle, this thinking can only have a 'thin', a-social concept of membership in a polity. In contrast, republicans define liberty as non-domination. Drawing via Machiavelli on Roman (and Greek) political thought, non-domination is conceptualized in stronger terms than non-interference; it requires security against interference. Such security stems at least in part from the ways in which citizens relate to each other, in other words: from their social bonds, so that there is a less sharp divide between the private and the public and a 'thicker' concept of membership than in liberalism (see Pettit 1997; Skinner 1998, for recent accounts).

Among historians of political thought today, there is broad – maybe even too broad, but this is not the space for further discussion – agreement that republicanism was by and large abandoned around the turn of the eighteenth-century, and liberalism, though it neither appeared particularly powerful nor coherent before, very soon emerged as the pivotal political theory in post-revolutionary polities. Despite being inspired by republican thinking, the revolutions aimed at combining two objectives that proved to be practically impossible to hold together. On the one hand, they aimed at transforming state sovereignty in the hands of the monarch into popular sovereignty, i.e. they worked with extended notions of citizenship and liberty. On the other hand, they held such a transformation of the polity to be conceivable only in the form of the existing territorial state and within its dimensions.

Such double transformation entailed, first, that the existing social bonds between the people, tainted with the suspicion of domination and privilege characteristic of feudal society, had to be weakened or abolished. Thus, however, a major available resource for a substantive, 'thick' grounding of a modern republic was rejected. Second, the idea of extending political rights widely cast doubts on the viability of a demanding, socially rich concept of liberty such as the one upheld in the republican tradition. Caution seemed to demand, not least for some more conservative observers, limiting the substance of the concept of liberty at the moment at which its reach was extended. As a consequence, the public realm, the polity, was robbed of most of its 'social' substance and the formal process through which common deliberations were reached was emphasized instead. The adoption of some kind of such a proceduralist, individualist liberalism is the main reason why the tradition of political philosophy declined. With the renunciation of any substantive, social foundation of the polity and 'a total grounding of government in self-interest and consent' (Wood 1998 [1969]: 614 and 612, about the founding of the USA), the conclusion seemed undeniable that, once the reasonable will of the human beings had been cast into institutions, the political order must be seen as intrinsically satisfactory (Manent 1994: 228–9).

The rise of social theory

Not everybody, though, was convinced that such solution was viable, in particular in Europe where the revolution towards self-determination seemed to be intrinsically connected to the possibility of terror. 'The effect of liberty to individuals is, that they may do what they please: We ought to see what it will please them to do, before we risk congratulations', as Edmund Burke (1993 [1790]: 8–9) famously put it in his reflections on the French Revolution. While individualist liberalism may be seen as providing the ('negative') concept of liberty as non-interference that may live up to Burke's requirements under the proviso that the state is capable of maintaining order for and above the individuals, there is another way out of the aporia of liberty, namely the attempt to arrive at knowing 'what it will please them to do' by other means. The American and French revolutions, thus, strongly suggested to study what held human beings together, how they would actually organize their lives – individually, in 'associations' (Alexis de Tocqueville) or 'social movements' (Lorenz von Stein), and in the polity and the 'nation' – and what kinds of regularities and orders could be expected, if people were permitted to do so on their own, without imposed restrictions. This is a new search for social bonds, which is simultaneously one major root of social theory and a politically motivated search.

It soon emerged that there was a variety of ways to conceptually determine 'what it will please them to do', and this variety forms precisely the social metaphysics that Boltanski and Thévenot chose as the starting-point for their reconstruction of practical political philosophy. Some strategies start out directly from the assumptions of individualist liberalism. The rights-endowed individual became in such views the only conceivable ontological as well as the methodological foundation of a science of political matters after the revolutions. Once the rights of man had been generally accepted as self-evident and unalienable, it seemed obvious, to Turgot and Condorcet for instance, that they were also 'the logical foundation of the science of society' (Baker 1975: 218). In rights-based liberalism, the individual is the only category that need not, often in fact – cannot, be debated.

Once this assumption was accepted, basically two avenues of constructing a science of the political had opened. Both these forms of theorizing connect modernist political philosophy, i.e. individualist liberalism, to a science of the political.[8] One possibility was to try to identify by theoretical reasoning the basic features of this unit of analysis, the individual human being, and its actions. Since this unit was conceived as an ontological starting-point, devoid of all specific, historical and social, ties to the world, its characterization was to proceed from some inherent features. From earlier debates, those features had often been conceived as twofold, as passions and as interests. In the late Enlightenment context, the rational side of this dichotomy was regarded as the one amenable to systematic reasoning. It thus allowed the building of a scientific approach to the study of at least one aspect of human activity, namely the production and distribution of material wealth.[9] This approach inaugurated the tradition of *political economy*, later to be transformed into *neo-classical economics* and, still later, into *rational choice theory*. The moral and political philosophy of the early modern period split into a political theory based on the idea of the social contract and a rationalized moral theory based on the idea of exchange. In both cases, the individual is the starting-point and unit of the analysis.

While political economy was based on a highly abstract, but for the same reasons extremely powerful, assumption of human rationality, the other conclusion from the individualist foundational principle was much more cautious. Avoiding any substantive assumptions on the driving forces in human beings at all, the statistical approach, often under the label of *political arithmetic*, resorted to the collection of numerically treatable information about human behaviour. The space of substantive presuppositions was radically emptied in this thinking, but the methodological confidence in mathematics increased in inverse proportion (Desrosières 1993).

Thus, two strands of political thought that had been proposed and elaborated for some time rose to new and greater prominence, political economy and political arithmetic. The denominations these approaches were known by in the late eighteenth-century referred explicitly to political matters. Both were to lose these attributes in the nineteenth-century when they had consolidated their ways of proceeding and when the application of these cognitive forms had established predominance over political deliberation in decision on common matters, at least in the view of many economists and statisticians. Mostly, this terminological change has been interpreted as an autonomization of cognitive approaches and as a differentiation of the sciences into disciplines. However, it is not exactly appropriate to say that *economics* and *statistics* separated from politics. Once the approaches of the former two are accepted as comprehensively valid, there is nothing political left to study. The common just emerges from assumptions about rationality or from aggregation.

The acceptance of the economic and the statistic ways of conceiving of the social world did not go without criticism; and they were never accepted as the only possible ways anywhere. However, the critiques and alternatives that were proposed most often accepted the fundamental change in political reasoning after the construction of a polity based on the assumption of free individuals.[10] After such a polity had begun to come into existence, new problems were identified. These were now essentially liberal problems; they resulted, one might say, from the observation that not everything that was needed for organizing a liberal polity could indeed be derived from an 'original position' (John Rawls 1971). Two main types of problems may be distinguished by reference to the hypothetical original position in which individuals meet under a veil of ignorance.

On the one hand, the range of conclusions that could be drawn from the assumption of free and equal individuals was too limited. These individuals' relations were structured by the existence of politically important 'pre-political' social facts, of orientations and links between human beings that were seen to already exist before individuals entered into political communication and deliberation. On the other hand, the working of the liberal rules would themselves produce new kinds of social relations, 'post-political' relations, which would have a structuring impact on the polity in turn.

Attempts to theorize 'pre-political' relations all start out from the critical observation that the human being who enters into political relations is not such a kind of individual as liberal political theory described it, and that the hypothesis of any original position would lead to serious flaws in the conclusions. This thinking emphasizes the rootedness of the singular human beings in *contexts* from which their ways of giving meaning to the world stem. The broadest intellectual movement of this kind has been the *cultural-linguistic theory* of the boundaries of the polity, which inaugurated culturalist thinking in social theory and also became one source of later nationalism. However, the contexts need not necessarily be defined in collectivistic terms; two major alternatives have been developed across the past two centuries. They can also be conceptualized as modes of *intersubjectivity* emerging from an idea of primary sociality and of interaction, such as in the early works by Hegel (see, e.g. Honneth 1992; Joas 1992), or they can start out from an original condition of being-in-the-world and of being-with, as developed by Martin Heidegger and his followers (see, e.g. Nancy 1986; 2001). In both cases, though such alternative assumptions do not lead as directly to ideas about the form of the polity as collectivistic theories do.

The other main line of post-revolutionary social thought started out from the insights, first, that the basic liberal assumptions, once they were cast into effective rules, would have durable and important *effects* on what social theorists would soon call the 'structure' of social relations. In this sense we can refer to those relations as being conceived as 'post-political'. And second, the question of such relations was forced on to the agenda of social and political thought by the fact that the liberal assumptions on their own did not suffice to create and justify a political order. The observation of structures of representation was used to enhance stability and certainty in political procedures that otherwise could appear to be opened to all contingencies by the abolition of any legitimacy of preordained orders. There are then again two main strategies for rediscovering certainties, systematic observation and reflective conceptualization. These two intellectual responses to the political *problématique* inaugurate two further modes of social theorizing, the *behavioural* and, based on a social-interest theory of representation, the *structural-functional* one. Unlike economics and statistics, they do not make individualistic assumptions but aim at grounding socio-political life in purely social forms.

The social and the political bond after the rise of social theory

Thus, all basic approaches to social theory can be regarded as ways of dealing with the problem of contingency after the assertion of human freedom. *Theories* of the *social* are proposed to make intelligible the possibilities and probabilities of actions and their consequences in the space of the political that was widely opened at the moment at which it was exclusively the free will of its members that should determine the polity. *Philosophies* of the *political* had long already known what is at stake, and from Greek political thought to Renaissance humanism they had tried to give reasons and means for both accepting the openness of the political and limiting its impact. Working generally with the view that politics is seen as a human activity that by its nature is open, plural and diverse (Arendt 1958), any strong cognitive linkage of free action and predictable outcome was inconceivable. But political philosophy had never before been required to develop its reasoning under the assumption of equal liberty of all members of the polity, and it was under these circumstances that, apparently paradoxically, 'the sociological point of view constitutes itself in the moment when the notion of liberty becomes the principal articulation of the human world', to paraphrase Manent again.

More recently, such social theorizing has come under strong attack, mostly because of its inherent determinism. Orderly outcomes can only result from planned or routine activities, work and labour in Hannah Arendt's terminology, over which certainty can be established before they are started. In contrast, political action in a context of liberty must go along with contingency of outcomes. From an Arendtian viewpoint, thus, social theory establishes an impossible connection. Trying to identify laws and regularities of human action and societal development, social theory necessarily abandoned the heritage of political philosophy, the emphasis on creative agency, irreducible diversity and the permanent possibility of unpredictable beginnings. It is in the light of such considerations that the closing decades of the twentieth century witnessed a revival of political philosophies of freedom, often going beyond concepts of liberty as held in liberal political theory. These works, by authors such as Claude Lefort, Pierre Manent or, more historically oriented, Quentin Skinner, are not merely contributions to political philosophy or its history. Rather, they challenge the very separation of social theory from political philosophy.

As much as the critique of social theory from such a perspective is highly valid, however, the mere return to political philosophy is no solution to the issues that are raised. Many of the contributions to the current debate fail to address the reasons for the historical decline of political philosophy and the concomitant rise of social theory. And those that do, most often conclude on a normative rejection of 'the invention of the social' (Donzelot 1984) because of the implied move towards the 'administration of the social' (Arendt 1958) without, though, fully appreciating the ways in which politics was transformed in response to actually problematic situations rather than merely because of misconceptions of the political. It is on those grounds that this essay needed to reconstruct, even if in all due brevity, the historical shift from the political to the social with a view to the specific conceptions of the political and of the social bond.

In our brief intellectual history, one key observation concerned the centrality of a notion of equal liberty in European (and North American) history of the past two centuries. This notion is closely related to the assumption of 'common humanity' made by Boltanski and Thévenot to identify the common principles of the social metaphysics. We may say that Boltanski and Thévenot only look at 'modern' modes of justification, or that they only draw on the resources of political modernity in their reconstruction. While they do thematize the boundary they thus create, for instance in their discussion of eugenics, they do not reflect on the conceptual relation of that assumption to the modes of justification that are reigned by it. In our reconstruction above, this assumption is seen as being at the core of individualist liberalism, the pivotal theory of political modernity. If it is accepted as in some way inescapable, there are then three ways to deal with this approach.

First, one can take individualist liberalism as self-sufficient for the normative underpinning of 'modern societies'. All one needs to posit is the equal freedom of rights-endowed human beings, and everything else can be left to those human beings' use of the liberties. This is the position to which Burke objected. In the terminology chosen here, it conceives of only a thin political bond between human beings and of no social bond of any interest at all. Second, one can argue that equal liberty is only the starting-point for reasoning about a political modernity that is furthermore characterized by the communicative interaction between human beings with a view to determine what they need to regulate in common and how they should do so. This is the republican position that has largely been found, even while attractive, implausible and unsustainable under conditions of large societies with complex forms of interaction. It works with a strong assumption about political bonds being woven and constantly rewoven in social interaction, but it says little to nothing about the nature of those bonds. Third, one can respond to the desire of knowing more about the bases on which humans interact by observing and conceptualizing their modes of interaction with various auxiliary means. This is the way social theory and the social sciences went, and it has been accused of socially over-determining human life. This approach works with a strong conception of the social bond, or rather: with a variety of such conceptions, and it has largely forgotten about the political question that stood at its origins.

A comprehensive political sociology that reopens the connection between social theory and political philosophy, and that can draw some inspiration from Boltanski and Thévenot's theory of justification, would stand between the second and the third position, while accepting elements of the first as a background. It allows for substantive assumptions, the application of which determines the outcome of interactions and the positions of human beings in society; in this sense it operates in the mode of social theory. But it also holds that the application of such assumptions is itself a possible concern of dispute and interpretation, thus requiring the kind of communicative deliberation that is at the centre of republican political philosophy. There is, thus, a possible theoretical position that integrates again what was separated in the intellectual history of the past two centuries, the conceptualization of the political and of the social. It still needs to be shown, in part contra Boltanski and Thévenot's own claims, that from this position a sociology of entire social configurations can be developed that sustains the concern for political forms. Lacking the space to demonstrate this in detail here, I will just use as an illustration the political history of post-Second World War Europe.[11]

Contemporary modern polities and their need for justification

The reconstitution of polities during this period was marked by a strong emphasis on civic liberty and the rule of law, stronger indeed than during the nineteenth-century and the first half of the twentieth-century. We recognize here the application of individualist liberalism as a normative political philosophy underlying these polities. A closer look, however, will also reveal that the relatively stable West European political orders of the 'thirty glorious years' (Jean Fourastié 2004) were indeed not based on the pure proceduralism of rights-based individualist liberalism. Domestically, as liberal-democratic nation-states with increasingly developed welfare policies, they rather showed signs of a compromise between liberal justifications and both those of a cultural–linguistic and a social-interest based nature. They, thus, combined a rational–individualist, a cultural–linguistic and a structural–functional socio-political theory – in common political terms known as liberalism, nationalism and socialism – into a viable arrangement, which was not theoretically consistent on any terms, but was seen as satisfactory by a large majority of the population, as increasing 'mass loyalty' seemed to demonstrate until the late 1960s. Vaguely aware of the inconsistency of this liberal–cultural–social foundational compromise, furthermore, these polities tied those justifications together by recourse to an empirical science of politics and society, using the tools of behaviourism and statistics, which was to guide the way on a path of wealth and loyalty, the employment of which was never free of technocratic undertones.

Historically existing polities can thus be interpreted as institutionalized compromises of a variety of basic modes of justification. Individualist liberalism provides the background, and also creates the basic *problématique*, against which the other modes of justification are being deployed. It allows the question of the constitution of a polity to be seen as indeed a political one, as the foundation of an agreement under conditions of liberty, but as one that cannot be resolved by the conventional means of political philosophy. Assumptions about the social bond, most importantly the cultural–linguistic one and the structural–functional one, then step in to deal with the *problématique* thus created. They are not just social theories; they support repertoires of justification of immediate political relevance. They may be used to determine, as a matter of principle, whether a human being is rightly a member of a given polity rather than a different one, and what her/his place within that polity is. Finally, these repertoires of justification are not sufficient on their own for such determination. For their use, their concepts need to be transformed into categories of action that allow the precise identification of a singular human being as indeed a 'case' in which the justification may be applied (see Wagner and Zimmermann 2003). This task can be accomplished with the help, most importantly, of law, in direct association with the rights-endowed individual of liberalism, and of statistics, in direct association with the cultural and social modes of reasoning. These tools permit the creation of those devices that can stabilize the complex institutional compromises between modes of justification that characterize contemporary polities.

The comparative study of modern polities from the perspective of such a conjoined social theory and political philosophy would then need to focus on three issues: the analysis of the variety of forms of political modernity on the basis of the observable range of institutionalized combinations of individualist liberalism as the inescapable groundwork of political modernity, with the socially richer interpretations of the human engagement with the world provided by what for want of a better word was just called cultural and social modes of reasoning (see Lamont and Thévenot 2000; Wagner 2005); the study of the 'cultural' variety of modernity in terms of existing combinations of these latter modes of reasoning as basic modes of societal self-understanding or, in Cornelius Castoriadis' terms 'imaginary significations of society'; and the study of the use of modes of justification, with a view to overcoming the antinomy between (political) voluntarism and (social) determinism, as actualizations of the commitment to liberty in situational contexts, or, as Charles Taylor (1975) would put it, as 'situated freedom'.

Notes

1 Translations are my own.
2 For an interpretation of the political discourse of modernity as the attempt to decrease this necessity, by way of 'immunizing' singular human beings, see Esposito (1998).
3 For a retrieval of the emergence of a 'society'-based terminology from an earlier 'politics'-based one, see Hallberg and Wittrock 2006; for a proposal to reweave the connections between the social and the political, see Karagiannis and Wagner 2005.
4 See very similarly Bruno Latour's observations on the separation of the natural and the social in *Nous n'avons jamais été modernes* (1991).
5 As Rorty (1989: 63), in a combination of complacency and lack of historical political knowledge indeed suggests: 'Western social and political thought may have had the last conceptual revolution it needs'; for a reflection on this phrase, see Gander (1999).
6 See Therborn (1976), for an earlier – Althusser-inspired – analysis of the emergence of sociology 'between two revolutions'.
7 For a detailed reconstruction of republican political thought in Europe now see van Gelderen and Skinner (2002).
8 They are versions of 'social theory' in our current understanding of the term, even though their view of the social is extremely thin, or maybe more precisely: their substantive interest in the social is very limited; the outcome of interaction is in the centre of interest.

9 As Albert Hirschman (1977) has shown, this reasoning also suggested a transformation of social configurations towards an ever-increasing importance of the 'commercial bond' at the expense of other forms of social bond.

10 Since nineteenth-century polities all worked with restrictions that are incompatible with a fully-fledged individualist liberalism, one should say more precisely that such a polity was put on the horizon of political debate through the revolutions, rather than made actual in institutional form.

11 One basic assumption that enables this step to be taken is the following: Under conditions of political modernity, the rules of political life are always in need of justification, or more broadly: they can be exposed to the requirement of justification.

References

Arendt, H. (1958) *The Human Condition*, Chicago: The University of Chicago Press.

Baker, K. M. (1975) *Condorcet: From Natural Philosophy to Social Mathematics*, Chicago: The University of Chicago Press.

Boltanski, L. and Thévenot, L. (1991) *De la justification*, Paris: Gallimard.

Burke, E. (1993 [1790]) *Reflections on the Revolution in France*, Oxford: Oxford University Press (ed. L. G. Mitchell).

Desrosières, A. (1993) *La politique des grands nombres: Histoire de la raison statistique*, Paris: La découverte. (Engl. tr. *The politics of large numbers. A history of statistical reasoning*, Cambridge, MA: Harvard University Press, 1998)

Donzelot, J. (1984) *L'invention du social: Essai sur le déclin des passions politiques*, Paris: Fayard.

Esposito, R. (1998) *Communitas: Origine destino della comunità*, Turin: Einaudi (French trans. 2002).

Fourastié, J. and Cohen, D. (2004) *Les Trente Glorieuses ou la Révolution invisible de 1946 à 1975*, Paris: Hachette Littératures, p. 288.

Gander, E. (1999) *The Last Conceptual Revolution: A critique of Richard Rorty's political philosophy*, Albany: SUNY Press.

Hallberg, P. and Wittrock, B. (2006) 'From koinonía politiké to societas civilis', in P. Wagner (ed.) *The Languages of Civil Society*, Oxford: Berghahn, forthcoming.

Heilbron, J. (1995) *The Rise of Social Theory*, Cambridge: Polity.

Hirschman, A. (1977) *The Passions and the Interests: Arguments for capitalism before its triumph*, Princeton: Princeton University Press.

Honneth, A. (1992) *Kampf um Anerkennung*, Frankfurt/M: Suhrkamp. (Engl. tr. *The struggle for recognition*, Cambridge: Polity Press, 1995).

Joas, H. (1992) *Die Kreativität des Handelns*, Frankfurt/M: Suhrkamp. (Engl. tr. *Creativity of action*, Cambridge: Polity Press, 1996).

Karagiannis, N. and Wagner, P. (2005) 'Towards a theory of synagonism', in *The Journal of Political Philosophy*, 13(1): 232–265.

Lamont, M. and L. Thévenot (eds) (2000) *Rethinking Comparative Cultural Sociology*, Cambridge: Cambridge University Press.

Latour, B. (1991) *Nous n'avons jamais étés modernes*, Paris: La découverte. (Engl. tr. *We have never been modern*, London: Harvester Wheatsheaf, 1993).

Lefort, C. (1986) 'Réversibilité: Liberté politique et liberté de l'individu', in *Essais sur le politique. XIXe-XXe siècles*, Paris: Seuil: 197–216. (Engl. tr. *Democracy and political theory*, Cambridge: Polity, 1988).

Manent, P. (1994) *La cité de l'homme*, Paris, Fayard. (Engl. tr. *The city of man*, Princeton: Princeton University Press, 1998).

Nancy, J-L. (1986) *La communauté désoeuvrée*, Paris: Bourgois. (Engl. tr. *The inoperative community*, Minneapolis: The University of Minnesota Press, 1991).

Nancy, J.-L. (2001) *La communauté affrontée*, Paris: Galilée.

Offe, C. (1998) 'Demokratie und Wohlfahrtsstaat: Eine europäische Regimeform unter dem Streß der europäischen Integration', in W. Streeck (ed.) *Internationale Wirtschaft, nationale Demokratie*, Frankfurt/M: Campus: 99-136.

Pettit, P. (1997) *Republicanism: A theory of freedom and government*, Oxford: Clarendon.

Rawls, J. (1971) *A Theory of Justice*, Cambridge, MA: Harvard University Press.

Rorty, R. (1989) *Contingency, Irony, Solidarity*, Cambridge: Cambridge University Press.

Skinner, Q. (1998) *Liberty Before Liberalism*, Cambridge: Cambridge University Press.

Taylor, C. (1975) *Hegel*, Cambridge: Cambridge University Press.

Therborn, G. (1976) *Science, Class and Society: On the formation of sociology and historical materialism*, London: New Left Books.

Van Gelderen, M. and Q. Skinner (eds) (2002) *Republicanism: A shared European heritage*, Cambridge: Cambridge University Press (2 volumes).

Wagner, P. (1998) 'Certainty and order, liberty and contingency; the birth of social science as empirical political philosophy' in J. Heilbron, L. Magnusson and B. Wittrock (eds) *The rise of the social sciences and the formation of modernity*, Dordrecht: Kluwer: 241–263.

Wagner, P. (1999) 'After *Justification*: Repertoires of evaluation and the sociology of modernity', in *European Journal of Social Theory*, 2(3), 341–357.

Wagner, P. (2001) *A History and Theory of the Social Sciences*, London: Sage.

Wagner, P. (2004) 'Soziologie der kritischen Urteilskraft und der Rechtfertigung: Die Politik- und Moralsoziologie um Luc Boltanski und Laurent Thévenot', in S. Moebius and L. Peter, *Französische Soziologie heute*, Konstanz: UVK/UTB, pp. 417–448.

Wagner, P. (2005) 'The political form of Europe: Europe as a political form', in *Thesis Eleven*, no. 80, February, pp. 47–73.

Wagner, P. and B. Zimmermann (2003) 'Nation: Die Konstitution einer politischen Ordnung als Verantwortungsgemeinschaft', in S. Lessenich (ed.) *Semantiken des Wohlfahrtsstaats*, Frankfurt/M.: Campus, pp. 243–266.

Wood G. S. (1998 [1969]) *The Creation of the American Republic 1776–1787*, Durham: University of North Carolina Press.

4

Social theory and theology

Austin Harrington

A consensus prevails among political theorists today about the salience of the theological dimensions and roots of such basic concepts of modern political thought as 'rights', 'representation', 'sovereignty' and 'equality before the law'.[1] Yet in the neighbouring field of *social* or *sociological* theory, rather less attention has been accorded to theological genealogies in recent decades. This neglect is surprising in view of some obvious areas of commonality between the two fields. While social theorists typically differ from political theorists in their concern with structures and dynamics of group behaviour rather than with more normative questions of obligation to sovereign powers, social theory's load of normative historical baggage is not fundamentally any different from that of political theory. If we can accept that the first modern thinkers of society were for the most part legal-political thinkers and that 'social' or 'sociological' thinking in the narrower sense only arrived somewhat later by way of a transformation in the mediating field of eighteenth- and nineteenth-century political economy, we should also accept that social theory evinces a genealogical relationship to theology of some kind.

Theological themes unquestionably mattered to the classical early twentieth-century social theorists, especially to German thinkers such as Max Weber, Ernst Troeltsch, Karl Jaspers, Alfred Weber, Karl Mannheim and Max Scheler. These writers were obsessed with the kinds of agonising metaphysical problems of disintegrating ultimate ethical value-schemes raised by the novels of Tolstoy and Dostoyevsky and by the theme of Faust's compact with the Devil, from Goethe to Thomas Mann. The early to middle decades of the century also saw an extraordinary wave of theologically informed engagements in social thought among Jewish exile intellectuals influenced by phenomenological and existentialist philosophy and by Hegelian Marxism. Among the most notable were Franz Rosenzweig, Martin Buber, Walter Benjamin, Gershom Scholem, Ernst Bloch, Theodor Adorno, Max Horkheimer, Hermann Broch, Karl Löwith and Hans Blumenberg, as well as Strauss, Voegelin and Arendt. But in the later twentieth century, much of the *élan* of this thinking appeared to slip out of the hands of scholars in the social sciences. In the 1970s and 1980s much of the impetus fell to the Latin American liberation theologians, taking their cue partly from earlier anti-fascist Christian intellectuals in Europe such as Bonhoeffer in Germany or Pasolini in Italy.

Only in very recent years have theological themes begun return to the forefront of the attention of social theorists. Heated controversies in the public sphere about the scope and limits of secularism in public policy have forced on to the table some thoroughgoing debates about the status of the Judaeo-Christian origins of modern Western universal validity-claims. Notable contributions have come from leading political philosophers such as Habermas (2001, 2002, 2004) and Charles Taylor (2002, 2004), from French phenomenological philosophers such as Marion (1991) and Janicaud (2000), from an array of German sociological scholars, philosophers and theologians such as Joas (1997, 2004), Theunissen (1991) and Graf (2004), from some leftist theorists such as Zizek (2000, 2003), Badiou (1997), Debray (2004) and Bhaskar (2002a, 2002b), and from scholars of non-Western ancient civilisations and cosmologies such as Assmann (1986) and Eisenstadt (2002) – to mention only a few authors. Particularly indicative of the times have been Habermas's statements since 11 September 2001 on the urgency of theological self-questioning in political philosophy, notwithstanding his own strict commitment to 'methodological atheism', in the spirit of the 'religiously unmusical' Max Weber.[2]

This essay surveys these developments by first identifying three broad frameworks of contemporary thinking about theology and social theory. These are labelled as:

1 'postmodernism';
2 'globalisation'; and
3 philosophical 'anti-Eurocentrism'.

The middle part of the essay draws together a range of epistemological issues about the relationship between theology and sociology. The final part concludes by distinguishing and evaluating five major types of argument about theology in social theory.

'Postmodernism' raises theological problems for social theory insofar as it thematises questions about the legitimacy of scientific reason as a modernist secular project. Scepticism about projects of autonomous rational inquiry highlight the hubris of ideas of enlightened emancipation from particularistic dogmas, traditions, creeds and authorities. Bacon's ban on 'idols of the mind' or Kant's 'courage in the use of one's own reason' 'without dependence on an other' suggest a will to banish certain styles of feeling, sensing, experiencing and cognising as alien to our idea of grounded knowledge. Theology in this sense appears to subtend modernising processes insofar as it systematises experience around a unified transcendental signifier but is at the same time expelled from the modern scientific imaginary to a realm of mythos. Alongside allegory, metaphor, parable and figuration, the theological appears to stand on the side of the occluded Other of a 'logocentric' order that is intolerant of all equivocation of sense.

For many postmodernist commentators, refusal of such binarism consists in imagining how Nietzsche's 'death of God' might imply a certain presence of the theological in its absence, in the secular 'traces' of its being (Blond 1997; Taylor 1984; De Vries 1999; Wernick 2001). It is along these lines, for instance, that postmodernist writers have reacted to the more militantly atheistic projects of the Enlightenment legacy, from the French eighteenth-century sensationists to the nineteenth-century British utilitarians and the twentieth-century Viennese positivists. Such movements appear haunted by a need to repress the theological as an inferior stage in the evolution of the human mind. Yet the theological typically takes revenge on its expulsion from these systems in a spectral form, in the form of a returning engulfing metaphysical telos. One of the most spectacular instances of a 'return of the repressed' in this sense seems to have been Comte's later slide into theology in his programme of the 'religion of humanity' – spurred on by sublimated erotic passion for the figure of the lady Clotilde de Vaux.

In thinkers such as Derrida, Levinas and Blanchot, or from a more Catholic direction by Klossowki, and more derivatively by a writer such as Bauman (1993, 1995), postmodernist sensibilities draw on motifs in Nietzsche and Freud about play, semblance, desire, loss and mourning, frequently in recombination with Jewish themes of exile, erring, wandering and desolation (cf. Derrida and Vattimo 1998; Derrida 2002). The thesis of a return of the theological famously formed part of Foucault's historicist critique of the 'anthropological slumber' of modern philosophical humanism, crystallising in his examination of the preconditions for a *pensée du dehors*. Much of Foucault's thinking here also drew on elements in French anthropological thought from Durkheim and Mauss to Callois and Bataille about sacred collective representations as structural preconditions of cultural reproduction, even in contexts of advanced societal differentiation and secularisation in the civic sphere. Some commentators also remark on a running preoccupation in French thought with the role of intellectuals in society as members of a certain kind of priesthood and with an associated ethos of communal regeneration and 'social effervescence' in moments of periodic revolutionary upheaval (Gane 2003). A particular sociological thinking about the semiotic valency of evil also appears in a writer such as Baudrillard, and in a more nuanced way in the work of Ricoeur. Both these writers mobilize themes in French aesthetic thought since Baudelaire and the Surrealists about the social meanings of the accursed and the execrated – such as prostitutes and gypsies or the urban dispossessed. More diffusely, we might regard a large swathe of French thinkers since Voltaire's satire on Leibnizian theodicy as exploring the scope and limits of an analysis of stratification in terms of quasi-theological existential constants. Even the militantly anti-obscurantist sociology of Bourdieu shows something of this preoccupation with the obduracy of inequality as something bordering on a theological order of things.[3]

'Globalisation' describes a second broad framework for renewed thinking about theology in social theory in the way it suggests doubts about the paradigmatic status of Western secularised understandings of the world and the possibility of different civilisational styles of sociological reasoning. Here the assumption of a single universal process of secularisation that starts from the premises of medieval European Judaeo-Christianity and gradually sheds its religious underpinnings as it passes through the watersheds of the European Renaissance and the eighteenth-century Enlightenment comes under fire. In its stead is a suggestion both of alternative religious sources of social and political thought, Judaeo-Christian as well as non-Judaeo-Christian, and of alternative courses of secularisation, each beginning from these different religious starting-points. Novalis's dualistic thematic 'Christianity or Europe' in this sense cedes place to an idea of multiple lines of descendancy between different civilisational sources of religious–theological understanding on the one hand and different cognitive styles of social and political thought on the other hand.

It is this way of thinking that appears in the thesis of 'multiple modernities' defended by Eisenstadt (2002) and others, building on Jaspers's thesis of the Axial Age civilisations. At a more dubiously relativist end of this thinking is a work such as Huntingdon's *Clash of Civilizations* – latter-day avatar of *The Decline of the West* by Spengler (Spengler 1932; Huntingdon 1996). At a more progressive end are the interventions of feminist, anthropological and anti-Orientalist critics of Western scientific self-images, represented by authors such as Harding (1998), Chakrabarty (2000), Rajan (1998) and Latour (1993), among others.

Allied to such work has been a distinctive consciousness of the theological dimensions of European ideas of 'world history'. Anti-Eurocentric critique evokes a sense in which many of the grand narratives of the eighteenth- and nineteenth-century philosophies of history substitute an idea of the agency of Europe for divine providence. Europe in these analyses is unmasked as the would-be god or demiurge dressed as universal 'subject of humanity'. The conceit seems at hand in the Napoleonic imperial project or in the Comtean vision of Europe as universal society of the future. As Paul Valéry spoke of Europe as a 'little head on the body of Asia', or as Hegel spoke of the state as 'the march of God through the world', or as Durkheim spoke of God as the self-projection of the social collective on the screen of the cosmos, so Europe figures itself in these narratives as deity of world history.

Yet ideas about postmodernism, globalisation and Eurocentrism in social theory take on an exaggerated importance unless they are informed by an awareness of the range of forms of internal self-criticism predominating in European thinking about religion, science, modernity and world history since the Enlightenment period. It is important to note an ethos of his-toricising self-questioning in European thinking since the nineteenth century, marked out by the names of outsider philosophers from Kierkegaard, Marx, Nietzsche and Heidegger to the Jewish phenomenologists and the Western Marxist humanists of the twentieth-century as well as the nineteenth-century German historical theologians after Schleiermacher. While all of these thinkers and their associated intellectual movements begin from Judaeo-Christian traditions, none of them in principle exclude non-Western cosmological ideas from possible sources of modern social and political self-understanding. All of these thinkers confront Western theology and philosophy with its Other and break down its claim to absoluteness, without at the same time countenancing any wholesale suspension of its normative validity-claim. It is in this sense that the early twentieth-century German historicist writers defended broadly cosmopolitan understandings of the religions and civilisations of the world, without at the same time embracing simple kinds of axiological eclecticism, relativism or nihilism. Troeltsch's *The Absoluteness of Christianity and the History of Religions* (of 1902), aimed, as the author saw it, to comprehend the claim of Christianity to absoluteness, not in spite of its relative position in history beside other world religions but precisely *in* this relative position, *in* its very relativity: Christianity's claim to absoluteness could and should be defended, but defending the claim did not imply a denial of the claims of other world religions to abso-luteness. In a similar way we can understand Lukács's famous 'transcendental homelessness' of modern man as implying not only the collapse of conventional Judaeo-Christianity into agonistic existentialist and materialist reasoning, but more particularly the confrontation of this reasoning with the residues of other ancient world religions equally secularised and dis-enchanted in their different ways.

All the above-named writers can be seen as wrestling with the aporias of the idealist phi-losophical systems of the early romantic period, above all in Hegel and Schelling. The his-toricist thinkers break open idealism's totalising logic, recognising in these systems a certain deeply Euro- and Christo-centric metaphysics that falls well short of an adequate sociological consciousness of its own material conditions of possibility. Marx was the first to demonstrate this inadequacy in his materialist radicalisation of Feuerbach's Christian humanism in *The German Ideology* – while Mannheim's *Ideology and Utopia* continued the interrogation in his analysis of the ways in which theological ideas of the absolute at once mobilise utopian social energies and traduce them by surrendering them up to earthly authorities. Yet on another level, the early twentieth-century historicists remained acutely aware of a kernel of truth in idealist philosophy that cannot be surmounted by any purely empiricist 'sociology of knowl-edge'. The Jewish Marxists recognised that social theory always stands in a certain relationship to theology and to the philosophy of history as intrinsically teleological projects, even as this relationship takes on a radically negative character, in the radical distance or absence or hid-denness or non-representability of God. Rosenzweig's *The Star of Redemption* of 1921 sug-gested that the project of a total critique of existing social relations with respect to ultimate values necessarily presupposed some ideal end state of the human species in reconciliation with itself and its world – a vision that cannot be entirely disentangled from conventional Judaeo-Christian doctrines of salvation, even as it rebels against such doctrines and their encrusted ideological shells. This was famously the sense of Benjamin's anti-progressivist messianism in the *Theses on the Philosophy of History*, as it was, too, of Bloch's *The Principle of Hope* and Horkheimer's and Adorno's *The Dialectic of Enlightenment*.

The critical theorists appreciated the significance of Hegel's conception of religion as an element in the domain of 'absolute spirit', and not simply in that of 'objective spirit'. Hegel had placed religion in a median position between the sensuality of art and the conceptuality of philosophy, insofar as religion not only reflects social practices at determinate times in history but also 'thinks about itself' or 'reflects on its reflection'. More than the 'spirit of the nation' or the 'spirit of the laws', art, religion and philosophy communicate truth at once *in* their time and world *and* in the transcendence of time and world. Although Dilthey's historicist extension of the category of objective spirit at the expense of the absolute in no way implied a simple retreat into objectifying relativism, the idealist gesture that the critical theorists sought to champion against positivism in the social sciences was that religion is already a form of thinking rationalisation of social affairs which contains within itself a certain theory of the social world, a certain *logos* of the social cosmos, or 'socio-*logos*'. It was in this sense precisely that Horkheimer and Adorno could see myth and theology as incipient forms of rationalising unification of social reality that at once recede under the impact of the disenchantment of the world and simultaneously return like ghosts from the grave – in Weber's famous image in *Science as a Vocation*.[4]

These reflections indicate that social theory's relationship to theology is a significantly more loaded matter than one merely about appropriate methodological rules for comprehending religion sociologically (in the sense of Weberian *verstehen*). At issue are questions not only about empirical social determinants of religious practices and beliefs but also about a certain two-way normative dialogue between sociology and theology. It would appear that theological and religious moments are in some sense 'preserved' or implicated as residues of the past in the very categories with which sociologists attempt to study them scientifically. Therefore we cannot speak of any simple diachronic progression from a stage of the theological to a stage of the metaphysical and finally to a stage of the scientific that might allow us to study them as external objects of detached investigation – such as in Comte's Law of Three Stages. Sociologists may instead have to adopt an attitude to theological ideas that regards them as normative sources of understanding about social life in their own right, which may compete with and possibly challenge or dispute the statements of social scientists about the place of religion in society.

Table 4.1 formalizes these considerations by distinguishing four distinct levels of analysis relevant to a sociological dialogue with theology. It suggests that questions about theology in social theory properly only obtain at a meta-level where the normative authority of social science to make statements about religion is problematized in certain ways. At an initial level, sociological study of religion implies a transition to sociological study of theology to the extent that religious practices are not adequately understood unless and until the sociologist gains an understanding of the theological thought-systems that inform these practices and give cognitive structure to them.

Here is a first implication of any hermeneutical approach to the understanding of religion in society; but there are arguably further, more radical implications. If theological propositions themselves imply theories about the social world, they potentially contain cognitive responses to the claims of social science, with which sociologists or social theorists ought to engage. At stake here is the capacity of theologians to think sociologically about their own

41

Table 4.1. Four levels of analysis relevant to a sociological dialogue with theology

	Level of analysis	Object of analysis	Some representative authors/schools
1	Sociology of religion	Social determinants of religious practices	Durkheim
2	Sociology of theology	Social determinants of the thought-systems of religious practices	Mannheim
3	Sociological theology	Sociologically self-conscious theology	Liberation theology/Feminist theology
4	Theological sociology	Unconsciously theological social theory	Authors in Table 4.3
		Consciously theological social theory	

propositions and to incorporate sociological considerations into their own normative doctrines. It is in this sense that numerous twentieth-century theologians have been able to answer back to the kinds of 'depth-hermeneutical' arguments associated with the critiques of Marx, Nietzsche and Freud. They have done so by arguing that while the validity of theological doctrines is not immune to criticism on grounds of observations about the social circumstances under which such doctrines are formed and disseminated, theological teaching can adapt itself consciously and reflexively to the problems posed by these circumstances. Thus South American liberation theologians have been able to re-frame Christian teachings about charity, humility and forgiveness precisely in a consciousness of the constant susceptibility of such teachings to ideological appropriation by ruling classes or advantaged groups (corruption and conservatism in the Catholic Church; egoism and hypocrisy in the Protestant ethic, and so on). Similarly, feminist theologians have been able to mobilise values of pastoral caring long associated with paternalistic ecclesiastical organisation against the effects of patriarchy in society at large.

Finally there is the idea of a possible counterpart to sociological theology in the form of certain kinds of 'theological sociology'. *One* interpretation of the range of conceptions at this last and most abstract level of analysis might take the form of a claim that most, if not all, modern social theories, reproduce theological structures of thought 'unconsciously'. In the middle years of the twentieth century one of the most notable exponents of this claim was Karl Löwith, in his influential book *Meaning in History* (1949). A more recent exponent has been the British theologian John Milbank, in his book *Theology and Social Theory: Beyond Secular Reason* (1990).

The reasoning behind this view typically begins with some reflections on Kant's statement that while God and the infinite are not possible objects of empirical knowledge, the theory of knowledge 'clears a space for faith'. Theologians of a postmodernist persuasion such as Milbank see Kant's statement and its influence on the classical founding figures of sociology as implying, or disguising, a form of rationalistic imperialism over religious faith: demarcation of the limits of the space in which faith is possible implies prior legislation over something that in essence refuses or rebels against all such legislation. Milbank in particular goes so far as to claim that Neo-Kantian epistemology in social science steps so extensively beyond its proper domain that sociology itself often becomes a form of unwitting theology. On this view, theology's own 'socio-logos' is both historically prior to, and epistemically more basic than, that of social science; and to the extent that sociologists neglect or forget this greater primordiality of the theological, they labour under illusions about the capacities of their own project.[5]

Milbank's claim would seem to be a fair comment about Comte's 'religion of humanity'. Perhaps it is also a fair comment about Durkheim's *The Elementary Forms of Religious Life*. (We may recall Evans-Pritchard's apothegm: 'It was Durkheim, not the Azande, who made a god out of society'.) Similarly, a common claim is that Marxism represents a form of secularised Judaeo-Christian eschatology, and that Soviet communism represented a form of ersatz-theocracy or 'ideocracy' (Raymond Aron, Solzhenitsyn). Table 4.2 suggests a range of ways in which contemporary sociological categories might be seen as in some sense echoing, resembling, recalling or possibly 'repeating' theological categories 'unconsciously', or at least in hitherto relatively untheorized ways.

The pairings in Table 4.2 might lend support to a thesis such as Milbank's that asserts an idea of the epistemic dependence of social-scientific concepts on pre-, post- or extra-secular contexts of thought and belief. However, claims such as Milbank's are open to some significant objections. It is one thing to establish that social scientists cannot operate without a consciousness of historical antecedents that might encompass theological thinking. It is demonstrably another to assert that social theory is 'nothing but theology under another name'. To say that all four levels of analysis in Table 4.1 implicate one another in an upward sequence is by no means to say that they entail one another in an irrefutable chain of transitions. We must clearly be careful with the kinds of pairings presented in Table 4.2. A pressing task is to establish how far, or in what sense, if any, we can say that the categories on the left represent 'secularised' forms of those on the right – and if they *do* represent secularised forms, to define exactly what follows from the observation. A further question would be to consider whether the proposition of the dependence of sociology on theology is pertinent to *all* or only *some* schools of social theory. Should a distinction be drawn between schools which most strive to be neutral with respect to 'ultimate values' (for example: functionalism) and schools which least strive to be neutral with respect to 'ultimate values' (for example: Marxism)?

Claims such as Milbank's are likely to be greeted with suspicion by many social theorists. Many are likely to suspect an attempt by theologians merely to appropriate social theory for the purposes of dignifying or apologising for their own fideism: aware of the ever-diminishing relevance and respectability of religious beliefs in the political arena, theologians feel a need for strategies of aggressive intellectual self-vindication. In Milbank's case this will to apologia takes the extreme form of a claim to deep-rooted prior ownership over the arguments of theology's staunchest contemporary critics.

It can be argued that one of the most engaging sources of resistance to such manoeuvres today still remains the argument developed by Hans Blumenberg in the 1960s in response to Karl Löwith's claims about the spiritual 'degeneracy' of the modern age. In *The Legitimacy of the Modern Age*, Blumenberg (1983) argued that modernization and rationalization cannot simply be thought in terms of a process of parasitic 'falling' from a prior condition of ontological oneness with the cosmos, represented by the theological teachings of Greek antiquity and Judaeo-Christianity. The demise of Platonic and Augustinian teachings in the early

Table 4.2. Sociological and theological categories

Sociological categories	Theological categories
Revolution	Salvation
Emancipation	Revolt of the slaves
Solidarity	Brotherhood of man
Justice as equality	'The first shall be last and the last shall be first'
Stratification	'The great chain of being'
Functionalist explanation	Theodicy
The State	Caesar
Society	God

modern period must be thought of as the outcome of an immanent impulse *within* these systems of thought towards critical self-validation in the light of constructive engagement with the earthly world. Subjectivization, or the falling back of human beings on their own capacities to reason for themselves, is not simply a 'malady' or tragic 'fate' of the modern age. Weberian disenchantment carries within itself processes of collective rational self-determination that are spontaneous expressions of social creativity and are more than sheer symptoms of, or mere compensations for, felt states of falling from grace or lack or absence of grace.[6]

A similar type of response can be made to Milbank: unless his thesis of the 'bankruptcy of secular reason' is to rest purely on some kind of 'leap of faith', it must be capable of justifying itself by philosophical and sociological *argument*; but if it *is* capable of justifying itself in this way, then it is, ipso facto, *self-refuting*. The very possibility of being able to frame the contention implies its own falsehood. Criticism of the self-consciousness of sociology with respect to theology is itself a work of sociological reasoning. Theological critique of the social sciences is itself an exercise in the reflexive self-justification of the scientific projects of modernity.

An alternative reading of the dispute between theology and sociology would therefore be to point to the significance of potentially *self-consciously* and *self-critically* theological forms of social theory – rather than simply naïve or 'unconscious' kinds. Table 4.3 identifies a range of ways of thinking along these lines.

The third, fourth and fifth positions in Table 4.3 suggest strategies for resolving the standoff between the radically anti-secularist claims of theologians such as Milbank on the one hand and the counter-claims of committed social scientists on the other. The challenge here is to see how far such strategies succeed, or whether we are stuck with the second position: the position of irreconcilable conflicts between value-systems famously represented by Max Weber.

The most promising strategy would seem to be the last position. This position recognises that social theory has theological origins but affirms that it seeks, and can achieve, critical

Table 4.3. Five positions on the relationship between social theory and theology

	'Social science . . .	Some representative authors	Provisional evaluation
1	. . . is secularised theology.'	Löwith Voegelin Milbank	Commits a genetic fallacy (X from Y; therefore X is Y)
2	. . . has nothing to do with theology and conflicts with it.'	Max Weber	Problem of incommensurability between value-systems
3	. . . interacts with theology dialectically.'	Bloch Benjamin Frankfurt School Žižek	Problem of totality: difficulty of unifying science and transcendence
4	. . . translates theology into secular discursive moral argument.'	Durkheim Parsons Habermas	Possible rationalistic imperialism over belief
5	. . . has theological origins but achieves critical distance from them without forgetting them.'	Troeltsch Blumenberg Ricoeur Theunissen Charles Taylor Joas	Open for consideration

distance from such origins without forgetting or 'repressing' them. Social theorists on this view become aware of certain debts to theology but nevertheless seek, and achieve, intellectual autonomy precisely in a consciousness of this indebtedness. The position holds that social theory retains a capacity and a need to criticise theology, even as it is, or becomes, conscious of its historical relationship to theology. It does not hold that social theory 'derives from' theology in any strongly genetic sense (Position 1). But nor does it hold that social theory interacts with theology in some kind of 'negative dialectic', such as in the work of Adorno or Bloch: it sees a problem in attempting to unify empirical knowledge with transcendence, even when this undertaking is conceived in terms of negative theology (Position 3). Furthermore, it does not hold that social theory seeks to 'translate' theology into some superior language of secular humanistic moral argument, allegedly better 'adapted' to contemporary conditions – the kind of position taken by Habermas, Parsons or Durkheim, following in the footsteps of Kant's philosophy of religion (Position 4). Instead, it recognises limits in the Habermasian project of the 'linguistification of the sacred': it recognises limits in the possibility of converting representations, lived feelings or pre- or semi-linguistic experiences of the sacred into abstractly universalising, procedurally fallible arguments about morality in the civic domain. It accepts an ineliminable presence of 'traces' or 'residues' of the sacred in the categorial structures of social theory and it tries to take account of these traces or residues without mystifying them. It thematises the process by which social science becomes at once aware of its roots in theological thought and able to seek and achieve distance and autonomy in relation to these roots through an internal labour of self-criticism and reflexive self-overcoming. Rather as Jacques Lacan came to speak of the autonomy of the Subject as consisting precisely in a consciousness of heteronomy, of dependence upon, and subjection to, an Other which must be negated in order that the Subject may form itself and give to itself its own law, so social science can be seen as achieving intellectual freedom from theological origins precisely through a labour of remembering and recognizing these origins.[7]

Notes

1 Carl Schmitt, Leo Strauss, Eric Voegelin and Hannah Arendt have been among the most influential twentieth century contributors on these matters. The locus classicus is Schmitt's repeatedly cited *Political Theology* of 1922.

2 Notable contributions from British writers in recent years have been John Milbank's *Theology and Social Theory: Beyond Secular Reason* (1990) (discussed further below), Gillian Rose's writings on Marxism, Judaism and critical theory (Rose 1981, 1992), and the extensions of Bhaskar's 'critical realist' epistemology to religion and theology by Archer *et al.* (2004) and Collier (2001, 2003), partly revisiting Alasdair Macintyre's earlier *Marxism and Christianity* of 1968. Also still valuable are the two earlier studies of Hegel, theology and critical theory by Theunissen (1969, 1970) and the many studies of Hegel's and Schleiermacher's theological conceptions by German scholars, especially by Dieter Henrich and Eberhard Jüngel. An informative account of Habermas's relationship to the earlier Frankfurt school's ideas about religion and theology appears in the collection edited by Eduardo Mendieta (Habermas 2002). Applications of the Habermasian discourse theory to theology beginning from Kant's philosophy of religion include McCarthy (1991) and Peukert (1986). More sociologically oriented studies have been Gill (1977), Martin (1997), Martin *et al.* (1980), and Herman *et al.* (2002).

3 Bourdieu scathingly dubbed Blairite Third-Way discourse a neo-liberal 'sociodicy' (Bourdieu and Wacquant 2001).

4 In passing it can be noted that Weber's image in turn recalls a passage in Heinrich Heine's poem *Die Götter Griechenlands* (or *Die Götter im Exil*), to which Freud refers in the essay on 'The Uncanny'. Freud writes: 'When all is said and done, the quality of uncanniness can only come from the fact of

the "double" being a creation dating back to a very early mental stage, long since surmounted – a stage, incidentally, at which it wore a more friendly aspect. The "double" has become a thing of terror, just as, after the collapse of their religions, the gods turned into demons' (Freud 1953–1974, vol. 17: 236). The Heine passage is:

> Das sind sie selber, die Götter von Hellas,
> Die einst so freudig die Welt beherrschten
> Doch jetzt, verdrängt und verstorben,
> Als ungeheure Gespenster dahinziehn
> Am mitternächtlichen Himmel
>
> . . .
>
> Wenn ich euch jetzt da droben schaue
> Verlassene Götter
> Tote, nachtwandelnde Schatten, . . .

5 Comparable to Milbank's work, in some respects, is Gerhart Wagner's *Gesellschaftstheorie als politische Theologie* (1993), which defends a rather exaggerated and contrived thesis about Parsonian functionalism as a form of unconscious political theology in the spirit of the Hobbesian sovereign power as an impersonated god or theological symbol of the unity of the social system. Note, however, Parsons's own explicit response to questions of theology in Parsons (1967).
6 For one discussion of the Löwith/Blumenberg debate, see Delanty (2000: 32–51).
7 A full working out of this position is beyond the scope of this essay. It is, however, the explicit aim of this author's forthcoming research papers.

References

Archer, M. S., Collier, A. and Porpora, D. V. (2004) *Transcendence: Critical Realism and God*, London: Routledge.
Assmann, J. (1986) *Theologen und Theologien in verschiedenen Kulturkreisen*, H. von Stietencron (ed.), Düsseldorf: Patmos.
Badiou, A. (1997) *Saint Paul: La fondation de l'universalisme*, Paris: Presses Universitaires de France.
Bauman, Z. (1993) *Postmodern Ethics*, Oxford: Blackwell.
Bauman, Z. (1995) *Life in Fragments*, Oxford: Blackwell.
Bhaskar, R. (2002a) *Reflections on Meta-Reality: Transcendence, Emancipation, and Everyday Life*, London: Sage.
Bhaskar, R. (2002b) *Beyond East and West: Spirituality and Comparative Religion in an Age of Global Crisis*, London: Sage.
Blond, P. (1997) *Post-Secular Philosophy: Between Philosophy and Theology*, London: Routledge.
Blumenberg, H. (1983) *The Legitimacy of the Modern Age*, trans. R. Wallace. Cambridge, MA: MIT Press.
Bourdieu, P. and L. Wacquant (2001) 'New Liberal Speak: Notes on the New Planetary Vulgate', in *Radical Philosophy*, 105: 6–7.
Chakrabarty, D. (2000) *Provincialising Europe*, Cambridge: Cambridge University Press.
Collier, A. (2001) *Christianity and Marxism*, London: Routledge.
Collier, A. (2003) *On Christian Belief: a Defence of a Cognitive Conception of Religious Belief in a Christian Context*, London: Routledge.
Debray, R. (2004) *God: An Itinerary*, trans. J. Mehlman. London: Verso.
Delanty, G. (2000) *Modernity and Postmodernity*, London: Sage.
Derrida, J. (2002) *Acts of Religion*, G. Anidjar (ed.), London: Routledge.
Derrida, J. and Vattimo, G. (1998) *Religion*, Cambridge: Polity Press.
De Vries, H. (1999) *Philosophy and the Turn to Religion*, Baltimore: Johns Hopkins University Press.
Eisenstadt, S. (ed.) (2002) *Multiple Modernities*, New Brunswick: Transaction.
Freud, S. (1953–1974) 'The Uncanny', in *The Standard Edition of the Complete Psychological Works*, Volume 17.
Gane, M. (2003) *French Social Theory*, London: Sage.

Gill, R. (1977) *Theology and Social Structure*, Oxford: Mowbray.

Graf, F. W. (2004) *Die Wiederkehr der Götter: Religion in der modernen Kultur*, München: C. H. Beck.

Habermas, J. (2001) *Glauben und Wissen*, Frankfurt am Main: Suhrkamp.

Habermas, J. (2002) *Religion and Rationality: Essays on Reason, God and Modernity*, E. Mendieta (ed.), Cambridge: Polity Press.

Habermas, J. (2004) 'Vorpolitische moralische Grundlagen eines freiheitlichen Staates', in *Zur Debatte: Themen der Katholischen Akademie in Bayern*, 34, ISSN 0179-6658.

Harding, S. (1998) *Is Science Multicultural? Postcolonialisms, Feminisms, and Epistemologies*, Bloomington, IN: Indiana University Press.

Herman, C. A. M., Immink, G., de Jong, A. and van der Lans, J. (eds) (2002) *Social Constructionism and Theology*, Amsterdam: Brill.

Huntingdon, S. P. (1996) *The Clash of Civilizations: and the Remaking of World Order,* New York: Simon & Schuster.

Janicaud, D. (ed.) (2000) *Phenomenology and the 'Theological Turn'*, New York: Fordham University Press.

Joas, H. (1997) *Die Entstehung der Werte*, Frankfurt am Main: Suhrkamp.

Joas, H. (2004) *Braucht der Mensch Religion? Über Erfahrungen der Selbsttranszendenz*, Freiburg: Herder.

Latour, B. (1993) *We Have Never Been Modern*, trans. C. Porter. Cambridge, MA: Harvard University Press.

Löwith, K. (1949) *Meaning in History: The Theological Implications of the Philosophy of History*, Chicago: Chicago University Press.

Macintyre, A. (1968) *Marxism and Christianity*, New York: Schocken.

McCarthy, T. (1991) *Ideals and Illusions: On Reconstruction and Deconstruction in Contemporary Critical Theory*, Cambridge, Mass: MIT Press.

Marion, J.-L. (1991) *God Without Being*, Chicago: University of Chicago Press.

Martin, D. (1997) *Reflections on Sociology and Theology*, Oxford: Oxford University Press.

Martin, D., Mills, J. O. and Pickering, W. (eds) (1980) *Sociology and Theology: Alliance and Conflict*, London: Harvester.

Milbank, J. (1990) *Theology and Social Theory: Beyond Secular Reason*, Oxford: Blackwell.

Parsons, T. (1967) Social Science and Theology, in W. A. Beardslee (ed.), *America and the Future of Theology*, Philadelphia: Westminster Press, 136–157.

Peukert, H. (1986) *Science, Action, and Fundamental Theology: Toward a Theology of Communicative Action*, trans. J. Bohman, Cambridge, Mass: MIT Press.

Rajan, S. (1998) *Beyond the Crisis of the European Sciences*, Shimla: Indian Institute of Advanced Study.

Rose, G. (1981) *Hegel Contra Sociology*, London: Athlone.

Rose, G. (1992) *The Broken Middle*, Oxford: Blackwell.

Spengler, O. (1932) *Decline of the West,* New York: Knopf.

Taylor, C. (2002) *Varieties of Religion Today*, Cambridge, MA: Harvard University Press.

Taylor, C. (2004) *Modern Social Imaginaries*, Durham, SC: Duke University Press.

Taylor, M. C. (1984) *Erring: A Postmodern A/theology*, Chicago: Chicago University Press.

Theunissen, M. (1969) *Gesellschaft und Geschichte: Zur Kritik der kritischen Theorie*, Berlin: de Gruyter.

Theunissen, M. (1970) *Hegels Lehre vom absoluten Geist als theologisch-politischer Traktat*, Berlin: De Gruyter.

Theunissen, M. (1991) *Negative Theologie der Zeit*, Frankfurt am Main: Suhrkamp.

Wagner, G. (1993) *Gesellschaftstheorie als politische Theologie? Zur Kritik der Theorien normativer Integration*, Berlin: Duncker & Humblot.

Wernick, A. (2001) *Auguste Comte and the Religion of Humanity: the Post-theistic Program of French Social Theory*, Cambridge: Cambridge University Press.

Zizek, S. (2000) *The Fragile Absolute, or, Why is the Christian Legacy Worth Fighting For?*, London: Verso.

Zizek, S. (2003) *The Puppet and the Dwarf: The Perverse Core of Christianity*, London: Verso.

Part 2

National traditions

5

Contemporary German social theory

Hauke Brunkhorst

The development of theory in postwar German sociology was initially shaped entirely by *philosophical anthropology*. In Germany, unlike in America, philosophy and sociology had not yet become distinct disciplines, and this is true both of the sociological theory of philosophical anthropology and of Marxism, or neo-Marxist trends such as the Frankfurt School. Of these, Marxism was only an indirect participant. Its presence was acknowledged in the first few decades after the war, but because of the division of Germany it was largely confined to the GDR until the late 1960s, while the Frankfurt School was not initially perceived as a form of Marxism at all. Marxism as such did not begin to make itself felt before the mid-1960s. From the end of the 1950s, however, a *new German sociology* started to emerge, one that was stimulated as much by a growing awareness of the increasingly vociferous American debate about Talcott Parsons' functionalism as by a new reading of Marx. For his part, Marx now began to be taken seriously not just as the anthropologist of human self-alienation and as an enlightened champion of ideological critique, but as a founding father of sociology and social theory. Thereafter the 1970s were increasingly defined by the *communication turn* in social theory, a trend that survives more or less undiminished down to the present. In its shadow a host of modernist and post-modernist *variants* have emerged, but scarcely any *alternatives* to the communication theories of society. At any rate, no real paradigm shift can be discerned; what we witness instead is a certain normalization and consolidation of the programme of communication theory.

Philosophical anthropology

In the 1950s, social theory was dominated by three writers of the Leipzig School who had earlier invested great hopes in National Socialism. These three were, first, Arnold Gehlen who had been born in 1904, a philosopher who no longer wished to be one and who now thought of philosophy as the empirical science of a mankind considered as a social being. Second, there was the considerably older Hans Freyer who was born in 1887. In 1925 Freyer, who described himself as a 'right-wing revolutionary' (Freyer 1931), was the first person to be appointed to a chair in sociology in Germany; in 1934, shortly after the National Socialist takeover, he was made president of the German Sociology Society. The third figure was Helmut Schelsky, who was born in 1912 and who became the star student of Gehlen and Freyer. At the end of his life, having seen sociology develop into a normal university subject, one that had fallen strongly under the influence of the political left, Schelsky was to declare himself an anti-sociologist (Rehberg 1999).

In philosophical anthropology, humanity ceased to be thought of in Aristotelian terms, as a 'political animal' who realizes himself through the organization of his own commonwealth. Instead, humanity was now conceived of as in the young Marx, namely as 'the ensemble of the social relations' (Marx 1960: 301 [Eng. 1976: 4]). Society now comes to take the place of community, whether conceived in Aristotelian terms or as transfigured in an archaic glow (Plessner 1924). For its part, social science can no longer, as in Aristotle and Hegel, gaze upon society and its history from an external theoretical or ethical point of view. Instead, it sees itself, as in Marxism and neo-Marxism (the Frankfurt School), as a science of society (sociology) which itself plays an active part in society whether it likes it or not (Freyer 1930: 228f., and also at around the same time, Lukács 1923; Korsch 1993; Marcuse 1930, 1932). In contrast to Marx, however, Gehlen understands society as a system of established dominant institutions, with a healthy core which has always remained archaically authoritarian and which can be altered only at the price of mankind's self-destruction.

In 1950 Gehlen's chief work, *Der Mensch* [Man], which had first appeared in 1940 and had at once come to occupy a dominant position, was reissued in a heavily revised version, and this was followed six years later by *Urmensch und Spätkultur* [Primeval Man and Late Culture]. In the intervening period he had studied American cultural anthropology in close cooperation with Helmut Schelsky. This resulted in the idea that man is not at home in his own body, but has always been outside himself, 'eccentrically' positioned (Plessner 1927). Because of this anthropologically conditioned distance from himself, man must objectify himself in society or else come to grief. He is a 'creature of lacks' (*Mängelwesen*) and these lacks can only be made good (and here the conservative Gehlen clearly diverges from the more liberal Plessner) by powerful, authoritarian institutions that will relieve him of the eccentric burden of constant reflection about himself (Gehlen 1950, 1956). The role of institutions is to take the place of the body armour and the instinct for self-preservation that ensure the survival of the crocodile in a 'world full of enemies' (Luther). In Gehlen, as in Freud and Durkheim, the archaic, primeval human being finds himself directly confronting a modern, functionally differentiated and technically neutralized society. This is the 'late culture' that Gehlen locates within the trajectory of a theory of decline (Gehlen 1956) in whose *post-histoire* nothing new will eventuate (Gehlen 1956, 1957). This motif will recur decades later as a fundamental theme of postmodern sociology and philosophy.

However, the unmediated confrontation of primeval man and late culture leads to a late-Protestant neglect of the evolution of human society. That society is the product not merely of a dialectic of age-old helplessness and the search for protection under authoritarian rule, but also of a long history of religious traditions, virtuous achievements specific to particular groups, and collective learning processes. Durkheim and the American pragmatists (Dewey and Mead) represent this as a step-by-step (phylogenetic and ontogenetic) internalizing and transforming of authority into autonomy. In contrast, Gehlen's philosophical anthropology precludes the possibility of such learning processes from the outset because of the way he has chosen and defined its complementary basic concepts, '*primeval man*' and '*institution*', since these postulate 'an eternal nexus of protection and obedience' (Schmitt 1950: 295).

Following directly in Gehlen's footsteps, Schelsky modifies his teacher's authoritarian institutionalism and, in a return to the philosophy of consciousness, he rehabilitates the reflective achievements of the autonomous subject. Operating through the medium of positive law, which is tendentially (intentionally?) capable of modification, the human subject can take a critical view of institutions and endow them with a growing flexibility appropriate to subjective freedom. These are ideas that Luhmann, who was Schelsky's student, was able to adopt. In Schelsky, modern society is marked by a dialectic of institutionalization and subjectivity that is not just repressive, but also productive and liberating (Schelsky 1965: 33ff. and 272f.). According to this view, authoritarian rule is no longer simply *transmitted* by means of secondary objective processes; instead, the institutionally established but justifiable rule of objects (including the rule of law) comes to *take the place* of an unquestioned institutionalized authority. Thus Schelsky understands the technical world not as human self-alienation, but as the realization of the constructive nature of man. However, this technical world is no longer reinserted into the horizon of human political activity or even, as in the optimistic social anthropology of the American pragmatists, made subject to growing democratic control. The dominance of 'material constraints' provides the rationale of the technocratic conservatism of the 'technical state' (Schelsky 1965: 439ff., 457, 459). This technical state seeks out its social foundations in would-be harmonizing assumptions about the welfare state and its ability to reproduce an increasingly 'levelled-down middle-class society' [*nivellierte Mittelstandsgesellschaft*], as well as a critical but unpolitical generation, one that Schelsky with his eye on the university-educated youth of postwar Germany had dubbed the 'sceptical' generation (Schelsky 1957). This thesis was refuted by social developments from the mid-1960s and it turned Schelsky himself into an 'anti-sociologist' critical of the cultural trend (Schelsky 1981).

New German sociology

The young Ralf Dahrendorf was one of the first sociologists to lodge a protest against the closed society of a functional technocracy, confronting the technical state with a sociology of conflict derived from a Marxian theory of class struggle (Dahrendorf 1957a, 1957b, 1959). Dahrendorf follows Marx in emphasizing the inevitability of conflicts, but instead of treating them as the motor of the revolutionary overthrow of bourgeois society, he takes Popper's view that they should be diverted along reformist paths leading to democratic parliamentary solutions by means of piecemeal engineering that in turn leads to further conflicts.

It is only when we reach authors such as Ralf Dahrendorf, Jürgen Habermas, Renate Mayntz or Niklas Luhmann, all of whom studied after the war, that we find sociologists exploring American sociology, philosophy, social psychology, psychoanalysis, Western Marxism and the political theory of modern democracy. Habermas, in particular, began by stoking up public controversy about the National Socialist past of the generation of those who had taught him, a highly sensitive subject at the time (Habermas 1953). Under the growing influence of the Frankfurt School, to which he himself had belonged in the late 1950s, Habermas spoke out in favour of the rediscovery of German-Jewish anthropologists, sociologists and philosophers who had been excluded and repressed. These included Plessner, Arendt, Marcuse, Wittgenstein and Löwith, all of whom had been driven out by the Nazis, with many finding refuge in the United States. Dahrendorf, Habermas and Luhmann all follow the anti-Aristotelian turn in philosophical anthropology from the political community to a differentiated society and think of social theory as an aspect of an ongoing social practice. At the same time, they dismiss the authoritarian theory of institutions and abandon the fixation with decadence that had been cultivated on such a lofty plane by the Leipzig School and that was typical of a defiant cultural critique from a conservative standpoint. Schelsky's technocracy thesis, which for all his insight into social differentiation remained tied to a homogenizing concept of stability, now makes way for a new dynamism, one that shifts heterogeneous conflicts, crises, fragmentations and frictions into the centre of society. Crisis and critique are now promoted to the status of permanent assumptions underlying function systems and organizations (Luhmann, Mayntz), or are recognized as the productive drivers of social advances (Dahrendorf) and declared to be the natural element of public discourses (Habermas). The apologias for domination that characterized Gehlen's anthropology are now dissipated and replaced either by critiques of domination (Habermas, Dahrendorf) or else by defences of system rationality (Luhmann).

However, Habermas takes his lead initially from the core realm of philosophical anthropology, transforming it with the aid of Kant, Peirce, Scheler and Gadamer into a cognitive anthropology of the labouring creature who uses his imagination and strives to understand himself. This cognitive anthropology culminates in a theory - developed together with Apel (1970, 1971) – of knowledge-shaping interests in technology, in an intelligence-based, practical orientation and an emancipatory practice. Integrating Hegel, Freud and Marx in his theory, Habermas understands this anthropology as the 'radicalization' of the 'cognitive critique' derived from the philosophy of subjective consciousness, transforming it into critical 'social theory' (Habermas 1968: 9 [1972: 11]). The concept that links anthropology and social theory is the concept of 'species history' that goes back to Hegel and Marx (Habermas 1968; for his self-criticism, see Habermas 1973a, 1973b, 2000). The purpose of this radicalization of cognitive critique at the hands of social theory is to liberate the concept of reason developed by Kant and Hegel from its idealism and lead it back to the centre of social reality. Once there, however, it no longer appears, as it did to Hegel, as objective spirit incorporated in institutions ('ethical spirit' [Sittlichkeit]), but as the public and intersubjectively effective form of coercion that forces society into the act of self-criticism (Habermas, as early as 1962). This element aligns Habermas with Marx, but by thinking of the societalization [Vergesellschaftung] of reason as that of *intersubjective* communication, he hopes to do away with Marx's positivistic or scientistic misconceptions together with the reduction of practice to technology that is closely associated with it (Habermas 1968).

The position with Luhmann is quite different. Luhmann is heavily indebted to Gehlen's theory of the role of institutions in unburdening human beings, but he pushes anthropology to one side and instead takes up the legal positivism of Hans Kelsen, the structural functionalism of the late Talcott Parsons and the work of Herbert Simon on the sociology of organizations. These writers led him to the idea of dispensing with anthropology by simply reversing the 'unburdening' thesis [Entlastung]. This led to an influential displacement of the idea of unburdening, transferring it from human beings to society itself. It is no longer human beings who unburden themselves through the societalization [Vergesellschaftung] of what Gehlen calls 'excesses of stimuli' (Gehlen 1950) and of the chaotic complexity of the social and natural world, but society that unburdens itself of the chaotic complexity of human beings and their environment (life world). From the outset Luhmann is clear in his own mind that, looked at sociologically, human consciousness and the human organism form part of the environment of social systems, where they are as indispensable as they are irritatingly dangerous.[1] These systems need to free themselves from their mental, technical and also their natural, organic environment, from the demands imposed by human motives and from the irritations caused by the perceiving and reflecting mind. They achieve this by reducing complexity (outward specialization and inner differentiation) so as to determine and sustain themselves by separating themselves from their environment. By a process of system-building, the indeterminate and unending complexity of the world flowing in from outside is transformed into a controllable and finite complexity inside a system (for an incisive and succinct formulation, see Luhmann 1987: 320). The basic idea is as simple as it is illuminating. If all the avenues of communication between twenty people are restricted by organizations, e.g. by separating out the roles of teachers and pupils, and by subject-matter prescribed by the syllabus, the effect will be that, in contrast to what happened previously, people will all stop speaking across each other and instead will all sing together, or, more likely, listen in silence to whoever is speaking at the front of the room.[2]

This switch from human beings to the social system in the unburdening process has an important consequence for the theory of freedom. Due to this, the increasing compatibility of subjective (or negative) freedom and systemic material constraints that Luhmann's teacher Schelsky had initiated, is now fully realized. The 'secondary systems' (Freyer), the 'material constraints' (Gehlen) and the 'technical state' (Schelsky) do not simply shed their intimidating authoritarian aura; they lose all hostility to, or tension with, the concept of freedom, which Luhmann – and here he follows Schelsky implicitly – continues to think of only subjectively (negatively). Seen from this angle, Adorno's 'administered world' looks like a veritable kingdom of freedom. From the outset Luhmann locates the reason for the growth in freedom through administration in the *modern* separation of the social system from the psychological one. In the course of modernization 'social integration ... and personal integration diverge more strongly than ever' – this was his view as early as 1964. Because of this, the separation of social and personal integration leads inexorably to growth in the individual's scope for subjective freedom. The complete compatibility of administration and freedom has an important polemical point, one that is directed in equal measure at Schelsky and Gehlen on the one hand, and Adorno and Marcuse on the other. If specialization, functionalization, organization and administration are turned into the preconditions of the possibility of untrammelled and equal subjective freedom, this spells the end (Luhmann 1964: 26) of every extravagant cultural-critical scenario of the birth of freedom from 'alienation' (Gehlen 1952; Horkheimer and Adorno 1997: 150 [2002: 101f.]) or of the interpretation of the subjective freedom of man as the 'loneliness' of Nietzsche's 'Last Men' or of 'heroic intellectuals' (Schelsky 1960).

Transferring the unburdening function from human beings to the social system has a fundamental influence on our view of subjective freedom. This freedom now ceases to appear as a lethal *threat* to the community, one that can only be banished by an unquestioningly accepted authority, as was repeated in ever new variants from Hegel down to Gehlen. Now, however, unless subjective freedom is unleashed, the function systems and organizations of modern society would be unable to stabilize themselves. They cunningly turn the chaos of the world to their own advantage by internalizing it. This shift from anthropology to systems theory results in a totally affirmative relationship between the theory of social systems and modern society. However, although Luhmann both perceived and endorsed the idea that *freedom is compatible* with institutions, systems and organizations, his approval was limited to a purely negative, voluntaristic notion of *subjective* freedom. For this reason, the *freedom* with which institutions are compatible does not necessarily imply *compatibility with democracy, political self-determination* or *self-legislation*.

On this issue, Habermas (and Dahrendorf) radically disagree with Luhmann. Admittedly, Habermas is just as positive about modernity as Luhmann, but less with regard to the *facticity* of functional differentiation than to the *normative value* of its practical, political project (Habermas 1981a; 1985, 1992). What unifies Habermas's work is that it may be seen as a single critical refutation of Schelsky's thesis that the modern, technical world no longer calls for legitimation by its citizens because 'politics in the sense of a normative decision-making process actually falls outside the framework (of the technical state) in principle', and is reduced to 'the status of an aid with which to correct its failings' (Schelsky 1965: 456f.). (This can be seen for the first time in Habermas (1962); and most recently in Habermas (2005: 37f.)) Conversely, what unifies Luhmann's work is his endorsement of Schelsky's thesis that the technical state does away with democracy, 'without being anti-democratic' (Schelsky 1965: 459). Where Habermas has been concerned from the outset with a repoliticization of society *without* abandoning the primacy of society over politics, Luhmann has always supported a radical downgrading of politics relative to society, with views sharply opposed to the state and sometimes with anarchistic implications. (On this point see Teubner 1997; Fischer-Lescano 2005.)

The young Habermas had begun by opposing institutionalized authoritarianism with a theory of non-coercive communication, while neglecting the power of constitutional institutions to guarantee freedom. Dahrendorf, in contrast, while neglecting what Foucault called the 'microphysics of power', looked to the fallible institution of parliaments to supply all the energy required to deal productively with the class and group conflicts that arise from the liberated subjective freedom of what Marx termed 'modern bourgeois society'. In contrast to this, Luhmann, ignoring the possibility of systemic crises, assumes that the complexity of functionally differentiated social systems is sufficient to neutralize the all-devouring complexity of the world around us and also to generate a controlled explosion of subjective freedom through the functionalization of authority *and* through greater egalitarianism. In this way he hopes to reconcile and even identify radical change with systemic restabilization for the first time (Luhmann 1997a: 499). Looked at from the standpoint of Habermas or Adorno, that would of course be false, a partial 'reconciliation under duress' (Adorno). This explains why in the course of his debate with Luhmann (Habermas and Luhmann 1971), Habermas argued for the rehabilitation of Marx's theory of crises, though in a more pluralistic, modern form (Habermas 1973a). In his analysis of functionalism, which was designed to render every strong form of democratic legitimation superfluous (Luhmann 1969), Luhmann joins forces with Schelsky (against Gehlen), while in his analysis of egalitarianism he agrees with Habermas. Unlike Habermas, however, Luhmann does not locate the energy to produce greater equality in democratic politics and the latent rationality of public debate, but in the (counter-) force of 'informal organization' (Luhmann 1964: 74; likewise Mayntz 1958: 59ff.; 1961: 37). Because of what was said above about the systematic reversal of the function of unburdening, informal organization can be made the precondition of the practical efficacy of formal organizations (Luhmann 1964: 30, 33, 52). In his conclusion that modern society devours all critique and all negation, transforming them into the motor that drives itself forward, Luhmann's positive image of this society resembles Adorno's negative concept of the totality. It is almost the identical image, but with radically opposed values attached to it (Brunkhorst 1988, Breuer 1995).

The communication turn of social theory

The concept of communication moves quite unobtrusively into the centre of theory formation in the early writings of Luhmann and Habermas. Until the early 1970s, in line with anthropology and the philosophy of the subject, Habermas retains the pre-evolutionary concept of human 'species history'. But thereafter, at quite an early stage, and in close cooperation with Apel (1971), he replaces the reflective nature of the subject with the reflective nature of colloquial language. This enables him to anchor the rationality of technical, practical and emancipatory knowledge in the continuum of rationality contained in everyday communication. Language used communicatively becomes the agent of an autonomous *evolution*, one no longer determined by the biological and psychological development of human beings. However, Habermas only arrives at this particular conclusion in the course of the 1970s. But as early as *Knowledge and Human Interests* (1968), he suspends the societalization [*Vergesellschaftung*] of the individual between the poles of coercive and non-coercive *communication*, whereas the Marxist-inspired critique of ideology is reduced to depending upon agreed criteria with which to demolish distorted communications.

Luhmann, too, became aware of the social significance of the concept of communication at an early stage. However, he is less concerned with the epistemic and emancipatory part played by communication in the reproduction of society than with its role at the intersections between *formal* and *informal organization*. Ultimately, communication is just as vital for Luhmann as it is for Habermas (one needs only look at his two main works: Luhmann 1984; 1997). His view, however, is strictly functional. It is indeed orientated towards freedom, but he attaches no emancipatory value to it; as he says using one of his favourite phrases, the function of the postal service is not the emancipation of the post office workers, but the conveying of letters, and for Luhmann, who comes from an administrative background, the postal service is a paradigm of modern society, as it was for Lenin. However, it is not simply a technical apparatus (as it was for Weber or Lenin), but a communication system. Thus as early as 1964 he writes that systems can only grow and maintain themselves 'through communication' because they 'consist' of communications that process meanings (Luhmann 1964: 190). What counts is the communicative energy with which meaning is processed. *Formal* organization arises from a reduction of the environment of complex actions to a network of transparent, verbal, and highly structured communications so that the *manifest* function of distributing communication opportunities unequally can be implemented. In contrast, the *latent* functions of systemic self-preservation in a constantly changing world can only be carried out through the 'informal intermezzi' (Luhmann 1964: 193) of covert, deviant, oppositional, faulty, illegal and innovatory communications. In organizations – by analogy with legal power and sub-legal counterforce in political systems (Luhmann 1981; see on this point Neves 2000) – formalized communication networks and loosely structured, informal communications form two independent circuits that come into collision with each other only on the margins of the system. At the same time, the spontaneous nature of informal communication has the function of moulding the boundaries of the system in a way adequate to the world around it and of facilitating flexible transition from a rigid vertical formalization to an elastic horizontal one and vice versa. To be sure, in the 1960s, Luhmann still operated with a technical transmitter–receiver model of communication that he later abandons under the influence of Bühler, Apel and Habermas (see below) (Luhmann 1984, 1997a, 2002). But even at that time he could see that the role of communication in the formation and maintenance of systems had to amount to more than the 'auxiliary function' of the simple 'conveying of messages'. He realizes that the transmitter's messages are so intertwined with the independent message processing by the receiver that information can be accepted, inspected and rejected or interpreted in innovative ways (Luhmann 1964: 191f.). Thus, *commmunication* and *function* have been seen to be equally fundamental since well before the autopoietic turn of the 1980s.

Thus for Luhmann the equally fundamental status of communication and function supplied the key to overcoming the old European ontology. For Habermas, however, this ontology was to be overcome by the complementary, but equally fundamental status of *communication* and *explanation* or *justification* (*Begründung*). Instead of replacing the ontological 'rationality of listening' (*Vernunft des Vernehmens*) by the functional 'rationality of comparison' (Luhmann 1965: 8), Habermas replaces it with the communicative rationality of reaching an understanding (Habermas 1981a). Beginning with the 1970s, Habermas finally severed his links with his early roots in anthropology and in the philosophy of subjective consciousness and actively developed the communication turn of social theory. This opened up the way to a fundamental paradigm shift in theoretical sociology. It began with *Preparatory Comments on a Theory of Communicative Action* (Habermas and Luhmann 1971: 101ff.). With Apel, Habermas makes use of the Bühler and Morris three-function scheme of communicative language (individual expression, cognitive representation and pragmatic yes/no responses) and elucidates it with the assistance of the distinction between the propositional content and intersubjective validity claim (illocutionary function, mode) of each individual speech act (Habermas 1981a, 1988; Habermas and Luhmann 1971).[3] In the course of time Habermas elaborated this theory into one of communicative rationality which he then used as the foundation for his socio-logical magnum opus, the *Theory of Communicative Action* (Habermas 1981a) in the intro-ductory chapters and the first Intermediate Reflection.

Luhmann at once recognized the significance of the communication turn and adopted it, at the same time directing it along a functionalist path in the *Introductory Remarks on the Theory of Symbolically Generalized Communication Media* (Luhmann 1974; see also his review of *The Theory of Communicative Action*: Luhmann 1982: 372). Generalized communication or communications articulated in such media as money, power, love, truth/reputation, law, beauty, and so on, and also in print media, electronic media, and so forth, have the *function* of making it easier to gain acceptance for such otherwise unpalatable communications as 'I order you to stand still' or 'I assert that p'. They aim to achieve this by replacing them with con-ditionals such as 'If you do not stand still, I shall force you to do so', or 'If you do not believe me I shall prove it to you, or refer you to authoritative sources'. From the standpoint of sys-tems theory the functional meaning of accepting speech act offers is quite independent of whether an assertion is actually true or a command really justified. Nor is this affected by the structural coupling of power and law in the constitutional state (Luhmann 1990). To be sure, power – unlike its position in Hobbes, Austin or Schmitt – is subject to law and changes in the law are subject to democratic decision-making processes, but the legitimacy of such pro-cesses, like the rightness of the law, is overshadowed by the duty of the constitution to guarantee the boundaries and the peaceful interaction of law and politics.

Habermas proceeds differently, since he attempts to show that even the performance of highly specialized functions is dependent upon the way in which the actors convey their justifications in colloquial language. The explanations and justifications involved in reaching an understanding in everyday encounters do become differentiated in the specialized dis-courses of the law, morality, science or art, each with its own *truth functions*, but the truth of scientific statements and the correctness of moral judgements is ubiquitous, in other words, *acceptable* in society as a whole and not just in its own specialist discourse. It is acceptable not just because it is *held to be* acceptable and because it can therefore guarantee the *sustained* ability of communications to 'link up' with other discourses (Luhmann), but because it *is* true or correct (until proved otherwise). This inter-subjective, social variant of a realist theory of truth and validity, with its dependence on reaching an understanding, is one that Habermas defends within the specialist discourse of philosophy (most recently in Habermas 1999), but – and this explains why it is so eminently suited to being a permanent irritant to a functionalist social theory – its point lies exclusively in its sociological (and political) implications. The truth-functional discourses of morality, law or science are highly tenacious social systems that nevertheless flow back into both the non-specialized communication of everyday and the political decision-making processes of a civic public sphere. And since in order to survive, they depend on the use of the colloquial language and constant reference to the events and practices of ordinary life, they form a *rational continuum* with everyday non-specialized communication. Even the diffuse background convictions of everyday communication and the expressions of the wishes of a politically focused, but not politically specialized public are – so the thesis goes – both *capable of truth and dependent upon it*. 'A "post-truth democracy" would cease to be a democracy at all' (Habermas 2005: 17). The redeeming of the validity claims of explicit performative speech acts is the indispensable prerequisite both for any changes in our background convictions and for the democratic decision-making process. The sociological thesis on this point is as simple as it is provocative. If the channels of truth-bearing communication are blocked, whether by the police or the power of capital, or if they are transformed by discursive hegemony into unobtrusive 'discourse power' (Foucault), the insulted communicative rationality of the people takes its revenge by withdrawing its loyalty, political apathy, eruptive violence, irrationalist actionism, populist voluntarism, projective fanaticism or, at best, protest movements and political revolutions (Habermas 1981a, vol. 2: 345, 350). The non-specializable stubbornness of truth-functional discourses consists in the fact that any damage they suffer must lead to disruptions and irritations in the self-production (or autopoiesis) of function systems, and this will express itself in economic crises, crises of rationality or legitimacy or motivation, and massive social pathologies, all of which can be researched empirically (Habermas 1973a, 1981a). In contrast to the traditional philosophy of subjective consciousness, the correctness of the core thesis of the inevitability and contra-factual *effect* of normative validity claims must be tested against values that actually operate in society. This means that their development or their refutation must be made subject not just to explanatory *philosophical* discourses but to theoretical *scientific* discourses and to the empirical findings of sociology and other disciplines.

Luhmann has always reacted with an ironical display of paradoxes to such arguments and, looking at the question from the point of view of a detached observer, has always responded by putting a question that is logically possible and even meaningful sociologically but quite unproductive philosophically. This is the question of the social *function* of truth, validity claims and discourse, a question he puts only in order to shelve the entire discussion. Nevertheless, at the conclusion of his entire monumental oeuvre, in the course of his search for a theory of a global society [*Weltgesellschaft*], he came across a problem to which he had previously attached no particular *theoretical* importance. Now, however, he had to acknowledge that the global exclusion of vast masses of the population from access to almost all function systems confronts a functionally differentiated global society with a symptomatic crisis *of its own making*, compared to which nineteenth-century problems of class conflict and exploitation are mere child's play (following Neves 1992; Luhmann 1994, 1997a, 1997b). It seems as if with the advance of globalization, all function systems themselves produce social exclusions and a fragmentation of populations into over-integrated and under-integrated strata. This fragmentation places all (constitutional) linkages between law, politics and the economy in jeopardy and leads to a collapse of the functional differences between the most important subsystems – above all, those existing in the huge periphery of the global society (Neves 1992). This in turn could be explained (by both Habermas *and* Luhmann) by arguing that modern societies can only stabilize *one* variant to cater for *all* the motives of communicatively active persons, since the function systems involved need to achieve the social inclusion of entire populations, but are incapable of doing this on their own (Brunkhorst 2002: 111ff., especially 124f.). Habermas surmises that the integrated world community with its human rights' claims will be unable to acquiesce in the moral scandal of the social exclusion of entire sections of vast populations and entire regions of the world. If he is right, then it might one day come to pass – almost as in Marx's original social critique – that the crisis in both the system and the legitimacy of the global society will come together and mutually reinforce each other – with a highly uncertain outcome.

However that may be, the new paradigm was able to prevail and to establish itself widely, thanks to the fortunate circumstance that the shift from the subject to communication was carried out simultaneously by both the rationalist and functionalist trends in sociology. In contrast, all other productive but deviant developments were overshadowed by the communication turn in the social sciences.

These changes have partly been inspired by Habermas and Luhmann or have occurred in reaction to them, but were partly independent of them and influenced them in their turn. With the advance of globalization in the sciences and the frantic pace of change in transport and the electronic media, it has become increasingly difficult to relate this paradigm change to national or regional schools and traditions. At the start of the twenty-first century what we find are closely interlinked globalized sciences with at best national or regional colouring. What began in the 1950s as new German sociology has long since migrated into the network of global discourses.

Variations and alternatives

In the highly politicized climate of the 1960s, the neo-Marxism that flourished at the time succeeded initially in resisting the turn to communication. However, in contrast to France or Italy, Marxism remained largely sterile in Germany, and its climactic points were confined to the revival of interest in Marx (Reichelt 1970). There are indeed a number of further developments up to and beyond the threshold of the twenty-first century, but they became possible only at the cost of massive revisions in the assumptions underlying Marxist orthodoxy. They include widely differing attempts to integrate Gramsci's concepts of hegemony and civil society as well as Adorno's concept of commodity fetishism. Or again, they follow the developments of the late Althusser school, latch on to the ideas of Foucault, Lacan, Anglo-Saxon cultural studies and the debate about Fordism, or else move straight on to the post-Marxism of Laclau, Mouffe, Butler and Zizek (Buckel *et al.* 2003; Hirsch *et al.* 2001). These revisions, while often highly productive, already reflect the impact of the communication paradigm. However, the concepts of communication, language and text are interpreted more broadly than in Luhmann and Habermas and have been extended to include every conceivable social and sub-social phenomenon, including phantasms, actions and body dramatizations, and so forth. Politics, the state and culture move into the centre of theory; dualist doctrines of 'being and consciousness' or 'superstructure and base' make way for ideas that are arranged in heterarchies rather than hierarchies. 'Class struggle' and 'material interests' are read as 'texts'; their 'meanings' are decoded and interpreted as 'discourses'. State and class power mutate into a pluralist tangle of hegemonial and counter-hegemonial power discourses. Materialism is assimilated into an all-inclusive concept of 'language'. Social conflict and communicative understanding are two sides of the same coin which as a rule – and in contrast to Habermas – can be displaced by any concept of reason, however formal, and neutralized by any assumptions of rationality, even functionalist ones.

Other alternatives to the turn to communication frequently follow in the footsteps of phenomenological sociology or rehabilitate philosophical anthropology. The disciples of Gehlen and Plessner have followed an independent course that continues an anthropological theory of society independently of phenomenology, critical theory and systems theory (Rehberg 2001, 2002; Fischer 2004; Lichtblau 2002). But even here we can say that although they have made a clean break with Gehlen's authoritarian view of institutions, they rely all the more strongly on intersubjectivist categories of reciprocal understanding and the formation of identity through communication. In this sense, the alternatives have survived hitherto only as variants on the periphery of the communication paradigm. The same paradigm can be found in Kuhn while a competing research programme can be seen in Lakatos.

The same may be said of phenomenological sociology. This latter sees itself as an alternative to the communication paradigm, but in the last analysis remains within its boundaries and even played an important part in establishing it. Luhmann borrows his concept of *meaning* (*Sinn*) from here, Habermas his concept of the *lifeworld*. Thomas Luckmann, who like Luhmann was born in 1927, but who did not return to Germany from the USA until the end of the 1960s, was largely instrumental in introducing the work of Alfred Schütz into German sociology (Berger and Luckmann 1966; Schütz and Luckmann 1975, 1984; Luckmann 1995). Luckmann follows Schütz in moving Husserl's concept of the *lifeworld* into the centre of a strictly phenomenological theory of *social constitution*, one that shifts from an ordinary notion of *meaning* to the social construction of reality. However, unlike Luhmann or Habermas, Luckmann avoids having any recourse to theory, so as to allow the *original* social nature of man to express itself directly from the point of view of the participant. At the same time, he overcomes the methodological individualism of Husserl and Schütz, replacing it with an *intersubjectivist* perspective wholly in line with the communication paradigm. In the same way, the advance from an ego-based subjectivity to communicative intersubjectivity enables phenomenological sociology to establish a *rival* research programme *within* the communication paradigm (Soeffner 1989). This once again leads social theory back closer to philosophical anthropology, and then develops its own proto-sociological methodology that integrates research and theory into one and the same act. Finally, it differs from Habermas through its value-neutral description and strictly objectivist reconstruction of the social constitution of the real, while distinguishing itself from Luhmann by its radical rejection of a theoretical, purely observer-based concept of system. The starting-point and crux are always the actors themselves. Using a very broad notion of 'constituting' – the actors constitute, create their social world simultaneously as political community and as unpolitical society. Since the *constitution* of society consists in the intersubjective production of socially orientating meaning, the typical modern phenomenon of distorted, faulty or absent meaning moves into the centre of attention in the shape of a *crisis of meaning and orientation* (Berger and Luckmann 1995).

In *direct* reaction to Habermas, Axel Honneth has attempted to appropriate the cultural anthrology of Gehlen and Plessner for Critical Theory, to integrate it in the framework of a Hegelian and Marxist theory of social conflict, and to absorb the ideas of interactionist and psychoanalytical identity theories. Whereas Luhmann is for the most part ignored, the early Habermas is emphasized at the expense of the later one (Honneth 1992). In the course of an intensive exchange with Honneth (Honneth and Joas 1980), Hans Joas, inspired for his part by the social anthropology of the American pragmatists and the recent communitarian debates, has tried to rescue the communitarian, expressive aspect and the innovative power of communication from the grip of hegemonial, rationalist and functionalist interpretations of the communication paradigm (Joas 1992).

Habermas's own pupil, Claus Offe, has also gone his own individual way. A child of globalization, he has long since published more in English than German, and has become better known in America and Australia than in Germany. He combines elements of Habermas's theory of communication with Elster's rational choice theory and Albert Hirschmann's dialectic of 'exit' and 'voice' to make a comprehensive theory of the political system of modern society. With his response to Putnam's discussion of social capital in America, Offe, who had always shown an interest in the development of economics, succeeded finally in establishing a connection between economics and social theory, links that have since been continued independently among academic poitical economists (Grözinger and Panther 1998).

In Offe's writings from the 1970s and early 1980s, the tension between capitalism and democracy stood at the centre of an ever-changing diagnosis of crisis. The secret end-point of that analysis was still the great transformation of 'late capitalism' (Offe 2003). However, in the 1990s his focus shifted to the internal workings of democracy and capitalism. The essay on 'Political Rule and Class Structures', which dated back to a lecture he gave in 1968, was notable for the theme of disparity that became so famous at the time. This contains in a nutshell almost everything that would later come to be written about the risk society and individualization (see below). The search for lines of conflict that intersect individual bio-graphies *despite* existing class structures, and that confront all citizens equally with fragmented, neglected and desolated spheres of life, is a consistent motif of Offe's writings. But in texts written in the 1990s he is no longer concerned with alternatives *to* capitalism but with its widely differing variants – whether beneficial to or destructive of democracy. Instead of 'Socialism or Capitalism' we now find, to cite the title of a work published in 1993, *Capitalism vs Capitalism* (Albert 1993), and as Offe continues to argue in a series of new attempts, the alternatives *within* capitalism are always concerned with society as a whole (Offe 2003). With the shift in focus from outside to inside, his theory likewise changes. Henceforth he is no longer interested in hopes of the 'spread' of crisis, but in the threat to democracy, in 'inno-vations' as opposed to 'retrograde steps' (Offe 2003). The evolutionary implausibility of modern democracy becomes evident. It is implausible that democracies should exist at all; even more implausible that there should suddenly be so many. Like Habermas, Offe still clings to the mediation of facts and values, but his overall message is far more defensive. With the passing of the years it becomes ever clearer to him that democracy is favoured by very specific contexts, and this raises doubts about whether it can be a candidate for globalization. It remains uncertain whether human rights and democracy can thrive beyond the endan-gered, porous frontiers of the nation state. What was once said about Hirschmann can also be said of Offe: he is the 'constructive sceptic' of contemporary social theory.

Within the communication paradigm we can see that, following both Habermas and Luh-mann, there was a certain turning away from abstraction towards the *material side of society*. It is not only post-Marxists or neo-Marxist disciples of Habermas such as Honneth who empha-size the role of the subject, human totality, an inclusive ethic and non-argumentative action. Authors more strongly dependent on Luhmann have also recently shown a striking interest in the material categories of space and region (Stichweh 2000), collectivity and the visibility of communication (Nassehi 2002).

The logical development of the idea of global society is predicated on the accessibility of every possible communication in its uniqueness. Since that is so, the fact of exclusion where it occurs brings to light the disappearance of *space*. The desire for space makes the 'structural coupling' of communication and space in periods in which society faces a radical despatiali-zation appear particularly painful. Communication systems depend on clean air. They are no longer able to exclude spatially all those denied access to communication and are forced to solve the problem within the system by converting it into a problem of time [*Verzeitlichung*]. When the bankers disappear to their suburban villas, the excluded take over the town centres at night. Every communicative act is both global *and* local – electronic post comes literally from nowhere, but is always written somewhere and read somewhere else. Since that is the case, so Stichweh argues, the global decentring of function systems seems to be followed by the compulsion to open up new *regional* spaces (such as 'Europe') beyond the old distinctions within global space ('First World'/'Third World') that had been shaped by the colonial, early modern division of the world into 'blocs' [*Großräume*] (Carl Schmitt). Just as the email address has become the smallest local unit of global communication, so individualized and personalized localities have once again succeeded in creating their own space in the heterarchy of the world's great regions (even down to the surprising renaissance of the registered share certificate). And note that these individual, local phenomena are no longer hermetically sealed off from the global society (as had been the case in the classical nation state). Whereas global causes lead to local catastrophes, the regions turn into catchment areas that are large enough to absorb the global effects of massively increased but functionally superfluous differentiations in space, ethnic identity, religion and stratification, and small enough to make a minimum of commonality perceptible at the political level (Stichweh 2000: 95ff., 191ff. and 226).

The global society and its regionalization are also core themes treated by writers as different as Willke, Scharpf, Münch or Peters, who have recently made attempts to overcome the sceptical attitude to control which is a feature of Luhmann's systems theory, and has been made widely publicized and applauded the increasingly conservative climate of the German press. These writers approach the subject from many different angles: systems theory (Willke 1987); decision theory (Scharpf 1989, 1999); a theory of integration that builds on Parsons (Münch 1991) or synthesizes Parsons and Habermas (Peters 1991, 1993). From these different starting-points, they put forward what are often complex models of control (Willke 1994, 1995), identify untapped control potential in both national and regional politics (Scharpf 1999), describe social evolution as consensus-dependent and hence by implication capable of being corrected (Münch 1991) or use the plural of national socie*ties* not merely as a counter-concept to the singular global society, but also so as to concentrate all normatively acceptable (i.e. public, democratic) control mechanisms in the national *society* (and not in the nation state). For Peters, the communication system represented by the 'national society' is not simply a subsystem of the global society, but rather the global society – unlike what it stands for in Willke and Stichweh – is simply a limiting context for the many national societies (Peters 2001). In contrast, Willke and Stichweh have radicalized Luhmann's notion of the global society and linked it to the theory of the global knowledge society. But they also take a further step beyond Luhmann when they assert that the global society is integrated not just by communicative accessibility, global media and decentred function systems, but also *normatively*, by a universally inclusive *public sphere* that has tended towards globalization from the very outset (i.e. since the eighteenth-century) (Willke 2001, Stichweh 2004). This makes it possible to establish links *between* the two competing approaches to research at the heart of the communication paradigm. There have now been a whole series of attempts to achieve novel syntheses of Habermas and Luhmann, focusing above all on politics and law and the context of the global society (Teubner and Willke 1984; Neves 2000; Brunkhorst 2002, 2005). Whereas one school emphasizes the *functional autonomy* of values in the lifeworld, spontaneously integrated in function systems, the other argues in favour of the *dependence of functional autopoiesis* upon the legitimating actions generated by a diffuse public decision-making process, even though the latter is unable to programme the social evolution to which it belongs.

Lastly, the enthusiastic and highly productive response of the political left to Luhmann (especially in Germany and Italy) has focused attention on the modernist and anarchist implications of his writings. For this reason, left-wing and postmodern writers have done away with the vestiges of state centrism (the state as the centre of a decentred political system) as well as the legal formalism derived from Kelsen and the legal positivism of Luhmann's sociology of law, replacing them with the radical, even anarchic pluralism of global self-help organizations (Teubner 1996, 1997; Fischer-Lescano 2005).

Finally, the postmodern impulse has given birth to the widely read books of Ulrich Beck. His theory of reflexive modernity and the risk society builds on Habermas and also the late Giddens, while ignoring Luhmann. We may regard his work as a further variant of the communication paradigm viewed from the standpoint of the global society (Beck 1986). Beck is interested in the renewal of political and democratic (cosmopolitan) forms of control beyond the nation state (Beck 1993; Beck and Grande 2004). In contrast, systems theorists emphasize the relatively slow progress of globalization in politics (Nassehi 2002) when compared with the frantic pace of globalization in the economy. However, it is unclear, particularly at a time when people talk not only of a global economy but of global (neo)-imperialism, whether the unparalleled development of the privatized economy is actually a structural reality or merely the product of the ubiquitous hegemony of neo-liberal semantics, i.e. whether it is an ideology. Furthermore, the theory of the *second modernity* is likewise conceptually fuzzy, and this may have systematic reasons. The 'reflexivity' of modernization (the second modernization of the first) and 'individualization' 'beyond class and status' are the chief pillars of the theory, together with 'risk', which overlays the older concept of 'crisis'. What is striking is that all these categories could be said to be characteristic features of this 'second modernity' just as much as of the first one, and that they have all been in circulation for a long time as *central* markers of modern society as opposed to the stratified society of 'old Europe'. They have put their stamp on the way this society has understood itself ever since the eighteenth-century. 'Risk' is as basic as the even older modern insurance industry, and in the middle of the nineteenth-century Charles Sanders Peirce could include the risks of the insurance business among the reasons for justifying pragmatism in taking leave from 'old Europe'. Even German idealism had defined the nature of modern society exclusively in terms of its reflexive and individualizing force, and when we read the *Communist Manifesto* we can see how individual autonomy, which begins beyond class and status, marks the divergence of modern capitalism from all previous forms of capitalism and class society. But beyond that, we gain the impression that the reflexive self-production of modern society does not just occur twice, but that it happens every day anew and every day it happens faster. Moreover, little seems to have changed since then. The repetition of the terminology of the 'first modernity' (here I mean words like 'reflexive' and so forth) in Beck's writings, as blunt as it is eye-catching, could equally be described in Gehlen's terms as the *exhaustion* of the potential for innovation in the *post-histoire*. However, such a description would miss the systematic point of a new description in the same terms, since this goes beyond the conservative laments about *post-histoire* and provides us with a progressive *insight* into the inescapable immanence of modern society. Its boundaries can indeed be transcended, though not the way Gehlen had supposed, but only performatively, from the inside and to the inside. And such transcendence is at the same time normative (see the use of 'cosmopolitanism' in Beck 1986), innovative (see the occurrence of 'Europe' in Beck and Grande 2004) and factually unavoidable (as in 'risk', see Beck 1986). To discover innovations in such self-transcendence calls for no new vocabulary, since the vocabulary of the self-description of modern society is the only one that is exclusively designed to generate such innovations.

(Translated by Rodney Livingstone)

Notes

1 This is already anticipated in Parsons. In Parsons' AGIL paradigm the Aristotelian and Weberian concept of action is broken down into a functionally differentiated system consisting of a variety of

components – Luhmann liked to quote Parsons' slogan '*action is system*' – while the person, culture and the organism are forced out into the environment of the social system.

2   Here, too, Luhmann takes up Parsons' idea of the autocatalysis of social systems through a twofold contingency.

3   Luhmann reduced the same three-function paradigm to the triadic model of communication, information and understanding.

References

Albert, M. (1993) *Capitalism vs. Capitalism*, New York: Four Walls Eight Windows.

Apel, K.-O. (1970) 'Peirces Denkweg vom Pragmatismus zum Pragmatizismus', in: K.-O.- Apel (ed.) *Charles Sanders Peirce, Schriften II*, Frankfurt: Suhrfkamp.

Apel, K.-O. (1971) 'Scientistik, Hermeneutik, Ideologiekritik', in: K.-O. Apel (ed.) *Hermeneutik und Ideologiekritik*, Frankfurt: Suhrkamp.

Apel, K.-O. (1971) *Transformation der Philosophie*, vol. 1, Frankfurt: Suhrkamp.

Beck, U. (1986) *Risikogesellschaft*, Frankfurt: Suhrkamp. [Eng. (1992) *Risk Society*, trans. Mark Ritter, London: Sage.]

Beck, U. (1993) *Die Erfindung des Politischen*, Frankfurt: Suhrkamp.

Beck, U. and E. Grande (2004) *Das kosmopolitische Europa*, Frankfurt: Suhrkamp.

Berger, P. L. and T. Luckmann (1966) *The Social Construction of Reality*, New York: Anchor Books.

Berger, P. L. and T. Luckmann (1995) *Modernität, Pluralismus und Sinnkrise. Die Orientierung des modernen Menschen*, Frankfurt: Gütersloh.

Breuer, S. (1995) 'Adorno/Luhmann: Die moderne Gesellschaft zwischen Selbstreferenz und Selbstdestruktion', in S. Breuer *Das Verschwinden der Gesellschaft. Von der Selbstzerstörung der technischen Zivilisation*, Hamburg: Rotbuch Verlag.

Brunkhorst, H. (1988) 'Die ästhetische Konstruktion der Moderne – Adorno, Gadamer, Luhmann', in *Leviathan*, 1: 77–96.

Brunkhorst, H. (2002) *Solidarität. Von der Bürgerfreundschaft zur globalen Rechtsgenossenschaft*, Frankfurt: Suhrkamp [Engl. trans. (2005) *Solidarity. From Civic Friendship to a Global Legal Community*, Cambridge: MIT Press].

Brunkhorst, H. (2005) 'Demokratie in der globalen Rechtsgenossenschaft. Einige überlegungen zur poststaatlichen Verfassung der Weltgesellschaft', in *Zeitschrift für Soziologie: Sonderheft Weltgesellschaft* (forthcoming).

Buckel, S., R-M. Dackweiler, and R. Noppe (eds) (2003) *Formen und Felder politischer Intervention. Zur Relevanz von Staat und Steuerung*, Münster: Westfälisches Dampfboot.

Dahrendorf, R. (1957a) *Soziale Klassen und Klassenkonflikte in der industriellen Gesellschaft*, Stuttgart: Enke.

Dahrendorf, R. (1957b) *Pfade aus Utopia*, München: Piper.

Dahrendorf, R. (1959) *Class and Class Conflict in Industrial Society*, Stanford: Univ. Press (new and revised edition of Dahrendorf 1957a).

Fischer, J. (2004) *Philosophische Anthropologie – Eine Denkrichtung des 20. Jahrhunderts*, Freiburg: Alber.

Fischer-Lescano, A. (2005) *Globalverfassung. Die Geltungsbegründung der Menschenrechte im postmodernen ius gentium*, Weilerswist: Velbrück Wissenschaft.

Freyer, H. (1930) *Soziologie als Wirklichkeitswissenschaft. Logische Grundlegung des Systems der Soziologie*, Leipzig: Teubner.

Freyer, H. (1931, 1st edn 1929) *Revolution von rechts*, Jena: Diederichs.

Gehlen, A. (1950) *Der Mensch. Seine Natur und seine Stellung in der Welt*, Bonn: Athenäum. [Eng. (1988) *Man, his Nature and Place in the World*, trans. C. Macmillan and K. Pillemer, New York: Columbia University Press.]

Gehlen, A. (1952) 'über die Geburt der Freiheit aus der Entfremdung', in *Archiv für Rechts- und Sozialphilosophie* 40, 338–353

Gehlen, A. (1956) *Urmensch und Spätkultur: Philosohische Ergebnisse und Aussagen*, Frankfurt/Bonn: Athenäum.

Gehlen, A. (1957) *Die Seele im technischen Zeitalter*, Hamburg: Rohwolt. [Eng. (1980) *Man in the Age of Technology*, trans. P. Lipscomb, New York/Guildford: Columbia University Press.]

Gehlen, A. (1960) *Zeit-Bilder*, Frankfurt: Klostermann.

Grözinger, G. and S. Panther (1998) *Konstitutionelle Politische ökonomie*, Marburg: Metropolis.

Habermas, J. (1953) 'Mit Heidegger gegen Heidegger denken. Zur Veröffentlichung von Vorlesungen aus dem Jahr 1935', in *Frankfurter Allgemeine Zeitung*, republished in: J. Habermas (1971) *Philosophisch-politische Profile*, Frankfurt: Suhrkamp.

Habermas, J. (1962) *Strukturwandel der öffentlichkeit*, Frankfurt: Suhrkamp. [Eng. *The Structural Transformation of the Public Sphere*, trans. T. Burger and F. Lawrence, Cambridge, Polity Press, 1989.]

Habermas, J. (1968) *Erkenntnis und Interesse*, Frankfurt: Suhrkamp. [Eng. (1972) *Knowledge and Human Interests*, trans. J. Shapiro, London: Heinemann.]

Habermas, J. (1973a) 'Nachwort', in J. Habermas, *Erkenntnis und Interesse*, Frankfurt: Suhrkamp, 367–417.

Habermas, J. (1973b) *Legitimationsprobleme im Spätkapitalismus*, Frankfurt: Suhrkamp. [Eng (1976) *Legitimation Crisis*, trans. T. McCarthy, London: Heinemann.]

Habermas, J. (1981a) *Theorie des kommunikativen Handelns*, 2 vols., Frankfurt: Suhrkamp. [Eng. (1986 & 1989) *The Theory of Communicative Action*, trans. T. McCarthy, Cambridge: Polity Press.]

Habermas, J. (1981b) 'Die Moderne – ein unvollendetes Projekt', in *Kleine politische Schriften I – IV*, Frankfurt: Suhrkamp, 444–466. [Eng. 'Modernity - An Incomplete Project', in M. P. d'Entreva and S. Bebhabib, *Habermas and the Unfinished Project of Modernity*, Cambridge: Polity Press, 1996.]

Habermas, J. (1985) *Der philosophische Diskurs der Moderne. Zwölf Vorlesungen*, Frankfurt: Suhrkamp. [Eng. (2000) *The Philosophical Discourse of Modernity: Twelve Lectures*, trans. F. Lawrence, Cambridge: Polity Press.]

Habermas, J. (1988) *Nachmetaphysisches Denken*, Frankfurt: Suhrkamp. [Eng. (1994), *Postmetaphysical Thinking*, trans. W. M. Hohengarten, Cambridge: Polity Press.]

Habermas, J. (1992) *Faktizität und galtung*, Frankfurt: Suhrkamp.

Habermas, J. (1999) *Wahrheit und Rechtfertigung*, Frankfurt: Suhrkamp.

Habermas, J. (2000) 'Nach dreißig Jahren: Bemerkungen zu *Erkenntnis und Interesse*', in S. Müller-Dohm (ed.) *Das Interesse der Vernunft. Rückblicke auf das Werk von Jürgen Habermas seit 'Erkenntnis und Interesse'*, Frankfurt: Suhrkamp 2000, 12-20.

Habermas, J. (2005) *Religion in the Public Sphere*, Manuscript.

Habermas, J. and N. Luhmann (1971) *Theorie der Gesellschaft oder Sozialtechnologie*, Frankfurt: Suhrkamp.

Hirsch, J., B. Jessop, and N. Poulantzas (ed.) (2001) *Die Zukunft des Staates Denationalisierung, Internationalisierung, Renationalisierung*, Hamburg: VSA.

Honneth, A. (1992) *Kampf um Anerkennung. Zur moralischen Grammatik sozialer Konflikte*, Frankfurt: Suhrkamp. [(Eng. 1995) *The Struggle for Recognition*, trans. J. Anderson, Cambridge: Polity Press.]

Honneth, A. and H. Joas (1980) *Soziales Handeln und menschliche Natur. Anthropologische Grundlagen der Sozialwissenschaften*, Frankfurt: Campus.

Horkheimer, M. and T. W. Adorno (1997) *Dialektik der Aufklärung. Philosophische Fragmente*, Ges. Schriften 3, Frankfurt: Suhrkamp. [Eng. (2002) *Dialectic of Enlightenmnent*, trans. E. Jephcott, Stanford, Cal.: Stanford University Press.]

Joas, H. (1992) *Die Kreativität des Handelns*, Frankfurt: Suhrkamp. [Eng trans. (1996) *The Creativity of Action*, trans. J. Gaines and P. Keast, Cambridge: Polity Press.]

Korsch, K. (1993) *Marxismus und Philosophie: Schriften zur Theorie der*, in M. Buckmiller (ed.) Arbeiterbewegung 1920–1923, Frankfurt: EVA. [Eng. (1970) *Marxism and Philosophy*, trans. Fred Halliday, London: NLB.]

Lichtblau, K. (2002) *Transformation der Moderne*, Berlin: Philo.

Luckmann, T. (1995) *Theorie des sozialen Handelns*, Berlin/New York: de Gruyter.

Luhmann, N. (1964) *Funktionen und Folgen formaler Organisation*, Berlin: Duncker & Humblot.

Luhmann, N. (1965) *Grundrechte als Institution*, Berlin: Duncker & Humblot.

Luhmann, N. (1969) *Legitimation durch Verfahren*, Frankfurt: Suhrkamp.

Luhmann, N. (1974) 'Einleitende Bemerkungen zu einer Theorie der symbolisch generalisierten Kommunikationsmedien', in: *Zeitschrift für Soziologie* 3, 236ff.

Luhmann, N. (1981) 'Machtkreislauf und Recht in Demokratien', in: *Zeitschrift für Rechtssoziologie* 2, 158–167.

Luhmann, N., (1982) 'Autopoiesis, Handlung und kommunikative Verständigung', in: *Zeitschrift für Soziologie* 47: 366–379.

Luhmann, N. (1984) *Soziale Systeme. Grundriss einer allgemeinen Theorie*, Frankfurt: Suhrkamp.

Luhmann, N. (1987) 'Autopoiesis als soziologischer Begriff', in: H. Haferkamp and M. Schmidt (eds) *Sinn, Kommunikation und soziale Differenzierung. Beiträge zu Luhmanns Theorie sozialer Systeme*, Frankfurt: Suhrkamp.

Luhmann, N. (1990) 'Verfassung als evolutionäre Errungenschaft', in *Rechtshistorisches Journal* 9, 176–220.

Luhmann, N. (1992) *Einführung in die Systemtheorie: Autobahnuniversität*, Heidelberg: Carl-Auer-Systeme Verlag, Lecture Notes from the Winter Semester 1991/92.

Luhmann, N. (1994) *Theorie der Gesellschaft: Autobahnuniversität*, Heidelberg: Carl-Auer-Systeme Verlag, Vorlesungsmitschnitt aus dem Sommersemester.

Luhmann, N. (1997a) *Die Gesellschaft der Gesellschaft*, Frankfurt: Suhrkamp.

Luhmann, N. (1997b) *Das Recht der Gesellschaft*, Frankfurt: Suhrkamp.

Luhmann, N. (2002) *Einführung in die Systemtheorie: Autobahnuniversität*, Heidelberg: Carl-Auer-Systeme Verlag, Vorlesungsmitschnitt aus dem Wintersemester 1991/1992.

Lukács, G. (1923) *Geschichte und Klassenbewusstsein. Studien über marxistische Dialektik*, Berlin: Malik. [Eng. (1971) *History and Class Consciousness*, trans. Rodney Livingstone, London: Merlin Press.]

Marcuse, H. (1930) 'Das Problem der geschichtlichen Wirklichkeit', in: T. W. Adorno, M. Horkheimer, and H. Marcuse *Kritische Theorie der Gesellschaft IV*, o.O., o.J.: Raubdruck.

Marcuse, H (1932) 'Zum Problem der Dialektik' I und II; in: T. W. Adorno, M. Horkheimer, and H. Marcuse *Kritische Theorie der Gesellschaft IV*, o.O., o.J.: Raubdruck, 243–282. [Eng. 'On the Problem of Dialectic', trans. M. Schoolman (Part I) and D. Smith (part II), in *Telos* 27, Spring 1976, 12–40.]

Marx, K. (1960) 'Thesen über Feuerbach', in: K. Marx and F. Engels, *Die deutsche Ideologie*, Berlin: Dietz. [Eng. (1976:4) K. Marx and F. Engels *The German Ideology*, in *Collected Works*, vol. 5, London: Lawrence & Wishart.]

Mayntz, R. (1958) *Die soziale Organisation des Industriebetriebes*, Stuttgart; Enke.

Mayntz, R. (1961) 'Die Organisationssoziologie und ihre Beziehungen zur Organisationslehre', in: E. Schnaufer and K. Agte (ed.) *Organisation*, Berlin/Baden-Baden: Deutscher Betriebswirte Verlag.

Münch, R. (1991) *Dialektik der Kommunikationsgesellschaft*, Frankfurt: Suhrkamp.

Nassehi, A. (2002) 'Politik des Staats oder Politik der Gesellschaft? Kollektivität als Problemformel des Politischen', in: K-U. Hellmann and R. Schmalz-Bruhns (ed.) *Theorie der Politik. Niklas Luhmanns politische Soziologie*, Frankfurt: Suhrkamp.

Neves, M. (1992) *Verfassung und positives Recht in der peripheren Moderne*. Berlin: Duncker & Humblot.

Neves, M. (2000) *Zwischen Themis und Leviathan: Eine schwierige Beziehung*. Baden-Baden: Nomos.

Offe, C. (2003) *Herausforderungen der Demokratie. Zur Integrations- und Leistungsfähigkeit politischer Institutionen*, Frankfurt: Campus.

Peters, B. (1991) *Rationalität, Recht und Gesellschaft*, Frankfurt: Suhrkamp.

Peters, B. (1993) *Die Integration moderner Gesellschaften*, Frankfurt: Suhrkamp.

Peters, B. (2001) *Deliberative öffentlichkeit*, Frankfurt: Suhrkamp.

Plessner, H. (1924) *Grenzen der Gemeinschaft. Eine Kritik des sozialen Radikalismus*, Bonn: Cohen.

Plessner, H. (1927) *Die Stufen des Organischen und der Mensch*, Berlin: de Gruyter.

Rehberg, K-S. (1999) 'Hans Freyer, Arnold Gehlen, Helmut Schelsky', in D. Kaesler (ed.) *Klassiker der Soziologie*, vol. 2, München: Beck.

Rehberg, K-S. (2001) 'Aktion und Ordnung. Soziologie als Handlungslehre', in C. Bohn and H. Willems (eds) *Sinngeneratoren – Fremd- und Selbstthematisierung in soziologisch-historischer Perspektive*, Konstanz: Univ. Verlag, 301–337.

Rehberg, K-S. (2002) 'Institution, Kognition und Symbole', in A. Maurer and M. Schmid (ed.) *Neuer Institutionalismus*, Frankfurt: Campus.

Reichelt, H. (1970) *Zur logischen Struktur des Kapitalbegriffs bei Marx*, Frankfurt: EVA.

Scharpf, F. (1989) 'Politische Steuerung und Politische Institutionen', in: *Politische Vierteljahrsschrift* 1, 10–21.

Scharpf, F. (1999) *Regieren in Europa – Effektiv und demokratisch?* Frankfurt: Campus.

Schelsky, H. (1957) *Die skeptische Generation*, Düsseldorf: Diederichs.

Schelsky, H. (1960) *Einsamkeit und Freiheit*, Münster/Westfalen: Aschendorff.

Schelsky, H. (1965) *Auf der Suche nach der Wirklichkeit. Gesammelte Aufsätze*, Düsseldorf: Diederichs.

Schelsky, H. (1981) *Rückblicke eines Anti-Soziologen*, Opladen: Westdeutscher Verlag.

Schmitt, C. (1950) *Der Nomos der Erde*, Berlin: Duncker & Humblot. [Eng. (2003) *The Nomos of the Earth in the International Law of the Jus Publicum Europaeum*, trans. G. L. Ulmen, New York: Telos.]

Schütz, A. and T. Luckmann (1975 and 1984) *Strukturen der Lebenswelt*, vol. 1 (1975) and vol 2 (1984) Neuwied: EVA [Eng. (1973) *The Structures of the* Life-World, trans. R. M. Zaner and H. T. Engelhardt Jr., Evanston (IL): Northwestern University Press.]

Soeffner, H. G. (1989) *Auslegung des Alltags – der Alltag der Auslegung. Zur wissenschaftssoziologischen Konzeption einer sozialwissenschaftlichen Hermeneutik*, Frankfurt: Suhrkamp.

67

Stichweh, R. (2000) *Die Weltgesellschaft. Soziologische Analysen*, Frankfurt: Suhrkamp.

Stichweh, R. (2004) 'Der Zusammenhalt der Weltgesellschaft: Nicht-normative Integrationstheorien in der Soziologie', in: J. Beckert, J. Eckert, M. Kohli, and W. Streek (eds) *Transnationale Solidarität. Chancen und Grenzen*, Frankfurt: Campus.

Teubner, G. (1996) 'Globale Bukowina. Zur Emergenz eines transnationalen Rechtspluralismus', in: *Rechtshistorisches Journal* 15: 255–290.

Teubner, G. (ed.) (1997) *Global Law Without a State*, Aldershot: Dartmouth.

Teubner, G. and H. Willke (1984) 'Kontext und Autonomie: Gesellschaftliche Selbststeuerung durch reflexives Recht', in: *Zeitschrift für Rechtssoziologie* 6: 4–35.

Willke, H. (1987, 1994, 1996) *Systemtheorie I-III*, 3 vols., Stuttgart: Lucius & Lucius.

Willke, H. (2001) *Atopia*, Frankfurt: Suhrkamp.

6

The age of epigones

Post-Bourdieusian social theory in France

Frédéric Vandenberghe

The French do not only produce high fashion, good wine and soft cheese; they also produce fine intellectuals and export their precious thoughts as valuable items for academic consumption and distinction. The highly centralised, elitist educational system of the *grandes écoles* is uniquely suited to produce well-trained cohorts of highly cultivated, polyvalent, original and provocative politicised thinkers, like Foucault, Bourdieu and Derrida, who set the intellectual agenda world-wide. Somewhat envious of the French spirit, sociologists from abroad often think of France as a country where every working sociologist is, by nature, a social theorist who combines elegance with depth and commitment. But, paradoxically, if the republic counts indeed an impressive number of internationally famous social theorists, it knows no social theory as such, at least not if one understands by social theory the relatively autonomous subfield of sociology that aims to construct a unified view of the social world through exegesis of the classics (Marx, Weber, Durkheim) and re- or deconstruction of the contemporary canon (Habermas, Giddens, Foucault, etc.).

In France, the sociologist is not supposed to work on theory for theory's sake. The scholar who submits sociological texts to an ontological, epistemological and ideological investigation is not doing social theory, but 'epistemology'.[1] Wary of the scholastic elaborations of the 'idealists without heart' and the speculations of the 'materialists without material', French sociology has remained Durkheimian in this respect. If one wants to tackle the great theoretical questions, one can do so, but only via case studies or investigative fieldwork. Bourdieu's work is exemplary in this regard, but not exceptional. Alain Touraine developed the actionalist perspective on historical action while doing research on working class consciousness in the factories of Renault; Michel Crozier theorised the 'vicious circles of bureaucracy' in the course of an analysis of the strategies of power in the administration of two public enterprises; Edgard Morin expanded his systemic theory of complexity in a multidimensional analysis of social change in the small village of Plozevet and, more recently, Albert Piette (1992) worked out a grand theory of theorising in the minor mode.

Three generations of sociology

In spite of the early institutionalisation of sociology around Durkheim, Mauss and the *Année Sociologique*, French sociology remained for a long time under the wings of philosophy. In fact, it is only after World War II that sociology would become fully recognized as an autonomous discipline with its own research agenda and teaching curriculum. Since then, three generations of sociologists have evolved. In the 1950s and the 1960s, the field was largely dominated (from right to left by) Raymond Aron, Claude Lévi-Strauss, Georges Gurvitch, Lucien Goldman and Louis Althusser. After 1968, Pierre Bourdieu, Alain Touraine, Raymond Boudon and Michel Crozier took over the main field of sociology.[2] The 'gang of four' would effectively control the field up till the end the 1980s, leaving the margins to post-modernising sociologists like Michel Maffesoli, Pierre Sansot and Jean-Claude Kaufmann who gather around Georges Balandier, a political socio-anthropologist, and publish in his journal *Cahiers internationaux de sociologie*.

If Bourdieu's 'genetic structuralism' and Touraine's 'actionalist sociology' are relatively well known abroad, the same cannot be said of Boudon's 'methodological individualism', and even less of Crozier's 'strategic analysis'. In the 1980s, Touraine proposed to reconceptualise social movements as Subjects searching for meaning rather than as carriers of 'historicity'. Since the 1990s, his thinking has taken a personalist turn and a tragic tone. He now conceives of 'late' (or 'low') modernity in terms of a dissociation of the system and the actor, while society, which used to constitute the link between both, has disintegrated into a global world of things and a tribal world of identities (Touraine 1997). 'Methodological individualism' represents the French variant of rational choice theory. In order to escape the strict utilitarianism of the latter, Boudon has opened up the concept of rationality. Taking a stand against relativism, his sociology of knowledge explores and explains 'wrong choices' in terms of 'good reasons'. Of late, the former collaborator of Lazarsfeld has even attempted to reconsider Weber's value-rationality along similar lines (Boudon 1995). While 'methodological individualism' appears as a reasonable remake of rational choice, 'strategic analysis' represents an application of Simon and March's analysis of 'bounded rationality' to the sociology of organizations. In *L'acteur et le système*, Crozier and Friedberg (1977) have developed a systematic framework for the analysis of the relations of power within organisations. Focusing on the 'margins of freedom' that social actors can strategically manipulate to advance their own interests, they analyse organisations as contingent and collective constructs of organised action.

In the 1980s and the 1990s, a new generation of sociologists, social theorists and political philosophers has emerged on the scene. Reacting against the post-structuralist 'masters of suspicion' (Bourdieu, Foucault, Lacan, Derrida), they have introduced a paradigmatic change in the social sciences – from structuralism and the critique of domination to pragmatism, phenomenology and the hermeneutics of interpretation.[3] The sociologists who turned to action insisted with Ricoeur, Habermas and Giddens – but against Bourdieu – on the reflexive capacities of the agent. Influenced by the 'linguistic turn' that took place in analytic and continental philosophy, they took up the lead of American pragmatism, symbolic interactionism, phenomenology and ethnomethodology, and tried to overcome the opposition between agency and structure through a constructivist analysis of situated interaction.[4] Even if the new sociologies are rather variegated, they nevertheless display some interesting 'family resemblances': Reaction against the determinism of Bourdieu's theory of reproduction and, to a lesser extent, the historicism of Touraine's sociology of social movements; strong influence of Anglo-Saxon philosophy, continental hermeneutics and American micro-sociology; multidisciplinary approach of the social world with particular attention to anthropology, history and economics; grand theory conjoined with minute ethno-philosophical analysis of action; insistence on the ordinary competence of actors coupled to attempts to introduce society, history and politics via a constructivist analysis of the concrete situation of action;

political engagement on the left and regular interventions in the public sphere or, at least, in the columns of the main quality newspapers.

There's no doubt that Bourdieu is the towering figure of French post-war sociology. His position in the French field can easily be compared to the one Parsons occupied in the American one up until the 1960s. Whether one likes it or not, his influence is such that one has to think either with or against Bourdieu. The most interesting developments in francophone sociology are definitely post-, though not necessarily anti-Bourdieusian. In the following sections of this chapter, I will first present the posthumous publications of Pierre Bourdieu; and next, I will proceed to post-Bourdieusian sociology as such. In sequence, I will expound the pragmatic sociology of Luc Boltanski, Laurent Thévenot and Eve Chiapello; the actor-network theory of Bruno Latour and Michel Callon; the mediation studies of Régis Debray; the political philosophy of Marcel Gauchet and the sociology of the gift of Alain Caillé; and, crossing the Atlantic, I will conclude with the Montreal School of Michel Freitag.[5]

Posthumous publications of Pierre Bourdieu

Some people are forgotten before they die, others, like Pierre Bourdieu (1930–2002), expire under the glare of publicity. Although the publication of the quasi-totality of his interventions in the public sphere – from the war of Algeria to the one in Bosnia and from the reform of the universities to his scathing attack on the media (Bourdieu 2002a) – show that he was always a 'political animal', it is only in the last decade of his life that he willingly assumed the role of the 'total intellectual' *à la* Sartre and became a national celebrity. In *La sociologie est un sport de combat*, a documentary film made by Pierre Carles (2001), one sees the leading sociologist touring the country to criticise the neo-liberal politics of globalisation, giving a voice to the 'no-no's' ('*les sans*'), those who have no voice, no job, no papers, no nothing. Since his death, Loïc Wacquant, his transatlantic interpreter who studies boxing, ghettos and prisons in America (Wacquant 2000/2003), seems to have inherited the pugilistic habitus of his master.

A few months after his death, Bourdieu's autobiography was published, not in French though, but in German (Bourdieu 2002b). *Outline for a self-analysis* extends the final lecture of the course on the reflexive sociology of science that he gave at the *Collège de France* (Bourdieu 2001) with a protracted socio-analysis of his intellectual journey. His ambivalence towards the intellectual world, which expresses itself in a strange, but comprehensible mixture of intellectual arrogance and self-depreciation, appears as a psychic sedimentation of the years of lonely suffering he spent at the boarding-school, a 'total institution' that almost broke him. Following his studies in philosophy at the Ecole normale supérieure, where he came under the influence of the 'historical epistemology' of Gaston Bachelard and Georges Canguilhem, the young philosopher from the province went to Algeria to fulfil his military service. During the war of independence, he did extensive fieldwork and became an anthropologist. The catalogue of the exhibition of the pictures he took in Algeria show that he had not only a sharp mind, but also a good eye for the details of everyday life (Bourdieu 2003). Having moved in the 1950s from philosophy to ethnology, the young anthropologist 'converted' in the mid-1960s to sociology. Throwing himself frenetically in all kinds of sociological researches on all kinds of objects and subjects (photography, comic strips, cultural taste, Heidegger, etc.), the sociological genius developed in the span of a few years (1966–1972) a total theory of the social world. Bourdieu was only in his mid-thirties when he formulated, at the highest level of abstraction and with the greatest conceptual precision, the interrelated theories of 'fields',

71

'the habitus' and 'symbolic violence' that form the backbone of his progressive research pro-gramme into the reproduction of the structures of domination.

The posthumous publication of three texts (Bourdieu 2002c), written at different times, in which he analyses the progressive exclusion of peasants from the matrimonial market, allows one to follow in detail how he successively developed and integrated his main concepts in a grand theory of social reproduction. In the first text, Bourdieu presents a total description of his native village in the south of France. He explains the celibacy of the peasant through a masterful description of his habitus – 'he drags his big wooden shoes or his heavy boots even though he's wearing his Sunday shoes' (Bourdieu 2002b: 114) – that can compare with Heidegger's. In the second text, the same problematic is treated once again, but this time the matrimonial practices are explained in terms of unconscious strategies of reproduction. In the third text, the symbolic dimension of the economic exclusion of peasants is covered through an analysis of the modernisation of rural regions. The book concludes with a violent postscript in which Bourdieu slams the urban representations of the rural and attacks Foucault in a footnote.

Since the 1990s, the international reception of his oeuvre has grown into a prosperous cottage industry, comparable perhaps to the field of Foucaldian and Habermasian studies. The publication of Bourdieu's completed bibliography (Bourdieu 2002d) thus comes in handy. In France as well, his work is now being seriously studied. Several books have appeared and, by the end of 2004, at least five edited collections had been published as a tribute to the departed sociologist. Whereas most critiques try to think 'with Bourdieu against Bourdieu', Bernhard Lahire (1998) is more ambitious and tries to think differently from him. Starting with an analysis of the ordinary practices of writing of shopping lists, travel plans, etc., he has intro-duced reflexivity into the habitus and developed an ambitious theory of plural actors in which individuals appear as the product of multiple, heterogeneous and conflicting process of socialisation. In his last book (2004), a remake of *Distinction* he has explained in detail how the heterogeneity of the habitus expresses itself in the sphere of cultural consumption.

Pragmatic sociology

Luc Boltanski, a sociologist, and Laurent Thévenot, an economist, are former colleagues of Bourdieu who were working on the social construction of socio-professional categories and groups when they fell out with the master.[6] Together, they have written *On Justification: The Economies of Stature* (Boltanski and Thévenot 1991, 1999), a major treatise on the pragmatics of justice in which they systematically link up the micro-sociology of ordinary conflicts to the 'economy of conventions', a heterodox school of institutional economy that analyses the role of social representations in the coordination of actions. Breaking with the structuralist assumptions of Bourdieu's critical sociology of domination, they have steadily moved towards a more hermeneutic sociology of critique and legitimation that redeploys Michael Walzer's theory of the spheres of justice in a pragmatist theory of situated action.

The theory of justification analyses short stretches of actions in which actors publicly denounce situations of injustice, and offers a 'grammar of disputes' in which different prin-ciples of justice are simultaneously at work. Disputes are analysed as conflicts in which the 'stature' of persons are at stake. In order to explicate the 'logic of inquiry' (Dewey) that allows for a qualification of the persons and the objects that make up the concrete situation of dis-pute, Boltanski and Thévenot construct a model, known as the model of the *Cités* or Com-monwealths, that formalises the argumentative and normative constraints that actors have to take into account if their critique is to be accepted as a valid one. *Cités* are axiological orders, built around a central value, in which a vision of 'the good life with and for others in just institutions' (to quote Ricoeur) is systematically worked out. Drawing on classic works of political philosophy (St Augustine, Bossuet, Hobbes, Rousseau, Saint Simon and A. Smith), they distinguish six orders of justification and their corresponding values: the Commonwealth of inspiration (grace and intuition), household (loyalty and trust), fame (opinion and recognition), citizenship (equality and solidarity), industry (efficacy and technical competence) or market (competition and economic performance).[7] The authors do not wish to suggest, of course, that ordinary people have read any of these authors. Rather their argument is that when actors proffer a critique, they necessarily act as practical metaphysicians and implicitly refer to philosophical vocabularies of justification that appeal to a common good.

Moving from the lofty heights of political philosophy to the commonplaces of everyday life, Boltanski and Thévenot follow actor-network theory (cfr. *infra*) and introduce ordinary objects into the model of justification. Unlike humans, who can aspire to greatness in any of the Commonwealths and can thus not be attached definitively to any of them, non-humans have a well defined character. A chronometer belongs to the world of industry, a poem to the world of inspiration, and a banknote to the world of the market. Those common objects play a central role in disputes. When they are activated *in situ*, a corresponding register of justification is automatically selected, and the stature of the actor can consequently be evaluated. An empty CV, tended to an employer, is enough to disqualify the candidate as a 'small player' in the job market, while one's appearance on the cover of a magazine defines one as a 'big fish' in the world of fame. Protagonists of a dispute also have the capacity to foreground objects, point to them to redefine the situation to their advantage or to clear compromises.

Focusing on micro-situations of conflict, *On Justification* does not really take macro-social structures of domination into account. In *The New Spirit of Capitalism*, Luc Boltanski and Eve Chiapello (1999) have extended the pragmatic model of the *Cités* to analyse the structural transformations of capitalism since the 1960s. The basic argument of this great book, already a minor classic in France, is that capitalism has successfully co-opted the anti-capitalist critique, with the result that capitalism is stronger than ever while the critique of capitalism seems rather disarmed. Capitalism, or the unlimited accumulation of capital by formally pacific means, cannot function without an ideology that justifies it in terms of the common good. Capitalism needs a spirit. Since the nineteenth-century, three spirits of capitalism have succeeded each other. The 'first spirit' corresponds to a predominantly domestic capitalism and focuses on the individual entrepreneur. The central values are the family and competition. Confronted with the social question, liberal capitalism reorganised itself in the 1930s along Taylorist, Fordist and Keynesian lines. The dominant figure of organised capitalism is the managing director. The forms of justification invoked by the 'second spirit' are of a civic and industrial nature and concern mainly security (of employment, promotion, indexed income, etc.). As capitalism could no longer 'afford' the neo-corporatist arrangement of the 'golden thirties', it started to restructure itself in the 1980s along neo-liberal lines.

Boltanski and Chiapello analyse the 'new spirit of capitalism' by way of a comparative analysis of literature of management of the 1960s and the 1990s. They distinguish two forms of critique of capitalism, the 'social' and the 'artistic' critique, and argue that the neo-liberal turn of the 1980s can be explained in terms of the progressive integration of the artistic critique of capitalism by capitalism itself. Social critique corresponds to the traditional critique of capitalism by the workers' movement. It denounces poverty, inequality and exploitation in the name of solidarity and justice. Artistic critique is post-modern. It criticises the alienating and dehumanising nature of organised capitalism in the name of spontaneity, creativity and authenticity. In May 1968, the two critiques were joined and capitalism was seriously challenged.

At first, the employers negotiated with the trade unions about wages. In the 1980s, they started to lend an ear to the artistic critique. Circumventing the unions, they gave a neo-liberal interpretation to the libertarian demands of creativity, introduced flexibility in the workplace, and transformed the organisation into a contractual network. Confronted with insecurity, the flexi-worker became a networker selling his self, his skills and his project on the market. Criticising the injustice of network capitalism, Boltanski and Chiapello call for a renewal of social critique.

Actor-network theory

Bruno Latour, a post-modern theologian and anthropologist, and Michel Callon, an engineer and sociologist, work at the *Centre de sociologie de l'innovation* (CSI) of the *Ecole des Mines* in Paris. Together, they have developed actor-network theory (ANT) as one of the most original, provocative and iconoclastic sociologies currently on offer. ANT started as a radical offshoot of the social studies of science of the 1970s and the 1980s that aimed to deconstruct the philosophies of sciences through an ethnographic study of science in the making.[8] Creatively drawing on the philosophy of translation of Michel Serres and the rhizomatics of Gilles Deleuze and Felix Guattari, Latour and Callon forcefully introduce objects into sociology, and analyse society in the making as an expanding socio-technical network that associates humans and non-humans into a 'seamless web'. Thanks to the good services of John Law in the UK, ANT is now becoming a global success story in academia.

The main tenets of ANT can be summarised in *three* sentences:

1 *Science is social* (Latour 1988). Through a technography of a scientific laboratory in California, Latour and Woolgar showed how scientific facts are literally constructed and fabricated by scientists. Working with 'inscription devices' that re-present nature on paper and reduce reality to a flat surface, scientists were busy transforming rats and chemicals into a series of blots, graphs and figures that could be integrated in their articles. As their vision of nature became generally accepted by colleagues, who quoted the article, the scientific representation of nature was progressively hardened and transformed into a scientific fact ('blackboxed'). When the square quotes around 'nature' were eventually removed, nature ended up appearing as something that was not made but discovered by the scientist. In spite of the radical constructivist assumptions, one should not conclude too quickly, however, that Latour is anti-science. His work on scientific inscriptions aims to show how scientists construct nature as a scientific fact through a 'cascade of representations' that describes nature more and more accurately.

2 *Society is natural* (Latour 1996). Scientific facts are socially constructed but cannot be reduced to the social because the social is also made up of objects mobilised to construct it. For too long sociologists have analysed society as a commonwealth of humans (subjects), without understanding that society is impossible without non-humans (objects) that stabilise social relations and keep society together. What distinguishes baboons from humans is the fact that the latter use objects to give material consistency to the social contract. Thanks to common objects (walls, doors, tables, televisions, etc.) – and contrary to ethnomethodologists, who treat humans as if they were baboons! – the social order does not have to be continuously renegotiated and constantly remade *in situ*. Non-humans do not only replace and stand in for humans – e.g. the traffic light replaces a policeman and the automatic door closer, a porter – but they can be considered

as actors in their own right. Drawing on Greimas' structural semiotics, Latour and Callon introduce the notion of 'actant' to refer to any actor, human or non-human – God, scientists, microbes, scallops, etc. – that intervenes in the construction of society as a heterogeneous network of humans and non-humans.

3 *Nature and society are co-constructed in and through socio-technical networks that associate humans and non-humans into a seamless web* (Callon and Latour 1981). Nature and society are not given, but always in the making; neither is a cause, both are a result and emerge out of the network that continuously transforms and performs reality. Mutually constitutive of each other, nature and society are co-produced and constituted in and through the heterogeneous network that associates humans and non-humans. Redefining sociology as the science of associations, ANT analyses how micro-actors become macro-actors by enrolling humans and non-humans alike in an expanding rhizomatic network. At this point, the sociology of science takes a political turn and science is analysed as politics by other means. Natural scientists (like Pasteur) who represent nature or social scientists (like Bourdieu) who represent society, speak in the name of others and give them a voice. Speaking in their name, they 'translate' their interests, associate them to their project, integrate them in a collective, and progressively compose the world as a network among networks that potentially covers the whole world.

Mediation studies

Like Boltanski, Thévenot and Latour, Régis Debray used to be close to Bourdieu, but expelled from the cenacle, he broke with him to go his own way. Former comrade in arms of Che Guevara, former consultant for the Third World of President Mitterand, staunch defender of the nation-state, this polymath, novelist and political theorist is a rather controversial figure. On his own, he invented mediology as the new science of mediations, launched a new journal *Les cahiers de mediologie*, and gathered some of the most interesting philosophers of technology (Bernard Stiegler, François Dagognet, Pierre Lévy, but also Bruno Latour and Antoine Hennion) around his project. Like Latour, Debray is a follower of Michel Serres, and conceives of technology as a socio-technical construct; unlike Latour, he is not influenced by Deleuze and Guattari, however, but by Paul Valéry (an essayist), André Leroi-Gourhan (a palaeontologist) and the Toronto School of Media Studies (McLuhan, Derrick de Kerckhove, Harold Innis).

Mediology or mediation studies broadens the notion of media so as to include all material and institutional vectors of communication – from the ways, the canals, the stations, the ports and the portals to the sects, the churches, the schools and the parties. It defines mediation as the totality of interactions between culture and technology that makes the diffusion (through space) and the transmission (over time) of ideas possible. Taunting communication scholars who work in the tradition of Roland Barthes, Debray presents the new interdiscipline as a successor science to media studies that integrates the semiotic analysis of contents in a more encompassing philosophy of the history of the technologies that transmit culture across generations.

At the most general level, mediology studies the material and institutional conditions of the symbolic transmission of culture and the (re)production of society. In *Critique of Political Reason,* Debray (1981) analysed the role of ideology in the structuration of collectives. He argued that religions (which unify) and nations (which divide) are not simply social representations of

75

reality; to the extent that they emotionally move people, they have a symbolic efficacy and a performative force that can transform people, society and history. *Cours de médiologie générale* (Debray 1991) is the foundational text of the study of mediations. It deepens the metapolitical analysis of ideologies and group formation with an analysis of the techno-social modes of the transmission of ideologies and ideas. Religions and ideologies may grip the masses, but it is only if the prophet and the ideologue can rely on an effective social organisation and a powerful system for the diffusion and the transmission of their ideas that they can possibly intervene as a force in history. Situated at the crossroads of philosophy, theology, anthropology, archaeology, history, sociology, political sciences, semiotics, media and cultural studies, mediology is a relatively autonomous discipline that analyses the totality of the processes of mediation that intervene between culture and agency, and transform ideas into a material force.

Following Serres and Latour, Debray conceives of mediation as a socio-technical process of hybridisation that interconnects culture (ideas and texts, such as the *Communist Manifesto*), people (like Marx, but also intellectuals and workers) and media (from printing to travelling) into an active network. To understand 'how one can do things with words', one has to open the black box of the medium and analyse mediation as a double process in which ideas are transmitted by technological vectors at the same time as people are organised into groups and societies.

Mediology conceives of the media not so much as material causes, but as formal causes, in the Aristotelian sense of the word. The media are not neutral vectors of cultural transmission, but they impose a certain worldview and configure a certain way of thinking, feeling and acting. In order to analyse the shifting impact of the spoken, the written and the audio-visual media on society and politics, Debray introduces the ecological notion of the 'mediasphere' as a masterconcept and analyses the successive development and integration of the logo- (writing), grapho- (printing) and videosphere (audio-visual).[9] The current passage from the logo- to the videosphere implies not only a shift of predominance from the power of words to the power of images, but this shift is also linked to a commercialisation of intellectual and political life. Somewhat nostalgic of the times when television did not rule politics, Debray deplores and criticises the current state of 'mediocracy' in a stream of books.

The recomposition of society through politics

Marcel Gauchet and Alain Caillé are both former students of Claude Lefort and critics of Pierre Bourdieu. Inspired by the critique of totalitarianism of *Socialisme et Barbarie* (Lefort, Castoriadis and Lyotard), they consider 'the political' as a fundamental dimension of social life. In opposition to socialism and liberalism, they insist on the potentials and the liabilities of radical democracy, and are looking at civil society to breathe new life into the atomised society of egoist individuals. One way or another, both are exploring the question of the social order from the perspective of comparative historical anthropology and insisting on the importance of symbolic representations for the structuration of society. Finally, both are public intellectuals on the left who animate a journal and seek to stimulate non-partisan public debate.

Marcel Gauchet is the editor in chief of *Le Débat*. In spite of his classicism, he might well be the successor of Michel Foucault. Like Foucault, he delves into the archives of the past in order to develop a 'history of the present'. What he wants to understand is the coincidence of the secularisation of religion, the advent of historicity and the invention of democracy that marks the protracted transition to modernity, as well as the consequent adventures of democracy in individualist societies like ours where individuals give themselves their own laws. Through a history of psychiatry, which is at the same a critique of Foucault's *History of Madness*; through the study of the French revolution and the invention of human rights; and, above all, through a political history of religion, Gauchet has investigated the transition from a holist, hierarchical and heteronomous conception to an individualist, egalitarian and autonomous conception of society.

In *The Disenchantment of the World*, a Weberian treatise in political theology, he interprets Christianity as the 'religion of the exit of religion' (Gauchet 1985: II). Following the invention of monotheism during the axial age, humanity projects itself in a transcendent personal God who offers a symbolic representation of the unity of society and thereby founds the social order. With the emergence of the State in traditional societies, the transcendental order becomes progressively 'introjected' into society in the form of worldly power. The symbolic representation of society is incorporated at first by the absolute king; later, with the French revolution, power will be democratized and represented by the Law. The democratic revolution marks the breakthrough of individualism and inverts the order of foundation from top to bottom. Henceforth, the coexistence of individuals and the unity of society will be the product of the individuals themselves. Through the democratization of power, societies renounce the idea of unity, depersonalize power, become pluralist and accept conflict as a fundamental given of social life. While totalitarianism tried to reintroduce by force the unity of holistic and hierarchical societies into individualist and egalitarian societies, liberalism endorses individualism and conceives of the social order as an order that spontaneously emerges from below.

In the long run the successes of liberal democracy and human rights undermine, however, the political foundations of society. Offering a critical evaluation of contemporary politics and societies, Gauchet (2002) points to the contradictions of democracy in different fields (religion, education, psychology, ecology, social movements, etc.). Convinced that societies cannot exist without a holistic reference, he warns a depolitisation and individualisation of society. The social order requires a symbolic and normative representation of its unity; without it, it decomposes into an atomised society of egoist individuals.

Less of a republican than Gauchet, Alain Caillé also calls for a democratic recomposition of society and puts his hope in the politics of associations. Caillé is the founder of the anti-utilitarian movement of the MAUSS – an acronym for *Mouvement Anti-Utilitariste dans les Sciences Sociales* – and the editor of the *Revue du MAUSS*, a bi-annual journal devoted to the study of the gift in which anthropologists, sociologists, economists and political philosophers on the left explore the contours of an alternative science and society that are not based on self-interest and egoism. Founded in 1981 to counter the hegemony of utilitarianism in the social sciences (rational choice) and society (neo-liberalism), Alain Caillé has worked out Marcel Mauss's classic essay on the gift into a full blown political sociology of associations that considers the triple obligation – 'to give, accept and return the gift' – as the bedrock of social life (Godbout and Caillé 1992; Caillé 2000).

Reintroducing symbols and agency into the sociologism of Durkheim, Mauss has outlined a generous sociology of social relations that overcomes the opposition between the individual and society. Free, yet obligatory, the 'spirit of the gift' is the catalyst of social relations that makes society possible as a primary network of associations out of which the market and the state will emerge as a secondary formation, which is currently being incorporated into a tertiary network of global relations. Caillé does not ignore the agonistic nature of the primitive gift; nor does he believe that contemporary societies are only driven by interest. To the contrary, he defends the primacy of the gift and conceives of it as a 'total social fact' that animates all institutions of society. It encompasses conflict and peace, obligation and freedom, interest and generosity. The gift does not only represent a third sociological paradigm between individualism and holism, but institutionalised into a third sector of voluntary associations, it also offers a genuine third way beyond liberalism and socialism. As politics is conceived as the continuation of the gift by other means, the local associations that implement the politics of giving can be understood as social movements that seek to uphold the moral economy against the market and the state. The associations do not aim to abolish the state or the market, but to rejuvenate the social tissue and to 'reembed' (as Polanyi says) the market and the state into the life-world. Against contractualist versions of workfare, the anti-utilitarian movement defends the basic income as a generalised expression of reciprocity that can regenerate solidarity. The idea is that when every citizen receives an unconditional 'demogrant', they will do something in return for the community and thereby contribute to the realisation of Mauss's dream of a cooperative or associative socialism.

The Montreal School

Meanwhile, in Francophone Canada, Michel Freitag, an old friend of Caillé and former student of Touraine, has developed a monumental neo-dialectical critical social theory (Freitag 1986, 2002). Freitag's theory of society has some affinities with Giddens's structuration theory, but through incorporation of Gauchet's history of the symbolic representation of societies, it redeploys the synchronic analysis of the conditions of production and reproduction of society into a larger dialectical framework that diachronically analyses the historical transformation of its mediations through the ages, from primitive and traditional societies to modern and post-modern ones. The result is a historical theory of the modes of the regulation of practices and the constitution of society that can easily compare with Habermas' theory of communication or Luhmann's theory of autopoietic systems. Be that as it may, the dialectical theory of society culminates in a militant critique of the desymbolising tendencies of the systemic mode of reproduction that characterises postmodernity.

The original project of *Dialectique et Société* comprised five volumes, only two of which have been published so far. In the first volume, the Swiss born sociologist presents a general theory of symbolic practice. Its basic idea is that practice is always already and inevitably caught in a web of symbolic representations and significations that functions as an *a priori* and transcendental order of determination that regulates and unifies the practices, which reproduce in turn society. By introducing culture as a virtual totality that a priori forms, informs and regulates the symbolic practices that produce and reproduce society, Freitag has successfully forged a dialectical connection between the regulation of practices and the reproduction of society. This 'double dialectic' between agency and structure forms the starting point of the developmental theory of the modes of formal reproduction of society that is presented in the second volume. Analysed in a historical and diachronic perspective, the ideal-typical description of a society that is conceived as a community of language reappears now, formally, as the first mode of reproduction of society, the 'symbolic-cultural' one, which, 'sublated', will be succeeded in modernity by the 'political–institutional' one and, subverted and tendentially abolished, in post-modernity by the 'decisional-operational' one. The 'cultural-symbolic' mode of reproduction of society characterises primitive societies. As soon as those societies become aware of themselves through an idealised projection of their symbolic representation in myths and religions (cf. Gauchet), the transition to the political–institutional mode of reproduction has already set in. Following the progressive detranscendentalisation of the Divine in traditional societies, modern societies start to reflexively produce their own mediations and regulations in the form of legitimate political institutions. With the transition to post-modernity and the advent of the 'decisional-operational' mode of reproduction, the transcendental mediations that give *a priori* unity to societies are progressively dissolved. As a result, societies are transformed into self-referential social systems that are unified *a posteriori* through adaptation and accomodation to its changing environment. Luhmann's analysis of the world system is empirically right, according to Freitag, but normatively wrong.

In a series of lengthy articles that have been published in *Société*, the organ of the Montreal School, Freitag has depicted post-modernity as a systemic decomposition of society that signifies at the same time the demise of culture, subjectivity and politics. His critique of post-modernity is anything but post-modern though. In the spirit of the Frankfurt School, it offers a systematic analysis and critique of the desymbolising and dehumanising tendencies of the contemporary world.

Conclusion

Since the waning of the 'new theoretical movement' of the 1980s, European social theory seems to have entered the age of epigones. The UK is post-Giddensian (R. Bhaskar, M. Archer, N. Rose), Germany is post-Habermasian (A. Honneth, H. Joas, U. Beck) and France is post-Bourdieusian. For twenty-five years, Bourdieu has dominated the field of French sociology and determined its agenda of research. Coming from philosophy, he introduced philosophical concepts into sociology and put them at work in concrete empirical research. Even Bourdieu's main opponents are influenced by him. Like him they pursue the great theoretical questions of the age by way of empirical research and use their research to make a political point. We can thus conclude this overview of French sociology at the turn of the millenium in the same way as Levi-Strauss (1945) concluded his fifty years ago. The dependence of French sociology on philosophy and its opening to politics may well turn out once again to be its greatest asset.

Notes

1   Passeron's (1991) systematic vindication of a non-Popperian, ideographic and illustrative method for the social sciences and Berthelot's (1990) mapping of the sociological 'schemes of intelligibility' can be considered as two examples of social epistemology in the strict sense. The *Revue du MAUSS* (2004, no. 24) has recently invited some of the main sociologists (Touraine, Boudon, Latour, Thévenot, Freitag, Quéré, Dubet) to debate about the possibility of a general sociological theory.

2   The four names refer, in fact, to four different schools with their own research programmes, centres of research and preferred journals (see Ansart, 1990). Bourdieu and his collaborators (P. Champagne, R. Lenoir, A. L. Pinto, L. Wacquant) work at the *Centre de sociologie européenne* of the E.H.E.S.S. and publish in the *Actes de la recherche en sciences sociales*. Alain Touraine and his associates (M. Wieviorka, F. Dubet, F. Khosrokhavar, D. Martuccelli) are members of the Cadis (*Centre d'Analyse et d'Intervention Sociologique*), also at the E.H.E.S.S. Crozier and his collaborators (A. Friedberg, J.C. Thoenig, R. Sainsaulieu) are affiliated to the *Centre de sociologie des organisations*, based at the *Institut de sciences politiques* and, like the Tourainians, they often write for *Sociologie du travail*. Boudon and other methodological individualists of the Sorbonne, like F. Chazel, M. Cherkaoui and B. Valade, control the *Presses Universitaires de France* and publish in the *Revue française de sociologie*.

3   For an influential account of French post-structuralism, see Ferry and Renault (1988). Dosse (1995) and Corcuff (1995) present good overviews of the most recent developments in the human sciences.

4   The influence of American micro-sociology (Goffman, Garfinkel, Sacks, Cicourel) on the new pragmatic sociologies of action of L. Quéré, L. Thévenot, P. Pharo, B. Conein and M. de Fornel cannot be underestimated. They publish in *Raisons pratiques* and *Réseaux* and, of late, under the influence of the analytic philosophy of action, some of them have rejoined the neo-positivist circle of the methodological individualists.

5   In the following, I draw on former work in which I discuss more extensively the writings of Bourdieu, Boltanski and Latour (Vandenberghe, 2005), Debray and Lévy (Vandenberghe, 2001) and Gauchet and Freitag (Vandenberghe, 2003).

6   Following Bourdieu's seminal work on classification and classes, the constructivist analysis of social groups (Boltanski), socio-professional categories (Thévenot) and statistics (Desrosières) has become a subfield of research at the crossroads of sociology and history with its own journal *Genèses. Sciences sociales et histoire*.

7   The number of *Cités* is not fixed. Thévenot and Lafaye have later added an ecological Commonwealth, while Boltanski and Chiapello (1999) introduced the Commonwealth of projects. Lamont and Thévenot (2000) present a comparative analysis of the vocabularies of justification in France and the U.S.

8   For an outstanding account of STS by one of its protagonists, see Lynch (1993).

9   Debray mentions the hyper- or cybersphere, but the analysis is left to Pierre Lévy (1997), a visionary who conceives of the internet as a living megabrain that produces a single, complex, evolving hypertext.

References

Ansart, P. (1990) *Les sociologies contemporaines*, Paris: Seuil.

Berthelot, J. M. (1990) *L'intelligence du social*, Paris: P.U.F.

Boltanski, L. and E. Chiapello (1999/2004) *Le nouvel esprit du capitalisme*, Paris: Gallimard [*The New Spirit of Capitalism*, London: Verso].

Boltanski, L. and L. Thévenot (1991) *De la justification: Les économies de la grandeur*, Paris: Gallimard.

Boltanski, L. and L. Thévenot (1999) 'The Sociology of Critical Capacity', in *European Journal of Social Theory*, 2(3): 359–377.

Boudon, R. (1995) *Le juste et le vrai*, Paris: Fayard.

Bourdieu, P. (2001) *Science de la science et réflexivité*, Paris: Raisons d'agir.

Bourdieu, P. (2002a) *Interventions politiques, 1961–2001: Sciences sociales et action politique*, Marseille: Agone.

Bourdieu, P. (2002b) *Ein soziologischer Selbstversuch*, Frankfurt/Main: Suhrkamp.

Bourdieu, P. (2002c) *Le bal des célibataires: Crise de la société paysanne en Béarn*, Paris: Seuil.

Bourdieu, P. (2002d) *Bibliographie des travaux de Pierre Bourdieu*, Paris: Le Temps des Cérises.

Bourdieu, P. (2003) *Images d'Algérie: Une affinité élective*, Paris: Actes Sud.

Caillé, A. (2000) *Anthropologie du don: Le tiers paradigme*, Paris: Desclée.

Callon, M. and B. Latour (1981) 'Unscrewing the Big Leviathan; or How Actors Macrostructure Reality, and How Sociologist Help Them to Do So', in K. Knorr and A. Cicourel (eds) *Advances in Social Theory and Methodology*, London: Routledge: 277–303.

Corcuff, P. (1995) *Les nouvelles sociologies: Constructions de la réalité sociale*, Paris: Nathan.

Crozier, M. and E. Friedberg (1977/1980) *L'acteur et le système*, Paris: Seuil [*Actors and Systems: The Politics of Collective Action*. Chicago: Chicago University Press].

Debray, R. (1981) *Critique de la raison politique ou l'inconscient religieux*, Paris: Gallimard [*Critique of Political Reason*, London: Verso].

Debray, R. (1991) *Cours de médiologie générale*, Paris: Gallimard.

Dosse, F. (1995/1999) *L'empire du sens: L'humanisation des sciences humaines*, Paris: La Découverte [*Empire of Meaning: The Humanization of the Social Sciences*, Minneapolis: University of Minnesota Press].

Ferry, L. and A. Renaut (1988/1990) *La pensée 68: Essai sur l'antihumanisme contemporain*, Paris: Gallimard [*French Philosophy of the Sixties: An Essay on Antihumanism*, Minnesota: University of Massachusetts Press].

Freitag, M. (1986) *Dialectique et société: Vol. 1: Introduction à une théorie générale du symbolique*, and *Vol. 2: Culture, pouvoir, controle: les modes de reproduction formelle de la société*, Lausanne: L'âge d'homme and Montréal: Saint-Martin.

Freitag, M. (2002) 'The Dissolution of Society within the Social', *European Journal of Social Theory*, 5(2): 175–198.

Gauchet, M. (1985/1997) *Le désenchantement du monde: Une histoire politique de la religion*, Paris: Gallimard [*The Disenchantment of the World: A Political History of Religion*. Princeton: Princeton University Press].

Gauchet, M. (2002) *La démocratie contre elle-même*, Paris: Gallimard.

Godbout, J. and A. Caillé (1992/1998) *L'esprit du don*, Paris: La Découverte [*The World of the Gift*, Montreal: McGill-Queen's University Press].

Lahire, B. (1998) *L'homme pluriel: Les ressorts de l'action*, Paris: Nathan.

Lahire, B. (2004) *La Culture des Invididus: Dissonances Culturelles et Distinction de Soi*, Paris: La Découverte.

Lamont, M. and L. Thévenot (eds) (2000) *Rethinking Comparative Sociology: Repertoires of Evaluation in France and the United States*, Cambridge, UK: Cambridge University Press.

Latour, B. (1988) 'Drawing Things Together', in M. Lynch and S. Woolgar (eds) *Representations in Scientific Practice*, Cambridge, MA: MIT: 19–68.

Latour, B. (1996) 'On Interobjectivity', in *Mind, Culture, and Activity*, 3 (4): 228–245.

Lévi-Strauss, C. (1945) 'French Sociology', in G. Gurvitch and W. Moore (eds): *Twentieth Century Sociology*, New York: The Philosophical Library: 503–537.

Lévy, P. (1997) *L'intelligence collective: Pour une anthropologie du cyberespace*, Paris: La Découverte [*Collective Intelligence: Mankind's Emerging World in Cyberspace*, Cambridge, Mass.: Perseus Press].

Lynch, M. (1993) *Scientific Practice and Ordinary Action: Ethnomethodology and Social Studies of Science*, Cambridge: Cambridge University Press.

Passeron, J. C. (1991) *Le raisonnement sociologique: L'espace non-popperien du raisonnement naturel*, Paris : Nathan.

Piette, A. (1992) *Le mode mineur de la réalité*, Louvain: Peeters.

Revue du MAUSS, 2004, 24(2) (*Une théorie sociologique générale est-elle pensable?*)

Touraine, A. (1997/2000) *Pourrons-nous vivre ensemble? Egaux et différents*, Paris: Fayard [*Can we live together? Equality and Difference*, Cambridge: Polity Press].

Vandenberghe, F. (2001) 'From Media to Mediation Studies. An Introduction to the Work of Régis Debray and Pierre Lévy', in *Crict Discussion Paper*, Series 2, Number 1, Brunel University (http://www.brunel.ac.uk/depts/crict/debray.pdf).

Vandenberghe, F. (2003) 'Review Essay: A Phenomenology of Spirit for Our Times', in *European Journal of Social Theory*, 6 (3): 357–365.

Vandenberghe, F. (2005) 'Construction et critique dans la nouvelle sociologie française', in *Complexités du posthumanisme: Pour une critique de l'économie bio-politique*, Paris: L'Harmattan.

Wacquant, L. (2000/2003) 'Corps et âme. Carnets ethnographiques d'un apprenti boxeur', Marseilles: Agone, *Body and Soul: Notebooks of an Apprentice Boxer*, Oxford: Oxford University Press.

7

The peculiarities of the British

Social theory in the United Kingdom

David Inglis

Any discussion of the development of social theory in the British context encounters a key question. Does there exist a distinctive entity called 'British social theory' that is sufficiently differentiated from other 'national traditions' in social theory to count as one in its own right (Kumar 2001)? Or is it the case that there exists merely a melange of different streams of social thought that have been influential at different times in the British context, some of which are more or less 'indigenous' but most of which are not?

The argument of this chapter is that answers to such questions can only be given in terms of a long-term historical consideration of the different phases through which what we can call 'social theory' has moved in Britain since the beginnings of modernity. A long-term historical analysis of the changing contours of social theory in Britain reveals two things. First, there has never been a wholly or purely 'British' tradition in social thought, partly because 'Britain' itself is a problematic idea that erases differences between its constituent national elements, but more importantly because there has always been a degree of 'international' exchange of ideas between 'British' intellectuals and those abroad. This has been the case since early modernity, but as we shall see, it becomes more accelerated in the nineteenth-century and then very greatly accentuated after the Second World War. Second, although there is certainly no 'pure' strain of identifiably 'British' social theory, nonetheless there are identifiably 'British' intellectual trends and traits, expressive of a philosophical and intellectual culture that was for a long time markedly empirical and anti-metaphysical in nature, that are frequently present not only in the social theoretical productions of many 'indigenous' intellectuals, but also in the ways that 'non-indigenous' ideas, mainly from France and Germany, have been appropriated in the British context.

The essence of this chapter, then, is a presentation of the historical genesis of social theory in a British context which rejects the idea that there has ever existed a homogeneous entity called 'British social theory', but which nonetheless recognises that there are certain recurring motifs and dispositions, centred around the imperative for empirical investigation, that have recurred throughout modernity, and although weakened in the present day, continue to be present to some degree in social theoretical endeavours.

We will begin the account with an examination of the varying assumptions as to the procedures of social investigation in seventeenth- and eighteenth-century England and eighteenth-century Scotland. We will then look at the, primarily but not exclusively, empiricist and individualist tenor of nineteenth-century social theories. At the beginning of the twentieth-century, this paradigm began to fragment, a process intensified greatly after the Second World War, as evidenced in the present-day diversity of social theoretical production in a British context that is increasingly systematically integrated into trans-national networks of knowledge production.

Beginnings – England and Scotland

It is fairly uncontroversial to begin outlining the genesis of modern social theoretical developments in Britain with the work of Thomas Hobbes (1588–1679), who was writing within the politically fractious conditions of the English civil war. This is in part because his work was the main stimulus behind what we may call the 'first phase' of social theory in Britain, and also because his work has clearly had ramifications internationally, especially given Talcott Parsons' (1961: 93) influential assertion that the 'Hobbesian problem of order' is at the root of sociological thought in general, and that Hobbes identified the problem of social order 'with a clarity which has never been surpassed'. As is well known, Hobbes in *Leviathan* (1651) asserts that life for humans in the 'state of nature' is characterised by unmitigated strife, as each seeks to impose his selfish will on all others. Social order occurs when individuals come to realise that it is in their interests to submit to a sovereign authority which will regulate all of them and thus maintain social peace and stability. Hobbes departs from older, ultimately Aristotelian, notions of political science in the following ways. For Hobbes:

1 analysis examines empirical human behaviours rather than ideal states of affairs;
2 human behaviours are to be regarded as 'naturally' self-interested and calculating, and analysis must reconstruct the ways in which individual action is based upon the calculation of self-interest;
3 'social' and 'political' phenomena are always the outcomes of individual actions, and the analyst must pursue a policy of rigorous methodological individualism;
4 the idea of 'natural' dispositions among humankind towards social order is to be dropped in favour of seeing anarchy as the natural condition, and social order as a fabricated, and therefore always fragile, human achievement.

As Levine (1995: 128) notes, so great was Hobbes' subsequent influence in his homeland that these analytical developments 'were to undergird the major philosophical efforts to construct sciences of human phenomena' in England 'for the next three centuries', as well as being important objects of critique abroad too. It is primarily from Hobbes that the strains of individualism, utilitarianism and empiricism in English social thought spring.

Most of Hobbes' subsequent English disputants can be seen as sharing his fundamental assumptions, whilst taking issue with his more concrete propositions. John Locke (1632–1704), writing in a period characterised by fears of Stuart absolutism, sought to refute Hobbes' emphasis on the necessity of unmitigated sovereign power by characterising political authority as being generated by contracts between sovereign and subjects, with the former agreeing to respect the property rights of the latter. Locke, like his near contemporary the Earl of Shaftesbury, also reasserted the view that humans are naturally social animals, and that even their most selfish dispositions can have socially benign consequences. Yet Locke and Shaftesbury shared Hobbes's more fundamental views, to the effect that the individual is the key unit of social analysis and that his actions are carried out on the basis of reasoning what his best interests are.

In fact, in some senses, Locke's overall philosophical position is even more focused on individual existence than Hobbes', insofar as he insists upon all knowledge being based on contingent individual experiences rather than on any innate dispositions. But somewhat contrary to the Hobbesian paradigm, the view of the mind as a *tabula rasa*, open to and shaped by the impressions of the outside world, is clearly an important antecedent of certain strains in modern anthropology and sociology. It opens up within individualist thinking the possibility of regarding the individual as socially-shaped, rather than as a monadic entity that, as it were, precedes social arrangements.

At a general level, we may say that eighteenth-century social and political thought in both England and Scotland reflected less and less the domestic turmoil of the age in which Hobbes and Locke lived, and expressed more the advantages and problems of a burgeoning commercially-based society. This was reflected in England by Bernard de Mandeville's (1670–1732) accounts of how the selfish 'private vices' of egoistic individuals could have general 'public benefits', for example how personal avarice can breed increases in general social wealth. The emphasis here is again on calculating individuals, in this account unintentionally creating a functioning social order.

But in Scotland, the analysis of an increasingly mercantile society proceeded on rather different grounds. The sense of the social shaping of individuals, unintentionally opened up in the English context by Locke, was one, and arguably *the*, key theme of social theoretical developments over the border in Scotland (Swingewood 1970). One of the earliest figures of the movement subsequently known as the 'Scottish Enlightenment', namely Francis Hutcheson (1694–1746), developed the theme of Locke and Shaftesbury that self-interest is but one element in a whole array of human dispositions, most of them oriented around sociability and fellow-feeling. Later thinkers, including Adam Ferguson (1723–1816), Adam Smith (1723–1790) and John Millar (1735–1801), not only worked within the framework of the inalienably 'social' nature of man, but added two important dimensions to it:

1 The empirically-based identification of different historically variable forms of human association. The induction of 'theory' from empirical data was especially important in a philosophical environment marked by empiricism and scepticism, as evinced most famously in the work of David Hume (1711–1793) (which in turn would later be a major stimulus to Kant's revolutionary contribution to the analysis of the nature of the human mind).

2 Accounts of social evolution, designed to understand how and why humankind had gone from an initial 'rude' state of social affairs up to the much more refined, complex and sophisticated social arrangements of the present day.

On this view, social analysis involved the identification of the laws of development of human society. It is important not to over-emphasise the differences between Scottish and English intellectual contexts at this time. After all, both Hutcheson and Hume are important figures in the development of utilitarian thought, working out models of costs and benefits, pains and pleasures. Nonetheless, within the Scots' shared emphasis on forms of human association, we see the emergence of a train of thought that, in opposition to the English emphasis on atomic individualism, is concerned to interrogate the nature and evolution of 'social structure', the main units of analysis being the group or institutions rather than individuals. The innovations involved can be seen clearly in the work of Smith, who was often subsequently regarded as simply an avatar of the individualistic trends of 'British political economy'. The distinctively 'Scottish' element in Smith's work lies in its focus on how the individual is formed within social relations. This involves both the actual reactions of others to the individual's behaviours and also the individual's anticipation of others' likely reactions to him or her, anticipated and actual reactions being a 'mirror' through which a sense of self is generated. This position is an important though frequently unacknowledged precursor of more recent development in interactionist sociology and psychology (Swingewood 1970).

The Scottish focus on social institutions regarded as *sui generis* entities, produced by the unintended consequences of (socialised) individuals' actions, can be seen in the work of Adam Ferguson. Anticipating Marx in some ways, Ferguson departs from both Hobbes and Locke in regarding notions of the 'state of nature' as mere analytical fabrications that are unnecessary to the work of social investigation, which must instead look at real examples of social formation. Ferguson shares Locke's emphasis on the importance of private property but unlike the latter, systematically locates the development of this institution historically, as both product of, and motive force behind, the development of different stages of social organisation. Ferguson, like many of the other Scots, was indebted to Montesquieu's analysis of different types of polity, but he broadened the analysis from purely 'political' forms of organisation to encompass the analysis of whole 'societies', each with their own peculiar political, social and economic structures. In a similar vein, Smith's focusing of analysis on the division of labour as an entity in its own right, and its compelling effects on both individuals and other social institutions, entailed a move away from narrower English individualistic conceptions of political and economic activities (Hawthorne 1976).

Nineteenth-century trends

Many of the ideas of the eighteenth-century Scots, with the notable exception of Smith's economic writings, were ignored by later social thinkers in Britain, until sociologists in the latter half of the twentieth-century rediscovered them in a self-conscious search for *bona fide* intellectual antecedents. The nineteenth-century primarily witnessed further developments of the individualist and utilitarian elements of earlier English writers. The key strains of what we can term 'mainstream' British social thought from the later eighteenth-century through to the later Victorian period, are (in rough chronological order of their appearance and dominance in the field) political economy, utilitarianism, social empiricism, and evolutionism, all of which were, generally speaking, 'positivist' in orientation.

In the first case, political economy took its cue not only from the work of Smith but also from the late eighteenth- and early nineteenth-century writings of figures such as Thomas Malthus (1766–1834) and David Ricardo (1772–1823). In the work of political economists such as Nassau Senior (1790–1864), a focus on rationally motivated individual actions was combined with Smith's (and Mandeville's) account of the unintended consequences of such actions, namely the workings of the 'invisible hand' of the market. The aim was empirically to discern both the 'natural laws' of wealth creation, and concomitantly, the brakes upon wealth creation by such factors as the laziness of the 'undeserving poor', through the collation of aggregated data about the activities of individuals.

Political economy's focus on the rationalising agent segues into the second key strain of British social thought in the period, namely utilitarianism. Jeremy Bentham (1748–1832), probably the first person to use the phrase 'social science' in English, revived Hume's ambition to create a scientific calculus to ascertain the costs and benefits of particular modes of action, regarding human nature as fundamentally involving the individual's avoidance of 'pain' in favour of 'pleasure'. From this point of view, morality is simply a matter of the degree to which a particular action causes more or less pain or pleasure to an individual or to an aggregate of individuals. Bentham's position is also strongly methodologically individualist, in that it regards any notion of 'society' merely as an analytic fabrication rather than as referring to a real entity. Bentham's work was promoted especially by the philosopher James Mill, and then, in a modified form by his son John Stuart Mill, thus helping utilitarianism to become one of the cornerstones of British social thought until the end of the century (Halévy 1966). The younger Mill's own version of social science expressed the general temper of the times well, in its stress on methodological individualism and data collection in the service of ascertaining the empirical laws of social functioning. The desire to mount the analysis of issues of moral and social concern on a rigorously scientific footing free of metaphysical assertions can also be found in the work of Alfred Marshall (1842–1924), who regarded economics as involving accurate measurement of human desires, through externally observable indices, most notably the prices individuals were prepared to pay for given goods. Marshall's work is an important staging post between the older English individualist traditions and twentieth-century liberal economics.

A third strain in nineteenth-century British social thought can be dubbed 'social empiricism'. This was a general and relatively loose grouping of government officials and social reformers, rather than a self-conscious intellectual movement, oriented around the collation of 'facts' about 'social problems', especially those concerning poverty, criminality and the 'condition of the working classes'. The especial emphasis here was on the collection of statistics through survey means, in the belief that statistics simply revealed the nature and extent of the 'problem' under consideration. At one level, we are barely here in the realm of what might meaningfully be called 'social theory' at all. As Abrams (1968: 5) puts it, the social statisticians of the period from the 1830s onwards instigated 'an empirical tradition of which the great monuments are government inquiries; massive but intellectually sterile levers of social reform'. But on the other hand, the hyper-empiricism of mid-nineteenth-century social statistics not only lies behind the streams subsequently dominant in British sociology until quite recently, namely demography and studies of poverty, it is also at the root of the social policy and social administration traditions, academically institutionalised, first at the London School of Economics, from the early twentieth-century onwards.

It should be added that social empiricism was widely bound up first with Christian, then liberal, and at a later date social democratic, policies and reform movements. Earlier in the century, social research was coupled with Christian moralising about the morally problematic characters of the poor. But as the century wore on, figures such as Charles Booth, Seebohm Rowntree and Beatrice and Sidney Webb reoriented the empirical tradition in the direction of evaluating the effects of social conditions on the habits and attitudes of those working class people under study. Empirical social research became much more analytically refined under the influence from the 1880s onwards of the research on working class family life of the Frenchman Fréderic Le Play. He took the family, rather than the individual, as the main unit of properly 'sociological' – as opposed to merely 'social' – research, and developed a typology of different sorts of family unit and their relations with wider social structure. His methodological innovations, such as detailing the habits and practices of particular family units, were transformative of British empirical work in the later nineteenth-century. Although Le Play was himself a political conservative, he came to have a great influence in a number of ways upon the liberal reforming researchers such as Booth and Rowntree, and these in turn continued to have a lasting influence in certain intellectual circles well into the twentieth-century.

The final element of mainstream nineteenth-century British social thought we will examine is evolutionism. As is well known, later nineteenth-century thought in a number of national contexts was highly marked by evolutionary principles, partly through the increasingly great influence of Darwinism, a doctrine that despite its highly controversial implications for organised religion nonetheless could be made to fit with the individualistic 'war of all against all' ideas deriving from Hobbes and influencing political economy.

In a more diffuse manner, the influence of the pre-Darwinian ideas of Comte may also be discerned. Harriet Martineau had brought out a shortened English translation of the *Course in Positive Philosophy* in 1853. It made little impact, Comtean notions as to the nature of the social order remaining little known until the 1870s, by which time John Stuart Mill had come to champion the methodological aspects of the Comtean system, whilst utterly rejecting what to English individualists seemed like prescriptions for totalitarian government. Comtean ideas as to the nature of sociology had certain elective affinities with notions firmly embedded in English liberal intellectual life, including the view that sociological analysis was a means whereby society could be improved without revolutionary upheavals.

The relation of Comte to that home-grown English giant of evolutionism, Herbert Spencer (1820–1903), is in the same vein: an abhorrence on the latter's part of Comtean political recommendations coupled with a general agreement as to the desirability of solid scientific foundations for social science. Spencer's evolutionism can be seen as a distinctive fusion of specifically 'British' intellectual dispositions with more general evolutionary ideas at play in other national contexts. On the one hand, Spencer, echoing Smith, infers that the primary motive force behind the development of the division of labour are individuals' actions. But on the other hand, he rejected one of the dogmas of most forms of British individualism, namely that 'human nature' is both static and primarily oriented around principles of egotism, since for Spencer human experience and disposition were historically variable. Likewise, he was prepared to reject the idea that social phenomena are only aggregates of individual actions, arguing instead for the view that society is in fact an organic entity, with certain structural and functional properties, a position that potentially is the direct opposite of any kind of methodological individualism, especially since Spencer himself argued that as social order became more complex, the unintended consequences of individual actions become ever greater in scope, a situation which in turn constricts the future actions of individuals (Abrams 1968).

Spencer's sociology is fundamentally one of movement, but, despite his individualist admonitions just mentioned, at the level of social institutions rather than individual actions. The level of analysis has been significantly shifted away from the individual to the level of the 'social structure'. Spencer's position is thus both in some ways 'native' to English traditions, but in more significant ways involves important departures from them. Despite its great analytic innovations, its apparent political implications – social ameliorism merely helps the 'unfit' to survive and is thus counter to evolution – meant that it seemed to stand against native traditions of social reform, and thus its effects on wider intellectual life were relatively restricted, except as a resource for early twentieth-century proponents of eugenics.

Early twentieth-century trajectories

Social thought in Britain in the first few decades of the twentieth-century can be seen as involving both extensions of, and departures from, the concerns of the later Victorian period. A general concern for evolutionism continued but in different ways, three of which we will mention here.

In the first instance, the development of Darwinian themes in both analytic and policy terms was developed by the eugenicists such as Francis Galton. Second, and opposed to a strong social biological line in favour of analyses of environmental effects on human behaviours, were the 'town planners', led intellectually by Patrick Geddes, whose work was informed in methodological terms by Le Play's survey methods and in theoretical terms by interpretations of both Comte and Spencer. In this analysis, the focus of political economy as to the fitness or otherwise of social arrangements vis-a-vis the promotion of wealth creation was dropped in favour of examining how well institutions allow people to adapt the physical environment to their needs and wants. The polemics between eugenicists and anti-eugenicists arguably profoundly oriented later British sociology in the direction of questions as to whether individual abilities or environmental forces play the larger part in determining patterns of educational achievement, social mobility, job allocation and so on (Halsey 2004). The class and mobility studies carried out from the late 1950s onwards by such figures as David Lockwood and John H. Goldthorpe, are particularly influential examples of this kind of work.

Beyond the eugenicists and the town planners, a third grouping, the 'ethical evolutionists', argued that far from being imprisoned forever in the mechanisms of natural selection, humankind had evolved in such a way as to be possessed not only of self-consciousness, but also, as a result of this evolution of mind, of abilities to formulate moral ideals that could regulate the struggle for survival. This position was formulated by L. T. Hobhouse, the occupant of the first dedicated Chair in sociology in Britain, created at the LSE in 1907. Here, then, was a way of squaring Spencerian evolutionism with the tradition of social amelioration, now in the guise of the Lloyd George Liberal Party's welfarism. By regarding social and mental evolution in Comtean and Hegelian terms (Hobhouse having garnered the latter from the Oxford Hegelian T. H. Green, active in the 1880s), they could be regarded as involving the triumph of superior – more rational and more altruistic – forms of mind over more primitive forms (Hawthorne 1976).

Hobhouse is today a largely neglected figure, but he is important in the present context not just because of his trail-blazing institutional position, but also because he may be seen as playing an important role in the ongoing development of English ethical socialist thought, which Dennis and Halsey (1988) trace back as far as Sir Thomas More. More specifically, the importance in British social science of the LSE-centred social reformist tradition, led the French sociologist Raymond Aron to comment in the 1950s that British sociology was primarily concerned with the intellectual problems of the Labour Party.

Certain of Hobhouse's preoccupations were carried on by his successor for the LSE Chair, the Lithuanian-born Morris Ginsberg (1889–1970), whose work on the interrelations between moral systems and social structure, and the need for building social institutions in rational and ethical ways, was influential until at least the 1960s. Locatable within the same political vein is the work of T. H. Marshall (1893–1981), the founder of modern citizenship theory. For Marshall, there had been a developmental process, whereby civil rights (e.g. freedom of speech) were achieved in Britain from the eighteenth-century onwards, political rights (in the form of enfranchisement of the whole adult population) had developed throughout the latter half of the nineteenth-century, and social rights (based around economic welfare) had been consummated by the post-1945 welfare state. The ameliorist strain in English social thought was here conjoined with a more sociological account of the possible and actual tensions between citizenship rights on the one hand and economic inequalities on the other. A further important figure in this tradition is Richard Titmuss (1907–1973), Professor of Social Administration at the LSE and adviser to the Labour Party, whose theorisation of welfare provision saw the latter as more than a safety-net for the most vulnerable in society, it being an expression, and mechanism for the promotion, of altruistic values and communal ways of life.

Internationalisation and diversification

The academic institutionalisation in Britain of sociology and related disciplines was pioneered before World War I at the LSE, with a plethora of new departments opening in both 'old' and 'new' universities throughout the 1960s (Halsey 2004). The effects of this institutionalisation on social theoretical debates has been widespread, not least in terms of further and more systematically opening up the 'indigenous' intellectual culture to 'foreign' influences, mainly in this case the French, German and American traditions in social theory and sociological methodology. The work of contemporary social theorists who are British by birth, such as Roland Robertson, John Urry and Mike Featherstone (and, for example, other British-born or British-based thinkers such as Scott Lash, and those associated in one way or another with the journal *Theory, Culture and Society*), draws upon a very wide-ranging set of intellectual resources from French, German, American and other 'national' traditions. Indeed, Robertson's pioneering work on the sociology of globalization has contributed a great deal towards endeavours to transcend nationally-based sociological traditions in favour of more ecumenical and 'global' paradigms of analysis.

Another good example of these tendencies concerns the work of Bryan Turner, until recently Professor of Sociology at Cambridge, whose writings have ranged over such terrains as Weberian theory, medical sociology, sociology of the body and theories of citizenship. In the latter work, we can see the 'internationalisation' of intellectual resources available to British-born or British-based social theorists in a number of ways: first, Marshall's account of citizenship is criticised for making universalising claims that are based too narrowly on specifically British political experiences; second, the British 'model' of citizenship, idealistically treated by Marshall, is juxtaposed against political experiences and understandings of the 'citizen' drawn from other national contexts; third, Marshall's account is identified as being too nation-state centred and thus inadequate within a context of globalising socio-political conditions; fourth, the range of analytical tools Turner has at his disposal is far wider ranging, in terms of both 'national origin' and conceptual reach, than that which figures like Marshall and Titmuss had at their disposal. The case of citizenship theory illustrates very well the broadening of intellectual resources available to those in the British context that occurred in the latter part of the twentieth-century, to the extent that we might better talk of 'social theory in Britain' rather than 'British social theory' *per se*, if the latter is taken in a narrow way.

Why has this situation come to pass? We can certainly say that the institutionalisation of sociology in universities has been a powerful mechanism for the 'internationalisation' of social theoretical discourse in Britain in the last several decades of the twentieth-century and beyond (Albrow 1990), to the extent that one might wish to talk of the 'globalisation' of social theoretical means of production in Britain. Certainly the internationalisation of theoretical resources has led to an intensification and complication of intellectual – and indeed institutional – lineages in social theoretical developments.

One might also add that, given recent intellectual mutations within and across disciplines, social theory is certainly no longer solely based, developed and used within departments of sociology, but has become important in a wide range of intellectual settings. For example, the influential work of the human geographer Nigel Thrift both draws upon social theoretical resources, and has also placed the geographer's concern with the social construction of space firmly on to the social theoretical agenda. Likewise, within academic history, the early modernist Peter Burke has been a British proponent of the broad movement called the 'new cultural history' associated with such continental cultural historians as Emmanuel Le Roy

Ladurie, Jacques Le Goff and Carlo Ginzburg. He has productively reflected upon the ways both in which the terms of social theory have thus far and could in future enrich empirically-oriented historiographical research (the work of Foucault, Elias, Sahlins and Braudel among others being important here) and also in which historiographical data can help deepen the empirical grasp of social theoretical models. Finally, in political theory and the history of ideas, Quentin Skinner has drawn upon positions in hermeneutics and the ordinary language philosophy of Wittgenstein and J. L. Austin, to contextualise political discourses, such as that of Hobbes, within their original contexts of production and dissemination, in order to show that what we take to be 'classic texts' containing eternal theoretical verities are in fact made up of webs of concepts that are only fully explicable in terms of their original historical locations of writing and reading.

It should be underlined that in addition to such relatively recent developments, 'foreign' input into social thought in Britain has always been a factor, as we have already seen in several cases. For example, in the case of what is called 'British social anthropology', not only was one of the most influential figures in the development of that form of anthropological functionalism an emigré Pole, namely Bronislaw Malinowski, it was also the case that the British-born structural-functionalists A. R. Radcliffe-Brown and E. E. Evans-Pritchard were greatly indebted to the French school of Durkheim and Mauss (Kuper 1999).

Moreover, the migration of Jews from Nazi-occupied continental Europe brought with it a number of distinguished and subsequently influential figures. These included the philosophers Karl Popper and Isaiah Berlin, both highly influential, the former in the philosophy of science and the other in the history of ideas; and the emigré Czech anthropologist Ernest Gellner, whose wide-ranging work was centred around the defence of rational inquiry against irrational orthodoxies. The great influence on debates in Britain on the philosophy of science of those hailing from central Europe is indeed quite striking. The work of the Viennese Ludwig Wittgenstein is crucial here, his work not only having become central in Anglo-American linguistic philosophy, but also being a key reference point in issues to do with the epistemological nature and status of scientific endeavours. The antagonism between Wittgenstein and Popper, both at the personal and theoretical levels, is well attested, with the contrast between an account of universal rationalistic procedures for theory-testing, and a relativising notion of localised forms of language production and meaning-making, being a marked one (Edmonds and Eidinow 2005).

To a great extent Popper and Wittgenstein are the background against which contemporary dramas in the philosophies of both natural and social sciences are played out, especially given the popularisation of a Wittgenstein position by Peter Winch's influential writings. For example, the 'Edinburgh School' of the sociology of science, led by David Bloor, draws upon Wittgensteinian themes to relativise the validity claims of natural scientists. Conversely, the development of the doctrines associated with 'critical realism', first by Rom Harré and then by Roy Bhaskar and other thinkers such as Margaret Archer, which seek to provide accounts of the generative structures which are said to underpin human social life, have had to engage with the issues elaborated by Popper, Wittgenstein and others of the previous intellectual generation.

Other notable central European emigrés to British shores have included the sociologist and educational theorist Karl Mannheim, whose sociology of knowledge brought together themes from both the French and German traditions; the sociologist Zygmunt Bauman, who fled from Soviet-era Poland, and who as Professor Emeritus at the University of Leeds has produced highly influential works on the ethical dilemmas of modernity; and the sociologists Ilya Neustadt and Norbert Elias, both at the University of Leicester in the 1960s, in a sociology department that housed figures who would later be influential in a range of areas, such as John Goldthorpe and Anthony Giddens. Elias's 'figurational sociology', which owes much to Germanic influences such as the work of Simmel and Alfred Weber, underwent various vicissitudes in terms of scholarly reception, from the first publication of *The Civilizing Process* in the ill-starred year of 1939 (Elias 1994), through to the fact that for all of the period of his tenure at Leicester, none of his German-language books were translated into English. The cumulative effect of all of this was that Elias was only recognised as a major thinker, particularly in Britain, Germany and the Netherlands, late in his lifetime. In Britain, advocates of Eliasian sociology, most notably Eric Dunning and Stephen Mennell, have done much to promote the Eliasian approach as a distinctive position in social theory.

Yet in many ways Eliasian approaches to social theory remain of interest more to certain specialist scholarly groupings rather than being widely regarded as part of more 'mainstream' social theoretical currents (as evidenced, for example, in the lack of coverage of Elias, as opposed to, say, Foucault and Bourdieu, in contemporary British undergraduate theory courses and textbooks). Nonetheless, there may be certain more subterranean ways in which Elias has influenced the parameters and nature of social theoretical production in Britain. Certain similarities of position on the vexed issue of relations between 'society' and 'individual' can be discerned between former Leicester colleagues Elias and Giddens, hinting at a tacit intellectual relationship between the sociology of figurations and structuration theory that has too rarely been remarked upon.

Giddens himself is probably the contemporary British social theorist most well-known outside Britain, his writings on structuration having brought him recognition in certain quarters in the United States, for example. Giddens' work is instructive in the present context in a number of ways. In the first place, while it clearly reflects the influence of Franco-German thinkers, it also makes use of Wittgenstein's ideas on rule-following and language games in manners – such as the focus on individual agents rather than on abstract 'structures' – that mark it out as in some ways distinctively 'Anglo-American' or even 'Anglo-Saxon' in nature, as opposed for example, to Luhmann's more Franco-German emphasis on language games as 'systems' of meaning. Second, the transition in Giddens' oeuvre from the more orthodox 'sociological' concerns of the early 1970s (e.g. class structure in advanced capitalist societies) through the structurationist writings of the 1980s, to the substantive work on 'late modernity' in the 1990s, stands as an expression of wider tendencies in British sociological circles. These involve moves away from classically 'sociological' theorising about 'social structures' towards the more heterodox dispositions of the genre of 'social theory', based around a wider set of philosophical resources and focused on a broader range of issues, including 'culture', 'identity' and 'selfhood'. The hitherto strongly empirical, if not in some ways empiricist, tendencies of British sociology, have in some senses, and in some institutional sectors, been usurped by 'social theory' as a distinctive genre of thought in its own right, with the paradigms within it having varying relationships with methodological and data collection issues. Third, and in a manner that locates Giddens more firmly in a more 'traditionally British' intellectual context, his ideas as to a political 'third way' between dirigiste socialism and unfettered capitalism, coupled with both his directorship of the LSE and his acting as an adviser to Tony Blair's New Labour government, locate him within the English left-liberal tradition associated with other LSE figures such as Hobhouse and Marshall (Studholme 1997). In various ways, then, Giddens' career is emblematic of both change *and* continuity in British intellectual life.

Re-indigenisation?

Since at least the 1960s, those in Britain who are in the business of formulating social theoretical positions have had a very wide range of international intellectual resources at their disposal, to the point where either the older 'indigenous' authors like Hobhouse have to a large degree been forgotten, or where their work has been refracted through the lens of non-British commentators, such as in the case of Talcott Parsons' presentation of Alfred Marshall, or American neo-functionalists' representations and developments of Spencer's evolutionism. (For a British-born thinker's recent attempts to purge social evolutionary thought of Spencerian errors, see the work of W. G. Runciman.)

Nonetheless, what can be described as (relatively speaking) distinctively 'British' appropriations and developments of 'international' materials can still be discerned. An interesting and important case here is that of variants of Marxist theory. The main currents of 'continental Marxism' have been both represented, and in some cases significantly developed, in Britain in ways more substantial than would be the case if these were just passing academic fads. A central figure here is the sociologist Tom Bottomore, who was not only an important Marxist analyst of class structure and political formations in his own right, but was also for several decades from the 1960s onwards highly influential in disseminating many of the main currents of Euro-Marxism, including Frankfurt critical theory and Austro-Marxism, to an Anglophone audience. William Outhwaite has done a great deal to promote Habermasian themes in British sociology and philosophy of science. In the same broad vein, Gillian Rose can be regarded not only as a British representative of Frankfurt-inspired critical theory, but also as an important ethical thinker in her own right. More recently, British thinkers have made important contributions to the dissemination and development of 'post-Marxist' paradigms. A notable case in point here is Nikolas Rose's deployment and extension of Foucauldian themes in his analyses of techniques of political, bio-political, psychological and other forms of governance.

In addition to the taking-root of these 'continental' variants of Marxism and post-Marxism, a discernible genre of 'British Marxism', which draws in some senses from the empirical and anti-metaphysical strains in 'traditional' British intellectual culture, has also been of international importance. Crucial here of course is the historian E. P Thompson, a key figure in the British 'New Left' political movement of the 1950s and 1960s (and an inspiration for some of the 'new cultural historians' such as Peter Burke mentioned above). He is best known in theoretical circles for his sustained polemic against the fetishisation of 'structures' in the work of Althusser and cognate thinkers, and his defence of micrological and empirical analysis of social and cultural conditions, as they are made and remade by historical actors. A similar controversy of the 1970s involved the English political thinker Ralph Miliband and the Greek Althusserian Nicos Poulantzas, with the latter claiming that the modern Western state was 'capitalist' for reasons of its social functions, and the former, armed with a barrage of empirical data, contending that the state was a capitalist institution only insofar as it had been 'captured' by politically organised bourgeois groups. Also important in Marxist debates in Britain has been the historian Eric Hobsbawm, another central European emigré and author of a wide range of Marxist analyses of modern history, whose most influential work in the social sciences has perhaps been his interrogation of how 'national traditions' were invented and reproduced for the purposes of elite power. The Scottish theorist of nationalism Tom Nairn also made his name through his interrogation of Marxian terms from the point of view of developments in nationalist politics in a range of countries, but most especially Scotland.

Another case of a certain 'indigenisation' of 'foreign' materials concerns the emergence of the (loose) discipline of 'cultural studies', which has come in some ways to rival sociology as the institutional site for the production of 'theory' in the social sciences. In its current phase in Britain, key cultural studies figures like Stuart Hall and Tony Bennett, having moved beyond the Gramscian dispositions they held in the 1970s and early 1980s, have enthusiastically embraced the linguistic and discursive models produced by French post-structuralist semiotics, taking these in specific directions (generally unanticipated by their progenitors) attuned to the analysis of 'hybrid identities' and other cultural studies concerns.

Yet the earlier, 'culturalist' phase of cultural studies, which predominated until the mid-1970s, and which still has isolated pockets of followers around the English-speaking world, was much more obviously 'English' in orientation, especially given its roots in the literary critical analyses of figures such as F. R. Leavis. The work of Richard Hoggart, for example, from the 1950s onwards could be said to be a quintessentially 'English' amalgam of social empiricism and literary-critical 'close readings' of cultural forms. Although the later (1970s and 1980s) Marxian and cultural materialist work of the Welsh theorist and critic Raymond Williams engaged with the main currents of European Marxism, his earlier writings are suffused with ideas drawn not just from English literary criticism, but from the wider English literary and cultural 'tradition', self-consciously identified in Williams (1958), that stems from the times of Edmund Burke in the late eighteenth-century, and develops through the nine-teenth- and early twentieth-centuries in the work of such literary intellectuals as S. T. Coleridge, Matthew Arnold and T. S. Eliot.

This genealogical line of thought about 'culture', and its relations to 'society', seems at first glance to be wholly 'native' in nature. But someone as well attuned to the closures on thought effected by national boundaries as Williams, knew very well that this was a line of thinking that had hybrid and non-indigenous elements. For example, both Coleridge and Arnold were highly influenced by German Idealist and Romantic currents, and despite the highly stylised 'Englishness' of (the American-born) Eliot, he was indebted to French anthropology for the important notion of culture as a 'whole way of life'.

Conclusion

This chapter has examined the historical genesis of social theoretical endeavours in Britain. It has taken a long-term approach in order to highlight the changing contours of social theoretical production – most importantly, from outside universities to within them, and from less intensive to more sustained 'international' influences. This has illustrated the point, which a shorter-term historical focus would have missed, that the conditions of production of social theory today in Britain, and thus to a great degree the nature of social theories themselves, are in certain respects much changed from the way they were 'traditionally' in Britain, at least until the early twentieth-century.

From that time on, the empirical – if not empiricist – and individualist dispositions of English (but not to such a great degree, Scottish) intellectual life were increasingly subjected to competition from, and then domination by, more 'holistic' and 'theory-friendly' epistemological assumptions, primarily generated outside the borders of the British state. The influence of emigré intellectuals in transforming the boundaries of theory production in Britain should not be underestimated, and should be understood as part of wider trajectories towards the internationalisation, if not globalisation, of theory generation throughout the latter part of the twentieth-century and on into the twenty-first. Yet even in the heyday of what is too simplistically known as 'English empiricism', there were not only important 'foreign' (and in the case of the Scots, 'not quite foreign') influences, but also counter-trends and other ways of thinking. In particular, consideration of the long-term genesis of con-temporary cultural studies illustrates the fact that, if we broaden the definition of 'social the-ory' to include theoretical accounts of 'culture' and the contributions of intellectuals outside of the social sciences, we can see that the 'British' contribution to social theory may rest as much, if not in fact more so, on thinking about the importance of 'culture' in social life, as of tendencies towards empirical checks on what are taken as theoretical flights of fancy.

References

Abrams, P. (1968) *The Origins of British Sociology*, Chicago: The University of Chicago Press.

Albrow, M. (1990) 'Introduction', in M. Albrow and E. King (eds) *Globalization, Knowledge and Society*, London: Sage/International Sociological Association, pp. 3–16.

Dennis, N. and A. H. Halsey (1988) *English Ethical Socialism*, Oxford: Clarendon Press.

Edmonds, D. and J. Eidinow (2005) *Wittgenstein's Poker*, London: Faber and Faber.

Elias, N. (1994) *The Civilizing Process*, Oxford: Blackwell.

Halévy, E. (1966) *The Growth of Philosophical Radicalism*, Boston: Beacon Press.

Halsey, A. H. (2004) *A History of Sociology in Britain*, Oxford: Oxford University Press.

Hawthorne, G. (1976) *Enlightenment and Despair: A History of Sociology*, Cambridge: Cambridge University Press.

Kumar, K. (2001) 'Sociology and the Englishness of English Social Thought', *Sociological Theory*, 19(1): 41–64.

Kuper, A. (1999) *Culture: The Anthropologists' Account*, Cambridge, MA: Harvard University Press.

Levine, D. H. (1995) *Visions of the Sociological Tradition*, Chicago: The University of Chicago Press.

Parsons, T. (1961) *The Structure of Social Action*, Glencoe: Free Press.

Platt, J. and S. Hopper (1997) 'Fragmentation, Social Theory and Feminism: Sociology in the United Kingdom', *Contemporary Sociology*, 26(3): 283–285.

Studholme, M. (1997) 'From Leonard Hobhouse to Tony Blair: A Sociological Connection?', *Sociology*, 31(3): 531–547.

Swingewood, A. (1970) 'Origins of Sociology: The Case of the Scottish Enlightenment', *The British Journal of Sociology*, 21(2): 164–180

Williams, R. (1958) *Culture and Society 1780–1950*, London: Chatto and Windus.

8

Everything changes and nothing changes

Change, culture and identity in contemporary Italian social theory

Monica Sassatelli

Generations of scholars of Italy have agreed, to the point of rendering it a conceptual com-mon-place, that there is no shared national culture and identity, and that what characterises Italy is precisely diversity, notably due to its late unification as a nation-state. However, it does not take much of a leap of (postmodern) imagination to then say that this pastiched diversity *is* Italy. Essentialism, thrown out of the door, tends to enter back through the win-dow: that very lack can eventually be taken as the essence of Italy, colouring every aspect of it. This includes its social theory, which struggles for some form of unitary hegemony (a well-known Italian contribution to the conceptual tool-kit of social theory) in order to be able to will into existence Italy as a unity. But it should hopefully be clear in these times of con-structivism that the issue is not so much that Italy is not a pre-existing nation whereas others were. Rather, that what elsewhere has been the successful imagination of a nation, or better its operationalisation for the purposes of a State (solidarity and spontaneous obedience), has been problematic in Italy, an otherwise quite culturally meaningful entity, that is to say something that shows relevant family resemblances and no homogeneity or 'purity' at all (Bedani and Haddock 2000; Barański and West 2001). The disappointing reality of unified Italy, the patent impotence of intellectuals to lead change and the apparent indifference of people for being made into Italians,[1] find expression in modern Italian social theorists' main preoccupation: the unresolved relationship of theory and practice (Bellamy 1987). This was variously addressed, but shaped a terrain of shared derivative themes, such as the relationship of elites and masses, the legitimating role of ideology and ideologues, and the formation of parties and the rational organisation of productive forces. These themes could also draw on a long tradition of Italian thought, extending back to Machiavelli, which dealt with ruling strata, non-rational action and the cyclicity of historical dynamics (Levine 1995). This is well epitomised, on the one hand, in the works of Vilfredo Pareto where he conceived of the relationship of theory and praxis, or ideology and political action, in terms of trailing justifi-cations for already accomplished actions, triggered by rather irrational residues and deriva-tions. On the other hand, in Antonio Gramsci we find a less cynical and yet more critical account, committed to an *engagé* attempt at reform(ulat)ing a new connection between politics and political culture and more explicitly assigning to intellectuals the role of agents of social change.[2] This self-attributed mission has been the underlying common thread of generations of Italian social theorists, and it can be said that in the 1960s Italian sociology was still mainly occupied with the changing nature of Italian society (Pinto 1981).

To avoid essentialism without overreacting to it, contemporary Italy[3] can be conceived as a signifying frame within which to highlight relations of proximity, to take account of the geo-historical embeddedness of theory (Wagner 2001). Weakened as it may be, the national context remains a meaningful entity, if nothing else to see how wider, smaller, cross-cutting instances are emerging through it. The problem with it is that it has tended to become an unquestioned ideal of social and cultural organisation, set once and for all. Now that the cultural unity of nations has long shown both its fragility and often imposed character, giving way to the thematisation of multiple and dynamic identities – notably in the shape of Europe desperately looking for a 'unity in diversity' that might be more than just an empty Eurospeak motto – Italy's difficult historical and intellectual gestation seems all the more interesting as a way of coming to terms with the marginal and anomalous aspects of mod-ernisation. Recent theoretical contributions emerging from Italy are thus well placed to contribute to the emerging problematisation of modernity as multiple or entangled (Eisen-stadt 2000; Thernborn 2003).

In fact, if social change, especially that subsumed in the term modernisation, has been both the (epistemological) seedbed out of which social theory emerged, and its primary (empirical) object, then it does not surprise that modern Italy's peculiar dynamics should show in its social theory. Italy has imported theories of social change much as it used to invite foreign masters to solve its internal problems.[4] Therefore we might detect a constant preoccupation with change that does not result so much in a theory of social change, but in a heightened sensibility for what can prevent it or detour its direction, making history look like a cycle rather than progress: from Pareto's non-logic action destabilising ration-ality, to Eco's *opera aperta* destabilising a hegemonic signification, Italian theories are linked mostly to a questioning of what really does change when we talk of change, and who can make it happen and for whom. 'If we want everything to stay the same, everything has to change' (Tomasi di Lampedusa 1960: 24): this notorious quote from the modern Italian literary canon, infamously concretised in the political practice of *trasformismo*, encapsulates Italian intellectuals' overarching preoccupation. If social change can be conceived as *the* topic of social theory, including as corollaries most of the others – social order, agency/structure, social identity (Noble 2000) – one can look at all this from another perspective, that is when change doesn't quite happen: not for all, not in the same way or with the same meaning, and not as a matter of rationalisation. That is when problems of elite *vs* mass, of quality and differentiation (from the high/low culture debate to recent theorisa-tions of postmodern global imaginaries), and of identity politics emerge. One could say that Italy's problematic relationship with change is reflected in its social theory as a concern with boundaries and roles; the boundaries of theory itself (from the theory of praxis to postmodern *pensiero debole*) and the role of its bearers, the intellectuals (as recently put, from Vico to Eco, from *philosophes* to pundits (Bellamy 2001)). This first overarching theme leads on in turn to a special focus on cultural formations, whose political import in a society that could never be seen as aproblematically self-regulating was always an issue and, finally, to a concern for how all this should lead to a consideration of individual and social identities. These themes, that are also the bedrock of those contemporary theories elaborated in Italy that have been mainly exported – postmodernism and social movements theory, together with a Gramscian revival, in particular within cultural studies[5] – provide a transversal insight across some of the main contemporary Italian contributions to social theory.

Organic, mediating and creative intellectuals between politics and culture

Making social theory implies an attempt to make history, mainly either by finding connection with established power elites or by trying to mobilise a revolutionary force (Lemert 1991). A more sociologically informed way to phrase this is to refer to the forms of collective activity that lie behind such abstract terms as theory and history, that is, the activity of the 'intellectuals'[6] and their often self-bestowed role as a factor of change of other people's beliefs and behaviours. In contemporary Italy, the intellectuals' search for relevance has been seen as both potentially more crucial and practically more difficult, thus rendering them particularly sensitive towards such a pragmatic sociology of intellectuals, uniting not only modern and contemporary thinkers, but tracing a link that could go as far back as the search for a social ethic in Machiavelli and Vico. Antonio Gramsci, writing from prison in the 1920s, can be seen as the modern turning point. Criticising the idea of the intellectual as abstracted from the concrete life of the state, Gramsci classified intellectuals according to their attitude towards their position within state and civil society. The practical conditions for the relevance of theoretical endeavours are thematised through his distinction between traditional and organic intellectuals. Traditional intellectuals are those who have a deluded vision of themselves (which they project outside) as autonomous and independent of the dominant social group. Instead, organic intellectuals acknowledge and embrace their rootedness, recognising that every group produces a specialised stratum whose role is to act as that group's consciousness: 'Every emerging social group, coming into existence on the original terrain of an essential function in the world of economic production, creates, together with itself, organically, one or more strata of intellectuals which give it homogeneity and an awareness of its own function not only in the economic but also in the social and political fields' (Gramsci 1971: 5). According to the revisited form of materialism that Gramsci held (thanks also to the idealist bent he owed to his Italian milieu) there is no such a thing as a raw fact, conceptual frameworks are always necessary to construct facts. Organic intellectuals do explicitly what common people do erratically and implicitly, in as much as mundane action always contains a theoretical worldview, however embryonic and hidden. The intellectual shapes this pre-existing material, theoretically making explicit the practical union of theory and practice.

This is a momentous stance as a number of developments have descended from it, and, from the point of view of the history of ideas, this particular combination of idealism and a Marxism devoid of any positivist overtones is what has granted Gramsci a place amongst sophisticated contemporary theories. The first implication is that the separation of theory and practice can only be fictitious, and not innocently so, as it encourages 'mental laziness' in the masses that are left on the passive, agency-deprived side of the divide. This is why, second, recognising the role of consciousness for action leads to highlighting the importance of what Gramsci called hegemony in the reproduction of social relations, as a consensual basis in civil society, which a political system can draw on to avoid open domination and the use of force. A revolutionary thinker, Gramsci thought therefore that the incumbent task was to free the masses from the hegemony the ruling class are able to maintain thanks to their control over the means of cultural (re)production. This could be done through exposing the falseness of ideology and substituting it with a new true ideology, that would itself be 'organic', as it would not be imposed from an exterior class of intellectuals–priests (like the traditional type) but developed internally as a conscious and advanced expression of the spontaneous philosophy of ordinary people. Two of the main dilemmas this brought up were clear to Gramsci: the difficulty of keeping the intellectuals, the 'permanent persuaders', both separated from and attached to their base, whose consciousness and way of life ended up being their main critical target, and the fact that the new ideology had to attain hegemony if it was to mean something, as its truthfulness, he thought, could only be judged in historical terms.

Gramsci's critics disagree on the degree to which he was able to solve these dilemmas. Before his original analyses of popular culture and hegemony were put to use within cultural studies and before the rethinking of political sociology in terms of cultural politics stimulated by the 'cultural turn' in social theory (Nash 2001), the debate on Gramsci was launched in Italy by the liberal legal philosopher Norberto Bobbio. Since the 1950s Bobbio (1955; 1993) has in fact formulated the terms of discussion as an opposition between 'cultural politics' and the 'politics of culture'. According to Bobbio, cultural politics, Gramsci's strategy for the intellectuals to create a new hegemony is but a way to subordinate culture to politics, letting the latter programme the former; whereas by the politics of culture he meant 'the politics of men of culture in defence of the conditions necessary for the existence and development of culture' (Bobbio 1955: 37). The intellectuals here are still *engagé*, for Bobbio never argued for apolitical intellectuals, inasmuch as they are seen as carriers of a specific form of power, but they become a mediating instance: which is what he has tried to be all his life, calling himself a mediating intellectual. In the actual cases of Gramsci and Bobbio their relevance may not have been so different – after all the latter has been called 'the civil conscience of Italy' – but in theoretical terms their approaches are divided by a significant shift towards increased detachment. Above all, this debate reveals that underneath its surface there is the question of culture's multiple instrumentalities and creative derivativeness (an apparent contradiction in terms, but it indicates that culture can be relatively autonomous and productive, beyond the economic and the political, and yet at the same time reflect them). In the 'fall' from legislators to interpreters (Bauman 1987) – a shift that has been detected in Gramsci as well (Walzer 1989) – the fact of (allegedly) being insiders is paid with a net loss in practical relevance; here the further move to intellectuals as mediators or observers seems to add a self-inflicted if unintentional aloofness.[7]

Rather than a conceptual shift, this progressive erosion of the role of intellectuals can be conceived as an historical one, originating from a social context of the erosion of the autonomy and significance of the specific form of power they carry. This is how the political sociologist Gianfranco Poggi has addressed the issue in the framework of a social theory of power (Poggi 2001; see also 1990). In the tradition of modern Italian social theorists (or indeed their forebears: Poggi has been defined a Weberian Machiavelli), Poggi considers intellectuals as an active force among others competing for influence. This goes back to a concern about how theory, what intellectuals do, is always also practice, a form of social construction of reality. The question is not whether one holds notions of ideas (ideologies) as derivative of 'material' conditions, or the contrary: tough-minded scholars as different as Marx and Pareto consecrated much effort in understanding the power of ideological phenomena, derivative as they might have thought they were. Starting from a tripartite notion of power, political, economic and ideological/normative, for which he refers to Weber but also to Bobbio, Poggi posits that there is a distinctive group with a monopoly over meaning, norms, and aesthetic and ritual practices, that is to say over ideological/normative power (Poggi 2001: 58–73). Within this group, and especially in modern conditions where the monopoly crumbles due to differentiation and secularisation, one can then differentiate a minority ideal type of creative intellectuals. Creativity here refers to a faculty to 'shape the generality's opinion, moral sensitivity and taste, to orient the collectivity, to make sense of individuals' circumstances … through discourse, through the mutual confrontation of the participants' competing views and preferences' (ibid. 101). Because the counterpart, the audience, is rarely as undifferentiatedly passive and readily responsive as this (self)definition presupposes, relevance is usually sought through a *do ut des* relationship with the state, that is the instance that can *enforce* its vision of what the proper goals and modalities of a good social existence are, but that needs legitimation, the imagination of a community, and also a well-entertained citizenry.

However, the differentiation and secularisation that rendered possible the existence of profane creative intellectuals, seems to have backfired on them. Poggi points to the fact that the pluralisation that substituted the monopoly of the sacred intellectuals also means a wea-kened relevance of each and all; and the widening of the public sphere is paralleled by a lost possibility of speaking a public language, thus of having a public relevance and a bargaining capacity with the state. But rather than favouring the latter, itself seen as challenged by globalisation, this development appears to favour a media/market domination of symbols, self-perception and forms of experiencing; that is of the imaginary. Paradoxically, just when the conditions for creative intellectuals to freely exercise their role have become favourable and the significance of the imaginary has increased, they have not accordingly become more influential, having instead lost control over the imaginary. The reasons for this lie at least partly beyond their reach, as a by-product of the same processes that gave them voice in the first place. Because, whilst creative intellectuals became internally over-differentiated and increasingly self-referential, the production of images and myths was becoming industrialised: today the media, and media intellectuals are those who make public language. This is seen as problematic not in moral or cultural terms, but because it makes the economic and political elites the shapers of the new global imaginary to the detriment of the intellectual elite, thus impoverishing the plural balance of the different elites. If today's global imaginaries apparently seem to lead to an explosion of ideological/normative power, when we look beneath the surface, to the social relations and forms of powers at its source, the apparently pluralistic world where the *imaginaire* is increasingly relevant appears instead increasingly homogenised. It is not a question of an essential, qualitative differential between the creative intellectuals with their (high?) cultural experimentalism and the media intellectuals with their (mass) cul-ture. What matters, in Poggi's view, is the threatening reduction of the plurality of pre-sumptively distinct power forms, as a paradoxical, often overlooked, by-product of modern differentiation: a postmodern de-differentiation, too often illusorily, and not innocently so, celebrated as a liberation from power *tout court*.

Postmodern global imaginaries and cultural theory for rethinking the project of modernity

A strong alliance of modern Italian intellectuals with 'high culture' has been detected as one factor in their lost battle for wider social relevance. The success of television in Italy (a decidedly market and politically oriented one for that matter), in achieving precisely what high culture had failed to do – making the Italians – seems to reinforce the idea of a trend towards the creation of an hegemonic mass imaginary dependent on the economic and poli-tical forms of power. With a continuity of themes from previous generations, and as a reac-tion to their solutions, contemporary Italian thinkers not only exposed this, focusing on the power relations that underlie the production of meaning, as we have just seen, but have also engaged in a cultural analysis from the side of consumption. This is the case of Umberto Eco's semiotics of reception. Eco's impact on the social sciences can be traced to *Apocalittici e Integrati* (1964), yet another classification of intellectuals, the frowning censor of culture's corruption and the enthusiastic champion and producer of mass culture: the apocalyptic announce the apocalypse coming, the integrated *make* it, both ignore a social analysis. The main objective of this volume is not so much in the catchy title, which has since become proverbial, but in the serious consideration of 'frivolous' matter – from comic strips to the meaning of kitsch – as a practical demonstration not only of the untenable division of high and low culture but, through that, of the equally untenable univocal interpretation of cultural products. This not only generated an impressive public debate in Italy at the time, but launched a perspective on popular culture and mass communication analysis in social theory that has been very influential internationally, in particular for postmodernism and cultural studies. Drawing critically on the Frankfurt school, but also on Gramsci's work on culture, and adapting Saussure through Peirce's semiology as his main theoretical framework, Eco showed the necessity for social theory to turn towards mass culture and the media from the side of reception. This means a conceptualisation of culture as multidimensional and ultimately *open*, such as the artistic avant-garde movements seen in *Opera aperta* (*The Open Work* 1989 [1962]): the art object is not the definitive and objective bearer of a closed meaning set once and for all, but is constantly recreated, like its meaning, by interpretation and reception. This, as Eco argued more recently, does not mean an absolute relativism of meaning, it is rather aimed at highlighting the *content nebula* of symbols, which is neither total arbitrariness nor unique hegemonic sense, precisely because 'the content of the symbol is a *nebula* of possible interpretations' (Eco 1984: 161), it always contains an unforeseen and unforeseeable result which is nevertheless a non-arbitrary one. Eco's use of the Peircean principle of interpretation and notion of unlimited semiosis lets him speak of the crisis of reason and weak thought[8] in affirmative terms, against the metanarrative of a globalising reason carrying a strong definitive vision of the universe and thus denying voice to the unlimited work of contextual intersubjectivity. If postmodern diffidence towards essences and *grands récits* has infiltrated social theory, spreading a suspicion for over-rationalized conceptions of society, this is linked to those theories, such as Eco's, that make the symbolic domain their principal target (or those, as we shall see in the next section, that emphasise identity over strategy, looking at the same issues from the side of agency), one that deserves a specific form of analysis.

Eco's extensive use of postmodern irony, however, carries the risk, shared by much interpretative sociology, often sensitive to these formulations, of overlooking social processes, with social action becoming derivative of discourse, narrative, text (Hałas 2002). If semiotics deals with the unexpected meaning, calling for an unmasking of the contradiction of all univocal and ideological positions – and, to go back to the previous section's theme, for a role of the intellectual limited to interpretative expertise – social theory has to engage in the question of agency. This has to be problematised well beyond a 'role of intellectuals', already empirically exposed as rather limited. The fading of the distinction between high and low culture questions the model which is almost always the necessary and implicit premise of cultural theories, of a diffusion of cultural trends from top to bottom. Following the Gramscian heritage, Eco put Marxism and semiotics to use in criticising that model. Showing the inescapability of an interpretative mediation implied by our linguistic access to reality carries not only a potentially 'liberating' effect for agency, but also an epistemologically undermining one, destabilising its founding principles. This 'condition' generated, a few decades ago now, two main opposed reactions: an apocalyptic pessimism (traceable in the neo-conservative critique of cultural modernity) and a kind of manic postmodernism (or, to build on Eco's distinction, integrated). More recently, in Italy as elsewhere, a new 'generation' of the reflection on postmodernity (rather than postmodern reflection) has developed, addressing the questions of influence and its subjects, and that of the foundation of validity.

In one instance the key issue has been seen as that of the production of a widespread imaginary – as the contemporary equivalent of the Weberian iron cage working as a form, at the same time highly abstract and interiorised, of control and determination, in a world now characterised by information economy – and the space for an alternative to it. The notions of empire and then of multitude, emerging from Italian radical thought (Virno and Hardt 1996) and defined by Michael Hardt and Antonio Negri (2000; 2004) are an attempt at doing this, thus addressing the question of influence and its subjects. The multiplicity that in recent dominant cultural theory is an effect of interpretation or even interactivity brought about by the digital revolution, in Hardt-Negri's radical and according to many utopian cultural theory is rather the multitude's confrontation with the unifying logic that underlies postmodern hybridisation and blurring of boundaries. The programme is that of a rehabilitation of (post-human) humanism and (non-hegemonic) universalism. It starts by highlighting and investigating how resistance can grow out of the interstices opened by the inherent contradictions of power; practical or discursive. As the last turn of phrase suggests, the main source of this approach is French poststructuralist, neo-Nietzschean, thought – in particular Foucault, for power, and Deleuze and Guattari, for rhizomes – grafted on to a reformed Marxist scheme reflecting the specificity of the Italian intellectual and historical context (Lumley 1990). In the framework of an otherwise anodyne view of globalisation entailing the informatisation (postmodernisation) of the economy, world market and declining national sovereignty, Hardt-Negri introduce these two concepts that have themselves struck the collective academic imaginary: *Empire* (2000) and *Multitude* (2004). The empire is the new global power structure: the comparatively limited power of the disciplinary society has been substituted by the overarching presence of the society of control, where through inclusion, differentiation and management the world market accomplishes the role that was that of Foucault's panopticon. But if postmodern capitalism transforms the processes of becoming human, there is the possibility for a further non-dominating transformation: the integration of culture and production in rhizomatic networks is what contains the emancipatory potential of globalisation. Against the new form of control, and within it, new forms of resistance and new commonalities immanent to the new economy of immaterial labour emerge. If poststructuralism's red thread is a critique of all kinds of transcendence, including metaphysics, universalism, meta-theory (Morris 2004), the negation of anything collective as a form of transcendence (of the individual) is not the only path recent theory has followed. There is a second path that connects the critique of transcendence to a collectively mediated experience, leading to actual strategies of resistance, without the collectivity becoming a transcendent identity. In Hardt-Negri a form of universality without transcendence is at stake, and it is sought through the concept of multitude, the productive subject fighting the Empire, via the creative power of its desire. The desiring multitude is conceived of as the global, postindustrial equivalent of the proletariat and as the only really generative, or creative, instance, that capital exploits, but that fires back on it. This avoids a fixed identity and remains plural: any formulation in terms of identification or representation would not only be untenable in the era of deterritorializing, informational global political economy, but would also reinforce the very logic of control of Empire.

Although from different premises and with different results, the definition of a space of resistance towards forms of dominations is similarly both the starting point and the normative underpinning of another type of cultural analysis amounting to a fully fledged social theory, namely critical theory. In its third generation, this has an Italian contemporary exponent in the sociologist and philosopher Alessandro Ferrara. He develops another postmetaphysical position that does not renounce universalism, this time directly addressing the issue of the

101

foundations of validity. Ferrara's programme, in line with this affiliation, is in fact to revalidate a form of universalism beyond the plurality of cultures, traditions, scientific paradigms and linguistic games brought about since the first half of the twentieth-century by the philosophical 'linguistic turn'. Here the struggle for the recognition of diversity and a different globality is substituted by an attempt at rethinking universalism, through retrieving theoretical varieties of it formulated in the past but which have never become dominant, in the conviction, along with Habermas, that the foundational role of universalistic principles cannot be totally substituted for the validation of sustainable forms of intersubjectivity. This programme is carried out via a reconstruction of the more neglected tradition informing modernity, the tradition of authenticity (Ferrara 1993), leading to a comprehensive rethinking of the modern project (Ferrara 1998), and to a more specific consideration of this approach's implications for political philosophy (Ferrara 1999). Starting from a reconsideration of Rousseau, and with him of an alternative 'tradition of authenticity' (that includes also Schiller, Kierkegaard, Nietzsche, Heidegger) opposed to the dominant 'tradition of autonomy' (Kant, Hegel, via utilitarianism up to Rawls and Habermas) that has monopolised the definition of modernity until recently, Ferrara proposes a concept of validity combined with authenticity. This means grounding validity in a form of universalism that, following Simmel in particular, is not generalising but exemplary, as well as accounting for what Ferrara calls postmodern *eudaimonia* (well-being), the shared normative ideal of authenticity towards which the postmodern pluralism of life-forms and life-styles is directed. Ours is an age of authenticity, that is best exemplified by the self-congruency of life-history in the life-world and of the work of art in expert practices. To deliberate about these means to express a judgement of taste, and see the universal in the particular, or the normativity without principles of Kant's reflective judgement, hence Ferrara's idea of reflective authenticity, that tries to bridge the gap between the two traditions. This makes Ferrara propose this conclusion: 'Paradoxically we are driven to, and at the same time we associate a sense of necessity with, our conception of the source of validity as *uniquely singular*, precisely because that is the best way of accommodating the transcontextual relevance of validity with our convictions regarding the genuine plurality of values. In this embracing of extreme singularity in order to reconcile plurality and universalism also lies the best chance for the project of modernity to finally come to work' (Ferrara 1998: 164). Putting him within the mentioned recent theorising of varieties of modernity, this conclusion also shows how further developments are above all a question of interrogating modernity's different variants, such as the traditions of autonomy and authenticity, in terms of the implications and unexplored possibilities for contemporary identities.

Identity matters, from social movements to the bare life (and Europe)

Different approaches in contemporary social theory point to identity both as a bearer of liberating potentialities and as a potential instance of control. If it is when it cannot any more be taken for granted that identity becomes an issue of social inquiry, it is no wonder that intellectuals – with their problematic relationship with their own ambiguous role and belonging – are fascinated by it, and that Italian intellectuals in particular have provided some major contributions to the theme. Alessandro Pizzorno and Alberto Melucci are the two Italian champions of identity and of its fundamental role as a tool to interpret the social world. Pizzorno, one of the founding fathers of Italian sociology, is best known as a political sociologist (Pizzorno 1993) and for his early work within Olivetti's Industrial Relations Research Service in the 1950s. As a political sociologist he engages critically with Hobbesian theory of social order and economic theories of democracy. Combined with an appropriation of Foucault, this provides Pizzorno's access to social theory as a concern for the conditions of possibility of a democratic polity and the status of subjects, furthering the Italian tradition of social theory as a search for 'categories that give order to the unruly multiplicity of experience' (Pizzorno 2000: 244). It is in direct and open contrast with the dominant paradigm of the last two decades, rational choice theory, that he develops his theory of identity as the basic explanation of social action.[9] It is identity seeking and not interest seeking that can explain collective action: there's no interest without an agent calculating it, and the existence and persistence of that agent cannot be taken for granted, it is instead that which has to be explained at the beginning, that is, problematising the processes of identity creation through recognition. Presupposing the intertemporal continuity of an individual's preferences, theories that put rationality at the centre of social action rather than identity fail to see that identity is the end of action: an action's aim is not to procure given goods, but to realize collective identification, that is precisely to secure continuity and avoid dissolution. If today this argument of identity *vs* strategy as a theoretical paradigm to interpret action, within social movements in particular, is more widely accepted, this is also due to Pizzorno's efforts since the 1980s in this direction, that showed how focusing on structural contradictions and social class is not enough to understand contemporary collective actors and thus social change (Cohen 1985). As a foundational concept identity has far reaching consequences, as it involves non-negotiable demands: when oriented to identity action is expressive rather than instrumental, requires participation rather than representation, or so it is for collective instances that are not yet institutionalised, such as the new social movements. Created in collective interaction and recognition, identity needs constant reaffirmation, or, to again use Pizzorno's favourite term, recognition. Identity is thus considered for its performative, public aspects where the internal dimension of actors is accounted for insofar as it is expressed, and thus observable from a sociological point of view, within action.

More willing to investigate the individual existential dimension is the sociologist Alberto Melucci, arguably in connection with his second professional career as a clinical psychologist. Especially in his late works, this emerges as an interest in aspects otherwise neglected by social theory, such as the corporeal and affective spheres. But from the beginning this specific attention for the entanglement of collective action and individual experience can be seen in his investigations of the relationship between movements, identity and individual needs, for which since the 1980s he has been known as a theorist of 'new social movements' (Melucci 1989). A pupil of Alain Touraine in Paris, Melucci studies social movements as networks of collective, solidary action sustained by specific cultural codes, investigating the *meaning* collective actors see in their action. He develops a constructivist approach that problematises the relationship between change and conflict and stresses the cultural rather than political nature of the NSM, always putting the question of identity construction at the centre of his theoretical framework.[10] Social movements are thus a good vantage point, because not being yet crystallised into social structures, they provide a lens to investigate the relational fabric of society *in action*, and, as we read in *The Playing Self* (1996a), the aim of both individual and collective action is the action itself, the construction of its own codes (1996b). It is thus through a microsociological and psychological analysis of action's specific ways grounded in the lived and embodied individual experience, that he builds a macrosociological historical picture of the development of contemporary social movements. As in Pizzorno, the now well known theme of multiple identities, to whose development they have both contributed, is addressed, notably with the famous definition 'nomads of the present' – clearly combining both the diachronic/temporal and synchronic/spatial nature of the subject's pluralisation and incertitude – but without consenting to the total fragmentation and dissolution of the subject. Rather he conceives of identity, against all essentialisms, as a field of opportunities and constraints: 'it appears evident that identity increasingly takes on the shape of a field rather than of an essence, a system of axes or vectors of meaning, with possibilities and limits that we can recognise and that we contribuite to define' (Melucci 2000: 108). Hence, with the tension constitutive of identity – the difficult coexistence of determination and freedom – emerges the paradoxical place of the individual, as the result of both a duty of freedom and opportunity of (self) determination.[11]

If Pizzorno's and Melucci's problem is that of the danger of dissolution of identity, seen as a necessary if paradoxical dimension of individuals and collectivities, other recent theories have a more radically critical and wary attitude to identity, as we have already seen emerging from some approaches dealing with global imaginaries and resistance: the question is increasingly less cultural and more biopolitical. Notably this is what can be found in Giorgio Agamben's different answer to the Foucaultian theme of the normatisation of subjectivity, articulated through the notions of 'coming community' (1993) and 'homo sacer' (1998). Here identity is seen chiefly as an essentialist, exclusivist tool of control. What is proposed in its place is the idea of being *whatever*: so is the coming community, without belonging and specificity, absolutely *inessential* – because what is common cannot be the essence of what is singular – yet not indifferent; and so is the coming being, neither individual nor universal in any received meaning. In terms of a traditional political order, this means becoming a totally irrelevant subject, a '*homo sacer*', that according to the archaic Roman law is doomed to death, excluded from the human world: a 'bare life' that cannot be sacrificed but that can be killed without committing homicide. This is the real challenge to power and to today's spectacularised society of control, because power, as expressed by the State, can always understand and eventually incorporate struggles of identity, contrasting as they might be, but it cannot accept that 'the singularities form a community without affirming an identity, that humans cobelong without any representable condition of belonging. . . . For the State, therefore, what is important is never the singularity as such, but only its inclusion in some identity, whatever identity (but the possibility of the *whatever* itself being taken up without an identity is a threat the State cannot come to terms with)' (Agamben 1993: 85). Hence, Agamben rejects the depoliticisation of subjectivity that characterises many postmodern approaches and sees in contemporary instances of refusal of institutional identities and traumatic encounter with the excluded 'bare life' the starting point for rethinking the subject of the political (Vighi 2003).[12]

The idea of coming community, as the struggle between empire and multitude evoked earlier on, can easily take, or be interpreted as taking, a messianic or utopian turn. This may be why some insightful – if sometimes frustrating – reflections on the same constellation of issues cluster around the all too concrete problem of European identity. This is a theme dear to many contemporary Italian thinkers, historians and philosophers in particular, often in connection to other sensitive identity issues such as gender or emotions (Passerini 1998). Well rooted in the geocultural and (bio?) political reality of Europe as a continent and as a developing polity, the question of European identity has become one of the major battlefields to engage with – rather than utopianly solve or postmodernly dissolve – the paradox of identity, which can be seen here, as it once was for Italy, at its highest degree. The philosopher Massimo Cacciari has claimed that the characterising feature of European identity, as of individual identity, is the struggle between irreducible components (Cacciari 1994; 1997). Europe is an 'absent homeland', not something to own and belong to, but something to reach for, something to experience; experience being conceived of as an exit from a closed and essential identity, and an opening to the Other. If this interiorisation of the other implies a danger, this too is not a disposable byproduct, but part and parcel of this attempt at redefining identity, European and other (see also Cassano 1996; Marramao 2003). It is the metaphor of the Archipelago that illustrates the double danger and necessity of the continuous struggle against oneself: 'The European Archipelago exists thanks to a double danger: that of finding a solution in a hierarchically ordered space or a dissolution in inhospitable, "idiotic" individualities, unable to attract and connect with each other, parts that have nothing left to share. In the Archipelago, instead, genuinely *autonomous* cities live in constant navigation *versus-contra* each-other, in indissoluble distinction' (Cacciari 1997: 21).

Levine talked of a paradox of the Italian tradition from Machiavelli to Gramsci in that 'inspired by a quest for the good society based on the findings of scientific reason, it concludes that the majority of people must be guided if not manipulated by acquiring beliefs that run counter to science' (Levine 1995: 250). The elitist tone of this paradox seems to have been superseded, but the paradox returns as that of ways of reconciling both determination and freedom (the modern constellation) and sameness and difference (the postmodern one) within the historical necessity and conceptual impossibility of social change (as the Italian, and now European, vantage points continue to show), precisely when elitist and exclusivist solutions – including 'cultures' and 'identities' – are no longer readily available.

Notes

1 The now trite *adagio* 'Italy is made, now we have to make Italians', first expressed by D'Azeglio, and today rendered both more trite and more relevant by its rediscovery with Europe and Europeans, underlines the widespread importance of the Italian 'anomaly' for contemporary geopolitics.

2 For accounts of earlier generations of the 'Italian tradition' see in particular Bellamy (1987) and Levine (1995). Reviews focusing more specifically on contemporary sociology are Pinto (1981), Ferrarotti (1996), D'Andréa (2000) and Rossi (2003).

3 The risk of essentialism is partly avoided thanks to the combination of geographical and historical specifications. If historicising protects against an otherwise possible ethnic implication of the geographical name, the reverse could also be said, the geographical specification protecting against a surreptitiously universal idea of what is 'contemporary'. The utility of considering a national context at a specific time is thus specified as to avoid thinning ideas into an abstract universal dialogue about a disembodied nature of the 'social' (Seidman 1994).

4 As Norberto Bobbio said, having never experienced a religious revolution, like Germany, or a political one, like France (England experienced both), and its industrial one late on, in Italy the word itself has been always mis- and overused, but a theory of revolution and of the revolutionary praxis has never been elaborated (Bobbio 1995 [1969]: 109).

5 One should add a specific reference to feminism: 'Two major areas in which contemporary Italian theory has begun to have more than a local effect amongst (primarily Western) intellectuals and academics are philosophical post-modernism and Feminism' (West 2001: 342). However, social theory at large does appear to remain 'boy talk' (Eadie 2001) as this view does not seem widely spread in the literature. For an overview of this emerging tradition of Italian feminism see Wood and Farrell (2001).

6 The term itself is notoriously a recent development, emerging, as often happens, with its object becoming problematic, as a way to both investigate the reasons of the crisis and new ways of gaining a crucial role in society (Bauman 1987). For a periodisation of the 'sociology of intellectuals', that poses its founding moment in the late 1920s see Kurzman and Owens (2002).

7 The dead end seems all the more inescapable as it is often phrased in terms of a shift from modern to postmodern epistemology, outruling any possibility of a claim to objectivity and universality (see Note 8). Gramsci himself was very wary of these terms, indeed he believed that since man is historical becoming, objectivity is a becoming as well, being thus possible only as what is 'humanly objective' (Gramsci 1977: 1415–1416).

8 For the originary formulation of the 'weak thought' (*pensiero debole*) see the book edited by Rovatti and Vattimo (1983). Subsequently, Gianni Vattimo has developed an hermeneutic approach to the 'transparent' society of generalized communication (Vattimo 1992).

9 Pizzorno has addressed identity in a series of articles since the 1980s. Identity, together with recognition and exchange, make up his pivotal concepts (for a detailed bibliography and commentaries see the edited book in his honour (Della Porta *et al.* 2000), that also contains a new essay on these themes and an autobiographical piece by Pizzorno.

10 See the recent volume in his memory, with essays by Touraine, Bauman and many others (Leonini 2003).

11 The theme of identity as the dialectical result of determination and its negation, within a reconsideration of social solidarity today, has been developed by Franco Crespi (1994).

12 A parallel path leading from community to a consideration of biopolitics can be found in Esposito (1998, 2004).

References

Agamben, G. (1993) *The Coming Community*, trans. M. Hardt, Minneapolis: Minnesota University Press.

Agamben, G. (1998) *Homo Sacer: Sovereign Power and Bare Life*, trans. D. Heller Roazen, Stanford, CA: Stanford University Press.

Barański, Z. G. and R. J. West (eds) (2001) *The Cambridge Companion to Modern Italian Culture*. Cambridge: Cambridge University Press.

Bauman, Z. (1987) *Legislators and Interpreters: On Modernity, Post/Modernity and Intellectuals*, Cambridge: Polity Press.

Bedani, G. and B. Haddock (eds) (2000) *The Politics of Italian National Identity: A Multidisciplinary Perspective*, Cardiff: University of Wales Press.

Bellamy, R. (1987) *Modern Italian Social Theory: Ideology and Politics from Pareto to the Present*, Stanford, CA: Stanford University Press.

Bellamy, R. (2001) 'From Philosophes to Pundits: Italian Intellectuals & Politics from Vico to Eco', *Journal of Modern Italian Studies*, 6(2): 151–156.

Bobbio, N. (1955) *Politica e cultura*, Torino: Einaudi.

Bobbio, N. (1993) *Il dubbio e la scelta: intellettuali e potere nella società contemporanea*, Roma: La Nuova Italia Scientifica.

Bobbio, N. (1995 [1969]) *Ideological Profile of Twentieth Century Italy*, trans. L.G. Cochrane, Princeton: Princeton University Press.

Cacciari, M. (1994) *Geofilosofia dell'Europa*, Milano: Adelphi.

Cacciari, M. (1997) *L'Arcipelago*, Milano: Adelphi.

Cassano, F. (1996) *Il pensiero meridiano*, Roma-Bari: Laterza.

Cohen, J. L. (1985) 'Strategy or Identity: New Theoretical Paradigms and Contemporary Social Movements', *Social Research*, 52(4): 663–716.

Crespi, F. (1994) *Imparare ad esistere: Nuovi fondamenti della solidarietà sociale*, Roma: Donzelli.

D'Andréa, F. (2000) 'La sociologie italienne', in P. Cabin and J-F. Dortier (eds) *La sociologie: Historie et idées*, Auxerre: Sciences Humaines éditions.

Della Porta, D., M. Greco, and A. Szakolczai (eds) (2000) *Identità, riconoscimento, scambio: saggi in onore di Alessandro Pizzorno*, Roma-Bari: Laterza.

Eadie, J. (2001) 'Boy Talk: Social Theory and Its Discontents', *Sociology*, 35(2): 575–582.

Eco, U. (1964) *Apocalittici e Integrati*, Milano: Bompiani.

Eco, U. (1984) *Semiotics and the Philosophy of Language*, London: Macmillan Press.

Eco, U. (1989 [1962]) *The Open Work*, trans. A. Cancogni, Cambridge, MA: Harvard University Press.

Eisenstadt, S. N. (2000) 'Multiple Modernities', *Dædalus*, 1291(1): 1–29 (monographic issue).

Esposito, R. (1998) *Communitas: Origine e destino della comunità*, Torino: Einaudi.

Esposito, R. (2004) *Bios: Biopolitica e filosofia*, Torino: Einaudi.

Ferrara, A. (1993) *Modernity and Authenticity*, New York: Suny Press.

Ferrara, A. (1998) *Reflective Authenticity*, London: Routledge.

Ferrara, A. (1999) *Justice and Judgement*, London: Sage.

Ferrarotti, F. (1996) 'Scienze sociali e politiche', in C. Stajano (ed.) *La cultura italiana del '900*, Roma-Bari: Laterza.

Gramsci, A. (1971) *Selections from the Prison Notebooks*, trans. Q. Hoare and G. Nowell Smith, New York: International Publishers.

Gramsci, A. (1977) *Quaderni dal carcere*, V. Gerratana (ed.), Torino: Einaudi.

Hałas, E. (2002) 'Symbolism and Social Phenomena: Toward the Integration of Past and Current Theroetical Approaches', *European Journal of Social Theory*, 5(3): 351–366.

Hardt, M. and A. Negri (2000) *Empire*, Cambridge, MA: Harvard University Press.

Hardt, M. and A. Negri (2004) *Multitude: War and Democracy in the Age of Empire*, New York: Penguin Press.

Kurzman, C. and L. Owens (2002) 'The Sociology of Intellectuals', in *Annual Review of Sociology*, 28: 63–90.

Lemert, C. C. (ed.) (1991) *Intellectuals and Politics: Social Theory in a Changing World*, London: Sage.

Leonini, L. (ed.) (2003) 'Indentita e movimenti sociali in una società planetaria' in *ricordo di Alberto Melucci*, Milan: Guerini.

Levine, D. N. (1995) *Visions of the Sociological Tradition*, Chicago: University of Chicago Press.

Lumley, R. (1990) *States of Emergency: Cultures of Revolt in Italy from 1967 to 1978*, London: Verso.

Marramao, G. (2003) *Passaggio a Occidente. Filosofia e globalizzazione*, Torino: Bollati Boringhieri.

Melucci, A. (1989) *Nomads of the Present: Social Movements and Individual Needs in Contemporary Society*, London: Hutchinson Radius.

Melucci, A. (1996a) *The Playing Self: Person and Meaning in the Planetary Society*, Cambridge: Cambridge University Press.

Melucci, A. (1996b) *Challenging Codes: Collective Action in the Information Age*, Cambridge: Cambridge University Press.

Melucci, A. (2000) *Culture in gioco: Differenze per convivere*, Milano: Il Saggiatore.

Morris, M. (2004) 'The Critique of Transcendence: Postructuralism and the Political', *Political Theory*, 32(1): 121–132.

Nash, K. (2001) 'The "Cultural Turn" in Social Theory: Towards a Theory of Cultural Politics', *Sociology*, 35(1): 77–92.

Noble, T. (2000) *Social Theory and Social Change*, Basingstoke: Palgrave.

Passerini, L. (1998) *Identità culturale europea: idee, sentimenti, relazioni*, Firenze: Nuova Italia.

Pinto, D. (1981) 'Sociology, Politics, and Society in Postwar Italy', *Theory and Society*, 10(5): 671–705.

Pizzorno, A. (1993) *Le radici della politica assoluta e altri saggi*, Milano: Feltrinelli.

Pizzorno, A. (2000) 'Risposte e proposte', in D. Della Porta and M. Greco *Identità, riconoscimento, scambio: Saggi in onore di Alessandro Pizzorno*, Roma-Bari: Laterza.

Poggi, G. (1990) *The State: Its Nature, Development, and Prospects*, Cambridge: Polity Press.

Poggi, G. (2001) *Forms of Power*, Cambridge: Polity Press.

Rossi, P. (2003) 'Il ritorno alla sociologia: Un confronto tra sociologia italiana e sociologia tedesca nel dopoguerra', *Quaderni di sociologia*, 33(3): 101–120.

Rovatti, P. A. and G. Vattimo (eds) (1983) *Il pensiero debole*, Milano: Feltrinelli.

Seidman, S. (1994) *Contested Knowledge: Social Theory in the Postmodern Era*, Oxford: Blackwell.

Thernborn, G. (2003) 'Entangled Modernities', *European Journal of Social Theory*, 6(3): 293–305.

Tomasi di Lampedusa, G. (1960) *The Leopard*, trans. A. Colquhoun. New York: Pantheon.

Vattimo, G. (1992) *The Transparent Society*, Cambridge: Polity Press.

Vighi, F. (2003) 'Pasolini and Exclusion. Žižek, Agamben and the Modern Sub-Proletariat', *Theory, Culture & Society*, 20(5): 99–121.

Virno, P. and M. Hardt (eds) (1996) *Radical Thought in Italy*, Minneapolis: Minnesota University Press.

Wagner, P. (2001) *A History and Theory of the Social Sciences*, London: Sage.

Walzer, M. (1989) *The Company of Critics: Social Criticism and Political Commitment in the Twentieth Century*, London: Peter Halban.

West, R. J. (2001) 'Italian Culture or Multiculture in the New Millenniun?', in Z. G Barański and R. J. West (eds), *The Cambridge Companion to Modern Italian Culture*. Cambridge: Cambridge University Press.

Wood, S. and J. Farrell (2001) 'Other Voices: Constesting the Status Quo', in Z. G Barański and R. J. West (eds) *The Cambridge Companion to Modern Italian Culture*. Cambridge: Cambridge University Press.

9

Contemporary Spanish social theory

Salvador Giner and Manuel Pérez Yruela

Any satisfactory interpretation of contemporary social theory in Spain must take into account the country's 'anomalous' modern history within Europe. Traditionally simplistic notions about nineteenth-century Spain's backwardness or failure to develop a substantial industrial and democratic revolution do not suffice to explain the country's supposed 'abnormality'. In some cases they are thoroughly misleading. Once a powerful political unit and the metropolis of a vast world empire, Spain entered the following century in a state of crisis, impotence and confusion. Moreover, though the Spaniards' artistic and literary faculties seemed never to have flagged, one crucially important dimension of their culture – science, philosophy and modern rational and critical thinking – had become extremely weak and unsatisfactory by normal European standards.

Spain, many thought, had ceased to count in a number of fields. One was social science. This judgement was harsh and even unfair at the time. Today, however, it would be groundless. Yet, largely as a result of this unfavourable perception, general surveys of modern sociology, economics, political philosophy, ethics, and social anthropology tend to lend little or no attention to Spain's contribution. An elementary acquaintance with the contents and achievements of those disciplines in Spain over the last century and a half yields a far less negative picture. Spanish scientific culture, especially in the social sciences, has had to pay an extremely high price for having developed within a country which had lost its central position in the Western world when others developed towards modernity at a much faster and firmer pace. During that period, Spain was relegated to a semi-peripheral position within it.

Spain's relatively recent and full reincorporation into the Western cultural core has not yet entirely corrected the former misrepresentation and lack of knowledge of its contributions in social science and theory. Spain is neither alone nor unique in this: though to a lesser extent, the contemporary social sciences in Italy, for instance, suffer from a similar lack of international recognition. Their international presence is not always commensurate with their achievements.

Marginalization or even the apparent non-existence of a nevertheless substantial national contribution within the world cultural sphere poses an interesting problem in the sociology of culture. We cannot go into it here. (Does political and economic peripherilization entail a parallel cultural subordination or ignorance by others?) This may be a neglected question within the current interest in globalization processes, where more attention is given to 'Westernization' and other 'convergence' problems than to serious imbalances occurring within the core areas of such processes.

A vivid illustration of the force of the negative perceptions just pointed out is that, as authors of this essay, we must now refer, albeit very sketchily, to the evolution of social theory in Spain since the nineteenth-century itself, so that the nature of the contemporary contribution can be properly described. Within a relatively brief account, German, French or English authors would certainly not feel the need to do so with their respective subjects.

The consolidation of modernity in Spanish social thought

Spain's troubled relationship with modern rationalist, secular and analytic thought sinks its roots as far back as the late Renaissance period, when it became a bulwark of the Counter-reformation as well as the chief political power within that movement. Despite early out-standing contributions to science and technology, and important innovations in fields such as international law, tight ecclesiastical and political control over thought and university life smothered critical and creative scientific thought since the late sixteenth-century.[1] It is most revealing, from the standpoint of the negative repercussions of marginalization, that Spain's later achievements in the fields of technology, science, and political economy during the Enlightenment period, its 'Eighteenth-century revolution' (Herr 1958) went almost unno-ticed abroad. The subsequent debacle – just at a time when the country was 'catching up', as it were, with the other Western European countries – in the form of the devastating Napo-leonic invasion and war of independence can hardly be exaggerated.

Spain's struggles with modernity throughout the nineteenth-century sank the country in a continuous state of confusion and, often, impotence. A serious preoccupation with 'Spain as a problem' occupied the minds and debates of the country's critics and intellectuals throughout the period. (Parallels with Russian or Italian social thought, at the time are not entirely mis-placed.) Interestingly, some conservative thinkers (Donoso Cortés) or reformist ones (Jaime Balmes) became quite influential abroad (Saavedra 1991: 33–76) but, on the whole, the country became again a backwater in the sciences and the humanities.

Intellectual modernization, however, finally materialized from at least one extraordinarily important focus of enlightenment and progress. That was the *Institución Libre de Enseñanza* created in Madrid in 1876 under the inspiration of a moral philosopher and educator, Fran-cisco Giner de los Ríos. Although other parts of Spain –notably Catalonia, with its capital city of Barcelona – had by then become thoroughly industrial, secular and progressive societies, the tensions between liberals and often anti-clerical professors and intellectuals and a repres-sively reactionary government came to a head in Madrid. Its policies forced the former to seek refuge in a private institution from which they attempted to carry out what they termed the 'moral and intellectual regeneration' of the country. Though the *Institución* was not the only cultural and scientific centre of modernization – positivism as a philosophy had already made many independent inroads in Spain – it certainly became the most influential one. Spanish sociology, at any rate, was born in it. And it was born as an essential element in the effort to modernize the country. Sociology and social science generally were seen by this movement as tools for the further secularization, democratization and prosperity of the country.

Early Spanish sociology fell under the double influence of positivism and organicism, the latter being a facet of the prevailing influence of the *Institución*'s philosophy, which combined an austere lay morality with an organic and well-ordered conception of the nation. The link between sociology and moral philosophy became firmly established in that tradition and lasted at least until the Civil War broke out in 1936. When sociology later recovered, in the 1960s, this tradition seemed to be lost, as Spain's social scientists became involved, almost *en masse,* in empirical social research.

Several members of the *Institución* introduced sociology into Hispanic culture, from the 1880s (González Serrano 2003; Giner 1963). Some of them also carried out notable empirical studies, from criminology to rural sociology. We shall mention here only three: Manuel Sales, Joaquín Costa and Adolfo Posada.

Manuel Sales y Ferré (1846–1910) was awarded the first chair in Sociology in Spain, at the University of Seville, in 1899. Among his several works, Sales published a massive four volume *Treatise of Sociology* which must be seen as one of the earliest efforts in the annals of European sociology to systematize and codify the sociological knowledge of the times (Núñez Encabo 1976). It is inspired by a judicious mixture of positivism and the moral reform ideals of the *Institución.* Joaquin Costa (1946–1911) on the other hand had a less discipline-oriented approach to social matters. Primarily interested as he was in the solution of 'social problems' and the reform of social conditions in Spain, his chief contribution was a now classical study of the relationship between the rural oligarchy and the political corruption of liberal democratic order (Tierno Galván 1961). Termed *Oligarquía y caciquismo como formas de gobierno* (*Oligarchy and political 'bossim' as government forms in Spain*) Costa's inquiry is much more than an extraordinary document of the age. While other social scientists elsewhere – from Thorstein Veblen in America to Werner Sombart in Germany – analysed the social structure and dynamics of modern capitalism, historically or otherwise, Costa turned his eye towards a stage in capitalist development where industrialism was weak and so were the entrepreneurial classes, the bourgeoisie and several key state institutions. While doing this, Costa also analysed forms of democratic rule and direct popular participation among the peasants in certain regions of the country. The importance for sociology of his work is thus double. On the one hand, he looked into a dimension of the relationship between politics and the economy which suffered much neglect by most of his contemporaries, understandably interested in a more mature and expansive capitalist development. On the other, Costa became a pioneer in what would become, much later, the fashionable sociological study of patterns of domination, political bosom and the corruption of liberal democracy which have been, and continue to be, widespread in several regions of the world.

Last, but not least, Joaquín Costa was the modern founder of one of the most outstanding currents in Spanish social science and theory: the study of agrarian society and the development of rural sociology. Its roots go back to the reformers and intellectuals of the Enlightenment period, some of whose studies were of the highest order.[2] Spanish rural sociology, following in the footsteps of this tradition and inspired by an 'agrarian reform' programme that was destined to become one of the substantial contributions to the field, as we shall see in due course.

For his part, Adolfo Posada (1860–1944) belonged to a later generation within the *Institución* tradition. A modern sociologist in every sense, Posada combined his socialist (and liberal) convictions with a truly cosmopolitan vision of the discipline (Laporta 1974). Freed from the predominance of any national sociological school, Posada surveyed European and American sociology with passionate detachment. He must be deemed one of the earliest sociologists to integrate contributions and schools – from Pareto's elite analysis to Marxism, from an interest in Durkhein which does not preclude a similar interest in the latter's adversary, Gabriel Tarde, to an admiring stance towards Herbert Spencer, Albion Small and Lester Ward. The last two were eminent American sociologists hardly known in Europe at the time.

He compounded all this with a keen interest in the centuries-old Spanish tradition of social reform proposals.[3] It would be wrong to dismiss Posada's work as a mere case of syncretism. Apart from his reformist interests (he wrote on feminism, democracy, education) Posada's sociology constitutes a pioneering and wholly conscious effort towards the elaboration of a cumulative social science, unequalled perhaps by anyone else anywhere at the time.

The tragic sense: modern Spanish social philosophy

Contemporary modern social theory in Spain cannot be understood without the contributions of a series of intellectuals and critics who produced their work beyond the confines of the then new social sciences, largely in response to what they saw as the dire situation of their country within the modernization process. Their reflections established for a long time the nature of the *problématique* to be confronted by both critics and ideologues, until an entirely new generation, partly as a reaction to their conceptions, turned towards an empirically oriented social science or, alternatively, to Marxist and radical interpretations.

The glaring shortcomings of Spanish modernization inspired a soul-searching philosophical movement in the country. The loss of the last imperial colonies in the Pacific and the Caribbean at the very end of the nineteenth-century intensified this preoccupation, and generated a stream of studies and reflections that would last for another century. Historians, essayists, and sociologists, joined in the debate at one time or another.[4]

Though the roots of this current can already be found in the Enlightenment period, its contemporary formulation found its first expression in Ángel Ganivet's 1897, *Ideárium español*.[5] Ganivet (1865–1898) analysed Spain's 'awkward' position within European civilization, and its duality – as it were – within it. Spain appears simultaneously as a historically crucial European society and yet seems to be somehow outside Europe in some essentially important respects, during long and significant periods. Ganivet also tried to explain Spanish exceptionalism and to find an answer as to why the country had taken so many 'wrong turnings' during its history. Being a major European country and yet marginal to the rest of Europe rested on peculiarities of character that lent its civilization and culture a certain tragic character. Ganivet's suicide in Finland at an early age, together with the serene and lucid tone of his writings gave a dramatic force to his conceptions and his unended quest about the frustrations of being Spanish.

His friend Miguel de Unamuno (1864–1937) accentuated the trends towards the interpretation of Spanish history and society in 'tragic' terms. An outstanding philosopher (and one of the pioneers of existentialism in Europe, after Kierkegaard) Unamuno chose to revel in contradictions and, as far as his social philosophy is concerned, to accept Spain's 'backwardness' and failure to integrate into a more rationalistic, scientific and positivist ways of thinking. This was, according to him, an expression of a certain moral superiority *vis à vis* the other varieties of Western European civilization. These had fallen prey to the vulgarities of the positivist and materialist conceptions of the age. His *Tragic Sense of Life* was often read abroad as the early existentialist essay that it certainly was, though, together with his other essays, it also meant something else to his fellow Spaniards. It entailed an austere and stoic acceptance of national failures and limitations, which were in turn the expression of other national virtues. However, neither Ganivet nor Unamuno revelled in backwardness. They rather thought of it as the byproduct of a culture oriented towards a set of very Western values which nevertheless neglected the more commercial, pragmatic and industrial spirit of capitalism.

If Unamuno managed to elicit a certain interest outside Spain, José Ortega y Gasset (1883–1955) was the first twentieth-century Spanish philosopher to attract a substantial philosophical attention abroad. Although his 'vitalistic rationalism' (or 'ratio-vitalism') found as much favour inside and outside the country as 'parallel' European intellectuals of not altogether different views, such as Bergson in France and Croce in Italy, his major influence was in the field of social philosophy. In this, the range of his work was considerable.

Ortega devoted a number of reflections and essays to Spain. From a *Theory of Andalusia* and *Invertebrate Spain* to *The Redemption of the Provinces* he explored the by then *loci classici* of an anguished intellectual establishment: the shortcomings of Iberian modernization, the paucity of secularization, and general backwardness were central to his preoccupations. In fact, Ortega's brilliant literary and essayistic approach to these problems was destined to be one of the causes that triggered the 'positivist' and 'empiricist' reaction against that sort of theorizing which became characteristic of many social scientists after his death.

From his *Dehumanization of Art* to his *Revolt of the Masses* (1929), Ortega published works on very diverse subjects. Read together, however, they amounted to a cogent critique of modernity, drawn up from the standpoint of a conservative, though clearly reformist and bourgois liberal thinker. His originality and forceful language captivated many minds and influenced sociological thought in more ways than one. (The once extremely popular 'mass society' conception of modernity owes him an inmense debt, not least for having coined the expression 'mass man' and having theorized his rise and alleged predominance in advanced societies. Interestingly, a number of radical sociologists in the C. W. Mills and the Frankfurt School traditions reformulated Ortega's theories about mass society to make them fit their own conceptions) (Giner 1976). Paradoxically for a thinker whose influence became felt in sociological thought, Ortega, in his last book *El hombre y la gente (Man and People)* took his distances from what he saw as the pernicious positivism of most sociology (in the Durkhemian tradition, essentially) in order to favour a more reflexive and philosophical approach to the analysis of social life. However, his most interesting observations – though often quite irritating to many of his more 'realistically' inclined readers – are probably those he devoted to his own country. Yet, both his immensely influential best seller *The Revolt of the Masses* and his other 'social' essays, written in the cosmopolitan vein, remain what must be deemed the internationally best-known Spanish contribution to social theory in the twentieth-century.

A significant philosophical work in social theory is also to be found in José Ferrater Mora (1912–1991) whose efforts to bridge the gap between the Anglo-Saxon analytical tradition and continental philosophy deserve more than the scant attention that his extraordinarily erudite work has received outside Spain. Ferrater's *Man at the Crossroads* (first Spanish edition, 1952) represents his chief contribution to the abundant 'crisis of our time' literature. Its originality lies in Ferrater's systematic comparison of the crisis and transformation of classical culture and thought during the Hellenistic period with that of advanced modernity. In both periods, syncretism, relativism and the multiplication of schools, together with an encyclopaedic and apparently cumulative culture, thrived and produced a number of parallel philosophies and conceptions of life and the world. His reflections on Spain (and Europe) were also abundant. One of them, written from exile in 1944, *The Elementary Forms of Catalan Life*[6] was a welcome and refreshing interpretation of his own native Catalonia which shed a different light on the more dramatic interpretation of 'eternal Spain' presented by other thinkers (Ferrater 1972). His writings on Spanish life, while never avoiding the issue of the troubled course of its recent history, produced a more level-headed vision than that of the by then established 'tragic view': a more serene vision which the prolonged existence of the Franco dictatorship would not allow to come easily to the fore.[7]

The exile of sociology

The proclamation of the Republic in 1931 coincided with a remarkable recovery of Spanish culture and science, including the social sciences. The first generation of sociologists following that of its founders and early pioneers came to maturity at the time. As sociologists tended to be democrats and republicans, however, the outcome of the Civil War, in 1939, meant exile for them. In contrast with Italy and Germany, in Spain fascism was not voted in: it conquered power only after a murderous and very prolonged armed conflict against the legitimate government. The resulting regime (about whose nature a rich sociological literature and research would eventually develop) was a military, right-wing dictatorship, supported by the Catholic Church and the Fascist movement.

Spain's loss was other countries' gain. Leaving aside the flight of eminent historians, scientists, humanists and intellectuals to other countries, several outstanding sociologists took refuge overseas. José Medina Echavarría (b. 1903) settled in Mexico, where he soon published *Sociología: teoría y técnica* (1941) a very competent introduction to the discipline destined to exercise much influence throughout Latin America. He also produced the first complete translation of Max Weber's *Economy and Society* in any language, during the 1940s. Also in Mexico settled Constancio Bernaldo de Quirós (1873–1959) who belongs to the already mentioned rural sociology tradition, to which we shall have to come back later.

For his part, Francisco Ayala (b. 1906) an outstanding novelist and essayist, and an assistant to Adolfo Posada, went to Argentina, and later to Puerto Rico and several American universities. In 1947 he published his *Tratado de Sociología* where he dealt with the main issues of the discipline from a fundamentally theoretical standpoint, skilfully combining a history of ideas approach with a systematic and conceptual one (Ayala 1958). Besides this very substantial treatise, Ayala produced influential theoretical essays on cultural sociology and the sociology of intellectuals (Ayala 1944, 1958). At a later stage, he abandoned the discipline to return to his more literary endeavours but the high quality of his sociological phase set considerable standards to sociological theorizing in the Hispanic world.

Few established sociological practitioners managed to remain in the country, while a first new generation of social scientists felt the need to study and settle abroad. (Some of the latter could be considered exiles also, in one way or another, sometimes because they had no real possiblities of finding work or expressing their views freely as sociologists; at other times because the dearth of intellectual life in their own country increased the lure of going abroad in order to study and, eventually, even to settle there more or less temporarily.) Amongst those who stayed Enrique Gómez Arboleya stands out, without any doubt the father of post-Civil War sociology in Spain.

Arboleya (1910–1959) came from the philosophy of law field and soon acquired an uncommon mastery of cultural history. A late disciple of the by now banned *Institución*,[8] he cautiously bridged the gap between the Republican period and the dictatorship. Teaching first in Granada and later from the newly established chair in sociology at Madrid University, he first entered the field from a history of ideas approach, with his *Historia del pensamiento y de la estructura social*, published in 1958 of which he only completed the first volume (Arboleya, 1957, 1958, 1962) This masterful treatise combines cultural history with the history of ideas, both looked at sociologically. It opened a line of enquiry later only followed by a handful of Spanish sociologists (Iglesias 1988). Just before his untimely death, Arboleya abruptly turned to empirical sociology and pioneered rigorous research in a functionalist and positivist vein. A significant number of contemporary Spanish sociologists claim him as their teacher.[9]

At the height of Arboleya's teaching and of his almost single-handed efforts at the reconstruction of sociology within Spain, a number of students managed to go abroad and study sociology at diverse European and American Universities, where several of them obtained their doctorates. Their later work was destined to influence Spanish sociology, social thought and public discourse from the early 1960s on, lending it a particularly cosmopolitan flavour which, paradoxically, can be said to be much more pronounced than that prevailing in several other European societies, probably for the very reason that training had taken place abroad. The temporary, though often very prolonged, diaspora[10] of Spanish sociologists can also be considered – without unduly stretching the imagination – as a second wave of exile. In some senses and in several personal cases that new exile was as dramatic as that of directly ensuing from the civil war. In others, of course, it took a much milder form. Many of the authors we shall now encounter belong to this diaspora.

Not a few of these sociologists remained abroad, but many began to return from about 1959, and filled the new chairs at several Universities and, soon, at the new Faculty of Political Science and Sociology at Madrid. (other Faculties, at Barcelona and Granada, were opened later.) In the following sections no attention will be lent to these and other academic developments in order to concentrate exclusively on some schools of thought and theoretical contributions.[11] We shall single out four relatively distinct approaches in which sociological thought in Spain has expressed itself quite forcefully, and made substantial contributions to the discipline, over recent decades. We could name them, quite loosely, under the convenient labels of 'functionalism–empiricism', 'Marxism', 'rural sociology' and 'political sociology'.

Empiricism and functionalism

In the late 1950s and early 1960s, the need for academic respectability, combined with the relatively strict surveillance of the right-wing dictatorship upon the universities, made the functionalist approach quite acceptable as the most viable sociological theory in Spain. Functionalism (writ large) went hand in hand with a sudden surge of interest in sociological studies, of a strictly empirical kind, in which social surveys and fairly uncensored opinion polls predominated. As a result, and against all predictions, Spain, though still very far from being an open society (political parties and free trade unions were strictly forbidden) soon acquired, from the early 1960s, a considerable stock of data (and expertise) about its social conditions. Surveys also included people's opinions and attitudes on a wide range of subjects. The setting up of an official Institute of Public Opinion in 1963, intended as a tool for gauging people's attitudes and possible responses to government policies – later transformed into the *Centro de Investigaciones Sociológicas*, or CIS – was one crucial event.[12] A number of other institutions – Catholic foundations, private economic and social research units – soon proliferated, and were more or less tolerated by the dictatorship. This is not the place to analyse their development, but their very visible presence formed a crucial background to the development of theory. Essentially, research institutes and the considerable flow of 'objective' surveys and studies that soon filled the public market place substantially changed the intellectual atmosphere of the country, as well as the economic and political discourse, with a new sort of 'realism' which blatantly contrasted with the regime's ideology and increasingly outdated rhetoric.[13]

The reception of 'functionalism', often identified by some of its critics with 'American style sociology', did not, on the whole, produce much original theory in Spain.[14] It was mostly derivative. However, the period of its apparent hegemony saw the expansion of sociology in the Universities, the development and subsequent multiplication of social research agencies, and the aforementioned development of social surveys and 'positivistic analysis' of what was then routinely termed 'social reality'. This was an oblique reference to the clearly biased 'unreal' or 'official version' of Spanish life, economy, culture and social and economic conditions. Many of these empirical surveys were rigorous and sophisticated, thus putting at our disposal a considerable mass of reliable data about Spanish society, under political conditions that were in principle hostile to then called 'positivistic' approach. (This flow of information has kept steadily growing to this day, stored at the just-mentioned CIS and later also at the *Instituto de Estudios Sociales Avanzados*, in Cordoba.) These developments must be recalled for the simple reason that it was against their background, as well as a reaction to the 'official' blessing 'functionalism' received, that much recent contemporary Spanish social theory must be explained.

Marxism and 'critical' sociology

'Francoism' lasted from 1939 till 1975. The effective and substantial support – *de facto,* but also *de jure* – it increasingly received from the Western democracies stimulated the development of Marxism among the disappointed intelligentsia of Spain, whose members had expected greater support and solidarity from their counterparts abroad. Generational changes, intense economic growth and prosperity in the absence of democracy, the rise of a new, more free-market economy, and the parallel collapse of fascist-style protectionism and autarky within the regime itself also played a role in the growth of a Spanish version of what has been termed 'Western Marxism'.[15]

Spanish Marxism soon became more a state of mind than a case of rigorous scholarship or a true philosophy. It was never confined to sociology. On the contrary, the apparent success of institutionalized sociology in Spain – which many plainly saw as a shameless form of 'collaborationism' with the regime[16] – prompted some Marxist intellectuals to castigate sociology as a 'bourgeois science' echoing the mood of the official Soviet slogan at the time. However, as time wore on, and more and more sociologists were attracted by Marxism, the possibility of a Marxist sociology took root and the earlier general hostility against the discipline considerably weakened. The Marxist approach to social matters kept steadily growing to the point that, by the mid-1960s, it practically became predominant within the ranks of the (always clandestine or illegal) opposition to the dictatorship. Despite this new, officially unacknowledged pre-eminence, the results of the research and theoretical work produced at the time only seldom reached the quality of their Marxist counterparts in other Western countries, with some outstanding exceptions in fields such as class conflict analysis and urban social movements.[17]

From a wider democratic and, unavoidably at the period, left-wing standpoint the results were more interesting. A *marxistisant* critique developed, often among critics of society lacking straightforward sociological credentials who nevertheless produced poignant analyses of Spain's social structure.[18] Their work was often widely read and in some ways eclipsed that of the 'functionalists' and more conventional sociologists. On the other hand, a vigorous critical analysis developed – often in exiled or foreign publications such as the Parisian *Cuadernos de Ruedo Ibérico* – which could be easily labelled, following the fashionable vocabulary of the times, as an expression of 'critical sociology' but which often analysed the situation from a non-Marxist standpoint, though certainly always from a 'conflict sociology' perspective.[19]

As in other countries, in the end, Marxism, instead of disappearing altogether, found some sort of continuation in the guise of 'analytical Marxism'. This perspective was to find considerable favour with a number of authors in the 1990s and first years of the twenty-first century. They attempted to establish a link between a radical view of society or social criticism – as inherited from Marxism – with the new interest towards rational choice theory and other forms of analysis, including methodological individualism (the latter approach had a scarce tradition in Spanish sociology, though certainly not in philosophy, as the work of both Unamuno and Ortega clearly show). However, the full story of the rise and fall of the once nearly all-pervading Marxism in Spain still remains to be written.[20]

Rural sociology

As already suggested the 'agrarian question' soon became one of the chief problems in the history of modern Spain and, consequently, a crucial theme for its thinkers and critics. Its centrality in public discourse and social theory have been felt until quite recently. Only the prosperity of the economy, after 1959, and the modernization of the methods of cultivation, together with a massive rural exodus to the cities and emigration abroad – from the 1950s till the 1970s – pushed it into the background. It left behind, however, a substantial tradition of scholarship, research and theory. For a very long time, the 'agrarian question' had stimulated a constant and original debate among the often called *agrarista* intellectuals. (Authors, in fact, including economists, sociologists, literary critics, philosophers, rural sociologists and, of course, agronomists.) It was thus that a genuine body of 'agrarian social thought' took shape in Spain.

Several of its outstanding contributions have been in the study of the agricultural factor in economic development, on rural social structures, social conflict as a result of land tenure and property inequalities, and the role of small owners or landless peasants in the social evolution or the politics of the nation.

Costa was, as we said, the fountainhead of this tradition. The *Institute for Social Reforms*[21] had inspired empirical research especially in the rural areas of the South at the turn of the century. Bernaldo de Quirós's work on peasant conflict in Andalusia stands out and must be considered a precedent of the qualitative research later carried out in Andalusia, during the 1970s. A key contribution within this tradition was that of Juan Díaz del Moral, who knew the social conditions and structure of the *latifundio* society better than anyone till then, and persuasively explained millenarist peasant movements in the Guadalquivir valley of Andalusia, linked to a mythical belief in the power of a 'general strike' in his 1929 *History of Andalusian Peasant Revolts*.[22] He put forward a hypothesis much later used by Eric Hobsbawm's justly famous *Primitive Rebels*. Díaz del Moral emphasized population dispersion, isolation and a landless peasantry of seasonal workers in order to explain the naïve belief that revolt would force the authorities to implement radical rural reform. The Spanish Republican government (1931–1939) was influenced by his work and started serious moves towards reform, along lines similar to certain reforms which were also taking place in Central Europe. These however were violently interrupted by the Civil War and its outcome. The American scholar Edward Malefakis' thesis about the agrarian revolution as an alternative to agrarian reform, leading to that tragic confrontation, remains a *locus classicus* of the sociological and historical literature on the subject.[23]

During the 1960s and 1970s academic interest once more turned towards these issues, when rural population had seriously begun to decline. This led to important work on the social disorganization generated by migration in the cities of destination but also to studies about rural adaptation to the new circumstances. Spanish sociology then took on board the discourse and analysis about the 'crisis of community' which concerned much Western sociology at the time, and in Spain were combined with an abiding interest in class domination patterns.[24] On the other hand the *latifundio* question, that so much interested Spanish and Italian sociologists studying their respective Souths – Andalusia, Sicily – had to be reconsidered. Juan Martínez Alier's work on the unexpected and newly acquired stability of *latifundio* society under conditions of modernity (extensive, but industrially managed land, needing much smaller workforce, with fewer landless peasants) came to fill a gap in the literature.

Much anthropological work developed in parallel to the more sociological study of Spanish rural society. Anthropology in Spain was lucky to produce a researcher of Julio Caro Baroja's stature whose work on the lore and myths of the peasantry, witchcraft, the magic mentality in the sixteenth- and seventeenth-centuries, the traditional tensions between urban and country life in Mediterranean societies, North African society, and several other topics influenced much Spanish ethnography as well as a number of foreign anthropologists (especially British) studying Southern Europe (Caro Baroja 1966, 1974).

Interest of Spanish social scientists for the 'rural dimension' has not decayed. From the 1970s on, however, it has shifted its attention towards new problems, such as agricultural modernization, rural development, agrarian neocorporatism, and the loss of influence of landowners and peasants as political actors.[25]

Political sociologies

Three crucial events have spurred Spanish political scientists and sociologists to develop what amounts to be a very original contribution to contemporary social analysis: the downfall of the Republic and the Civil War, the 'atypical' semi-fascist dictatorship under General Franco, and the country's remarkably skilful and peaceful transition to democracy around 1975.

The Civil War in Spain elicited a massive amount of historical, political and journalistic literature throughout the world. It still continues to attract attention. The Spanish historiographical contribution has been considerable. On the whole, however, it took slightly longer to develop, given the initial difficulties for free access to the archives and documents about the conflagration. Yet, the fall of the Republic and the civil war soon inspired important debates among exiled historians – notoriously the exchange between Claudio Sánchez Albornoz in Buenos Aires and Américo Castro in Houston – about the nature of Spanish history and its possible 'exceptionalism' within Western patterns of development. In more senses than one, the 'essentialist' debate inherited the classical preoccupations described at the beginning of this chapter, though the discussion and diverse interpretations were now enriched by further data and scholarship. Unfortunately, the new disputes did not go beyond what had by then become classical obsessions. An important exception to this trend was the work of Jaume Vicens Vives (1910–1960) an economic historian, who looked at Spanish history from the point of view of Catalonia and introduced a more sober interpretation and a far less 'Castilian oriented' perspective into the usual key themes about the relative lack of an industrial bourgeoisie, Spanish 'backwardness' and such like.[26] Other contemporary historians of his generation have revolutionized historiography and made a serious contribution to a much less speculative and 'existentialist' view of past and present in Spain.[27]

While historians grappled with a new, more realistic vision of their country's history, political sociologists began to concentrate their attention upon the causes and, especially, the 'odd' nature of the Franco regime itself. Juan Linz's efforts to find an explanation and a theoretical framework for it are well-known in the annals of contemporary social science. His notion of the 'authoritarian regime' came to the rescue of those analysts who were unders-tandably reluctant to subsume the Spanish variety of modern dictatorship under a straight-forward ideal type called 'fascism'. The fact that Linz's model of 'authoritarian regime' could be easily extended to other regimes (especially in Latin America) lent it much credibility and usefulness.[28] Quite a few political scientists in several countries found it convincing. Until then most attention had gone in the direction of either democracy or totalitarianism (fascism and communism) and too little to dictatorships such as Spain's. Linz drew attention to regimes under which great part of mankind lived, and yet were often neglected by political science.

Linz' interpretation was soon found to be excessively benign by some of his fellow Spa-niards, who produced an alternative and 'tougher' view of the regime's nature[29] without, however, entirely rejecting all of his contribution. (For instance, some of them retained Linz' notion of 'restricted pluralism' in order to explain the varieties of factions at the dictatorship's top). They described Francoism as an expression of 'modern despotism' – by using Mon-tesquieu's notions about despotic rule – and linked it to the idea of 'modernization from above' and class domination patterns. While Marxist and *marxistisant* interpretations, and in at least one case, libertarian views, also vied for attention, much interest was elicited by these contrasting views.

Most sociologists of Francoism naturally paid attention to the role of 'fascist' corporatist structures in the regime and later to the rise of 'neocorporatism' during the transition to democracy and its role in making it possible. The international 'neocorporatist' literature which became quite ubiquitous in the 1970s not only found a strong echo in Spain, but also had a true Spanish component, as its representatives had also their voice heard in the general debate.[30] Perhaps the prevailing view among Spanish writers on corporatism was that of 'societal' corporatism, in contrast with those who elsewhere restricted their analysis to the study of 'social pacts' and agreements between governments, trade unions and employers' associations. Without rejecting the former view, some social scientists today continue the study of neocorporatist relationships in the traditional way, i.e. as the processes produced by the interaction between pressure groups, professional associations, employers, government and trade unions within the 'societal' perspective.[31]

After the rise of the first 'corporatist' literature, much attention was turned to the texture of civil society itself in Spain, to its alleged weaknesses and its role as part of the democratic process as well as in its role in final modernization of the country. Víctor Pérez Díaz, among others, put these issues within the wider perspective of contemporary theory.[32] Still others, such as José Maria Maravall continued interest in the investigation of regime transitions to democracy, but expanded it to a comparison between Southern and Eastern Europe, with their very different backgrounds, capitalist or communist (Maravall 1995).

The latest and quite strong trend in the field of political sociology in Spain has been linked to rational choice theory and methodological individualism. Josep Maria Colomer's analysis of the political transition to democracy from a game theory perspective can be said to have opened the trend[33] and to have in some ways renewed the more 'classical' approach pre-dominating in transition studies. Colomer has extended his interests to the 'art of political manipulation' in general and then on to electoral system choices in several countries.[34] Rational choice theory has been extremely successful. After some pioneering work,[35] a small but very active group of rational choice scholars has made its presence strongly felt.[36] To a certain extent the rise of this new generation of political sociologists has announced the end of the social theory predominant during the first two decades after the advent of democracy in 1975, and the beginning of a new period in Spanish social science.

Some concluding remarks

Only a few aspects of the Spanish contribution to contemporary social analysis and theory could be chosen – rural sociology, corporatist and civil society interpretations, political sociology – in order to illustrate a much wider and complex field, which cannot be covered within the bounds of this essay.[37]

Over the last three decades Spanish social theory, and very particularly sociology, have shifted from a set of very specifically Iberian preoccupations to a much more cosmopolitan and general interpretations of social reality. Although Spaniards in the 1960s and 1970s often used 'international' perspectives – functionalism, Marxism – they understandably tended to be bound in their interests by the pressing and sometimes very serious problems of their own society. A few, however, took a more 'cosmopolitan' or world view of the contemporary world at an early stage (Giner 1976). Later, attention was turned, as in other countries, and very much in the same vein, to the so-called crisis of modernity (Rodríguez Ibáñez 1978). It was in this direction that the internationally well-know work of Manuel Castells, which had begun in the field of urban sociology, developed. His *Information Age*, in several volumes, which attempted to chart and diagnose the state of the world in the age of globalization, received much attention.[38]

Works such as Castells' clearly epitomize the passage of Spanish social theory from its classical preoccupation with the peculiar (and tragic) conditions of the country in its struggle for modernity (and 'against' modernity!) and the full entry of the Spanish social science community into the international community. Spanish social theory today is, if anything, open, cosmopolitan, competent and, if we are allowed to state so, often vigorously original as well. Some of the *genius loci* is still felt in its texture, of course. At least in one field of social theory – the widespread interest for moral philosophy and ethics in general – the weight of history is still felt.

Although Spanish moral philosophers have long embraced contemporary international trends, the considerable flourishing of the philosophy of law and democratic philosophy (led by Elías Díaz) and ethics (led by Javier Muguerza) is still linked it seems to us, to the age-old Spanish tradition of combining social theory with moral concerns.[39] In a way, the recent upsurge of works on republicanism in political theory in Spain and that of civic studies, participatory democracy, and social policy is also clearly linked to contemporary moral philosophy, and through it, to the classical Iberian tradition. It is seldom that the selfsame authors work simultaneously in all these fields.[40]

By and large, Spanish social theory today shares with that produced in other countries a clear trend towards 'denationalization' and cosmopolitanism. Its problems, answers and solutions to today's problems are not always particularly Spanish. They are preoccupations shared by many others, anywhere. A better knowledge abroad, however, of what the Spanish intellectual community has to say about those issues, given the frequent rigour and originality of its contribution to contemporary social science and theory, would benefit all.

Notes

1 However, see J. Linz (1972), for a nuanced sociological assessment about this crucial episode in Spanish cultural history.
2 The works of Gaspar Melchor de Jovellanos and Pablo de Olavide, both ministers in the *ancien régime* stand out.
3 Cf. A. Posada (1990), 1st edn. 1899.

4 This intellectual current can be said to start with Mariano José de Larra (1809–1837) and finish with Pedro Laín Entralgo (1908–2001). An important episode within it, which we unfortunately must ignore, was the debate among prominent historians exiled after the Civil War, essentially Claudio Sénchez Albornoz (from Buenos Aires) and Américo Castro (from the USA).

5 No precise English translation of this title seems possible, that of '*The Spanish Ideology*' being unacceptable.

6 In the original *Les formes de la vida catalana*.

7 A significant number of works appeared both within and outside Spain about the suppoosedly tragic nature of the country and its history. Cf. the crucial debate between exiled historians Claudio Sánchez Albornoz (Argentina) and Américo Castro (USA, whose work was used by Talcott Parsons in his historial considerations on social change); or essays such as Lain Entralgo's.

8 He was a student of Fernado de los Ríos. He was also the secretary of Manuel de Falla, the composer had himself to flee the country.

9 Among them Francisco Murillo, Salvador Giner, Luis González Seara, Salustiano del Campo and José Castillo.

10 A list by no means complete of those who for one reason or another left at an early stage would include: Juan Linz (PhD, Columbia) (later professor at Yale); Francisco Marsal (Princeton, PhD, taught University Buenos Aires); Salustiano del Campo (studied at Chicago, worked at the UN, won chair at Barcelona, 1962); José Jiménez Blanco (Michigan); Salvador Giner (MA, PhD, Chicago); Esteban Pinilla de las Heras (Paris), Manuel Castells (Doctorate, University of Paris, later taught in California), Ignacio Sotelo (Berlin). A second and later 'wave' included: Emilio Lamo de Espinosa (Berkeley); José Maria Maravall (PhD, Oxford); Manuel Pérez Yruela (Lancaster); Gregorio Rodríguez Cabrero (Lancaster).

11 There are quite a few sources that describe and analyse the growth of the profession, its academic avatars, and the political and cultural conditions of the sociological community in Spain. Cf. S. Giner and L. Moreno, Eds. (1990); S. del Campo, (ed.) (2001); A. de Miguel (1972, 1973).

12 C. Torres, (ed.) (2003).

13 The general survey *Informe sociológico sobre la situación social en España* (1966), published under the auspices of the FOESSA Foundation was a crucial landmark in the new stream of sociological surveys. The *Informe* (despite the elimination of a whole chapter by the censorship) was periodically followed by several others with the same title.

14 See, however, J. Zarco (2001).

15 Cf. For instance E. Lamo de Espinosa (1981).

16 Giner, S (1965)

17 Cf. Alfonso Ortí (1992, 2002), Manuel Castells (1974, 1975).

18 Comín, A.C. (1965).

19 Cf. Giner (1972), Preston (1976).

20 Cf. however, J. R. Capella (2005) for an account of the influential philosophical Marxist school founded by Manuel Sacristén in Barcelona.

21 Created at the turn of the century, as a development of the nineteenth century Commission for Social Reforms (cf. *Información oral y escrita practidada en virtud de la Real Orden de 5 de Diciembre de 1893*, 5 vols. Ministry of Labour, facsimie re-edition, 1983.

22 Díaz del Moral 1987 [1929].

23 Malefakis, E (1970).

24 Pérez Díaz, V (1966), Pérez Yruela (1979), Sevilla, E (1978).

25 From 1975 to 1997 the journal *Agricultura y Sociedad*, edited by the Ministry of Agriculture (and unfortunately discontinued) published many articles devoted to the analysis of social and economic changes in Spanish rural society. See also García Sanz, B (1999), Gómez Benito, C. and González Rodríguez, J.J. (1997) and Moyano Estrada (1984).

26 J. Vicens Vives (1984).

27 Dominguez Ortiz for Andalusia and the seventeenth-century, Ramón Carande for Charles the V and the Empire's bankers, deserve to be mentioned along Vicens Vives in this context. The following generation includes economic historian Jordi Nadal, and contemporary historians such as Juan Pablo Fusi and Javier Tusell. Important foreign influences – Braudel and the Annales school, John Elliott, Raymond Carr and Angus Mackay have helped shape Spanish historiography, though it is fair to say that a two-way relationship has become firmly established.

28 Linz, J. (1976).

29 Giner, S., Pérez Yruela, M., and Sevilla, E. (1978).
30 Pérez Yruela, M. and Giner, S. (eds) (1988); for a critical and very well-balanced overview of the 'neocorporatism' debate in Spain see Rodríguez, Ibáñez, J. E. (1999).
31 Cf, for example, Moyano, E. (1993)
32 Pérez Díaz, V (1987).
33 Colomer, J. M. (1990).
34 Colomer, J. M. (2004).
35 Giner, S. (1978) based on a earlier publication of 1977.
36 Cf. Aguiar, F. and Francisco A. de (2002).
37 For a much more complete coverage of the Spanish contribution to social theory cf. V. Camps (ed.) (2000) and S. Giner (2003); also S. Giner and L. Moreno (eds) (1990).
38 Castells, M. (1998).
39 Díaz, E. (1984) and (1998), Camps, V. (ed.) (2000).
40 Cf. Giner, S. and Sarasa, S. (eds) (1997) *Buen gobierno y política social* Barcelona: Ariel, and S. Giner (2003).

References

Aguiar, F. and Francisco, A. de (2002) 'Rationality and Identity' *European Journal of Sociology*, 41, 119–131.
Anon. (1971) *Sociología española de los años 70* Madrid: Fondo para la Investigación Económica y Social.
Arboleya, E. Gómez (1957) *Hisotria del pensamiento y de la estructura social*, Madrid: Instituto de Estudios Políticos.
Arboleya, E. Gómez (1958) *Sociología en España*, Madrid: Instituto de Estudios Políticos.
Arboleya, E. Gómez (1962) *Estudios de teoría de la sociedad y del estado*, Madrid: Instituto de Estudios Políticos.
Ayala, F. (1944) *Razón del mundo: un examen de conciencia intelectual*, Buenos Aires: Losada.
Ayala, F. (1958) *El escritor en la socidad de masas*, Buenos Aires: Sur.
Ayala, F. (1984) *Tratado de sociología*, Madrid: Espasa Calpe (1st. Edn. 1947).
Bonal, R. (1995) 'La sociologia de Catalunya: aproximació a una història', *Revista Catalana de Sociologia*, 1(Nov.), 11–34.
Campo, Salustiano del (ed.) (2001) *Historia de la sociología española*, Barcelona: Ariel.
Campo, S. del (2001) *Historia de la sociología en España*, Barcelona: Ariel.
Camps, V., (ed.) (2000) *Historia de la Etica*, Barcelona: Crítica, 3 vols.
Caro Baroja, J. (1966) *La ciudad y el campo*, Madrid: Alfaguara.
Caro Baroja, J. (1974) *De la supersticiónh al ateismo*, Madrid: Taurus.
Capella, J. R. (2005) *La práctica de Manuel Sacristán*, Madrid: Trotta.
Castells, M. (1975) *La teoría de las crisis económicas*, Madrid: Siglo XXI.
Castells, M. (1974) *La cuestión urbana*, Madrid: Siglo XXI (1st French edn., 1972).
Castells, M. (1998) *The Information Age: Economy, Society and Culture*, Oxford: Blackwell, 3 vols.
Colomer, J. M. (1990) *El arte de la manipulación política*, Madrid: Anagrama.
Colomer, J. M. (2004) *Handbook of Electoral System Choice*, London: Palgrave Macmillan.
Comin, A. (1965) *España del Sur: aspectos económicos y sociales del desarrollo industrial de Andalucía*, Madrid: Tecnos.
Díaz del Moral, Juan (1987 [1929]) *Historia de las agitaciones campesinas andaluzas,* Madrid: Cinco Dias.
Díaz, E. (1984) *De la maldad estatal y la soberanía popular*, Madrid: Debate.
Díaz, E. (1998) *Estado de derecho y sociadad democrática*, Madrid: Taurus.
Ferrater Mora, F. (1952) *El hombre en la encrucijada*, Buenos Aires: Sudamericana (2nd edn, 1965).
Ferrater Mora, J. (1972) *Les formes de la vida catalana*, Barcelona: Selecta.
García Sanz, B. (1999) *La sociedad rural ante el siglo XXL*, Madrid: MAPA.
Giner, S. (1963) 'El pensamiento sociológico de Eugenio María de Hostos', *Revista de Ciencias Sociales*, Puerto Rico., VII(3), September, 215–230.
Giner, S. (1965) 'Sociologia dirigida', *Promos*, 33, January, 18-20. (Text partly censored.)
Giner, S. (1972) 'La estructura social de España' *Horizonte Español*, Paris: Cuadernos de Ruedo Ibérico, pp.1–44.
Giner, S. (1976) *Mass Society*, London: Martin Robertson; New York: Academic Press.

Giner, S. (1978) 'Intenciones humanas y estructuras sociales: aproximación crítica a la lógica situacional', in J. Jiménez Blanco and C. Moya Valgañón (eds) *Teoría sociológica contemporánea*, Madrid: Tecnos, pp. 465–500.

Giner, S. (2003) *Carisma y Razón,* Madrid: Alianza

Giner, S., Pérez Yruela, M. and Sevilla, E. (1978) 'Despotismo moderno y dominación de clase', *Papers Revista de Sociología*, no. 8, pp. 103–141.

Giner, S. and Moreno, L. (eds) (1990) *Sociology in Spain* Madrid: CSIC.

Gómez Benito, C. and González Rodríguez, J. J. (eds) (1977) *Agricultura y sociedad en la España contemporánea*, Madrid: CIS.

González Serrano, Urbano (2003) *La sociología científica* Madrid: CIS (1st edn, 1884).

Herr, R. (1958) *The Eighteenth Century Revolution in Spain*, Princeton: Princeton University Press.

Iglesias, J. (1988) *Homenaje a Enrique Gómez Arboleya*, Ayuntamiento de Granada and University of Granada.

Lamo de Espinosa (1981) *Teoría de la reificación: de Marx a la Escuela de Francfort*, Madrid: Alianza.

Lamo de Espinosa, E. (1990) *La sociedad reflexiva*, Madrid: CIS.

Laporta, Francisco (1974) *Política y sociología en la crisis del liberalismo español*, Madrid: Edicusa.

Linz, J. (1972) 'Intellectual Roles in Sixteenth- and Seventeenth-Century Spain', *Daedalus,* Summer, 59–108.

Linz, J. (1976) 'An Authoritarian Regime: Spain' in S. Payne (ed.) *Politics and Society in Twentieth Century Spain*, New York: Frank Watts, pp. 160–207.

Malefakis, E. (1970) *Reforma agraria y revolución campesina en la España del siglo XX*, Bardcelona: Ariel.

Maravall, J. M. (1995) *Los resultados de la democracia: Un estudio del sur y este de Europa*, Madrid: Alianza.

Medina Echavarría, J. (1941) *Sociologíca: teoría y técnica*, Mexico: Fondo de Cultura Económica

Miguel, A. de (1972) *Sociología o subversión*, Barcelona: Plaza & Janés.

Miguel, A. de (1973) *Homo sociologicus hispanicus*, Barcelona: Barral Editores.

Moyano, E. (1993) *Las organizaciones profesionales agrarias en la Communidad Europea*, Madris: MAPA.

Moyano, E. and Pérez Yruela, M. (eds) (1999) *Informe social de Andalucía 1978–1998*, Córdoba: IESA.

Moyano Estrada, E. (1984) *Corporativismo y agricultura: Asociaciones professionales y articulación de intereses en la agricultura española*, Madrid: Instituto de Estudios Agrarios Pasqueros y Alimentarios.

Núñez Encabo, M. (1976) *Manuel Sales y Ferré y los orígenes de la sociología en España*, Madrid: Edicusa.

Ortí, A. (1992) 'De la guerra civil a la transición democrática' in J. Ibáñez (ed.) *Sociología*, Madrid: Universidad Complutense.

Ortí, A. (2002) 'Fundación, límites de clase y crisis de hegemonía', in various authors *Centenario de la Información del Ateneo de Madrid*, Madrid: Ateneo and Editorial Fundamentos.

Pérez Díaz, V. (1966) *Estructura social del campo y éxodo rural*, Madrid: Tecnos.

Pérez Díaz, V. (1987) *El Retorno de la Sociedad Civil*, Madrid: Instituto de Estudios Económicos.

Pérez Yruela, M. (1979) *La conflictividad campesina en la provincia de Córdoba, 1931–1936*, Madrid: Ministerio de Agricultura.

Pérez Yruela, M. and Giner, S. (1988) *El Corporatismo en España*, Barcelona: Ariel.

Posada, A. (1990) 'La sociología en España', (first published, 1899) *REIS*, 52 (Oct–Dec.), 162–192 (introduced by R, Gutiérrez).

Preston, P. (ed.) (1976) *Spain in Crisis*, London: Harvester.

Rodríguez Ibáñez, J. E. (1978) *Teoría crítica y sociología*, Madrid: Siglo XXI.

Rodríguez Ibáñez, J. E. (1999) *Un nuevo malestar en la cultura?*, Madrid: CIS (pp. 49–75 contain his discussion of the debate, published earlier in the journal *REIS*. On 'Posfranquismo y corporatismo').

Rodríguez Zúñiga, L. and Salcedo, J. (1991) 'Veinte años de sociología', *Sistema*, 100, 103–108.

Saavedra, L. (1991) *El pensamiento sociológico español*, Madrid: Taurus, 1991.

Sevilla, E. (1978) *La evolución del campesinado en España*, Barcelona: Península.

Tierno Galván, E. (1961) *Costa y el regeneracionismo*, Barcelona: Barna.

Torres Albero, C. (2003) *IOP/CIS, 1963–2003*, Madrid: CISç.

Vicens Vives, J. (1984) *Notícia de Catalunya*, Barcelona: Destino (1st Edn, 1956).

Zarco, J (2001) 'El funcionalismo y la "sociología empírica"' in S. del Campo (ed.) *La sociología en España*, pp. 161–203.

10

Nordic social theory

Between social philosophy and grounded theory

Lars Mjøset

Let us understand social theory as a notion of theory which spreads among social scientists under growing influence from the humanities.[1] We find such a pattern of influence in Nordic social science in the 1980s and 1990s. We distinguish this period from two earlier ones. Through the postwar period before the 1960s, the term 'social theory' was not used at all. Theory was linked to disciplines and mainly legitimated with reference to an ideal derived from the natural sciences. In the next period – roughly from the early 1960s to the late 1970s – Nordic words for the German term 'Theorie der Gesellschaft' were now and then employed. But only very recently, a direct translation of 'social theory' into the Nordic languages has occasionally been used, as an emulation of an increasingly popular Anglo-American terminology.

Thus, in the two earliest periods it is impossible to delimit a separate group of Nordic contributions to social theory. We shall instead focus on the emergence, growth and consolidation of the social science disciplines (sociology in particular, but also anthropology and political science) within which a style of argument that might today be counted as 'social theory' emerged. Our periodization provides a context for this analysis. It refers both to internal social change in the Nordic area, and to changing impulses from the broader western social science community. But its focal point is the relationship between social science and the humanities – how close it is and in which direction the influence goes.

The early postwar phase – positivism, the humanities and upstart social science

In the early postwar period, the dominance of the natural science ideal was close to total. Physics was seen as the paradigm science, varieties of the deductive–nomological model provided master examples of scientific explanations, and the measurement of correlation between variables was seen as the self-evident empirical foundation of social science. We shall refer to this as the *standard attitude* (approach, view, etc.) in social science and even in certain parts of the humanities (Mjøset 2003, forthcoming).

Aiming to gain credibility for their disciplines, the upstart social sciences adopted this approach, inspired mainly by US social science. But the universal validity of the natural science ideal was challenged already in the mid-1950s. The 'critique of positivism' was a response to the spread of this unity of science ideal in the humanities, particularly via the philosophy departments.

That critique is by now familiar, and clearly relevant to the conduct of social science: research into society is different from research into nature. For the sciences involved in the 'study of man', the object consists of interactions between fellow subjects, and these have the capacity to challenge whatever knowledge science would produce about them. The philosophical emphasis was on meaning/understanding as opposed to causality/explanation, an incarnation of the Neo-Kantian *Natur-/Geisteswissenschaften* dualism, pitting phenomenological understanding against explanation by law.

In Norway, this criticism was first launched by philosopher Hans Skjervheim (1957) and by philosophically oriented sociologist Dag Østerberg (1961). They had some influence in Norden more broadly, but inspiration also came from international sources, such as the early work of Habermas and Apel in Germany, Sartre in France, Winch's work in the Wittgensteinian direction and the Anglo-American debates on historical explanations. In Finland, Georg Henrik von Wright had a similar influence, but his was more of an internal criticism of philosophies projecting the natural science ideal on historical explanations (von Wright 1971).

In the 1960s, such inspirations seeped into humanities faculties across Norden. The debates were less heated in Sweden and Denmark: Sweden already had a quite broad social science tradition within economics, and sociology developed from within philosophy (Segerstedt in Uppsala). In Denmark, German immigrant T. Geiger sustained interest in German, non-standard sociological traditions, but he died in 1952 before sociology had become an autonomous academic discipline.

Only a small number of researchers were active as empirical researchers in the upstart social sciences in the 1950s and early 1960s. Whether these knew about the philosophical criticism or not, they did not relate to it in their own research. Typical of this period, then, is the gap between humanities and the social sciences. Presenting critical theory, Skjervheim (1976 [1962]: 219–20) explicitly made sociology into a 'philosophical discipline', and he later (1973: 190f) stated that it was 'outside the scope' of his analysis to discuss various types of empirical research. The natural science oriented notion of theory was countered by a humanities oriented notion of theory as the transcendental conditions of the sciences of man. The critique of positivism pitted one high-level notion of theory (transcendental conditions) against another one (explanation by laws). The unfortunate consequence was that quite a share of the empirical researchers simply regarded their work as 'positivist' or at least 'atheoretical' only because it was empirical.

In fact, the researchers who really tried to live up to strong versions of the standard ideal, produced the least successful empirical research. Who today considers the work of K. Svalastoga – notably *The Social System* (1974 [1969]) and *On Deadly Violence* (1982) – to be important parts of the knowledge accumulated by Nordic social scientists? Svalastoga was the first sociology professor in Copenhagen, trying to practise the gospel of the arch-positivist US Lundberg school.

Paradoxically, then, work that is still remembered and looked back upon as lasting contributions to Nordic sociology, fit neither the humanities – nor the natural science-inspired high level notions of theory. We shall mention three examples of such seemingly non-theoretical, but highly influential contributions.

In 1965, Vilhelm Aubert published *The Hidden Society,* a collection that can be seen as the first empirically oriented 'social theory' in Norwegian sociology. Describing common features of his essays, Aubert (1965: 3) conveys a self-denying disinterest: 'they lack reference to an explicit methodology, a clearly defined set of relevant data, and a precise theoretical framework. I have, in principle, no preference for this kind of "unscientific" approach and feel no need to defend the mode of sociological thought which the essays exhibit'. Still, he regards it as a 'mode of sociological thought'!

Like Aubert, the Danish sociologist Verner Goldschmidt was educated in law. His research in the 1950s related to the formulation and implementation of a criminal code in Denmark's former colony, Greenland (Bentzon and Agersnap 2000). Such research explicitly participated in the development of society, but its notion of theory was unclear. That social science should be useful was also Svalastoga's ambition, but given his absurdly crude social-engineering approach, nothing in his research – e.g. on deadly violence – was of any value to planners or decision makers!

Third, Norwegian political sociologist Stein Rokkan (1970) made a pioneering effort to move out of the 'national empiricism' of variables-oriented survey research, towards a comparative approach that relied as much on 'intensive nation-specific' case studies as on national data archives. Contact with Rokkan's networks played a crucial role for Erik Allardt, who was the most important figure in Finland's early postwar sociology. Rokkan pioneered a tradition of research that started from analysis of local cases, using these (and/or other Nordic cases) as analogies that inspire the comparative mapping of cases within a broader region. This strengthened their ability to get to the crucial aspects of their own country's development.

Mobilization and revolt – the social sciences gains an independent and offensive role

The second phase, from the early 1960s to the late 1970s, is marked by early welfare state expansion and reforms of higher education that (unexpectedly) led to major inflows of students into the upstart social sciences. Academic reorganization created separate social science faculties. Experiencing turbulent times, the new social sciences became the core location of the student revolt, which launched notions of critical (participatory) social science. Despite internal tensions, social scientists here played an offensive role, influencing the humanities, rather than the other way around. Ahead of the student revolt, an educated, leftwards-leaning public sphere emerged, including a number of publishers. This was an important precondition of the student revolt, but that revolt soon turned dogmatic, creating generational tensions within Nordic social science. The student revolters radicalized the philosophical critique against the standard view, but given their concern with oppressed groups, they turned it in an empirical direction.

This empirical turn, paradoxically, also led the student movement intellectuals towards convergence with the humanities, and thus away from empirical studies! The student revolt expressed revolutionary romanticism: it identified the working class as an essentially revolutionary critical subject. Reformist social democracy was the main target of their attack. They projected an image of the mid-nineteenth century working class on to Norden's postwar social compromise mass consumption society, a society regarded as legitimate by most workers. The main proof that capitalism was breaking down was thus *not* drawn from empirical studies, but from classical texts. The student revolters read the mid-nineteenth century works of Marx – together with Hegel and Lukacs, adding various other secularized philosophies of history – with a degree of philological precision only possible after years of higher eduction. There is the impressive case of two Danish translations of Marx's *Grundrisse*: the far-left publisher finding the mainstream publishers' translation unreliable!

When the student movement faded in the mid-1970s, this paradox of revolutionary romanticism gave way to a polarization between two different ways of practising social science: we shall call them the reformist/empirical and social-philosophical/reconstructionist approaches.

The latter line extended the student movement's philological concern with one classic (Marx) to a larger selection of sociological and philosophical classics. Institutionally, these social scientists worked in universities. Their style of research was very similar to that of the humanities: reading and commenting classical texts. They continued the criticism of the standard approach by developing the humanities-inspired notion of high-level theory already promoted by the philosophers of the earlier phase. This yielded a social-philosophical notion of theory ('Theorie der Gesellschaft').

In Norway, Dag Østerberg (1971, 1974) turned from a purely philosophical critique of positivism to essayistic treatment of topics such as power, material structure and social classes in the early 1970s. Simultaneously, he published on both Marx and Durkheim. His classical reader in 'sociological theory' (Østerberg 1978) contained excerpts from both European and American classic texts. It may well have been the first Nordic reader in 'social theory', widely used as a textbook.

There were a number of parallel works in the other Nordic countries. In Sweden, Göran Therborn (1976) surveyed the relationship between sociology and Marxist historical materialism. Jukka Gronow in Finland and Torben Hviid Nielsen (1977) in Denmark focused on the relationship between Marxism and reformist politics, which also implied close attention to the 'bourgeois Marx', Max Weber. In Finland, a main trend – exemplified by the work of Arto Noro – was to investigate whether Marxist analysis could be fused with formal analysis of daily life interaction, particularly as analysed by Simmel.

In Denmark, French structuralism was absorbed within the humanities since the late 1960s (Ditlevsen *et al.* 1972). Danish linguist Louis Hjelmslev had already made important contributions to that tradition. Physicist, peace researcher and philosopher of science Anders Boserup worked on 'structural dialectics', fusing inspiration from the Hegelian–Marxist tradition with the Bachelard–Canguilhem-tradition in French history of science, including followers such as Althusser and Foucault. Ethnographer Thomas Højrup made it his task to continue what Boserup started. The structuralist influence was also marked in Sweden, where, in the early 1980s, a group of educational sociologists began to publish and comment on Bourdieu's work (Broady 1991).

The other group, the reformist researchers were concerned with problem areas of the welfare state, relying on links between academia, the expanding sector of research institutes and the state apparatus, often mediated through research programmes of the national research councils. Many of them sensed the irrelevance of the philosophical criticism as well as the romanticism of the student revolters and returned to the standard attitude. Some relied on mainstream techniques of statistical generalization, working with large datasets of relevance to the management of an increasingly generous welfare state.

Others realized the weaknesses of pure behaviourism, and turned to rational choice theory, which allowed them to combine far-reaching formalization with a focus on action. Norwegian philosopher Jon Elster emerged from Oslo's left-leaning intelligentsia (Mjøset 2000b) to be an internationally acknowledged pioneer in this line of study. Given the links to neo-classical economics this understanding of theory became a branch of the standard view. Another influential Norwegian social scientist, anthropologist Fredrik Barth (1966), had already earlier promoted modelling inspired by game theory and evolutionary genetics, but emphasized that the models' logical operations should represent empirical processes. Thanks to this requirement he could retain grounding in the situated interaction that the anthropologist experiences during fieldwork (Barth 1981).

The upgraded versions of the standard approach were criticized by the reconstructionist social philosophers: one notion of high-level theory pitted against another. But before we evaluate this controversy, we shall ask again as we did for the first period: were there trends in empirical resarch that were not captured by the two high-level notions of theory?

Smaller groups of scholars resisted the 'methodological nationalism' of reformist empirical research. The content of their studies – topics such as the welfare state, consensual labour relations, egalitarian social relations – often parallelled the reformists, but the comparative focus on peculiarities of Nordic political and economic structures led them to specify context rather than to search for high-level generalities. Already in the late 1970s, one could see the contours of a comparative political economy research frontier combining typological thinking and historical periodization.

The ambition to map diversity by means of comparisions parallelled Rokkan's efforts (Rokkan (1999) contains his work from the 1970s) to establish taxonomic maps that would provide context enough to allow the explanation of the various trajectories of state formation and nation building in Western Europe. Many of Rokkan's followers (Kuhnle, Østerud, Aarebrot, and others, cf. Mjøset 1998) made important contributions to the comparison of Nordic state formation and welfare state policies. Therborn (1977) combined political economy and the comparative study of Western European political systems in the Rokkan tradition. The political economists could also hook on to the work of Walter Korpi (1983), who followed up his large 1978 monograph on Sweden with ambitious variables-oriented, but comparative, work on strikes, industrial relations and class politics in Western Europe.

Another set of empirical studies escaping current notions of theory was conducted by researchers who – unlike the student revolters – related to real existing critical subjects. The feminist movement is a major case in point. Reflecting the rising female educational attainment and labour force participation, a main focus was the double labour of women, their non-paid work and the specific rationality of the caring work at the domestic level and in the welfare state (Wærness 1982). Only the *standpoint* – standpoint theory is another term for critical theory – of women could make visible patterns of male domination (Holter 1996).

Feminist social science experienced a split similar to that between reformists and political economists. It developed its own reformist branch which produced nationally oriented research that supported 'state feminists' who through political parties influenced legislation e.g. on self-determined abortion and maternity leave provisions. But in academia, groups of scholars opposed the reformist turn by going for case-based, often participatory, action-based research linked to feminist grassroots mobilization. This research seldom discussed the macro level. The political economy situation was seen as a background (Holter (ed.) 1975) to the focus on female experiences.

This case-/action-oriented trend extended more broadly than the feminist movement. In line with Aubert's focus on the 'hidden society', several studies focused on the many 'underdog' groups both in modern national welfare capitalism and at the international level. In Norway, Thomas Mathiesen's and Nils Christie's research on prisoners, control, and violence extended to activism within movements for prison reform, but also yielded reflections on the principles of action research. There were similar studies, e.g. in criminology, across Norden. These studies all fit the broader literature on 'social construction' of social problems, an established branch of sociology's symbolic interactionism/ethnomethodology traditions.

At the international level, peace research turned to development problems and at the national level, social scientists adressed the problems of uneven regional development.

There is no room here for a detailed survey of Nordic varieties, nor for a discussion of its distinct methodological properties (see Mjøset forthcoming). Common was their aim at participatory interaction with the 'objects' of study in order to promote legitimate claims to social change. In Norway, both feminists and other action researchers joined to criticize the so far most prestigious project of reformist research: the government-sponsored study of power. But they left the theoretical critique to reconstructionist social philosophers (cf. Østerberg in Andenæs, *et al.* 1981). Even if both political economists and action researchers were empirically oriented, none of them discussed the kind of theory that was really involved in the empirically most successful individual studies. They lived up to Aubert's (1969: 194) statement: 'I prefer to do sociological work rather than talking *about* sociology'. They accepted that theoretical debates took place at the high level: social philosophers versus the standard view. This created a vicious circle between philosophical criticism of 'neo-utilitarianism' and the revised standard approach of rational choice.

Failing to address the question of whether empirical work could be done also on non-standard conditions, the critical alliance undercommunicated the differences between humanities/ social philosophy and social science. In the humanities, research is basically work on written texts and in history, on archival sources. In the social sciences, the research process is more diversified, involving participant observation, interviewing, and/or analysis of large data-sets. In the humanities and philosophy, both sources and research work come out as personal works, while generation of empirical knowledge in social science largely is a collective project.

Recent decades – differentiation of social science, parts of which moves closer to the humanities

The reconstructionist turn in Western sociology culminated in the early 1980s, as a cluster of works (by Habermas, Münch, Luhmann, Giddens and Alexander) took up the old Parsonian project of writing 'the history of theory with a systematic purpose': the goal was a transcendental theory of action, structure and knowledge – of relevance not just to sociology, but to social science as a whole.

Through the late 1980s and early 1990s, the interaction between higher living standards and emphasis on education as a way to postpone entry into a slack Nordic labour markets led to the most rapid expansion in higher education since the late 1960s. Social science expanded both in terms of students and personnel in higher education and research. With a multitude of disciplines, academic social science became a big 'education factory', as ever larger shares of Nordic youth aspired to gain higher education. A share of the large, recently graduated cohorts of social scientists engaged in rereading, translating, editing, writing introductions to and teaching about older and more recent classics.

An independent Nordic contribution to this literature was Østerberg (1988). It is obvious from that book – as from many similar surveys – that controversies were emerging within the social philosophical camp. In the early 1980s, a Franco-German tension had surfaced: Habermas responded to the French post-structuralists, in continuation with his critique of Luhmann in the 1970s. These tensions were imported into the Nordic area. Østerberg chose to go with Touraine and Bourdieu against Luhmann and Deleuze–Guattari, retaining a focus on practice (rather than discourse) and on knowledge about structures of material power (rather than seeing all knowledge as expressions of the will to power).

Post-structuralism was not unknown in the Nordic area, but now became more influential. In the Western world, rising living standards among the majority of the population implied a culture where consumption choices became increasingly important in identity-formation. In Norden, furthermore, the upwards trend in public service employment faltered, while private services picked up: publishing houses, new privatized media, marketing, and 'communication' consultancies, the latter an addition to the more well known social science related fields of management and labour relations consultancies. Concerning the lower end of the labour market, the population inflows from the Third World increased: both immigrants, refugees and asylum seekers became more marked features of urban life. As for international high politics, the end of the Cold War 1989–1991 was a major historical juncture. This implied the decline of 'arms race'-focused international relations, and a resurgence of ethno-nationalist mobilization, especially secession movements in the former Eastern bloc.

In this situation, post-structuralism was added to the portfolio of what was now more often called social theory. The reception was broader than in sociology only. Given the exposure to social science thinking in the earlier period, humanities scholars all over the Western world had rid themselves of their ties to 'national legacies', reaching a 'post-national' stage. Post-structuralism came via Anglo-American humanities and publishers, strengthening the influence of the humanities on social science.

The impact of post-structuralism differed by discipline: in fields like political science and international relations, where the earlier philosophical criticism had not gained much ground, it became a substitute for earlier varieties of criticism against the standard approach. In these disciplines, the role of the sociological classics was obviously less crucial than in sociology itself. But the French influence paved the way for impulses from a broader literature on 'construction of social problems', decades after its postwar rehabilitation in sociology with action-/case-oriented research. Emerging from the social science side, being committed to empirical research, these approaches did not go as far towards a relativist sociology of knowledge as the French post-structuralists, but defenders of political science's standard views would often identify any challengers as complete relativists. In a situation where the 'unholy alliance' between rational choice and variables-oriented approaches represented the standard approach, the stage was set for dramatic clashes along several dimensions of the *Natur–Geisteswissenschaften* dualism.

The Danish penchant for structuralism here developed into the Copenhagen school of international relations (Buzan *et al.* 1998), innovatively applying the philosophy of speech acts to the interaction between decision makers and public spheres: under certain circumstances, a field may not just be politicized, but *securitized*, meaning that measures are legitimated with reference to an 'existential threat'. This approach linked the post-structuralist focus on feelings and desires to the older tradition of social problems construction in sociology.

In anthropology, case-orientation has always been crucial. As immigration made multi-culturalism a challenge (first in Sweden, then in Denmark and Norway, now possibly even in Finland), anthropologists could increasingly do their fieldwork at home. The study of ethnic relations has been a strong field for the kind of constructionism that came with the post-structuralist impulse. Generally, the absorption of post-structuralist ideas was much smoother in anthropology than in political science. In Sweden, for instance, Ulf Hannerz (1996) turned from urban anthropology to investigate transnational connections – the many flows that cross nation-state borders – focusing recently on the production of foreign news, bringing anthropology closer to both international relations and sociology.

In sociology, with an established tradition for criticism of the standard view, post-structuralism was added alongside reconstructionist social philosophy. An important basis for its influence was the split within feminist social science. The reconstructionist turn was less interesting to feminists who embarked on careers in academia. The classics of social science were overwhelmingly male, as were the reconstructionists. The split within 1970s feminism had been between reformists and action researchers, now there was even a split within the academic sphere. The focus increasingly turned to private relations, e.g. persistence of patriarchy in the domestic division of labour, on rights and conflicts in a situation of increasing divorce rates, and on darker sides such as violence against women. This was also the stuff of literature and psychology. Many feminist social scientists felt at home in the borderland between humanities and social science. To the extent they related to classics, these were found in the humanities. In Paris was one grand classic, Simone de Beauvoir, and more recent forerunners: the Parisian turn to post-structuralism had taken place within the 'sciences humaines', in the borderland between aesthetics, linguistics and psychology, and several female intellectuals had participated. The works of Kristeva, Irigaray, Cixous and others, were now translated into English, making feminism a strong faction in the post-structuralist movement.

Also other new interdisciplinary fields emerged, some with the ambition to become new disciplines. The field of science, technology and innovation studies illustrates how practical concerns in the mixed economies (how to retain industrial employment in a high wage context) combined with the academic process of closer humanities/social science ties. History and political economy showed how technological development was path-dependent, and that social institutions influenced the innovative success of firms, regions and countries. From the humanities side, US feminist philosophers turned to science studies, asking to what extent science expressed male ideals and whether there was feminist science. From Parisian post-structuralist circles, the work of Latour inspired such studies.

Whether these new interdisciplinary fusions emerged within the humanities or social science faculties, differed between countries and universities. A general phenomenon was the coming of separate fields named 'cultural studies', more or less dependent/independent of older ethnography/history of ideas disciplines.

There have also been important contributions to science studies independently of the feminist movement. In Denmark, two scholars with a background in the humanities have published surveys that do not mainly reconstruct classical contributions, but relate their work (cf. Olsen and Köppe 1981, Olsen 1988) to single natural science disciplines, or simply give impressive interpretations of the recent development of such disciplines (Köppe 1990). In Norway, psychiatrist Svein Haugsgjerd (1986, 1990) has published surveys of modern trends in psychiatry, including the work of Lacan, but seen in the context of therapeutic work, not in a high-level philosophical setting.

In Finland, the move via Simmel towards cultural studies led to an interest in consumption. Post-structuralism always had a focus on the cultural construction of desires and wants, and its debt to psychoanalysis and surrealism. Falk (1994) combined case-based studies with psychoanalytic and linguistic frameworks. Gronow (1996) emphasizes fashions and 'taste communities' as important creators of order in present day society. These studies exemplify an interplay between the two social-philosophical branches, but more often, post-structuralism challenged reconstructionism. The former pointed out that the string of social philosophical syntheses remained personal ones, indicating that the search for fundamentals was an 'essentialist' fallacy. This was a deconstructionist criticism, returning a scepticist sociology of knowledge inspired by Nietzsche. We see here the contours of a pendulum movement between two social-philosophical positions: back and forth between re- and de-constructionism.

The reconstructionist line of defence was already indicated in Habermas' combination of his fundamental notions of lifeworld and system into an interpretation of the present as a case of 'colonization of the lifeworld'. Also the other proposed transcendental frameworks (including Giddens) were followed by reflections on the kind of society that gave rise to such a search for basic concepts. After all, from the start the philosophical criticism had implied that social researchers were participants, thus bound to interpret their own presents. The present was periodized as 'modernity', a term from art history and the history of ideas. The present was thus stretched out, covering all of modern history, equating the classics' present with our own, retaining thus a connection to the classics' fundamental concepts. While already the student revolters had taken Marx' statements on class struggle and the 'impoverishment' of the working class under capitalism as a direct interpretation of the postwar present, social philosophers now related in the same way to statements on rationality (Weber), anomie (Durkheim), and selected other statements (mostly) of cultural criticism.

This led social philosophers towards empirical studies, converging with a broader tradition of social scientists adressing critically contemporary developments. Some of these works relate to modern Western civilization (Beck, Baumann, Castells – to mention just a few). Other works relate to particular countries, trying to eke out the 'national identity', or pinpointing 'what is wrong with' one's own country. Such works cross the boundaries between the scientific community and the public sphere. Some of these scholars become 'stars' in Western or national culture as their broad descriptions of the present as 'risk society', 'information society', 'knowledge society', 'globalization', or the like, promote transdiscursive concepts (Miettinen 2003) adopted by broader strata outside of research, inspiring both public debates and legitimation of political strategies.

Even post-structuralists make this turn, just altering the periodization. Given their criticism of Western enlightenment, they regard the present as a state of post-modernity, recounting relativist small stories that undermine essentialist 'grand narratives'. Even this ideal had French roots, in the work of Lyotard, although only loosely linked to the central post-structuralist concerns with the arbitrary nature of the sign. But it also has a foundation in Anglo-American developments, typically in the arts, especially in architechture.

Another effect of the post-structuralist inspiration was the turn to discourse analysis and conceptual history, bolstering the alliance between post-nationalist humanities and social science. The analysis of texts was extended to the analysis of rhetoric in specific settings, implying some cross-fertilization with interactionist approaches to e.g. conversation analysis. A Nordic literature containing tools for such analysis emerged.

All over Norden, scholars reflected on modernity. There is no space here for a detailed survey. Generally, the varieties of such studies can be related to three dimensions: the kind of historical periodization involved, what specific social philosophers they rely on, and what specific fields of social science (local research frontiers) they draw on. In Norway, Østerberg (1999) published a history of ideas account of modernity starting from the mid-eighteenth-century, covering Western cultural history, noting his debt to Cassirer, Parsons and Sartre. Swedish political scientist Bjørn Wittrock (1999) studies the history of Western knowledge-institutions, starting from the same period of transition, noting his debt to Koselleck and Foucault. In Denmark, Lars Qvortrup (2003) claims that the paradigm of hypercomplexity characterizes present-day society since the start of the twentieth-century. His dominant inspiration is Luhmann and he mainly relates to the field of education and information/communication technology.

The controversies within social philosophy goes between theory as either fundamental concepts *or* as deconstruction of such concepts. Relying *either* on a high-level notion of theory or on no notion of theory, they claim capacity to analyse the present situation of modernity – post, late or whatever. But such a scope – different delimitations of modernity or post-modernity – allow only the most general, existential questions to be asked. Reconstructionist social philosophers run the risk of repeating the weaknesses of older philosophy of history: they fly way above any substantive research frontiers. Deconstructionist social philosophers run the risk of crashing below these frontiers – they often claim that any notion of theory as accumulated knowledge can be reduced to quite temporary strategies of elites striving to retain power.

However, through this period, we find several studies of considerable importance to the interpretation of the present, but linked to one or more local research frontiers. They study specific situations, in particular regions in historically delimited periods. Thus, like for the two other periods, we need to survey some studies with no high-level notion of theory to go with them.

In comparative political economy, a number of studies worked further from the French regulation school, which emphasized that British nineteenth-century capitalism was in important ways different from twentieth-century US capitalism. The latter – sometimes dubbed Fordism – had influenced postwar development in Western Europe, and Nordic scholars spelt out the specific patterns of capitalism that resulted when these international impulses interacted with specific Nordic conditions (Mjøset 1987). Therborn (1986, 1995a) did comparative work on national variations in unemployment and on Europe's postwar development more broadly. Danish sociologist G. Esping-Andersen compared Swedish and Danish social democracy in 1980. He then joined Korpi's project of establishing a detailed cross-national database allowing fine-grained analysis of trends and structures of contemporary OECD welfare states. This led first to a study of Nordic social democracy and finally to his famous typology of three families of Western European welfare states (Esping-Andersen 1990). Studies in several other, related fields contributed to the specification of inter-Nordic, Nordic and European specificities (Mjøset 1998).

The comparative focus separates these studies from reformist work. Systematic work on qualitative factors led to higher sensitivity of context, strengthening local research frontiers in areas of relevance to social development. Analyses of ongoing restructuring in OECD welfare states put the achievements of the Nordic type welfare states into perspective. Also the 'Nordic model' became a transdiscursive concept, but a more grounded one than those coined by the social philosophers.

The comparativists were good at explaining interesting present developments, but did not fit current notions of theory. Most of them were in practice agnostic about high level notions of theory. Like the political economists earlier, they did not ponder the question of why contextualization by means of typologies was a main feature of their work. Their work neither fit the social-philosophical notion of theory as reconstructions of classics, nor the standard ideal of decontextualized correlational exercises, or – equally decontextualized – rational choice models. Testing of formal sequences or patterns (or mechanisms) was only done *inside* of the various types! In contrast, adherents of high level notions of theory do not take such types seriously, and thus remain caught in a vicious circle between 'methodological nationalism' and decontextualization.

Space prevents an equally detailed survey of studies at other levels, except for two Danish works from this period. Both scholars combine research on specific questions of regional planning with ambitious theoretical considerations. Thomas Højrup (1983) studied how life modes in a Danish region adapted their permanent features to structural pressures for change. Bent Flyvbjerg (1991) studied political participation and urban planning in a middle-sized

Danish city. In contrast to the agnosticism of the political economists mentioned above, these scholars actually did write extensive sections (in fact separate volumes!) on questions of theory and method, even reaching back to the great philosophers. We shall soon return to these works.

Conclusion

Considering curricula and teaching in the broadest social science discipline, sociology, a certain pluralism has been institutionalized: standard views dominate courses on quantitative methods, while theory classes provide samples from the many personalized social philosophies. In the courses on qualitative methods, notions of theory are often ambiguous.

Followers of the standard approach are no longer in a position to impose their practical philosophy of social science as a normative canon for all researchers. The social philosophers, on their part, accept the inclusion of a rational choice position. Although they criticize it, they also fit it into the reconstructionist notion of theory as derived from the classics: rational choice is simply a 'neo-utilitarian' reconstruction of older utilitarian, liberal theory. Variables-oriented studies, on the other hand, are met with the same disinterested scepticism as any other empirically oriented 'hyphenated sociology' – perhaps even reproducing the view that empirical research can only be done in the variables-oriented way.

At times, the two positions clash in debates on fundamentals, reproducing the *Natur-/Geisteswissenschaft*-polarization. Such debates tend to reproduce the consensus that at the very least, *theory* is knowledge at a very high level. The possibility that social science could develop a notion of theory based only on its own experience, is lost. This is an unfortunate stalemate situation in which social philosophers and followers of standard views have divided the field between them. Through this essay, we pointed to empirical research that does not fit any of the high-level notions of theory. It is now the time to ask whether there is also a notion of theory for comparative and participation-oriented case-studies.

To find such a notion, let us reject the dualism by turning its two poles into two out of three practical philosophies of social science (Mjøset forthcoming). Besides the standard and the social-philosophical attitudes, we define a third attitude, a practical philosophy of social science which is based on reflection on the participation of social science itself in social development. We call this a pragmatist/participatory attitude. It rejects the imposition of ideals both from the natural sciences and the humanities. Among its recent spokesmen we find those who argue that the impulses of American pragmatists and the Chicago school of sociology actually represent a viable alternative for social science as a whole (Mjøset 2003, referring to the work of Abbott and Ragin). But this attitude also has European roots, namely critical theory understood as the standpoint theory.

Social philosophers might call this 'neopragmatism', since they are inclined to link theory not to substantive findings, but to new permutations of ideas from older schools. But this programme was above all a reflection on the substantive success of comparative historical social research. Furthermore, the link to the Chicago-school programme was not based on a wish to reconstruct core notions of action, structure and knowledge. The pragmatist attitude only involves a thin notion of action: that all interaction is historically situated in a concrete context, and that generalization must be grounded in case-studies of such situated action/interaction. The point was rather to revive social science that had explanatory relevance.

Through the three periods discussed above, we have emphasized influential contributions to empirical research that does not fit high level notions of theory. Our major point is now that the pragmatist attitude yields notions of theory that fits these kinds of research. A classic account of such a notion, synthesizing the Chicago-school tradition, is Glaser and Strauss's (1967) grounded theory. It is possible to chose a neutral term also, such as explanation-based theory.

Whether macro or micro, the concern for the situated nature of action is common to these styles of empirical study. Consider macro-comparisons: they yield theories developed from below (from specific explanations) and these are at a clearly lower level than the social-philosophical reconstructions, but they are more general than social-philosophical decon-structions. They challenge the social-philosophical project of making *modernity* (high, late or post) as such the contextual framework, and also the standard view of theory as decontex-tualized, so far unfalsified knowledge. Both these notions are unable to account for the kind of knowledge that we possess, e.g. in the typologies found in Rokkan or Korpi/Esping-Andersen's work. These must be seen as general substantive theories which aid the researchers in the complicated task of establishing context. They generalize, without loss of context.

Grounded theory comes in two versions: substantive and formal. A substantive theory would be an explanation that – at the present local research frontier – is accepted by the research community as a valid account with reference to a specified context, such as e.g. the Nordic welfare states in the 1990s. A formal theory, in contrast, would be a module (some prefer the term 'mechanism') that can apply in various contexts (e.g. 'the strength of weak ties' in net-work theory), but one that only becomes explanatory when used in a context (a set of scope conditions). Despite the fact that Jon Elster's early work belong to the rational choice tradition, his recent emphasis (Elster 1998) on mechanisms as tools of explanation are quite close to such a notion of theory.

Social philosophers might object that such formal theory is not rooted in a 'transcendental theory of action, structure and knowledge'. But it is a promising thought that such formal notions of theory can be developed from an interdisciplinary venture centred on recent cognitive science. This is a too complex topic to explore further here, but it is an important one, presently being adressed by several research groups, also in Norden. Within education, a group of Finnish scholars, led by Y. Engestrøm (1999), has already done a lot of work along these lines. More will follow as economists turn more of their attention to cognitive economics.

A number of scholars agree that context is important, and advocate modified versions of the standard approach (Merton's 'middle range theories'). But they accept the natural science prodecure as their – however distant – ideal. The search for law-like relations bias their notions of theory to what looks like formal grounded theory. But only substantive grounded theory gives meaning to a notion of the scope of theory. Importantly, this is not a question of testing, since a researcher can test competing (explanatory) theories only *within* a set of scope conditions. Neither can scope conditions be deduced from more general theory, they must be established in pragmatist terms, through the participation of researchers in society (local research frontiers), since scope must be a function of what we want to know, that is, our 'knowledge interests'. This is different from explanation by laws: we rather have explanation by causal constellations which establish the context for individual or collective actors. The understanding/explanation-dichotomy is here irrelevant. The analysis of causal constellations is at the core of the more pragmatic sciences such as psychology (as therapy), law and history. Such arguments lead us to conclude that the notion of general theory should *not* be linked to formal theory, but to substantive theory. To be simultaneously general and explanatory, theory must consist of comparison-based contextual factors that are of value to several local research frontiers. Such general theory is not converging in one direction, there may be sev-eral general theories, related to clusters of research questions. A general substantive grounded theory unites a number of local research frontiers (for instance industrial relations, welfare states, political development, ethnic mobilization), but never all.

There are other approaches that emphasize formal theory without invoking explanation by law-like relations. Evolutionary theory (March and Olsen (1989)-type organization theory, evolutionary economics) often search for smaller sets of explanatory modules. This position is quite close to the notion of formal grounded theory, but from a pragmatist standpoint one would not give any priority to analogies drawn from evolutionary biology.

The search for lower level notions of theory has precedents in Nordic social science. Such a programme can look back at and learn from scholars who – as shown – in practice ignored high-level notions of theory (for the case of Rokkan, see Mjøset 2000a). Although Aubert was disinterested in 1965, he put out a Norwegian translation of *The Hidden Society* in 1969, adding an essay on theory and methods, with statements that are very close to the idea of grounded theory. Barth (1981: 1–2) looked back at his programmatic discussion of models in anthropology and noted that his main emphasis was always on generative processes (situated action in Goffman's terms figure importantly in his writings), and that his main background was not other theorists, but his own fieldwork. His plea for 'naturalism' in later writings also brings him close to grounded theory.

To this can be added the rediscovery of classical (as opposed to neo-realist) geopolitics and political geography in political science/international relations, and the (however marginal) efforts to learn from the German historical school, evolutionary and cognitive science in economics.

As for Denmark and Sweden, there are interesting examples of scholars balancing between grounded studies and social-philosophical reflections. Both Wittrock and Therborn have addressed the question of disaggregating modernity. Therborn (1995b) has explored four routes to modernity. As for the Danish scene, we mentioned the grounded case-studies of Højrup and Flyvbjerg. Still, there is a strong element of social philosophy in their work, especially in their reliance on selected classical philosophers. A telling example is Højrup's rediscovery of the idea of the state system by reading Clausewicz. The importance of the state system is after all obvious from numerous geopolitical studies, and Højrup (2003: 2f) is of course, at the margins, aware that he here converges with a broader tradition of comparative historical sociology. Flyvbjerg (1991, 2001) invokes both antique philosophers, as well as the cognitive science of Dreyfus, and Foucault's post-structuralism to arrive at his notion of 'the science of the concrete'.

These elements of social philosophy are strikingly indicated by the lack of cross-referencing between Danish scholars who are actually all suggesting grounded theories as inventive redirections of post-structuralist impulses. The Copenhagen school's work on regional security complexes (Buzan and Wæver 2003) clearly leads to grounded theories about aspects of the state system, but there is no Wæver–Højrup cross-referencing. Højrup and Flyvbjerg both have a connection to regional studies, but show no awareness of contributing to a common research frontier. Different disciplinary location may be part of the explanation of such mutual disregard (Wæver/political science, Flyvbjerg/planning, Højrup/ethnography). But in welfare state research, we see a research frontier to which Nordic and other researchers are contributing, independently of their disciplinary locations. This indicates that the persistence of high level social philosophical understandings of theory – above all in Flyvbjerg and Højrup – weakens the ability of scholars to consider the specific local research frontiers that they relate to. They run the danger of erecting personal theoretical frameworks, rather than contributing to the collective efforts at specific research frontiers.

The question of whether what we have described here as a pragmatist attitude should be seen as yielding *social theory*, or simply *social science theory,* can be left for the reader to decide.

As for the relation to the humanities, our conclusion is that influence from the humanities should be balanced by close attention to the actual practice of social research. The natural science ideal may have been weakened in social science under inspiration from the humanities, but we must build our notions of theory with reference to what we do in substantive social research, not to what scholars do in other lines of academic work.

Notes

1 I am thankful for comments at various stages of this work from Lars Bo Kaspersen, Jukka Gronow, Ann Nilsen and Ole Wæver.

References

Andenæs, K. Johansen, T. and Mathiesen, T. (eds) (1981) *Maktens ansikter*, Oslo: Gyldendal.
Aubert, V. (1965) *The Hidden Society*, Totowa: Bedminster Press. (Revised Norwegian edn, 1969.)
Barth, F. (1966) *Models of Social Organization*, vol. 165, The Royal Anthropological Institute of Great Britain and Ireland.
Barth, F. (1981) 'Models reconsidered', in F. Barth, *Process and Form in Social Life*, London: Routledge.
Bentzon, A. W. and T. Agersnap (2000) 'Verner Goldschmidt: Danish Sociologist of Law and Culture', in *Acta Sociologica*, 43(4): 375–380.
Broady, D. (1991) *Sociologi och epistemologi*, Stockholm: HLS Förlag.
Buzan, B., Wæver, O. and Wilde, J. de (1998) *Security*, Boulder: Rienner.
Buzan, B. and Wæver, O. (2003) *Regions and Powers: the structure of international security*, Cambridge: Cambridge University Press.
Ditlevsen, T., Mønster Petersen, J. and Svindborg, B. (eds) (1972) *Tegn Tekst Betydning*, Copenhagen: Borgen.
Elster, J. (1998) 'A plea for mechanisms', in P. Hedstrøm and R. Swedberg (eds), *Social Mechanisms*, Cambridge: Cambridge University Press.
Engeström, Y., Miettinen, R. and Punamäki, R-L. (eds) (1999) *Perspectives on Activity Theory*, Cambridge: Cambridge University Press.
Esping-Andersen, G. (1990) *The Three Worlds of Welfare Capitalism*, Cambridge: Polity.
Falk, P. (1994) *The Consuming Body*, London: Sage.
Flyvbjerg, B. (1991) *Rationalitet og magt*, Århus: Akademisk.
Flyvbjerg, B. (2001) *Making Social Science Matter*, Cambridge: Cambridge University Press.
Glaser, B. and A. Strauss (1967) *The Discovery of Grounded Theory*, New York: Aldine/De Gruyter.
Gronow, J. (1996) *The Sociology of Taste*, London: Routledge.
Hannerz, U. (1996) *Transnational Connections*, London: Routledge.
Haugsgjerd, S. (1986) *Grunnlaget for en ny psykiatri*, Oslo: Pax.
Haugsgjerd, S. (1990) *Lidelsens karakter i ny psykiatri*, Oslo: Pax.
Holter, H. (ed.) (1975) *Familien i klassesamfunnet*, Oslo: Pax.
Holter, H. (ed.) (1996) *Hun og han*, Oslo: Pax.
Højrup, T. (1983) *Det glemte folk. Livsformer og centraldirigering*, Copenhagen: Statens Bygforsknings Instituts Forlag.
Højrup, T. (2003) *State, Culture and Life-Modes*, Aldershot: Ashgate.
Köppe, Simo. (1990). *Virkelighedens niveauer*, Copenhagen: Gyldendal.
Korpi, W. (1983) *The Democratic Class Struggle*, London: Routledge.
March, J and Olsen, J. P. (1989) *Rediscovering Institutions*, New York: Free Press.
Miettinen, R. (2003) *National Innovation System*. Helsinki: Edita.
Mjøset, L. (1987) 'Nordic economic policies in the 1970s and 1980s', in *International Organization*, 41(3): 403–456.
Mjøset, L. (1998) 'Nordic Comparative Historical Macrosociology', in M. Bertilsson and G. Therborn (eds) *From a Doll's House to the Welfare State: Reflections on Nordic Sociology*, Madrid: International Sociological Association.

Mjøset, L. (2000a) 'Stein Rokkan's thick comparisons', in *Acta Sociologica*, 43(4): 381–398.

Mjøset, L. (2000b) 'Et barn av gullalderen', in *Vardøger*, 26: 15–37.

Mjøset, L. (2003) 'Versuch über die Grundlagen vergleichenden historischer Sozialwissenschaft', in H. Kaelble and J. Schriewer (eds) *Vergleich und Transfer – Zum Stand der Komparatistik in den Geistes- und Sozialwissenschaften*, Frankfurt and New York: Campus.

Mjøset, L. (forthcoming) 'Six notions of theory in the social sciences'.

Nielsen, T. H. (1977) *Borgerskabets reformer og marxismen*, Århus: Modtryk.

Olsen, O. A. (1988) *Ødipus-komplekset*, Copenhagen: Reitzel.

Olsen, O. A. and S. Köppe. (1981) *Freuds psychoanalyse*, Copenhagen: Gyldendal.

Østerberg, D. (1961) *Den sosiale realitet*, Oslo: Institutt for sosiologi, Universitetet i Oslo.

Østerberg, D. (1971) *Makt og materiell*, Oslo: Pax.

Østerberg, D. (1974) *Essays i samfunnsteori*, Oslo: Pax.

Østerberg, D. (ed.) (1978) *Handling og samfunn*, Oslo: Pax.

Østerberg, D. (1988) *Metasociology*, Oslo: Norwegian University Press.

Østerberg, D. (1999) *Det moderne*, Oslo: Gyldendal.

Qvortrup, L. (2003) *The Hypercomplex Society*, New York: Lang.

Rokkan, S. (1970) *Citizens, Elections, Parties*, Oslo: Universitetsforlaget.

Rokkan, S. (1999) *State Formation, Nation-building, and Mass Politics in Europe*, Oxford: Oxford University Press.

Skjervheim, H. (1957) *Objectivism and the Study of Man*, Oslo: Dept. of Philosophy: University of Oslo.

Skjervheim, H. (1973) *Ideologianalyse, dialektikk, sosiologi*, Oslo: Pax.

Skjervheim, H. (1976 [1962]) 'Sosiologien som vitskap: positiv eller kritisk disiplin?', in Skjervheim, *Deltakar og tilskodar og andre essays*, Oslo: Tanum Norli.

Svalastoga, K. (1974 [1969]) *The Social System*, Copenhagen: Academisk Forlag.

Svalastoga, K. (1982) *On Deadly Violence*, New York: Columbia University Press.

Therborn, G. (1976) *Science, Class and Society*, London: New Left Books.

Therborn, G. (1977) 'The Rule of Capital and the Rise of Democracy', in *New Left Review*, 103: 3–41.

Therborn, G. (1986) *Why Some Peoples are more Unemployed than Others*, London: Verso.

Therborn, G. (1995a) *European Modernity and Beyond*, London: Sage.

Therborn, G. (1995b) 'Routes to/through modernity', in M. Featherstone, S. Lash, and R. Robertson (eds), *Global Modernities*, London: Sage.

von Wright, G. H. (1971) *Explanation and Understanding*, Ithaca: Cornell University Press.

Wærness, K. (1982) *Kvinneperspektiver på sosialpolitikken*, Oslo: Universitetsforlaget.

Wittrock, B. (1999) 'Social Theory and Intellectual History', in F. Engelstad and R. Kalleberg (eds) *Social Time and Social Change*. Oslo: Scandinavian University Press.

11

Contemporary East Central European social theory

Arpad Szakolczai and Harald Wydra

This chapter attempts to present the most important ideas of contemporary East Central European social theorists. It will have three particularities. While most of the best-known thinkers from the region were originally Marxists, little space will be devoted to them, as their prominence was due not so much to their ideas, rather to matters of political and ideological supply and demand. For much the same reasons, more than usual space will be devoted to historical and biographical background, or existential-experiential concerns. In compensation, the ideas presented hopefully still sound fresh, even anticipating recent developments in social theory – illustrating the thesis of Hadot and Foucault that philosophy, or theorising, is not just a matter of doctrine but also a way of life.

East Central Europe is hardly even present on the map of contemporary social theory.[1] Most students of sociology, even those well versed in theory, would be hard pressed were they asked to name an East Central European theorist.[2] The case is different for art, be it cinema, theatre or novels. Such a situation is as self-evident as it is deeply puzzling. It is self-evident, as the Iron Curtain functioned particularly well in social theory, preventing the mutual exchange of ideas in both directions. But from two interlinked perspectives it is deeply perplexing. Since the early nineteenth-century Central Europe, especially Germany, was the centre of European thought. Since the time of Kant and Hegel, through Kierkegaard, Marx, Nietzsche, Freud, Simmel, Weber, Husserl, Wittgenstein, Heidegger, the most important centres of thinking were Central European: Berlin and Jena, Heidelberg and Frankfurt just as Vienna, Prague and Budapest. Nobody would consider the difference between Husserl and Heidegger, Elias and Schutz, or Mannheim and Adorno in terms of an East–West contrast.

Due to the heavy impact of world wars and totalitarian regimes a certain loss of standards would be understandable. However, due to this same reason one would also expect the gestation of particularly important ideas. Social theory is not simply the product of abstract thinking, performed under leisurely conditions. Quite on the contrary, from Socrates and Plato through Augustine, Machiavelli, Hobbes or Hegel, it was the result of reflections, under considerable stress, on events personally lived through. The combination of these two aspects should have produced a particularly important tradition in social thinking.

The apparent anonimity of East Central European social theory, far from being self-evident, is thus deeply problematic. What is the reason for this silence? And were there important thinkers in or from the region after 1945 who belong to a relatively coherent school of thought but who are not yet known to the wide world?

The explanation lies in the particularly overwhelming, double impact Marxism exerted on thinking in the region after World War Two, on two different levels. The first was official Marxist-Leninist ideology, used to brainwash entire generations. While such indoctrination is bad enough in itself, it became truly devastating through the second level, critical intellectual discourse. Marxism was a radical critique. Under Communist power, a certain version of Marxism became the official ideology. At the same time, it also pretended to be the most important idiom of criticism; and this combination proved to be lethal.

This happened for two reasons. First, it implied that official ideologists and their critics shared a common language. Instead of two camps, one should rather talk about a continuum, ranging from crude party hacks to sophisticated European intellectuals, represented most clearly by György Lukács and his school, where the boundary between official Marxist dogma and heretic ideas, formalised in Hungary by György Aczél in the infamous trio 'támogatott, türt and tiltott' (supported, tolerated and forbidden) continuously shifted. The exact nature of personal and intellectual connections alongside this continuum is highly controversial. However, it is beyond controversy that anybody who did not share the common idiom of Marxism was twice excluded from discussion.

Still more important was the impact which – due to the 'double bind' of official and critical thinking – a certain Marxist 'mentality' or 'spirit' exerted on the intellectual life in the region, strengthening and magnifying, almost without limit, the most problematic aspects of Marx's thought. This is an excess of critique, a situation in which the destructive tendencies of a purely negative spirit that sees every single human act only from the reverse ran amok, unchecked.

The clearest embodiment of this tendency was György Lukács, the most visible social theorist behind the Iron Curtain in the 1950s and the 1960s; a figure who – both in his activities and impact – was deeply ambivalent. Lukács was an extremely well-educated person with a brilliant mind, managing to enchant even Max Weber. Due to his standing and contacts, he became a privileged interlocutor. But he had personal shortcomings, which came to the surface in the most important events of his life, and which were best captured by two important artists: by Thomas Mann in the figure of Naphta in *The Magic Mountain*, one of the keys novels of the twentieth-century (Mann and Kerényi 1975: 13); and in a poem written in the 1950s by György Faludy, a major Hungarian poet, who spent years in Recsk, the Hungarian Gulag. For decades Lukács used his intellectual capital abroad to white-wash the regime, while at home presenting Marxism as the only possible language of 'immanent criticism', topped with his notorious slogan according to which even the worst socialism is better than the best capitalism. As he lived during the worst Stalinist times in the Soviet Union, none can argue that he did not mean what he said. As much of *The Magic Mountain* was about the education of its hero, Hans Castorp, in the literal sense of a struggle for his 'soul', Hungary represents the spectacle, terrifying for any reader of the novel, of a country where the most promising young intellectuals for generations came under the spell of Naphta.

As a result, many of the best and most sensitive minds in Hungary, and to some extent also in Poland or Czechoslovakia, came to believe that Marxism was not only the official ideology, but also the only possible language for genuine critique. Their energies were spent on hair-splitting discussions between 'good' and 'bad' Marxism, performing spectacular somersaults over ideological positions, until they either burned out to cynicism or – making the final somersault – became legalistic liberals or rational choice theorists.

Hungary

The most important Hungarian thinkers in the twentieth-century were one-time friends Károly Kerényi (1897–1973) and Béla Hamvas (1897–1968). They belong to the same World War One generation as Elias and Borkenau, or Voegelin and Schutz, and in their lives and works, ideas and friendship were just as intertwined as for the other two pairs. In 1935 Kerényi and Hamvas started a periodical entitled *Sziget* (*Island*), with the aim of renewing Hungarian intellectual life. The journal attracted as contributors some key intellectuals, but had to close down after a few years. After this experience, Kerényi became increasingly distanced from the centre of Hungarian intellectual life, emigrating to Switzerland in 1943, while Hamvas withdrew into internal emigration. Their friendship ended bitterly.

Kerényi studied classical philology and wrote his dissertation on Plato. He was in close contact with key intellectual figures, especially Carl Jung and Thomas Mann. For decades he was a core member of the Eranos circle, but never secured a proper university appointment.

His life-work took up and extended Nietzsche's contrast in *Birth of Tragedy* between the Apollonian and Dionysian. Kerényi's first major mature book was *Apollo: The Wind, the Spirit, and the God: Four Studies* (Kerényi 1983 [1937]), and his last was *Dionysos: Archetypal Image of Indestructible Life* (1976). In between, he added a third dimension to the Nietzschean dichotomy: the Greek trickster demi-gods, Prometheus and especially Hermes.

Kerényi had a fundamental role in calling attention to the figure of the Trickster, this strange creature surfacing in mythologies all around the planet, even holding a key to contemporary politics (Horváth 1998). The classical anthropological work of Paul Radin was resumed in a book published with two essays by Jung and Kerényi (Radin 1956).[3] The most important ideas of Kerényi are contained in *Hermes the Guide of Souls*, written in 1943, at a highly liminal moment of his own life, inspired by the writings and personality of Thomas Mann.

Kerényi introduces Hermes negatively, by a series of contrasts. In opposition to Walter Otto's idealised, classicist picture, Kerényi presents the complete figure, including its 'revoltingly repulsive' aspects. Contrasting the *Iliad* and the *Odyssey*, he also brings out the opposition between charisma and the trickster. The Iliad is the world of charismatic heroes, where Hermes is only a master thief. In Odyssey, devoted to the endless wanderings of the cunning Ulysses, the trickster flourishes, feeling at home in the homelessness. Finally, Kerényi also compares Hermes to Apollo and Dionysus.

Positively, Hermes is first of all a messenger of gods and guide of souls. His interest extends to all spheres of communication: economy and commerce, transport and traffic, language (hermeneutics) and eloquence. His activities are everywhere ambivalent. Hermes is the god of commerce, but also a master thief; the god of speech, but also a liar. He not only guides souls, but steals them as well, transporting them to the underworld. This is where the prankster ambivalence of the figure ends. Hermes is a lethal deity, being particularly quick and merciless, even laughing at his hapless victims.

Ambivalence belongs to the heart of Hermes, including age: Hermes is depicted as a youth, but also as a bearded man; and in gender Hermes epitomises virility, having phallic images, but is also a hermaphrodite. It is best visible in his intimate link with night. It is in the uncanny[4] and undifferentiated darkness, in the movement of the shadows, conjuring dangers, that the trickster is truly at home. Through Hermes, Kerényi warns about the dangers involved in opening up unconscious forces.

Using recent perspectives in social theory, Kerényi's analysis could be taken further. Hermes the 'homeless' god of thresholds is the *par excellence* god of liminality; but also, as a deity of communication, commerce, language, speed and sexuality, impersonating ambivalence, is a paradoxical 'deity of modernity'.

In his posthumous masterwork Kerényi went a step further, giving new impetus to the understanding of Dionysus. In the *Birth of Tragedy* Nietzsche argued for the centrality of Dionysian experience for Greek and consequently of European culture, a vantage point to criticise modern nihilism. The claim went against the entire tradition of classical philology, convinced of the cult's foreign origins. The situation only changed with the archaeological discovery of the ancient Minoan civilisation, and especially the breaking of the linear B script and the decoding of the name of Dionysus among the inscriptions. This led Kerényi to recognise the Minoan origins of Greek culture. This included the joyful affirmation of existence, celebrating the indestructible forces of life, the pleasures of sociability acquired through wine, and the discovery of a general 'grace of life' for which Minoan civilisation became famous.

Kerényi also reinterpreted the central, enigmatic Cretan symbol, the Labyrinth. Beyond the late interpretation as an impenetrable maze, the events associated with the Labyrinth were rituals that took place at the Palace court. Its central motive was spiral, not maze; those entering it were not supposed to get lost there, rather to go through the spiral, entering bravely its centre, turn around there, and leave afterwards. The Labyrinth was the stage of initiation rituals, comparable to religious experiences of conversion, close to Plato's famous cave metaphor and the experience of turning around. The Minotaur at the centre represented the perilous passage of such rituals.

Even here, Kerényi did not hide away the dark aspects, related to excess and suffering. Dionysus is associated with the most elementary forces and experiences – fertility, drinking, sociability, erotic. However, as these are also most dangerous, they require particular care. Cult rituals were always on the edge of being transformed into something sinister, even horrifying. It is due to this reason that Dionysus also became the god of suffering: the god who had to die, and in the most terrible manner, so that it could be born again.

These dark aspects can be harmonised with the joyful grace of Cretan culture by returning to conversion. Dionysus is the god who overcame suffering, having a second birth, thus renewing life. Pentheus ('the suffering one'), however, failed to go through, continuously tearing up and licking his wounds, becoming identical with suffering. The Graces assisted Dionysus in the rituals, assuring that the intoxicated celebration did not overspill into uncontrolled frenzy. The Furies, deities of hatred and vengeance, expressed and transmitted the experiences of Pentheus, pulling anybody they could reach into their vortex of raging destructiveness.

Béla Hamvas was a philosopher of the religious tradition of mankind. Being disenchanted with academic and public life under 'Christian nationalist' Hungary, he left university, working in a library while accumulating mountains of notes and manuscripts, many of which were destroyed in the Second World War. After 1948, he was thrown to the street, and in his 50s and 60s worked in desolate socialist plants around the countryside.

His work departed from the 'crisis literature' of the 1920s and 1930s, highlighted by Jaspers, Mannheim or Huizinga, that was strongly influenced by Nietzsche. On this basis his work extended in time and space to cover the entire history of the planet. In this he was helped by prodigious erudition and the mastery of seventeen languages, including Greek, Hebrew, Arabic, Persian, Sanskrit and Chinese.

His two most important works are the three-volume *Scientia Sacra*, an overview of the wisdom contained in the sacred tradition of mankind, of which the first two volumes were written during the Second World War, and a third and unfinished volume in the early 1960s;

and the two-volume *Patmosz*, a collection of essays dating from the 1960s. A collected edition of his works, planned for twenty-six volumes, is currently being published.

Scientia Sacra advanced Jaspers's 1949 thesis on 'axis time', while offering a different perspective (see Szakolczai 2005). Hamvas argues that the spiritual events around 500 BC were not a transcendental breakthrough, offering new perspectives on human life, rather efforts to mobilise the entire tradition under new conditions of distress. Hamvas assigned equal importance to Chinese, Indian, Hebrew or Greek spirituality, underlining the common message, and emphasised the unique role of Plato for Europe. Central to this Ancient 'crisis literature' is a diagnosis of the times as 'the meaningless and disordered swarming of individual "I"-s', stimulated through the imposed formation of images on the mind (Hamvas 1995/6, I: 62, 303–04; II: 48), and the call for 'awakening' or 'illumination' (Ibid., I: 30–33, 45, 190), a return to true inner order.

The third, fragmentary volume, together with Patmosz, offers a new perspective. It is devoted to Christianity, hardly present in the first volumes. Hamvas sees Christianity not as a radical departure, rather as a return to tradition. The New Testament added only one new element, the power of love as 'the measure of being' (Ibid., III, 169). This superior power, however, is highly vulnerable. Due to its very virtues – its sensitivity and receptivity – it can be attacked, slandered and defiled. Still, while demonic forces might seem to gain the upper hand in their struggle against love and the idyllic, such efforts are ultimately hopeless, as 'the corruption of being simply doesn't stand a chance' (Hamvas 1992, II: 242).

The intellectual activities of István Bibó (1911–1979) were intertwined with political involvements. With a background in public administration and law, in the 1940s he published a series of highly influential articles on the historical and socio-political situation of the entire Central-European region. Deprived voice in the darkest Communist times, he became a leader of the 1956 uprising, narrowly escaping the death penalty. Marginalised again until death, in the 1980s he became a main source of inspiration for the dissident movement, especially through the famous Bibó Festschrift.

In order to understand the political events in which his world became entangled, he situated them on a broad historical panorama. The results of his studies are resumed in a long 1971–1972 essay on 'The meaning of European social development' (Bibó 1986, III: 5–123). While not producing astonishing insights on the rise and dynamics of Western civilisation, the work is interesting at the level of perspective and judgement. It accords positive importance to the Middle Ages, refusing the caricatures of Renaissance humanism and the Enlightenment, but without idealisation. It also identified in an ideological reading of history – due especially to Marxism but also rooted in aspects of Christianity – the loss of a proper sense of distinction and judgement characteristic of contemporary Western intellectual life.

Bibó's essays on the specific historical path of the region, and its reasons, remain strikingly fresh, offering wider validity. Bibó argues that the catastrophes which Central Europe, from Germany through Hungary up to Yugoslavia, brought to itself and to the entire world in the twentieth-century were not results of inherent backwardness, as usually assumed, but of a misdirected development path for which he coined the term 'zsákutcás fejlödés' (dead-end-street development). He analysed the tragic consequences of this situation using a terminology recalling both medicine and his favourite Greek classics (diagnosis, hysteria, crisis, balance), one of the most evident symptoms being an excessive nationalist.

Bibó's core theoretical interest was the question of power. Given his life experiences, he could not avoid being confronted with the 'one-sided concentration of power'. He unconditionally supported democracy as the technique to prevent such a concentration and the resulting, humiliating and life-debilitating experiences of 'védtelenség' (defencelessness) and 'kiszolgáltatottság' (this term expresses the experience of being exposed to the mercy of more powerful others, built up from the common Hungarian root for 'service' and 'serf'). On this basis Bibó reflected on the inherent links between politics and ethics. Far from identifying them, he claimed that a rigid separation of the two spheres, characteristic of modern positivist science and legalist political practice, is untenable, even nihilistic.

The position can be illustrated by a 1942 article entitled 'Elite and social sensibility' (Bibó 1986, I: 221–241). According to Bibó it is impossible to give a 'value free' definition of the elite, and no democracy can function without a genuine elite. The term is not restricted to structural position within existing hierarchies, as the tasks of the elite include the formulation of communal goals and the ennobling of social and cultural life. Furthermore, radically reversing the Marxist paradigm, Bibó argued that the solution of the social problem requires not the elimination of the elite, rather the education of an elite endowed with 'social sensibility'. The 'calm and creative' activity of the elite assumes self-confidence, and requires a social consensus behind elite selection mechanisms. The elite of a society can only perform its tasks if it has stable conditions for its activity, and if its qualities are generally recognised.

Here the argument joins the analysis of the sources of the 'collective hysteria' that stimulated the disasters of the twentieth-century. In the broad region, including Germany, the self-confidence and consciousness of the elite was broken. This led to a serious crisis of conscience, a deepening socio-political crisis, and the resulting elevation into high position of individuals who were not members of an elite in any meaningful sense, and whose activities further magnified the crisis. Marxist criticism, far from providing a way out, merely expressed and exacerbated the crisis. A solution can only lie, argued Bibó in 1942, unfortunately without political effect, in restoring the disturbed harmony of the community – the condition of possibility for a new elite.

Bibó's ideas were taken up by the historian Jenö Szücs, especially in his essay on the 'Three Historical Regions of Europe' (Szücs 1988). Szücs argued that the peculiar features of the region are due not to issues of content – historical events and structural characteristics that rendered the region unique, and therefore restricting understanding to area specialists, rather the form of this development, marked by a long experience of transitoriness. Szücs also studied the long-term historical processes leading to the rise of the nation state and nationalist movements, of special importance being his conceptual history of 'nation' (Szücs 1984: 464–502).

One of the most important books produced beyond the Iron Curtain, *Intellectuals on the Road to Class Power* was again the joint effort of two friends: György Konrád (b. 1933), a writer who worked some time as a social worker, and Iván Szelényi (b. 1938), a sociologist with a background in Weber. They argued that transcending all internal differences, the intellectuals as a whole were about to acquire class dominance in the region. The thesis was just as innovative as requiring courage, and on two counts: it not only went against the official position, bound to provoke repression, but also questioned the self-understanding of the intellectuals. These reactions did not fail to materialise: the authors were arrested, and the book was repeatedly debated with rare passion.

It is clear now that – just as it happened with every forecast done or inspired by Marx – the thesis proved to be wrong. The intellectuals did not gain class power in East Central Europe, and are not 'on way'. Two questions remain to be posed: what was the real content of the insight, or its experiential basis? And in what way was this betrayed by the terminology used to express it?

Concerning the first, in a narrow sense the book was a semi-internal critique of East European Marxism, more particularly the Lukács circle. It recognised the fact that while Marxists fancied themselves to be the only 'authentic' opponents of the system, they were the only ones who could afford to do so. In a broader sense, this situation was shared by many of the educated people. While the first years of Communist power witnessed a radical, and tragic, sweeping of the administrative and intellectual elites, by the late 1960s access to elite positions was channelled through education. Whether through family or school friends, all members of the educated strata became connected and could arrange matters in ways which ordinary mortals could not even dream of.

The insight, involving perceptiveness, soul-searching and courage, was real. Unfortunately, it was formulated in the language of Marxist class theory, which undermined its analytical and prognostic power and sidetracked it.

As often happened in the region, the fates of Konrád and Szelényi were radically separated. After their arrest in 1974, Szelényi accepted to leave the country, emigrating to Australia, while Konrád chose internal exile. Konrád developed his 'anti-politics' thesis, close to Havel and Michnik, while Szelényi became one of the most important contemporary figures of world sociology, building up departments first in Australia and then in the United States (Madison, UCLA, Yale).

The best known theorist of the Lukács school is Agnes Heller (b. 1929). One of her earliest books, *Renaissance Man* (1978), illustrates perfectly both the merits and the shortcomings of the school. It is the product of vast erudition and sharpness of mind. But it is written not as a collection of ideas, rather in an oracular manner of passing sentences, judging ideas and theorists on the basis of general, ideological theses, and using the hardly penetrable idiom of the master. In her later work Heller came to be influenced by Heidegger's ideas, emphasising the conflict in modernity between everyday life and institutional developments, whether driven by capitalism or the state; and the central role played by technology (see Delanty 2005: 276–278 and her contribution to this volume).

Like for many others, Nietzsche was the single most important source of inspiration for Elemér Hankiss (b.1928) as well. Educated in philosophy and writing his dissertation on the reception of Hamlet over the centuries, Hankiss became a sociologist in the 1970s, even pioneering the application of survey research methods. His rise to prominence as a main public intellectual was due to a series of penetrating analyses of everyday life that first appeared in Valóság, the most important intellectual periodical then, and subsequently in bestselling books.

Norbert Elias argued that the European civilizing process was instigated by a situation of 'transition' in which everyday conduct has become problematic and was consequently remodelled. Due to the decivilising impact of Communism these aspects became visible again by the 1970s in Hungary. Going beyond the taken for granted wisdom of both regime and critics, just as Konrád and Szelényi did, Hankiss recognised that the most important and problematic effect of communism lies not at the level of high politics or ideology but in the most trivial everyday practices.

The first such article, 'Deformities in our behaviour culture', appeared in mid-1978, and was immediately striking by its style (in Hankiss 1983: 157–204). It was 'our' behaviour culture and not 'theirs' that was deformed, while in the language of both communists and their opponents it was always 'they' who had problems. Substantively it was an almost 'ethnomethodological' analysis of Communism, making individuals face the all-too familiar but rarely noticed details of everyday life, like the fact that there were hardly any forms left in which one could properly address another person.

A year later Hankiss published 'The Crisis and Absence of Communities' (in Hankiss 1983: 205–240). Though more directly political, the attack was not ideological but sociological, questioning the self-image of the regime. While the Party fancied itself as the promoter of collective life, Hankiss argued that it was rather an instrument of forced individualisation or atomisation. 'Infantilism' (Hankiss 1983: 396–446) was first presented at the Institute of Sociology. It was vehemently denounced by critics as blaming suffering victims and by apologists as untenable slander, and publication in Valóság this time was declined. The paper analysed five plays recently performed in Budapest, each showing adults being treated and eventually behaving as children. Hankiss argued that the hiding away and emptying of values by the 1970s became a commonly shared social game. This is the stage when the regime became autopoietic; when it no longer needed communists to perpetuate itself, constituting a vicious circle.

After 1989, Hankiss became the consensus choice of the new political parties to lead Hungarian Television. The consensus soon evaporated, and he faced difficulties similar to those of Havel. His most recent work focuses on the experience of fear and anxiety and its symbolisation, instigated by the question of whether we are at home in this world, or whether it is an alien place (Hankiss 2001).

Czechoslovakia

Jan Patočka (1907–1977), by far the most important contemporary Czech thinker, was a philosopher. He studied abroad with Husserl, writing his dissertation on the phenomenology of the 'natural world', and also became acquainted with Heidegger. Still, he considered Nietzsche as the 'philosopher of our times' (Tucker 2000: 108), due to his diagnosis of nihilism and prophetic foresight of the world wars. Patočka's interpretation of all three master thinkers, while authoritative, was both different from the course of Western reception and highly original.

After the Second World War, Patočka received a chair and lectured on Socrates, Plato and Aristotle. Demoted to a librarian post by the Communists, Patočka responded by one of his most important essays, 'Negative Platonism', questioning the 'death of metaphysics' thesis (Patočka 1989a), and continued working. His time came again in the mid-1960s, with the 'Prague Spring', ending after the Soviet invasion. This time his response was different. He formulated his ideas programmatically in his 1973 Varna lecture (Patočka 1989b), of which the first, public section reassessed Husserl and Heidegger, while the second, not pronounced part argued for a philosophical attitude of (self-)sacrifice, referring also to Christianity.

This was followed, in quick succession, by his two most important works: *Heretical Essays on the Philosophy of History* (1996) and *Plato and Europe* – a book identified by his translator as 'a rare gift' (Lom, in Patočka 2002: xiii). The first was delivered as a private seminar, part of an underground university, containing the astonishing thesis that Europe as a civilisation grew out of the Platonic idea of the care of the soul. The significance and actuality of the idea is increasingly recognised by some of the most important contemporary thinkers. A pioneering role was played by Michel Foucault, who in his last *Collège de France* lectures identified Patočka as the only philosopher who interpreted the history of European philosophy in the same way as himself (Szakolczai 1994). It was continued by Gadamer, Derrida or Giovanni Reale – not to forget Ricoeur, who helped the first French publication of Patočka's works.

Patočka soon got the chance to put his ideas into practice, becoming one of the three spokesmen of Charta 77, the dissident human rights movement. The first case taken up was defence of a mystic-Christian Czech rock music group Plastic People of the Universe (Tucker 2000: 57) – exactly at the moment when the Sex Pistols inaugurated the 'punk revolution'. Patočka died of cardiac symptoms after exhausting police investigations, in March 1977.

145

Being a philosopher, Patočka's aim was not to say something new and interesting on the actual course of Western history, rather to alter the perspective from which this history is usually viewed. This was done partly by reassessing the importance of the Middle Ages in European history. Much more important, and original, are his ideas concerning the care of the soul.

Patočka adamantly asserts that his is not an idealist thesis. On the contrary, the care of the soul is a practice, and a specifically philosophical practice. Far from escaping the world, it grows out of a certain attitude firmly located in it. Its starts by a recognition or 'wondering', a wake-up to the realisation that the world is in a particular 'situation'; a state of crisis. This crisis is so all-encompassing that it can only be resolved by a turn towards the inside, by strengthening and forming the inner self, or the soul, through a series of philosophical practices (originally called askesis), a type of conversion. These practices, and the resulting strengthening of the soul, shape personalities capable of standing up to the crisis and finding a solution. It is to the formation of individuals through such techniques, in philosophical schools and then through the rise of Christianity, that Patočka traces the origins of Europe. A genuine answer to the contemporary crisis can only be a return to the care of the soul.

The formation of individuals through the care of the soul can only start among a small group of people. This poses the problematic link between elites and democracy – an issue not always understood even by experts on Patočka. The conflict, however, only appears by ignoring that the build-up and maintenance of a democratic society requires a genuine elite.

His position can be glimpsed through his merciless assessment of Czech history. In opposition to mythical accounts, the origins of the modern Czech nation should not be searched in fourteenth-century Hussites or seventeenth-century Protestants, rather in the liberation of serfs that took place in the late eighteenth-century, due to the Enlightenment. This meant that the Czechs, in opposition to their neighbours, including Poles and Hungarians, lacked both nobility and upper bourgeoisie, having only peasantry and petty bourgeoisie.[5] Such lowly origins, while being conducive to a democratic mentality, also explain the pettiness of Czech society, its lack of ability to generate leadership, thus succumbing in 1938, 1948 and 1968 to external and internal conquerors and oppressors, without putting up a fight. Such socio-political shortcomings were undermined by spiritual factors, especially a romanticised misreading of the past, which render nineteenth-century Czech spirituality a fake (Tucker 2000: 108). The only person attempting to rise above provincialism was Masaryk, both as a politician and a thinker, but even he failed to produce a single important idea, partly due to his positivism.

While in the 1990s Patočka was an iconic figure in Czech culture, the reception of these ideas was reserved, as 'Czechs [did] not feel comfortable with their greatest philosopher's derogatory evaluation of them' (Ibid.: 113). Just as it happened in Hungary with Hamvas or Bibó, even with Szelényi and Hankiss, the (post-)Communist intellectual pseudo-elites only went with the ideas of their most important thinkers in so far as it did not require the alteration of their own self-understanding as suffering martyrs deserving more.

For Patočka, as for the entire non-Marxist East Central European dissenting literature, founding human rights was of central concern. Significantly, both Marxist apologues and critics argued that human rights were merely an ideology of capitalism, only to adhere later to a purely legalistic understanding. Patočka dissented from both positions, relying on three of the most influential contemporary thinkers, while presenting a new synthesis.

He started from Husserl's phenomenology and the primacy of consciousness, but instead of bracketing the world, in an *epoché*, as the precondition of phenomenological analysis, he started by recognising the problematicity of the world, and identified as the core of the human person – something Husserl was not able to conceive of – the ability of the soul of self-movement, thus to transcend, exactly when stressed, in an act of (philosophical) conversion, the limitations of time and place and reach out to truth – not simply in the epistemological sense of true knowledge, but more importantly as true life.[6]

Relying on Heidegger, especially his critique of inauthenticity and technology, and the concern with care, but moving beyond the anti-humanism of *Dasein*, Patočka posed the care of the person, or of the soul, at the centre, thus overcoming the 'critique of metaphysics' tradition in which Heidegger's thought was still entrapped. Finally, while recognising the significance of Nietzsche, he argued that the overcoming of nihilism lies not in the overman and his 'will to power', rather in a return, through the practice of the care of the soul leading to metanoia, to the divine in the human being (Patočka 2002: 50, 68).

Václav Havel, as he was ready to admit, was hardly a thinker of Patočka's standing. But he was converted to philosophy on the basis of an encounter with Patočka, in police headquarters, shortly before he died (Tucker 2000: 88, 135), in order to become the leading politician of his country for over a decade, providing a test case for Plato's 'philosopher king'.

Havel's best-known and most important work is 'The Power of the Powerless' (from 1978). The essay is driven by reflections on minute aspects of everyday life under Communism – strikingly close to Hankiss's essays written at the same moment. The powerful starting image is the slogan displayed in a greengrocer's window: 'Workers of the world, unite'. Similar signs pervaded everyday life beyond the Iron Curtain – but Havel suddenly reflected on the significance of such acts, and their effects. Continuing Patočka's reflections on 'living in truth', Havel put the emphasis on the ethical foundations and implications of everyday acts.

The assessment of Havel's presidency cannot be the task of this chapter. One can conjecture, however, that his most evident failings might be connected to a stronger adherence to a Heideggerian position, without Patočka's balance and wisdom.

Poland

Given Poland's particular history, Marxism had an effect quite remarkably different from that in Hungary, and partly, in Czechoslovakia. 'Social theory' in post-Second World War Poland was in a continuous tension between the dominant Marxist project and the concern for national independence. As Poland was deprived from independent statehood between the late eighteenth-century and 1918 – the crucial period of the formation of nation-states and civil societies in the West – the Polish term for 'society' (społeczeństwo) generated in opposition to foreign domination, implying that concern for society has been almost equivalent to confessing identity with the nation. Adam Michnik, the influential dissident and social thinker, described his fundamental identity as that of a Polish patriot because he wanted to identify with something that is weak, beaten and humiliated. Therefore, społeczeństwo can be regarded primarily not as a sociological but a political concept. This identification with society as the bearer of cultural autonomy and political sovereignty favoured a focus on collective and macrosociological concerns at the expense of individualist or psychological approaches.

The evolution of social thought has been tightly linked to several political crises between 1956 and the early 1980s. After the workers' revolt in Poznań in October 1956, the initially radical Marxist critique assumed important national overtones, attempting to reconcile a socialist project with the 'national road to socialism'. The wave of workers' protests in March

1968 was followed by a nationalist anti-Zionist campaign, which would lead to the emigration of two of the most distinguished thinkers of the humanist Marxist tradition, the philosopher Leszek Kołakowski (born 1927), and the sociologist Zygmunt Bauman (born 1925). Inspired by Kant and Sartre, Kołakowski's work especially after 1956 developed an increasingly disenchanted critical Marxism that claimed the moral responsibility of the individual against any determinism. After criticising the party's policies he was expelled from the Communist party in 1966. His major three-volume work on the main currents of Marxism (1978) presented an authoritative intellectual history of Marxism whose concluding suggestion was that Marxism neither interprets nor changes the world but has become a repertoire of slogans for the organisation of various interests. Unlike the standard discussion of 'good' and 'bad' Marxism, Kołakowski's 'creativity in dogma', as Milovan Djilas put it, did not remain 'radical' but inspired the younger generation of the leftist intelligentsia to seek an alliance between their social criticism and the guarantor of national consciousness, the Catholic Church. His article 'Theses on Hope and Hopelessness' (1971), published in the exile literary review *Kultura* just after the bloody suppression of the workers' strikes in Szczecin in December 1970, marked the fundamental split with attempts to reform the party from inside. This essay embraced the idea that only ceaseless, peaceful pressure on the basis of self-organised associations could diminish Poland's dependence on the Soviet Union. In his essay 'A New Evolutionism' (1976) (Michnik 1985), Adam Michnik (born 1946) summarised this practical social philosophy in the claim that the desired democratic socialism should not be primarily based on an institutional and legal structure but should emanate from real communities of freed individuals. In practical terms, this radical appeal for building independent and a-political enclaves from below led to the foundation of the Committee for the Defense of Workers (KOR) in 1976 that became the crucial institutional link where leftist intellectuals engaged with legal protection of workers. The election of Karol Wojtyła to Pope John Paul II in 1978 raised the spirits of countless Poles and his first visit to the country in June 1979 became the dress rehearsal for society's revival.

Unlike the 'ethical individualism' in Czechoslovakia or the radical detachment from society propagated by 'anti-politics' in Hungary, the emergence of an independent, self-organising trade union movement Solidarność in summer 1980 came to constitute a 'second Poland' where the sheer size of almost ten million Poles provided a unique platform for affirming the subjectivization of the Polish nation (podmiotowość społeczeństwa). On the one hand, the political impact of such a broad movement prompted the definition of a self-limiting revolution (samoograniczająca się rewolucja). On the other hand, the attempt to introduce the distinct aspect of civil society (społeczeństwo obywatelskie) was burdened with the 'second reality' of an anticipated condition of full freedom. The self-defence of społeczeństwo from the communist system rested upon the separation of the spheres of 'us' against 'them', thus replacing the collective symbolism of Marxism with the collective symbolism of a utopian, national romanticism. Solidarność was less a community of similar-minded citizens but rather a collective subject that pre-existed individual choices and whose major point of attraction was a consciousness of belonging.

The strongest impulses for theorising the paradoxes of the Polish condition between the search for freedom and the necessity of belonging to the nation came from a group of writers in exile, all attached to its unique mouthpiece *Kultura*, a monthly literary review published in Paris by Jerzy Giedroyc since 1947. In his essay *The Captive Mind* (Zniewolony Umysł 1953) the Noble-prize winner Czesław Miłosz (1911–2004) denounced how communism controlled the individual's mind and thus not only generated public acquiescence with the system but a profound schizophrenia in public and intellectual life. The most consistent body of a social theory informed by existential–experiential thought can be found in the work of Witold Gombrowicz (1904–1969), a writer, essayist, and philosopher who left Poland right before the outbreak of the Second World War for Argentina before coming to France in the early 1950s. His philosophical anthropology was initially developed in novels such as *Ferdydurke*, *Trans-Atlantyk*, or *Kosmos*, and most systematically pursued in his extensive diary that spans the period from 1953 to 1969. His short course on philosophy, written in 1969, provided a re-interpretation of philosophy, from Kant to Nietzsche and Heidegger, from a stance of a critique of existentialism. Similar to Miłosz's analysis of the violation of human minds by communism, Gombrowicz's social thought denounced the subjective dependence of the Polish nation on a 'second reality'. Liberating man from the yoke of the second reality meant for Gombrowicz to substitute the we-identity of the national form by countless identities generated in historically concrete life-experiences.

As a self-proclaimed 'grand-grand-nephew' of Kierkegaard, Gombrowicz aimed to liberate the historical process from the dependence on constructions of objective theories such as Marxism, psychoanalysis, or existentialism. All three theoretical traditions contrive a mechanisation of existence, where the formation of reality through consciousness appears as a theoretical construction from a distant viewpoint 'outside' the concrete experiential conditions of humans. Psychoanalysis treated humans as objects, while the collective god propagated by Marxism only reinforced the collective idolatry of the Polish nation. Aware of the condition of man as a sufferer, victim, martyr, and slave, Gombrowicz was also sceptical of individual consciousness as presented by existentialists. Even the existentialism of Albert Camus had objectivising tendencies as it postulated that a high degree of self-consciousness would make experience more authentic. Existentialism, therefore, turns existence into an essence, which lies beyond experienced historical existence. Against this essentialism, Gombrowicz's view of the riddle of reality accepted the tension that concrete experiences produce.

A further central concern was to elucidate the reasons for Poland's formlessness and the problems of identity-formation attached to it. He understood the condition of his times as an existential crisis rooted in the social and cultural phenomena of immaturity and infantilism. Deprived of certainties such as God or moral and legal boundaries, collective goals such as fatherland, race, or the proletariat become possible. Immaturity also generated the narrow-minded provincial political culture that placed the nation as the highest value. Poland's historical position as a transitional country between East and West suggested backwardness, disintegration and an 'inferiority complex' as essential characteristics of the Polish national tradition. The mental dependence of the Poles on their weak and deformed past reinforced the identification of a people with its condition of gradual degradation. Gombrowicz's social criticism aimed to replace the pathological genetic burden of the 'fatherland' by the 'sonland'. It sought to arrive at a complete detachment and distance from the Polish style of collective idolatry of the nation, which communist ideology perverted and the Catholic Church did too little to overcome. Yet, while Gombrowicz rejected the stereotypical, quasi-totalitarian anti-communism professed by the Catholic Church, he much agreed with its acute awareness of evil in man, in the fear of an excessive dynamism of humanity. Despite the lack of distance between Polish Catholicism and the nation as a collective value, the Church's support for Solidarność put the human being into the centre of attention. After the proclamation of martial law in 1981, small and de-centralised communities were maintained under the shelter of the Church, whose appeal to continue an ethically truthful way of life proved decisive for keeping the spirit and memory of Solidarność alive.

The revolution of 1989 introduced a new type of formlessness in Polish politics and society, which put the self-construction of the subject at the centre of attention. Piotr

Sztompka (born 1944) has conceived of the transformations as a civilizational break, which shattered not only institutional realities but also produced an epistemological anarchy reversing values, meanings, and traditions. His sociological theory of trust (1999) postulates the need for a culture of trust where ethical principles and community values underlie civilisational competence as the essential cultural resource for political participation, self-government, and the development of a democratic society.

The cultural foundations of forms of power are also central to Zygmunt Bauman's work, whose 'universal' appeal has been tightly related to distinctive 'Polish' elements such as its sociological tradition or the memories of his wife Janina as a survivor of the Holocaust. While the ideological and practical constraints in the Poland of the 1950s put Polish sociology 'behind' Europe, it was also 'ahead' of Europe. Its relative isolation taught Bauman to focus on problems to solve rather than to profess reverence of canonical texts or sociological schools of thought. His life as a refugee scholar after his forced emigration in 1968 had its problems in terms of academic career but provided also a degree of freedom to draw from any inspiring source that he would not trade off for the comforts of belonging.

Bauman's focus on culture sees human life as both being structured by society and structuring it. In his view, sociology has no other sense and utility than that of an ongoing commentary on human 'lived experience', as transient and obsessively self-updating as that experienced itself. Despite his criticism of positivist approaches in the 'Durksonian tradition' and the stress on the cultural basis of action, however, Bauman did not abandon the Marxist tradition that focused on the constraints imposed by society. As a mediator between East and West, Bauman saw clearly that the revolutions of 1989 came down to the dissolution of the West's own past, in the ultimate failure of the Enlightenment tradition of constructing a perfect, rationally ordered 'total' system of society.

Bauman's concern with modern forms of power rests upon the insight that the rationalizing spirit of the Enlightenment was culturally creative of mechanisms of disciplinary power that harbored potentially self-destructive consequences. In *Modernity and the Holocaust* (1989) Bauman linked the civilising power of the modern state to the 'decivilizing' techniques, the split consciousness, and the efficiency necessary for the mass extermination of Jews. More recent works such as In *Search of Politics* (1999) and *Liquid Modernity* (2000) address central questions such as how the 'privatization' of public man and the dissolution of the classical space and place of politics have affected the possibility of agency in politics by expropriating citizens of their powers. Against the ideological 'totality', such as in communism and fascism, but also rejecting the sober rationality of communitarianism, Bauman's cultural approach pleads for the creation of community in the continuous dialogue of a republican setting.

Conclusion: an East-Central European tradition?

During the Cold War the East-Central European countries were significantly cut off from the rest of the world, while being intellectually isolated even from each other. Yet, in spite of everything, or rather exactly due to this fact, one can recognise elements of a distinct tradition that draws both on earlier achievements and later experiences; a tradition that, while relying on some of the same sources as contemporary Western thought, focusing on existentialism (especially Nietzsche and Heidegger) and phenomenology (especially Husserl), nevertheless takes a direction radically different from existentialism, post-modernism or post-structuralism. East European thinkers had a passionate interest in the course and direction of world history, especially the question of Europe. While recognising the significance of Renaissance humanism or the Enlightenment, they dissented from mainstream Western social theory by the positive evaluation assigned to the medieval period, and especially by questioning the tenability of the entire 'critique of metaphysics' tradition. While Nietzsche, Heidegger and Derrida each tried to outdo each other by further radicalising this critique, accusing their predecessors of still falling pray to metaphysics, the best East-Central European thinkers found a way back to the Western metaphysical tradition, especially to Plato.

The difference also extended to the assessment of phenomenology. In the West, Husserlian phenomenology was interpreted fundamentally in an epistemological sense. In the Eastern side of Central Europe, it was read more in an ethical key, in an attempt to discover the ethical foundations of politics in the human person. The close involvement with political events and the reliance on personal experiences explain two further characteristics: the importance attributed to everyday life, and – as another radical difference from Western social theory – the recognition of the crucial role genuine elites play, and should play, in society, in opposition to a generalised critique of 'elitism' that for them certainly would have seemed deeply nihilist.

Notes

1 By East Central Europe the chapter means Hungary, Poland and the former Czechoslovakia (while the Czech Republic and Slovakia are separate states today, they were joined in much of the twentieth-century). In the Conclusion we'll return to the question of whether one can talk about an East Central European 'tradition' in social theory.
2 Zygmunt Bauman is the exception confirming the rule.
3 On the importance of Radin, see also Bauman (1990).
4 In German *unheimlich*, meaning both uncanny and homeless, capturing Hermes being at home in the homelessness.
5 Patočka compares this to Belgium, the Baltic States and the Balkans; one could easily add Ireland.
6 These ideas are strikingly close to the philosophical writings of Karol Wojtyla. For details, see Szakolczai (forthcoming).

References

Bauman, Z. (1989) *Modernity and the Holocaust,* Cambridge: Cambridge University Press.
Bauman, Z. (1990) *Modernity and Ambivalence,* Cambridge: Polity.
Bauman, Z. (1999) *In Search of Politics,* Cambridge: Polity.
Bauman, Z. (2000) *Liquid Modernity,* Cambridge, Polity.
Bauman, Z. and K. Tester (2001) *Conversations with Zygmunt Bauman,* Cambridge: Polity.
Bibó, I. (1986) *Válogatott tanulmányok* (Selected essays), 3 volumes, Budapest: Magvető.
Delanty, G. (2005) 'Modernity and Postmodernity: Part II', in A. Harrington (ed.) *Modern Social Theory,* Oxford: Oxford University Press.
Gombrowicz, W. (1969/1982) *Dzieła zebrane,* 11 vols, Paris: Instytut Literacki.
Gombrowicz, W. (1995) *Cours de philosophie en six heures un quart,* Paris: Rivages.
Hamvas, B. (1992) *Patmosz,* 2 volumes, Szombathely: Életünk.
Hamvas, B. (1995/6) *Scientia Sacra,* 3 volumes, Szentendre: Medio.
Hankiss, E. (1983) *Társadalmi csapdák/Diagnózisok* (Social Traps/ Diagnoses), Budapest: Magvető.
Hankiss, E. (2001) *Fear and Symbols,* Budapest: CEU Press.
Havel, V. (1985) 'The Power of the Powerless', in J. Keane (ed.) *The Power of the Powerless: Citizens Against the State in Central Eastern Europe,* London: Hutchinson.
Heller, A. (1978) *Renaissance Man,* London: Routledge and Kegan Paul.
Horváth, Á. (1998) 'Tricking into the Position of the Outcast', *Political Psychology* 19: 331–347.
Kerényi, K. (1976) *Dionysos: Archetypal Image of Indestructible Life,* Princeton: Princeton University Press.
Kerényi, K. (1983 [1937]) *Apollo: The Wind, the Spirit, and the God: Four Studies,* Woodstock, CT: Spring.

Kerényi, K. (1984) *Hermész, a lélekvezetö* (Hermes, the guide of souls), Budapest: Európa.

Kołakowski, L. (1971) 'Theses on Hope and Hopelessness', *Survey*, 17(3), 35–52.

Kołakowski, L. (1978) *Main Currents of Marxism: its Origins, Growth, and Dissolution* (translated from the Polish by P. S. Falla), Oxford: Oxford University Press.

Konrád, G. and I. Szelényi (1979) *The Intellectuals on the Road to Class Power*, New York: Harcourt.

Mann, T. and K. Kerényi (1975) *Mythology and Humanism: The Correspondence of Thomas Mann and Karl Kerényi*, New York: Cornell University Press.

Michnik, A. (1983) 'Nowy ewolucjonizm' in *Ugoda, praca organiczna, myśl zaprzeczna*, Biblioteka Krytyki: Warszawa, 140–148.

Michnik, A. (1985) 'A New Evolutionism' in A. Michnik, *Letters from Prison and Other Essays*, Berkeley, CA: University of California Press, pp 41–63.

Miłosz, C.(1953) *The Captive Mind,* New York: Alfred A. Knopf.

Patočka, J. (1989a) 'Negative Platonism', in E. Kohák (ed.), *Jan Patocka: Philosophy and Selected Writings*, Chicago: University of Chicago Press.

Patočka, J. (1989b) 'The Dangers of Technicization in Science according to E. Husserl and the Essence of Technology as Danger according to M. Heidegger', in E. Kohák (ed.), *Jan Patocka: Philosophy and Selected Writings*, Chicago: University of Press.

Patočka, J. (1996) *Heretical Essays on the Philosophy of History*, La Salle, IL: Open Court.

Patočka, J. (2002) *Plato and Europe*, Stanford: Stanford University Press.

Radin, P. (1956) *The Trickster: A Study in American Indian Mythology*, with commentary by K. Kerényi and C. G. Jung, New York: Schocken.

Szakolczai, À. (1994) 'Thinking Beyond the East West Divide: Foucault, Patočka, and the Care of the Self', *Social Research*, 61(2), 297–323.

Szakolczai, À. (2005) 'Between Tradition and Christianity: The Axial Age in the Perspective of Béla Hamvas', in J. P Arnason, S. N. Eisenstadt and B. Wittrock (eds) *Axial Civilizations and World History*, Leiden: Brill.

Szakolczai, À. (forthcoming) 'Moving Beyond the Sophists: Intellectuals in East Central Europe and the Return of Transcendence', *European Journal of Social Theory*.

Sztompka, P. (1999) *Trust: A Sociological Theory*, Cambridge: Cambridge University Press.

Szücs, J. (1984) *Nemzet és történelem* (Nation and history), Budapest: Gondolat.

Szücs, J. (1988) 'Three Historical Regions of Europe', in J. Keane (ed.) *Civil Society and the State*, London: Verso.

Tucker, A. (2000) *The Philosophy and Politics of Czech Dissidence from Patočka to Havel*, Pittsburgh: University of Pittsburgh Press.

Wydra, H. (2004) 'Naród polski między mitem a rzeczywistoscią. Trans-Atlantyk Gombrowicza i psychologia polityczna Polaków', in Marek Zybura (ed.), *Patagonczyk w Berlinie. Witold Gombrowicz w oczach krytyki niemieckej* (Cracow: TAWPN: Universitas, 2004), 451–475.

12

Contemporary Russian social theory

Alexander Dmitriev

The question as to what exactly Russian social theory represents immediately raises a multitude of problems, concerning both methodology and its object. What exactly is so specific about the scholarly attempts at social theory undertaken in Russia throughout the twentieth-century? In how far does this local context allow us to speak of an independent and significant variant of modern social theory that stands out against the backdrop of social theory at large? Or are all these theories simply mechanical adaptations of theoretical constructs from the outside (from Europe or the West), refitted to match the specificity of Russian social condition and its local intellectual tradition?

The evolution of social theory is usually separated into two main 'waves'. The first of these is connected to the ascendance of a general social–philosophical orientation in thinking, while the second is conditioned by the formation of the welfare state and the growing expert–consultant function of predominantly empirical social sciences (Wittrock *et al.* 1989: 35-38). The first of these 'waves' can be dated to the late nineteenth-/early twentieth-century, while the second 'wave' rose during the 1950s–1970s. In terms of chronology, in Russia these phases roughly coincide with similar developments in Western Europe. However, the political pressure exerted by either autocratic or state-socialist regimes supplied Russian social theory with a special 'compensatory' and 'totalistic' character. In Russia and the USSR, both the process of societal development in and of itself, and the parallel 'scientific rationalization of the social' (Raphael 1996) did not take place by virtue of the immanent developments in social and economic spheres, but rather through state-intervention. These conditions caused the special concentration of Russian social theory on the themes of power, the state, etc. (Vucinich 1976). In conceptualizing the *problematique* of modernity, Russian social thought from the mid-nineteenth century onward did not only touch upon questions such as the reforms of Peter the Great, the influence of the French revolution or the 'imported' nature of Russia's educational institution. Beginning with Chaadaev and the controversies between Westernizers and Slavophiles (*zapadniki* and *slavyanofili*), its attention was primarily devoted to the question of the relationship between Russia's singular, distinctive identity and the universalism of the West (Schein 1977; Walicki 1975). This dilemma had a decisive influence on the further development of Russian social theory in the century to come. (For more on the roots of the identity and social role of the Russian intelligentsia, see Confino 1972; Clowes *et al.* 1991).

153

The origins of Russian social theory

The development of sociology in Russia was intimately connected to both the social modernization of the Russian Empire and the rise of liberal and radical political movements. As many scholars and publicists of the time acknowledged, the subject of pre-revolutionary sociology was not to be found in the academic field, but rather in the 'most advanced' and most active stratum of the Russian intelligentsia (see also positivist and critically revised Spencerian theoretical framework of such populist thinkers as Nicolaj Mikhailovsky and Peter Lavrov). This resulted in a deep but indirect ideological connection between sociology and the technologies of directed social transformation, and, in the final analysis, with socialism, a connection which was also characteristic of the situation in Western Europe during the first half of the twentieth-century. (For more on the connection of economic scholarship with social theory and revolutionary movements see Stanziani 1998.) Before 1917, sociology remained on the periphery of the academic world (as it did in Germany, in contrast to the USA or France, where academic interest in sociology was particularly high). Russian universities had no special departments or institutes of sociology; the discipline was little more than the incidental, occasional occupation of historians, jurists, economists and, to a lesser degree, of philosophers. It was only with the development of non-governmental institutions of higher education after 1905 that sociology in Russia gained an independent albeit peripheral academic status (Nowikow 1988; complete bibliography for Russian sociology and translations before 1917 see: Golosenko 1995, 1997).

Another landmark in the formation of political sociology can be found in the famous work *Democracy and Political Parties* (1898) by M. Ya. Ostrogorksy, which was close to the analysis of oligarchical trends in modern democracy, as outlined outlined by Michels and Weber. Similarily Maxim Kovalevsky's comparative-historical work on the history of legal institutions in Russia, or the economic history of medieval Europe pointed towards the real absence and the future question of the mechanism of representative democracy, which only began to emerge after 1905. The generation of social scientists to follow Kovalevsky and De Roberti, such as the Peter Struve-circle and the 'Westernizers' of the 1910s, was no longer oriented towards organistic sociology and positivism (of the French or English varieties), but was far more influenced by German scholarship, primarily in Sombart and Simmel, with its focus on philosophical-methodological problems, (Nowikow 1988: 179–182). In this sense, the work of two jurists close to Neo-Kantian methodology, Lev Petrazhitsky and Bogdan Kistiakovsky, is especially significant. The former, was a proponent of the psychological interpretation of norms, while the latter, consistently opposed 'organistic' sociology. The positivist approach was developed in early works of Pitirim Sorokin, who was disciple and personal secretary of Maxim Kowalewsky. His political activism and firmly anti-Bolshevik position led to his banishment from Soviet Russia in 1922 along with the philosophers of the 'Vekhi' group – Struve, Frank, Berdyaev.

While the 'Russian school' of sociology was already a term as early as the late nineteenth-century, the views of Lenin are often understood as synonymous to 'Russian Marxism'. In *What is to be done?* (1902) (Christman, ed. 1987), Lenin was able to formulate his main innovation to Marxism by outlining a conception of the party as an organization of professional revolutionaries. As a socialist intelligentsia, its goal was to 'bring socialist consciousness' to the working class from the outside. *What is to be done?* still figures as one of the key works on the sociology of political movements to this very day. On the whole, the complex of Lenin's ideas relied upon Engels' version of Marxism and the 'orthodox' faction of the Second International: however, its most important political innovations consisted in its heightened attention towards the peasantry on the strength of conditions in Russia, as well as a growing interest in the philosophy of Hegel as a direct predecessor to Marx, although this interest arises a little later in Lenin's work during the 1910s.

For Russian social theory, the revolution and the ensuing civil war were extreme experiences. In particular, inequality became an important theme of scholarly tractates and political publicism (by the positivist radical Sorokin or the idealist Berdyaev, for an example), often openly contradicting the utopian hopes of the triumphant Bolsheviks (Burbank 1986). At the same time, Sergei Bulgakov's *Philosophy of Household* (1912) served as a résumé of sorts for the social philosphy of Russian neo-idealism (Evtukhov 1997). Notwithstanding the work's similarity to the ideas of H. Freyer, J. Habermas, and the philosophical efforts of the late Parsons (noted by Russian commentators of the early 1990s), its attempt to rethink the pre-conditions of political economy from the vantage point of Solovyov's idealism proved fruitless in the final analysis and found no continuation, neither in Bulgakov's later work, nor in Russian social philosophy at large. The programme of the Vekhi-group in relation to the revolution was sketched out by Pyotr Struve in his editorial preface to the new anthology *Iz glubiny* (*From the Depths*) (1918). It underlined the author's 'conviction that the *positive* principle of social life is *rooted* in deep religious consciousness and that any interruption of this root-work is a disastrous crime. They feel that this interruption as an incomparable moral-political defeat facing our people and our state' (Vekhi 1991: 209).

The primacy of the religious principle could also be felt in books by Semyon Frank such as *A Sketch of Social Science* (1922) and even more so in *Spiritual Foundations of Society* (1930). In this sense, they are largely irrelevant to the development of social theory, since they were primarily concerned with examining interpersonal and social-hierarchical relationships through the idea of serving God against the backdrop of a 'free theocracy' (Boobbyer 1995). (On the 'self-orientalisation' of Russian thought in exile see: Williams 1972: 272). The evolution of Berdyaev was more complex in comparison, leading from the prophecy of the new 'middle ages' during the mid-1920s to the recognition of the immediate relevance of the social question for the modern world and the necessity for a positive rethinking of the social shock to philosophical-religious thinking during the 1930s–1940s. The activity of the journal *Novy Grad* was very significant in developing a interpretation of the new reality that arose during the revolution. Published in Paris during the 1930s, it too attempted to respond to the socio-political challenges of modernity (Raeff 1985). Aside from Berdyaev, the historian and philosopher Georgij Fedotov played an crucial role as one of the journal's most important contributors. In comparison, the sociologist Nikolai Timashev took a far more conservative-liberal position with regard to the social transformations of the 1920s to 1940s. In 1946, he was able to formulate his idea of the 'Great Return' in a book of the same name, through which he described the gradual and inexplicit return of the Soviet Union's elites and rank-and-file to the norms, values, and structures of social relations characteristic for pre-revolutionary Russia.

Notwithstanding their indisputable ideological influence and their parallels to the main tendencies of Western thinking during the crisis of positivist social theory, studies undertaken by former so-called 'legal Marxists' such as Pyotr Struve, Semyon Frank, Sergei Bulgakov or Nikolai Berdiaev, were not able constitute a representation of the Russian idea as such, as both these writers themselves as well as many subsequent commentators have noted. Instead, it remained yet another variant of Russian thinking during the first half of the twentieth-century (cf. Read 1979).

The émigré tradition and the emergence of Eurasianism

Noteworthy is that the Western sources of these ideologized oppositions – Russian thought versus Western subjectivism – were connected to romanticism and were analysed by a number of émigré authors, including Alexander Koyre, Dmitri Chizhevskij and Alexander von Schelting, whose work also touched upon the re-interpretation of this tradition (Koyre 1929; Čyževs'kyj 1934; Schelting 1948). However, most of its characteristics – the surmounting of 'gnoseological' aspirations, the exit beyond the boundaries of positivism and Neo-Kantianism, the search for and combination of ontological principles and historicism – are obviously hardly original or specific specialities of Russian thinking as such. They are rather characteristic of a general intellectual turn, experienced by the philosophers and theorists of the humanities in both Europe and America at the time. It was hardly coincidental that this turn was connected to the interpretation of the catastrophic social transformations that took place in the period of 1914 to 1923. In my view, it is the recognition and reflection of the link between the epistemological turn and social upheaval that supplies social theory with its 'contemporary' status. Both the Russian revolution and the later rise of Stalinism and Nazism in the 1930 are extremely important aspects of this general social upheaval (Kotkin 2001). It is highly revealing to compare the intellectual legacies of two waves of emigration of equal strength in the social sciences and humanities, namely the exodus of intellectuals from the Russia of the 1920s and Germany of the 1930s: why did the former remain a fact of the intellectual history of one country, while the latter formed some of the most important identificatory images for all contemporary social theory? The leading thinkers of Russian emigration attempted to explain the painful tensions and contradiction of modern society from the outside vantage of a cultural, religious or national ideal that was incapable of taking shape in reality. In contrast, German thinkers used the immanent logic and the perspectives of their concrete socio-historical reality as a point of departure, be it through the analysis of contemporary mass-society, through the pessimistic critique of the 'cultural industry' or through the search for a synthesis of liberal values and collectivist principles (see, for example, Srubar 1988).

It is hardly coincidental that Marxism underwent a transformation in the 1920s: what was once a positivist approach to the development of nature and society became an activist philosophy of the revolutionary proletariat, geared towards lifting the inborn alienation of the human being. This change fits well into the overall shifts taking place at the time. One central event that determined this metamorphosis of Marxism was the appearance of Georg Lukács's *History and Class Consciousness* (1971 [1923]). Yet all of these shifts also had their Russian dimension. The revolution supplied social thought with new possibilities, as it took on a new role in culture and avant-garde aesthetics. In my view, it would be very fruitful to compare the turns towards sociality of the so-called Budapest circle around Lukács (Adalbert Fogarasi, Karl Mannheim, Arnold Hauser) and the so-called 'Nevel School', which decisively formed the philosophy of Bakhtin and the theoreticians of his circle (Matvej Kagan, Valentin Voloshinov, Pavel Medvedev, Lev Pumpyanskij) during the 1910s and 1920s (Nikolaev 1991; Gluck 1985).

The obvious Marxist and less obvious phenomenological orientation of Bakthin's thinking during the second half of the 1920s was built on an unarguably Neo-Kantian foundation. Both Georg Simmel's notion of the conflict of modern culture and Max Scheler's material value-ethics also exerted an immediate influence on Bakhtin's early writings, which were dedicated to the 'philosophy of the act' and the relationship of the author with the hero in the world of aesthetics. During the 1920s, both the spiritualized messianic thinking of Hermann Cohen and Max Scheler's philosophy of love sketched out the socio-philosophical interests of Bakhtin and his friend Matvej Kagan, who had studied under Cohen in Germany (Coates 1998). At the same, two other authors extremely close to Bakhtin, namely Volshinov and Medvedev, demonstrate a substantially different trajectory from Neo-Kantian 'theoretism' to concreteness, to speak in the language of the young Bakhtin. (One should not forget that it has yet to become clear in how far Bakthin participated in the writing of 'Freudianism', *The Formal Method in Literary Scholarship* (Bakhtin and Medvedev 1991), and *Marxism and the Philosophy of Language* (Voloshinov 1986 [1929]). In underlining of multiplicity of social accents in discourse, considering ideological projections as refractions (and not simply reflections) of social life, and criticizing both the 'abstract objectivism' of Saussure and the 'material aesthetics' of Russian formalism, these rather Marxist works from the Bakhtin circle build a connecting bridge from Bakhtin's early personological aesthetics to his work on the theory of novel in the 1930s (Brandist 2002).

Bakhtin's extremely broad trans-historical (synchronistic) interpretation of the novel's essential quality, its *romannost'*, within the framework of the typology of artistic culture contained an implicit controversy with Lukács' canonized, diachronic vision of the novel as a bourgeois epic, exclusively limited to the age of modernity. Yet still, this collision between two theorists and their historically specific and essentialist views of art takes place on common ground: both interpretations understand culture as the organon of social communication, seen through the problem-prism of creativity, subjectivity, and modernity (Tihanov 2000b: 65–111). In this way, Russian debates on the social determination of art and culture – both in Soviet Russia and in the émigré diaspora – displayed close connections to a broad field of socio-philosophical discourse, most of which took place in the German language. The evolution of Karl Mannheim, for an instance, during the 1920s–1930s is quite close to that of Bakthin, in that it too leads from idealist-philosophical aesthetics to a sociology of culture (Morrow 1998).

Eurasianism was another extremely important current of émigré thought. In contrast to the Vekhi-group, the Eurasianists attempted to consider the lessons of the October Revolution and the First World War. In doing so, they closely followed the conclusions of the nineteenth-century Russian philosopher Nikolai Danilevsky, as presented in his *Russia and Europe*, which narrated the incommensurability of different national cultures. Beginning in the 1920s, the linguist Nikolai Trubetskoy and his supporters asserted the developmental originality of Russian culture, citing the simultaneous presence of both European and Asian-'Turanic' elements (Schlacks 1997). The Eurasianists – aside from Trubetskoy, these included the geographer Peter Savitskiy, who had studied under Struve, and the musicologist Peter Suvchinsky – did not only see the Russian revolution as the necessary conclusion of the 'false' Petersburg period in Russian history, but also as the assertion of a spontaneous folk-principle, albeit in a distorted, atheistic form (Riasanovsky 1967). They assumed that the base for the ideal social system for Russia would be constituted by the principle of the (Russian-Orthodox) church. This 'ideocracy', as they called it, stood in stark contrast to the corrupted and selfish regimes of Western democracy that dominated their time. However, it would be a mistake to consider the early structuralist ideas of Jakobson and even Trubetskoy as a pure projection of Eurasianism on to the scholarly plane. Instead, we are actually dealing with a rather varied spectrum of attempts at the ideological legitimation – or reflexive meta-description – of scholarly innovations (Gasparov 1987). The key concept of structure was considered as the predetermined teleological totality of deep interrelation, and not as the hypothetical principle for explaining this or that collection of facts, which the Russian structuralists of the Prague Circle actually saw as a deficiency in the structuralism of the Saussurian school of linguistics (Toman 1995).

The comparative analysis of Eurasianism and the German conservative revolution as anti-democratic ideological formations shows how far both intellectual currents were based on a programme of negating contemporary Western individualism, liberalism and democracy (Luks 1998). In this sense, Peter Savitsky's approach corresponded to basic geopolitical assumptions of Ratzel and Haushofer; Nikolai Alekseyev's philosophy of law had a great deal in common with the views of Carl Schmitt and Hans Freyer, especially in terms of its negation of Kantian normativism and its emphasis on the category of 'the people'; Trubetskoy's ideocracy is reminiscent of Othmar Spann's notion of the *Stände-Ordnung* ('order of estates'). However, it was Leo Karsavin who most completely personified the continuity between between pre-revolutionary neo-idealism and Eurasianism. Karsavin was a talented historian and medievalist who already became a religious philosopher during the early 1920s. His philosophical writings formulate an aggregate version of the the Slavophile notion of *sobornost'* as the special spiritual–political community principle of the Russian people's social life, which included an understanding of the nation as a 'collective personality'. By the late 1920s, Karsavin had become one of the leaders of the Eurasianist movement's left wing, which only existed rather briefly. In the pages of *Eurasia*, the periodic organ of this faction, he polemicized with the young emigrant Aleksandr Kozhevnikov (Kojève), who wrote his dissertation on the religious philosophy of Solovyev at Heidelberg. Although the Russian sources of Kojève's social philosophy remain rather obscure until today (Aufrett 1990: 129–155), his direct projections of the idea of the end of the history onto the political reality of the late 1930s, and the arbitrary rapprochement of the figures of Napoleon and Stalin (which so shocked Walter Benjamin) clearly testify to the stability of his Left-Eurasian world view, which remained intact well into the 1950 and 1960s (Tihanov 2002).

In examining the resonances between ideas of Eurasianism and the thinking of Bakhtin, Galin Tihanov turns his attention to the penetrating aspirations and hegemonial features of Bakhtin's novelistic discourse. (Notwithstanding characteristic similarities, it must be said that Bakhtin's ideas were far more moderate in comparison to the imperial cultural ambitions of Eurasianism.) Tihanov also argues that the well-known notion of the chronotope displays significant analogies with Savitsky's notion of *mestorazvitie* ('development-place'), which he applies to the principles of cultural evolution in a similar way (Tihanov 2000a). Nevertheless, if we examine the disputes of the 1920–1930s in retrospect, it becomes obvious that – despite all their apparent differences – the Formalists, Jakobson, and Bakhtin all found themselves on one side of an ideological boundary as far as the *problematique* of secularization and modernity were concerned, while the Vekhi-group and the Eurasianists were on the other.

In Soviet Russia, the two thinkers to come closest to the ideological and sociopolitical doctrine of Eurasianism were the philosopher-priest Pavel Florenskij and Aleksey Losev, an important historian of antique thought and original philosopher. Losev's synthesis of neo-Platonism and phenomenology and the rigid non-acceptance of Kantianism in Florensky's thought make it possible to locate their explorations in the same current of 'right-wing' ontologizations of the epistemological turn described above. The similarities in their ideological doctrines – such as clerical anti-Semitism and sympathy towards anti-liberal and theocratic constructions in the spirit of Plato's 'State' – make these two thinkers rather vivid representatives of those 'new Middle Ages' that Berdayev had written about in the 1920s (though not in their atheistic-Bolshevik version) (cf. Agursky 1987; Hagemeister 2001). Florensky died in a Stalinist Gulag in the 1930s. Losev, having returned from banishment, was to become the informal teacher of a number of nonconformist Moscow intellectuals, among whom the famous historian and Byzantologist Sergey Averintsev, the historian of sociology Yuri Davydov and the philosopher Victor Bibikhin are most noteworthy.

The legacy of academic Marxism

Until the late 1920s, a great many empirical social studies were carried out in the USSR, although the number of academic institutions for the reproduction of sociology as a scholarly discipline had actually decreased (Tschernych 1995). The different attempts to conduct research in the Marxist spirit all also took place under the banner of a general turn away from positivism and Kantianism to a Hegelian historicism, socially sharpened and honed by Marx. This 'academic Marxism' of the 1920s was historically represented by Aleksandr Neusykhin's subtle interpretations of Weber, or by Andrey Shebunin, an informal successor of Plekhanov and scholar of 1820s ideology. In philosophy, the work of Valentin Asmus is one of the most striking examples. Asmus's main work, *Marx and Bourgeois Historicism* (1933), shows how far he was influenced by Lukács' *History and Class Consciousness*, even if he was forced to formally join the criticism of Lukács by A. Deborin (For more on the history of Soviet philosophy as special 'in-place-of-philosophy' see: Van der Zweerde 1994). The Marxist reformulation of key issues in psychology is also of special interest. In parallel to the efforts of Georges Politzer in France (and to the Gestalt psychologists and to Piaget, at least in part) Lev Vygotsky attempted a Marxist solution to the conceptual crisis in sociology, which he complemented by the development of a cultural–historical approach to human activity. Vygotsky's theory of interiorization displayed interesting parallels with ideas on the social nature of world-view in Mauss and Durkheim (*The Elementary Forms of the Religious Life*, for an example (Durkheim 1995 [1912])). Other significant versions of Marxist psychology in the USSR of the 1930s can be found in Sergey Rubenstein's effort to turn towards the newly discovered manuscripts of the young Marx, or a little-known work on the sociology of thinking by the Georgian philosopher Constantine Megrelidze, who died at an early age. Much like the approaches of Vygotsky and his school, they all rested on the principle of activity and the social nature of consciousness (Wertsch 1985, Joravsky 1989). The programme of the Bakhtin circle made it possible to connect these searches with the general *problematique* of structuralism: 'consciousness is composed and achieved through sign material, which is created in process of the organized collective's social interactions.' (Voloshinov 1986 [1929]: 20)

From the 1890s to the 1910s, the development of Russian social theory (including the abundance of the translations of books by many different Western scholars into Russian) was 'synchronized' to the development in Western Europe. Even if the 1920s were probably the most fruitful period in terms of producing original Russian social theories, the 'Great Break' of 1929 was followed by three decades of almost total isolation. This created a situation of delay and even backwardness in the development of Russian social theory, which resulted in a need to 'catch up' that has not been fully satisfied to this very day. During the 1930s, the narrowing of the possibilities for Russian social theory were primarily caused by direct state-intervention in the social-scientific sphere: most empirical social studies had, in fact, been discontinued, and the field of interaction with Western and American scholarship was sharply reduced. During the second half of the decade, the institutional field of Soviet social studies had, for all intents and purposes, been unified. (For more on the general tendencies of this period, see Fitzpatrick 1978). One of the last echoes of the fruitful expansion of Marxist ideas into the traditional fields of the humanities during 1920s can be found in Boris Gessen's formulation of the main postulates of the so-called 'externalist' approach to the history of science (in his famous report on Newton at the Second International Congress for the History of Science and Technology in London in 1932). Robert Merton's famous work about science and religion in seventeenth-century England (Merton 1973 [1938]) can be understood as a polemical answer of sorts to Gessen (Graham 1985). It should also be noted that Pitirim Sorokin was actually one of the first scholars to oppose the approach taken by Merton, who was his student at the time. But Sorokin's global diagrams of sociocultural dynamics soon yielded their intellectual superiority to the re-conceptualization of the classics of European

159

sociology, which the young Talcott Parsons presented in his early theory of social action (Johnston 1995).

When the revolutionary experiment was finally internally reborn in the forms of state-socialism, this system of forced modernization only required official, propagandistic legit-imations, rather than any independent social-scientific reflection (Marcuse 1957). In Soviet Russia of the 1930s aesthetics became an important vent for those thinkers trying to avoid the terror; it was here, on the aesthetic field, that they were able to implicitly examine the main social and ideological contradictions of their epoch. In the mid-1930s, for an example, the Moscow circle around Lukács discussed the problem of the Thermidor using the material of nineteenth-century Germany (Fichte, Hegel, Hölderlin). Unlike Trotsky or Ustryalov, the leader of the emigrant current of 'Smena Vekhi', the Marxist theorists around the journal 'Literaturnyj kritik' – besides Lukács, these also included Mikhail Lifschitz – followed Hegel in considering both terror and the temporary recoil of revolution as dialectical phases of the general revolutionary process, rather than the bureaucratic regeneration or inevitable restoration of capitalism (cf. Sziklai 1992; Hardemann 1994). The revolutionary and experi-mental activisms of the 1920s were transformed into state-mobilized collectivity; aside from the totalitarian ossification of the regime, this also reflected the general civilizatory imperative of the interwar period, which called for the construction of a mass-society on an industrial basis. For an example, many researchers clearly discern reflections of the Stalin-period's ideological atmosphere in Bakhtin's book on Francois Rabelais and the unofficial culture of the carnivalesque. Going further, the contemporary Russian theorist Mikhail Ryklin inter-prets the notion of speech genres and discourses in Bakhtin (and in Voloshinov, during the late 1920s) as a paraphrase of the logic of terror that dominated the time. From Ryklin's point of view, this conception was an irreflexive socio-linguistic doctrine, oriented towards the primacy of coercive statements, of totally social and absolutely conscious vocal activity, where the statement's authorship belonged to the collective personality, and not to the individual who had broken away from it (Ryklin 1993).

The revival of independent theoretical thought in the USSR began immediately after Sta-lin's death in 1953, even if it was almost exclusively limited to Marxism. For an instance, a group of young researchers from the philosophical faculty of Moscow State University (MGU) launched a study of the logic of Karl Marx's *Das Kapital* that, in many respects, anticipated analogous explorations by Louis Althusser and his disciples during the 1960s. Approximately between 1953 and 1957, an informal discussion group known as the 'Moscow methodological circle' united a number of theorists who would go on to become well-known thinkers in the future. These included the logician and writer-dissident Aleksandr Zinov'ev, the philosopher Merab Mamardashvili, the sociologist Boris Grushin, and the ori-ginal theorist of the 'social technologies' Georgiy Shchedrovitsky. Ewald Il'enkov, a close informal student of Mikhail Lifschitz, was also in close contact with this circle during this period. It was Il'enkov who redirected the attention of Soviet postwar philosophy towards Hegel; his anti-naturalist theory of the ideal was especially popular at the time (Bukhurst 1991). In his innovative work on the Marxian concept of consciousness (1986), Mamar-dashvili depicted Marx as a non-classical philosopher, who exceeded the limits of the tradi-tional reflexive philosophy of consciousness by introducing the concept of the 'converted forms' of the social agent's consciousness, for example (Mamardashvili 1986). Although Mamardashvili displayed a lively interest in social philosophy until his death in 1990, his later work was increasingly oriented towards the existentialist and stoic ideas of personal act, coming close to the studies of the late Foucault, and also, to an even greater degree, to Bakhtin's philosophy. Il'enkov and Shchedrovitskiy, on the other hand, worked in close contact with the students of Lev Vygotsky from the 1950s well into the 1970s. Mamardashvili had close ties with the semiotic movement in the USSR through a friend of Yuri Lotman's, the philosopher and Buddologist, Aleksandr Pyatigorsky (his original post-structuralist theory of observation displays many interesting parallels with analytical philosophy in general, and with Niklas Luhman's in particular). In many respects, the Moscow–Tartu school, arguably the highest achievement in the late Soviet humanities, constructed its positions on the implicit negation of the Marxist thesis on the social conditionality of culture. The Kantian and Saussurian foundations of structuralism helped Yuri Lotman and his followers in their battle against the ideological presumptions of historical materialism and the vulgar 'theory of reflection' (Shukman 1977). At the same time, the other historical background of late Soviet structuralism – Mukařovsky, Bakhtin, and in particular the late formalist efforts of Boris Eikhenbaum towards a theory of the literary environment ('byt') – prompted the appearance of a series of very promising studies focused on the poetics of everyday behaviour by Lotman during the 1970s. These studies addressed the material of Russian literary history of the nineteenth-century's first half. In recent years, contemporary Russian observers have noted the proximity of these studies by Lotman to 'new historicism' or to Clifford Geertz's programme of 'thick description'. However, during the 1980s, Lotman became increasingly interested in the idea of synergy or the production of a general 'culturological' discipline (Zorin 2001). The transformations and degeneration of this latter-day sub-discipline after the death of Lotman are currently under examination (Engelstein 2001; Scherrer 2003).

After 1968, the decline of real socialism left little place for the methodological development of Marxism itself in unofficial Soviet thought – in contrast to the neo-Marxian turn in Western social and cultural theory of the time. This divergence is especially significant in that it effected the formation of two incompatible views of Bakhtin during the 1980s and 1990s: one of these, rooted in Slavonic philology, saw Bakhtin as the implicit heir of Russian-Orthodox *sobornost'* and Solov'ev's idealism, while the other view, emerging from the post-Soviet humanities, understood him as a close collocutor of Lukács, Gramsci, Althusser and E. P. Thompson in the development of the Marxist theory of ideology and superstructure for cultural studies. During the 1970s, however, Mikhail Lifschitz and Ewald Il'enkov remained faithful to the ideals of authentic Marxism and high realism and enlighted rationalism in the spirit of the 1930s. Despite their prestige in semi-official and unofficial circles, they remained nearly completely isolated, tragically and consciously out-of-time (Jones 1994). (This position could be compared to the final divergence of Lukács with his students from the so-called Budapest School.) The intellectual biography of Yuri Davydov, the most prominent Soviet historian of sociology, is highly symptomatic for the changes that were taking place at the time. Setting out from an enthusiastic fascination with the young Marx, following Il'enkov, Davydov had already moved to a consciously neo-conservative position (in the Western sense) by the late 1960s, becoming one of the chief critics of the neo-Marxism of the Frankfurt School. From the second half of the 1980s onward, he began to make attempts at combining the development of the theoretical heritage of Max Weber with the ideological horizon of the authors of the Vekhi-group, primarily of Sergey Bulgakov (Davydov and Gaidenko 1995). In this sense, one might say that the philosopher Vladimir Bibler and the historian Mikhail Gefter were far truer to the spirit of the Soviet post-Stalinist renaissance of 'real Marxism'. During the second half of the 1960s, both worked in the innovative Sector of the Methodology of History at the Historical Institute of the Academy of Sciences of the USSR (Markwick 2001). Turning to Bakhtin (but not to Habermas!) and to Marx's division of 'joint' and 'universal' labour, Bibler was able to develop a general theory of the contemporary transformation of scientific rationality into pluralistic rationality, becoming a 'logic of culture' (Bibler left behind an entire school of talented researchers and teachers). Gefter, by contrast, developed ideas on the plurality and the systemic interrelation of historical worlds, multi-temporality, and the alterity and subjectivity of contemporary history. In part, his ideas were similar to the philosophies of history propounded by Ernst Bloch or Sigfried Krakauer. References to Gefter can be found in the majority of contemporary domestic theories of the historical development of Russia (Vichnevski 2000).

The main theoretical problem of Soviet sociology soon became its delimitation from historical materialism (Weinberg 1974). In the final analysis, the 1970s affirmed – with implicit references to the ideas of Merton – three theoretical levels: while historical materialism was afforded the highest, philosophical ground, the realm of sociology did not only cover the lowest, empirical level but also broke into an 'intermediate' space of theoretization. Largely concentrated on surveys, quantitative indices and mathematical methods, this sociology soon moved towards major American theoretical literature and the collaboration with social psychology as its main point of reference. In this situation, it becomes clear why Talcott Parsons – and not the loquacious Pitirim Sorokin or the nuanced Robert Merton – was actually 'the main Soviet sociologist', as a recent joke tells us: Parson's theory of self-sustaining social systems with a matching collection of values, needs and motivations corresponded quite well to the demands of the stable society of the Brezhnev era. Towards the late 1960s, it was Yuri Levada who proposed the most refined version of theoretical sociology based on the theoretical groundwork laid by Parsons. However, his work was immediately subject to staunch ideological attacks for the absence of any class approach and for its tendency to usurp the methodological functions of historical materialism (Shlapentokh 1987). Nevertheless, Levada's colleagues and collaborators from the 1970s – such as Boris Dubin, Leo Gudkov and Leonid Sedov – remain the most important analysts and theorists of the processes of post-totalitarian transformation to this day, especially insofar as the sociology of culture and literature are concerned.

Social theory after Communism

Although the revolutionary changes of 1989 to 1991 alleviated the pressure of official Marxist dogma, the last decade has not produced any explosion or boom of independent sociological theory – despite the rise of newly established research institutions in the social sciences (for a general survey see Batygin 2004). The apology of an 'open society', which dominated the first post-Soviet years, was soon replaced with a return to the ideals of statehood and centralism during the first years of the new millennium. At the same time, the theoretical paradigms of totalitarianism, modernization or 'transitology', which most Russian researchers subscribed to as their main methodological tools, clearly seem insufficient, even from the point of view of the scholars themselves. A symptomatic example for the growing rift between theory and its object can be found in the discussion of the relationship between Western theory and domestic reality, held by major Russian theorists on the pages of authoritative political-science periodical 'Pro and Contra' in 2000–2001. Here, Aleksandr Kustarev, Vadim Radayev, Aleksandr Filippov, Vladimir Pantin discussed possible reasons for why post-Soviet Russia, in contrast to Europe or the USA, had – as of yet – failed to produce any comprehensive theories or at least partial hypotheses to explain the Russian 'scenario'. It seems clear that this inexplicability does not fit into the local specificity of the 'decomposing empire', belated modernization, or compensatory development etc. At the same time, it seemed obvious that most researchers had reached a consensus as far as the impossibility of turning towards 'depleted' traditions in explaining contemporary Russian realia was concerned. This impossibility even applied to any potential return to the lost historical models of Berdyaev, Sorokin, Bakhtin, or even Eurasianists, for that matter. One exception can be found in the attempts made by Victor Bibikhin, a student of Losev's and a talented interpreter of Heidegger (Bibikhin 2003). Bibikhin made an attempt to lean on the heritage of Solovyev and the tradition of high modernism in the spirit of T. S. Eliot, in order to engage in social-philosophical reflection of the Russian transformation and its historical sources. Nevertheless, it should be noted that these original theoretical efforts are hardly convertible to the positions of even the most philosophically saturated social theory. In one way or another, the majority of eminent Russian social scientists from the mid-1990s oriented in their research towards this or that prevailing paradigm from contemporary ('Western') social theory, substantially modifying it with their own additions and innovations. Aleksandr Filippov, for an instance, referred to Luhmann's systems-theory, recasting it in the light of problems such as empire, space and social event. Yuri Kachanov, on the other hand, based his work on Bourdieu's socio-analysis, which he combined with the reconsideration of Heidegger's fundamental ontology and self-reflection in the field of intellectual production and expert-communities of modern Russia. Yet another researcher, Andrey Fursov found his grounding in the world-system approach of Immanuel Wallerstein, which he augmented by the search for the social subject of the transformations that had taken place in Russia and the rest of the world.

In any event, the original theoretical work of contemporary Russian social theorists cannot be only reduced to the 'adaptation' of contemporary social theory to the analysis of Russian reality. The material of the Russian history often becomes a testing ground for the development of social theory: thus, Oleg Kharkhordin analysed the evolution of the collective and the singular personality in Russia in a spirit close to Stephen Kotkin and the nascent school of analysing 'Soviet subjectivity' (Jochen Hellbeck, Igal Halfin). For Vadim Volkov the study of the public sphere in Russia of the nineteenth-century or the idea of the Eliasin 'civilizing process' ('*kulturnost*') under Stalinism led to further reflections – together with Oleg Kharkhordin – on theory of social practices in general, following in the footsteps on analytical philosophy and a pragmatic reading of the early Heidegger (Kharkhordin 1999). Volkov's analysis of the contemporary Mafia and the 'return of the state' in Russia at the brink of the new millennium (Volkov 2000) corresponds to Kharkhordin's studies on the practices of 'living together' and the problems of the connecting sociality and corporeality in the context of the *res publica* (which also draw upon the approaches of Bruno Latour and Laurent Thevenot).

The 'French' intellectual revolution in Russia during the 1990s – which equated the 'high' and the 'low' and affirmed the 'crash' of any and all 'great narratives' – should be considered as an import of post-modern ideology, rather than any fundamental concretization of the methodologies used in post-structuralist scholarship to date (see Swiderski 1998). At the same time, from the second half of the 1990s onward, key figures of this revolution – such as the philosophers Mikhail Ryklin and Valery Podoroga – turned to the *problematique* of the event and its character, to the non-classical analysis of the body and its corporeality, and – especially in the case of Ryklin – to the reflection on the collective phantasms of utopia lost (for an accurate chronological account, see Buck-Morss 2000: 214–278). Having become the object of prognosis through sociological and politological analysts, the decline and fall of the system of state socialism, the disintegration of Soviet empire and the formation of a new social order, remained an important event-related context, but never really became the key object of any contemporary Russian social theory. The 'compensatory' character of early twentieth-century Russian sociology, especially as far the general society's general intellectual backwardness, as well the variety of interpretations given to the revolution and the interwar 'uprising of the masses' – be it through the Bakhtin-circle or Lukács–Lifschits group – all this provide testimony for the deep connection of social theory in Russia with its local, cultural 'chronotope' (see: Uffelmann 1999). In many respects, this was connected with the presence of this social theory's palpable subject and addressee, which consisted of the radical or liberal pre-revolutionary intelligentsia and its heirs. For the Lifshchits or Il'enkov, these consisted in the ideological avant garde of Communism, while Nikolai Trubetskoy and the Eurasianist saw it as the 'ideocracy' to come after the revolution; for the post-Stalinist sociology, this referent is obviously the dissident and semi-dissident intellectuals of the 1950s–1980s (see Beyrau 1993). In post-Communist Russia, it is precisely this social layer of the former intelligentsia that experienced the most significant and radical transformations and changes, so that it simply no longer exists in its previous form. After a boom of public debates on historical or sociopolitical issues during the *Perestroika* and its aftermath during the 1990s, the entire field of social reflection in the very general meaning of the word was soon confined to the very narrow space of professional sociological communication. In the light of the obvious and explicable predominance of 'imported' Western methodologies on the domestic market of ideas, it is hardly surprising that many of Russia's most important contemporary researchers question the very existence of Russian social theory as an independent and integral phenomenon. The most sceptical point of view was taken on by Alexander Filipov, who claims that there is, in fact, 'no such thing as theoretical sociology in Russia today... [T]here are no extensive and constant discourses on fundamental sociological theory, nor are there are any extensive conceptual constructions in particular fields (branched theory)... [T]here are no significant claims towards the creation of any original theoretical project at large' (Filipov 1997: 247). By contrast, Yuri Kachanov has taken a far more positive approach in evaluating the potential prospects for Russian social theory, openly disputing Filipov's views. Yet at the same time, historian Nikolai Koposov identifies a general crisis of the social sciences, which defines all efforts taking place today and does not see theoretical production in Russia as any exception to this problem at large.

One way or another, the future discussion will not simply about be able to focus on the specifically Russian social theories – ranging from those articulated by Pitirim Sorokin or Bakhtin to those produced in our own time – but will focus more and more on the common space for communication, which is an integral part of international social science, reflecting this global albeit fragmentary intellectual horizon together with the tendencies which oppose it. Both in their individual research and in their collective existence (as an academic community, for example), contemporary Russian researchers will need to face the problem of developing firm institutional ground for reflection, where a critical and polemical re-thinking of both their own intellectual tradition as well as its unconditional roots in local social and political conditions.

References

Agursky, M. (1987) *The Third Rome: National Bolshevism in the USSR,* Boulder, CO: Westview Press.

Auffret, D. (1990) *Alexandre Kojeve. La philosophie, l'Etat, la fin de l'Histoire,* Paris: Bernard Grasset, pp. 129–131, 153–155.

Bakhtin, M. M. and Medvedev, P. N. (1991) *The Formal Method in Literary Scholarship: A Critical Introduction to Sociological Poetics,* Baltimore, MD: Johns Hopkins Press.

Bakhurst, D. (1991) *Consciousness and Revolution in Soviet Philosophy. From the Bolsheviks to Evald Ilyenkov.* Cambridge: Cambridge University Press.

Batygin, G. S. (2004) 'Social Scientists in Times of Crisis: The Structural Transformations Within the Disciplinary Organization and Thematic Repertoire of the Social Sciences', *Studies in East European Thought*, 56(1): 7–54.

Beyrau, D. (1993) *Intelligenz und Dissens: die russischen Bildungsichten in der Sowjetunion 1917 bis 1985*, Göttingen.

Bibikhin, V. (2003) *Drugoe nachalo [Another Beginning]*, St Petersburg: Nauka (in Russian).

Boobbyer, P. (1995) *S. L. Frank. The Life and Work of a Russian Philosopher 1877–1950*, Athens, OH: Ohio University Press.

Brandist, C. (2002) *The Bakhtin Circle: Philosophy, Culture and Politics*, London and Sterling: Pluto Press.

Buck-Morss, S. (2000) *Dreamworld and Catastrophe: The Passing of Mass Utopia in East and West*, Cambridge: Cambridge University Press.

Burbank, J. (1986) *Intelligentsia and Revolution. Russian Views of Bolshevism 1917–1922*, New York: Oxford University Press.

Christman, H. M. (ed.) (1987) *Essential Works of Lenin*, New York: Bantam Books.

Clowes, E. W., Kassow, S. and West, J. L. (eds) (1991) *Between Tsar and People: Educated Society and the Quest for Public Identity in Late Imperial Russia*, Princeton: Princeton University Press.

Coates, R. (1998) 'Two of a Small Fraternity ? Points of Contact and Departure in the Work of Bakhtin and Kagan up to 1924', in D. Shepherd (ed.) *The Context of Bakhtin*, Amsterdam: Harwood Academic Publishers, pp. 17–28.

Confino, M. (1972) 'On Intellectuals and Intellectual Traditions in Eighteenth- and Nineteenth-Century Russia', *Daedalus*, 101(1), 117–449.

Čyževs'kyj, D. (1934) 'Hegel in Russland', in D. Čyževs'kyj (ed.) *Hegel bei den Slawen*, Reichenberg: 145–397.

Davydov, J. and Gaidenko, P. (1995) *Rußland und der Westen. Heidelberger Max-Weber Vorlesungen 1992*, Frankfurt am Main.

Durkheim, E. (1995 [1912]) *Elementary Forms of Religious Life* (trans. K. E. Fields), New York: Free Press.

Engelstein, L. (2001) 'Culture, Culture Everywhere: Interpretations of Modern Russia, across the 1991 Divide', *Kritika* 2(3), 363–393.

Evtukhov, C. (1997) *The Cross and the Sickle: Sergei Bulgakov and the Fate of Russian Religious Philosophy*, Ithaca: Cornell University Press.

Filipov, A. F. (1997) 'Theoretical Sociology' (in Russian), *Soziologicheskie Chtenija*, vol. 2: 247–269

Fitzpatrick S. (ed.) (1978) *Cultural Revolution in Russia 1928–1931*, Bloomington, IN: Indiana University Press.

Gasparov, B. (1987) 'The Ideological Principles of Prague School Phonology', in K. Pomorska (ed.) *Language, Poetry and Poetics. The Generation of 1890's: Jakobson, Trubetzkoy, Majakovskij*, Berlin: Mouton de Gruyter, pp. 49–78.

Gluck, M. (1985) *Georg Lukács and His Generation, 1900–1918*, Cambridge (Mass.) and London: Cambridge University Press.

Golosenko, I. (1995) *Russian Sociological Works from Middle of XIX Century to Beginning of XX Century: A Bibliography*, St Petersburg: Onega.

Golosenko, I. and Skorokhodova, A. (1997) *The Works of Western Sociologists in Russian Print and Periodical Press from the Middle of XIX Century to Beginning of XX Century: A Bibliography*, St Petersburg: Institute od Sociology RAS.

Graham, L. R. (1985) 'The Socio-Political Roots of Boris Hessen: Soviet Marxism and the History of Science', *Social Studies of Science*, 15(6): 705–722.

Hagemeister, M. (2001) '"Wiederverzauberung der Welt: Pavel Florenskij Neues Mittelalter"', in Pavel Florenskij – Tradition und Moderne: Beiträge zum Internationalen Symposium an der Universität Potsdam, 5 bis 9 April 2000', Frankfurt am Mein: 21–41.

Hardeman, H. (1994) *Coming to Terms with the Soviet Regime. The 'Changing Signposts' Movement among Russian Émigrés in the Early 1920's*. De-Kalb, IL: Northern Illinois University Press.

Harding, N. (1977, 1981) *Lenin's Political Thought*, Vols. 1, 2, London: Macmillan.

Hecker, J. F. (1915) *Russian Sociology: A Contribution to the History of Sociological Thought and Theory*, New York: Columbia University Press.

Johnston, B. V. (1995) *Pitrim A. Sorokin. An Intellectual Biography*, Lawrence, KS: University Press of Kansas.

Jones, P. E. (1994) 'Evald Ilyenkov and the history of Marxism in the USSR', *History of the Human Sciences*, 7(2): 105–118.

Joravsky, D. (1989) *Russian Psychology. A Critical Survey*, Oxford, Oxford University Press.

165

Kharkhordin, O. (1999) *The Collective and the Individual in Russia: A Study of Practices,* Berkeley and Los Angeles: University of California Press.

Kotkin, St. (2001) 'Modern Times: The Soviet Union and the Interwar Conjecture', *Kritika: Explorations in Russian and Eurasian History*, 2(1): 111–164.

Koyré, A. (1929) *La philosophie et le problème national en Russie au début du XIX siécle,* Paris: Honoré Champion.

Lukács, G. (1971 [1923]) *History and Class Consciousness*, Cambridge, MA: MIT Press.

Luks, L. (1998) '"Eurasier" und "Konservative Revolution". Zur antiwestlischen Versuchung in Russland und Deutschland' in G. Koenen and L. Kopelew (eds) *Deutschland und russische Revolution 1917–1924,* München: Fink Verlag, pp. 219–239

Malachov, V. (1995) 'Ist Philosophie auf Russisch möglich?', *Deutsche Zeitschrift für Philosophie*, 43(1), 63-73.

Mamardashvili, M. K. (1986) 'Analysis of consciousness in the works of Marx', *Studies in Soviet Philosophy*, 32, 101–120.

Marcuse, H. (1957) *Soviet Marxism. A Critical Analysis*. New York: Columbia University Press.

Markwick R. D. (2001) *Rewriting History in Soviet Russia: the Politics of Revisionist Historiography, 1956–1974,* New York: Palgrave.

Merton, R. K. (1973 [1938]) *Science, Technology and Society in Seventeeth Century England*, New York: Harper.

Morrow, P. (1998) 'Bakhtin and Mannheim : An Introductory Dialogue' in. M. Bell and M. Gardiner (eds) *Bakhtin and the Human Sciences*, London: Sage, pp. 145–162.

Nikolaev, N. (1991) 'The Nevel School of Philosophy (Bakhtin, Kagan and Pumpianskii) between 1918 and 1925: Materials from Pumpianskii's Archives', in D. Shepherd (ed.) *The Contexts of Bakhtin: Philosophy, Aesthetics, Reception*, Amsterdam: Harwood Academic, pp. 29–41.

Nowikow, N. (1988) *Die Soziologie in Rußland. Ihre institutionelle Entwicklung von den Anfängen bis zur Oktoberrevolution 1917:* Wiesbaden: Harrassowitz.

Raeff, M. (1985) Novyj Grad and Germany: A Chapter in the Intellectual History of the Russian Emigration, in I. Auerbach, A. Hildgruber and D. Schramm (eds) *Felder und Vorfelder russischer Geschichte. Studien zu Ehren von Peter Schreibert,* Freiburg: Rombach.

Raphael, L. (1996) 'Die Verwissenschaftlichung des Sozialen als methodische und konzeptionelle Herausforderung für eine Sozialgeschichte des 20. Jahrhunderts', *Geschichte und Gesellschaft* 22(2), 165–193.

Read, C. (1979) *Religion, Revolution, and the Russian Intelligentsia, 1900–1912: The Vekhi Debate and Its Intellectual Background,* London: Macmillan.

Riasanovsky, N. (1967) 'The Emergence of Eurasianism', *California Slavic Studies*, 1: 39–72.

Ryklin, M. K. (1993) 'Bodies of Terror: Theses Towards a Logic of Violence', *New Literary History*, 24(1): 51–74

Schein, L. B. (ed.) (1977) *Readings in Russian Philosophical Thought: Philosophy of History*, Waterloo, Ontario: Wilfrid Laurier University Press.

Schelting, A. von. (1948) *Russland und Europa im russischen Geschichtsdenken. Auf der Suche nach der historischen Identität*, Bern: Franke Verlag.

Scherrer, J. (2003) *'Kulturologie'. Russland auf der Suche nach einer zivilisatorischen Identität*, Göttingen: Wallstein-Verlag.

Schlacks, C. (1997) 'Exodus to the East: Forebodings and Events. An Affirmation of the Eurasians', in I. Vinkovetsky and C. Schlacks (eds) *Exodus to the East: Forebodings and Events. An Affirmation of the Eurasians*, Marina del Rey: Charles Schlacks, Jr.

Shlapentokh, V. (1987) *The Politics of Sociology in the Soviet Union*. Boulder: Westview Press.

Shukman, A. (1977) *Literature and Semiotics: A Study of the Writings of Yu. M. Lotman*, Amsterdam: Elsevier, North Holland.

Srubar, I. (ed.) (1988) *Exil, Wissenschaft, Identität*, Frankfurt am Main: Suhrkamp.

Stanziani, A. (1998) *L'économie en révolution. Le cas russe, 1870–1930*, Paris: Albin Michel.

Swiderski, E. M. (1998) 'Culture, Contexts, and Directions in Russian Post-Soviet Philosophy', *Studies in East European Thought*, 50(4): 283–328.

Sziklai, L. (1992) *After the Proletarian Revolution. Georg Lukács's Marxist Development, 1930–1945,* Budapest: Akadémiai Kiadó.

Tihanov, G. (2000a) 'Cultural Emancipation and Novellistic: Trubetzkoy, Savitsky, Bakhtin', *Bucknell Review*, 43(2): 47–67.

Tihanov, G. (2000b) *Master and Slave. Lukács and Bakhtin in Ideas of their Time*, Oxford; Oxford University Press.

Tihanov, G. (2002) 'Regimes of Modernity at the Dawn of Globalisation: Carl Schmitt and Alexandre Kojève', in D. Kadir and D. Löbbermann (eds) *Other Modernisms in an Age of Globalisation*, Heidelberg: Universitätsverlag C., 75–93.

Toman, J. (1995) *The Magic of a Common Language. Jakobson, Mathesius, Trubetzkoy and the Prague Linguistic Circle*, Cambridge, MA and London: The MIT Press.

Tschernych, A. (1995) 'Eine andere Macht – ein anderes Wissen. Das Schicksal der Soziologie in Sowjetrußland in den 20er Jahren', in B. Balla and A. Sterbling (eds) *Soziologie und Geschichte – Geschichte und Soziologie. Beiträge zur Osteuropaforschung*, Hamburg: Krämer, pp. 151–167.

Uffelmann, D. (1999) *Die russische Kulturosophie. Logik und Axiologie der Argumentation*, Frankfurt am Main: Peter Lang Verlag.

Vekhi (1991) *Landmarks* [1909], *De Profundis* [1918], (ed.) A. A. Jakovlev, Moscow: Pravda (in Russian).

Vichnevski, A. (2000) *La faucille et le rouble. La modernisation conservatrice en URSS*, Paris: Gallimard.

Volkov, V. (2000) 'The Political Economy of Protection Rackets in the Past and the Present', *Social Research*, 67(3), 709–744.

Voloshinov, V. N. (1986 [1929]) *Marxism and the Philosophy of Language*, Cambridge, MA: Harvard University Press.

Vucinich, A. (1976) *Social Thought in Tsarist Russia. The Quest for a General Science of Society 1861–1917*, Chicago and London: Chicago University Press.

Walicki, A. (1975) *The Slavophile Controversy: History of a Conservative Utopia in Nineteenth-Century Russian Thought*, Oxford: Clarendon Press.

Weinberg, E. A. (1974) *The Development of Sociology in the Soviet Union*, London: Routledge.

Wertsch, J. (ed.) (1985) *Culture, Communication and Cognition: Vygotskian Perspectives*, Cambridge: Cambridge University Press.

Williams R. (1972) *Culture in Exile. Russian Emigres in Germany, 1881–1941*, Ithaca and London: Cornell University Press.

Wittrock B., P. Wagner, and Wollman, H. (1989) 'Social Science and Modern State: Policy Knowledge and Political Institution in Western Europe', in P. Wagner (ed.) *Social Sciences and Modern States. National Experiences and Theoretical Crossroads*, Cambridge: Cambridge University Press,pp. 35–38.

Zorin, A. (2001) 'Ideology, Semiotics, and Clifford Geertz: Some Russian Reflections', *History and Theory*, 40(1), 57–73.

Zweerde, E. van der (1994) 'Soviet Philosophy – the Ideology and the Handmaid. A Historical and Critical Analysis of Soviet Philosophy, with a case-study into Soviet History of Philosophy' (PhD text), Nijmegen.

Part 3

Intellectual traditions

13

How to criticize? Convergent and divergent paths in critical theories of society

Stefan Müller-Doohm

The concept of 'critical theory' first emerged in 1937 in an essay Max Horkheimer published in the *Zeitschrift für Sozialforschung*, where it figured as a description of his own research programme. Horkheimer was the director of the Institute of Social Research and was in essence in charge of the direction and contents of its research activities. At the time, the Institute had been associated with Columbia University in New York for a good three years.[1] Following the seizure of power in Germany by the National Socialists, Horkheimer emigrated to the city on the Hudson River, taking with him the majority of his Institute colleagues, including Leo Löwenthal, Herbert Marcuse, Erich Fromm, and Fritz Pollock. With their Jewish origins and their own oppositional stance as left-wing intellectuals and Marxists, they were obviously at risk in Hitler's Germany and had to leave the country as quickly as possible.

One reason why Horkheimer had chosen the term 'critical theory' had been to distinguish his own brand of social theory from what he called 'traditional theory'. By this he understood a tradition of science-based 'positivism' which led from Descartes to Carnap. In contrast to this philosophical trend, but also by way of differentiating himself from the purely speculative currents of idealist philosophy, Horkheimer defined his own theory as (self-)critical because it set out to account for its own function within a given society. Instead of going in search of knowledge that was technically useful and readily applicable, it was concerned to focus on society and its antagonisms as objects of reflection. 'Actual circumstances do not appear to it as givens simply to be noted and to be calculated in advance according to the laws of probability.' (Horkheimer 1988: 217; cf. McCarthy 1993 [1991]: 211f.). The critique Horkheimer had in mind was directed both against the restrictions of the individual sciences in their different approaches (critique of science) and against an unconscious, self-destructive society that was drifting blindly towards catastrophe (critique of society). The two essential preconditions of critical thinking are on the one hand an insight into the causes of oppression, i.e. the economic mechanisms that determine repressive social structures, and on the other hand, empathy in the sense of a compassionate experiencing of social suffering. What a critical theory seeks is a knowledge of the individual and collective emancipation that will lead to a non-exploitative society.

However, Horkheimer's intention in using the term 'critical theory' was not simply to sum up Marxist approaches to the analysis of society and to clarify the scientific status of his own

171

critical method. It is rather the case that critical theory's new understanding of itself also sig-nalled a new direction for the future work of the Institute of Social Research in the United States.[2] Towards the end of his programmatic essay, Horkheimer comes on to the question of the current position of critical theory and writes that in a historical situation 'in which the entire power of existing reality presses forward to the abandonment of all culture and to the darkest barbarism' there can be no universal 'criteria for critical theory as a whole'. It follows that 'Critical theory ... has no specific authority in its favour apart from its interest in the abolition of social injustice, an interest with which it is anyway linked. Reduced to an abstract statement, this negative formulation is the materialist content of the idealist concept of reason' (Horkheimer 1988: 216). Even though Horkheimer attempts to link his right to criticize with the belief that he is asserting an objective truth, an assertion justified by the self-reflexive status of his own thinking, this cannot prevent his growing doubts about the historical and practical effectiveness of critical reason.[3] In effect his new programme was to interpret critical theory as a specific form of reflection that would criticize social reality from the vantage point of a possible alternative existence.[4] This development brought him closer to what Adorno had always had in mind when he emphasized what he thought of as the crucial common strands in their philosophical approaches. Theodor W. Adorno was eight years younger than Horkheimer, and from their very first meeting in Frankfurt during the 1920s, he had always attached great importance to the similarities in their way of thinking, even though at this particular point in time there were considerable differences of opinion between them.[5] However, in the Postscript to his influential essay of 1937 Horkheimer emphasized the phi-losophical nature of critical theory and came to the conclusion that its aim and meaning was not the 'increase in knowledge' but a philosophical reflection that attempted to answer the question 'to what purpose' and, more generally, to encourage a self-reflective stance. In putting forward this argument he came much closer to the ideas that Adorno associated with critical knowledge as an open process of antithetical thinking, as determinate negation.[6]

Adorno: binding statements without a system

As early as his inaugural lecture as a lecturer in philosophy in the summer of 1931, Adorno had emphasized the idea of 'philosophical interpretation' and rejected the attempt to grasp 'the totality of the real' with the assistance of the sciences or a philosophical system.[7] Instead he proposes an interpretative approach, the point of which is to develop a series of varying models of interpretation and then to integrate these models in 'changing constellations'. The aim of these interpretations, which are to be inspired by 'an exact imagination', is 'to con-struct keys before which reality springs open' (Adorno, *The Actuality of Philosophy* in 2000: 35 and 37). However, no key is able to provide a valid solution with which to unlock the con-stitutive 'riddle–character' of intentionless reality. For if there were a definitive answer to the riddle of existence, it would mean we were living in a different world from our historically existing reality whose contingent nature constantly calls for new interpretations which can do no more than 'light up the riddle-*Gestalt* like lightning' (Ibid., 31 and 34). This conception of an experimental critique that interprets the world with the aid of a variety of interpretative models, none of which are able to attain to ultimate truth, since truth is thought of as a never-ending process, was one that Adorno retained right up to and including his philosophical magnum opus, the *Negative Dialectics* of 1966. Throughout his entire life he concentrated on criticizing various objects as a frank attempt to decipher their 'internal texture'. He held that this mode of immanent critique was to be distinguished from instrumental forms of thought that are based on subsumption theory and so are designed with purposiveness and the taming of nature in mind. Critique in his view is a process of making the possible visible, of opening things up through the determinate negation of assumptions, whether about givens, statements or forms of behaviour. The truth content of critical thinking is demonstrated in the visible nature and the depth of what is known. But the interpretative process does not result in knowledge that is 'absolutely correct, irrefutable and watertight' (Adorno 1974b: 71). Knowledge that is expressed in the form of precise statements about the nature of reality is tautologous in Adorno's view. It follows that the truth criterion of critical propositions can consist neither in the correspondence of judgements to factual reality (correspondence theory) nor in the logic or systematic nature of justifications (coherence theory). Critique makes use of conscious, and in that sense, controlled exaggerations that go beyond the mere depiction of the given. And in general, interpretation only makes sense as exaggeration or over-interpretation. 'It has nothing to hold onto – not even the agreement between interpretation and its object, since in that event the interpretation would be no interpretation but mere reconstruction. Thus Adorno only adheres to a notion of truth, only discerns the truth, where the interpretation takes risks and does not simply stick to what it finds in front of its nose.' This means that Adorno's principle of overshooting and exaggeration implies an awareness of the contingent nature of the process of understanding 'while maintaining the critical impulse behind its own interpretative activity. For it is critical because it envisages change. And looked at epistemologically, it is only this contingent nature of interpretation that creates the possibility of different models of interpretation and hence of changing the social world itself.'[8] It is not for nothing that Adorno calls dialectics 'the consistent sense of nonidentity'. In other words, 'dialectics amounts to thinking in such a way that the form of thought will no longer turn its objects into immutable ones, into objects that remain the same. Experience shows that they do not remain the same' (Adorno 1973: 5 and 154).

Adorno's interpretations of cultural and social phenomena lay bare their concrete determining factors as mediated by society. However, 'mediacy is not a positive assertion about being but rather a directive to cognition not to comfort itself with such positivity. It is really the demand to arbitrate dialectic concretely' (Adorno 1982: 24). In Adorno's view, people and things in society do not have to be the way they happen to be in fact. Since they have been shaped by history, they contain the potential for change, as does everything that is social. For this reason Adorno defines critique as 'resistance to everything that is merely posited, that justifies itself with its existence' (Adorno, 'Critique', in Adorno 1998: 282).

However, because of the power of what exists, the scope for freedom, for whatever is different, is not self-evident. To make it visible calls for the deconstructive energies of criticism. Criticism constantly brings forth alternative interpretations and opens up spaces for 'what is distant and different' (Adorno 1973: 192). The type of criticism advocated and practised by Adorno can be described as a particular 'form of world-disclosing criticism'. According to Axel Honneth, the meaning of such criticism is that 'it provides such a radically novel account of social conditions that at one fell swoop everything acquires the new meaning of a pathological state' (Honneth 2000b: 81; see also Honneth 2000a: 729ff).

Two features are characteristic of such a disclosing critique. First, the idiosyncratically provocative linguistic form that places the accustomed in a new light. Honneth refers here to such devices as 'narrative illustration', the 'chiastic positioning of words or clauses', or 'exaggerated emphasis' (Honneth 2000b: 84ff.). Second, the argumentation is based on a conception of truth that rejects the primacy of deductive logic, but at the same time wishes to be more than 'either verification or speculation' (Adorno 1974b: 74). Adorno's dialectics is open-ended in principle and it proposes as its maxim that 'the value of a thought is measured by its distance from the continuity of the familiar. It is objectively devalued as this distance is reduced; the more it approximates to the pre-existing standard, the further its antithetical function is diminished, and only in this ... are the claims of thought founded' (Adorno 1974b: 80).

As a fully fledged example of what he meant by this disclosing critique, Honneth rightly adduces the first book that Horkheimer and Adorno wrote jointly, the *Philosophical Fragments* of 1944 that was then published with the title *Dialectic of Enlightenment* in 1947. The intention of this book is to reconstruct the rise and fall of western thought. In their attempt to rethink the process of enlightenment and the principle of rationality and trace them back to their origins, the authors dispense with the coherent unity of a logical narrative. Instead, in keeping with the spirit of Adorno's methodology, they present a series of interpretative models, three main sections together with two excursuses, grouped around their central thesis that 'human beings purchase the increase in their power with estrangement from that over which it is exerted' (Horkheimer and Adorno 2002: 6; cf. Müller-Doohm 2004a).

The concept of enlightenment does not serve to characterize an epoch in the history of philosophy, but to describe a specific modern state of consciousness. Enlightenment signifies the continuous expansion of freedom in the spheres of what can be done pragmatically, what ought to be done morally and people wish to do emotionally. The flipside of flight from (the irrationalities of) myth and into the freedom of the (rational) shaping of the world for the purpose of self-preservation is the autocratic appropriation of nature and society, as well as the control of the human subject. In the same way, the concept of reason is likewise understood in a dichotomous fashion as both operational and intuitive rationality (cf. Schnädelbach 1983: 72). It means both instrumental power and self-reflective contemplation. In the view of the authors, these two aspects of a unified rationality at the vanishing point of the process of enlightenment have become destabilized. The fact that reason can be equated with self-preservation is a one-sided development whose roots can already be discerned, according to Horkheimer and Adorno, in myth, the primeval form of enlightenment. For in their view stories about events in prehistory are already primitive attempts at explanation that serve to secure control over the forces of nature for the human subject. Just as myth is already enlightenment, so enlightenment regresses to mythology. The mythological or ideological element of the enlightened consciousness of modernity consists in the idea that *Homo faber* makes use of his reason so as to bend the universe to his will. The reason for man's desire to control the world with the aid of reliable knowledge, for the fusion of enlightenment and domination, is his fear of the actual superiority, the overwhelming force of nature. His 'attempt to break the compulsion of nature by breaking nature' means only that thought 'succumbs more deeply to that compulsion. That has been the trajectory of European civilization' (Horkheimer and Adorno 2002: 9). In order to escape the fate of civilization that is tied up with the subjugation of nature both internal and external, and with the imperative of instrumental reason, what is called for are the powers of resistance of dialectical thinking. For Adorno and Horkheimer this is the only way to make sure of the rationality of reason on a broader front. In *Minima Moralia*, which he was writing at the same time, Adorno speaks of the feat of Baron Münchhausen 'of pulling himself out of the bog by his own pigtail'. It is this that has 'become the pattern of all knowledge' (Adorno 1974b: 74). For Adorno dialectics is more than a way of thinking in opposites (thesis, antithesis) that arrive at a compromise (synthesis) in the middle. Instead, between the opposites there is an inner mediation without middle; a mediation of the opposites among themselves. It consists in the fact 'that the analysis of each of the opposites points to its other'. 'This could be called the principle of dialectic as opposed to a merely external, dualistic or disjunctive, mode of thinking' (Adorno 1974a vol., 2: 142).

The idea that this form of dialectical thinking calls for a specific mode of expression is something that Adorno tried to demonstrate and to practise in his *Reflections on Damaged Life*, as *Minima Moralia* is subtitled. The most striking feature of that book is its style, its attempt to bring out the literary or aesthetic dimension of philosophical and sociological concepts while at the same time doing justice to the rules of discursive logic. Thus alongside allegorical allusions, evocative stylistic devices, disjunctive comparisons, and conscious exaggerations, we find rigorous conceptual analyses, such as those of the historical nature of the individual, the function of the culture industry, relations between the sexes or the effects of dabbling in the occult. The very 'element of exaggeration, of over-shooting the object, of self-detachment from the weight of the factual'[9] points to the abandonment of any attempt to restrict language to its descriptive function. All this points to a mode of knowledge that seems tailor-made for the process of thinking against oneself. For Adorno such a stylistic method is the alternative to the conceptual discourse based on subsumption logic that ministers to man's domination of nature and himself. Thanks to the artistry of his writing Adorno shows how critical knowledge can be constructed as contrapuntal, antithetical thinking at the stylistic level. What characterizes his aphoristic miniatures is the way in which they create a force field out of paradoxes. 'Only by the recognition of distance in our neighbour is strangeness alleviated: accepted into consciousness' (Adorno 1974b: 182). Knowledge grows out of the contradictory form of argumentation. Arguing in antitheses enables each point of view to expose the one-sided excesses of its opposite. By shedding light on the extreme aspects of a question, Adorno generates an altogether provocative surplus of meaning, one that must give the reader pause. For no sooner has he understood something than he finds further questions raised about it. This is why Adorno states: 'True thoughts are those alone which do not understand themselves' (Adorno 1974b: 192).

In his *Negative Dialectics* of 1966 Adorno summed up the idea informing his mode of reflection: 'The utopia of knowledge would be to use concepts to unseal the non-conceptual with concepts, without making it their equal' (Adorno 1973: 10). The most important precondition of the realization of this utopian goal is *unregimented* experience: 'for the human subject to entrust himself passively, without anxiety, to his own experience' ('On Subject and Object', in Adorno 1998: 254). The first step in *interpretation* is to make an experience accessible. This is achieved by means of *conceptual* thought. It is 'the attempt to make experience or rather, the wish to express something ... authoritative' (Adorno 1974a vol. 1: 83). According to Adorno, to make something authoritative or binding (*verbindlich*) means constructing a theory that culminates in the unity of theory and practice. Just as interpretation mistrusts the 'deceit of appearances', so too '... the more smoothly the façade of society presents itself, the more profoundly does theory mistrust it. Theory seeks to give a name to what holds the machinery together' ('Sociology and Empirical Research', in O'Connor 2000: 176).

However, we should not overlook the fact that this type of theory aims at the formulation of 'binding statements without a system' (Adorno 1973: 29). This maxim undoubtedly contains methodological principles, principles Adorno finds embodied in a concept he calls 'thinking in constellations'. This 'constellational' thinking involves a particular approach to interpretation that strives to avoid the classification of phenomena, their subsumption under higher concepts. Instead, it aims to use interpretation in order to open up the diverse qualities of an object, the plenitude of its characteristics. This attempt at a hermeneutic unlocking of the phenomena to be interpreted does not confine itself to exact description but moves from analysing elements on the surface to deciphering elements of their deep structure. 'What is, is more than it is' (Adorno 1973: 160). This 'more', the wealth of variants in any matter under scrutiny, can be opened up by 'immersion in the interior', a mode of interpretation[10] that mobilizes theoretical constructs and variant readings that have to be strictly relevant so as to try and articulate whatever phenomenon one wishes to explain by examining it in the light of ever new reference points, points of view and perspectives.

Thus the critical theory of society as Adorno conceived it is no theory with a systematic aim. It consists rather of a variety of individual analyses. This explains why he speaks explicitly of thinking in models: 'The model captures the specific, and more than the specific, without dissipating it in its superior concept' (Adorno 1973: 29, alternative translation). The truth of theory, then, consists not simply in matching propositions to the given realities to which they refer, but it lies in the linguistic expression, i.e., in uttering 'what one perceives in the world'. Just as the world itself is contradictory and divided, so too the process of acquiring knowledge cannot but be painful, a process that while conscious of the possibility of a life rightly lived is able to give an account of the absurdity of the course of the world (Cf. Adorno 1974a: vol. 1: 86ff. and 160ff.).

Jürgen Habermas: the linguistic turn of critical theory

Honneth regards the *Dialectic of Enlightenment* as the exemplary model of a world-disclosing social critique whose meaning consists in 'provoking a changed perception of the inventory of our seemingly familiar life-world such as will enable us to become aware of its pathological nature'.[11] Habermas, in contrast, classifies that document as its joint authors' 'blackest book' (Habermas 1994: 106). His fundamental analysis of the radical critique of both enlightenment and rationality in the *Dialectic of Enlightenment* leads to significant conclusions. Proceeding from the thesis that their totalizing critique became ensnared in a performative self-contradiction,[12] Habermas attempts to establish a new rationale for the core of critical theory, namely criticism itself. In this sense, he remains part of the tradition of critical theory itself. However, when he looks for answers to a question Adorno and Horkheimer had left open, he goes beyond the 'basic concepts of its philosophy of consciousness' (Habermas 1982: 7). This question is: how is critical thinking itself to be legitimated? Habermas discovers the foundations of critique not by analysing the deficiencies of older critical theory, but through the systematic examination and productive appropriation of the analytical philosophy of language and pragmatic action-theory.[13] These inputs were a factor in his definition of language as a social 'meta-institution'. Since his 'turn from the theory of knowledge to the theory of communication' (Habermas 1982: 10) he works on the assumption that critique is embedded in the structure of language because it opens up the path to dissent. For Habermas the true locus of critique is the practice of non-coercive argument. This is based on the premise that Habermas systematically elaborates in the course of his attempt at linguistic self-clarification: 'Reaching understanding is the inherent telos of human speech' (Habermas 1984 [1981]: 287).

Having established that the precondition of the entry of rationality into social existence lies in a linguistically mediated communication process, Habermas then passed a second crucial 'junction' [*Weichenstellung*]: If human beings reach an understanding with one another through language, then claims make themselves felt – he calls them 'validity claims' – that are open to inspection and can therefore be criticized in principle. As long as an exchange of views allows for the expression of reasons and counter-reasons we are justified in expecting that what will finally prevail is the non-coercive force of the superior argument. For 'reasons are made of a special stuff; they force us to say Yes or No to a particular viewpoint. This means that an element of unconditionality enters into the conditions of action oriententated towards reaching an understanding. And it is this element that distinguishes the validity we claim for our own views from the merely social acceptance of conventional practices.' (Habermas 1990b [1981]: 19 [alternative translation]). Thus Habermas overcomes the perspective that has hitherto prevailed in European philosophy of consciousness, namely that of the purposive activity of the isolated subject. It is superseded by the interaction of people who speak and act with one another.

This leads him to pass a third significant junction: in the course of these interactions, the actors, apart from their pursuit of specific goals, lay claim to an agreement that is related in its turn to the recognized norms and values of society. At its most basic level, this agreement consists in people speaking the truth, behaving rightly and representing themselves in a truthful fashion. This premise enables Habermas to build a bridge to the diagnosis of the age. What he foregrounds is the situation of the communicative process. The social dynamics of the development of modern society can be disrupted at a fundamental level if the everyday practice of communication is replaced by calculations of a purely instrumental or strategic nature.

In his principal work, *The Theory of Communicative Action* of 1981, Habermas presents a programme that is designed to do justice to the increased complexity of modern societies. From the standpoint of the observer – and this is Habermas's fourth crucial 'junction' – societies are antagonistic unities consisting of the basic elements of 'the system' and 'the life-world'. These two fundamental categories comprehend, on the one hand, the institutions and organizations of the economy and the state that attempt to wield influence with the aid of money and power. On the other hand, the concept of the life-world serves to accentuate the autonomy of the communal sphere of intuitive certainties. It is once again the 'logos of language' that establishes 'the intersubjectivity of the life-world' in which we find ourselves informed in advance so that we may encounter one another face to face as subjects, as subjects, moreover, whose soundness of mind is presupposed, in other words, our ability to base our actions on transcendent validity claims' (Habermas 1991: 155). The life-world is the realm in which three processes take place through interactions orientated towards reaching an understanding:

1 the transmission of cultural knowledge;
2 the integration into society through individuals' mutual recognition of each other; and
3 the formation of responsible persons with a developed sense of their own identity.

In view of the fact that each of these two realms, the life-world and the system, is governed by its own laws, social critique amounts to a process of enlightenment about tendencies for the life-world to be colonized by the abstract functional mechanisms of the system. Society must be analysed by a diagnosis with a significant theoretical and an empirically substantial content. Such an analysis functions as an 'early-warning system'. Social criticism raises its voice when everyday communicative processes find themselves under attack from money and power, since their encroachments threaten the existence of the meanings underpinning the socio-cultural life-world. This can be seen whenever cultural practices are regulated by financial factors and the conditions of life are subjected to administrative constraints. Habermas warns that meaning can be neither purchased nor acquired by force. The goal of social criticism in Habermas's view 'is no longer simply the elimination of a system of domination consisting of an independent capitalist economy and an equally independent bureaucracy', as was the case in Adorno and Horkheimer, 'but the democratic rolling back of the colonizing *assaults* of the system on realms of the life-world.'[14]

This review of the architecture of Habermasian theory shows that he concretizes critique as enlightenment with the aid of the central concept of an argumentative practice. This form of critique has no certainties to fall back on, nor is it motivated by any supposedly authoritative conception of a good life. The social theory that is confident enough to venture evaluative propositions, that is to say, statements about what can be judged to be true and false within a society that is to be structured rationally, is not able on its own to ensure that what ought to be done can be made into the principle informing social practice. It was Marx who had originally advanced the idea that social theory should become practice. But however self-critically it is formulated, this idea is an illusion (Habermas 1999: 233ff.), in Habermas's view, an illusion incidentally whose seductive power in a world of instrumental thinking Adorno warned about.[15] Social theory can only become effective in practice as critique if the social scientist is able to convince anyone who suffers from questionable social trends that he has good reason to accept that these trends are questionable. Social criticism can only have practical consequences if the validity claims associated with it are able to withstand critical scrutiny in the autonomous realm of social reality. Two aspects of criticism are available to social theory. It convinces us as a critique *of* states of communication if analysis enables it to expose systemic distortions of communication; and social theory is fruitful *in* communication situations if the theoretician is able to assume the role of the public intellectual,[16] the expert in practical discourse,[17] and to captivate us with his arguments. In both cases, social criticism depends on moral knowledge that 'consists of a supply of convincing reasons for the consensual resolution of the kind of conflicts that occur in the life-world' (Habermas 1999: 304). This means that while Habermas considers his own social theory to represent a new beginning, a break with the tradition of Horkheimer and Adorno, his defence of a fallibilistic consciousness means that he retains their critical project.

If we attempt to sum up a response to the question of how critical thinking can be justified, we can emphasize three points. First, we may note that the definition of critique as the exposure of the factors that inhibit it, i.e. the structures of systemically distorted communication, is a constant theme of Habermas's work. He understands this programme as an extension of the critical theory of society. There is a further continuity on the question of critical authority: it is fundamentally those who are affected who must convince themselves and be able to reach agreement about what they wish to accept or reject. This strips criticism of its exclusiveness and so means that it acts out the role of one good argument alongside other good arguments. It can be shown to be superior only by the weight of the arguments in its favour. A further aspect is that within the framework of the philosophy of language (formal pragmatics) Habermas has succeeded in developing a general theory of criticizability. The critical function of this theory, which reconstructs the possibility of critique in principle, consists in the ability to differentiate between what is factually the case and what can lay claim to validity.

From the theory of criticizability to the rehabilitation of social critique

Jürgen Habermas's grounding of social critique in the pragmatics of language has proved to be too abstract for a younger generation of social theorists who began by accepting his *Theory of Communicative Action* as their starting-point, but then tried to overcome his paradigm of reaching understanding. Pride of place here goes to the social philosopher Axel Honneth. Honneth has succeeded to Habermas's chair in Frankfurt and is the current director of the legendary Institute of Social Research. He represents what has recently been termed the 'recognition' turn in critical theory. This focuses on the question of the paths taken by groups and individuals to secure their social significance within the contexts of their own lives. What are the prelinguistic processes that enable people to become conscious of who and what they would like to be in society? Is it possible to realize one's own aspirations? Will they be respected or disrespected? According to Honneth, social theory must respond to experiences in which people give expression to the fact that their claims have been slighted, that their aspirations have been disrespected in society and by it. Coming from this perspective of disrespect, he focuses on deep-seated anthropological perceptions of justice that, as he says, 'are intimately bound up with the respect due to one's own dignity, honour or integrity' (Honneth 2000c: 103).

Honneth's critical debate with critical theory as represented variously by Horkheimer, Adorno and Habermas is marked by his wish to rescue its core element:[18] that of critique as a normative, context-transcending procedure. In his reconstruction of the elements common to the different conceptions of critical theory,[19] Honneth singles out six features. In the first place, there is 'the idea of a deficient rationality in society' and the 'idea of a socially effective rationality', both of which constitute central elements of the different critical theories (Honneth 2004: 10f.). In the second, Horkheimer, Adorno and Habermas all 'assumed that the cause of the negative state of society must be sought in a deficiency of social rationality' (Honneth 2004: 12). At the same time, their positions are all determined by the premise that 'the socialization of human beings can only taken place under the conditions of free cooperation' (Honneth 2004: 15). Lastly, these different approaches shared the conviction that the structural power relations in society could not become visible as such because their own dynamics effectively obscure them, making them appear to operate according to natural laws. 'This means that because in critical theory a relationship of cause and effect is presupposed in the connection between social evils and the absence of negative reactions [on the part of those affected], a normative critique has to be supplemented by an element of historical explanation' (Honneth 2004: 19). According to Honneth, all critical theorists are convinced that the capitalist economy has created structures that are incompatible with the realization of a rational society. In its turn, this patholological situation is the cause of the social sufferings which feed the desire for self-determining forms of life.

In Honneth's view the greatest failing of the critical theorists lies in their inability to provide meaningful empirical evidence of the ways in which conflicts arising from social evils and the experience of subjective suffering can be converted into the practical action that must be seen as the precondition for the elimination of degrading circumstances. 'On the contrary, the question of the motives and attitudes that might spur people to act, a question that ought to be central here, is largely ignored because reflection on the conditions for the practical application of ideas is not seen as falling within the remit of critique' (Honneth 2004: 25, cf. also Roth 1994: 422ff). This blank space is one Honneth would like to fill with a new orientation towards a practice-related philosophy or sociology. Starting from the premise that the gaining of social recognition is the normative precondition of communicative action, the task of a modern critical theory of society must be to examine the historical roots and the social causes of the ways in which the claims of individuals and social groups to their own identity have been violated as a consequence of the lack of mutual recognition in the course of their ordinary life together. The focus of critical analysis is no longer the communication situation, as it was with Habermas, but the circumstances surrounding recognition, or alternatively the social causes leading to its systematic violation. Honneth's starting-point is the belief that 'there is an intimate connection between the damage done to the normative assumptions of social interaction and the moral experience of individuals in their everyday interactions: if these assumptions are undermined because a person is denied the recognition he deserves, he will generally react with the moral feelings that accompany the experience of disdain, in other words, shame, outrage or indignation.'[20] The variant of critical theory developed by Honneth retraces the path back to the criticism of actual society whose pathological features are analysed as deformations and deficiencies in the sphere of social recognition. In support of this idea of providing a normatively substantive diagnosis of the age by examining empirical forms of disrespect, Honneth differentiates between three patterns of mutual recognition: first, affection in the realm of friendships or love relationships; second, one's right to legal recognition as a person defending one's own legitimate interests; and finally, the social value placed on personal achievements which enable the members of society to give proof of their specific skills. This conception of social criticism sets out to thematize the moral experiences of individuals who have found their claims to an emotional life, legal security and social esteem disrespected.[21]

No doubt, Honneth remains fundamentally committed to critique as a strong form of social analysis. Its task is to diagnose the social pathologies of modernization that have not yet manifested themselves in actual conflicts and crises, so that it has not become possible to get a handle on them. They persist as latent forms of anomie that can lead to visible disturbances, and dangers, distorted ways of seeing and false estimates of one's own value. If these social and cultural deficiencies are to be made visible, we need a radically new account of our accustomed view of the circumstances of people's lives, one that opens the eyes of those affected to whatever it is that consciously or unconsciously causes them suffering. According to Honneth, the *Dialectic of Enlightenment* is the prototype of such world-disclosing critique. It persuades us not so much by virtue of its normative and rational cogency, but thanks to its mode of expression. Its purpose is to contribute to changes in social life-practices. Honneth has vigorously defended this quite specific model of critique, and he has sought to supplement and expand it by adding a genealogical way of thinking to the method of reconstruction as immanent critique that was practised by Horkheimer, Adorno and Habermas. He interprets reconstruction as an immanent method that makes it possible to expose the emancipatory ideals that are embedded in society, but are repressed. These ideals can then come into play as the reference points of a 'context-transcending' critique because what they express is the latest historical stage of social rationality or the latest possible degrees of freedom. With genealogy he establishes a link with the project that goes back to Nietzsche 'of criticizing a social order in such a manner as to demonstrate historically the degree to which its determining ideals and norms are employed to legitimate a disciplinary or repressive practice' (Honneth 2000a: 733 and 735). Thus Honneth retains the idea of a *world-disclosing* socio-philosophical critique that attempts to transcend and sublate routine values, but he also adds to it an immanent *reconstructive* and *genealogical* principle. This latter reminds society of its own ideals and their faults, while the former shows how those ideals turn into their opposite, namely into practices that stabilize systems of domination. 'Thus a social critique that has learnt from the *Dialectic of Enlightenment* circumscribes the norms available to it from two different sides. On the one hand, as socially embodied ideals these norms have to satisfy the criterion of expressing the process of social rationalization; on the other hand, they must be scrutinized to determine whether in their social practice they still retain their original meanings.' No social critique can survive today unless it conducts genealogical researches to track down changes in the meanings of its ruling ideals' (Honneth 2000a: 737).

Even if this conceptual distinction allows us to grasp the distinct modes of critique in critical theory with greater precision, and therefore test their limits, their rational basis, the question of the relations between world-disclosing, reconstrucive and genealogical critique still remain open.

Outlook: putting an inheritance to good use

Despite Habermas's and Honneth's efforts to overcome the older critical theory of Horkheimer and Adorno, striking continuities persist. Thus the critical element in their differing theories of society remains sensitive to social abuses and to injustice. Just as Horkheimer had insisted on critique as the moral insight that manifests itself in compassion, and Adorno wanted his form of critique to help those who experienced real suffering in history to give expression to it, so Habermas linked his thinking with the negative idea of the abolition of discrimination and suffering. In a similar vein, Honneth understands critical theory as a morally inspired form of thinking that must basically be concerned to eliminate every conceivable form of disrespect and humiliation.

Although this striking consensus with regard to their moral point of view is very evident, we can nowadays speak of critical theory only in the plural, since over the past fifty years it has generated different varieties of critique. Whereas the older generation envisaged a historical state of affairs in which, in Adorno's words, 'people can be different without fear' (Adorno 1974b: 103), Habermas and Honneth have come to focus more on the conditions of reaching an understanding or obtaining recognition. What potential for the further development of critical theory can we discern in this heterogeneous picture? 'To the degree to which social and political structures remain what they were, it seems sensible to retain the insights of the *older generation* and to continue their analyses. Where they have changed, new theoretical efforts will be needed that can follow where the classics had led. Instead of precipitately labelling the earlier versions "obsolete" and ignoring them, *all* approaches should be preserved and continued. Instead of playing individual thinkers off against each other, critical theory should be concerned to relate to the *entire* tradition' (Roth 1994: 444f.). Compared to the older critical theory, the younger generation is considerably more cautious about the political and practical dimensions of critique. In particular, the modesty of Habermas's claims is very striking. He refuses to grant the sciences a privileged role. Social criticism is not able to change the world on its own, however conceptually sophisticated it may be. In reality, there is no such thing as a World Spirit to which the representatives of critical theory have privileged access and to whose authority they could appeal. The key idea that the critical critic has a special insight, a special position, has to be abandoned, just as there is no reason to believe either that the necessary development of critical theory must involve the denunciation of others, or that it need be harmless in principle.

(Translated by Rodney Livingstone.)

Notes

1 Thanks to his own political foresight Horkheimer had made sure that the funds of the Institute of Social Research were safely removed from Germany and at the same time he made preparations to set up Institute branches in Geneva, Paris and London. Julian Gumperz, a member of the Institute and a native American, was able to establish personal contacts with Columbia where he was given a highly encouraging reception by its president, Nicholas Murray Butler, as well as such leading sociologists as Robert S. Lund and Robert MacIver. It was this fact that led Horkheimer to decide fairly promptly in favour of the USA.

2 The idea of critique also extended to the dogmatic element in Marxism. Dubiel notes quite accurately: 'The choice of the term "critical theory" arose not simply from a wish to disguise [its Marxist roots – trans.] in emigration in North America. It desired also to convey the message that here was a different political theory at work' (Dubiel 1995: 70).

3 This somewhat defensive description of Horkheimer's own project as social theorist implies that the most he could achieve in an age of 'inhumanity' (Horkheimer 1988) was to preserve the rational and the just in the form of a correct theory. With this Horkheimer effectively abandoned his original programme as he had conceived it in 1931 as the youthful director of the Institute of Social Research. The speech he had given six years previously on taking up his duties as director still envisaged that the Institute's work would have as its main focus the long-term interdisciplinary collaboration of the traditional departments – economics, sociology, psychology, history and law. Simultaneously, the individual disciplines together with their own methodologies were to feed into the formation of socio-philosophical theory. At the time, two years before Hitler came to power, Horkheimer was chiefly interested in applying the most progressive empirical research tools to explore the factors conditioning the formation (or the distortion) of human consciousness, and to analyse the connections between the economy, the psychological development of individuals and cultural change. However, following the triumph of fascism and the subsequent spread of totalitarian governments, his programme was narrowed down to ensuring the survival of critical theory as an alternative philosophical praxis. The small circle of thinkers who continued to assert the claims of social criticism within sociological theory had now become the representatives of the cause of emancipation with the idea of a self-determining society as its focal point, a cause that, given the condition of the world as a whole, had now become homeless.

4 Cf. Bonß (2003: 368). See also Müller-Doohm (2000: 71ff).

5 See Müller-Doohm (2003: 112ff. and 203ff); see also Müller-Doohm (2004b).

6 Nevertheless, the differences of opinion between Horkheimer and Adorno are plain to see. 'Whereas Adorno reflected on the problem [of critique] in *methodological* terms, and put in a plea for analytical strategies that would be exemplary and take monograph form . . . Horkheimer argued more strongly in terms of the *organization of scientific thought*' (Bonß 2003: 375, his emphasis).

7 Adorno, Theodor, 'The Actuality of Philosophy' (trans. Benjamin Snow), in O'Connor (2000: 25).

8 Bonacker (2006). Bonacker develops the thesis that Adorno's concept of interpretation satisfies the requirements of his own conviction that interpretation is contingent in principle, and that it does so simply and solely because of the paradoxical presuppositions of the hermeneutic process. See also Bonacker (2000: 153ff); cf. Garcia Düttmann (2004).

9 Adorno (1974b: 126). Elsewhere he writes: 'All thinking is exaggeration, in so far as every thought that is one at all goes beyond its confirmation by the given facts.' 'Opinion Delusion Society', in Adorno (1998: 108).

10 Adorno's hermeneutic approach should be distinguished from an intentionalist (subjective) hermeneutics that is concerned to reconstruct a subjectively intended meaning: 'But since it is scarcely possible to determine what someone may have thought or felt at any particular point, nothing essential is to be gained through such insights. The author's impulses are extinguished in the objective substance they seize hold of' Adorno (1991: vol. 1, 4). There are striking resemblances between Adorno's dialectical method, which was only developed in rudimentary fashion and the methods of an objective hermeneutics developed by Ulrich Oevermann over recent decades. See Oevermann (1983: 234ff); and also Oevermann (1991: 267ff.).

11 Honneth (2000b: 84); contrast Honneth (1985: 54ff., 65ff. and 74ff.) Given the premises of the *Dialectic of Enlightenment*, how is critical theory 'able to make justifiable assertions about reality, if it is initially able to disclose reality only with the aid of conceptual knowledge?' (Honneth 1991: 63).

12 Ibid. 119ff. Objections to Habermas's critique of *Dialectic of Enlightenment* can be found in Bonacker. See Bonacker (2000: 130ff.).

13 Cf. Bonacker (2000: 115ff.). He distinguishes there between Habermas's social turn, as expressed in *Knowledge and Human Interests*, and the linguistic and pragmatic turns.

14 Habermas (1990a: 36) Preface to the new edition; cf. Habermas (1994: 362ff.).

15 Adorno, 'Marginalia to Theory and Praxis', in Adorno (1998: 259ff.). There he writes: 'The goal of right practice would be its own abolition.' [translation altered] (267). Against this background Seel was right to emphasize the contemplative aspects of Adorno's philosophy. 'The centre of gravity of Adorno's entire philosophy can be found in states of non-instrumental behaviour that are presented as those of a free and easy subjective and inter-subjective existence' (Seel 2004: 35).

16 In his role as public intellectual the [social] scientist abandons his professional role and appeals to a functioning political public sphere. Habermas's own activity as an intellectual demonstrates that what the intellectual wants is not to exert a strategic influence on the political power struggle, but to communicate, i.e. reach an understanding with an autonomous, pluralistic public sphere. The intel-

lectual can gain recognition as a moral authority through the quality of his arguments which have to prove their worth as stimuli for public debate amidst the hurly-burly of political discussion. See Müller-Doohm (2005).

17 Habermas defines discourse as a form of communicative action that has become reflexive, i.e., a form of argumentative practice in which problematic validity claims are treated as hypotheses: 'Among the necessary presuppositions of argument as an activity must be mentioned the complete inclusiveness of the participants, the equal distribution of rights and duties in argument, the non-coerciveness of the communication situation and the open-mindedness of the participants' Habermas (1999: 310f.).

18 Honneth arrives at different conclusions in an earlier discussion of the critical theory of Adorno and Horkheimer, conclusions that are closer to the objections raised by Habermas. Cf. Honneth (1985: 12ff. and 307ff.).

19 One would reach other conclusions if, instead of emphasizing the features common to Adorno, Horkheimer and Habermas, one were to highlight the differences between them. What emerges is that critique is grounded and implemented in very different ways. Cf. Müller-Doohm (2000: 71ff.).

20 Honneth (2000c: 100); cf. also Honneth (2000d: 180ff.) and also 1995. Here the author attempts for the first time to elaborate his idea of recognition on the basis of Hegel's theory of recognition in his Jena writings.

21 Klaus Roth (1994: 442) rightly asks: 'It remains an open question whether the doctrine of recognition can be upheld independently of its foundations in the philosophy of consciousness. The human desire for recognition finds gratification today not only in the contradiction-free and unproblematic forms of social intercourse, informal conversation, love, friendship and solidarity, etc. It is expressed not only in the various forms of cooperation, discursive will-formation and non-coercive communication, but continues also to be realized predominantly in the course of disagreeable activities and less than harmonious forms of life.'

References

Adorno, T. W. (1973 [1966]) *Negative Dialectics*, trans. E. B. Ashton, London: Routledge.

Adorno, T. W. (1974a) *Philosophische Terminologie*, vols. 1 and 2, Rudolf zur Lippe (ed.), Frankfurt am Main: Suhrkamp.

Adorno, T. W. (1974b [1951]) *Minima Moralia*, trans. E. Jephcott, London: NLB.

Adorno, T. W. (1982 [1970]) *Against Epistemology: A Metacritique*, trans. W. Domingo, Oxford: Basil Blackwell.

Adorno, T. W. (1991 [1958, 1961, 1965 and 1974]) *Notes to Literature*, trans. S. Weber Nicholsen, New York: Columbia University Press.

Adorno, T. W. (1998 [1963 and 1969]) *Critical Models*, trans. H. Pickford, New York: Columbia University Press.

Adorno, T. W. (2000) *The Actuality of Philosophy*, Cambridge: Polity Press.

Bonacker, T. (2000a) 'Ungewissheit und Unbedingtheit. Zu den Möglichkeitsbedingungen des Normativen', in S. Müller-Doohm (ed.), *Das Interesse der Vernunft. Rückblicke auf das Werk von Jürgen Habermas seit 'Erkenntnis und Interesse'*, Frankfurt am Main: Suhrkamp, pp. 107–143.

Bonacker, T. (2000b) *Die normative Kraft der Kontingenz. Nichtessentialistische Gesellschaftskritik nach Weber und Adorno*, Frankfurt am Main: Campus.

Bonacker, T. (2006) Erschließende Kritik. Über zwei Arten des Umgangs mit der Kontingenz des Verstehens bei Adorno. [English trans. 'Disclosing Critique: The Contingency of Understanding in Adornos Interpretative Social Theory', *European Journal of Social Theory*, 8(4).]

Bonß, W. (2003) 'Warum ist die kritische Theorie kritisch? Anmerkungen zu alten und neuen Entwürfen', in A. Demirovic (ed.) *Modelle kritischer Gesellschaftstheorie*, 366-392, Stuttgart and Weimar: Metzler.

Dubiel, H. (1995) 'Die verstummten Erben. Kritische Theorie in der Krise', in *Die Neue Rundschau*, S. 64-75, Frankfurt: Fischer.

Garcia Düttmann, A. (2004) *Philosophie der Übertreibung*, Frankfurt am Main: Suhrkamp.

Habermas, J. (1981) *Kleine politische Schriften* (I-IV), Frankfurt am Main: Suhrkamp.

Habermas, J. (1982) *Zur Logik der Sozialwissenschaften*, Frankfurt am Main: Suhrkamp.

Habermas, J. (1984 [1981]) *The Theory of Communicative Action* vol. 1, trans. T. McCarthy, Boston: Beacon Press.

Habermas, J. (1990a) *Strukturwandel der Öffentlichkeit*, Frankfurt am Main: Suhrkamp.

Habermas, J. (1990b [1983]) *Moral Consciousness and Communicative Action*, trans. C. Lenhardt and S. Weber Nicholsen, Cambridge, MA: The MIT Press.

Habermas, J. (1991) *Texte und Kontexte*, Frankfurt am Main: Suhrkamp.

Habermas, J. (1994 [1985]) *The Philosophical Discourse of Modernity*, trans. F. Lawrence, Cambridge: Polity Press.

Habermas, J. (1999) 'Noch einmal: Zum Verhältnis von Theorie und Praxis', in J. Habermas *Wahrheit und Rechtfertigung*, S. 319-334, Frankfurt am Main: Suhrkamp.

Honneth, A. (1985) *Kritik der Macht. Reflexionsstufen einer kritischen Gesellschaftstheorie*, Frankfurt am Main: Suhrkamp.

Honneth, A. (1991 [1985]) *The Critique of Power*, trans. Kenneth Baynes, Cambridge, MA and London: The MIT Press.

Honneth, A. (1995 [1992]) *The Struggle for Recognition*, Cambridge: Polity Press.

Honneth, A. (2000a) 'Rekonstruktive Gesellschaftskritik unter genealogischem Vorbehalt. Zur Idee der 'Kritik' in der Frankfurter Schule', in *Deutsche Zeitschrift für Philosophie*, 729-737, Berlin: Akademie Verlag.

Honneth, A. (2000b) 'Über die Möglichkeit einer erschließenden Kritik. Die 'Dialektik der Aufklärung' im Horizont gegenwärtiger Debatten über Sozialkritik', in A. Honneth, *Das Andere der Gerechtigkeit. Aufsätze zur praktischen Philosophie*, 70-88, Frankfurt am Main: Suhrkamp.

Honneth, A. (2000c) *Die soziale Dynamik von Missachtung*, Frankfurt am Main: Suhrkamp, pp. 88–110.

Honneth, A. (2000d) *Zwischen Aristoteles und Kant. Skizze einer Moral der Anerkennung*, Frankurt am Main: Suhrkamp, pp. 171–193.

Honneth, A. (2004) 'Eine soziale Pathologie der Vernunft. Zur intellektuellen Erbschaft der kritischen Theorie', in C. Halbig and M. Quante (eds) *Axel Honneth: Sozialphilosophie zwischen Kritik und Anerkennung,* Münster: Lit-Verlag.

Horkheimer, M. (1988) *Gesammelte Schriften* (GS), vol. 4, ed. Alfred Schmidt, Frankfurt am Main: Fischer.

Horkheimer, M. and Adorno, T. W. (2002 [1987, 1947]) *Dialectic of Enlightenment*, trans. E. Jephcott, Stanford, CA: Stanford University Press.

McCarthy, T. (1991) *Ideals and Illusions: on Reconstruction and Deconstruction in Contemporary Critical Theory*, Cambridge, MA and Cambridge, England: The MIT Press.

Müller-Doohm, S. (2000) 'Kritik in kritischen Theorien. Oder wie kritisches Denken selber zu rechtfertigen sei', in S. Müller-Doohm (ed.), *Das Interesse der Vernunft. Rückblicke auf das Werk von Jürgen Habermas seit 'Erkenntnis und Interesse'*, 71-107, Frankfurt am Main: Suhrkamp.

Müller-Doohm, S. (2003) *Adorno. Eine Biographie*, Frankfurt am Main: Suhrkamp. [English trans. *Adorno. A Biography*, Cambridge: Polity Press, 2005.]

Müller-Doohm, S. (2004a) *Sagen, was einem aufgeht. Sprache bei Adorno – Adornos Sprache* in Reinhard Schulz (ed.) *Philosophie in Literarischen und ästhetischen Gestalten*, Oldenburg: BIS.

Müller-Doohm, S. (2004b) 'Vom Niemandsland aus denken. Leben und Werk von Theodor W. Adorno', in *Swiss Journal of Sociology* 30(1), 21–24.

Müller-Doohm, S. (2005) 'Theodor W. Adorno and Jürgen Habermas: Two Ways of Being a Public Intellectual', *European Journal of Social Theory*, 813: 269–280.

Müller-Doohm, S. (2005) 'Thinking from No-man's land: The Life and Work of Theodor W. Adorno', *Social and Political Thought*, 11: 91–103, Sussex University.

O'Connor, B. (ed.) (2000) *The Adorno Reader*, Oxford: Blackwell.

Oevermann, U. (1983) 'Zur Sache. Die Bedeutung von Adornos methodologischem Selbstverständnis für die Begründung einer materialen soziologischen Strukturanalyse', in Ludwig von. Friedeberg/ Jürgen Habermas (eds), *Adorno Konferenz 1983*, 234–289, Frankfurt am Main: Suhrkamp.

Oevermann, U. (1991) Genetischer Strukturalismus und das Problem der Erklärung und Entstehung des Neuen, in S. Müller-Doohm (ed.), *Jenseits der Utopie. Theoriekritik der Gegenwart*, 267–336, Frankfurt am Main: Suhrkamp.

Roth, K. (1994) 'Neue Entwicklungen der kritischen Theorie', in *Leviathan*, 3: Westdeutscher Verlag, pp. 422–445.

Schnädelbach, H. (1983) 'Dialektik als Vernunftkritik. Zur Konstruktion des Rationalen bei Adorno', in L. von Friedeburg and J. Habermas (eds), *Adorno-Konferenz 1983*, Frankfurt am Main: Suhrkamp, 66ff.

Seel, M. (2004) *Adornos Philosophie der Kontemplation*, Frankfurt am Main: Suhrkamp.

14

After dialectics

Postmodernity, post-Marxism, and other posts and positions

Göran Therborn

The broken triangle

The classical Marxist triangle of social science, politics, and philosophy – constituted by the oeuvre of Marx and Engels and continued for the major part of the past century – has been broken, most probably irredeemably. Socialist politics, as politics for a different, socialist society has not disappeared. Where the electoral system allows its expression, it oscillates between 5 and 20 per cent of the national vote. It may well become much larger. Political ideologies and orientations have their ups and downs, and post-socialism may soon be over-shadowed by some new socialism. But the underdeveloped Marxist political theory and the social restructuration of capitalist societies make it unlikely that an ascendant Socialist politics would be very Marxist. The zenith of the industrial working-class has passed, while many previously neglected political subjects are entering the front stage.

Under non-repressive conditions, Marxism is unlikely to be attractive as *the* social science or historiography of committed Socialist scholars. By the standards of physics or biology, the advances of social science and of historical scholarship may look modest, but they nevertheless represent enormous strides forward compared to the times of Marx. However, it is also true, that each generation of social scientists tends to find new springs of inspiration among the classics of social thought. Therefore, it seems to be the best bet that Marx will be re-discovered many times over in the future, novel interpretations will be made, and new kinds of inspiration may be found – but conducive to little ism-ic identification.

Philosophers, on the other hand, are usually, rather than occasionally, bent over their pre-decessors. Whether Marx will have the same longevity of up to 2,500 years which Plato, Aristotle, and Confucius have already achieved, is still an open question. But the grounds for ruling it out look flimsy. A ghost never dies, as Derrida (1993: 163) said. The history of philosophy tends to generate ever new techniques of reading. Even the 1990s of triumphant neoliberalism saw two new remarkable readings of Marx, *Spectres of Marx* by Jacques Derrida (1993), and *The Postmodern Marx* by Terrell Carver (1998). (The decade also saw two huge retrospectives on Marx and his social and political thought, namely Jessop and Malcolm-Brown 1990 and Jessop and Wheatley 1999.)

Both new readings saw Marxes in plural and both underlined, in a sympathetic-cum-critical way the political meaning and significance of Marx, but as a historical individual political figure out of joint with any Marxism of contemporary movements. Derrida (1993: 151) placed his own whole oeuvre of deconstruction 'within a certain tradition of Marxism, within a certain spirit of Marxism', while flashing literary fireworks over his serious reading. (cf. the discussion of Derrida's book in Sprinkler 1999). Carver's (1998: 2) postmodernism was a 'mild' one, which did not confront modernity and the Enlightenment, and manifested itself mainly in a perceptive analysis of Marx's language and writing strategies in various texts and on different topics. Through cultural journalists and university graduate students, even rather abstruse Marxist political philosophers can establish some conduits to, minoritarian but not necessarily insignificant, political discourse.

The challenge of postmodernity

While 'post-Marxism' first of all has a political background, it is also part of a cultural shift, the rise of postmodernism and denial of modernity in the name of postmodernity. Post-modernism has at least two, very different roots (see further the unrivalled critical archaeology of Anderson 1996). One aesthetic is a mutation of the modernist succession of avant-gardes, having its most articulate base in architecture, reacting against the austere High Modernism of Mies van der Rohe and the 'International Style'. The other is a social philosophy, a mani-festation of ex-Leftist exhaustion and disillusion. The key figure here is the late French phi-losopher Jean-François Lyotard (1984 [1979]), a disillusioned former militant of the far-left grouplet *Socialisme ou Barbarie*.

Why did postmodernism become such a formidable challenge? Why was postmodernity 'badly needed, intuitively longed for, and desperately sought', as a wise old early devotee put it, from a recently acquired somewhat more sceptical hindsight (Bauman and Tester 2001: 71). The aesthetic attraction is easily understandable. Above all, it is another manifestation of the relentless modernist drive for innovation, while its specific forms may seen as influenced by opposition to its immediate predecessor/enemy, as well as by its socio-cultural context (cf. Jameson 1991; Anderson 1998: ch. 4). But that does not take us very far with respect to the theoretical and political significance of postmodernism.

To get at that, we have to start from noting that outside specific audiences of architecture and art, postmodernism originated from and spoke to the Left and the ex-Left, including left wing Feminism. Therefore, it did not even notice, or pay any serious attention to, the simultaneous rise of right wing modernism, in the form of neoliberalism or assertive capitalism. Instead, postmodernism fed on the demoralization and uncertainty of the Left after the brief euphoria of the late 1960s–1970s. Its critique of reason and rationality thrived on the 'machinery of images' of television society (Anderson 1998: 88), which provided academic sustenance to 'cultural studies'. But there were more two more pillars of the new edifice of postmodernity.

One was the social re-structuration following from de-industrialization, which undoubt-edly was an epochal social change. Another was the critique of modernist progress that arose from ecological considerations, which were greatly boosted by the oil crises of the 1970s and early 1980s. Environmentalism has had a difficult entry into the esoteric air of postmodernist philosophizing, but it did provide a receptive soil to the latter. In brief, mass communicated imagery, de-industrialization, and ecological blowbacks provided a social echo chamber to the postmodernist discourse of (ex-)Left disorientation.

But what was challenged? Modernity, the target of postmodernist attacks, has been defined in a number of ways. The most fruitful definitions are the least arbitrary and idiosyncratic, which usually implies a respect for etymological meaning and an abstention from loading the definition with aprioristic connotations. Modernity should then be seen as a temporal orientation only. Modernity is a culture claiming to be modern, in the sense of turning its back on the past – the old, the traditional, the *passé* – and looking into the future as a reachable, novel horizon (cf. Kosellek 1979: 314ff; Habermas 1985: 14–15). Modern man/woman, society, civilization have a direction, 'forward'. As it was put in the old GDR, 'Forward always, backwards never' (rhyming in German, *Vorwärts immer, rückwärts nimmer*). In order to keep its analytical edge, modernity should not be trivialized by attempts at translating it into concrete institutions, whether of capitalism or of politics, nor dressed up for easy philosophical targeting as a particular conception of rationality or of the subject. It had better be used only as a temporal signifier.

Marx and Marxism were very much modern in this sense, invoking it again and again in the *Communist Manifesto* and in the *Capital,* the 'ultimate purpose of which' was to 'disclose the economic law of motion of modern society', as Marx put in his preface to the first edition of the first volume (cf. Berman 1983). However, and this was crucial, it was a dialectical conception of modernity, as inherently contradictory. The modernity of capitalism and of the bourgeoisie was hailed, but at the same time attacked as exploitative and alienating. This dialectical conception of modernity was, in a sense, the very core of Marxian thought – in ways many would now find insensitive to, for instance, the colonial victims – affirming the progressivity of capitalism, of bourgeois, and even of capitalist imperialist rule, while at the same time, not only denouncing them, but organizing the resistance to them. In broad cultural-historical terms Marxism may be seen as Her Majesty Modernity's Opposition (cf. Therborn 1996). In order to catch a core cultural meaning of Marxism, and of the recent challenges to it, one has to locate it in its dialectical conception of modernity.

Let us first record the most important of the different 'master narratives of modernity' (see Table 14.1).

The first of these perspectives was how Kant defined Enlightenment. After its successes it has lost a good deal of its appeal. But it is today at the centre of controversies about how to explain, prevent, and cope with HIV-Aids and other lethal diseases in Africa and in other parts of the poor world. Is witchcraft a major source of sickness and death? Is penetration of a virgin a cure of Aids?

Collective emancipation/liberation has undergone a remarkable mutation recently, as part of postmodernization. On the whole, it has lost most of its social referents, the working-class, the colonized, women, gay and lesbian people. Above all, it has lost its Socialist horizon of emancipation from capitalism. But it has not disappeared, Instead, it has cropped up in militant liberal-democratic discourse – in right wing modernism, referring to political liberation from a select group of authoritarian political regimes, Communist, post-Communist, or otherwise anti-'Western'. In Indo-Latin America, on the other hand, emancipation has acquired a new social urgency, with the rise of new demands by indigenous populations.

The horizon of growth and progress governs all economies, and is emphatically worshipped by reigning neoliberalism. It is also the continuing story of science. Neoliberal globalization

Table 14.1. Master narratives of modernity

The Past was	The Future will be
Ignorance, superstition, subservience	Emancipation: rational, individual
Oppression, unfreedom	Emancipation/liberation: collective
Poverty, disease, stagnation	Growth, progress, development
Conditions of no/less competition	Survival of the fittest
Rule-bound, Imitative	Creative vitality

has given a new impetus to Social Darwinism, after its post-Fascist quarantine, and the hard struggle for survival. The collapse of rule-bound artistic academicism has left artistic modernism without a target, other than older modernists. The modern conflict of avant-garde and tradition has been replaced by a succession of fashions.

Marx was committed to all the above perspectives, although collective human emancipation and economic development were most central to him. However, what distinguished Marx and Marxism from other strands of modernist thought was a focus on the contradictory character of the modern era, and on these contradictions and conflicts as its most important dynamics (see Table 14.2).

Marxism put a dialectical perspective of emancipation against the linear liberal project of rationalization, progress and growth, explicitly affirming that capitalism and colonialism were exploitation as well as progress. The Marxist perspective also differed from the Weberian disenchantment with the modern rationalization of markets and bureaucracies as an 'iron cage'. The contradictions of modernity, according to Marx, were harbingers of radical change.

Postmodernism attacked all the grand narratives of modernity, while usually ignoring the dialectic conception of Marxism. But all its socio-political advances were against the Modernist left. At the same time, right wing Modernism defeated almost all its traditionalist conservative rivals, most successfully in Thatcher's Britain. Neoliberalism is right wing High Modernism, and it was never hit by postmodernist arguments. The re-invigorated American right is a vivid illustration of modernity entangled (cf. Therborn 2003). While recruiting its storm troopers from Christian fundamentalists, the hegemonic tenor of the American right is its 'willingness to embrace the future', which it believes is their's (Micklethwait and Wooldridge 2004: 346ff). (The theological celebration of worldly success by the mainstream of the new Christian Evangelical fundamentalism facilitates, of course, this powerful brew of secular modernism and religious fundamentalism.)

Modernity has not become an abandoned intellectual position (see, e.g. Habermas 1985; Callinicos 1989; Beck *et al.* 1994; Eagleton 1996). Ulrich Beck has even tried a prophetic mantle proclaiming a 'Second Modernity' in a special book series at Suhrkamp, a theme still being elaborated, incorporated into a still ongoing well-funded research programme. But the socio-political challenge across the whole left-right spectrum has not been really faced up to.

Ulrich Beck's (1992) *Risk Society*, first appearing in German in 1986, is a major theoretical work of the last decades. It did also provide a possible basis for a new conception of modernity. 'Risk may be defined as a systematic way of dealing with hazards and insecurities induced and introduced by modernization itself. Risks ... are politically reflexive' (p. 21, italics omitted). This is an important conceptualization, also finding a political resonance among Green parties and wider ecological concerns. However, the critical edge of it is blunted by two features. First, its basic blindness to what was happening on the right-of-centre of the political scale, the rise of right wing liberal modernism – never as strong in Germany as in the Anglo-Saxon world but politically triumphant since 1982. Second, by

Table 14.2. The Marxian dialectics of capitalist modernity

Progress	Contradiction/Conflict
Individualization	Atomization, alienation
Productivity development	Distributive polarization
	Fettering relations of production
Capitalist extension	Proletarian unification
Globalization	Anti-imperialist revolts

filling his New, later Second Modernity with specific institutional content, with the demise of class, full employment, of nation states, with individual 'release' from industrial institutions, laying his perceptive grasp of a changed time frame open to charges of arbitrary selectivity, bias or empirical unreliability.

Postmodernist discourse has something important to teach, but it should be subjected to a symptomatic rather than a literal reading, as a questioning of non-dialectic conceptions of modernity, as symptoms of disorientations of the (ex-)Left, and as expressions of myopia or blindness, to the world outside the North Atlantic (ex-)Left.

The postmodernization of the world is very uneven. In the frenzied pace of aesthetic discourse, postmodernism may even be 'over', as one of its once most successful presenters put in a second edition epilogue (Hutcheon 2002: 166). Zygmunt Bauman (2000), in advanced age wonderfully tuned in to the shifting sirens of the times, has turned to peddling 'liquid modernity' instead of postmodernity. But, shred of all the narcissistic and vitriolic hyperbole, the two decades of postmodernism, the 1980s and the 1990s, did, as symptoms of their politico-economic times, produce a caesura in left wing social thought, which has not been overcome. The future, as novelty, as difference, disappeared behind a smokescreen.

The ambiguity of social theory

Having laid out the parameters of recent social theorizing and of its changes, before moving on there is another beginning question to be answered: 'What is social theory?' – which this volume is supposed to accompany. Because of editorial licence, the individual author has to finds his/her own answer. To me, social theory is hung up between two ambitious poles, between providing a comprehensive explanation or explanatory framework to a set of social phenomena, and, on the other hand, something 'making sense of' a large set of social phenomena. In other words, the ecumenical conception of 'theory' applies here both to *Sinnstiftung*, (constitution of meaning) and to explanation, the more wide-ranging the more important.

The importance of philosophy in the classical Marxist triangle of social science, philosophy, and politics, and the far greater resilience of philosophy to empirical developments mean that the contributions of political and social philosophy are very important to an overview of recent social theory of 'post-Marxism and the left', as the editorial assignment went. At the other end, of empirical social science, theory is not a separate field or a sub-discipline, an armchair thinking without research, but the guiding compass of empirical investigation. That was the way Pierre Bourdieu (e.g. 1992: 86, 136f), for instance, viewed social theory. Attention will be given also to that kind of social theory in scientific action.

Modes of response

The challenges to left wing social thought, posited by postmodernity and by post-socialism have been met in very different ways. Disregarding cases of flight from radical thought, which have occurred but which fall outside the task of this article, the responses of scholars left-of-centre have varied in thematic content as well as in socio-political stance. Given space allows neither lengthy expositions nor elaborate analyses of the wide-ranging variation, in this situation, the present writer has opted for an area road map, rather than a few selected house reportages. In this vein, the modes of response have two basic axes, thematic content and theoretico-political positioning.

Themes of Theoretical Change

The theological turn

The most striking and surprising theoretical development in left wing social philosophy in the past decade has been a theological turn. In the main, this has not meant an embrace of a religious faith – although some former left wing intellectuals have come to affirm an ethno-religious Jewishness – and although a particular personal relation beyond belief to religion or to a religious figure is often pointed to. 'Three things have occupied my life [as a writer], war, art, and religion' Régis Debray (2004a: 7) wrote recently. Rather, the theological turn has manifested itself in a scholarly interest in religion, and in a use of religious examples in philosophical and political argumentation.

The principal work here is that of Debray (2003, 2004b), who has brought his extraordinary talent as a writer to original scholarly investigations into the structures of the Judeo-Christian holy narratives and religious 'procedures of memorization, displacement, and organization' (Debray 2004b: 6), and to the re-lit fires of religion around the world.

Debray developed a religious eye from his *Critique of Political Reason* (1983), bringing to light the religious unconscious in politics and political forms of the sacred, after having begun his adult religious studies – starting with a biography of the eleventh-century Pope Gregory VII – while imprisoned (as a revolutionary *guerillero*) in Bolivian Camiri, where Christian literature was the only non-censored (Debray 1983: 7ff).

Alain Badiou (2003: 2), a former Maoist but still active left militant as well as philosopher, turns to Saint Paul, in his 'search for a new militant figure ... called upon to succeed the one installed by Lenin', referring to an old poetic personal relation to Saint Paul. Badiou's apostle supposedly laid the 'foundations of universalism' in his letter to the Galateans: 'There is neither Jew nor Greek, neither slave nor free, neither male nor female'.

Slavoj Zizek (2001) elaborates the parallels of Paul and Lenin into three pairs of guides Christ/Paul, Marx/Lenin, and Freud/Lacan. But his main point in *On Belief* is to argue the authentic ethical value of unconditional belief – political rather than religious – making no compromises and including what Kierkegaard called 'the religious suspension of ethics'. The ruthlessness of Lenin, and of radical religious fundamentalists are thereby presented as admirable. The Book of Job has also become a fascination of Zizek, 'perhaps the first modern critique of ideology' (Zizek and Daly 2004: 161).

A milder religious example is held forth by Michael Hardt and Antonio Negri (2000: 413) as an illumination 'of the future life of communist militancy: ... Saint Francis of Assisi'. In his own sober way Jürgen Habermas (2002: 24) has also paid his respect to religion: 'As long as better words for what religion can say are found in the medium of rational discourse, it [communicative reason] will ... coexist abstemiously with the former, neither supporting it nor combating it.'

This widespread fascination with religion and religious examples, mainly Christianity, may be taken as an indicator of a broad cultural mood, for which postmodernity appears a good label. A future disappears, and roots, experience, background become important. A classical European education and a maturation in a non-secular milieu make Christianity a natural historical experience to look at.

Homages to networks

At another end of thematic change, far away from the connotative complex of religious history, is a purely conceptual re-orientation, this time into something novel. That is the replacement of structure and/or organization with network. Classical, nineteenth-century sociological theory focused on modes of social connectivity, distinguishing 'association' and 'community'. Mid-twentieth-century sociology concentrated on the 'group'; 'primary groups' and 'secondary groups', or organizations.

Network analysis of social connectivity has a background in social psychological, so-called sociometric studies of friendships in school milieux, and in some post-World War community studies by anthropologist and family sociologists. It was also a tool in US studies of diffusion of ideas. From the 1960s on it developed into mathematical models of access, diffusion, and power structures in an expanding number of areas, from vacancy chains to sexual contacts and global city pattern. The key theoretical figure has been Harrison White (1992) and his students (cf. Rule 1997: ch. 5).

The public influence of the concept, however, was carried largely by new managerial thought attempting to grasp and to generalize the success of Toyota and other Japanese corporations, and interest was, of course, fed by the electronic revolution, from corporate steering to internet communication.

It was the post-Marxist sociologist, Manuel Castells (1996–1998), who made the 'network society' into a central concept of a magisterial work of social analysis, setting out from new management conceptions and from information technology, without trying to relate it to previous sociological theory. 'Network' has then become a key analytical concept of the most influential neo-Marxist enterprise, Michael Hardt and Toni Negri's *Empire* (2000) and *Multitude* (2004). Both the world-ruling 'Empire' and its global opposition 'multitude' are presented as networks.

On the other hand, while crucial to recent post- and neo-Marxist social theorizing, network itself has no political affiliation. Nor has it been subjected to any analytical critique, scrutinizing its relative acumen and the boundaries of its indubitable fruitfulness. It is a concept still enjoying its unmolested honeymoon.

The displacement of class

Class has become a displaced concept in recent left and left-of centre discourse, defeated, by capitalist class struggle ironically, pushed into decline by post-industrial demography, and dislodged from its previous location of theoretical centrality. Class is still around but without a secure abode and with a contested right to exist. Its social appearance has become almost unrecognizable after being dropped into an acid of pure politics, as in the political philosophy of discursive hegemony by Ernesto Laclau and Chantal Mouffe (1985), arguably the intellectually most powerful contribution of post-Marxist political theory. When Slavoj Zizek (2000) invokes class and the class struggle, Laclau (2000: 205) dismisses it as 'just a succession of dogmatic assertions'. 'Antagonism', 'struggle without classes' become central, although it may also occur between classes (cf. Balibar 1988).

'Multitude is a class concept', Hardt and Negri (2004: 103) tell us, but it is not a class, it is 'meant to repropose Marx's political project of the class struggle' (p. 105). Castells' (1996–1998: I: 475–476) more empirically grounded but occasionally also apocalyptic conclusion is that: 'Capital tends to escape in its hyperspace of pure circulation, while labor dissolves its collective identity into infinite variations of individual existences.'

There is as yet no global class analysis corresponding to the many national class maps produced by Marxists of the 1960s and 1970s (although see, e.g. Pijl 1998; Sklair 2001; Silver 2003), and the pictures referred to may well be seriously challenged. The re-articulation of

191

class with race and nation, largely suspended after the generation of Lenin and Otto Bauer, is a theoretical advance (Balibar and Wallerstein 1988/1997), while the postmodernist onslaught has largely put an end to Feminist articulation of sex and gender with class. Typically, a recent overview of 'Third Wave Feminism' has no reference to class whatsoever (Gillis *et al.* 2004).

Exits from the state

1 From the national class-state to the global network, not (yet) to the World Bank concept of global governance, though, a great deal of Marxist theorizing in the 1960s and 1970s was concerned with the state, the national capitalist state and its modes of operation as class rule. Most of that interest has melted away, although Claus Offe's (1996) post-Marxist critical analyses make a significant exception. Political interest has turned to globalization and global 'Empire' networks, under assumptions that the nation-state, or at least its 'sovereignty', has lost its significance (Castells 1996–1998: III: 355; Hardt and Negri 2000). Insofar as the analysis of political steps out of the nation and of its North Atlantic context, out of 'methodological nationalism' (Beck 2002: ch.II), this shift is warranted. However, the bold claims of state sovereignty loss have so far never been properly empirically argued. In a time perspective somewhat longer than a couple of decades it may even be seriously questioned.

2 Alternatively, the move away from the state turned to civil society as a basis of opposition to authoritarian states, and, in more utopian visions as the best site for new social constructions (Keane 1988). The old concept – whose distinction from the state goes back to Hegel – was revived, by anti-Communist dissidence, in the final years of decomposition of Eastern European Communism, and soon received a worldwide reception, left and right, as a reference for many different movements and strivings for civic autonomy. In Eastern Europe, the civil society discourse also had the function of keeping out any serious discussion about political economy and a restoration of capitalism – till the latter was already installed. The concept has continued a programmatically idealistic career, instead of furthering analyses of variable patterns of sociability, association, and collective conflict.

3 A third exit from state theory was provided by moving to a more abstract philosophy of politics. The autonomy or specificity of the political, in relation to modes of production and to class structures has been a central theme of several major thinkers. A seminal work here was the already mentioned *Hegemony and Socialist Strategy* by Ernesto Laclau and Chantal Mouffe (2000), with their sophisticated treatment of the classical problem of political philosophy of universalism and particularism, and their discursive substitution of hegemonic struggles of particular interests for the struggle of classes.

From completely different sources of philosophical inspiration came the normative programme of a universalistic dialogical politics out of Jürgen Habermas' (1984–1987) grand theory of communicative action. In an interesting abstention from argument, Laclau and Mouffe (2000: xvii) dismiss Habermas' ideal of a non-exclusive public sphere of rational argument as a 'conceptual impossibility'. A tyranny of concepts?

Former disciples of Louis Althusser have made distinctive new contributions to radical political philosophy (Balibar 1994, 1997; Rancière 1998; Badiou 2001). The most circumspect and the most influential among them, Étienne Balibar (1994) has applied his skills at textual reading to political philosophy before Marx (Spinoza, Rousseau, Locke, Fichte), but also to a political theory for coping with violent antagonisms. Alongside the traditional left wing politics of emancipation and transformation, Balibar (1997: ch.1) reflected on a politics of 'civility', regulating 'the conflict of identifications'. Violence has become more physically tangible and much more ambiguous, even dubious, of meaning than its cathartic appearance to Sartre and Fanon.

While his anti-capitalist political project is very explicit and his philosophical edge and erudition conspicuous, the political philosophy of Slavoj Zizek (1999) appears more a stance than a reasoned conclusion. A compulsively productive writer, a formidable polemicist, and an intellectual with a seemingly inexhaustible supply of cinematic and other contemporary cultural aperçus, Zizek has become an emblematic figure of radical thought. His Slovenian Eastern European experience and his background as a former ex-Communist turned anti-Communist dissident provide him, as a current radical iconoclast, at the same time with a classical left wing political formation and with impeccably respectable liberal credentials from which to operate. This combination has made Zizek (2002b) the only Leninist with an admiring Western following in recent years.

But his admiration of Lenin is accompanied by a seemingly equivalent admiration of 'an authentic conservative', who like the forceful Conservatives of the British Empire, admired by Kipling, were not afraid of the 'necessary dirty work' (Zizek 1999: 236; 2004: 50–51).

Return of sexuality

The distinction of biological sex and social gender – first elaborated by Anne Oakley (1972) – and a focus on the construction and the re-construction or transformation of gender, constituted a key orientation of Socialist, and of mainstream, Feminism of the 1970s and 1980s. But the givenness of sex has more recently come under attack, sometimes in ways similar to the questioning of any non-discursive givenness of class. The intellectual thrust of sexuality has come from the American philosopher Judith Butler – 'sex itself is a gendered category' (Butler 1990: 7) and from French theorizations out of a battleground of Feminist philosophy and psychoanalysis (Oliver 2000; Cavallaro 2003). Oakley (1997) herself has conceded the non-tenability of the sex-gender distinction. Politically, the givenness of sex has been powerfully challenged by assertive homosexuality. The latter has managed a certain specific theoretical presence in Anglo-Saxon academia under the banner of 'Queer Theory' (e.g. Morland and Willox 2005).

The surge of literary-philosophical postmodernism in Feminist discourse broke most of the links between intellectual Feminism and the Left, previously summed up as Socialist Feminism (cf. Oakley and Mitchell 1997; Gillis *et al.* 2004). Scandinavian welfare-state oriented Feminists experienced the encounter with postmodernist Feminism as a shock (Hildur Ve and Karin Waerness oral communication). The cosmopolitan literary theorist Toril Moi (2005) saw herself forced to explain in writing 'What is a woman' to intellectual Feminist milieux gone lost. It is also striking how more deeply currently prominent Feminism is still rooted in the Euro-American corner of the world, much more so than the male Left or Left-of-centre (Therborn 2004.)

Enduring distance to political economy

Political economy was always distant to 'Western Marxism', so it was to be expected that that distance should endure. Exceptions to the rule have also remained, like the ecological global economic analyses of Elmar Altvater (1992). But two points should be added. One comes from the British House of Lords, to which the Indian-British economist Meghnad Desai has been elevated, and with the help of whose library he wrote a spirited history of the dynamics of capitalism in relation to economic analyses. Originally inspired by a re-reading of Lenin and of the classical modernist Marxist economists, Desai's (2002) *Marx's Revenge* is a rehabilitation of Marx the social scientist of capitalist political economy, while taking an agnostic position on the question whether there is socialism after capitalism.

The other point comes from radical lines of thought outside Marxism. It is rather from them that most critiques of liberal economics and most alternative economic analyses have stemmed in recent years. It might be summed up as institutionalist or sociological economics. In France, where the main label is 'theory of regulation', Robert Boyer is a currently central representative (Boyer and Saillard 1995; Hollingsworth and Boyer 1997), in Britain post-Marxist Geoffrey Hodgson (1991; Hodgson *et al.* 2001).

The last major work of Pierre Bourdieu (2000) was devoted to a penetrating sociological investigation of the French housing market, deploying some of his key concepts, like the 'habitus' of dispositions and the 'field' of force and conflict, in the empirical research as well as in a generalizing theoretical critique.

The Repertoire of Positions

Social theorizing is still related to, nay committed to, specific political positions. While staying clear of apologetic as well as of denunciatory temptations, a sociological history of social theorization will have to pay attention to political commitments and to their motivation. Understanding the recent history of leftwing thought, there are two poles in relation which positions may be located (see Figure 14.1). One is theoretical, Marx and Marxism as an intellectual tradition. The other is social and political, Socialism, as a society and as a political goal distinctively different from capitalism. (Socialism is used in looser meanings too, but they do not pertain here.) The two axes form a system of coordinates, which may be put up as a heuristic device of searching, but which had better not be seen as a permanent address book.

The picture should, of course, be seen as a very approximate map, aiming at conveying relative positions correctly but making no claims about the scale of distances.

What it shows is perhaps first of all that theory and politics are two different dimensions, even among politically committed social theorists. Second, it indicates a new distance from Socialism, as a distinctive type of society. A conception of a Socialist alternative has become a minority view among the intellectual left, without, in most cases, meaning a step into the capitalist fold. The editorial assignment puts the relationship to Marx and Marxism at the centre here, but a wider perspective has to be brought in to situate the former.

Post-socialism

A certain 'post' distance to any explicit Socialism has pervaded most of the Euro-American Left recently, but an elaborate post-Socialist left-of-centre agenda is a specific project. In this particular context, the location is defined by non-Marxism in theory and absence of anti-capitalism in politics.

The Waste Land of triumphant Thatcherism was a natural breeding-ground of 'post-socialism'. One effort was John Keane's (1988) celebration of 'civil society', as scornful of 'Social Democracy' – and its unworkable model of 'state-administered socialism' (p. 26) – as of 'totali-

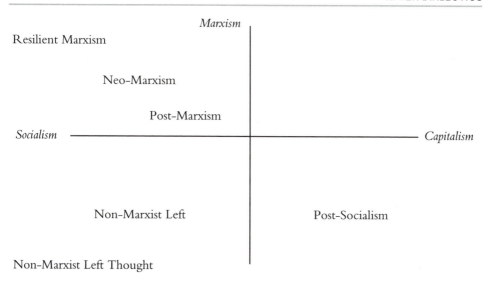

Marxism

Resilient Marxism

Neo-Marxism

Post-Marxism

Socialism ———————————————————————— *Capitalism*

Non-Marxist Left   Post-Socialism

Non-Marxist Left Thought

Figure 14.1. Current Left Theoretico-Political positions

tarian' Communism. For a good decade it was riding high on the hot air of Eastern European anti-Communist liberalism. A decade of capitalist immiseration of large parts of the Eastern European population called for no qualification, or even comment by the author (Keane 1998).

A few years later, the most successful Anglophone sociological theorist of the outgoing century proclaimed his bold step of moving 'Beyond Left and Right' (Giddens 1994), with a number of ideas but also full of Thatcherite sneers at Social Democracy and the welfare state (73ff). This book, which brusquely dismissed 'there is no Third Way' – between 'welfare socialism' and 'Communism' – soon turned out to having prepared the ground for a short-lived but nevertheless contemporarily unique politico-theoretical alliance of a post-socialist 'Third Way' (Giddens 1998). For some years, Giddens became the officious theoretician of the British Prime Minister and his 'New Labour' regime. Giddens could give an intellectual gloss to a Labour Party which had lost – or rather severed – any connection to First Way Social Democracy, because of traumatizing defeats by ruthless (though always civicly minoritarian) neoliberalism. In these projects there was for a time, a relation of social theory and politics, of a different kind than the classical Marxist-Socialist one. Ideological controversy apart, Anthony Giddens (2000) defence of the Third Way is in some sense exemplary, with a brief but fair presentation of important criticisms and a programmatic use of a wide range of social scientific knowledge. It may be added, though, that at least in Europe (while there is still an East Asian interest), the attraction of the Third Way ended similarly to the Czechoslovak 'socialism with a human face', with the *Realpolitik* of invading tanks (this time into Iraq).

Post-socialism also had its emotional generational dimensions, highlighted, in public scripture. In 1994 Ralph Miliband died, an elder statesman of the 1968 generation, a prominent Marxist theoretician of politics and the state (Miliband 1968). An unrepentant volume on *Socialism for a Sceptical Age* was published posthumously (Miliband, R. 1994). In the same year his son David (Miliband, D 1994), who was to become a senior staff figure of Prime Minister Tony Blair, put out a collective volume, where Giddens tabled a post-socialist agenda.

Ulrich Beck (1992, 2002) is a radical cosmopolitan democrat, very much concerned with the 'sub-politics' of critical professionals and dissident groups and individuals, to whom Communism and Socialism of European First Modernity are 'used up' ideas (2002: 407).

The non-Marxist left

Social Democracy, by far the major component of the non-Marxist left, has recently had few if any social theoreticians of wide-ranging ambitions. The Swedish sociologist Walter Korpi is mainly an empirical analyst of social policy institutions, but his explanatory theorizations of power resources and of the 'democratic class struggle' (Korpi 1983), and his scientifically robust defence of the welfare state (e.g. Korpi and Palme 1998) are important contributions to social theory. In the face of them, the anti-welfare state railings, including by theorists seeing themselves as on the left, appear jejune.

French sociology has always mainly stayed left-of-centre, and Alain Touraine (1992, 2001) is a typical example. The outstanding contribution is, of course, that of Pierre Bourdieu. While out of the spotlight in the heydays of rue d'Ulm Marxism, Bourdieu built up a formidable reputation as a top-class social researcher, from where he late in life emerged as the foremost intellectual spokesman of the anti-capitalist left, in Europe as well as in France. He brought a powerful voice against the capitalist 'misery of the world' (Bourdieu 1993, 1998). He did not hold out a Socialist horizon, but nor did he ever condone existing capitalism.

Resilient Marxism

The recent trajectory of Marxism also includes a mode of resilience, cutting its path through thickets of adversities and altered unmapped terrain. What has become the generally recognized flagship of left wing social thought, at least in the Anglophone world – and in fact *hors pair* in other language areas, including Francophony – the London-based *New Left Review*, successfully relaunched itself in 2000 with a manifesto of intransigence, of 'uncompromising realism' (Anderson 2000: 14). The guiding spirit of the *NLR* for more than forty years, who was also in charge of the re-launch operation, Perry Anderson, is a major Marxist historical scholar as well as a master of intellectual critique, including intra-Marxist (e.g. Anderson 1976, 1983, 1992, 1998).

Historically the *NLR* might best be called a neo-Marxist journal, always keen on theoretical innovations, with a muted enthusiasm for straight political economy, and plainly uninterested in exegesis and in exegetical polemics. Brilliance and radicalism have been the *NLR* criteria of publication, never orthodoxy of whatever kind. This comes at a price of short-term political insignificance, although the journal has always cultivated contributions from and on radical social movements, from the student movement of the 1960s to the anti-capitalist globalization movements of the 2000s. And its outspoken political radicalism has not prevented the journal's entry into the Social Science Citation Index.

Some other important mouthpieces of European Marxism have also survived; above all, the two German publications *Das Argument* and *Prokla*, also the Stalian *Critica Marxista* and some new ones have emerged, like *Historical Materialism*.

Post-Marxism

Post-Marxism is used here in a loose sense, as referring to writers with an explicit Marxist background, whose recent work has gone beyond Marxist problematics, and who do not publicly claim a continuing Marxist commitment. It is not tantamount to ex-Marxism. Post-Marxism does not include rupture, denunciation, renegacy; development and new desires, yes, maybe even divorce, but only on amicable terms. Laclau and Mouffe (2000: ix), accepting a post-Marxist label, refer to 'the reappropriation of an intellectual tradition, as well as the process of going beyond it'.

Hegemony and Socialist Strategy by Ernesto Laclau and Chantal Mouffe (1985) may be regarded as the most important contribution of post-Marxism. The authors plod through a Marxist tradition of political theory from classical German and Russian Social Democracy to Gramsci, by way of formidable abstractions. But their project remains hung up on the French Revolution – in itself a venerable tradition from Marx via Lenin to Gramsci – arguing a project of 'radical democracy', in which there is a 'socialist dimension', by 'deepening the democratic revolution' (ch. 4).

The boundaries between post- and neo-Marxism have become blurred in recent times, and my use of it is mainly practical, for reasons of disposition. Some important writers may well be put under both rubrics, Etienne Balibar is perhaps the best example (most succinctly manifested in his ch. 10 to Balibar and Wallerstein 1988/1997). Here no critical evaluation at all is invested into the grouping. But the term neo-Marxist has been used only for new theoretical projects with explicit Marxist aims.

German Critical Theory was arguably the first major current of post-Marxism, implied in the frozen silence of Adorno and Horkheimer after the Second World War, explicit in the overtowering work of Jürgen Habermas. As a post-Marxist, Habermas has remained an intellectual and a theoretician of a Liberal (in the American sense) left, becoming a left-of-centre conscience of the West German nation, much less radical than Sartre but more widely listened to. In recent years groping with moral issues of genetic engineering and of the increasingly violent implications of a *Westbindung* to the USA, to which Habermas as a German anti-nationalist has always been committed. In the latter respect there occurred an interesting, more Europeanist rapprochement between Habermas and Jacques Derrida (Borraderi 2003). In the context of this overview, Habermas' programme of dialogical politics, laid out in his magnum opus on communicative action (Habermas 1984–1987), and his defence of modernity as an 'unfinished project' (Habermas 1985), have to be underlined.

Claus Offe (1996), once Habermas' *Assistent* and a longtime post-Marxist, is one of the few who, as a prominent political scientist has continued the 1960s–1970s Marxist preoccupation with the state, among other things taking it into the post-Communist states of Eastern Europe. Axel Honneth is the current professorial successor of the Frankfurt School. His main philosophical elaboration has concerned the struggle for recognition, once launched into modern social philosophy by Hegel and his analysis of the dialectic of the constitution of the master-servant relations, differentiated by Honneth (1992, 1995) into three spheres, of love, law, and solidarity. In a debate with the American philosopher Nancy Fraser, who was spurred by strident US 'identity politics' into defending redistribution (Fraser and Honneth 2003), Honneth has argued a broader normative theory of experiences of injustice than the 'more or less utilitarian anthropology' of Marxism (p. 127). From an egalitarian perspective, 'recognition' may, in my opinion, be seen as a crucial aspect of existential equality, one of three fundamental dimensions of (in)equality (Therborn 2006). Given Honneth's background, his modernist optimism may be noticed, in his observations on modern 'moral progress' (186ff).

Post-Marxism is not necessarily textual re-interpretations. It may also take forms of new empirical forays or of social commentary. The two most extraordinary works coming out of a Marxist background are undoubtedly the three-volume sociological landmark analysis of contemporary world society by Manuel Castells (1996-1998), and the breath-taking historical 'mediology' of Régis Debray, starting from a critique of the Marxist concept of ideology, but also inspired by the Althussserian discussion of 'ideological state apparatuses' out on to a long historical exploration of the materiality of mediated communication, or the 'mechanics of [cultural] transmission', of Judeo-Christian religion in particular (Debray 1996, 2000, 2004a,b). While skilfully and originally crafted theoretically, these works are first of all contributions to social analysis rather than to social theory. As such they are outstanding achievements.

There is also the prolific output of social commentary by Zygmunt Bauman (1992, 1999, 2000), which has received a strong transnational resonance. The centre of it is a sociological variety of postmodernism. Bauman's recent writings travel light, burdened neither by research nor by any kind of theoretical analytics, carried by an unusual life wisdom, a trained observer's eye, and a fluent pen.

Neo-Marxism

For all its political defeats, the creativity of Marxism has not ceased. The last decade has seen the emergence of at least two very original, hard-hitting discourses, explicitly deriving from and building upon a Marxist legacy. On one hand, there is the irreverent philosophical politics of the Slovenian thinker Slavoj Zizek, who has not only kept alive but who has also renovated the radical Marxist cultural critique, and who vigorously defends Marxist radicalism against the powerful 'conformist liberal scoundrels' (Zizek 2002a: 4). Zizek's oeuvre includes a spirited defence of classical modernity (1999) and the most extensive use of film in cultural–philosophical commentaries. Zizek has gone against current conventional wisdom to the point of editing, introducing, and commenting on a new selection of Lenin's writings, from 1917 (Zizek 2002b). The sense of Zizek's exhortation to 'repeat Lenin' was to look out for possibilities of radical social change in a hopeless situation after a disastrous defeat, in Lenin's case the First World War and the break-up of the II International.

The second major manifestation of neo-Marxism claims to have found the revolutionary exit of the twenty-first century: 'This is a revolution that no power will control – because biopower and communism, cooperation and revolution remain together, in love, simplicity, and also innocence. This is the irrepressible lightness and joy of being communist' (Hardt and Negri 2000: 413, italics omitted). 'The possibility of democracy on a global scale is emerging today for the first time'; 'After this long season of violence and contradictions ... the extraordinary accumulation of grievances and reform proposals must at some point be transformed by a strong event, a radical insurrectionary demand. ... In time, an event will thrust us like an arrow into that [already] living future' (Hardt and Negri 2004: xi, 358). Toni Negri and Michael Hardt also refer to Lenin, to his *State and Revolution*, as an inspiration for a 'destruction of sovereignty', but combined with the American Federalist James Madison and his conception of checks and balances.

These two contributions have several features in common, apart from their upbeat radicalism and their international publishing success. They are both works of political philosophy – Zizek's main books are probably *The Sublime Object of Ideology* (1989) and *The Ticklish Subject* (1999) – rather than of social theory. Negri and Zizek are both professional philosophers, while Negri's former Paris student Hardt is a literary theorist with a philosophical orientation. Both sets of authors write with verve and gusto, in a Baroque style of *assemblages*, displaying an impressive erudition and capacity of association from a great number of fields and traditions, at a fast pace with little time for historical contexts or empirical investigation. Different variants of dissident Communism – and a more similar mainstream Communist family of origin – form the political background of Negri as well as of Zizek, the spontaneist and violent Italian far left, and meandering Slovenian Communism-cum-dissidence, respectively.

They are also in line with the tradition of Western Marxism in the sense of reading and using Marx through the lenses of other great European intellectual traditions, first of all the psychoanalysis of Lacan but also through a philosophical spectrum with Heidegger in the middle in the case of Zizek, the philosophy of Spinoza for Negri. Their dazzling intellectual style has attracted readers far beyond their own political stance – and their intellectual complexity.

While Zizek (Zizek and Daly 2004: 32) may say 'that I have nothing whatsoever to do with sociology', the work of Hardt and Negri does directly pertain to social analysis, in spite of their Franco-Italian philosophical mode of writing. It is hung up on two key concepts, empire and multitude, both taken from the seventeenth-century philosophy of Spinoza. 'Empire' to Hardt and Negri, has nothing of the material concreteness of, say, the Roman or the British empire. It is a global network whereto sovereign power has gone from the nation-states, and in Spinoza's Latin, 'imperium' meant just sovereign government. This 'Empire' is 'a step forward', the authors of a self-proclaimed postmodernity assert in a typically modernist way (Hardt and Negri 2000: 43).

The accompanying opposite to Empire is the 'multitude', which has taken the place of the proletariat in classical Marxism and the people in classical democratic theory. It is 'the mass workers' of Negri's ultra-left Italy of the 1960s and 1970s now writ globally large, as 'mass intellectuality'. The multitude is similarly made up of all workers and poor people of the world, now increasingly interrelated all over a 'smoothed' world space of withering civil society and declining national boundaries (Hardt and Negri 2000: 336), by common knowledge and common relationships (Hardt and Negri 2004: 348–350). This multitude will bring global democracy, 'a future that is already living' (2004: 358). Socialism is left out of the prophetic vision.

In their emphasis on information or knowledge, on networks generally and on nation-state sovereignty being lost to multilateral networks in particular, there is a diagnostic similarity between Hardt and Negri, on one hand, and the empirically well-grounded end of millennium analysis by Castells (1996–1998), on the other. Their most importance difference of assessment concerns social differentiation. In contrast to one global multitude 'in an expanding, virtuous spiral' of commonality (Hardt and Negri 2004: 350), Castells (1996–1998: III; 346, italics omitted) finds 'truly fundamental social cleavages of the Information Age . . . : first, the internal fragmentation of labor between informational producers and replaceable generic labor. Secondly, the social exclusion of a significant segment of society made up of the discarded individuals whose value as workers/consumers is used up, and whose relevance as people is ignored.'

While the bestsellers of Hardt and Negri, like those of Zizek, testify to a continuing creativity and attractiveness of the Marxist tradition, sociologically minded readers are likely to be somewhat sceptical of the former's invocation of Spinoza's claim that 'the prophet can produce its [sic] own people' and their belief in 'prophetic desire as irresistible' (Hardt and Negri 2000: 65).

In lieu of conclusion

Even in times of right wing triumph, sociology remains largely left of centre, like economics mainly staying right of centre. Political defeats have not prevented theoretical creativity and innovation. Marx and Lenin are still inspiring bold and fascinating intellectual enterprises. However, the current global patterns of power, of disadvantage, and of resistance have not been given their proper due of investigation and analysis.

Historically, there is no reason to believe that there is no world beyond capitalism. Whatever their field of work, a number of students of society are likely to keep that horizon of difference in their hearts.

References

Altvater, E. (1992) *Der Preis des Wohlstands oder Umweltplünderung und neue Welt(un)ordnung*, Münster: Westfälisches Dampfboot.

Anderson, P. (1976) *Considerations on Western Marxism*, London: Verso.

Anderson, P. (1983) *In the Tracks of Historical Materialism*, London: Verso.

Anderson, P. (1992) *A Zone of Engagement*, London: Verso.

Anderson, P. (1998) *The Origins of Postmodernity*, London: Verso.

Anderson, P. (2000) 'Renewals', *New Left Review*, 1, 5–24.

Badiou, A. (2001) 'Politics and Philosophy: An Interview with Alain Badiou', appendix to A. Badiou, *Ethics*, London: Verso.

Badiou, A. (2003) *Saint Paul*, Stanford: Stanford University Press.

Balibar, E. (1988) 'De la lutte des classes à la lutte sans classes?', in E. Balibar and I. Wallerstein *Race, nation, classe*, Paris: La Découverte, pp. 207–246.

Balibar, E. (1994) *Masses, Classes, Ideas*, New York and London: Routledge.

Balibar, E. (1997) *La crainte des masses*, Paris: Galilée.

Balibar, E. (2003) *L'Europe, l'Amérique, la guerre*, Paris: Galiliée.

Balibar, E., and Wallerstein, I. (1988/1997) *Race, Nation, Class*, 2nd edn, Paris: La Découverte.

Bauman, Z. (1992) *Intimations of Postmodernity*, London: Routledge.

Bauman, Z. (1999) *In Search of Politics*, Cambridge: Polity Press.

Bauman, Z. (2000) *Liquid Modernity*, Cambridge: Polity.

Bauman, Z. and Tester, K. (2001) *Conversations with Zygmunt Bauman*, Cambridge: Polity.

Beck, U. (1992) *Risk Society*, London: Sage.

Beck, U. (2002) *Macht und Gegenmacht im globalen Zeitalter*, Frankfurt: Suhrkamp.

Beck.U., Giddens, A. and Lash, S. (1994) *Reflexive Modernization*, Cambridge: Polity Press.

Berman, M. (1983) *All that Is Solid Melts into Air*, London: Verso.

Borraderi, G. (ed.) (2003) *Philosophy in a Time of Terror*, Chicago and London: University of Chicago Press.

Bourdieu, P. (1992) *Réponses*, Paris: Seuil.

Bourdieu, P. (1993) *La misère du monde*, Paris: Seuil (English edn. *The Weight of the World*, Stanford: Stanford University Press, 1999).

Bourdieu, P. (1998) *Contre-feux*, Paris: Liber-Rasions d'agir.

Bourdieu, P. (2000) *Les structures sociales de l'économie*, Paris: Seuil.

Boyer, R. and Saillard, Y. (eds) (1995) *Théorie de la regulation, l'état des savoirs*, Paris: La Découverte.

Butler, J. (1990) *Gender Trouble*, New York: Routledge.

Callinicos, A. (1989) *Against Postmodernism*, Cambridge: Polity.

Carver, T. (1998) *The Postmodern Marx*, Manchester: Manchester University Press.

Castells, M. (1996–1998) *The Information Age: Economy, Society, and Culture*, 3 volumes, Maiden MA and Oxford: Blackwell.

Cavallaro, D. (2003) *French Feminist Theory*, London and New York: Continuum.

Debray, R. (1983) *Critique of Political Reason*, London: Verso.

Debray, R. (1996) *Media Manifestos*, London: Verso.

Debray, R. (2000) *Transmitting Culture*, London: Verso.

Debray, R. (2003) *Le feu sacré*, Paris: Fayard.

Debray, R. (2004a) *Chroniques de l'idiotie triomphante*, Paris: Fayard.

Debray, R. (2004b) *God, an Itinerary*, London and New York: Verso.

Derrida, J. (1993) *Spectres de Marx*, Paris: Galilée (English edn. *Spectres of Marx*, New York and London: Routledge, 1994).

Desai, M. (2002) *Marx's Revenge*, London: Verso.

Eagleton, T. (1996) *The Illusions of Postmodernism*, Oxford: Blackwell.

Fraser, N. and Honneth, A. (2003) *Redistribution or Recognition?*, London: Verso.

Giddens, A. (1994) *Beyond Left and Right*, Cambridge: Polity Press.

Giddens, A. (1998) *The Third Way*, Cambridge: Polity Press.

Giddens, A. (2000) *The Third Way and Its Critics*, Cambridge: Polity Press.

Gillis, S., Howie, G. and Munford, R. (2004) *Third Wave Feminism*, Basingstoke: Palgrave.

Habermas, J. (1984–1987) *Theory of Communicative Action*, 2 vols, Boston: Beacon Press.

Habermas, J. (1985) *Der philosophische Diskurs der Moderne*, Frankfurt am Main: Suhrkamp (English edn: *Lectures on the Philosophical Discourse of Modernity*, Cambridge MA: MIT Press).

Habermas, J. (2002) *Religion and Rationality*, E. Miendieta (ed. and intro.), Cambridge MA: MIT Press.

Hardt, M. and Negri, T. (2000) *Empire*, Cambridge MA: Harvard University Press.

Hardt, M. and Negri, T. (2004) *Multitude*, New York: Penguin.

Hodgson, G. (1991) *After Marx and Sraffa*, Basingstoke: Macmillan.

Hodgson, G., Itoh, M. and Yokokawa, N. (2001) *Capitalism in Evolution*, Cheltenham: Edward Elgar.

Hollingsworth, R. and Boyer, R. (eds) (1997) *Contemporary Capitalism: The Embeddedness of Institutions*, Cambridge: Cambridge University Press.

Honneth, A. (1992) *Kampf um Anerkennung*, Frankfurt am Main: Suhrkamp.

Honneth, A. (1995) *The Struggle for Recognition: The Moral Grammar of Social Conflict*, Cambridge MA: Harvard University Press.

Hutcheon, L. (2002) *The Politics of Postmodernism*, 2nd edn, London and New York: Routledge.

Jameson, F. (1991) *Postmodernism*, Durham NC: Duke University Press.

Jessop, B. and Malcolm-Brown, C. (eds) (1990) *Karl Marx's Social and Political Thought*, 4 vols, London and New York: Routledge.

Jessop, B. and Wheatley, R. (eds) (1999) *Karl Marx's Social and Political Thought*, 4 vols, London and New York: Routledge.

Keane, J. (1988) *Democracy and Civil Society*, London: Verso.

Keane, J. (1998) 'Introduction to the New Edition', *Democracy and Civil Society*, rev. edn, London: University of Westminster Press.

Korpi, W (1983) *The Democratic Class Struggle*, London: Routledge.

Korpi, W. and Palme, J. (1998) 'The Strategy and Equality and the Paradox of Redistribution', in *American Sociological Review*, 63/5, 661–687

Kosellek, R. (1979) *Vergangene Zukunft*, Frankfurt: Suhrkamp (English edn: *Futures Past*, Cambridge MA: MIT Press, 1985).

Laclau, E. (2000) 'Structure, History, and the Political', in J. Butler, E. Laclau, and S. Zizek, *Contingency, Hegemony, Universality*, London: Verso.

Laclau, E. and Mouffe, C. (1985) *Hegemony and Socialist Strategy*, London: Verso.

Laclau, E. and Mouffe, C. (2000) *Hegemony and Socialist Strategy*, 2nd edn, London: Verso.

Lyotard, J.-F. (1984 [1979]) *The Postmodern Condition: A Report on Knowledge (Theory and History of Literature)*, Manchester: Manchester University Press.

Mickletwait, J. and Wooldridge, A. (2004) *The Right Nation*, London: Allen Lane.

Miliband, D. (ed.) (1994) *Reinventing the Left*, Cambridge: Polity.

Miliband, R. (1968) *The State in Capitalist Society*, London: Weidenfeld & Nicholson.

Miliband, R. (1994) *Socialism for a Sceptical Age*, Cambridge: Polity.

Moi, T. (2005) *Sex, Gender and Body*, Oxford: Oxford University Press.

Morland, I. and Willox, A. (2005) *Queer Theory*, Basingstoke: Palgrave/Macmillan.

Oakley, A. (1972) *Sex, Gender and Society*, London: Temple Smith.

Oakley, A. (1997) 'A Brief History of Gender', in A. Oakley and J. Mitchell (eds) *Who's Afraid of Feminism?*, London: Hamish Hamilton, pp. 29–55.

Oakley, A. and Mitchell, J. (eds) (1997) *Who's Afraid of Feminism?*, London: Hamish Hamilton.

Offe, C. (1996) *Modernity and the State*, Cambridge: Polity Press.

Oliver, K. (2000) *French Feminism Reader*, Oxford and New York: Rowman & Littlefield.

Pijl, K.van der (1998) *Transnational Classes and International Relations*, London and New York: Routledge.

Rancière., J. (1998) *Aux bords de la politique*, Paris: La fabrique.

Rule, J. (1997) *Theory and Progress in Social Science*, Cambridge: Cambridge University Press.

Silver, B. (2003) *Forces of Labour*, Cambridge: Cambridge University Press.

Sklair, L. (2001) *The Transnational Capitalist Class*, Oxford: Blackwell.

Sprinkler, M. (ed.) (1999) *Ghostly Demarcations*, London: Verso.

Therborn, G. (1996) 'Critical Theory and the Legacy of Twentieth-Century Marxism', in B. Turner (ed.) *The Blackwell Companion to Social Theory*, Oxford: Blackwell.

Therborn, G. (2003) 'Entangled Modernities' *European Journal of Social Theory*, 6(3), 293–305

Therborn, G. (2004) *Between Sex and Power: Family in the World, 1900–2000*, London: Routledge.

Therborn, G. (2006) 'Introduction. Understanding and Explaining Inequality', in G. Therborn (ed.), *Inequalities of the World*, London: Verso.

Touraine, A.(1992) *Critique de la Modernité*, Paris: Fayard.

Touraine, A. (2001) *Beyond Neoliberalism*, Oxford: Polity.

White, H. (1992) *Identity and Control*, Princeton: Princeton University Press.

Zizek, S. (1989) *The Sublime Object of Ideology*, London: Verso.

Zizek, S. (1999) *The Ticklish Subject*, London: Verso.

Zizek, S. (2000) 'Class Struggle or Postmodernism? Yes Please', in J. Butler, E. Laclau and S. Zizek, *Contingency, Hegemony, Universality*, London: Verso.

Zizek, S. (2001) *On Belief (Thinking in Action)*, London: Routledge.

Zizek, S. (2002a) *Did Somebody Say Totalitarianism?*, London: Verso.

Zizek, S. (ed.) (2002b) *Revolution at the Gates*, London: Verso.

Zizek, S. and Daly, G. (2004) *Conversations with Zizek*, Cambridge: Polity

15

Hermeneutics, phenomenology and philosophical anthropology

Hans-Herbert Kögler

Hermeneutics holds substantial promise for social theory. Many of the most influential and productive theories are unthinkable without hermeneutic insights. The influence of existential and philosophical hermeneutics is pertinent in the theory of communicative action (Habermas 1983/1987), in structuration theory (Giddens 1984), and even the French tradition in Foucault (1990) [1966], Bourdieu (1977, 1990), and Castoriadis (1998). Yet the current potential is especially grounded in the emergence of a new, essential issue in social theory: *the challenge to produce a theoretical framework capable of mediating the need for a macro-theory of global processes and structures with a cultural sensitivity toward the local, regional, and contextual modes of human agency and understanding.* It is in this context that we must return to hermeneutics, now strengthened and expanded by social phenomenology and philosophical anthropology. This chapter lays out, in historical-systematic fashion, the core insights that can serve as building blocks for a larger theoretical approach not yet existent. It outlines how conceptual, methodological, and normative reflections in the hermeneutic, phenomenological, and anthropological approaches can advance the current context of social theoretical discourse.

In particular, there are three issues with regard to which hermeneutic reflections can help establish our quest for a productive framework for understanding social phenomena. Keeping in mind that we must move on a high level of abstraction if our reconstruction is to serve as a guide for diverse cultural contexts, these issues include:

1 the return of the subject and the need for a new theory of human agency;
2 intersubjectivity and the irreducibility of culture to objective social factors such as economics and power; and
3 a general account of the relation of situated agency to social and cultural institutions, including structural power.

In order to provide the most comprehensive and convincing account of the promise of hermeneutics, each section first lays out the central conceptual paradigm of the position at stake to then address its contemporary relevance for social theory. Concretely this means that we show in the first section how the phenomenological concept of intentionality is transformed into a hermeneutic account of agency, which in turn provides the foundation for a social or critical hermeneutics. This critical-hermeneutic approach allows for a dialectic approach of human agency according to which the situatedness of subjects in power-defined contexts is acknowledged yet a reflexive transcendence of social constraints is equally deemed possible. In the second section we employ the hermeneutic conception of a linguistically mediated understanding as a foil against which we can highlight some of the currently most pressing issues in social theory, especially with regard to intersubjective understanding and cultural interpretation. In this context, further differentiations in the field of social hermeneutics are introduced, including besides the critical approach also feminist hermeneutics, intercultural hermeneutics, and the hermeneutics of race and identity. Finally, we present philosophical anthropology as a conceptual link between hermeneutic understanding and social institutions. This approach, for one, allows for a broadening of the concept of human nature to include biological and bodily grounds of agency, yet it also connects the culturally situated sub-jectivity to its necessary dependence of socially constructed institutions that provide both enabling and potentially undermining background structures for human agency.

Systematically, the article explores the following issues: How should we conceive of situ-ated human agency? How is human understanding constituted? What are the grounds on which an agent can understand another human agent? What is the role of language and cul-ture in understanding human agency? How is human agency shaped and mediated by social and cultural institutions? By drawing on both classic and current perspectives in hermeneu-tics, phenomenology, and philosophical anthropology, the article suggests possible answers and approaches to these questions.

A hermeneutic approach to human agency

With regard to *the subject*, social theory of late and postmodern conviction has been driven by the urge to overcome the 'philosophy of consciousness', to deconstruct the meaning-conferring transcendental ego, to wash away the anthropological episteme like a face drawn in sand (Foucault 1990 [1966]; Derrida 1978; Habermas 1987). Accordingly, the subject's place is, as an ultimate foundation of knowledge, truth, and freedom, to be given up – but its former motivational grounds, such as the establishment of a society based on free and equal relations, or the just struggle against power and domination, are to be continued. Language, either as communication or as a structural semiotic or discursive framework, was to provide a new perspective for either reconstructing or deconstructing human agency (McCarthy 1991). But against those radical attempts at paradigm change, recent developments point to another option.

Hermeneutics allows for a reconceptualization of the situated subject that preserves the insights of the communicative and discursive turn in social theory without succumbing to the unjustified reduction of the self to larger intersubjective or social forces. Subjectivity is here seen as intrinsically grounded in a prior sphere of symbolically and socially mediated struc-tures, but those structures are seen as specifically enabling conditions for the realization of an intentional and self-reflexive agent. Hermeneutic social theory accomplishes thus the feast of mediating the macro-social background with the micro-intentional foreground, since both factors are taken to mutually depend on one another; they are considered a functional unit. The meaning-constituting background, which can be analyzed as transcending the intentional awareness of the situated self, is nonetheless directly tied to providing rules and resources for the consciously acting and reflecting subject. Symbolic mediation as in semiotic, discourse-analytic, or praxeological accounts are thus not methodologically disconnected from the intentional agent, but rather conceived as actualization-grounds for a concrete self. Similarly, the background structures that provide meaningful contexts are not hypostasized into a transcendental *a priori* that determines universal truth or absolute meaning. Rather, the grounded subject finds herself situated in historically and culturally changing background contexts that as such provide renewable resources for the productive self-construction of its situated agency.

The phenomenological project and the hermeneutic turn to agency

It was Husserl who, by drawing on Brentano's pioneering work, redirects philosophy by putting the notion of *intentionality* at its center (Husserl 1970). Intentionality is an act, a feature of consciousness, the directedness toward something that is understood by the experiencing mind or self. Yet while being the activity of a conscious understanding, this intentional directedness goes to *the things themselves*, it understands or experiences the content not as a mental or cognitive entity, but directly as it is given in the conscious experience. Intentionality is thus not conceived as in modern epistemology, grounding the act of understanding in a separate mental sphere of transcendental forms and constructs. Rather, the intentional experience is a *bridging* act between a subjective pole and an objective pole that cuts across the mind/body split, it reaches out to the world, the things themselves. What we see when we see something is not the idea, the mental image, the scheme, but the object itself, the tree, the house, the person. Phenomenology as a philosophical project, accordingly, sets out to describe this process of intentional understanding. It thus rediscovers, following the very understanding of the object or world in the act of understanding, the 'what' of the experience *as real*. At the same time, phenomenology sets out to describe how exactly the intentional objects are understood, it similarly attempts to get at the *subjective* 'how' of the experience.

What thus becomes possible is the mediation between the intentional claim to objectivity (the things themselves) and the acknowledgment of the mediating subjectivity (the how of understanding). However, the phenomenological project itself opens up a gap, a new separation between the mediating factors of the subjective pole, the disclosure of the world, and the claim toward its objective content, the orientation at the things themselves. Phenomenology is grounded in the self-reflexivity of the subject. Intentional knowledge is knowledge of something, and always knowledge of itself as that knowledge. We know that we know what we know (Sartre 1956). Phenomenology can draw on this resource to focus on the 'How' of understanding, to bracket the reality-assumption of our intentional object-pole and to carve out how the content is disclosed, how it is mediated. Husserl suggests two methodological steps, the transcendental and the eidetic epoche (Husserl 1962 [1913]). In the first move, we bracket the reality assumption to lay bare the pure rays of intentional orientation. In the second move, we focus on what essences are to be found in the immediacy of the now-separated sphere of pure intentional meanings. Yet Husserl succumbs, seduced by the methodological purity of separating the everyday immediacy of experience from a meta-reflexive effort at reconstruction, to the Platonic temptation (Heidegger 1982). He reifies what is a mediating background structure of intentional consciousness, which pre-directs consciousness in its everyday understanding of self, world and others, into eidetic structures that are taken to inhere in intentional consciousness as such (Husserl 1962 [1913]). But to make this claim, the mediation between the subjective and the objective pole in intentionality is broken apart again. One now needs to posit a transcendental ego in which such essences inhere. The grounding of intentional agency in a real context of objects and practices is lost; the Cartesian trap has snapped again.

Not so in Heidegger. In *Being and Time* (1962 [1927]), Husserl's former assistant redefines phenomenology both methodologically and regarding its object matter, and thus provides the ground for a hermeneutic theory of agency. In a seemingly reductive move, phenomenology is reconceived solely as a method to get to the phenomena, to reconstruct without bias that which presents itself *as itself* in understanding. However, as this excludes any transcendental-reflexive presupposition regarding an *a priori* mental ground, that which presents itself must now be analyzed in its most 'immediate' setting: *the social lifeworld of everyday agents* (Heidegger 1962 [1927]; 1985). Phenomenology thus becomes hermeneutic in a first sense, being redefined as a 'hermeneutics of facticity'. The agent's everyday existence, her practical orientation toward tools and objects, her mediated relation to other humans and herself, the structure of care and concern at the bottom of all her embedded endeavors and projects now come into focus as that which grounds all understanding and existence.

But hermeneutics is also redefined in a second, more critical and 'deconstructive' sense, as the rejection of distorting ontological assumptions about specific realms of being, such as those about our own existence. In this critical hermeneutics of our ontological self-understanding, Heidegger most prominently deconstructs the Western tendency toward reifying and objec-tifying conceptions of intentionality and human existence, as in the famous passage on Descartes in *Being and Time* (1962 [1927]: 122 f.). From now on, a situated and reflexive reconstruction of human agency has to both analyze the everyday meanings of agents situated in the lifeworld and the misguided schemes of self-interpretation that make an adequate and authentic self-understanding impossible. This double-edged approach toward understanding human agency has lost nothing of its systematic relevance.

The contemporary relevance of hermeneutics

The methodological transformation of phenomenology into a critical social hermeneutics is mirrored in the content definition of its object, i.e. human agency. Within the larger frame of reopening the question of being, Heidegger presents a theory of human existence that encompasses both its factual and its transcendent elements, and equally addresses its individual and its social dimension. Human agency is thus thematized in terms of an essential existential tension – a drama spun out from its situatedness which aims at self-realization and transcendence. The hermeneutics of *Dasein* (Heidegger's term for human existence) must project a general fore-understanding to reconstruct its object, which it is always also itself. *Dasein* is that being which has an understanding of its being (Heidegger 1962 [1927]; Sartre 1956). Similarly, *Dasein* is always irreducibly unique, defined by *Jemeinigkeit*. The dialectic of existence emerges since both dimensions depend on a previously acquired, an 'always already' existing pre-understanding of the world. Heidegger's main contribution consists in the reconstruction of this dimension of *pre-understanding* operating in the back of agents, which pre-structures what is consciously understood. The 'immediate' understanding is thus highly mediated, it is derived from a ground, or better, a pre-ground that structures what can possibly become an object of experience. But the mediating ground is, contrary to the Cartesian tradition, not an absolute ground or *a priori*, but rather the 'groundless ground' of contingent and historically changing background contexts (Lash 1998). Since human agency is defined by intentionality, the understanding of being is always about something. As such it is always *practical*, arising from an embedded know-how in referential contexts of tools and equipment-use; it is always *social*, as others are encountered in the use of tools and objects and shine forth through co-used objects and their general functions; and is also potentially *distorted and alienated*, as social knowledges and discourses have the capacity to place themselves in between an authentic (though always mediated) encounter between my projects and the social contexts within which they emerge.

The limits of early Heidegger's approach have numerously been recorded: a quasi-romantic pragmatism of the direct handling of tools and work, the absence of a sophisticated analysis of the intersubjective encounter of agents with one another, and the conservative overtones of a cultural criticism of alienation and modernity. Yet what remains highly suggestive here is precisely the *ambiguity* of the social background on which the intentional subject necessarily depends. On the one hand, this background is a quasi-transcendental condition for meaning, since it is indispensable as a holistic context in which particular acts can articulate and define themselves. On the other hand, the background is considered as the anonymous voice of 'the One' or 'the They,' as a social unconscious that normalizes, disciplines, disconnects from any rebellious, decisive, self-determining agency. The herme-neutic background of intentionality is thus *both* enabling and distorting, it is a resource for productive meaning and self-understanding *and* the source of power-shaped constraints and concepts.

With this move, the relevance and influence of social power for the agent's self-understanding and projects is thus pushed to a new level, as the meaning-constituting background itself is infused with social domination. And this is achieved, essentially, without reducing the agent to those external power structures, since the background is one to be tested, reflected, and transformed by concrete agents. The fine-structure of this background reveals itself as internally differentiated into layers of meaning; dimensions of a fore-understanding that allow for a productive reconnection with social theory and analysis. What Heidegger calls the *fore-structure* of all understanding entails a practical-social, a symbolic-conceptual, and a personal-biographic dimension, which together form shaping modes for anything that the social self understands (Dreyfus 1993; Kögler 1999). Heidegger's existential hermeneutics thus prepares the ground for a dialectical theory of human agency. Its major contribution is the internal connection between the social and cultural background – which is open to objective social analysis and reconstruction – and the intentional consciousness of the situated agent – which preserves the necessary and normative relation of social theory to the situated self-understanding of the concrete individual.

The Heideggerian double-edged conception of intentional agency (as dependent on a both enabling *and* power-infected background) has reemerged in contemporary social theory under the label of critical hermeneutics. While one of the earliest uses of the term goes back to a study on Habermas and Ricoeur (Thompson 1981), critical (or genealogical) herme-neutics recently acquired new meaning in authors who fuse critical theory with the best of hermeneutic intuitions. By drawing on poststructuralist thought as well as Gadamerian her-meneutics, the ambiguity of a contingent and holistic background that is both enabling and distorting is combined with the ethical ideals of self-determination and a critical analysis of power (Hoy and McCarthy 1994; Kögler 1999; Hoy 2004; see also Zuidervaart 2004). This approach not only reactualizes one of critical theory's most valid assumptions, namely that the theoretical categories employed to diagnose society must themselves be conceptually specific to the historically changing social and political realities (Horkheimer 1992 [1937]). Moreover, this project's historical consciousness includes a hermeneutic sensitivity for the cultural dif-ference of other agents who are recognized without succumbing to a postmodern celebration of mere difference and diversity. Rather, fusing the critique of power with a contextual recognition of otherness means that every critical-interpretive act needs to find a precarious balance between reconstructing constraining sources of power and the misguided imposition of one's own local and contextual value-judgments onto the other's self-understanding – which would in itself amount to an act of symbolic power. This fusion of critical power analysis with the recognition of concrete otherness defines a new frame for a general theory of the situated human being's potential to realize the moral and political ideals of reflexive self-determination, critical resistance to power, and the dialogical recognition of the other in mutual understanding (Hoy 2004; Mandair and Zene 2005; Kögler 2005).

The articulated conception of such a theory, however, requires attention to the essential medium in which the mediation between background and intentionality occurs: *language*. And the move to language prepares the ground for a hermeneutic theory of the relation between intersubjectivity and culture.

Intersubjectivity, language, and the cultural mediation of experience

With regard to the relation between culture and human agency, hermeneutics is able to provide an approach both richer and more dialectic than the most sophisticated social theories around. This is not surprising as hermeneutics developed from the methodological issues related to interpreting symbolic expressions from different historical and cultural settings. Contemporary social theory recognizes, in all its different branches, the limits of Marxism (and Neo-Marxism) in things cultural (Castoriadis 1998; Bourdieu 1990; Habermas 1987). But the replacement of the base-superstructure model with accounts that do justice to culture proved difficult and a continuing challenge. This is not to say that hermeneutic theory can claim to present a full-blown social theory of culture. But its reflections on the fine-structure of language and meaning, foregrounding the dependence of intentional understanding on a symbolically structured and socially situated background, will help to set such a theory on the right tracks. To do justice to culture in social theory will ultimately mean more than replacing the subject-object model with an interactionist subject-subject approach (Schütz 1967), or to situate communicating agents in a cultural background of taken-for-granted assumptions (Habermas 1983/1987). Equally, the turn from a Marxist and objectivistic model of labor or economic structure to culture will not be served with an equally objectivistic model of discourse, symbolic fields, or practical-linguistic habitus formations (as in Althusser 1969; Foucault 1979 [1975]; Bourdieu 1990). What is needed is a more versatile model that realizes that the cultural turn implies a *hermeneutic turn* in the sense that the what of culture, its meaning, will only be understood through some *intentional or first-person access, without losing sight of a general theory of how cultural competence is acquired under objective social and historical conditions.*

The significance of language for intersubjective understanding

The promise of hermeneutics consists in its unique fusion of two assumptions. On the one hand, no intentional object is given to experience *in an unmediated manner*. This means that interpretive schemes are employed that constitute or disclose something as something. These schemes are sedimented or crystallized forms of cultural experience that provide shared contexts of meaning according to which situated agents understand themselves, objects and others. On the other hand, hermeneutic theorists are especially interested in the way in which intersubjective understanding occurs. Traditionally, it was the objectified meaning in classic texts and artworks, but since Dilthey (2004 [1910]) and Heidegger (1962 [1927]) it is the everyday understanding as well that is the focus of analysis. The second major assumption thus involves that intersubjective understanding, as it is oriented toward another intentional agent, is different in kind from the explanation of non-intentional natural events. What is at stake is the adequate reconstruction of the other's intended meaning, the meaning which the interpreter or agent is encountering in the objectification of a text, artwork, speech act, or social act. This means that any understanding of another agent and her symbolic expressions is:

(a) based on some mediating interpretive scheme; and
(b) nonetheless bound by the presupposition that we are dealing with an intentional expression.

The question is how intersubjective understanding is affected by the fact that all understanding is mediated by some symbolic pre-construction of the object, or, inversely, what the general pre-schematization of experience means if we are dealing with another agent's symbolically mediated acts.

The decisive move toward an answer to this question consists in the discovery of the *world-disclosing function of language*. It was prepared and anticipated by the philosophy of language of German idealism, especially through Herder (1966) and Humboldt (1988), which remains grounded in a philosophy of mind (compare Cassirer 1955). At stake is the displacement of the constituting subject by shared language, which helps in overcoming the most sticky philosophical issues plaguing phenomenology with regard to intersubjectivity (Schütz 1967; Husserl 1991). If intentional thought is mediated and articulated through language, and language is an intrinsically social and cultural phenomenon, the problem regarding the transcendental constitution of the other becomes obsolete. The impossible deduction of the reality of the other mind from the immediacy of my own representation of the other – which is always *my* representation and thus never apodictic evidence *vis-à-vis the other* – can now be replaced by the shared embeddedness of my own and the other's experience in a socially constituted and linguistically mediated context (Gadamer 1989 [1960]; Habermas 1983/1987). My thoughts are mediated by symbolic structures, which means that the access to my own thoughts and identity takes place in a medium that is *socially structured*. The words and rules, meanings and references, values and norms are picked up in social contexts, and as such exemplify their function as a medium for communication and shared reference. Thus the access to myself is no less 'mediated' than the access to the other, who is essentially given as another with whom I can speak and communicate about something in a shared world.

However, it remains true that I never know *a priori* what another agent concretely believes, assumes, intends, projects, or feels. The linguistic grounding rules out a global skepticism toward other minds, one that makes the other as hypothetical as the 'object' in transcendental idealism. But it does not overcome the interpretive predicament that to make sense of another shall always involve some projective attribution, a 'hermeneutic circle' where I assign the most plausible and rational meanings to the other's symbolic expression on the basis of my own background assumptions. What is now gained is the focus on the *adequacy of the cultural interpretation*, the assessment of what defines the concrete meaning expressed by the symbolic act of another subject.

Language as the shared medium of understanding holds the key to an analysis of the intersubjective relation between my own and the other's intentional meaning. In phenomenology, the late Merleau-Ponty recognizes that a full account of human understanding requires a more central role for symbolic mediation within which all experience and perception occurs (Merleau-Ponty 1964). After his pioneering work on the role of the body, in which Bourdieu's notion of habitus is conceptually carved out, Merleau-Ponty discovers, prior to the post-structuralists, the importance of Saussure's semiotics. The linguistic mediation of thought is thus made crucial, and a semiotic reconceptualization of the notion of the field in which a bodily-situated perception is located is made possible. In hermeneutics, Heidegger gives up his earlier focus on the socially and practically situated subject (*Dasein* as Being-in-the-World) and emphasizes the transsubjective event-character of linguistic world-disclosure (Heidegger 1977). Indeed, the late Heidegger's discovery of language as the medium of understanding and experience not only repositions the situated subject, as it is now seen as largely dependent on a holistic background that 'discloses' reality according to some prior, yet historically contingent perspective. More importantly, it aims at redefining the substance of language itself. According to Heidegger, understanding language as a medium of subjective expression or as a tool for objective representation both misconceives the reality of language itself, its disclosing, constructing, world-constituting force (Heidegger 1971). Finally, to reject a view that makes language a mere mirror of some objective or subjective reality parallels the critique of positivism undertaken by the late Wittgenstein (1953). In a radical departure from his own earlier views, Wittgenstein deconstructs the notion of linguistic meaning as based on objective representation, and proposes as an alternative a quasi-phenomenological, hermeneutically sensitive view that attends closely to the multiple, contextual, and socially malleable ways in which human agents construct intersubjective worlds through signifying practices. The notions of 'language games' and 'forms of life' that are to capture meaning-constitution deserved their widespread impact on how to rethink meaning and understanding (Hollis and Lukes 1982; Habermas 1988; Winch 1991).

Current issues and approaches in hermeneutic social theory

To be sure, the most fruitful approach for social theory is Gadamer's Philosophical Hermeneutics, as the world-disclosing role of language is here concretely explored with regard to intersubjective understanding (Gadamer 1989 [1960]). In what we could call a 'phenomenology of the interpretive act,' Gadamer reconstructs the dialogical character of all understanding and interpretation. Understanding a text or symbolic expression is always oriented at some subject matter. Indeed, all linguistic comprehension consists in grasping a meaningful intentional content, *die Sache selbst*. What a word or sentence means involves knowing what it stands for, what the speech act is about. Yet making sense of some symbolic expression further involves that I must be able to connect it to my previous beliefs and assumptions concerning the subject matter. All understanding is interpretation of the subject matter in light of my pre-understanding of the issue at stake. This necessary dependence on pre-assumptions highlights the historical nature of all understanding, as it is the particular cultural background that provides the 'horizon' of my interpretation. This horizon or interpretive perspective, only part of which is consciously attended to, is itself the expression of an effective history (*Wirkungsgeschehen*) that has hitherto shaped the guiding prejudgments. If I am thus compelled to get at what a text or speech act expresses about a subject matter, but am also dependent on my own historically situated background assumptions, understanding a symbolic expression becomes the hermeneutic dialectic – indeed, the essential hermeneutic dialogue – between my pre-projections and the meaning of the text itself. Both meet, so to speak, in the comprehension of the text's message. Understanding is thus always an interpretive process in which my own horizon and the other's perspective encounter one another. Or rather, since the text's alterity can only profile itself in such a process *as* another's meaning, interpretation is always a 'fusion of horizons' (*Horizon-*

tverschmelzung) in which the shared assumptions as well as the topical differences are worked out.

Hermeneutic theory thus effectively overcomes the Cartesian legacy. The global skepticism regarding the reality of the other is replaced by the interpretive challenge to understand and explain the other's intentional action. Understanding oneself and understanding another are both interpretive endeavors, with different levels of pre-knowledge involved, but not distinguished by absolute access and self-transparency on the one side, and insurmountable opacity on the other (Schütz 1967). Indeed, understanding others and understanding oneself emerges as a co-dependent process within which the cultural and social identity of both self and other are constructed (Ricoeur 1992; Mandair and Zene 2005).

In particular, hermeneutic insights have advanced the discussion with regard to the following three issues. First, it is now better understood that interpreting human agency involves some kind of *normative orientation at the self-understanding of the other* as it exists in its culturally complex and thick descriptions. Leaving behavioristic or functionalist models on the side, classic empathetic or formally rationalistic models both miss the relevance of the pre-existing cultural context in which human agency and meaning is formed (Kögler and Stueber 2000). Understanding the other involves a process of perspective-taking deriving from one's own background, in which the interpreter is forced to work out the unique identity of the other's beliefs and assumptions in a to-and-fro movement between her prejudices and the other's assertions (Kögler 1999).

Second, discussion concerning the cultural differences revealed through this process of interpretation made clear that *incommensurability* should not be confused with absolute incomprehensibility or radical untranslatability. Incommensurability, understood as the impossibility to establish shared criteria and standards to assess evidence and facts with regard to a common conceptual framework, is a hermeneutic phenomenon. This means that it is based on *understanding* different yet incommensurable frameworks, not on remaining shut out from their meaning (Rorty 1979; Kögler 1999; Valadez 2001). This approach suggests a more pluralistic and multicultural understanding of social agency, one that is not premised on the substantive shared agreement of basic assumptions, but rather relies on the formally shared hermeneutic competence to make sense of cultural difference and situated agency (Taylor 1993; Benhabib 1999a; Valadez 2001).

Third, as the focus in cultural understanding is now less on consensus and more on difference, a new view toward the *reflexive potential* concerning intercultural dialogue becomes possible. Responding to a vast cultural need for the reflexive grasp of hitherto neglected perspectives and narratives, an explosion of discourses dealing with a critical reconstruction of our cultural identities has begun to emerge in social discourse (Bhabha 1994). New and increasing interest in the cultural dimension of political struggles for freedom and recognition testify to the critical need for hermeneutic theory in this regard (Warnke 2002; Baum 2004).

Alongside those thematic foci, we currently witness the development of subfields in a broadly defined social hermeneutics, including phenomenological, critical-theoretical, and poststructuralist modes of inquiry. Yet what is unique to the hermeneutic approach is the attempt to establish a theory of *situated subjectivity*, one that establishes a kind of middle-ground between universalist theories on the one hand and contextualism on the other hand (compare also Frank 1989). In this vein, several important anthologies have recently set out to redefine the grounds of a subject that, while historically and socially grounded, is nonetheless capable of self-determination and critical reflexivity (Deines *et al.* 2003; Kadi and Unterthurner 2005). A new generation of authors happily fuse poststructurally informed theories of social identity and power with a hermeneutic conception of self and identity.

This particular angle regarding situated subjectivity is further worked out in more specifically focused areas of inquiry. In feminist thought, many begin to see the choice between a Habermasian defense of universal-moral presuppositions and a poststructuralist endorsement of inescapably power-shaped social identities to be wrongheaded. Instead of the stale opposition between 'normativity or power,' an interest in the social, symbolic, and interpretative resources for identity-construction becomes visible (Stoller *et al.* 2005). The resources of a *feminist hermeneutics* include a new textual model of self-identity that opposes both a rigid social constructionism and the fully performativist turn of Judith Butler (Warnke 2004; Benhabib 1999b). It also includes a more open-ended and context-sensitive model of ethical recognition. Moreover, in *intercultural hermeneutics* a whole new set of issues and themes regarding the understanding of cultural difference and otherness is staked out. While close in its theoretical grounds to philosophical hermeneutics, this perspective is normatively less focused on consensus or the integration of texts and meanings into an existing traditional context. Rather, issues such as the implicitly power-driven function of cultural interpretation, the potential of intercultural understanding for reflexive identities, and the philosophical challenge of a tenable (that is: non-relativistic) theory of epistemic pluralism are at stake (for England and the US, see Mandair and Zene 2005; Dallmayr 1996; for Germany, see Renn 1999; Rosa 1999; Straub 1999; Kogge 2001; 2003; Straub *et al.* 2004). Finally, hermeneutically inclined authors have recently turned their analytic gaze toward issues of race and ethnic identity (Bernasconi 2001; McCarthy 2001). In what we could call a critical hermeneutics of racial identity, eminent thinkers and their theories are challenged with regard to their underlying racial bias. Most prominent is perhaps the case of Heidegger, whose personal and temporary attachment to fascism must concern anyone influenced by his ideas. At stake is the relation between the potential racism of theories developed by racist authors, or more dramatically still, the challenge whether philosophical thought can ever escape and transcend its power-shaped existential or national context of production. The power-ingrained background on which every interpreter and thinker *willy nilly* depends thus forces us to develop a theory of racially and ethnically shaped influences on thought that dialectically mediates between assessing the potential shaping-power of ethnic biases on theory – including critical social theory – without succumbing to a reduction of critical thought to social contexts.

All these endeavors have in common that they take seriously the situatedness of agency, and that they set out to develop both the social-theoretical and the normative tools to come to grips with this situation. While the hermeneutic dimension justly foregrounds the need for interpretive contextual sensitivity, social situatedness is incompletely theorized without an articulated connection between human agency and social institutions.

Agency and the power of social institutions

In philosophical anthropology, we encounter a concept of human agency not only broadened by the inclusion of the bodily basis of human existence. In addition, this discourse advances the hermeneutic notion of agency toward a theory of social institutions. To be sure, the conservative and rigid concept of social institutions proposed by philosophical anthropology must also be critically discussed in light of hermeneutic assumptions. The result of this discussion will be the outline of a hermeneutic theory of institutions in which the holistic pre-understanding provides a mediation between intentional agency and social structures.

Human nature and social institutions

Philosophical anthropology's theory of human nature is based on a double methodological reduction. In a first abstraction, Darwinistic or socio-biological theories of life are set aside as they project an inadequate conception of the roots of human life. Instead of accepting animal life-forms as the paradigm for biological sources, human existence must be understood on its own, uniquely biological grounds. Instead of being defined by instincts and fixed drives, human existence rather emerges from the *absence of pre-determined instincts and drives*. The human being is defined, in a word of Nietzsche, as the 'not yet determined animal' (Gehlen 1988). While all animals are pre-adjusted to the particular environments (Umwelt) in which their survival is at stake, the human being lacks such context-specific adjustments or adaptations, and is thus forced to create its own world (Welt). In a related move, this theory abstracts second from all social and cultural meanings within which human agency is historically embedded (Gehlen 1988; see also Plessner 1970). The project of an 'empirical philosophy' (Gehlen) sets out to lay bare the *universal biological roots* of all human agency, and thus brackets the *particular cultural contexts* within which such agency objectifies itself. Positing a universal need to survive, the human challenge consists in developing the yet-to-be-specified tools and capabilities that ensure the particular group or member the survival in a particular context. Instead of instinctual predetermination, human agency is thus defined by *world-openness*. The lack of specific tools to deal with a concrete context are taken to put an extreme challenge on the organism to develop strategies for survival, which involves at the same time an immense flexibility to adapt and adjust to an infinite range of different habitats.

The absence of pre-determining instincts and the positive counterpart of world-openness *together* define the relation between the human subject and its world. The first suggestive feature of philosophical anthropology is thus that the creative and world-disclosing capabilities of humans are directly related to their biological constitution. What one could call a notion of malleable or flexible agency involves that human agents must, as it were, spin out of themselves (but in interaction with the environment) the tools and schemes that allow them to cope successfully. As Gehlen argues in his major work *Man: His Nature and Place in the World* (1988), philosophy thereby overcomes the sterile opposition of a determined body and a free mind, and rather sees the intentional human mind as the outcome of an environmentally embedded, physiologically embodied human agency. Agency itself becomes a bridging concept, as it involves by definition the situatedness of the non-adapted body and the uniquely human capacity to forge the means to cope with the world. This, in turn, implies that knowledge and culture ultimately consist in tools to cope and adjust successfully. Culture is seen as a *compensation* for the absence of pre-adjusting instincts; its main function is to provide a new set of organized responses, that is, to structure, articulate, and orient the individual according to an ordered context of rules and schemes. By fulfilling this essential function, accumulated and sedimented schemes of cultural knowledge provide *relief* (*Entlastung*) with regard to the unpredictable, new, and challenging environment. Thus, the basic role of culture is to establish stability and order, to accomplish what nature failed to give the human being: a fixed set of responses and acts (Gehlen 1980, 1988).

The hermeneutic notion of language as a medium between social-historical contexts and intentional agency can thus be related:

(a) to our biological constitution; and
(b) to a functional concept of social institutions.

213

Language mediates between the lower, vegetative and sensory-motor functions of human understanding on the one hand, and the higher, cognitive and representational functions on the other hand (Gehlen 1988; see also Mead 1934). The lower functions are undetermined, and as such make the essential function of language possible: that the sign detaches something from its immediately present context. The further crystallization of an identifiable content in the repeatable and shared sign (or name) allows this experience to be 'kept in mind' (Cassirer 1955). It can now be represented and identified as a determined and stable content independent from particular contexts. Language thus both detaches and estranges the subject from its immediate environment *and* creates a new organizing medium through which the world is encountered (Gehlen 1988; Gadamer 1989). What Plessner (1970) coins the *eccentric positionality* of human existence involves this essential alienation from direct experience, including the capacity for self-distanciation and creative world-construction of our understanding.

To be sure, even though the lower functions ground higher intellectual activities, the different levels of mental capabilities cannot simply be understood in a hierarchical scheme, as if instinct, habit, practical intelligence and abstract thinking constitute separate steps in a developmental ladder (Scheler 1961). Rather, the lower functions form a permanent underground, or better, a background for higher cognitive functions, without thereby reducing mental or moral content to lower skills and habits. Indeed, the very relation between a practically acquired and culturally mediated background of skills and habits and the higher intentional acts is one of the most promising aspects of philosophical anthropology. This is because the necessary habitual schematization of a stable background of understanding is essentially tied to *cultural practices*; this process and condition thus connects higher intentional thought to the historical undercurrents of power and social institutions. As the habitual schemes and structures are acquired in hierarchically organized social settings, the background of understanding provides agents with a power-based sense of reality and identity, thus connecting an *irreducible* intentional understanding to power-based social identities and scientific constructs (Foucault 1994 [1976]; Hacking 2000). Philosophical anthropology thus allows us to integrate a power-sensitive concept of social meaning with intentional agency via the notion of the necessary background understanding of all meaning (Moss and Gutmann 2006).

Philosophical anthropology and social theory

However, in order to unleash philosophical anthropology's potential for social theory, we need to reconceptualize this thought with regard to three issues. First, the biological starting-point led especially Gehlen to exaggerate the function of stability and order as essential factors of human agency (Gehlen 2004 [1956]). The foil of a lack of natural instincts makes Gehlen and others assimilate human institutions to the biological function of creating stability and order as their *foremost function*. Since the poverty of instincts leaves the human being without order, culture – and thus the social institutions on which its reproduction depends – are conceived almost entirely as compensation *vis-à-vis* this lack of organized adjustment. This, in turn, puts an overblown emphasis on the internal structure of cultural schemes and institutions, and neglects the possible self-ideal in which the creative and reflexive adjustment is itself pursued and endorsed as an open-ended, flexible, and transformative project.

Second, philosophical anthropology abstracts from particular social and cultural practices to reveal the universal essence of human agency based on its biological nature. But the abstraction from particular cultural forms does not justify the abstraction from shared universal forms of culture, especially with regard to language. While language is productively introduced to bridge nature and culture, and habits and intentions, the internal resources that language as such entails need to be reconstructed. When it comes to the relation between habitual background and intentional agency, the symbolic background must be internally connected to its reproduction in intersubjective practices. Linguistic features such as the reflexivity of symbolic acts and the intersubjective assumption of a shared referential or intentional content that can be put into question and defended through reasons are systematically to be taken into account (Habermas 1983/1987). This is because those value-constituting reflexive acts shape the intentional self-understanding of agents in different symbolically structured contexts (Cassirer 1955).

Third, emphasizing the stability of cultural institutions without analyzing forms of linguistic reason fails to capture the critical-reflexive resources that inhere in all symbolically mediated human agency. In the cultural-diagnostic writings of these authors, the breakdown of stable and ordered institutions leads, as it were necessarily, to the destruction of an autonomous personality (Gehlen 1980; Plessner 1999). Similar in some respects to both the early Frankfurt School (Horkheimer and Adorno 1972) and to Foucault (1979 [1975]), modern subjects are delivered, almost without defense, to autopoeic social institutions that are taken to form the psychological material according to their own functional imperatives. The individual becomes the mirror-image of the macro-institutions, and as such itself an (externally formed) institution (Gehlen 1980). Employed for detecting social pathologies, the crystallization of habitual schemes of understanding is an indispensable tool of critical theory. Yet this perspective must conceptually be tied to the possibility of reflexive and interpretive acts of potentially autonomous agents. Social pathologies can thus be diagnosed as the *alienating interruption* of reflexive and creative agency from its cultural and institutional background. It is not the mere existence of a stable background of social institutions, but rather the capability to make use and draw on background resources in a productive manner that makes autonomous agency possible. If understood in this way, the anthropological focus is able to broaden our horizon. Hermeneutics can then fruitfully relate its conception of human agency to a theory of social institutions understood as *both enabling backgrounds of intentionality and institutional structures of power.*

References

Althusser, L. (1969) *For Marx*, New York: Pantheon Books.
Baum, B. (2004) 'Feminist Politics of Recognition', *Signs*, 29, 1073–1102.
Benhabib, S. (1999a) *The Claims of Culture*, Cambridge: Harvard University Press.
Benhabib, S. (1999b) 'Sexual Difference and Collective Identities: The New Global Constellation,' in *Signs*, 24(2), 335–361.
Bernasconi, R. (ed.) (2001) *Race*, Oxford: Blackwell Publishers.
Bhabha, H. (1994) *The Location of Culture*, London and New York: Routledge.
Bourdieu, P. (1977) *Outline of a Theory of Practice*, Cambridge: Cambridge University Press.
Bourdieu, P. (1990) *The Logic of Practice*, Stanford: Stanford University Press.
Cassirer, E. (1955) *Philosophy of Symbolic Forms, Vol. 1*, New Haven: Yale University Press.
Castoriadis, C. (1998) *The Imaginary Institution of Society*, Cambridge, MA: The MIT Press.
Dallmayr, F. (1996) *Beyond Orientalism*, Lanham, MD: Rowman & Littlefield.
Deines, S., Jaeger, S. and Nünning, A. (2003) (eds) *Historisierte Subjekivität/Subjektivierte Historie*, Berlin and New York: Walter de Gryter.
Derrida, J. (1978) *Writing and Difference*, Chicago: University of Chicago Press.
Dilthey, W. (2004 [1910]) *The Construction of History in the Human Sciences*, Princeton: Princeton University Press.
Dreyfus, H. (1993) *Being-in-the-World: A Commentary on Heidegger's Being and Time*, Cambridge MA, The MIT Press.
Foucault, M. (1979 [1975]) *Discipline and Punish*, New York: Pantheon Books.

Foucault, M. (1990 [1966]) *The Order of Things*, New York: Vintage Books.

Foucault, M. (1994 [1976]) *History of Sexuality: An Introduction*, New York: Vintage Books.

Frank, M. (1989) *What is Neostructuralism?* Minneapolis: University of Minnesota Press.

Gadamer, H.-G. (1989 [1960]) *Truth and Method*, New York: Crossroads.

Gehlen, A. (1980) *Man in the Age of Technology*, New York: Columbia University Press.

Gehlen, A. (1988) *Man: His Nature and Place in the World*, New York: Columbia University Press.

Gehlen, A. (2004 [1956]) *Urmench und Spätkultur*, Frankfurt/Main: Klostermann.

Giddens, A. (1984) *The Constitution of Society:* Berkeley and Los Angeles: University of California Press.

Habermas, J. (1983/1987 [1981]) *Theory of Communicative Action, Volumes 1 and 2*, Boston: Beacon Press.

Habermas, J. (1987) *The Philosophical Discourse of Modernity*, Cambridge, MA: The MIT Press.

Habermas, J. (1988) *On the Logic of the Social Sciences*, Cambridge, MA: The MIT Press.

Habermas, J. (1992) *Postmetaphysical Thinking*, Cambridge, MA: The MIT Press.

Hacking, I. (2000) *The Social Construction of What?* Cambridge: Harvard University Press.

Heidegger, M. (1962 [1927]) *Being and Time*, New York: Harper & Row.

Heidegger, M. (1971) *On the Way to Language*, San Francisco: HarperCollins Publishers.

Heidegger, M. (1977) *Basic Writings*, San Francisco: HarperCollins Publishers.

Heidegger, M. (1982) *The Basic Problems of Phenomenology*, Bloomington: Indiana University Press.

Heidegger, M. (1985) *History of the Concept of Time*, Bloomington: Indiana University Press.

Herder, J. G. and Rousseau, J.-J. (1966) *On the Origin of Language: Two Essays*, Chicago: University of Chicago Press.

Hollis, M. and Lukes, S. (1982) *Rationality and Relativism*, Cambridge, MA: The MIT Press.

Honneth, A. and Joas, H. (1988) *Social Action and Human Nature*, Cambridge and New York: Cambridge University Press.

Horkheimer, M. (1992 [1937]) *Traditionellle und kritische Theorie: Fünf Aufsätze*, Frankfurt: Fischer Verlag.

Horkheimer, M. and Adorno, T. W. (1972) *Dialectic of Enlightenment*, New York: Herder and Herder.

Hoy, D. (2004) *Critical Resistance*, Cambridge, MA: The MIT Press.

Hoy, D. and McCarthy, T. (1994) *Critical Theory*, Oxford: Blackwell Publishers.

Humboldt, W. von (1988) *On Language: The Diversity of Human Language-Structure and its Influence on the Mental Development of Mankind*, Cambridge: Cambridge University Press.

Husserl, E. (1962 [1913]) *Ideas: General Introduction to Pure Phenomenology*, London: Collier Macmillan Publishers.

Husserl, E. (1970) *Logical Investigations*, London: Routledge.

Husserl, E. (1991) *Cartesian Meditations*, Dordrecht and Boston: Kluwer Academic Publishers.

Kadi, U. and Unterthurner, G. (2005) *Sinn, Macht, Unbewusstes*, Würzburg: Köngishausen & Neumann.

Kogge, W. (2001) *Verstehen und Fremdheit in der Philosophischen Hermeneutik: Heidegger und Gadamer*, Hildesheim: Olms Verlag.

Kogge, W. (2003) *Die Grenzen des Verstehens*, Weilerswist: Velbrück.

Kögler, H.-H. (1999) *The Power of Dialogue: Critical Hermeneutics after Gadamer and Foucault*, Cambridge: The MIT Press.

Kögler, H.-H. (2005) 'Constructing a Cosmopolitan Public Sphere: Hermeneutic Capabilities and Universal Values', *European Journal of Social Theory* 8(4), 297–320.

Kögler, H.-H. and Stueber, K. (eds) (2000) *Empathy and Agency: The Problem of Understanding in the Human Sciences*, Boulder, CO: Westview Press.

Lash, S. (1998) *Another Modernity, A Different Rationality*, London: Blackwell Publishers.

Mandair, A. and Zene, C. (eds) (2005) 'Dialogue as the Inscription of "the West"', in J. McCumber, S. Sakai, R. Bernasconi, H.-H. Kögler, A. Lingis, C. Venn and T. Tosselini, *Social Identities*, special issue, 11(3), May 2005, London and New York: Routledge.

McCarthy, T. (1991) *Ideal and Illusions*, Cambridge, MA: The MIT Press.

McCarthy, T. (2001) 'Political Philosophy and Racial Injustice: From Normative to Critical Theory' unpublished manuscript.

Mead, G. H. (1934) *Mind, Self, and Society*, Chicago: University of Chicago Press.

Merleau-Ponty, M. (1964) *Signs*, Evanston, IL: Northwestern University Press.

Moss, L. and M. Gutmann (eds) (2006) *Philosophical Anthropology: Reviewed and Renewed*, Cambridge: The MIT Press.

Plessner, H. (1970) *Philosophische Anthropologie*, Frankfurt am Main.

Plessner, H. (1999) *The Limits of Community*, Amherst, NY: Humanities Books.

Renn, J. (1999) 'Der Tod des Captain Cook', in *Handlung/Kultur/Interpretation,* 8, Heft 2, Universität Hannover.

Ricoeur, P. (1992) *Oneself as Another,* Chicago, IL: Chicago University Press.

Rorty, R. (1979) *The Mirror of Nature,* Princeton: Princeton University Press.

Rosa, H. (1999) 'Lebensformen vergleichen und verstehen' in *Handlung/Kultur/Interpretation,* Heft 1, 8 Jg., Universität Hannover.

Sartre, J.-P. (1956) *Being and Nothingness,* New York: Simon & Schuster.

Scheler, M. (1961) *Man's Place in Nature,* New York: Noonday Press.

Schütz, A. (1967) *The Phenomenology of the Social World,* Evanston, IL: Northwestern University Press.

Stoller, S., Vasterling, V. and Fisher, L. (eds) (2005) *Feminsitische Phänomenologie und Hermeneutik,* Würzburg: Königshausen & Neumann.

Straub, J. (1999) *Verstehen, Kritik, Anerkennung,* Göttingen: Wallstein.

Straub, J., Renn, J. and Shimada, S. (eds) (2004) *Übersetzung als Medium des Kulturverstehens und sozialer Integration,* Frankfurt am Main: Campus Verlag.

Taylor, C. (1993) *The Politics of Recognition,* Princeton: Princeton University Press.

Thompson, J. (1981) *Critical Hermeneutics,* Cambridge: Cambridge University Press.

Valadez, J. (2001) *Deliberative Democracy, Political Legitimacy, and Self Determination in Multicultural Societies,* Boulder, CO: Westview Press.

Warnke, G. (2002) 'Hermeneutics, Ethics, and Politics', in R. Dostal (ed.), *The Cambridge Companion to Gadamer,* Cambridge: Cambridge University Press, 79-101.

Warnke, G. (2004) 'Hermeneutics or Postmodernism', *APA Newsletter,* University of Delaware, Spring 2003, 2(2), p.214.

Winch, P. (1991 [1959]) *Philosophy and the Idea of a Social Science,* London: Routledge.

Wittgenstein, L. (1953) *Philosophical Investigations,* Cambridge: Cambridge University Press.

Zuidervaart, L. (2004) *Artistic Truth,* Cambridge: Cambridge University Press.

16

Contemporary European cognitive social theory

Piet Strydom

Largely unnoticed, the cognitive approach has been moving slowly but surely towards the core of social theory during the past two decades. The reasons for this shift are, on the one hand, the increasingly visible vulnerability of modern societies and hence the mounting uncertainty about macro-processes and their outcomes, and, on the other, the cognitive revolution's exposure of the major sociological traditions as having, in one way or another, confounded the different dimensions of social reality and their relations.

The advance of this approach coincided with the increasing acceptance of constructivism, which epistemologically does not necessarily mean idealism since realism is equally compatible with it. The fact that constructivism focuses on the cognitive processes whereby structures are formed, ontologically leads a number of theorists to adopt naturalism, some celebrating the autonomy of events beyond individuals, human beings or social practices, and others acknowledging a weak, non-reductive naturalism which by no means disallows the knowledgeable agent, intersubjectivity and social practices. Opposed to the naturalists are those actionists who insist on the priority of the – sometimes rational – actor and intentional action. By the same token, humanists and anti-humanists are often embroiled in contestation. Cutting across these divisions, however, is the shared attempt to establish new relations among previously isolated disciplines. Indeed, the cognitive approach has entered the fray in the debate about which new transdiscipline is the most appropriate to meet the demands of the current post-disciplinary situation. It is against the foil of such considerations, which I am compelled to leave in the background, that I propose to attend here to some of the current theoretical and metatheoretical issues concerning cognitive social theory.

The international scope of the cognitive field of contestation suggests that a variety of traditions, schools and directions can be distinguished. Historically, the different cognitive strands in Europe and America are bound together at a deeper level by a subterranean background stretching back to Kant, Hegel and Simmel in Germany, Peirce, James and Mead in the USA, and Durkheim and Mauss in France. As this entwinement, invigorated by the cognitive revolution, continues to this day, the ideal thing would be throughout to bear in mind the various connections and relations. Here I am charged with giving an account of contemporary European cognitive social theory and, therefore, will not be able to offer such a contextualisation. The best I can do is to open with a brief overview of the distinct traditions and schools against the background of the cognitive revolution, and then to give a stylised account of the two major competing directions in contemporary European cognitive social theory.

The cognitive revolution

Traditionally, the study of cognition and knowledge had been the preserve largely of epistemology and psychology. Sociology also made a contribution, yet in the guise of the sociology of knowledge it focused, despite Durkheim, Simmel, Adorno and Schutz, on knowledge rather than the cognitive dimension. The cognitive revolution, however, decisively reconstituted this traditional concern.

Following a period of gestation dating from the 1940s in which cybernetics, information theory, psychology and neuroscience had played a role, the cognitive revolution occurred in 1956 on the basis of computer science, linguistics and psychology, but also neuroscience and epistemology. The subsequent maturation of the cognitive sciences between 1960 and 1985, in which artificial intelligence as well as Chomsky's linguistics and cognitive psychology were prominent, took place around a computational model according to which the mind was assumed to process information through the manipulation of symbols in accordance with rules. Of importance, however, was also Searle's so-called 'Berkeley approach', the concurrent critique of the narrow computational view in terms of a linguistic theory forming part of a theory of action. During this phase, the social sciences at best played only an ancillary role. By the early 1980s, however, the computer model became supplemented and even challenged by an alternative one based on the brain, not as a rule-governed central information processing unit, but as a neural network which changes through experience. So-called 'parallel distributed processing' or 'connectionism', entailing questions of networks, their self-organisation and production of emergent properties, now tended to take the place of the initial, rather narrow 'cognitivism'. This phase opened the door for the social sciences to play a more influential role in the interdisciplinary interactions shaping the future of the cognitive sciences.

In the current phase, where cognitive science is seeking a new identity, the door has opened still more widely for the social sciences. Whereas the original cognitive science model had been broadened first in the direction of the brain, it was now extended to the environment which is increasingly understood in terms of use in context, particularly due to the development of pragmatics and the not unrelated renewal of pragmatism. Neuroscience and cognitive psychology assumed the leading role, yet the impact of the sociological and anthropological understanding of situated and mediated action on the cognitive sciences is quite remarkable. Simultaneously, however, the cognitive transformation of the social sciences also intensifies, while the different cognitive science models import tensions into the cognitive understanding of social theory.

Social theory after cognitive science

The invigorating impulse of the cognitive revolution stimulated the development of distinct traditions or schools of cognitive social theory in parallel with the phase-like unfolding of the cognitive sciences since 1956.

Starting already in the 1960s, a number of theorists independently established platforms for distinct cognitive traditions. The most significant, all drawing in some way on the cognitive sciences, are: Habermas (1971, 1972) and Luhmann (1973) in Germany; Bourdieu (1977) in

France; Nowotny (1973) in Austria; Knorr (1977) spanning Europe and the USA; and Cicourel (1973) and Goffman (1974) in the USA. The critical theory, systems theory, practice theory and sociology of science of Habermas, Luhmann, Bourdieu and Nowotny and Knorr respectively contained cognitive elements sufficiently significant to provide starting points for distinct cognitive traditions in social theory. Cicourel and Goffman's contributions were more explicitly and systematically presented as cognitive social theory – the former speaking emphatically of 'cognitive sociology' and the latter putting forward cognitive 'frame analysis' – and as such would be the basis not only for a varied American tradition represented by Snow and associates, Gamson, Powell and DiMaggio, Zerubavel and Saferstein, but would also make itself felt on the Continent, particularly in France.[1]

With the change of the cognitive science model in the early 1980s, Luhmann (1995) revised his systems theory by basing it on the neuroscientific view of the brain as an operationally closed unit. The concurrent input of cognitive biology led him to expound the cognitive character of autopoietic theory in unprecedented detail (Luhmann 1990, 1992). This gave authors drawing on his work the twofold opportunity of focusing on the independent and autonomous system in terms of cognition interpreted either more biologically or more socially. As for Habermas, the alternative shift to action-oriented world creation and engagement with reality in an environment, reinforced his pursuit of the theory of communicative action (1984/1987) and, closely related to it, various cognitively important topics. In this context, Habermas (1996) through the 1980s and 1990s brought out aspects of the pragmatic cognitive dimension which had been present in his work from the 1960s. Since the early 1980s, a number of authors in Germany, the British Isles and Sweden working in more or less close proximity to Habermas started to focus on the cognitive dimension in a way that led to systematic results in the 1990s. In France, the introduction of cognitive sociology in the early 1980s was paralleled by the rise from Bourdieu's work of so-called 'pragmatic sociology' which is the currently most prominent vehicle of cognitive social theory there. These advances were helped, among other things, by the concurrent diagnosis that sociology is undergoing a 'cognitive turn' (Knorr-Cetina and Cicourel 1981) and a groundswell of interest in the cognitive dimension in various substantive areas, including the sociology of science, mass media, social movements, neo-institutional organisational analysis and discourse analysis.

Against this background, two major competing directions stand out in Europe today – what may be called metabiological and pragmatic cognitive theory.

Metabiological cognitive theory

Luhmann's wide-ranging oeuvre encapsulates a multi-level cognitive approach spanning a social systems theory (1992, 1995) and a constructivist epistemology (1990, 1992) which find application at more modest theoretical levels.

Luhmann's cognitive approach is signalled by his emphasis not on knowledge, but rather on knowing. The specificity of this approach becomes comprehensible only against the backdrop of his replacement of the traditional concept of the knowing subject by the concept of autopoietic system. Luhmann's original intuition derives from Wiener's militarily inspired cybernetics, particularly the idea of an autonomous combinatory communication process represented by a missile pursuing an enemy aircraft beyond the human agents involved. The autopoietic qualification is borrowed from biology in which cognition is extended to cover the life-maintaining operations of an organism – for which reason Luhmann's systems theory could be regarded as a 'metabiology' (Habermas 1987). Instead of subject-object, therefore, Luhmann's principal distinction is the conceptual pair 'system-environment'. Through its own cognition, any and every system, including societal functional systems as well as science (e.g. sociology), constructs a model of its own reality, masters the complexity of its environment and thus secures its own reproduction. Luhmann's shift to systems theory is supplemented by an anti-ontological and empiricist strategy. In the former case, he breaks with positions affirming the existence of a reality about which we could obtain knowledge formulable in statements. What counts alone, for him, is the organisational level of society understood analogous to organic life in terms of communication in the sense of an independent and self-sufficient process of the constant flow of information, selection and connection through time. Luhmann's empiricist strategy results in the dissolution of unitary concepts, such as society, culture, ideology and public opinion, by asking what operations such descriptions presuppose. From this standpoint, cognitive systems emerge only in the plural, and they relate to as many system-relative environments.

At a lower level, Luhmann (1999) offers glimpses of his more concrete conceptualisation of the cognitive organisation of society. Drawing directly from the cognitive sciences, particularly transposing the psychological concepts of memory, schema and script to the social level, he conceives of systems as being able to free themselves from their past so as to gain virtually unlimited operational possibilities and freedom to deal with new situations. A system activates memory to selectively recollect the past for the purposes of recognition and simultaneously generates redundancy and variety in anticipation of contingencies in the future. This is possible through cognitive schemata or categories making possible the recognition of something as something which themselves could be transformed into scripts leading to action upon, or intervention in, what is thus grasped. Schemata and scripts organise not merely theoretical-empirical or causal knowledge and action, but also norms and values as well as even the emotions. For example, first, the government agrees to support an unprofitable industry with subventions and takes corresponding action since it is convinced according to its schematisation of such situations that unemployment can thereby be curtailed; second, the UN applies human rights also to cultures which do not use the term and, when a violation is perceived in terms of this schema, the organisation embarks on humanitarian intervention; finally, rather than having a structuring effect, both private and public emotions follow in the wake of the transformation of normative or causal schemata into scripts actualising them.

His later work indicates that Luhmann (1999) regards public opinion and, related to it, the mass media as being of importance for the cognitive organisation and hence autopoiesis of society. Referring to the psychological theory of memory explaining the interrelation of forgetting and remembering, Luhmann defines public opinion as public memory. On the one hand, public opinion supports social and political communication which is able to take for granted the schemata and scripts it preserves. On the other, public opinion allows individuals to participate in collective memory, if only they are willing and able to follow mass media communication. While the mass media thus make possible a continuous integration of individual and social memory, public opinion serves the more specific function of establishing and developing cognitive schemata. By exercising this cognitive function, public opinion makes possible sense-making or form-giving processes which could relate to one another. The repertoire of schemata kept available by public opinion creates the conditions for controversies and free reasoning, and to the extent that public opinion articulates these schemata through the mass media it focuses actual controversies and mobilises participation. The application of a schema to reality allows values, emotions and engagements to crystallise, so that different groups are able to get excited about some script and compete over it. Simultaneously, the schemata put the participants in a position to observe each other and to assess the degree of approval or disapproval each schema attracts, as well as the strength of the support behind it. In controversies, Luhmann characteristically submits, schemata largely leave open the question of consent and dissent. There are therefore no grounds for insisting that the result of public communication is a correspondence of opinions or shared meanings. The distillation process of public communication leads to the fixing of a range of opinions by means of corresponding schemata and scripts, as attested by the fact that politically relevant opinions remain controversial.

Without exception, those inspired by Luhmann adopt his cognitive systems theory and, consequently, are emphatic that social systems consist of communication, thus representing an autonomous and independent level of organisation requiring its own theory and mode of analysis. While assuming this cognitive theory, however, his followers go in different directions, depending on the particular field of interest. Those who focus on science and technology (e.g. Leydesdorff 1993, 2000) explicitly take a cognitive view by conceiving of social systems in terms of parallel distributed processing or connectionism. Others (e.g. Bora 1997; Kneer 1997; Schneider 1997; Sutter 1997), whose more general interests include social and political communication, seek to strengthen systems theory's analytical ability by incorporating conversation or discourse analysis. Notably, the name of Miller, later discussed under pragmatic theory, is linked to this endeavour (Sutter 1997: 9). Nevertheless, these authors strictly confine sequentially organised temporal processes, structure securing operations and structure formation, which are central to their endeavours, to the systems level and it alone.

Typically, Luhmann's followers adumbrate his oft repeated argument against the concept of intersubjectivity due to its alleged identification of interaction and communication and, particularly, of understanding and agreement (Luhmann 1995; Hörning et al. 1997; Sutter 1997). The most pointed version of this argument, directed against Habermas, is that since systems theory consistently treats mass communication and subjective reception as separate domains, unlike interaction theory which insists on the intersubjective coordination of interlocutors, it is able to avoid the fallacy of the transfer of identical meanings and the control of mutual understanding. This argument is based on Luhmann's basic axiom of the separation of psychic and social systems. Although Bora (1997) acknowledges that both these systems are 'cognitive systems', he disregards the fact that cognitive structures are available at both these levels and, indeed, are in principle interrelated. Radical constructivists who are close to Luhmann's later version of cognitive systems theory, by contrast, take pains to warn against the transfer of concepts applicable to biological systems directly to social systems. Whereas Luhmann strictly separates psychic and social systems and his traditional sociological opponents regard communication as a cognitive operation or action, some radical constructivists therefore discover structural properties of a cognitive kind, yet of different levels and scope in both domains which allow their mediation and hence interrelation (Hejl 1993; Rusch 1999). But this points beyond metabiological cognitive theory.

Pragmatic cognitive theory

Two distinct lines of pragmatic cognitive social theory with only minimal interaction through their fountainheads, yet many remarkable similarities, can be distinguished – one French and the other German-led.

French cognitive sociology

The beginnings of an emphatic 'cognitive sociology' in France can be traced to Conein's introduction of Cicourel's sociology in the early 1980s (Corcuff 1995). Since then, a variety of cognitive approaches appeared (Boudon *et al.* 1997; Borzeix *et al.* 1998), for example, Pharo pursuing a Weberian actionist approach, Boudon an extended rational choice model relating action via 'axiological rationality' to collectively shared moral values, Bouvier a cognitivist argumentation analysis, Trépos an interactionist version focusing on the interpersonal construction of orders of evaluation and justification, and Conein progressing to a non-reductive naturalistic cognitivism.[2] Bourdieu (1984) severely criticised the cognitive approach for its subjectivism and idealism, yet his own work contained a significant cognitive dimension which provided a starting point for an alternative pragmatic and realist line of cognitive social theory. He assumed that historical classificatory schemata are common to the agents in a given society who internalise them as embodied cognitive structures, but due to social divisions the agents use or implement them in different and even antagonistic ways in their various practices. Accordingly, he insisted that the social scientist must include in the object of study the cognitive structures of the agents in such a way that he or she is able to appreciate the contribution those cognitive structures make to the object.

Coinciding with the introduction of cognitive sociology, Boltanski and Thévenot initiated a new line of constructivist enquiry which served as a vehicle for the advancement of cognitive social theory. Starting from Bourdieu but adopting a more systematic constructivist approach, Boltanski (1982) analysed the social group as being formed in and through a sociohistorical process of naturalisation rather than as something substantive. Together with the discursive, symbolic and institutional, the cognitive dimension formed an important, if as yet somewhat submerged, part of this process. If symbolic and institutional forms bring about a union in the course of the historical dialectic, then clearly the cognitive must be at the core of what becomes so unified, namely the preconstituted and reconstituted heterogeneous elements and forms. This cognitive component includes instruments for the construction of social reality, what Thévenot (1984) calls 'investment of forms', or what Boltanski (1984) regards as preconstituted 'social technologies' such as modes of collective action, juridical techniques and procedures of 'de-singularisation'. Crucial is that these instruments or technologies allow the bridging of the gap between individual and collective action. For through them the 'equivalences' among those involved emerge in the course of the process of construction as a 'common interest'.

Whereas the cognitive dimension did not enjoy the explication it deserves in the constructivist inquiries, the renewal of the Durkheimian tradition provided the impetus for a closer investigation during the 1980s into collective representations, particularly categories and forms of classification. Boltanski and Thévenot's (1983) study of the relation between everyday and learned practices of classification and Desrosières and Thévenot's (1986) work on social categorisation in the history of statistics led to a simultaneously more focused and more situationally-sensitive account of general forms of classification, evaluation and justification underpinning contemporary practices and institutions. Boltanski and Thévenot's *De la justification* (1991), one of the most important social scientific texts published in France in the 1990s, is the best example of this phase. Although a tendency is still observable here to confine the cognitive dimension to the individual or micro-dimension, i.e. the cognitive as competence, this work in fact presents a more general cognitive framework which by the mid-1990s would benefit the articulation of French cognitive social theory.

Observing the relation between action and reflection in the context of crisis and closure, which allows actors to deploy their actions communicatively and through the recognition of the obligation to arrive at tolerance, accommodation, agreement or compromise, Boltanski and Thévenot develop a high resolution pragmatic process model. Of all the phases through which the process passes, they focus on the moment of public justification elicited by the critique of a claim advanced in a public dispute. Not only does it capture both the instant of reflection on action and the correction or reorientation and hence the return of action to itself, but it also reveals the socio-historically constructed cultural forms, registers or schemes of justification to which the actors appeal. Rejecting any implication of relativism, the authors identify six of the most legitimate cultural models according to which actors in contemporary society seek to justify their claims in the public sphere. As different notions of the common good, the authors expound each of the schemes of justification with reference to its appropriate context and principle. Such forms of justification as inspiration, the domestic, opinion, the civic, merchant and industrial have their contexts in religion/art, personal relations, public relations, community relations, commerce and production respectively where they, again respectively, depend on the principles of creativity, trust, recognition of others, equality, the market and efficiency.

These orders of justification are derived from a model, the 'model of the city' (Boltanski and Thévenot 1991), which is based on the assumption that a variety of actors engaged in different kinds of practices in pursuit of distinct notions of the common good need to come to some understanding and eventually a compromise if the city is to be able to coordinate and sustain the mutual coexistence, practices and lifestyles of each. Legitimacy in a complex society such as ours, in which different orders of justification are available, depends on the fulfilment of two conditions. The first is the recognition and securing of the common humanity of all the members, and the second the establishment of the acceptability through a public discursive test of an order allowing the differential distribution of resources and the coordination of the actions of the members. This test is redeemed through the construction of a compromise between the conflicting justifications so that they are rendered compatible by being oriented towards the common interest. In his subsequent research, Thévenot (1998, 2001) has undertaken, with explicit reflection on the relation of sociology to cognitive science, to locate cognition within the dynamics of the coordination of humans' engagement with others, things and themselves, with the environments within which this occurs, according to the relevant conception of the good. This allowed him not only to cognitively differentiate pragmatic regimes of engagement of different levels of complexity such as 'familiarity' and 'regular planned action' beyond the regime of public justification on which he and Boltanski focused earlier. Simultaneously, it also enabled him to reconstruct the cognitively organised process of the interplay of common pragmatic regimes and the coordination of knowledge, the environment and information whereby social order is generated.

Thanks to the increasing interest in cognitive sociology and the accumulation of significant contributions, French cognitive social theory reached a nodal point in 1995, when special events at the Sorbonne (Boudon et al. 1997) and the Société française de sociologie (Borzeix et al. 1998) marked the rise of a framework systematically bringing together such topics as cognition in action, categorisation or classification, cognitive semantics, ideology, error, argumentation, cognitive adjustment in collective mobilisation, the constitution of collective action, and the diffusion of representations.

The Habermasian tradition

Although it is neither emphasised nor systematised in its own right due to its subordination to a normative approach, the cognitive dimension pervades Habermas's work in all its developmental phases and at all its levels.

Initially, Habermas introduced the cognitive dimension under the title of 'cognitive interests' in an epistemological inquiry into the conditions making knowledge possible (1972), but the direct impact of the cognitive sciences on his thinking through Chomsky and Searle became manifest at the outset of the 1970s in his 'theory of communicative competence' (1971) or 'universal' – later 'formal' – pragmatics' (1971, 1979) which presupposed his appropriation of the linguistic-pragmatic turn more generally. Whereas communicative competence refers to performance entailing the cognitive capacity to execute speech acts, universal pragmatics focuses on the pragmatic conditions or cognitively significant structures of communicative situations which are established in the course of the execution of speech acts. At this stage, Habermas also cognitively differentiated the concept of communication into interaction (or communicative action) and discourse, thus making a crucial distinction which would become central to the cognitive concern. Through his exposition particularly of discourse as involving such matters as the breakdown or problematisation of assumptions, crisis, dispute or public debate, argumentation, making and criticising validity claims, interpreting and defining common problems, providing grounds or reasons, justification, legitimation, universalisation and the generation of mutual understanding and agreement, Habermas contributed outstandingly to cognitive social theory. And he took the transposition of cognitive scientific insights to the social theoretic level yet a step further. On the one hand, leaning on cognitive psychology, he explicated the nature of the competent agent and its development of a complex ego identity, and, on the other, he generalised the illocutionary binding force of speech acts to public discourse, in which the collective learning embodied in social movements contributes to societal learning in the sense of the generation of structures of rationality and their universalisation and institutionalisation (Habermas 1979).

The early 1980s saw Habermas (1984/1987) consolidating his achievements by bringing his new position to bear on the sociological tradition. While the above-mentioned cognitively important matters remained central, Habermas here drew on a venerable line of cognitive social theory to complement his earlier account. Schutz, Durkheim and Mead combined enabled him to develop a communicative concept of the lifeworld and thus to clarify the situational structures, making possible the embedding and hence the structuration of interaction and discourse. Of particular importance is the threefold cognitive concept of culture Habermas put forward here – i.e. a componential or particulate rather than holistic concept consisting of cognitive structures of an intellectual (or cognitive in the narrow traditional sense), normative and aesthetic kind allowing the generation, structuration and application of theoretical-empirical, moral-practical and aesthetic-practical knowledge. Simultaneously, however, he also clarified the highly dynamic yet structured relations among personality, institutions and culture. The dynamics remind us of the basic nature of the process of the interactive-discursive practice of social life in and through which structures of different levels and scope are generated and established in such a manner that they in turn structure the process as it continues on its way. In the early 1990s, Habermas (1996) analysed this complex with reference to morality, law and politics, and then demonstrated it sociologically in terms of the conflict-ridden process of value and opinion formation, or the building and setting of agendas around issues and decision-making, in the context of the public sphere which could be either in a normal state of rest or in an agitated state of crisis consciousness.

The link Habermas forged between social theory and the cognitive sciences, even if curiously under-utilised, opened a space for a number of more or less closely related authors to contribute to the emerging pragmatic cognitive social theory.

Although not explicitly laying claim to cognitive sociology or social theory, Miller made a decisive contribution towards refocusing Habermas's wide-ranging yet largely normative approach in a cognitive direction. Drawing on cognitive psychology and linguistics, he started in the mid-1970s by investigating language acquisition and its pragmatic conditions, but by the early 1980s he advanced to inquiries into the relation of argumentation to both intellectual and moral learning as well as the development of collective moral interpretative frameworks. These studies culminated in the publication of a major work with the unmistakable cognitive theme of collective learning (1986), which cleared the way for various other publications, notably one dealing with discourse and morality (1992). Miller's achievement lies in his having provided detailed clarification of situations of social conflict or dispute, of the nature of discourse or what he prefers to call 'collective argumentation', the different levels of cognitive structure formation in and through discourse, and the principles of discursive procedure for generating a rational or coordinated dissent, if not a final consent. This entailed the demonstration that while Habermas's theory of communicative action and discourse shows that societally beneficial structure formation will result from discursively informed action, it fails to clarify how such an outcome could come about.

Eder took up the challenge of analysing and empirically demonstrating the modalities of such structure formation. Having investigated the formation of normative structures in the context of the emergence of state-organised societies, Eder with some dependence on Miller from the early 1980s started to focus on the cognitively significant topic of collective learning, which he combined with constructivism. This line of development reached its first systematic formulation in 1988. Here the cognitive dimension was explicitly broached, yet Eder still tended to understand it in the narrow traditional sense of the intellectual or theoretical-empirical, as attested by his contrast of cognitive and moral learning processes as well as his distinction of the cognitive, normative and symbolic construction of nature. Studies eventually published in book form in 1993 led Eder by 1990 to develop an increasingly explicit cognitive approach. Among them were analyses of social movements, the formation of collective actors, and social class involving a merging of Touraine's concept of 'cultural model' and Bourdieu's concepts of 'classification struggles' and 'habitus' understood as class-specific schemata of experiencing, perceiving and interpreting with the Habermasian concepts of discourse and learning. Having reached a nodal point with his reconstruction of the schemata used to justify social class positions in contemporary society with appeal to the modern cultural model of equality, his commitment to cognitive social theory was reinforced by the concurrent cultural or, more specifically, cognitive turn in organisational and social movement analysis in Europe, especially Eyerman and Jamison (1991). The theoretical insight gained into the process of the construction of cognitive schemata of the social world, in which classificatory practices permanently serve as the mechanism for defining and redefining the discursively mediated cultural and social context and hence transforming society, would subsequently stand Eder in good stead. Particularly relevant here is research in the early 1990s on the making of environmental issues in Europe which provided him with the opportunity to publish a translation of a revised and considerably supplemented version of an earlier book under the title of *The Social Construction of Nature* (1996). This work contains Eder's most systematic contribution to cognitive social theory. The newly added research-based part exhibits not only a shift from the narrow traditional concept of the cognitive to a comprehensive concept partially inspired by Habermas's cognitive concept of culture, but also a willingness to adopt the 'cognitive paradigm' as a presupposition of the normative one, thus stressing a constructivist theory of the social classification and definition of the world. Accordingly, three 'cognitive orders' – the social world of norms, the objective world of facts and the subjective world of experiences – provide cultural tools or 'cognitive resources' in the form of schematising or 'framing devices' used by actors to construct cognitive schemata or 'frames', which in turn are strategically communicated in the public sphere where the resulting discourse at best finally gives rise to a collectively accepted yet differentially and even antagonistically interpreted cognitive 'masterframe' (e.g. Enlightenment, industrialism, ecology).

My own contribution, which is close to Eder and Miller's, over many years grew out of participation in the cognitive transformation of Habermas's work and thus paralleled the above trajectory. Simultaneously, however, my aim was and still is to develop the cognitive approach epistemologically, theoretically and substantively in a more explicit, consistent and systematic manner than is to be found in my fellow travellers. I have been pursuing a cognitivist communication and discourse theory (Strydom 1987, 1992, 1999a, 1999b, 2000, 2002) taking the form of a pragmatic realism on a weak naturalistic basis (Strydom 2002; Delanty and Strydom 2003) that focuses on cognitive forms, from the micro- to the macro-level, which are central to the dynamic process of construction of the social world (Strydom 1999c, 2000), yet have their origin in natural historical developments. In various works, Delanty (e.g. 1999, 2001) develops closely related ideas. In a study devoted to the analysis of the formation of new macro-level cognitive structures in the late twentieth-century through the discursive conflict of the frames of environmental movements, politicians, industry, scientists and others (Strydom 2002), I, for example, showed that the modern macro-structures which had emerged previously from natural historical processes to make possible the production of risks and the authoritarian paternalism through which they were managed were themselves questioned and altered by the reaction of nature in the form of the environmental crisis and the related contestation of frames in the course of the risk debates. Analysing knowledge in the context of the changing framework of the university through the ages, Delanty (2001) for instance traced the process of the development and redefinition of knowledge up to the point where the late twentieth-century constellation of the knowledge society with its new relation to nature gave rise to a diversification and pluralisation of competing frames all trained on the contested object of knowledge.

It is notable that while those inspired by Habermas all engage in severe critiques of the Luhmannian metabiological confinement of cognitive theory, they have been willing to learn from their adversaries. Above all, the systems concept and critique of interaction theory or intersubjectivity have assisted in the elaboration of a more robust concept of discourse and structure formation in a discursive framework (e.g. Eder 2000; Miller 2002; Strydom in press).

Conclusion

While having roots in older traditions, European cognitive social theory has undergone a remarkable efflorescence during the 1980s and 1990s due to impulses deriving from the cognitive revolution. Besides a plethora of new ideas, the extension of the computer as a cognitive science model to the brain and the environment introduced a new productive tension into social theory. It gave rise to two major theoretical directions, the metabiological and the pragmatic, which do not merely compete with one another, but simultaneously define and redefine the context and thus drive the development of cognitive social theory forward, indeed, closer and closer to the very core of the social theoretic enterprise.

Notes

1   While the Americans fall outside the parameters of this overview, I lack space to discuss the new
    sociology of science Nowotny and Knorr-Cetina helped to found.

2   Since I chose to contrast the comparable French and German pragmatic versions with metabiolo-
    gical cognitive social theory, I am unable in the present context to do justice to these varied,
    carefully argued and undoubtedly important French contributions. Given the present concern with
    pragmatics, however, it is noteworthy that Boudon (Boudon *et al.* 1997) takes what he calls
    'axiological rationality' to imply a trans-subjective 'system of reasons' which makes possible a
    'practical syllogism'.

Acknowledgement

This chapter benefited from a research grant under the third cycle of the Irish Higher Education Authority's Programme for Research in Third Level Institutions. I wish to thank
Robert Mooney for his valuable research assistance.

References

Boltanski, L. (1982) *Les Cadres*, Paris: Minuit.
Boltanski, L. (1984) 'La dénonciation', *Actes de la recherche en sciences sociales*, 51, 3–40.
Boltanski, L. and Thévenot, L. (1991) *De la justification*, Paris: Gallimard.
Bora, A. (1997) 'Sachhaltigkeit versus Verfahren?', in T. Sutter (ed.) *Beobachtung verstehen, Verstehen
    beobachten*, Opladen: Westdeutscher.
Borzeix, A., Bouvier, A. and Pharo, P. (eds) (1998) *Sociologie et connaissance: Nouvelles approches cognitives*,
    Paris: CNRS.
Boudon, R., Bouvier, A. and Chazel, F. (eds) (1997) *Cognition et sciences sociales: La dimension cognitive
    dans l'analyse sociologique*, Paris: PUF.
Bourdieu, P. (1977 [1972]) *Outline of a Theory of Practice*, Cambridge: Cambridge University Press.
Bourdieu, P. (1984 [1979]) *Distinction*, London: Routledge.
Cicourel, A. V. (1973) *Cognitive Sociology*, Harmondsworth: Penguin Books.
Corcuff, P. (1995) *Les nouvelles sociologies*, Paris: Nathan.
Delanty, G. (1999) *Social Theory in a Changing World*, Cambridge: Polity.
Delanty, G. (2001) *Challenging Knowledge*, Buckingham: Open University Press.
Delanty, G. and Strydom, P. (eds) (2003) *Philosophies of Social Science*, Maidenhead: Open University
    Press/McGraw-Hill.
Desrosières, A. and Thévenot, L. (1988) *Les Categories socioprofessionelles*, Paris: Découverte.
Eder, K. (1988) *Die Vergesellschaftung der Natur*, Frankfurt: Suhrkamp.
Eder, K. (1993) *The New Politics of Class*, London: Sage.
Eder, K. (1996) *The Social Construction of Nature*, London: Sage.
Eder, K. (2000) *Kulturelle Identität zwischen Tradition und Utopie*, Frankfurt and New York: Campus.
Eyerman, R. and Jamison, A. (1991) *Social Movements: A Cognitive Approach*, Cambridge: Polity.
Goffman, E. (1986 [1974]) *Frame Analysis*, Boston: Northeastern University Press.
Habermas, J. (1971) 'Vorbereitende Bemerkungen zu einer Theorie der kommunikativen Kompetenz',
    in J. Habermas and N. Luhmann, *Theorie der Gesellschaft oder Sozialtechnologie,* Frankfurt: Suhrkamp.
Habermas, J. (1972 [1968]) *Knowledge and Human Interests*, London: Heinemann.
Habermas, J. (1979) *Communication and the Evolution of Society*, London: Heinemann.
Habermas, J. (1984/1987 [1981]) *The Theory of Communicative Action*, vol. 1-2, London and Cambridge:
    Heinemann/Polity.
Habermas, J. (1987 [1985]) *The Philosophical Discourse of Modernity*, Cambridge: Polity.
Habermas, J. (1996 [1992]) *Between Facts and Norms*, Cambridge: Polity.
Hejl, P. M. (1993) 'Culture as a Network of Socially Constructed Realities', in A. Rigney and D.
    Fokkema (eds) *Cultural Participation*, Amsterdam: Benjamins.
Hörning, K. H., Ahrens, D. and Gerhard, A. (1997) *Zeitpraktiken*, Frankfurt: Suhrkamp.
Kneer, G. (1997) 'Beobachtung, Verstehen und Verständigung', in T. Sutter (ed.) *Beobachtung verstehen,
    Verstehen beobachten*, Opladen: Westdeutscher.
Knorr, K. (1977) 'Producing and Reproducing Knowledge', *Social Science Information* 16, 669–696.

Knorr Cetina, K. and Cicourel, A. V. (eds) (1981) *Advances in Social Theory and Methodology*, London: Routledge.

Leydesdorff, L. (1993) 'Structure/Action Contingencies and the Model of Parallel Distributed Processing', *Journal for the Theory of Social Behaviour* 23, 47–77.

Leydesdorff, L. (2000) 'Luhmann, Habermas, and the Theory of Communication', *Systems Research and Behavioural Science* 17, 273–288.

Luhmann, N. (1973) *Zweckbegriff und Systemrationalität*, Frankfurt: Suhrkamp.

Luhmann, N. (1990) 'The Cognitive Program of Constructivism and a Reality that Remains Unknown', in W. Krohn, G. Küppers and H. Nowotny (eds) *Selforganization*, Dordrecht: Kluwer.

Luhmann, N. (1992) *Die Wissenschaft der Gesellschaft*, Frankfurt: Suhrkamp.

Luhmann, N. (1995 [1984]) *Social Systems*, Stanford: Stanford University Press.

Luhmann, N. (1999) 'Öffentliche Meinung und Demokratie', in R. Maresch and N. Werber (eds) *Kommunikation, Media, Macht*, Frankfurt: Suhrkamp.

Miller, M. (1986) *Kollektive Lernprozesse*, Frankfurt: Suhrkamp.

Miller, M. (1992) 'Discourse and Morality', *Archives Européennes de Sociologie* 33(1), 3–38.

Miller, M. (2002) 'Some Theoretical Aspects of Systemic Learning', *Sozialer Sinn* 3, 379–421.

Nowotny, H. (1973) 'On the Feasibility of a Cognitive Approach to the Study of Science', *Zeitschrift für Soziologie* 2(3), 282–296.

Rusch, G. (1999) 'Eine Kommunikationstheorie für kognitive Systeme', in G. Rusch and S. J. Schmidt (eds) *Konstruktivismus in der Medien- und Kommunikations-wissenschaft*, Frankfurt: Suhrkamp.

Schneider, W. L. (1997) 'Die Analyse von Struktursicherungsoperationen als Kooperationsfeld von Konversationsanalyse, objektiver Hermeneutik und Systemtheorie', in T. Sutter (ed.) *Beobachtung verstehen, Verstehen beobachten*, Opladen: Westdeutscher.

Strydom, P. (1987) 'Collective Learning', *Philosophy and Social Criticism* 13(3), 265–281.

Strydom, P. (1992) 'The Ontogenetic Fallacy', *Theory, Culture and Society* 9(3), 65–93.

Strydom, P. (1999a) 'Hermeneutic Culturalism and its Double', *European Journal of Social Theory* 2(1), 45–69

Strydom, P. (1999b) 'Triple Contingency', *Philosophy and Social Criticism* 25(2), 1–25.

Strydom, P. (1999c) 'The Challenge of Responsibility for Sociology', *Current Sociology* 47(3), 65–82.

Strydom, P. (2000) *Discourse and Knowledge*, Liverpool: Liverpool University Press.

Strydom, P. (2002) *Risk, Environment and Society*, Buckingham: Open University Press.

Strydom, P. (in press) 'Intersubjectivity – Interactive or Discursive? Reflections on Habermas' Critique of Brandom', *Philosophy and Social Criticism*.

Sutter, T. (ed.) (1997) *Beobachtung verstehen, Verstehen beobachten*, Opladen: Westdeutscher.

Thévenot, L. (1984) 'Rules and Implements: Investment in Forms', *Social Science Information* 23(1), 1–45.

Thévenot, L. (1998) 'Pragmatiques de la connaissance', in A. Borzeix, A. Bouvier and P. Pharo (eds) *Sociologie et connaissance*, Paris: CNRS.

Thévenot, L. (2001) 'Pragmatic Regimes Governing the Engagement with the World', in T. R. Schatzki, K. Knorr Cetina and E. von Savigny (eds) (2001) *The Practice Turn in Contemporary Theory*, London: Routledge.

17

Civilizational analysis, social theory and comparative history

Johann P. Arnason

The term 'civilizational analysis', as used in recent research and debate, refers to civilizations in the plural and is commonly linked to comparative perspectives on their patterns and transformations. It seems preferable to 'civilizational theory', inasmuch as it stresses the need to merge theoretical discussion with more concrete comparative-historical inquiry. The plurality of civilizations can, in the first instance, be understood in light of macro-cultural units that are frequently mentioned in accounts of world history and have – on a more reflective level – figured in proposals for alternatives to the dominant models: Western European, Byzantine, Islamic, Indian (or Indic) and Chinese (or Sinic) civilizations are the key cases in point. Their distinctive dynamics are, for example, central to Marshall Hodgson's critique of William McNeill's more linear approach to Afro-Eurasian history (Hodgson 1993). Civilizational analysts do not agree on the use of such categories; some of them suggest more extensive additions and differentiations than others, but the above-mentioned scheme of Eurasian subdivisions may be seen as a shared starting-point. It cannot be dismissed as a premature or speculative construct. Those who prefer to interpret world history as a development of increasingly global networks of interaction between smaller units are also making far-reaching assumptions which have to be justified through confrontation with models centred on macro-units.[1]

If the above-mentioned aggregates of cultures and societies can serve to concretize the idea of civilizations in the plural, a brief look at conceptual history will alert us to changing interconnections with other ideas. The eighteenth-century notion of civilization, mostly formulated in the singular and closely linked to Enlightenment visions of progress and liberation, seems to have been used – much less frequently and less definitely – in a plural sense, reflecting a growing awareness of global cultural diversity (Starobinski 1983). But further elaboration of the pluralistic perspective tended to rely on the concept of culture, and thus to defuse the question of the twofold meaning inherent in the idea of civilization. Both aspects were, however, reactivated and explored in classical sociology. Although the conception of sociology as a 'science of civilization', suggested by Comte, was overshadowed by more familar approaches, a distinctive understanding of civilization in the singular can be reconstructed from classical sources: it centres on growing control over nature, the development of a broad spectrum of human abilities and ways of relating to the world, and the differentiation of socio-cultural frameworks for corresponding activities. Such views of civilization are clearly formulated in works of Marx and Durkheim, and they overlap in part with Weber's problematic of rationalization. At the same time, the idea of civilizations in the plural reappeared as a necessary complement to other sociological themes. This was most explicitly stated by Durkheim and Mauss, who defined civilizations as socio-cultural units transcending the limits within which the concept of society had proved applicable. These large-scale but less determinate formations were to be analysed and compared in terms of basic components as well as overall forms. Durkheim and Mauss did not go beyond programmatic sketches; Max Weber, who went much further in linking his sociological perspectives to substantive analyses of civilizational patterns (and was therefore a more obvious source of inspiration for the post-classical revival of civilizational analysis), did not use the term 'civilizations'. In line with an older German tradition, he referred to 'cultural worlds' and 'cultural areas'.[2]

As will be seen, issues raised by the classics are still relevant to the agenda of civilizational analysis. More specifically, the question of the relationship between civilization in the singular and civilizations in the plural remains on the agenda. But the classical legacy must now be linked to new problems arising from later developments.

The rediscovery of civilizations

The revival of civilizational analysis in the last decades of the twentieth-century went hand in hand with other changes to the agenda of the social and cultural sciences. Most obviously, it was an integral part of the broader 'historical turn' in the human sciences. The growth and differentiation of historical sociology highlighted the diversity of socio-cultural units and the need for conceptual distinctions to match them; in that context, civilizations appeared as macro-units in space and time, with unifying patterns and developmental dynamics of their own. They were not always the most important frames of reference: for example, Wallerstein's world system theory added a civilizational perspective to its earlier, more fundamental and much more clearly defined models of global economic structures.

S. N. Eisenstadt's work represents the most systematic attempt to theorize the civilizational dimension of the social-historical world. In this case, civilizational perspectives are crucial to a comprehensive restructuring of sociological theory (although this does not entail claims to the status of a definitive and self-contained paradigm, such as those of Parsonian or Luhmannian systems theory), and inseparable from specific reinterpretations of key themes. Drawing on the experience of long involvement in controversies about modernization theory, Eisenstadt had already been reworking the basic concepts of tradition and modernity before the civilizational turn became fully apparent, but the new context gave a more radical twist to these efforts. As critics of modernization theory have repeatedly pointed out, its postwar pioneers used the concept of tradition in a levelling and residual sense, referring to cultures and societies that lack the attributes of modernity or resist modernizing changes. Eisenstadt takes this critique to constructive conclusions by identifying traditions with the complexes of meanings and institutions that make up the cores of civilizational formations. Seen from this angle, traditions have their distinctive internal problems, conflicts and dynamics. On the other hand, Eisenstadt argues that it may be useful to think of modernity as a new civilization. Its expansion can then be compared to the spread of the world religions that have in the past taken off from civilizational bases. A civilizational view of modernity centres on cultural premises, more precisely on a new vision of human autonomy and on concomitant changes to the whole mode of human being in the world.

The civilizational turn is also linked to reconsiderations of basic ontological assumptions about society and history. The plurality of civilizational patterns, with their respective dynamics of internal differentiation and historical transformations, casts doubt on evolutionary conceptions of social change. It may still be possible to speak of general trends at work across historical divides and cultural boundaries (as will be seen, this question is bound to arise in connection with the idea of civilization in the singular), but the rediscovery of civilizations has certainly undermined the strong evolutionism that posited law-like sequences and regularities throughout diverse cultural areas and historical epochs. Eisenstadt's emphasis on creativity as the key theme of civilizational analysis – and of social theory in general – reflects this anti-evolutionistic stance. By the same token, it serves to reinforce a radical critique of functionalism, developed on several analytical levels. In contrast to the structural–functionalist conception of culture as a systemic code, the civilizational approach stresses the order-transforming impact of cultural patterns no less than the order-maintaining one; this double-edged dynamic is grounded in emergent meanings that transcend existing social frameworks, allow for the articulation of alternatives and add a cultural dimension to social conflicts. In view of all this, Eisenstadt's use of the term 'cultural programme' seems misleading (and reminiscent of the structural–functionalist paradigm that he had done much to discredit) – 'cultural problematic' would be a more adequate expression.

Closer examination of Eisenstadt's theoretical project may begin with key formulations used in a recent programmatic statement. As he sees it, the 'central analytical core of the concept of civilization ... is the combination of ontological or cosmological visions of transmundane and mundane reality, with the definition, construction and regulation of the major arenas of social life and interaction' (Eisenstadt 2003 vol. 1, 34). The emphasis on comprehensive interpretations of the world, on their variability, and on their role as frameworks for institutional formations, stands in clear contrast to the one-sided structural-functionalist stress on values and their institutionalization through norms. The civilizational approach, as defined by Eisenstadt, takes a broader view of culture and its role in social life, but it is also designed to avoid cultural determinism: the interpretive dimension is an opening to indeterminacy. Eisenstadt goes on to argue that although this civilizational dimension is an integral aspect of human societies in general, it has throughout much of human history been 'embedded in the concrete institutional organizations of collectivities without being the object of specific institutional formations or bearers thereof' (ibid.: 35). More explicit articulations of civilizational patterns and dynamics resulted from major historical changes. For Eisenstadt, the decisive breakthrough occurred during the 'Axial Age' that encompasses a few centuries around the middle of the last millennium BCE. During this period, intellectual and religious innovations in separate civilizational settings – Ancient Greece, Ancient Israel, India, China, and perhaps Iran – transformed the cultural frameworks of social life and opened up new horizons for global history. The epoch-making implications of these developments had been recognized by earlier writers on world history (most notably Karl Jaspers), but Eisenstadt was the first to redefine the Axial Age in the language of historical sociology.

The idea of a civilizational potential or dimension, latent in tribal and archaic societies but brought to the fore and raised to the level of reflexive awareness in a more advanced historical phase, can be understood as a synthesis of two classical approaches. The reference to pre-literate cultures links up with Marcel Mauss's broad conception of civilizational formations, whereas the emphasis on great traditions and their world-historical destinies invokes the Weberian programme of comparative civilizational studies. From another point of view, the distinction between implicit and explicit civilizational dimensions may seem reminiscent of Hegelian models: a pattern-in-itself would mature into a pattern-for-itself. But this analogy is of limited value. The Axial Age mutations were, as Eisenstadt sees it, not so much outcomes of evolutionary progress as new openings for socio-cultural creativity; in that sense, they represent divergent approaches to further articulation of the civilizational dimension. Their common denominator is a new mode of world-interpretation, more precisely an ontological differentiation between higher and lower orders of being (Eisenstadt often uses the terms 'transcendental' and 'mundane'). This interpretive reordering of the world translates into new perspectives on the social order: it can now be more clearly separated from cosmic contexts, and at the same time confronted with standards inherent in the higher order of reality. The restructured world-view thus opens up new possibilities for legitimation as well as protest. Both the expanded ontological horizons and the new reflexive distance from social practices broadens the scope of rival interpretations, and interpretive conflicts add a new dimension to social ones. One of the central themes in Eisenstadt's comparative studies is the polarization of orthodoxy and heterodoxy, much more pronounced in some civilizational settings than in others, as well as its long-term ideological, political and social effects. Another key question concerns the varying structures and roles of intellectual elites that act as the bearers of new cultural visions and enter into more or less effective coalitions with political forces.

The innovations of the Axial Age are, in short, conducive to higher levels of reflexivity, more creative interaction of historical forces, and more articulate forms of social conflict. Shared problems, interpreted in light of comparable cultural premises, are solved in different ways that translate into divergent historical trajectories and developmental patterns. In particular, responses to new demands for the definition and legitimation of social order – in relation to new conceptions of ultimate reality – vary from one civilizational context to another. The reconstruction of a general pattern, accounting for basic affinities as well as possibilities of differentiation, has led Eisenstadt to stress the typological rather than the strictly historical aspect, and to speak of 'axial civilizations', without specific reference to the Axial Age. Later developments, such as the emergence of Islam, can then be subsumed under the axial type, and it becomes an empirical question whether crystallizations of this type were particularly frequent during the period with which they were at first identified. Axiality would, on this view, be a civilizational paradigm that can, in principle, take shape in diverse situations and at different junctures.

Eisenstadt's reflections on the theoretical assumptions and orientations of civilizational studies are closely linked to analyses of the axial type. But the cases that exemplify this privileged model also illustrate the difficulties faced by research programmes in this field: decisive progress could only be made through comparative inquiry on a scale that calls for extensive cooperation of historians, sociologists and area specialists. In other words, civilizational analysis needs interdisciplinary work of a hitherto unprecedented kind.

The shift from a historical to a typological understanding of axiality is, however, accompanied by another move which complicates the issue. Eisenstadt's growing interest in different patterns of modernity – for which he coined the term 'multiple modernities' – led him to reconsider the question of unity across the spectrum of diverse forms. To distinguish and compare varieties of modernity is to posit some kind of common denominator. Eisenstadt proposes to theorize it in terms of a new civilization, open to variations in changing historical settings. A more emphatic statement refers to a 'new type of civilization' (Eisenstadt 2003 vol. 2, 493), which suggests a more radical break. Irrespective of such nuances, the axial model also serves to clarify the new understanding of modernity: the decisive novelty consists in a radicalization of reflexivity, linking up with the axial breakthrough but going much further. This results in an unprecedented affirmation of human autonomy, expressed in the exploration and domination of nature, the construction and reconstruction of social orders, and conceptions of self-defining subjectivity. Higher levels of autonomy mean growing uncertainty, all the more so since the visions of autonomy are – at all levels – open to rival interpretations: individualistic and collectivistic, totalizing and pluralistic, rationalistic and anti-rationalistic. These divergent orientations – Eisenstadt refers to them as antinomies – are central to the dynamics of modernity as a civilization.

All these aspects are summed up in the description of modernity as 'a second axial Age' (Eisenstadt 2003 vol. 2, 494). Here the historical category is used again, alongside the typological one. But Eisenstadt also notes analogies between the global diffusion of modernity and the expansion of world religions that took off from civilizational bases, and this raises further questions. Only some of the axial transformations gave rise to world religions, and a comparison of the three main cases in point (Buddhism, Christianity and Islam) shows that the relations between religious communities and civilizational contexts varied in significant ways. If this line of thought is to be taken further, we thus need a more detailed account of contrasts and affinities between modernity and axiality. Moreover, the emphasis on autonomy sets limits to any parallels with world religions. When the modern visions of autonomy spread across civilizational boundaries, they are always to some degree translated into projects of self-affirmation and self-strengthening against their original inventors and propagators. This is one of the constitutive paradoxes of modernity; no similarly clear-cut pattern is inherent in the expansion of world religions.

In brief, a closer look at connections, similarities and differences between axial and modern transformations suggests that there is a vast field of problems and experiences to be tackled. The complexity of the issues makes it easier to understand why Eisenstadt's most detailed and systematic case study of civilizational dynamics (and probably the most comprehensive work of its kind so far) deals with a non-axial tradition, as well as with its role in shaping a corresponding pattern of modernity (Eisenstadt 1996). The exceptionally self-contained character of the Japanese trajectory (including its interaction with other civilizations, and therefore not to be mistaken for isolation) helps to bring its distinctive features into focus, and the reconstruction of a non-axial pattern is – *ex negativo* – a detour towards better understanding of the axial ones from which it has borrowed on its own terms, and to which it can be compared from a broader analytical perspective. As for the specific traits of Japanese non-axiality, they centre on continuity in more than one sense of the word. The ontological continuity of traditional Japanese modes of thought stresses the mutual embeddedness of nature and culture. Structural continuity has to do with the containment of institutional formation and change within a unifying framework: the powers and principles central to various areas of social life were continuously 'embedded and incorporated within the broad framework of the Japanese collectivity and its central symbols' (ibid.: 421). Finally, the historical continuity between tradition and modernity is – however partial – marked enough to set the Japanese pattern apart from others: the cultural premises challenged by modernity could be re-articulated and translated into modern projects of integration and legitimation.

Alternative approaches

The above discussion singled out some central problems in Eisenstadt's civilizational theory. To outline the case for another approach, let us briefly return to the starting-point. Eisenstadt's seminal re-interpretation of the Axial Age has sparked an extensive debate which does not seem to be drawing to a close (for the most recent round, see Arnason *et al.* 2004); rather, the most obvious results are a growing insight into the diversity of axial contexts and directions of change, as well as a clearer demarcation of different perspectives on the field in question. At this point, a shift from historical to typological terms of reference seems premature: there are too many unresolved issues on the historical level. The crucial importance of the Axial Age is not in doubt, but the ongoing controversies about its meaning would seem to argue against treating it as an ultimate cornerstone of civilizational analysis. Moreover, Eisenstadt's interpretation – equating the axial breakthrough with a first articulation of of the previously latent civilizational dimension – bypasses an earlier landmark. The more critical and less evolutionistic versions of modernization theory had come to see the modern transformation as a radical break, rather than an acceleration of universal trends, and to compare it with the emergence of civilization (which also meant the formation of the first civilizations in the plural). As I will try to show, a reconsideration of this earlier global divide may throw light on the theoretical framework of civilizational analysis.

There are good reasons to regard the emergence of civilization – and more specifically its key aspect, the rise of the state – as a world-historical mutation of the first order. This idea has been convincingly defended by scholars of otherwise different persuasions (see Clastres (1977) and Gauchet (1997), on the one hand, and Mann (1986) on the other). According to Michael Mann, the emergence of civilization represents a break with the previously operative logic of general social evolution. The decisive components of the new pattern were 'three social institutions, the ceremonial center, writing, and the city' (Mann 1986: 38); it seems clear that sacred rulership was integral to the earliest ceremonial centres, although its forms as well as its relations to priesthoods and other potential counterweights varied from case to case.

The first point to be noted is that this brings us back to the concept of civilization in the singular, which does not figure prominently in Eisenstadt's frame of reference. As we have seen, a working definition of this concept can be extracted from the classics: it refers to an ongoing transformation of the human condition. This was what Comte and Durkheim had in mind when they described sociology as a 'science of civilization', and Marx applied the same criteria to highlight the civilizing achievements of capitalism. Norbert Elias added the crucial insight that processes of state formation are – because of their direct and indirect effects in all areas of social life – central to the whole civilizing dynamic. On the other hand (and independently of developments within the sociological tradition), historians and anthropologists tended to redefine the concept of civilization in more specific terms: as coextensive with a macro-historical period that began with the changes mentioned above. It seems appropriate to follow this usage, and to take a corresponding view of civilizations in the plural. Statehood, incipient urbanization and the formation of written traditions add up to an epoch-making civilizing breakthrough, in the sense adumbrated by the classics; the early civilizations integrate these common trends into divergent socio-cultural frameworks, linked to different modes of thought and ways of interpreting the world. Later transformations take off from this original differentiating turn.

Taking the crystallization of the early civilizations as a starting-point, the scope and domain of civilizational analysis can be clearly demarcated. It focuses on the interplay of meaning and power that begins with the emergence of the state as a separate power centre. This is not a logical continuation of any trends or patterns inherent in primitive societies. Following the authors quoted above, the new constellation is best understood as a break with earlier forms of social life; it occurs in specific situations and in response to particular problems, rather than on the basis of cumulative evolution. The power structures that embody the break combine political and ideological factors in varying forms. In this context, one of Max Weber's passing remarks is worth quoting: as he pointed out, early developments of the relationship between kings and priests, often due to contingent events more or less lost to collective memory, can have a lasting impact on civilizational patterns. The contrasts between Egypt and Mesopotamia, as well as between China and India, illustrate this point. In other settings, the two forms of power underwent major changes that also redefined their mutual relations. The formation of the Christian empire in late antiquity, followed by different transformations in three successor civilizations (Byzantine, Western Christian and Islamic), is a particularly striking case. Durable constellations do not exclude tensions and divisions; rivalries between sacred and secular power – or between different mixtures of both – can interact with other socio-cultural conflicts in complex and innovative ways. Medieval Western Christendom, with its interdependent but competing imperial and papal versions of universal monarchy, is perhaps the most instructive example.

Archaic configurations of political and ideological power – both of them embedded in sacral frameworks – can thus serve as historical anchors for more wide-ranging comparisons and genealogies extending to later periods. Forms of economic power in the early civilizations seem to have been less specific. They were built on foundations laid by an earlier mutation of economic life (the neolithic revolution), and their core institutions reflect both constraints and opportunities inherent in local settings for agricultural development, but they did not transform economic practices as radically as the political and ideological ones. New forms of centralized and coercive cooperation (Lewis Mumford's 'megamachines') were geared to goals set by the political centre and did not reshape the overall pattern of economic organization. Attempts to explain the rise of civilization and the state in terms of irrigation agriculture and its functional dynamics have failed (the same would seem to apply to the notion of the 'Sumerian temple-state' as a total institution). This observation can be adapted to a more general perspective. The premodern world was, as Marshall Hodgson put it, divided into, and dominated by, 'agrarianate' civilizations, i.e. socio-cultural formations that combined an agrarian basis with more or less developed urban centres of trade and handicrafts. Although these limiting infrastructures should not be mistaken for a closed circle of simple reproduction, they were less open to historical variations and cultural specifications than were the political and ideological patterns of social life. Only the industrial–capitalist revolution – a key part of the transition from early to advanced modernity – brought about economic change on a scale comparable to the neolithical precedent. This is not to deny that the question of the political and ideological preconditions of the economic mutation – posed in paradigmatic terms by Max Weber – remains on the agenda. But comparative civilizational perspectives have clearly proved less directly applicable to the economic sphere as such. It is a well-established fact that civilizations differ in regard to the dynamic of technological progress, the development of commercial networks in general and long-distance trade in particular, and the conditions for capitalist activity; beyond such general considerations, specific links between civilizational contexts and the forms of economic life are perhaps best traced through the processes of state formation.

Elias and his followers have analysed the ramifications of state formation throughout all socio-cultural spheres, not least the economic one. The consolidation of state structures opens up social spaces, mobilizes social forces and provides foundations for social strategies. Although this line of argument operates with the concept of civilization in the singular, its results can be integrated into a pluralistic conception and adapted to a comparative framework. On the other hand, the reference to civilizations in the plural brings reflexive and interpretive aspects of state formation to the fore. Elias tended to neglect them, but their importance becomes obvious when differences in long-term directions and dominant projects are taken into account. Political cultures and traditions of political thought take shape through the interaction of civilizational premises and processes of state formation; they serve to articulate goals and guidelines that link state-building strategies to other concerns, and the scope for unilateral rationalization of state interests depends on the context. Chinese Legalism, with its extreme emphasis on state control and mobilization of human and non-human resources, is perhaps the earliest example of a breakthrough in that direction. It was one of the most distinctive products of the Chinese Axial Age, and left its mark on the Chinese imperial tradition, even if it was officially overshadowed by other currents more suited to legitimizing purposes. At a more basic level, we can distinguish underlying cultural definitions of power that structure the political problematics of their respective civilizations. As has been noted, the archaic form of sacred rulership lent itself to variations, and further transformations resulted in new images of power. On the one hand, the nexus between kingship and the sacred could – as in China – be rationalized into a model of the ruler as an accountable intermediary between the cosmic and the social order. On the other hand, the fundamentally different innovations of the Axial Age in Ancient Greece and Ancient Israel converged in a rejection of sacred kingship. The anti-monarchic turn institutionalized in the Greek *polis* transferred power to a political community whose social basis could be broadened; the Jewish transfer of sovereignty to a legislator god, linked to his chosen people through a covenant, imposed new criteria of meaning and legitimacy in the domain of political power. But these transformations did not destroy the imaginary of sacred kingship. Rather, they channelled it into new contexts. Revivals and redefinitions, some more momentous than others, shaped the post-axial course of history in the cultural worlds influenced by Greek and Jewish tradition. The *sacrum imperium* of late antiquity, mentioned above, stands out as the most important case in point.

As these reflections show, the historical experience of early civilizations can serve as a guide to general questions that also concern later developments. The same applies to interpretations of the Axial Age: if the archaic backgrounds are given their due, the breakthroughs will appear in a new light. Eisenstadt does not deny that axial transformations have a prehistory: he refers to 'important steps in that direction . . . in some archaic civilizations' (2003 vol. 1, 35). But a full recognition of the historicity of the archaic world must go beyond the search for mere approximations to the pre-established axial model. The civilizations in question had their own distinctive trajectories, diverged in regard to interpretive and institutional patterns, and created different preconditions for further innovations. Given these diverse settings, closer examination is likely to show that the contextual meanings of axial transformations varied from case to case. However, historical scholarship on early civilizations is unevenly developed, and faces more formidable obstacles in some cases than others. Jan Assmann's work on Ancient Egypt is the most ambitious and instructive venture into this field (Assmann 2000, 2003); Leon Vandermeersch's work on China (1977–1980) has been amplified and nuanced by some recent interpretations (see e.g. Pines 2002). The particular obscurity of early Indian history invites speculative constructions (see Heesterman (1993) for a fascinating but extremely controversial alternative account of the axial turn).[3]

The issue of civilizational dynamics and differences before the Axial Age is linked to another aspect of our problematic: the question of intercivilizational encounters. This concept was coined by Benjamin Nelson (1981); the historical phenomena to which it refers are still among the least explored themes of civilizational analysis, but a more adequate understanding of them would help to counter the recurrent misconception of civilizations as closed worlds. Intercivilizational encounters are as multi-dimensional as the internal patterns of civilizations: they include commercial integration, imperial conquest and religious expansion across civilizational boundaries, as well as the crystallization of core structures through contact with other civilizations that can both transmit models to be emulated and provide a negative focus for self-definition. For Nelson, twelfth- and thirteenth-century Western Christendom

237

was a particularly interesting example of the latter kind. The encounters with the Byzantine and Islamic world were important for its most formative phase, not least because they led to the rediscovery of a shared classical legacy that could then be put to more creative use in the West.

Encounters of this type seem to have been involved in the two most widely discussed axial transformations. Close contact with and extensive borrowing from the older cultures of the Near East were crucial to the emergence of Archaic Greece as a distinctive civilization, but at the same time, the Greeks invented a new form of political life, eminently conducive to self-reflection and increasingly central to Greek identity when the contrast to Eastern neighbours became more salient. Following Assmann's interpretation, the Jewish invention of mono-theism may be understood as a rejection of the Egyptian model of sacred kingship; the new conception of divine authority and its relationship to the human world was to some extent articulated in a languange that drew on Mesopotamian traditions. In both cases, positive and negative relations to other civilizations are thus intertwined with more autonomous trends. Indian and Chinese developments during the Axial Age seem to have been much more self-contained.

Closer examination will reveal other contrasts between different versions of axiality. In particular, a comparison of Jewish and Chinese transformations highlights a basic conceptual problem: the distinction between civilizational patterns and civilizational complexes. The direct institutional expression of Jewish monotheism did not go beyond a peripheral theo-cratic regime (the Second Temple), but monotheism as a civilizational pattern underwent further changes, was embodied in multiple civilizational complexes (notably the Western Christian, Byzantine and Islamic ones), and translated into universalist claims that transcended civilizational boundaries. The Chinese transformation occurred during a prolonged crisis of a civilizational complex which then drew on the axial innovations to reconstruct itself on a larger scale and establish a regional model without an unambiguously universalist self-image. As for the two other paradigmatic cases, the Greek experience seems closer to the Jewish one: the patterns unfolding within the *polis* framework had a more significant impact than Jewish monotheism within its original environment, but the flowering of Greek civilization went hand in hand with an aggravation of internal conflicts, culminating in a struggle perhaps best described as a civilizational schism (the Peloponnesian War) and a self-destructive dynamic that paved the way for foreign conquest. The Greek legacy then became a formative resource for later civilizations, coexisting as well as successive, but in a more diffuse and discontinuous way than the monotheistic traditions. Finally, India seems closer to China in that axial trans-formations entered into the long-drawn-out making of Hindu civilization, but Buddhism – in some ways the most accomplished product of the Indian Axial Age – may be seen as an incipient civilizational alternative that failed in its homeland and realized some of its potential in other contexts, where its relative weight varied greatly.

The two categories distinguished above coincide with two sociological perspectives. Dur-kheim and Mauss used the concept of civilizations in the plural to denote macro-historical units, more or less clearly bounded in space and time; within the present frame of reference, such formations constitute civilizational complexes that combine cultural orientations with institutional configurations of power and allow for more or less extensive variations of their core structures. Eisenstadt's civilizational theory focuses on a more analytical model of inter-connections between world-views and institutional formations. This is the level of civiliza-tional patterns that realize their potential most adequately on the scale of civilizational complexes. But as we have seen, the relationship between the two aspects is subject to very significant variations.

The civilizational status of modernity

The above discussion took off from Eisenstadt's use of the axial model as a key to theoretical understanding of the civilizational dimension in general; it went on to suggest that a different world-historical perspective would translate into theoretical alternatives. To conclude, a few words should be said about the other main theme of Eisenstadt's civilizational theory: the much less developed idea of modernity as a new civilization. For Eisenstadt, this is obviously an answer to an inescapable question: what is the common denominator of 'multiple modernities'? His proposal to theorize the underlying unity in civilizational terms raises a series of further questions. To begin with the most basic one, the idea of a generalized and practically effective reflexivity – going beyond axial limits and resulting in a wholesale relativization of all socio-cultural patterns – is more easily associated with civilization in the singular than with civilizations in the plural. In fact, it seems to be rooted in the self-understanding of the Enlightenment at its most radical, and thus in the very set of ideas that gave rise to an universalist notion of civilization. Unrestrained reflexivity as such is not translatable into the specific combinations of interpretive and institutional orders that Eisenstadt had singled out as the defining theme of civilizational analysis. For both aspects, further contextualizing is needed. New levels of reflexivity gain operative meaning in conjunction with specific institutional principles and world-making orientations. Such considerations might lend support to another view of the modern transformation: as a new breakthrough for civilization in the singular, perhaps with inherent possibilities of diversification analogous to those that emerged at the beginning of recorded history.

Eisenstadt is of course well aware of contextual diversity in the modern world – the idea of 'multiple modernities' was designed to do justice to that part of the story. As noted above, the multiplying turn begins with the antinomies built into the cultural problematic of modernity. At its most radical, their mutual exclusion entails the negation or neutralization of the unrestrained reflexivity with which Eisenstadt equates the modern breakthrough: only thus can they achieve the closure needed to establish separate projects with ideological and institutional implications. Their antagonistic uses of shared cultural sources mark them as modern alternatives. But by the same token, the articulation and the interplay of antinomies define modernity as a new kind of civilizational formation. There are other cases of conflicting but less polarized cultural orientations, and the internal coherence of civilizational patterns is an open question for comparative analysis, rather than a defining feature.

The divergences thus grounded in the very core of modernity interact with a variety of forces that come into play when modernity expands beyond its original civilizational setting and acquires global dimensions. Although the cultural dynamic of modernity – as distinct from but not unrelated to power differences – undermines premodern civilizations, their legacies play a crucial role in the making of multiple modernities. Such connections emerge on several levels: in the strategic use of traditions, the unreflected influence of civilizational backgrounds on ways of adapting or reinventing modern institutions, and the explicit incorporation of civilizational identities into reconstructed self-images. After the modern transformation, there can be no clash of intact civilizations, but civilizational factors enter into the disputes and conflicts between alternative modernities.

The contextualizing line of argument may be taken one step further. Drawing on the insights of – broadly defined – hermeneutical currents in contemporary philosophy, reflexivity can be understood as always already and inherently contextual. The radical reflexivity that Eisenstadt seems to posit as a civilizational premise would then be a secondary de-contextualizing construct, one among other interpretations of a more complex set of premises, and when taken to ultimate conclusions, it generates its own versions of closure and fundamentalism. Its off-shoots include the ideas of a society dissolved into sovereign individuals and a totalized scientific world-view, embodied in a vanguard. In short, the antinomian character of modernity reasserts itself, at a level where it seems to cast doubt on the notion of a unitary civilization. To return to a point made above, the modern transformation can plausibly be described as a restructuring of the relationship between civilization in the singular and civilizations in the plural, but in such a way that the new openings to diversity have a more direct bearing on the common ground and are therefore more mutually contested than at comparable junctures in the past. This would seem to leave us with two possible interpretations. Modernity might represent a *civilizational transition*, with the structure of a new balance between unity and plurality still open to theoretical and practical dispute. But it could also – and this hypothesis seems more challenging – be seen as a *civilizational paradox*, in the sense that its cultural premises break through civilizational boundaries in a previously unknown fashion, yet remain too indeterminate and adaptable to conflicting interpretations for the idea of one distinctive civilization to be applicable. Modernity would thus be both more and less than a civilization. For both theoretical and historical reasons, it would be premature to try to close the debate on this issue.

Notes

1   William McNeill's work is the most representative example of global history striving to move beyond the civilizational perspective without abandoning it altogether. His magnum opus (McNeill 1992 [1963]) focuses on intercivilizational exchanges and learning processes; in later essays (including prefaces to new editions of *The Rise of the West*), the emphasis shifts towards the successive ecumenic worlds that encompass multiple civilizations, whereas the civilizations as such tend to shrink to elite constructions of cultural and behavioural codes.
2   For a more detailed discussion of classical sources, see Arnason (2003: 66–124).
3   The interpretation of civilizational patterns as perspectives on the human condition can – among other sources – draw on analyses of the early civilizations (particularly Egypt and Mesopotamia); the most ambitious elaboration of this idea can be found in the writings of Jaroslav Krejčí (see especially Krejčí 1993 and 2004). His version of civilizational analysis merits more attention than it has so far received. Because of the limited space available, it cannot be discussed here.

References

Arnason, J. P. (2003) *Civilizations in Dispute. Historical Questions and Theoretical Traditions,* Leiden: Brill.
Arnason, J. P., Eisenstadt, S. N., Wittrock, B. (eds) (2004) *Axial Civilizations and World History,* Leiden: Brill.
Assmann, J. (2000) *Herrschaft und Heil. Politische Theologie in Altägypten, Israel und Europa,* München: Hanser.
Assmann, J. (2003) *The Mind of Egypt,* Cambridge, MA: Harvard University Press.
Clastres, P. (1977) *Society Against the State,* Oxford: Blackwell.
Eisenstadt, S. N. (1996) *Japanese Civilization: A Comparative View,* Chicago: Chicago University Press.
Eisenstadt, S. N. (2003) *Comparative Civilizations and Multiple Modernities,* vols 1 and 2, Leiden: Brill.
Gauchet, M. (1997) *The Disenchantment of the World: A Political History of Religion,* Princeton: Princeton University Press.
Heesterman, J. C. (1993) *The Broken World of Sacrifice: An Essay in Ancient Indian Ritual,* Chicago: Chicago University Press.
Hodgson, M. (1993) *Rethinking World History: Essays on Europe, Islam and World History,* Chicago: Chicago University Press.

Krejčí, J. (1993) *The Human Predicament: Its Changing Image*, New York: St Martin's Press.
Krejčí, J. (2004) *The Paths of Civilization: Understanding the Currents of History*, New York: Palgrave-Macmillan.
Mann, M. (1986) *The Sources of Social Power*, vol. 1, Cambridge: Cambridge University Press.
McNeill, W. (1992 [1963]) *The Rise of the West*, Chicago: University of Chicago Press.
Nelson, B. (1981) *On the Roads to Modernity*, Totowa, NJ: Rowman and Littlefield.
Pines, Y. (2002) *Foundations of Confucian Thought: Intellectual Life in the Chunqiu Period (722–453 BCE)*, Honolulu: University of Hawai'i Press.
Starobinski, J. (1983) 'Le mot civilisation', in *Le temps de la réflexion*, Paris: Gallimard.
Vandermeersch, L. (1977–1980) *Wangdao, ou: La Voie Royale. Recherches sur l'esprit des institutions de la Chine archaïque*, Paris: Ecole Française de l'Extrême-Orient.

18

Cosmopolitanism

A social science research agenda

Robert Fine

Introduction

Cosmopolitanism is a way of thinking that goes back to the ancient Greeks, whence the word arises. It refers to the consciousness of being a citizen of the world whatever other affiliations we may have. In modern times the attainment of such a consciousness has been a repeated aspiration of enlightened thought, and from the classics of sociology to the present it has always been on the agenda of social theory. In recent years cosmopolitanism has become a widespread intellectual and political movement within the social sciences (Cohen 1996; Cheah and Robbins 1998; Breckenridge and Pollock 2002; Vertovec and Cohen 2003; Archibugi 2004). It has taken off in many disciplines including international law, international relations, political philosophy and political theory, sociology and social theory (Fine 2003b). Its boundaries are not always distinct and internally it is traversed by all kinds of fault lines. Yet it is an identifiable intellectual and political movement united by a threefold set of commitments: first, a shared critique of the methodological nationalism that prevails in social science disciplines; second, a shared diagnosis of the present as an age of cosmopolitanism that in some sense has broken from the past; and third, a shared normative-philosophical commitment to the primacy of world citizenship over all national, religious, cultural, ethnic and other parochial affiliations. In seeking to understand the cosmopolitan outlook, we should see it more as a research agenda informed by these conceptual, historical and prescriptive considerations than as a body of fixed ideas.

The critique of methodological nationalism

In Sociology the rise of cosmopolitan thinking in has been expressed in attempts to dissociate the core concepts of sociology, especially that of 'society', from the presuppositions of the nation state (Smelser 1997; Wagner 2001; Urry 2002). Here the critique of 'methodological nationalism' goes back to the 1970s when a number of sociologists argued that a major defect of existing social science was the treatment of nation-states *as though* they were closed, autonomous and self-contained units, and that this led to purely endogenous explanations of social change (Wagner 1994: 30–31; Chernilo 2004). Today the critique of methodological nationalism has been considerably radicalised, particularly in the path-breaking work of Ulrich Beck, and it has become a *leitmotif* of the cosmopolitan outlook (Fine and Chernilo 2004; Chernilo 2006a, b).

In a co-ordinated series of works Beck (1998a, 2000a, 2002a, 2002b) has argued that traditional sociology generally equated the idea of society with that of the nation-state and assumed that humanity is naturally divided into a limited number of nations: 'It is a nation-state outlook', he writes, that 'governs the sociological imagination' – including the classics of sociology (Beck 2002b: 51–52). He maintains that this fusion of 'society' and the 'nation-state' was the result not only of national consciousness within the discipline, but also of the historical fact that sociology arose at a time when nation-states were in fact becoming the 'normal' form of political society and when nation-states had an interest in reinforcing an image of their own solidity and self-sufficiency. Beck maintains that this image of solidity and self-sufficiency has now been shattered. He formulates this epochal change in various ways – for example, as a transition from nation-state to world risk society, from the first age of modernity to the second, from the national to the cosmopolitan state – but he argues that in every case this rupture places on social science a responsibility to re-invent itself as 'a transnational science ... released from the fetters of methodological nationalism' (Beck 2002b: 53–54). If social theory is to escape from the traditional 'container theory of society', its research-agenda and conceptual tools must match the ways in which the world itself is being transformed. Beck writes of the 'obsolescence' of traditional social theories and their 'zombie categories' and defends a new 'methodological cosmopolitanism' able to tackle 'what had previously been *analytically* excluded' (Beck 2002b: 52).

Looking back to the past, Beck's thesis raises two key questions. The first is: has social theory been as dominated by methodological nationalism as the cosmopolitan outlook suggests? Beck himself concedes that we find partial arguments in the 'classics' that point beyond methodological nationalism. Kant's political writings (1991), written around the time of the French Revolution, bear witness to the fact that in political philosophy cosmopolitanism has been around as long as modern nationalism, indeed as long as the modern nation-state. Kant reconstructed cosmopolitan thinking for the modern age precisely at the time when the sovereign nation-state was becoming the 'imaginary community' *par excellence* of social and political thought – the fulcrum on which world history was turning (Bohman and Lutz-Bachmann 1997; Doyle 1993; Fine 2003a; Flikschuh 2000). A hundred years later Emile Durkheim continued to appeal to cosmopolitan moral foundations in his account of the political state:

> If each State had as its chief aim not to expand or to lengthen its borders, but to set its own house in order and to make the widest appeal to its members for a moral life on a ever higher level, then all discrepancy between national and human morals would be excluded. ... The more societies concentrate their energies inwards, on the interior life, the more they will be diverted from the disputes that bring a clash between cosmopolitanism – or world patriotism, and patriotism ... Societies can have their pride, not in being the greatest or the wealthiest, but in being the most just, the best organised and in possessing the best moral constitution.
>
> (Durkheim 1992: 74–75)

To be sure, Durkheim's fusion of *la patrie* and cosmopolitanism proved to be no obstacle to his anti-Germanism during the First World War, but this may say more about the nature of cosmopolitanism – that the cosmopolitan state too can construct its own enemies and seek to destroy them – than it does about the partiality of Durkheim's own cosmopolitan commitments. The cosmopolitan outlook is not as new within social theory as present-day cosmopolitans might like to think and we can still learn much from the difficulties classical writers had in defining and applying it for their own times and places. Indeed, one of the great strengths of the critique of methodological nationalism today is that it enables us to reinterpret and rediscover the classics in this new light.

The second question in relation to Beck's critique of methodological nationalism is this: was the nation state as solid and secure in the first modernity as Beck's cosmopolitan outlook suggests? Beck's representation of the history of the nation-state strangely mirrors the methodological nationalism he criticises by overstating the primacy of the nation state in the first modernity. He maintains that methodological nationalism was right for its own times though obsolete for ours. A more radical cosmopolitan outlook would go further and demonstrate that a methodological nationalistic social science was *never* able to provide a satisfactory account of nation-states *even* during the first age of modernity. Enchantment by the nation-state meant that sociology rationalised its existence, presented it in the manner of a teleology and imposed it conceptually on political formations, like empires and totalitarian regimes, that had little to do with nation states or even actively opposed them. It is not enough to say, with Beck, that 'national organization as a structuring principle of societal and political action can *no longer* serve as a premise for the social science observer perspective' (Beck 2002b: 51–52, my italics), if it is maintained that sometime in the past this national principle was an appropriate premise.

To understand what is happening in the present, it is not helpful to exaggerate the solidity and omnipresence of nation-states in the past. It is a limitation of the contemporary cosmopolitan outlook to mimic what it most opposes. One aspect of the cosmopolitan research agenda accordingly is to develop the critique of methodological nationalism so that we no longer mirror its projection of national characteristics on to non-national forms or echo its mythical view of the nation-state as a universal and harmonious socio-political form in modern times.

We find similar issues arising in political philosophy and international relations (Bartelson 2001). In both disciplines the cosmopolitan outlook has tended to follow Kant in representing the old international order of sovereign nation states (that is, the order of the 'first modernity') as a Hobbesian state of nature writ large, a perpetual war of all states against all in which no state could be secure. Paradoxically, it has also presented this order of nation-states as remarkably stable – enduring for over three hundred years from the Peace of Westphalia of 1648 to our own times. It acknowledges that this 'Westphalian order', as it is called, assumed different shapes and forms over time but its basic premise is that no fundamental change to the system of nation-states occurred until recently. Events as momentous as the eighteenth-century political revolutions, the growth of imperialism in the nineteenth-century, the collapse of mainland European empires after the First World War, the formation of a raft of newly independent nation-states out of their fragments, the rise of totalitarian regimes with global ambitions in the inter-war period, the collapse of overseas empires after the Second War, the formation of two 'camps' during the Cold War, etc. – all these events are presented as mere punctuation marks in a continuous and expanding 'Westphalian' narrative. Even the forms of international co-operation established among nation-states and the emergence of a *world system* of independent nation-states, are seen as consolidating the principle of national sovereignty and its accompanying *Realpolitik* (Giddens 1985). In this representation of history all events prior to the rise of the new cosmopolitan order seem only to reproduce or reinforce or enlarge the Westphalian order. It is as if the old adage, *le plus ça change, le plus c'est la même chose*, is all that holds sway in this sphere of life.

What the cosmopolitan paradigm is doing in this account is paint a reified image of the nation-state in the past in order to produce a spectacular image of its extinction in the future. In other words it remains dependent on the methodological nationalism it seeks to overcome. It too assumes a rupture between tradition and modernity dated in the mid-seventeeth century and then the inexorable rise of the nation-state. It differs only in that it refuses to see the nation-state as an end of history and proposes a second rupture: one that brings into being the postnational or cosmopolitan constellation (Wagner 2001: 83). This approach to history falls into the very historicism it denounces. Its 'dialectical' logic might be formulated like this: the thesis is the *traditional unity* of morality and politics; the antithesis is the *modern diremption* of morality and politics; the synthesis or moment of reconciliation is the *reunification* of morality and politics under cosmopolitan auspices. The inadequacy of this formulaic time-consciousness prevents us from capturing the troubled history of nation states throughout modernity. It does not invalidate the cosmopolitan critique of methodological nationalism. On the contrary, it calls for its radicalisation by exploring the actual history of the nation state in a way that includes its own internal instabilities and its external conflict with imperial, totalitarian and other modern forms of political community. Today the research agenda of the cosmopolitan outlook is, in part, to pursue further its emancipation from national presuppositions.

The age of cosmopolitanism

Beck's cosmopolitan manifesto (1998b) is not predominantly about what the world of nation states was like and how the social sciences misapprehended it, but rather about what the world is becoming and how the social sciences must change if they are to grasp it. It is more about the future than the past. A second set of questions addresses, therefore, whether there is in fact an epochal change of such proportion as to introduce an age of cosmopolitanism and whether the cosmopolitan outlook succeeds in understanding the advent of this age. The cosmopolitan outlook certainly posits the arrival of a new era in which, to cite Beck, *reality itself has become cosmopolitan*. This refers in part to a kind of banal, everyday and perhaps forced cosmopolitanism that arises out of social factors connected with the phenomenon of globalisation and corrosive of the national framework that prevailed in the first modernity. These social forces include the movement and mixing of people in ways that create heterogeneous, hybrid and diasporic populations in all modern societies and defy the 'nationalisation' of populations in the traditional sense of the term; the proliferation of economic, political and cultural connections across national boundaries in ways that both eat into national sovereignty and construct the potential for some form of global governance; and the explosion of global risks – economic, ecological and terrorist – that cannot be addressed adequately by nation-states acting independently and thus create inescapable pressures to co-operate across national boundaries.

The cosmopolitan outlook is a response to this perceived reduction of the nation-state's functional capacities. A remark of Jürgen Habermas, that 'national politics have dwindled to more or less intelligent management of a process of forced adaptation to the pressure to shore up purely local positional advantages' may be taken as exemplary of this outlook (Habermas 2001a: 61). In this context cosmopolitanism is a collective effort to rethink the traditional locus of *political* decision-making and address the normative-philosophical implications of this social change. The common cosmopolitan thematic, particularly among German writers, is

245

that the memory of Nazism has robbed nationalism of its last traces of innocence and high-lights the central fact of our times: that nationalism is no longer possible as an ethical norm and that national identity, defined by the unity of cultural and historical forms of life, can no longer coincide with the form of the state. Alongside the devaluation of nationalism the cosmopolitan outlook looks forward to the development of core features of Kant's cosmo-politan ideal: his restriction on *jus ad bellum* – the right to go to war, his commitment to legal norms guiding interstate relations, and his articulation of cosmopolitan citizenship based on universal rights. The idea that all people in the world are in principle rights-bearing citizens implies that a legal order cannot be regulated *solely* around nation states since they have proved to be unreliable guarantors of rights, and that mechanisms must be brought into existence to entrench the legal status of cosmopolitan citizens on a world stage (Habermas 1996; 1998).

None of these socio-political observations is as solidly based as they might at first sight appear. The cosmopolitan outlook continues to face difficult questions concerning whether nation-states retain the *capacity* to create political unity among rights-bearing citizens coming from diverse cultures, languages, religions, backgrounds, ethnicities, etc., and whether nation-states can still strengthen the steering power of democratic assemblies in the face of global market pressures. There are further questions to be addressed on the relation between the experience of catastrophes in the twentieth-century and the normative value of the nation-state. Hannah Arendt has amply demonstrated that totalitarianism was not so much an extreme form of nationalism (notwithstanding the name of 'National Socialism') as an essen-tially anti-national movement with global ambitions to destroy the European system of nation-states and the parochial nationalisms they generated (Arendt 1979).

Finally, and perhaps most importantly of all, we have to reflect further upon what is meant by 'the age of cosmopolitanism'. When Kant referred to his own times as an 'age of enlight-enment', he did not claim that his was an enlightened age but rather that enlightenment was, as it were, the intellectual project of his age – its social imaginary. In *What is Enlightenment* Kant wrote as follows:

> If it is now asked whether we at present live in an *enlightened* age, the answer is no, but we do live in an age of enlightenment. As things are at present, we still have a long way to go … But we do have distinct indications that the way is now being cleared for them to work freely in this direction … Men will of their own accord gradually work their way out of barbarism so long as artificial measures are not deliberately adopted to keep them in it.
>
> (Kant 1991: 58)

The age of cosmopolitanism may be understood analogously: more a philosophical perspec-tive for viewing the potentialities of our age and acting ethically within it, than an objective characterisation of the age itself. It might be helpful to say, in the spirit of Benedict Anderson (1983), that the cosmopolitan outlook expresses a new 'imaginary community' in the minds of men and women that does have actually existing references but whose virtual existence transcends anything yet established in fact.

Such difficulties of understanding give life to the cosmopolitan research agenda. Let us consider a further one of its claims; namely, that elements of a cosmopolitan order can be *imperfectly* detected in current legal and political reforms. The beginnings of this process are not as clearly pronounced as the inauguration of the Westphalian order in 1648. Some commentators, among whom I include myself, cite the Nuremberg Charter and trials as an important index of the emergence of a cosmopolitan outlook after the war (Fine 2000).

Nuremberg stipulated that individuals acting within the legality of their own state can still be held culpable of crimes against humanity; that service to the state does not exonerate any official in any bureaucracy or any scientist in any laboratory from their responsibilities (Finkielkraut 1992); that the excuse of 'only obeying orders' or indeed of 'only giving orders' does not absolve those who violate human rights. Nuremberg introduced the offence of 'crimes against humanity' into international law. It signified that atrocities committed against one set of people, be it Jews or Poles or Roma, are an affront not only to these people but to humanity as a whole, and that humanity would find the means to punish the perpetrators. In 1945 the philosopher, Karl Jaspers (1961) prefigured the contemporary cosmopolitan outlook when he heralded the Nuremberg Tribunal, notwithstanding its national limitations, as a realisation of the idea of cosmopolitan right first enunciated by Kant (Levy and Sznaider 2002).

These first shoots of post-war cosmopolitan law proved to be short lived. The deficiencies of the Nuremberg trials have often been rehearsed and the tribunal was in some respects vulnerable to the charge of 'victors' justice' (Douglas 2001). The more important point, though, is that the cosmopolitan precedent set at Nuremberg was abandoned with the onset of Cold War. For forty years or more cosmopolitan ideas went on to a backburner, preserved only among a few radical intellectuals and civil society associations. Hannah Arendt's dissenting cosmopolitanism from this period makes her work particularly attractive to the current generation of cosmopolitan thinkers. In the preface of her *The Origins of Totalitarianism*, published in 1950, she remarked that antisemitism, imperialism and totalitarianism

> have demonstrated that human dignity needs a new guarantee which can be found only in a new political principle, a new law on earth, whose validity this time must comprehend the whole of humanity, while its power must remain strictly limited, rooted in and controlled by newly defined territorial entities.
>
> (Arendt 1979: ix)

In her study of the Eichmann trial, Arendt wrote in a similar vein of her sense of lost opportunity that the universalistic import of crimes against humanity was being corralled back into a national frame of reference. She held, for example, that the charge of 'crimes against the Jewish people' levelled at Adolph Eichmann reinforced the very situation that the idea of crimes against humanity had sought to correct – the breaking up of the human race into a multitude of competing states and nations. The court, she said, failed to understand that 'the physical extermination of the Jewish people, was a crime against humanity perpetrated on the body of the Jewish people, and that only the choice of victims, not the nature of the crime, could be derived from the long history of Jew-hatred and antisemitism' (Arendt 1994; Hirsh 2003).

Most current advocates of the cosmopolitan outlook maintain that after the fall of the Berlin Wall in 1989 a new configuration of cosmopolitan practices actually began to change the character of the epoch. They point to a broad array of 'cosmopolitan' reforms since 1989: human rights conventions turned into enforceable international laws; international criminal tribunals established to prosecute violators of humanitarian laws; human rights laws diffused through the European Convention on Human Rights; military interventions set in motion to stop genocides; cosmopolitan criticism levelled at the failure of the 'international community' to prevent atrocities in Srebrenica and Rwanda; and so forth (Ignatieff 2000). The nub of their case is that such reforms are neither short-term nor contingent but visible expressions of a deeper social transformation. This claim remains open to further investigation. The important point, however, is not to confuse the wish for the reality by identifying equivocal and uncertain cosmopolitan moments with the attainment of a cosmopolitan order as such.

Types of cosmopolitanism

We can identify a number of different inflections within the contemporary cosmopolitan outlook. They depend on where there appears to be the greatest normative potential within already existing institutions and practices for cosmopolitan development. I shall mention here four inflections in the literature which I shall call for the sake of argument: liberal, democratic, civil society and transnational.

Cosmopolitan liberalism

A tempting route for the cosmopolitan to take is to advocate a form of cosmopolitan justice responsible for the protection of basic rights *without* requiring anything more than a formal democratic mandate. This idea of cosmopolitan right fits with a Lockeian form of liberalism. It upholds cosmopolitan institutions, such as international courts, to protect human rights through legally coercive measures. It presents us with an image of a benevolent grouping of powerful, well-ordered states acting in the best interests of individual rights-bearers. It defines a form of right that is imposed on sovereign legislators as an external constraint. In his *The Law of Peoples* John Rawls argues roughly in this vein when he makes the case that 'a constitutional regime must establish an effective Law of Peoples in order to realise fully the freedom of its citizens' and elaborates the principles that should inform this law (Rawls 1999: 10). The principles he outlines are basically abstract re-formulations of well-established principles of international law. They emphasise the independence and self-determination of peoples, respect for treaties and agreements between peoples, non-intervention in the internal affairs of other peoples and norms regulating the conduct of war. In line with more recent developments in international law they also advance more distinctively Kantian themes: that peoples are bound to honour human rights, that the principle of non-intervention may be suspended in the case of major human rights abuses, and that these principles should provide a frame of reference for international organisations such as the United Nations. Rawls also follows international law in appealing primarily to security considerations in defence of human rights. This defence remains hostage to the empirical criticism that rights-violating states may not pose a serious threat to international security and to the moral criticism that rights should be defended irrespective of their utility in preserving global security.

Cosmopolitan democracy

Any political theorist who advocates cosmopolitan politics has to confront whether the cosmopolitan outlook can be reconciled with existing national communities. The cosmopolitan outlook should not be confused with a doctrine of dissolution of the nation-state and the tension between national sovereignty and cosmopolitan right should not be overstated (Hollinger 2001). The key move here is to say that respect for constitutionally regulated politics at the national level can be *reconciled* with respect for the authority of supra-national institutions. Habermas, for instance, argues that there is no essential conflict between national and transnational forms of 'constitutional patriotism' inasmuch as both are based on universal principles of right (Cavallar 1999; Habermas 2001a, b). It is only when a nation-state is based on radically different principles of order and justice from those of cosmopolitan law, if for example it is based on ethnic exclusion or pursues genocidal policies, that the conditions for conflict will be mobilised. Generally, the cosmopolitan outlook looks for reconciliation between national and cosmopolitan institutions, *supplemented* by the possibility of cosmopolitan intervention where reconciliation is absent (Habermas 1999, 2001a).

The principle of the nation-state is that it offers citizens the chance to be both recipients and authors of the laws that govern them. They are at once bearers of private rights, members of civil society and participants in political procedures of lawmaking that distribute rights to citizens. In this conception of political community any system of rights presupposes they are substantiated through democratic deliberation. The question is whether this conception of democracy still holds when we move from a national to international frame of reference. A number of cosmopolitan writers have argued that the attainment of democracy in the cosmopolitan arena is as desirable as in the national, and they have engaged in a collective intellectual effort to give substance to this idea both through reform of existing international institutions and through the creation of new institutions and norms (Archibugi 1995, 2000; Held 1995, 2004; Achibugi *et al.* 1998). Without going into any detail here, it is fair to say that they encounter major difficulties in realising such large-scale democratic praxis. The idea of cosmopolitan democracy has been vulnerable to the empirical criticism that existing international organisations are *fundamentally* antithetical to democratic norms (Zolo 1997, 1999), and to the conceptual criticism that the all-inclusive character of cosmopolitan institutions may exclude democracy *in principle* since any democracy must at least distinguish between members and non-members (Habermas 2001a: 107).

Cosmopolitan civil society

In the face of difficulties in reconciling cosmopolitanism with democracy, a compelling response has been to look to 'global civil society' as a source of de-centred authority based on horizontal networks of interconnected 'nodes', capable of co-ordinating action by means of information and communication technology and acting independently of the state and the market (Walzer 1995; Castells 2000; Rosenau 2002). Global civil society is said to encompass transnational non-governmental organisations, social movements and other formal and informal associations that contribute to the growing emphasis on human rights and social justice in the international arena and to the democratisation of international legislation. An example might be the role civil society played in the Ottawa Convention on Banning Landmines or in the creation of the International Criminal Court (Kaldor 2003). The strength of this perspective lies in its recognition that civil society can bring issues of public concern to the top of the international agenda and influence otherwise resistant representative bodies by turning to international support and transnational advocacy networks. Yet civil society associations arise out of the same political economy as other international institutions, they are subject to the same pressures of cooptation by powerful interests, and their own policy making structures are often just as remote from the deliberations of representative bodies (Lupel 2004). Within nation-states democratic legitimacy normally comprises *two* moments: formal processes of democratic will formation in representative bodies and informal processes of opinion formation within civil society. If formal procedures are not to become detached from public life, there must be scope for creative interaction between the two spheres. Civil society takes on quite another meaning if it is converted from being one element of a two-track theory of democracy into a single track (Fine and Smith 2003).

Cosmopolitan Europe

Among European intellectuals there has been to turn to one of the few genuine examples of a transnational political community, the European Union, as a bearer of cosmopolitan values. Habermas has led the way to the re-conceptualisation of the European Union as a new kind

249

of polity – neither federal nor confederal, but with a binding constitution, an elected parliament, an impartial executive, a rule of law, a bill of rights for all citizens, a vibrant civil society, separation between members and non-members, and a dedication to social justice and welfare. It remains arguable whether this transnational body can replicate the democratic legitimacy attained at the national level. Will Kymlicka takes it as fact that 'transnational organisations exhibit a major "democratic deficit" and have little public legitimacy in the eyes of citizens' (Kymlicka 2001: 312). Habermas too concedes that the larger units of political decision-making required to control global economic forces, may have *less democratic legitimacy* by the standards of democracy he has elaborated in the context of the nation-state. One way in which he hopes to solve this difficulty is to say that transnational bodies may strengthen the *informal* moment of democratic legitimacy and that the participation of non-governmental organisations in the deliberations of the European Union will make formal decision-making processes more transparent and reconnect them to the grassroots level (Habermas 2001a). This approach mirrors that of global civil society at the transnational level.

The key to the turn to 'Europe' within European cosmopolitanism lies elsewhere (Derrida 1994). It is to be found in a representation of 'Europe' as the bearer, or at least a potential bearer, of cosmopolitan values. This idea of 'Europe' presents it as a locus of solidarity that can recover the re-distributive policies of the social welfare nation-state; as a source of human rights and of indignation over violation of human rights committed by others (Habermas and Derrida 2003; Habermas 2004); as the political ground on which citizens see themselves as members of an international community; as a political culture and form of life that supersedes all forms of conventional identity, including any 'Carolingian' appeal to a Christian Europe. This Europe is, to be sure, an 'imaginary community' – a transnational polity that comprises a plurality of distinct national cultures, revels in polyethnicity, challenges exclusive differentiations such as that of foreigner and native, opens itself to the world and institutionalises cosmopolitan values. Like any 'imaginary community' it occupies a space between past and future, between what is and what ought to be, between the empirical and the normative.

The strength of this turn to Europe is to ground cosmopolitanism, in Rawls's term, as a 'realistic utopia'. It nurtures a cosmopolitan vision for the European Union and finds a real political subject for its cosmopolitan vision. It risks, however, reverting to a new nationalism, a kind of transnational or pan-European nationalism, that treats Europe in the manner of a universal nation whose particular values and interests correspond with the universal values and interests of humanity in general. This way of thinking has a history. For the French enlightenment and its successors the universal nation (the nation without nationalism, as Julia Kristeva has dubbed it) is identified with France (Kristeva 1991); for official Communism it was Russia; for Maoism it was China; for neo-liberalism today, perhaps, America has become the universal nation. The idea of a universal nation, no less than that of a 'universal class', has in the past been used to justify all manner of violence. To be sure, this is not the intent of European cosmopolitans who want Europe to be the vehicle for cosmopolitan law, human rights and perpetual peace. If they are to be faulted, it is not for wishing to 'cosmopolitanise' Europe but for brushing over its equivocal history and identifying it with cosmopolitanism.

Between the nation and world government

These four inflections of the cosmopolitan outlook focus respectively on cosmopolitan law, cosmopolitan democracy, cosmopolitan civil society and cosmopolitan political community. They are not in principle incompatible with one another and we can certainly imagine a cosmopolitan strategy that works flexibly at all these levels. They have in common that in no case is the cosmopolitan outlook identified with world government or a world state. Hannah Arendt has pointed out that the idea that 'right' is what is good for the whole is *essentially* barbaric and does not lose its destructive force whether the whole is the German people or the proletariat or as Arendt puts it, 'if the unit to which "the good for" applies is as large as mankind itself':

> It is quite conceivable, and even within the realm of practical political possibilities, that one fine day a highly organized and mechanized humanity will conclude quite democratically – namely by a majority decision – that for humanity as a whole it would be better to liquidate certain parts thereof.
>
> (Arendt 1979: 299)

What is crucial is that 'the right to have rights, or the right of every individual to belong to humanity, should be guaranteed by humanity itself' (Arendt 1979: 298). At the time of Arendt's writing, international law still operated largely in terms of treaties and agreements between sovereign states; declarations of human rights had been made by international organisations but a sphere of authority above that of nations barely existed; and people who had lost all other protections except that of their human rights were scarcely less vulnerable than they had always been. Edmund Burke's idea, that the rights we enjoy spring as an entailed inheritance from within the nation, still appeared as a sound pragmatism rooted in the manifold experience of the age. Today it is an open question how much the world has changed and whether this national outlook remains the enemy that cosmopolitan consciousness still has to face.

Conclusion

The cosmopolitan outlook should be conceived as a radically incomplete research project rather than a body of fixed ideas (Calhoun 2002). In identifying ways in which actually existing cosmopolitanism still mimics the methodological nationalism it seeks to overcome, the aim is not to dismiss the cosmopolitan critique but to demonstrate that there is much work to be done in pursuit of its research agenda. There is no magic potion that can turn national prejudice into cosmopolitan enlightenment. Kant sometimes wrote as if he had found such a potion in the formation of 'a human legislative power of universal character and world-wide extent' (Kant 1991). His argument was that existing international laws were without the slightest legal force *because* they lacked a higher legal authority to enforce them, and that the formation of the federation of nations would provide the alchemy to transform lawlessness into law, perpetual war into perpetual peace, and usher in a new cosmopolitan order. It was not to be. The transition from one period to another does not annihilate the past and a higher form of law does not do away with the contradictions present in the lower forms.

The achievement of the cosmopolitan outlook does not lie either in its dismissal of classical social theory, or in its depiction of our age as cosmopolitan, or in its elevation of cosmopolitanism into an abstract ideal. In all three respects it has perhaps been premature in its conclusions. Its achievement lies in its collective effort to understand what is the idea of cosmopolitan right, how it is brought into existence and why it is important for the world. Cosmopolitan right is real. It is a definite social form – one of the various forms of right that constitute modern political life. It is a social product of the modern age that has already given rise to private rights, reflexive morality, romantic love, civil society and the nation-state. It can be studied with the same objectivity as other forms of right and their connections can be explored without privileging it over these other forms. Cosmopolitan is not absolute, but one

251

element in the ceaseless turmoil of passions and interests that defines our times. Like all forms of right, cosmopolitan right contains the potential for violence against those who violate it. The argument, however, that it is now growing in theoretical, empirical and normative importance, is one that is difficult to refute.

The *cosmopolitan outlook* is not to my mind a doctrine that substitutes methodological cosmopolitanism for methodological nationalism. It is an essay first and foremost in understanding. It does not raise cosmopolitanism above society, it explores its place in society. It does not cut itself off from social theory, it draws on the difficulties traditionally faced by social theory. It does not maintain the innocence of cosmopolitan social forms, but it certainly perceives their necessity. The cosmopolitan outlook faces up to the fact that the fraudster who rationalises his own violence in the name of cosmopolitan values and the cynic who dismisses cosmopolitanism as a fraud, are two sides of the same coin.

References

Anderson, B. (1983) *Imagined Communities: Reflections on the Origin and Spread of Nationalism*, London: Verso.

Archibugi, D. (1995) *Cosmopolitan Democracy: An Agenda for a New World Order*, Cambridge: Polity.

Archibugi, D. (2000) 'Cosmopolitical Democracy', *New Left Review*, 4, July/August, 137–150.

Archibugi, D. (ed.) (2004) *Cosmopolitics*, London: Verso.

Archibugi, D., Held, D. and Kohler, M. (eds) (1998) *Re-imagining Political Community: Studies in Cosmopolitan Democracy*, Cambridge: Polity.

Arendt, H. (1979) *The Origins of Totalitarianism*, New York: Harcourt Brace.

Arendt, H. (1994) *Eichmann in Jerusalem: A Report on the Banality of Evil*, New York: Penguin.

Bartelson, J. (2001) *The Critique of the State*, Cambridge: Cambridge University Press.

Beck, U.(1998a) *Democracy Without Enemies*, Cambridge: Polity Press.

Beck, U. (1998b) 'The Cosmopolitan Manifesto', *The New Statesman* 20, 38–50.

Beck, U. (2000a [1997]) *What is Globalization?*, Cambridge: Polity Press.

Beck, U. (2000b) 'The Cosmopolitan Perspective: Sociology of the Second Age of Modernity', *British Journal of Sociology*, 51(1): 79–105.

Beck, U. (2002a) 'The Cosmopolitan Society and its Enemies', *Theory, Culture and Society*, 19(1–2), 17–45.

Beck, U. (2002b) 'The Terrorist Threat: World Risk Society Revisited', *Theory, Culture and Society*, 19(4), 39–55.

Beck, U. (2003) 'Toward a New Critical Theory with a Cosmopolitan Intent', *Constellations*, 10(4): 453–68.

Bohman, J. and Lutz-Bachmann, M. (eds) (1997) *Perpetual Peace: Essays on Kant's Cosmopolitan Ideal*, Cambridge, MA: MIT Press.

Breckenridge, C. and Pollock, S. (eds) (2002) *Cosmopolitanism*, Durham, NC and London: Duke University Press.

Calhoun, C. (2002) 'The Class Consciousness of Frequent Travellers: Toward a Critique of Actually Existing Cosmopolitanism', in S. Vertovec and R. Cohen *Conceiving Cosmopolitanism*, Oxford: Oxford University Press, pp. 86–109.

Castells, M. (2000) *The Rise of the Network Society*, second edition, Oxford: Blackwell Publishers.

Cavallar, G. (1999) *Kant and the Theory and Practice of International Right*, Cardiff: University of Wales Press.

Cheah, P. and Robbins, B. (eds) (1998) *Cosmopolitics: Thinking and Feeling Beyond the Nation*, Minneapolis: University of Minnesota Press.

Chernilo, D. (2004) 'Sociology, Society and Nation-states: Toward a Sociological Understanding of Epochal Changes', PhD, University of Warwick.

Chernilo, D. (2006a) 'Social Theory: Methodical Nationalism and its Critique', in G. Delanty and K. Kumar (eds) *Handbook of Nations and Nationalism*, London: Sage.

Chernilo, D. (2006b) 'Social Theory's Methodological Nationalism: Myth and Reality', *European Journal of Sociology*, 9(1), forthcoming.

Cohen, J. (ed.) (1996) *For Love of Country: Debating the Limits of Patriotism - Martha Nussbaum and Respondents*, Cambridge: Beacon Press.

Derrida, J. (1994) *The Other Heading: Reflections on Today's Europe*, Bloomington: Indiana University Press.

Douglas, L. (2001) *The Memory of Judgement: Making Law and History in the Trials of the Holocaust*, New Haven and London: Yale University Press.

Doyle, M. (1993) 'Liberalism and International Relations' in R. Beiner and W. Booth (eds) *Kant and Political Philosophy: The Contemporary Legacy*, New Haven: Yale University Press.

Durkheim, E. (1992) *Professional Ethics and Civic Morals*, trans. by C. Brookfield, London: Routledge.

Fine, R. (2000), 'Crimes Against Humanity: Hannah Arendt and the Nuremberg Debates', *European Journal of Social Theory*, 3, 3.

Fine, R. (2003a) 'Kant's Theory of Cosmopolitanism and Hegel's Critique', *Philosophy and Social Criticism*, 29(6), 609–630.

Fine, R. (2003b) 'Taking the "ism" out of Cosmopolitanism: An Essay in Reconstruction', *European Journal of Social Theory*, 6(4), 451–470.

Fine, R. and Smith, W. (2003) 'Jürgen Habermas's Theory of Cosmopolitanisn', *Constellations*, 10(4), 469–487.

Fine, R. and Chernilo, D. (2004) 'Between Past and Future: the Equivocations of the New Cosmopolitanism', *Studies in Law, Politics, and Society*, 31, 25–44.

Finkielkraut, A. (1992) *Remembering in Vain*, New York: Columbia.

Flikschuh, K. (2000) *Kant and Modern Political Philosophy*, Cambridge: Cambridge University Press.

Giddens, A. (1985) *The Nation State and Violence*, Cambridge: Polity.

Habermas, J. (1996) *Between Facts and Norms*, Cambridge, Polity.

Habermas, J. (1998) *The Inclusion of the Other: Studies in Political Theory*, Cambridge, MA: MIT Press.

Habermas, J. (1999) 'Bestiality and Humanity: A War on the Border Between Legality and Morality', *Constellations*, 6(3), 263–272.

Habermas, J. (2001a) *The Postnational Constellation: Political Essays*, Cambridge: Polity.

Habermas, J. (2001b) 'Why Europe needs a Constitution', *New Left Review*, 11 (September/October), 5–26.

Habermas, J. (2003) 'Interpreting the Fall of a Monument', *Constellations*, 10(3), 364–370.

Habermas, J. (2004) 'America and the World: A Conversation with Eduardo Mandieta', *Logos*, 3(3).

Habermas, J. and Derrida, J. (2003) 'February 15, or What Binds Europeans Together: A Plea for a Common Foreign Policy, Beginning in the Core of Europe', *Constellations*, 10(3), 291–297.

Held, D. (1995) *Democracy and the Global Order*, Cambridge: Polity Press.

Held, D. (2004) *Global Covenant*, Cambridge: Polity Press.

Held, D. and McGrew, A. (eds) (2002) *Governing Globalization*, Oxford: Polity Press.

Hirsh, D. (2003) *Law Against Genocide*, London: Glasshouse Press.

Hollinger, D. (2001) 'Not Universalists, not Pluralists: The New Cosmopolitans Find their own Way', *Constellations*, 8(2), 236–248.

Ignatieff, M. (2000) *Virtual War*, London: Chatto and Windus.

Jaspers, K. (1961) *The Question of German Guilt*, New York: Capricorn.

Kaldor, M. (2003) *Global Civil Society: An Answer to War*, Oxford: Polity.

Kant, E. (1991) *Political Writings*, Cambridge: Cambridge University Press.

Kristeva, J. (1991) *Strangers to Ourselves*, New York: Columbia University Press.

Kymlicka, W. (2001) *Contemporary Political Philosophy: An Introduction*, Oxford: Oxford University Press.

Levy, D. and Sznaider N. (2002) 'The Holocaust and the Formation of Cosmopolitan Memory', *European Journal of Social Theory*, 5(1), 87–106.

Lupel, A. (2004) 'Democratizing Global Governance: Popular Sovereignty and Transnational Politics', American Political Science Association 100th Annual Meeting, Chicago, Illinois, 2–5 September.

Rawls, J. (1999) *The Law of Peoples*, London: Harvard University Press.

Rosenau, J. (2002) 'Governance in a New Global Order' in D. Held and A. McGrew (eds) *Governing Globalization*, Oxford: Polity Press.

Smelser, N. (1997) *Problematics of Sociology*, Berkley and Los Angeles: University of California Press.

Urry, J. (2002) 'The Global Complexities of September 11th', *Theory, Culture & Society*, 19(4), 57–69.

Vertovec, S. and Cohen, R. (2002) *Conceiving Cosmopolitanism: Theory, Context and Practice*, Oxford: Oxford University Press.

Wagner, P. (1994) *A Sociology of Modernity: Liberty and Discipline*, London and New York: Routledge.

Wagner, P. (2001) *Theorising Modernity*, London: Sage.

Walzer, M. (1995) *Toward a Global Civil Society*, Providence, RI: Berghahn.

Zolo, D. (1997) *Cosmopolis: Prospects for World Government*, Cambridge: Polity.

Zolo, D. (1999) 'A Cosmopolitan Philosophy of International Law? A Realist Approach', *Ratio Juris*, 12(4), 429–444.

Part 4

Themes and Narratives

19

European master narratives about freedom

Agnes Heller

In this chapter I employ the concept of master narrative in the spirit of the History and Memory school initiated by Pierre Nora. I will speak of stories, histories, fantasies, patterns of imagination which play the role of a kind of 'arche' in a given culture. I mean culture in the broadest interpretation of this many faceted and complex concept as did Clifford Geertz. He defined culture as 'a historically transmitted pattern of meanings embodied in symbols, a system of inherited conceptions expressed in symbolic forms by means of which humans communicate, perpetuate and develop their knowledge and attitude towards life' (Geertz 1973: 89). One can point at a concrete, singular culture in the case of, at least, one shared master narrative.

A master narrative can be termed an 'arche' of a culture in both interpretations of the Greek word. The 'arche' stories are stories to which we always return, they are the final, or ultimate foundations of a type of imagination. Yet as the guides of imagination they also rule, control, and are vested with power. Direct or indirect references to master narratives provide strengths and power to new stories or new images, they lend them double legitimacy: legitimacy by tradition and by charisma, for in case of master narratives tradition itself is charismatic. References to a shared tradition are not just cognitively understood but also emotionally felt, without footnotes, without explanation or interpretation. It is not even necessary for single men and women to be familiar with the master narrative itself, for they are living in a world where a host of memories and interpretations are imbued by their spirit. Several allusions refer to master narratives, irrespective of their evaluation. That Homer's two epic poems have been the master narratives of the ancient Greek culture, is beyond question. Yet Plato almost always makes negative references to them, since he is deeply dissatisfied with the culture which has been built around the Homeric master narratives. Yet he cannot avoid referring to them, to be properly understood by his contemporaries.

Which narratives will become master narratives of a culture and which not, is not decided at the very start, and it does not even necessarily depend on the quality of the narrative or of the kind or imagination. What would have happened, so a few scholars ruminate, if instead the orthodox Catholic Christianity heretic Gnosticism would have become the master narrative of the late Roman Empire. Perhaps, it could have become a master narrative, yet of a different culture, not ours. Our culture with a Gnostic master narrative would have been impossible. Gnosis is now an interesting topic of inquiry, a worthy object of scientific curiosity, yet an esoteric issue. References to eons, thirty-two emanations, or to the sin of Sophia were not legitimating even a single idea, image or story in European history and they do not do it now. References to the snake of Eve or to the death of Socrates, however, did and still do.

Every culture – in the broadest sense of the word culture – has its own master narratives, mostly myths, foundational stories, religious visions. Thus by 'European Culture' I mean the master narratives shared by different people and nations on the European subcontinent. Certainly, all people of Europe have also their own master narratives unshared by other European people. Moreover, non-European people can also share one or the other story of the European master narratives. In what follows, however, I restrict my interpretation to the shared European master narratives alone.

The European master narratives are the Bible on the one hand, and the Greek/Roman philosophy and historiography on the other hand. They are texts. We have no access to happenings or acts or to the spoken words but through texts. Or if we do today, due to archeological excavations and founds, this newly gained knowledge does not affect in the slightest our relation to the master narratives. The texts, not the archeological finds, are still constantly reinterpreted, presented and worked upon in literature, painting, philosophy, politics and also in daily life.

In what follows I will speak of the European master narratives exclusively from the vantage point of freedom and liberty. I want to give some thought to the importance of the issue that our European thinking of freedom, our imaginary institutions of liberty and freedom drew constantly on the sources presented and represented by the Bible on the one hand, and by the Greek/Roman philosophy and history writing on the other hand.

The biblical master narrative of freedom

Let me start with the Bible. The concept of freedom makes its first appearance in the Bible in its interpretation of free choice or free will. In this text no distinction was made between choice and will. Eve and Adam have picked a fruit from the tree of knowledge and tasted it. As we learn, it is from this moment that humans have the chance to choose between good and evil.

Nothing determines them at the outset to choose one rather than the other. For one person it is easy to choose the good, for the other it is difficult, yet for no one is it impossible. The possibility to choose is the human condition is general. It means to taken responsibility for the others and for oneself. Cain was the first human born from the mother's womb. He already 'inherited' the possibility of free choice. God has warned him such: 'Why art thou wroth? and why is thy countenance fallen? If thou doest well, shall it not be lifted up? and if thou doest not well, sin coucheth at the door, and unto thee is its desire, but thou mayest rule over it' (4: 7). Cain, as we know, failed to rule over his desire, but in a later chapter of Genesis, in a somehow similar situation, Esau succeeded. Instead of killing his brother he embraced him.

From the Christian fathers until Kant, Hegel and Kierkegaard the great philosophers constantly returned to this paradigm, Kant even twice. The European literature, both drama and novel are breast-fed on this master narrative. The serpent, the tempter, who is entirely absent from Greek tragedy, will play here also a central role. Macbeth is seduced into sin by the witches and by his Lady, Rastignac and Rumepre by the daemonic Vautrin, Rasokolnikov by the mythological image of Napoleon. Philosophers and theologians have dicsussed for two thousand years the essence of free will or whether it exists at all, but whichever conclusion is drawn, the discussion is never ending, and the text remains a master narrative.

The second fundamental biblical story of freedom is the narrative of liberation, the liberation from the Egyptian slavery. 'Let my people go', the biblical quotation, became the refrain of the song of the African slaves in America, who gave voice by this quotation to their desire and resolve for liberation. Nietzsche was right when wrote – albeit critically – in his *On the Genealogy of Morals* (1996 [1887]), that without this liberation story there would be neither modern democracy nor socialism. Instead of claiming descent from gods, a people claimed that they were descended from slaves, thereby upturning the hierarchy of values.

The central, the most emphatic, reference to liberation can be found in the passages about divine revelation at Mount Sinai. God, the giver of the law, makes himself known to the people of Israel not as the creator of the world, but as the liberator, as the God who brought them out from the land of bondage. God makes the people immediately aware of their liberty, since Law can be given only to free people, because only free people can obey the law as well as infringe it. After having revealed himself first as the liberator, God commands that people should not have other gods before him. They should not serve things as if they were gods, and above all no humans or their statues. The King of Kings stands above all Kings, as the victims of despotism in Shakespeare so frequently declare. Every Pharaoh or Emperor, just like a Hitler or a Stalin, are idols, and their worship is idolatry.

And the narration goes on with the paradigmatic story of the golden calf. This story became also a European master narrative. People do not want to be free, they prefer the flesh pots of Egypt. We may think, among others, of the encounter between Christ and the Grand Inquisitor in Dostoevsky's novel *The Brothers Karamazov*, as a kind of replay of the controversy between Moses and Aaron after the golden calf episode.

The third European master narrative of freedom is entailed in the story of Jesus of Nazareth, the fourth in the creed of Christ, the Redeemer. The two stories are connected, yet not identical.

The claim for the freedom of religion, the freedom of conscience and faith, appears first in the person and teaching of Jesus of Nazareth. Freedom of religion, of faith, is the first among all liberties claimed, and remained the first liberty claimed even in modern times. Jesus of Nazareth, did not invent a new religion, yet, thus the Gospels tell us, has interpreted the religion of his fathers in his own and new way, while surrounding himself with disciples who learned to share his interpretation. Jesus of Nazareth, a free spirit, refused to abandon his own radical and free thinking about religious observance for the sake of institutionalized interpretations. Thus he provoked the wrath of the Sadducean officials of the Temple and won the loving enthusiasm of many people. One can also interpret his martyr's death, first of all, as a sacrifice for the freedom of faith, religion and speech. Christian heretics have interpreted the Gospels also in this spirit. Yet they were not the only ones who did. A master narrative is a master narrative because it transcends the boundaries single communities of faith. For example, Sartre told the story of the birth of Jesus also in this sense, in his early drama *Bariola* which was staged first in a Nazi prisoner of war camp.

Christ is believed to be the Redeemer of humankind. This creed also entails, among others, a freedom narrative, the radicalization of the Genesis story about free choice and free will. The original story suggests, that one can always choose the good, that one is never ever determined to sin. Yet the promise of salvation goes further: it is, indeed, a promise. It does not only warn the faithful about responsibility, but also promises an entirely new beginning. It suggests, that even if one has chosen the evil path, this will not seal finally and forever one's character or fate. One can liberate oneself from sin, from one's own past, from all bad decisions, and become an entirely new person. One can be born for the second time. The Saulus/Paulus story is perhaps the first paradigmatic exemplification of this promise. European imagination returns to it again and again.

The Greek and Roman narrative of freedom

Now I turn to Greek and Roman stories which will become, just like the stories of the Bible, European master narratives. I repeat, that one does not need to know all those stories, perhaps not even one of them, and still keep them alive as master narratives, for they have already been absorbed by the series of imaginary institutions on the European continent.

Yet, interesting as it is, the Greek and Roman mythology does not belong to the European master narratives. Surely, one can return to them, revive them from time to time. This happened in painting from the late Renaissance to the Baroque or in the curriculum of the gymnasium in the nineteenth-century. But this culture was based on subtle knowledge and remained esoteric. There are exceptions, such as the image of Aphrodite/Venus and of Eros/Amor, yet their function rather than their stories became paradigmatic. As far as the freedom narratives are concerned, the sole remaining hero is Prometheus, the rebel, symbolizing not the relevance of mythology yet rather the uprising against the tyranny of a god. There is an absence of Greek and Roman mythology in the European master narratives, despite the repeated attempts to revive them and make them work. But monotheistic tradition excludes all kinds of mythology. The Bible is not mythological, and early Christian mythologies, such as gnosticism, were esoteric and have disappeared. In Europe, at least roughly during the last 15,000 years, there is no story of Theomachia, gods do not begets god, they do not make love, they do not metamorphose. The old gods are with us, yet not as gods: they do not dwell on the Olympus but in the museums.

True, in the nineteenth-century a radical change was attempted. The conviction that the Jewish/Christian God is dead, voiced by Heine, yet made popular by Nietzsche, became widely accepted. It took time to realize, that the conception was based on a false analogy. Greek and Roman gods died with their culture, thus, the conclusion presented itself, that modernity, as an entirely new culture or civilization, has, or will have, the same effect, the death of the Jewish/Christian God. What was not understood, yet is today emphasized, by excellent cultural historians like Jan Assmann, that the Jewish and Christian religions are not culture specific, they have already accommodated themselves to entirely different cultures and will continue to do this in all possibility also in the future. Yet as long as the creed in the coming demise of the Jewish Christian God remained widespread, at least in Europe, a few artificial attempts have been made to replace the old God with other gods, mostly borrowed from the world of ancient mythologies. Nietzsche for example tried to revive the figure of the prophet Zarathustra/Zoroasther, although rather allegorically, and also the god of wine Dionysus. Needless to say, that all the attempts to make old mythologies relevant to the modern European mind, were doomed to failure. There were some pagan racist fantasies like in the minds of some Nazis, to celebrate a cult around Germanic deities, especially Wotan, yet finally this idea became restricted to the cult of Wagner and his Ring cycle, where the mythical figures themselves served just as allegories for something universal, according to the composer. Yet even if Greek and Roman mythology has not bestowed Europe with master narratives, Greek and Roman philosophy and historiography has bequeathed several, among others three master narratives of freedom.

The foundational text of the first master narrative is the oration of Pericles according to Thucydides, and even if not exactly this oration, yet at least its spirit, among others in the definition of Aristotle's Politics: 'the city is the sum total of its citizens'. Just as the master narrative of liberation was bequeathed by the Bible, so was the narrative about the constitution of liberties by the Greeks and the Romans. Israel received the Law from God, the free Athenian citizens have themselves constituted the laws they were ready to obey. And they created also the fundamental law, the law of all the laws, the constitution. The Latin word constitution already suggests that we are talking about an artifice created by men. Aristotle even called constitution-making a kind of techne. In most variations of this master narrative, which one after the other transformed the original descriptions into a master narrative, the men who created the constitution are under the protection of the constitution, they preserve and enjoy their liberties. They are the free citizens. They are the city, all others are aliens. Let me refer again to the Biblical concept. There the Law is not of human making, it is not constituted, but bestowed as the gift of God, although its addressee are the free human persons. Here every one is equally subject to the law, not just men, yet also women, servants, slaves, and the Law includes even obligations towards the strangers. And everyone is equally in duty bound to obey the commandments.

One encounters at this point already one of the characteristic features of the European culture: there are tensions between various master narratives so that one master narrative or one interpretation of a master narrative can be played off against the other. This is not a kind of shortcoming but inheres in the dynamic character of this culture. Without a tension between certain master narratives one single interpretation of one master narrative would become in all probability fossilized. The tension prompts constant reinterpretations. Sometimes a kind of 'okumene' can be established between them, although the narratives are not to be fused. Still they can enter into conversation with one another and implant certain features from the one into the other. Typical examples of such mutual accommodations are the so-called social contract theories, and even the slogan of the French Revolution: liberty, fraternity, equality. That the mutual accommodation of the master narratives in political theories and slogans do not also eliminate tensions and contradictions in pragmatic political life has been brilliantly documented in Tocqueville's famous book on American democracy. Tocqueville discovers the dilemma and concentrates – among others – on the two master narratives, their messages and the difficulty of their coexistence.

Hobbes, the first author of a representative social contract theory goes very far in his attempt of thinking the two master narratives together, and not just in the second part of *Leviathan*, one of the first writings in political theology. The idea of the Contract or the Covenant itself attempts to fuse the Biblical tradition with the Greek/Roman idea of a good constitution. Although the contract is devised among humans, men are entering into contract with one another, yet they alienate their freedom to the Sovereign. Moreover, although humans are the makers of their own laws, they are still under the guidance of the laws of nature, which are on their part divine and serve as uncontestable sources of, and limits to, the human act of constituting.

Before the social contract theory reached its most republican version in Rousseau, different types of mediation between the two master narratives were attempted, even other narratives were called in for an complementary service, like the story of Adam and Eve by Locke. Rousseau came up with another kind of mediation. Although his republic was based entirely on the ancient model, or rather on a strong interpretation of the ancient anti-liberal Greek – rather Spartan – citizenship, he still needed God, the Supreme Being as the authority above and behind a constitution, which on its part, has been created solely by citizens. God is by no means the source of Law, but obedience to the Law is warranted by a commonly shared faith, the faith in God. Needless to say: the tension between the two master narratives on freedom always assumes different forms and meanings. For example today it makes its appearance in the feverish controversies between American communitarians and liberals.

The second European master narrative inherited from the Greek polis is the story of Socrates in the form as we know it from Plato's dialogues. It is the story of freedom of conscience. This story has been constantly retold, referred to by philosophers, writers, political actors, and it was deeply cherished by people who held freedom of speech and of conscience dear. The story was understood without footnotes. For example, during the Second World War, Steinbeck wrote *The Moon is Down*, a play about a man who was unwilling to betray his conscience and, as a result, he was condemned to death by the Nazis. Standing before his judges, he simply recited the words of Socrates from Plato's Apology. The audience was weeping.

European philosophers and other storytellers have frequently compared the fate of Jesus and the fate of Socrates. In times of the Renaissance they incidentally almost merged the two characters, for example in exclamations like: 'Holy Socrates, pray for us!' If we consider the master narratives of freedom alone, the comparison is justified. Both Jesus and Socrates died because they refused to act and to speak in discordance with their faith and conviction.

Still, the two stories convey also different messages, and the interpretations of the master narrative 'Socrates' were emitting those specific messages. The Socrates story is not the master narrative about freedom of religion, religious practices and faith, it is rather the master narrative about freedom of thought, expression, opinion, and of personal conscience. It is also the story about freedom of disbelief and about the dignity of personal and oppositional judgment and opinion in matters of state, constitution and tradition. Socrates, in Plato's narrative, died in defense of a new language game, in defense of being free to say things like 'what you consider true is in fact not true, what you consider just is in fact not just, something else is good or just' in discussing any topic, such as politics, poetry, ethics, and especially wisdom. The question concerning the philosophy of Socrates, the never-ending dispute about the possibility or impossibility of discerning Plato's philosophy from that of Socrates, interests us philosophers deeply, yet it does not make a difference in the master narrative of freedom. Socrates, this funny old sage who treated his accusers with irony, defied the prejudiced judges and the crowd, who defended himself and his truth with a sense of superiority and dignity, is and remains the hero of the European master narrative about the freedom of personality and of personal thinking, of moral autonomy. Especially about the defense of all these freedoms against tyranny: the tyranny of the tyrant, of the masses, of public opinion. Kant also spoke in the spirit of this tradition, in inventing the formula of the categorical imperative. The moral law, so he suggested, represents humankind within us, and not outside us.

Master narrative of republicanism

The third European master narrative on freedom that works on the Greek/Roman heritage is a complex one. It revives, applies and retells several stories about political and other institutions, their creation, survival and vicissitudes. The texts of philosophers, writers, yet first and foremost the texts of historians, are the essential sources of this complex master narrative. Let me mention only one of the sources, *Parallel Lives* by Plutarch. The social and political imagination of European historical actors has been deeply influenced and shaped by those stories until the full development of modernity.

Here are for example the foundation stories and the histories of the mythological 'founding fathers' from Lycurgos to Romulus and Remus. Machiavelli, the first modern political author, dwells – Discorsi – in length at the narratives of founding fathers, including Moses, of course. Needless to say, the United States has also its own founding fathers, this time not mythological ones. The gesture of foundation is said to be always a free gesture and as such creation out of nothing.

An entirely new political entity is thus created and established not just by laying foundations, but also by establishing basic institutions which will secure the longevity and the stability of the political entity, standing institutions, which allow change without changing themselves and which will protect the political body against tyranny. The protection of the great standing institutions against external and internal enemies requires heroic deeds. Greek and Roman master narratives provide Europeans with role models, among other role models of 'defenders of freedom' such as Brutus – both of them – the Gracchus brothers, Cato and so on.

Machiavelli's story, however, continues, and the continuation of the story is also an essential aspect of this master narrative. The continuation of the story sounds roughly this: times go on and people get accustomed to their liberties, they cease to care for them; they get richer, they become used to luxuries, morals sink from bad to worse, the tyrant stands before the door. Perhaps the story will end with the establishment of tyranny, and perhaps not. There is an alternative, namely revolution. Revolution is but the return to the beginning, to the gesture of foundation where the story can begin again. This master narrative is kept alive in political theory until the present day, from Rousseau to Hannah Arendt. Arendt's concept of new beginning, natality, modernizes the traditional freedom narrative, whereas in her book *On Revolution*, she also expresses her hope that perhaps even America might return to the glorious past of its foundation, the constitution of liberties (Arendt 1991).

Yet it is not just the story about establishing/losing/regaining freedom that gets constantly worked upon and re-told. Several concrete institutions presented in ancient philosophy and history book serve as models for new, and even for modern institutions. The drive to repeat is a well-known drive presented in the stories, yet it characterizes actors also in relation to the stories. The new is nowadays not rationally legitimated as something that has already been tried with success as in pre-modern times, yet reference to the old still makes the new emotionally more acceptable. Here is for example the story about the Roman Republic, the idea of the republic and republicanism included. The Latin term, *res publica*, 'the common thing' rings a bell also today. Here are the people's tribunes, that is, the emergence of the institution of representation, an institution which remains until the present day, one of the major pillars of modern democracy. Napoleon became first a consul, then an emperor, according the script of the master narrative, although he claimed the second step also as the continuation of the master narrative of freedom. Americans have their Senate, like the Romans, 'senatus populusque romanus' mutated into Senate and Congress. The function and the content of those institutions change, they are not copy-cat institutions.

Yet, there is a lesson in this old European master narrative, which constantly returns even in times of hereditary monarchies, first in free cities, in the institutions of the nobility, later also in the institutions of some protestant denominations, which will occupy the central place in modernity. And this is the following lesson or creed: the highest power is not enjoyed during one's whole life, for one is selected or elected for a limited time, power is thus temporary. It turns out, that the idea of the freedom of choice we are familiar with as the first master narrative on freedom from the Bible, is not only relevant in moral matters. One can freely choose in politics too, and what is true in the case of a moral decision, is true also in politics. One can regret one's choice and might choose next time differently and better.

The master story of republicanism is the master story of pluralism as well. It is also the story about the fragility of political freedom. The demise of the Roman Republic confronts us with the most horrifying spectacle: mass murder, mass executions, proscription, theft, civil wars, debauchery, fundamentalism – all in one. And, at the end comes the Empire, despotism. Others stories can also be told, and are told about the Imperial Rome, the stories of pluralism, of diversity, of early Christianity, yet as far as the freedom narrative is concerned, the outcome is the loss of republican freedom. Emperor Nero became the hero of the master narrative of the absolute loss of freedom, the European master narrative about despotism. For almost two thousand years the name Nero became identical with the freedom lost, the metaphor for the unlimited power of one single person who uses it for murder out of lust and whim. Nero's story is the indirect freedom story. It works as a warning: Freedom can be a burden, but the loss of freedom is the unlimited disaster itself. Only in the twentieth-century did Nero lose his pride of place as a metaphor of European despotism, for this place has been since occupied by Hitler and Stalin.

All master narratives of freedom speak also about the fragility of freedom. Freedom is burdensome, it goes with too much responsibility, liberty is difficult, as Levinas put it. Freedom does not promise immediate wish fulfillment, happiness, nor even personal security. If we start to rethink all the European master narratives about freedom we can draw a fairly pessimistic picture. Let me rehash the stories. Cain was free to choose between good and evil, and he chose evil. The people of Israel abandoned the God who liberated them from bondage and worshipped instead the golden calf. Jesus of Nazareth was crucified. Socrates drank the hemlock. After having flourished for a while, free republics wither and despotism prospers.

But the presentation of defeat has nothing to do with pessimism. If we ask the question whether it was, whether it is, worth the while, all the master stories on freedom give an unambiguous answer: yes it was, it is absolutely worth the while. Only those things that are worth having can be lost. Life is dear because my life and those who are dear to me will be certainly lost. Freedom is dear, because my freedom and the freedom of those dear to me can be eventually lost. Yet not certainly lost. Working on the master narratives on freedom is to work on freedom.

Conclusion

I have told a very short story about the European master narratives on freedom. These are the stories which are interpreted, used, applied, exploited, remade by thinkers, actors and storytellers who are living in this tradition. These are the texts in which we recognize ourselves, whether we are dwelling on the subcontinent called Europe or have carried the sweet burden of master narratives with us to the new world, whether we are Catholics, Protestants or Jewish, rich or poor. These are the fundamental principles of the European culture.

Yet, let me repeat, each and every national culture or culture of an ethnicity, a people, a religion, even a human group, a profession, a sect, a family, has its own little master narratives which they understand without footnotes, yet others do not. And what is obvious without even saying: the great ancient civilizations of India, China, Japan and others have their own universal master narratives, and so have all cultures and all people. 'Humankind as such': has however none, although one narrative can be translated into the language of the other with more or less success, and the different interpretations of various narratives can enter into a dialogue with each other. An *okumene* of the master narratives in general is not likely to be formed and it is, perhaps, not even desirable, yet an *okumene* of freedom narratives would be desirable, and, I hope, not entirely beyond reach.

I spoke only about those master narratives – the European master narratives on freedom – which, I hope, could perhaps form an *okumene* with other master narratives on freedom. Yet European master narratives are far broader and far more variegated and multifaceted than the master narratives on freedom. I mention only a few. One of the fundamental master narratives, termed metaphysics, has centered and still centers it inquiry around the question: 'whether there is something rather than nothing'. There is the master story of time, temporality, including eschatology, messianic message, there is the master story of incarnation or embodiment and the master narrative of friendship from Aristotle through Shakespeare to Derrida. The master narrative of 'amour passion', the master narrative on art, religion and philosophy, the master narrative of fate, good and bad luck, the master narrative of necessity and of contingency. And so on. I do not think that in case of those and other European master narratives an *okumene* of cultures would be desirable, even if it were possible. Let us remain different and let us remain curious.

At the end I quote the title of a wonderful book by Hans Blumenberg, *Work on Myth*. I think that as far as European culture is concerned, the title is a misnomer since European culture exists – and it has not existed in times of ancient Greeks and Romans, only since the times of the combination of the two sources of master narratives – we never work on myths, we work on master narratives (Blumenberg 1988). European culture is conspicuously void of myths. This is why Greek and Roman mythologies do not belong to our master narratives. Whether to live without myths, yet with master narratives, is an asset or a shortcoming, I cannot decide. No one can decide. One makes just emotional judgments, confessions of love or hatred, or both. This is why I have to end this essay with a confession. I love master narratives more than myths.

References

Arendt, H. (1991) *On Revolution*, Harmondsworth: Penguin.
Blumenberg, H. (1988) *Work on Myth*, Cambridge, MA.: MIT Press.
Geertz, C. (1973) *The Interpretation of Cultures,* New York: Basic Books.
Nietzsche, F. (1996) *On the Genealogy of Morals: A Polemic: By Way of Clarification and Supplement to My Last Book Beyond Good and Evil*, Oxford: Oxford University Press.
Steinbeck, J. (1995) *The Moon is Down*, Harmondsworth: Penguin.

20

Modernity and the escape from Eurocentrism

Gerard Delanty

The notion of modernity is a major preoccupation of recent social theory. The new thinking on modernity, which is a response to the postmodern/postcolonial critique and the growing consciousness of cosmopolitan currents in the world today and diverse expressions of globalization, represents one of the most exciting and important prospects for a cosmopolitan and critical social theory. The turn to modernity since the late 1980s can be explained by a dissatisfaction with the older ideas of modernization, on the one hand, and on the other capitalism as the key features of modern society (Haferkamp and Smelser 1992). The idea of modernity indicated a concern with issues and dimensions of modern society that were largely ignored by the allegedly functionalist, teleological and Eurocentric assumptions of modernization theory. World-Systems Analysis had already brought about a major theoretical change, which was critical in shaping the turn to globalization. As Marxist theory with its primary concern with the overcoming of capitalism went into abeyance, the focus on modernity suggested a more fruitful theoretical approach to interpret modern society. Influenced by the cultural and historical turn in the social and human sciences, a much strengthened social theory of modernity has endured the postmodern attack on modernity. Unable to announce a new departure, the postmodern moment can now be seen to be merely modernity in a new key, as Bauman has argued (Bauman 1987). Ever more numerous reinterpretations of modernism have also contributed to the relevance of modernity (Bernan 1982; Calinescu 1987; Kumar 1995; Childs 2000; Jameson 2003). What has emerged out of these developments is a new interest in 'cultural modernity' a counter-movement in modern society, but also in historical semantics (Koselleck 1984; Turner 1990, Yack 1997; Friese and Wagner 2000). If modernity is now more likely to be seen as an 'incomplete project', to use Habermas's formulation, it is also one that is on 'endless trial', to cite Kolakowski, and in Eisenstadt's terms has multiple forms (Habermas 1987b; Kolakowski 1990; Eisenstadt 2003). In the terms of Koselleck's historical semantics, it is the constantly changing interpretation of the present by reference to its past and to the open horizon of its future (Koselleck 1984).

The critical question today as far as the social theory of modernity is concerned is its relevance to global transformations and whether it can escape Eurocentrism (Kahn 2001). One of the main objections to the notion of modernity – and which was the basis of the postmodern and postcolonial critiques – was its allegedly Eurocentric nature. While the teleological, linear and functionalist assumptions of modernization theory became less central, the idea of modernity in the view of many critics was not a fundamental advance; failing especially to question the separation of tradition and modernity, the impact of colonization and various processes of localization, such as indigenization, vernacularization and hybridization. Modernity, its critics argued, was based on exclusion and was a Eurocentric construct by which the world could be intellectually mastered by the West. Habermas's vision of modernity, itself one of the more influential ideas, in the 1980s was almost entirely based on an 'Occidental understanding of the world', tied as it was to the completion of the eighteenth-century European Enlightenment project (Habermas 1984: 44; Delanty 1997). This is also true of Giddens's social theory and the notion of reflexive modernization (Giddens 1990; Beck *et al.* 1994). However, current developments in social theory, including Habermas's own social theory, seem to suggest that in fact modernity can be reconciled to a critical and non-Eurocentric social theory and that much of the accusations of orientalism are unfounded and even confused (Dallmayr 1996; McLellan 2000, 2003). This is reflected in theories of multiple modernities, alternative and even counter modernities, global modernities, hybrid and entangled modernities.

In this chapter I will attempt to assess critically the claim that modernity is Eurocentric and what the limits of Eurcentrism are, especially in relation to European modernity. A good place to begin with is to define the notion of Eurocentrism and to explore some possible alternative visions of modernity.

Eurocentrism – myth or hegemonic design?

The concept of Eurocentrism refers to certain assumptions of western social and political thought. In the most straightforward and literal sense of the term, Eurocentrism is the assumption that Europe or the West constitutes the centre of the world (Amin 1989; Young 1991; Blaut 1993; Latouche 1996; Wallerstein 1996; Chakrabarty 2000). The contrary to Eurocentrism would presumably be the view that there are many centres and the West is only one such centre. The difficulty with this position is that while it can be argued the world consists of many centres, the West has been particularly successful in imposing, in the form of westernization, its model on much of the rest of the world. So the term Eurocentrism does not mean anything not contained in the concept of imperialism.

A related usage of the term is the notion of western universalism, the claim that western modernity is universally valid. The counter position to this is the argument that there are different 'universalisms' and that therefore European/western univeralism must be relativized. While being an argument advanced by postcolonialism, anti-Eurocentrism can be related to much of modern European thought, which has argued for the relativity of all values. Indeed, it could be argued that anti-Eurocentrism is inherent in European culture (Brague 2002).

In a stronger sense, the term is an attack on the claim to the inherent superiority of Europe over the rest of the world. Identifying imperialism as the dark side of European civilization, proponents of anti-Eurocentricism argue that there is nothing morally superior about the West. There are certainly some academics who argue that West is morally superior to the non-Western world and in the view of others Eurcentrism is embedded in everyday life as well as in populist notions such as the 'clash of civilizations' (Shohat and Stam 1994). However, since most scholars do not promulgate such claims concerning the superiority of the West, an anti-Eurocentric position would be at most a reflexive awareness rather than a theoretical or methodological approach.

There is little doubt that the notion of Eurocentrism is generally used in the sense intended by Edward Said to mean 'orientalism' (Turner 1994). Said argued the Orient was a construction of the West, which cannot 'know' the Orient since the Orient was invented by the West and served as an intellectual strategy to legitimize colonialism (Said 1978). In this sense, then, Eurocentrism is an ethnocentric way of thinking about the Other. Although greatly influential, the orientalist critique, has been hotly contested. Among the criticisms are that all western views on the non-western world cannot be included in the same category (for example, German Enlightenment writings on the Orient certainly cannot be equated with late nineteenth-century French and British colonial writings for instance). The orientalist thesis also ignores the existence of Occidentalism, which is another expression of ethnocentrism (Buruma and Margalit 2004; Carrier 1995).

Within the social sciences, Eurocentrism has often been expressed in criticisms of the 'rise of the West' debate. For example, Max Weber's famous opening sentence to *The Protestant Ethic and the Spirit of Capitalism* (1930 [1904–1905]) – 'A Product of modern European civilization, studying any problem of universal history, is bound to ask himself to what combination of circumstances the fact should be attributed that in Western civilization, and in Western civilization only, cultural phenomena have appeared which (as we like to think) lie in a line of development having universal significance and value' – has often been an invitation to denounce Eurocentricism in modern scholarship. Aside from Weber's qualification, 'We like to think', the study with its thesis that modern science and Protestant ethic developed in Europe due to circumstances specific to the West can be criticized on empirical grounds as well as on normative grounds as lacking in self-critique and its tendency to see the non-European world in terms of deficiencies. A non-Eurocentric approach would thus be one that seeks to identify those features of modernity that can be found in non-Western parts of the world and where the explanation for the phenomena does not lie in western influences, but in autonomous logics of development. This is certainly one of the more positive developments in recent comparative scholarship and the basis of a great deal of new historical sociology. A non-Eurocentric, as opposed to anti-Eurocentric scholarship, would seek to identify those features of all civilizations and societies that display internal logics of development and where a western normative standard is not used as a measurement.

In sum, the concept Eurocentrism is not theoretically clear and does not suggest a particular methodological approach to modernity; it is best seen in the context of a reflexive discourse of anti-Eurocentrism entailing to varying degrees a critique of the West and in particular a critique of ideologies that distort the relation of the West to the rest of the world (see McLellan 2000). This would suggest that there is nothing inherently Eurocentric about modernity if the concept is defined in methodologically reflexive terms. However, to fully escape the charge of Eurocentrism, the notion of modernity must be considered in what might be called a cosmopolitan direction, that is a way that does not take the western route to modernity to be the universal model of development. This suggests a post-universalist notion of modernity. Moreover, as will be argued in this chapter, a cosmopolitan approach, as opposed to either an Eurocentric or an anti-Eurocentric approach, requires a conception of modernity that stresses the critical role of the interaction of different modernities under the conditions of globalization.

Modernity – the very idea

What is modernity? The term signals a condition of self-confrontation, incompleteness and renewal in which the localized past is reshaped by the present; it expresses a self-confidence in the transformative project of the present time as a liberation from the past. The word itself comes from the Latin *modus*, meaning now, but has come to taken on the stronger meaning of the belief in the possibility of a new beginning based on human autonomy. In Agnes Heller's words modernity means: 'Everything is open to query and to testing; everything is subject to rational scrutiny and refuted by argument' (Heller 1999: 41). The emergence of modernity in Europe is to be principally attributed to Christianity, which has given to it its most distinctive and abiding characteristic as a condition that is defined by a time consciousness (see Blumenberg 1983). The term 'modern' was first used – allegedly by Pope Gelasius, who could be considered the first modernist – in the fifth-century to distinguish the Christian era from the pagan age, although the term did not gain widespread currency until the seventeenth-century French 'Quarrel of the Ancients and the Moderns' on whether modern culture is superior to classical culture. But the term 'modernity' as opposed to 'modern' did not arise until the nineteenth-century. One of the most famous uses of the term was in 1864 when Baudelaire defined it: 'By modernity I mean the transitory, the fugitive, the contingent' (Baudelaire 1964: 13). This motif is also expressed in the *Communist Manifesto* as the condition 'all that is solid melts into air'. Modernity may be described simply as the loss of certainty and the realization that certainty can never be established once and for all. Whatever examples we take, modernity in the most general refers to a transformative project by which the present time defines itself by reference to a past that has been surmounted.

According to Habermas, the project of modernity entails the progressive extension of a potentially emancipatory communicative rationality to all parts of society (Habermas 1984, 1987a, 1987b). This leads to a fundamental tension at the heart of modernity between communicative rationality and instrumental rationality. It is this tension that provides the basic animus for the evolution of societies. In this view, modernity cannot be reduced to one particular structure, but is a societal condition formed out of the ongoing contestation of power. The modernity of modern societies is thus to be found in the learning processes of societies as they find communicative solutions to problems. So long as societies are in some way integrated through social processes that involve communication, modernity is incomplete. Many social theorists have stressed, what Johann Arnason aptly terms, modernity as a 'field of tensions' (Arnason 1991). Perhaps the most striking example of this is Castoriadis's characterization of modernity in terms of a radical imaginary confronting the institutional imaginary, which tries to domesticate it (Castoriadis 1987). The self-articulation of society is made possible by the radical imaginary which projects an image of an alternative society. This is such a constitutive feature of societies that even the tendency towards domination and instrumental mastery does not eliminate. This approach has been developed into a more elaborated theory of modernity by those influenced by his work, such as Johann Arnason and Agnes Heller (Heller 1999; Arnason 2003). Such approaches also give prominence to the creative dynamics and tensions in modernity which result from the pursuit of the goal of autonomy, on the one side, and on the other the pursuit of power and material accumulation. Emerging out of these dynamics are self-transformative tendencies and a conscious reflexivity. This way of theorizing modernity avoids an approach, which can be variously associated with Weber, Adorno and Horkheimer, and Foucault, that reduces modernity to the single dimension of a disciplinary apparatus of power which becomes more and more total. Avoiding this one-side approach, many theorists of modernity look instead to a double logic, which Peter Wagner has described as a relation of liberty and discipline or in Alain Touraine's terms can be seen as a struggle of Reason and the Subject (Wagner 1994, 2001; Touraine 1995; see also Delanty 1999). Another illustration of this tension within modernity is Adam Seligman's characterization of modernity in terms of a 'wager' over the nature of authority: modernity staked everything on reason and the indiviudal as opposed to the sacred. There is some evidence to suggest this bet has not been won, given the return of ethnic and religious identities (Seligman 2000: 32–33). Whether or not this bet has been won or lost, this is one way of seeing modernity as a tension that put risk at the centre of its consciousness.

We have then many examples of ways of theorizing modernity as a condition that is distinctive from a particular historical age or civilization. This view of modernity emphasizes processual aspects, especially tensions and dynamics. The forms, inter-relations and dynamics of modernity are varied and uneven, but underlying them is the most basic impetus towards self-transformation, the belief that human agency can radically transform the present in the image of an imagined future. This view of modernity as a break from the past seems to accord with the major philosophical and cultural understandings of modernity as a dynamic process that has made change itself the defining feature of modernity. Modernity is thus a particular kind of time-consciousness which defines the present in its relation to the past, which must be continuously re-translated; it is not a historical epoch than can be periodized. Modernity unfolds in different ways, according to different paces, and can take different societal forms. As a transformative process, modernity can be seen in terms of a model of translation: translations of past and present; translation of self and other; translations of the local and the global.[1]

The notion of modernity is clearly influenced by the cultural turn in the human and social sciences and contains within it resonances of modernism. It is not however, a purely cultural concept. Modernity must be differentiated into three broad dimensions: political modernity (including democratization, the law governed state, secularization, state building), cultural modernity (differentiation of science, art, morality), and the social orders of modernity (wealth creation, capitalism, technology, militarism).

Modernity or postmodernity?

The notion of a radical rupture between modernity and postmodernity must be rejected. Modernity is an on-going process that has many dimensions. There has been a notable tendency in recent times to view postmodernity as part of modernity rather than a radical break from it, a development that it is evident in the work of Zygmunt Bauman (1987). This is also true too of Frederic Jameson, who, in one of the most influential works on postmodernism, sees postmodernism as a reflection of the 'cultural logic' of capitalism in its current phase and not an entirely new kind of society (Jameson 1991). Thus in recent postmodernist influenced works, the idea of the end of modernity is not to be taken too literally. Indeed, as Baudrillard (1994) has argued, the very idea of 'the end' is an illusion. It makes sense to distinguish postmodernism as an intellectual movement from the idea of postmodernity or a postmodern society. In this view postmodernism can be viewed as a critique of certain tendencies within modern thought. This is certainly the way Foucault and Lyotard understood their projects.

Postmodernism suffered from an over-emphasis on society as text which had to be simply deconstructed. Over-relying on literary influenced approaches to the reading of texts, postmodernism reached certain limits as far as social theory was concerned. While it opened social theory to new dimensions it failed to provide a theory of the distinctive nature of social processes. However, it can be noted that the concern with purely cultural discourses has even within postmodern thinking been questioned. Increasingly, we find postmodernist thinkers writing about new conceptions of the social as opposed to the purely cultural. There is also increasingly a recognition that society can no longer be seen as discursive, as in the work of Foucault. Scott Lash thus sees postmodernist categories as less relevant to the new kinds of informational power that exist today and argues for a reinterpretation of the idea of modernity (Lash 2002: 3).

It is worth bearing in mind that postmodernism as a term was primarily a theory of culture and while it was compatible with certain epistemological developments in French post-structuralism it was never intended to be a social theory as such. Postmodernism was strictly speaking a movement within architecture and the arts, principally literature, that expressed a revolt against the rigid formalism of modernism, which it sought to revitalize in the form of an emphasis on emancipating 'content' from the structured and ahistorical 'form' of the modernist aesthetic. In bringing art and life closer together, postmodernism brought the aesthetic imagination to the brink of radical politics. Postmodernism received a philosophical basis in the poststructuralist revolt against Lévi-Strauss and the prevailing systems of thought in post-Second World War philosophy. Postmodernism was, in general, a revolt against just one tendency within modernity, but was not itself a movement against modernity. Indeed, Michel Foucault, who in the view of many exemplifies postmodern thought, never used the term postmodernism and saw his work as a search for what he called 'counter-movements' within modernity (Foucault 1997: 312).

The idea of postmodernity has now clearly entered a new phase in which the notion of a 'cultural modernity' has given rise to the idea of 'alternative modernities' (Gaonkar 2001). Central to this shift in the conceptualization of modernity is the question whether modernity must be theorized in the plural or singular. Until now the notion of an alternative modernity was generally discussed as part of the wider European cultural modernity. It was generally in these terms that the debate about postmodernism was discussed. The notion of 'alternative modernities' did not enter the picture. In that sense, postmodernism was an expression of western late or contemporary modernity. Is there one or many modernities; or, it possible to conceive of modernity in way that does justice to these dimensions?

The idea of multiple modernities?

There is general agreement that modernity does not take one form but many. But beyond that acknowledgement of the plural nature of modernity there is little agreement on methodological implications or even clarity on the nature of the problem. Is there one model of modernity or are there several forms? The search for a non-Eurocentric theory of modernity leads to a number of possible models, which can be briefly assessed.

The idea of an alternative modernity is one of the most obvious solutions to the tendency to see modernity as uniformity. This notion has been implicit in, for example, the *Sonderweg* [exceptional path] thesis of German modernity. According to this view, the path to modernity embarked on by Germany was a divergent one based on delayed modernization and ultimately regression. Another instance of this tendency to look for alternative routes to modernity is the notion of 'American exceptionalism' (Lipset and Marks 2000). The main problem with this approach to modernity is the assumption that there is a universal norm and everything that does not accord with it must be understood as aberrant. Yet, the notion of an alternative cannot be too easily dismissed, as this is essential for a critical perspective (Eder 1985). There is clearly some value in seeing Soviet communism and fascism as anti-modern movements if by that we mean movements that reacted to certain currents in modernity (Furet 1999). But the assumption that these movements are not just alternatives but counter-modernities, which arose and declined in the twentieth-century, and were not in fact modern at all is highly questionable. Johann Arnason has argued persuasively against this tendency,

271

claiming that Soviet communism was not merely 'anti-modern' but was a failed experiment with modernity (Arnason 1993). Communism and fascism were modernist projects, animated as they were by some of the most captivating of modern ideas – for example the belief that it is possible for elites to reconstruct society in the image of the state and bring about a new order, the vision of – what Toulmin calls – a total cosmopolis (Toulmin 1994). While there is indeed something unsatisfactory about the idea of an 'alternative' or divergent path to a successful or underlying modernity that has become dominant, the debate on alternative modernities had the virtue of pointing to different societal paths to modernity.

A second approach is to abandon altogether the idea of an alternative modernity that has emerged in opposition to a dominant one. The most interesting, but under-theorized, approach is the idea of 'multiple modernities' or – to use a term some authors favour – 'alternative modernities'. In this view associated with the work of a very broad spectrum of scholars, modernity is pluralized into a numerous societal and cultural forms (Al-Azmeh 1993; Taylor 1999; Gaonkar 2001; Eisenstadt 2000a, 2000b; Delanty 2003; Kaya 2003; Kamali 2005). When generalized to the wider world, modernity needs to be radically de-historicized, it is argued; it cannot be conceptualized in terms of some of the western processes of modernization. Islamism can be seen as a different expression of modernity (Sayyid, 2003). When viewed in this light, it would even appear that the notion of a singular modernity has in fact inherited too many of the assumptions of modernization theory, for instance certain assumptions about nation-state formation, capitalism and secularization. The idea of multiple modernities points to an epistemic break from a conception of modernity as a historical condition that with some delays and modifications has been generalized to the rest of the world; it also avoids a purely institutional conception of modernity, as entailing, for example, the separation of state and church. One of the leading proponents of the idea of multiple modernities is S. N. Eisenstadt.

Following in the footsteps of the comparative historical sociologies of Weber and Nelson, Eisenstadt (1986, 2000a, 2000b, 2001, 2003) has argued that the origins of modernity go back to the great civilizations of the world whose universalistic cultures the Great Revolutions of the early modern period partly took over and transformed. European civilization provided the major entry into modernity, which has become a global civilization today, he argues. Eisenstadt sees modernity as global but not necessarily universal, in the sense that modernity is culturally appropriated in different ways: 'The actual developments in modern or – as they were then designated – modernizing societies have gone far beyond the homogenizing and hegemonic assumptions of the original European or western programme of modernity' (Eisenstadt 2001: 329). Eisenstadt's thesis is that the 'multiple and divergent modernities' crystallized during the nineteenth- and twentieth-centuries; modernity was a process of continued revolution and upheaval arising out of its contradictions and antinomies. Eisenstadt remains convinced that modernity is not just global, but is a new civilization and that this is primarily one shaped by the initial impetus of western modernity.

Eisenstadt's writings on multiple modernities have established a basis for future scholarship. Other developments in 'historical sociology beyond orientalism' also suggest many important directions to a reconceptualization of East and West in a direction that also avoids the 'modernity versus tradition' dichotomy.[2] Among the many questions that this opens up, a central one is this: was there a particular historical moment or phase when a parallel development occurred across the eastern and western parts of the Eurasian macro-region? (see Arnason 2003). Such a perspective might help to analyse the diverse – but also, to a degree, the convergent – trends in earlier epochs and, in addition, might be able to specify the nature of a later 'great divergence' leading to the rise of the West (McNeill 1980). But how useful is the idea of multiple modernities? What conceptual advances does it make?

One of the main problems with the idea of multiple modernities is that modernity becomes the functional equivalent for nations. How many modernities can there be? The danger is that modernity becomes a numerical condition that can be infinitely pluralized to the point that it is devoid of analytical clarity and explanatory power. Thus we have an Islamic modernity, a Japanese modernity, an African modernity, a Turkish modernity, an Iranian modernity. The result is that we are not much better off than we were with a comparison of different patterns of nation-state formation. Eisenstadt (2000b) and Wittrock (2000) caution against such tendencies, arguing that modernity itself refers to the features that are common to the diverse forms of modernity. However, the debate on multiple modernities does not appear to have advanced beyond a general recognition that modernity takes more than one form. A second problem is that the idea of multiple modernities might reinforce a view of different modernities isolated from each other and being static, rather than processual, transformative and interpenetrating. In sum, the transformative logic within modernity tends to be neglected in favour of a multiplicity.

Modernity cannot be reduced to a cultural or national context as such without rendering the concept meaningless. For this reason Wolfgang Knöbl argues that modernization theory is not quite superceded by the new social theory of modernity (Knöbl 2003). Several sociologists have found that not all of the central tenets of functionalist theory have been rendered irrelevant, especially when divested of teleological notions (Mouzelis 1999; Holmwood and O'Malley 2003; see also Bendix 1967). For example, Ernst Gellner, who operated within this tradition, favoured an emphasis on uneven modernization to comprehend the diverse development of modernization in many countries. His argument, which reflected a questioning of earlier modernization theory, was that uneven modernization created conditions for nationalism and various backlashes to modernity (Gellner 1983). Neo-functionalism, sought to give stronger attention to the role of agency in responding to modernization (Alexander and Colomy 1990) and, albeit from the perspective of 'late modernity', Beck et al. (1994) introduced the notion of 'reflexive modernization' to refer to a condition in which modernity is now essentially concerned with the problems generated in an earlier phase of modernity.[3] Mouzelis (1999) has argued that modernity is not westernization and its key processes and dynamics can be found in all societies. But the implications of these ideas for an understanding of the plural nature of modernity are far from clear.

Given that we are back to modernity again, an alternative some authors have proposed is the notion of 'entangled modernities' to indicate the enmeshed, interconnected nature of modernities and that there is not just multiple but overlapping ones (Arnason 2003a; Therborn 2003). Such a position has clear advantages over the idea of a postmodern non-Western world because of the obvious fact that, with few exceptions, most of the non-Western world has been to varying degrees colonized by the West. It has also had the advantage of seeing modernity as something that can exist in different forms within particular nations and cultures. However, the notion, while being interesting, offers no major advance beyond the idea of multiple modernities, since it assumes the fact of different modernities, which simply become intertwined, leading to hybrid forms (see Nederveen Pieterse 2004). The suggestion that modernity exists not just in multiple but overlapping, entangled forms points to something previously neglected in the social theory of modernity and which was always central to the older modernization theory, namely an emphasis on transformative processes and, as Johann Arnason, argues, interconnections (Arnason 2003). No account of modernity in global perspective can neglect the interactive mechanisms and processes that lie at the root of modernity as a transformative process. 'Modernities' do not simply exist as coherent or stable units, but are in a constant process of change and this is due to the nature of the particular forms of interaction, selection, combination, adaptation and processing of cultural codes, resources, imaginaries, etc.

In sum, what recent work in social theory and historical sociology points to is a conception of modernity as global, but entailing diverse paths and different kinds and degrees of realization. The debate on multiple modernities has been very fruitful in advancing the social theory of modernity beyond the limited 'Occidental understanding of the world' that was central to Enlightenment influenced theory of modernity from Kant through Weber to Parsons and Habermas. It would appear to be the case that aside from a plural dimension into the notion of modernity, the most interesting implication is the interactive dimension by which modernity emerges. By pluralizing modernity into multiple modernities, the concept is in danger of being emptied of its specificity and, taken to an extreme, it comes indistinguishable from nations; restricting it to a singular form, on the other hand, it runs the risk of failing to address the diversity of societal models and civilizational contexts. An emphasis on interactive processes suggests a cosmopolitan approach to modernity.

Towards a cosmopolitan interpretation of modernity

The argument of this chapter is that modernity should be defined neither in the singular nor in the plural; it is a condition that arises as a result of the encounter of the local with the global, but is not itself reducible to the latter. Modernity is specifically defined by a mode of transformation in which translation plays a major role. The encounter of the local with the global takes multiple forms, determined largely by the forms of cultural translation influenced by civilizational patterns and historical interactions and conflicts arising out of institutional arrangements, cultural and political factors.

This suggests a view of modernity in terms of structurations, mechanisms, translations and processes rather than a condition that is simply either heterogeneous or homogeneous. Such a view of modernity refers to a uniformity only in socio-cognitive structures, forms of consciousness, legitimation processes and certain kinds of practices and rationalities; in sum, particular modes of translation. Modernity entails common ways of doing things, certain universalistic values such as democracy; but uniformity does not extend beyond these levels since the global is appropriated, or translated, differently by the local. This might explain how modernity emerges in different places, at different times, and in different societal forms without recourse to either an inexplicable notion of heterogeneity (where the stress will be on differences) or an over-deterministic notion of homogenization (where the stress will be on similarities). The multiple crystallizations of modernity cannot be explained monocausally by reference to a homogenizing and linear evolutionary process of modernization to which all societies adapt. It is neither a question of convergences nor of divergences, but one of the diffusion of globality in different societies by social actors as a result of civilizational and cultural encounters. Modernity is not constant but evolving, since the translations it brings about are never static, for people continuously reinterpret their situation in light of their ongoing encounters with others.

Modernity, then, is necessarily global in outlook; while it first emerged in western Europe, it is not western, American or European, but is an expression of cosmopolitanism (see Appadurai 1996; Breckenridge et al. 2002). This does not mean modernity is fully globalized or is to be equated with universality. Perhaps the best example of modernity as cosmopolitan is the world-wide aspiration for democracy.

A notion of modernity as cosmopolitan as opposed to global avoids the ambiguities of notions of multiple modernities and even of 'global modernities' (Featherstone et al. 1995).

The subject of a useful volume, the idea of 'global modernities' is clearly a response to the recognition that globalization is the primary reference point for modernities as a plural condition. However, in this volume the concept is not explained and remains a vague term to indicate the diverse response to globalization and fails to distinguish globality from modernity. In the most valuable contribution to the disparate collection of chapters, Göran Therborn has argued for a notion of global modernity that stresses the routes 'to/through modernity' (Therborn 1995). Rather than begin with the premise of diversity, he argues for a notion of modernity as global but which expresses itself in major macro-regional variations, of which he lists four (the European gate of revolution or reform; the American route of independence; a route represented by Iran, Thailand and Japan based on external threat and selective imports; the route of conquest experienced by much of Africa and Asia). This is a helpful way out of the impasse of multiple modernities and succeeds in making a link with globalization as the main explanation of different responses to modernity. It also avoids the danger of reducing modernity to national trajectories. But a limiting factor is that it stresses too much globalization as the condition of modernity. Nevertheless the idea of global modernity has the advantage of avoiding purely cultural explanations of the various forms of modernity, an argument that is also reflected in Arlif Dirlik's claim that modernity is a global and that it makes little sense arguing there are non-global modernities (Dirlik 2003). We need to reconcile the diversity of societal forms with a conception of modernity that acknowledges the consequences of globalization. The proposal I am making, then, is to see globalization – as a process that intensifies connections, enhances possibilities for cultural translations and deepens the consciousness of globality – as the principal motor of modernity. But modernity is not a global condition as such, or in Eisenstadt's terms a new civilization, but a transformative condition which can be called cosmopolitan due to its plural nature and interactive logics.

If modernity arises in the encounter of the particular with the universal, the local with the global, it can be found in many historical contexts.[4] The European Renaissance, Enlightenment, the social movements of the nineteenth-century were all expressions of this movement, which today has spread across the globe in a process of continuous social transformation. The forms, inter-relations and dynamics of modernity are varied and uneven, but underlying them is the most basic impetus towards self-transformation, the belief that human agency can radically transform the present in the image of an imagined future. This view of modernity as a break from the past seems to accord with the major philosophical and cultural understandings of modernity as a dynamic process that has made change itself the defining feature of modernity. Modernity is thus a particular kind of time-consciousness which defines the present in its relation to the past which must be continuously recreated; it is not a historical epoch than can be periodized. Modernity unfolds in different ways, according to different paces, modes of translation and can take different societal forms.

Viewed in this light, there is a solution to the question of whether modernity had an independent origin in the non-Western world. For example is there a tradition of civil society and the public specific to Muslim societies? While historical instances can be found of tendencies towards modernity, the inescapable conclusion is that although modernity in Muslim societies evolved in the encounter with the West – whether through colonization or cultural diffusion – it is possible nevertheless to speak of independent societal forms of modernity; that is, diverse local responses to globality (see Kamali 2005). This is also true of debates about human rights and other discourses of rights in the rest of the world. Universalistic notions of rights and particularistic cultural traditions are today mutually elucidated in each other's discourses (Cowan *et al.* 2001).

Conclusion: a post-universalist notion of modernity

The conception of modernity outlined in this chapter emphasizes the interactive dimension, both in terms of the relation between particularity and universality, on the one side, and on the other between globality and locality. Rather than define modernity as a singular or as a multiple condition it can be defined in terms of a logic of transformation. 'Modernities' do not simply exist as coherent or stable units, but are in a constant process of change. This is due to the nature of the particular forms of interaction, selection, combination, adaptation and processing of cultural codes, resources, imaginaries etc. The tendency to multiplicity within modernity was always present, but it has taken on an advanced significance today as a result of globalization which has led to the growing consciousness of modernity in many parts of the world. With this comes different cultural expressions of modernity and new conflicts between different societal and civilizational models of modernity. It should be noted, as Eisenstadt has argued, that the tensions produced by modernity can be both creative as well as destructive. Modernity, which itself is based on tensions, takes different forms, which in turn produced conflicts, including creative outcomes and new models of modernity. Viewed in this way, modernity is not Eurocentric but is post-universalistic since it entails ongoing pluralization and contestation. While it is driven by globalization, modernity arises when the particular and the universal meet; or, where the local and the global interact. It is this interactive dimension that constitutes the cosmopolitanism of modernity since through it different modernities interact.

Notes

1 For a more extensive discussion on modernity as translation, see Delanty (2005).
2 See various contributions to Delanty and especially Arnason (2003b) and Isin (2003).
3 In this work, the notion of a new age of 'reflexive modernization' is almost exclusively based on late western modernity and suffers from an inadequate theory of tradition as prior to modernity.
4 It also makes sense to speak of 'early modernities'. Modernity refers to a particular kind of con-sciousness or socio-cognitive form that has now become global but takes different social, political, economic and cultural forms (Eisenstadt and Wittrock 1998).

References

Al-Azmeh, A. (1993) *Islam and Modernity,* London: Verso.

Alexander, J. and Colomy, P. (1990) *Differentiation Theory and Social Change*, New York: Columbia University Press.

Amin, S. (1989) *Eurocentrism*, London: Zed Books.

Appadurai, A. (1996) *Modernity at Large: Cultural Dimensions of Globalization*, Minneapolis: University of Minnesota Press.

Arnason, J. (1991) 'Modernity as a Project and as a Field of Tension', in A. Honneth and H. Joas (eds) *Communicative Action*, Cambridge: Polity.

Arnason, J. (1993) *The Future that Failed: Origins and Destinies of the Soviet Model*, London: Routledge.

Arnason, J. (1997) *Social Theory and Japanese Experience: The Dual Civilization*, London: Kegan Paul International.

Arnason, J. (2003) *Civilizations in Dispute: Historical Questions and Theoretical Traditions*, Leiden: Brill.

Baudelaire, C. (1964) 'The Painter of Modern Life', in C. Baudelaire *The Painter of Modern Life and Other Essays*, London: Phaidon Press.

Baudrillard, (1994) *The Illusion of the End*, Cambridge: Polity Press.

Bauman, Z. (1987) *Legislators and Interpreters: On Modernity, Postmodernity and Intellectuals*, Cambridge: Polity.

Beck, U., Giddens, A. and Lash, S. (1994) *Reflexive Modernization*, Cambridge: Polity Press.

Bendix, R. (1967) 'Tradition and Modernity Reconsidered' *Comparative Studies in Society and History*, 9(3), 292–346.

Berman, M. (1982) *All that is Solid Melts into the Air: The Experience of Modernity*, New York: Simon and Schuster.

Blaut, J. D. (1993) *The Coloniser's Model of the World: Geographical Diffusionism and Eurocentric History*, London: Guildford Press.

Blumenberg, H. (1983) *The Legitimacy of the Modern Age*, Cambridge, MA: MIT Press.

Brague, R. (2002) *Eccentric Culture: A Theory of Western Civilization*, South Bend, IN: St Augustine's Press.

Breckenridge, C., Pollock, S., Bhabha, H. K. and Chakbarty, D. (eds) (2002) *Cosmopolitanism*, Durham, NJ: Duke University Press.

Buruma, I. and Margalit, A. (2004) *Occidentalism: The West in the Eyes of its Enemies*, London: Penguin Press.

Calinescu, M. (1987) *Five Faces of Modernism*, Durham, N.C.: Duke University Press.

Carrier, J. G. (1995) *Occidentalism: Images of the West*, Oxford: Oxford University Press.

Castoriadis, C. (1987) *The Imaginary Institution of Society*, Cambridge: Polity.

Childs, P. (2000) *Modernism*, London: Routledge.

Chakrabarty, D. (2000) *Provencializing Europe: Postcolonial Thought and Historical Difference*, Princeton: Princeton University Press.

Cowan, Jane K, Dembour, M.-B. and Wilson, R. A. (eds) (2001) *Culture and Rights: Anthropological Perspectives*, Cambridge: Cambridge University Press.

Dallmayr, F. (1996) *Beyond Orientalism: Essays on Cross-Cultural Encounter*, New York: SUNY Press.

Delanty, G. (1997) 'Habermas and Occidental Rationalism: The Politics of Identity, Social Learning and the Cultural Limits of Moral Universalism', *Sociological Theory*, 15 (3), 30–59.

Delanty, G. (1999) *Social Theory in a Changing World: Conceptions of Modernity*, Cambridge: Polity Press.

Delanty, G. (2000) *Modernity and Postmodernity: Knowledge, Power and the Self*, London: Sage.

Delanty, G. (2003) 'Japan and Modernity' in U. Beck, N. Sznaider and R. Winter (eds) *Global America: The Cultural Consequences of Globalization*, Liverpool: Liverpool University Press.

Delanty, G. (2005) 'Cultural Translations and European Modernity', in E. Ben-Rafael and Y. Sternberg (eds) *Comparing Modern Civilizations: Pluralism versus Homogeneity*, Leiden: Brill.

Delanty, G. and Isin, E. (eds) (2003) *The Handbook of Historical Sociology*, London: Sage.

Dirlik, A. (2003) 'Global Modernity? Modernity in an Age of Global Capitalism', *European Journal of Social Theory*, 6(3), 275–292.

Eder, K. (1985) *Geschichte als Lernprozess? Zur Pathogenese politischer Modernität in Deutschland*, Frankfurt: Suhrkamp.

Eisenstadt, S. N. (ed.) (1986) *The Origins and Diversity of the Axial Age Civilizations*, New York: SUNY Press.

Eisenstadt, S. N. (1995) *Japanese Civilization: A Comparative View*, Chicago: University of Chicago Press.

Eisenstadt, S. N. (2000a) 'The Civilizational Dimension in Sociological Analysis', *Thesis Eleven*, 62, 1–21.

Eisenstadt, S. N. (ed.) (2000b) Special Issue on Multiple Modernities, *Daedalus*, 129(1).

Eisenstadt, S. N. (2001) 'The Civilizational Dimension of Modernity', *International Sociology*, 16(3), 320–340.

Eisenstadt, S. N. (2003) *Comparative Civilizations and Multiple Modernities*, vols 1 and 2, Leiden: Brill.

Eisenstadt, S. N. and Wittrock, B. (1998) *Daedalus*, Special Issue on Early Modernities vol. 127(3).

Featherstone, M., Lash, S. and Robertson, R. (eds) (1995) *Global Modernities*, London: Sage.

Friese, H. and Wagner, P. (2000) 'When the Light of the Great Cultural Problems Moves on: On the Possibility of a Cultural Theory of Modernity', *Thesis Eleven*, 61, 25–40.

Foucault, M. (1997) 'What is Enlightenment?' in P. Rabinow (ed.) *Michel Foucault: The Essential Works* vol. 1, *Ethics*, London: Allen Lane.

Furet, F. (1999) *The Passing of an Illusion: The Idea of Communism in the Twentieth Century*, Chicago: Chicago University Press.

Gaonkar, D. P. (ed.) (2001) *Alternative Modernities*, Durham, NC: Duke University Press.

Gellner, E. (1983) *Nations and Nationalism*, Oxford: Blackwell.

Giddens, A. (1990) *The Consequences of Modernity*, Cambridge: Polity Press.

Habermas, J. (1984) *The Theory of Communicative Action*, vol 1, Cambridge: Polity Press.

Habermas, J. (1987a) *The Theory of Communicative Action*, vol. 2, Cambridge: Polity Press.

Habermas, J. (1987b) *The Philosophical Discourse of Modernity*, Cambridge MA: MIT Press.

Haferkamp, H. and Smelser, N. (eds) (1992) *Social Change and Modernity*, Berkeley: California University Press.

Heller, A. (1999) *A Theory of History*, Oxford: Blackwell.

Holmwood, J. and O'Malley, M. (2003) 'Evolutionary and Functionalist Historical Sociology', in G. Delanty and I. Isin (eds) *Handbook of Historical Sociology*, London: Sage.

Jameson, F. (1991) *Postmodernism, or, the Cultural Logic of Late Capitalism*, Durham, NC: Duke University Press.

Jameson, F. (2003) *A Singular Modernity: Essays on Ontology of the Present*, London: Verso.

Kahn, J. (2001) *Modernity and Exclusion*, London: Sage.

Kamali, M. (2005) *Multiple Modernities, Civil Society, and Islam: The Case of Iran and Turkey*, Liverpool: Liverpool University Press.

Kaya, I. (2003) *Social Theory and later Modernities: The Turkish Experience*, Liverpool: Liverpool University Press.

Knöbl, W. (2003) 'Theories that Won't Pass Away: The Never Ending Story of Modernization Theory', in G. Delanty and I. Isin (eds) *Handbook of Historical Sociology*, London: Sage.

Kolakowski, L. (1990) 'Modernity on Endless Trial', in L. Kolakowski *Modernity on Endless Trial*, Chicago: Chicago University Press.

Koselleck, R. (1984) *Futures Past: On the Semantics of Historical Time*, Cambridge, MA: MIT Press.

Kumar, K. (1995) *From the Post-Industrial Society to Post-Modern Society*, Oxford: Blackwell.

Lash, S. (2002) *Another Modernity; Another Rationality*, Oxford: Blackwell.

Latouche, S. (1996) *The Westernization of the World*, Cambridge: Polity Press.

Lipset, M. and Marks, G. (2000) *It Didn't Happen Here: Why Socialism Failed in the United States*, New York: Norton.

McLellan, G. (2000) 'Sociology's Eurocentrism and the "Rise of the West" Revisted', *European Journal of Social Theory*, 3(3), 275–291.

McLellan, G. (2003) 'Sociology, Eurocentrism and Postcolonial Theory', *European Journal of Social Theory*, 6(1), 69–86.

McNeill, W. (1980) *Poly-ethnicity and National Unity in World History*, Toronto: University of Toronto Press.

Mouzelis, N. (1999) 'Modernity: A Non-European Conceptualization', *British Journal of Sociology*, 50(1), 141–159.

Nederveen Pieterse, J. (2004) *Globalization and Culture*, New York: Rowman & Littlefield.

Robertson, R. (1992) *Globalization: Social Theory and Global Culture*, London: Sage.

Said, E. (1978) *Orientalism*, Hardmonsworth: Penguin.

Sayyid, S. (2003) *A Fundamental Fear: Eurocentism and the Emergence of Islamism*, 3rd edition, London: Verso.

Seligman, A. (2000) *Modernity's Wager: Authority, the Self, and Transcendence*, Princeton: Princeton University Press.

Shohat, E. and Stam, R. (eds) (1994) *Unthinking Eurocentricism: Multiculturalism and the Media*, London and New York: Routledge.

Taylor, P. (1999) *Modernities: A Geopolitical Interpretation*, Cambridge: Polity Press.

Therborn, G. (1995) 'Routes to/through Modernity', in *Global Modernities*, M. Featherstone, S., Lash and R. Robertson (eds), London: Sage.

Therborn, (2003) 'Entangled Modernities', *European Journal of Social Theory*, 7(3), 293–305.

Toulmin, S. (1994) *Cosmopolis: The Hidden Agenda of Modernity*, Chicago: Chicago University Press.

Touraine, A. (1995) *Critique of Modernity*, Oxford: Blackwell.

Turner, B. S. (ed.) (1990) *Theories of Modernity and Postmodernity*, London: Sage.

Turner, B. S. (1994) *Orientalism, Postmodernism and Globalization*, London: Routledge.

Venn, C. (2000) *Occidentalism: Modernity and Subjectivity*, London: Sage.

Wagner, P. (1994) *A Sociology of Modernity: Liberty and Discipline*, London: Routledge.

Wagner, P. (2001) *Theorizing Modernity*, London: Sage.

Wallerstein, I. (1996) 'Eurocentrism and its Avatars: The Dilemmas of Social Science', *New Left Review*, 226, 93–108.

Weber, M. (1930) *The Protestant Ethic and the Spirit of Capitalism*, London: Allen & Unwin.

Wittrock, B. (2000) 'Modernity: One, None, or Many? European Origins and Modernity as a Global Condition', *Daedalus* 129(1), 31–60.

Yack, B. (1997) *The Fetishism of Modernities*, Notre Dame: University of Notre Dame Press.

Young, R. (1991) *White Mythologies: History Writing and the West*, London and New York: Routledge.

21

European transformations

William Outhwaite

The title of this chapter is neatly ambiguous between at least three processes:

1 transformations in/of Europe, whatever we take this to be;
2 transformations by Europe of other parts of the world;
3 transformations of a European (or originally European) character which may take place in Europe itself or elsewhere in the world.

I shall concentrate mainly on the first of these, but we shall have to look also at the second, and in reflecting in particular on what I take to be the defining feature of Europe in the past few centuries, namely what is usually called modernity, we shall have also to address the third.

The question 'What is Europe?' can be given a very short geographical answer and a very long historical one. The geography need not detain us long. What we call Europe is a Western peninsula of Eurasia, mostly surrounded by sea (and some islands, including the one I happen to live on) and with a land frontier conventionally located at the Ural mountains and somewhere between the Black and Caspian Seas. At the borders of Europe, both Turkey and Russia have small 'European' parts and much larger parts outside Europe, but both are often included as a whole.

The historical answer, as I threatened a moment ago, is necessarily much longer and more complex, since 'Europe' is a historically developing and 'imagined' entity. It is clearly anachronistic to talk about 'Britain' or 'France' in the Stone Age, and by the same token also to talk about 'Europe'. Logically, then, if not necessarily chronologically, Europe's first transformation is perhaps its definition by itself or by its outside as European. And this definition can of course be questioned (see Delanty 1995). If we think of the defining structures and events of what we now call Europe, we need to reflect on which of them, singly or in combination, are distinctive of Europe. Ancient Greek polyarchy as a form of intra- and interstate organisation clearly deserves a mention, as do the Macedonian and, much more importantly, Roman empires. The latter of course intersects with a third crucial element, the somewhat unexpected rise of Christianity in the Empire and subsequently as a defining element of Europe as a whole, just as Islam became a defining element of the 'middle east'.

Yet just as it is artificial to separate out English history from the rest of European history before the fifteenth-century, it is similarly anachronistic to think of Europe as a distinct entity before that time. Charlemagne's empire of the early ninth-century may have covered the territory of the original European Communities and lent his name to a building and a prize, but it had nothing to do with Europe as such. The Crusades of the thirteenth-century are resented, with some justification, as inaugurating Europe's continuing domination of the 'middle east', but they are more appropriately seen, like the rest of the history of that half-millennium (and arguably the following one too), in a broader Eurasian context. A recent popular book (Aust and Schmidt-Klingenberg 2003: 89) contains a map of the trading network of the Hanseatic League around 1400 labelled 'The EU of the middle ages', but the irony is of course intentional.

In what Europeans call the fifteenth- and sixteenth-centuries, however, something distinctively European begins to emerge, marked by the conjuncture, roughly speaking, of the Renaissance, the Reformation and the beginnings of the voyages (anticipated of course by the Vikings) of discovery and conquest. These were not, to say the least, unique or endogenous 'European' developments, but they do initiate a distinctive path: a line of development from the Renaissance to the scientific revolution and the Enlightenment, from the Reformation to the religious wars and the 'European' state model consecrated in 1648 after perhaps the first genuinely European war, and from Columbian adventures to the European colonial and semi-colonial empires of the eighteenth-, nineteenth- and twentieth-centuries. The 'discoveries' were reflected in the culture shock of Europeans confronted by alterity, otherness, and perceiving themselves in its mirror.[1] A different form of alterity closer to home was provided by the Turkish victory at Mohács, Hungary in 1526.

We might, then, roughly mark out three interlocking spheres of transformation marked by the crude labels of Renaissance/Enlightenment, Reformation/state-formation and world-system/imperialism. The first directs our attention to ideas, which, as Marx (1975 [1844]) said of theory, 'becomes a material force when it seizes the masses'. The second refers us to the European national-state model, seen both in its domestic aspect and as part of a system of such states, and the third to Europe's economic and political domination of much of the rest of the world in the second half of the last millennium. The interrelations between the first and second spheres have been fairly well discussed, though there is little agreement over the relative power of ideas or more material political or economic processes. The relations between the first two and the third, however, have received much less attention and are finally getting it under such rubrics as postcolonial theory and critiques of Eurocentrism (see Gerard Delanty's contribution to this volume). Did Europeans colonise America and Australasia, almost all of Africa and much of Asia because they had a sense of intellectual or cultural superiority and believed that the particular middle-eastern religion which they had adopted as their own was the Truth, to be disseminated as widely as possible, or because of economic and/or military-strategic interests and capacities arising out of their particular state-forms?

Let us trace these processes rapidly down to the present. It is difficult to escape from the haze of self-congratulation in which intellectual developments in Europe over the past half-millennium have tended to be discussed. In the late twentieth-century there was a long overdue corrective movement, marked by a number of works which showed the dependence of Greek thought on regions to the east and south (Bernal 1987), of the Renaissance on past and contemporary Islamic scholarship, of Chinese anticipations of much of what has been attributed to the 'scientific revolution' of the seventeenth-century (Needham 1969) and of movements outside Europe and its settler colonies paralleling the European religious reformation and Enlightenment. For all that, there did develop in Europe a powerful set of syntheses of practical and speculative thought inspiring transformations in science and technology on the one hand and forms of political rule on the other.

One quite plausible attempt to explain the dynamism of a region which had previously been rather backward stresses the combination of a common ideological and political framework (Christendom and, for much of the region, Roman Law) with the political diversity of relatively small emergent states (Mann 1986, 1993, 1998). The creative tension between religious and secular power and the multiplicity of competing jurisdictions may have encouraged the development of individualistic ways of thinking and liberal political thought. The etymology of the word 'liberties' and its equivalents points to this: initially meaning privileges or exemptions, it comes to have a more universalistic sense in which, as the anarchist Bakunin put it, I can be free only if all others are free. Whether or not it is appropriate to include under the heading of transformations the rather diffuse development of European conceptions of individualism and of human and political rights and freedoms, the French Revolution clearly deserves a central place as the defining feature of the European political imaginary (Best 1988; Furet 1989). This is no less true of the conservatives who rejected it, brilliantly characterized by Mannheim (1986 [1925]), or of the socialists and communists for whom it was just a prelude to a full social democratic and anti-capitalist revolution.

Concurrently, the American Revolution inaugurated another form of republican constitutional government and, perhaps more importantly, the first major post-colonial state, what the American political sociologist Martin Lipset (1964) called 'the first new nation'. For progressive Europeans, this was one more victory over the old aristocratic order, and the French aristocrat Alexis de Tocqueville found in the US in the 1820s what he expected to be the democratic and egalitarian future of France and Europe. Geopolitically the American Revolution marked the beginning of the provincialisation of Europe, the relativisation of its power in between the United States and Russia, which Tocqueville also foresaw less than forty years after the Revolution (and an even shorter time since Napoleon's short-lived European empire) and when Europe's imperial power was still on the rise.

Imperialism was of course a European transformation both of Europe itself and of much of the rest of the world, running alongside the generalisation, within Europe itself, of capitalist production and industrialisation. From now on, though no-one was yet thinking in these terms (except perhaps in relation to the contrast between the old and the new worlds), there were multiple modernities and a post-European future. What Fernand Braudel and Immanuel Wallerstein called the capitalist world economy or world-system largely pre-dated systematic imperial conquests, though not of course the middle eastern 'Crusades'. Debates still rage over whether imperialism should be seen primarily as what Lenin (1964 [1916]) called the highest stage of capitalism or more as a matter of geopolitical competition, with economic interests secondary. (The neo-imperialist adventurism of the US in the early twenty-first-century provokes of course similar disagreements.) Imperialism and colonialism also transformed the European societies themselves. On the whole they got substantially richer, whatever happened to the wealth that was accumulated; the poorer and more peripheral states such as Spain and Portugal acquired or preserved a great power status. Germany started two world wars in large part out of *ressentiment* at its lack of a 'proper' overseas empire and the attempt to catch up (WWI) or to colonise Russia instead (WWII). Domestically, many states (not just the fascist ones) re-imported military and policing tactics tested in the colonies. Finally, the former colonial powers tended to attract (and often to recruit) immigrants from 'their' territories in the 'thirty glorious years' of capitalism from the late 1940s to the mid-1970s. As a result of these flows both from outside Europe and from its poorer peripheries,

Europe became more substantially multicultural, though not without a good deal of resistance and denial on the part of the 'natives'. (Conservative politicians in Germany, for example, solemnly announced that the Federal Republic was 'not a country of immigration'.)

Back at home, Europe experienced three further transformations, all in one way or another associated with notions of citizenship. First, there was the slow extension of political democracy, finally reaching adult women in most parts of Europe in the early twentieth-century. Second, the nationalism which was already implicit in the political structures of much of Europe became more forceful across the continent as a whole, in part as a reaction to Napoleon; this development, culminating in the post-First World War settlement, consolidated the (Western) European nation-state model. This model, with its prioritisation of nation-state citizenship as a defining identity, swept the world wherever the European states had not established colonies or, as in South America, were expelled from them. (In the second wave of decolonisation in the mid-twentieth-century, it was considered automatic that the colonial territories, already carved up into what Europeans considered state-sized chunks, would be set up as European-style states. Half-hearted supranational economic arrangements, in East Africa and elsewhere, rapidly succumbed to political contingencies.) Third, there was the dual response to the 'social question' in the form of welfare states (Donzelot 1980 [1977], 1984) and social democracy. The former is the beginning of the 'European social model' and social conceptions of citizenship (Marshall 1950), the latter of what can be called the European political model, the left-right division between ostensible opponents and all too real defenders of capitalism which structured European politics and tendentially the politics of much of the rest of the world at least until the end of the twentieth-century. As early as 1906, Werner Sombart was taking this as the norm and asking 'Why is there no socialism in the United States?'. Despite the current vogue of 'third way' politics in the UK, Germany, and much of the rest of Europe, it is far from certain that European politics is moving 'beyond left and right' (Giddens 1994).

In Russia, of course, after the Bolshevik Revolution, there was only the left left. The thoroughly European ideology of Marxism took hold in Russia, China and elsewhere outside Europe, with the Russian export model (Stalinist Marxism-Leninism) re-imported into much of Europe in the aftermath of the Second World War. Russia's land empire had of course been a classic case of European 'internal colonialism', the securing of control over peripheries. The Soviet Union also presided over the last quasi-imperial structure in Europe, with the so-called 'Brezhnev doctrine' of the limited sovereignty of Warsaw Pact states. This differed from the 'normal' imperial relation in that here it was the hegemonic power which supplied its more developed client states with cheap energy and raw materials in exchange for relatively advanced consumer goods.

Europe in its place

The world wars of the twentieth-century were quintessential expressions of Europe at its worst, practising techniques of warfare often tried out earlier on colonised populations. Europe had certainly transformed warfare, from the use of gunpowder, which in China had been used only for fireworks, to the massive Fordist operations of the First World War. Earlier European wars had of course been fought outside Europe, but now wars could only be fought as world wars. The (nuclear) third world war which we escaped more by luck than anything else would of course have been a further and no doubt final example, using weapons probably capable of destroying all human life on the planet. As Adorno (1973: 320 [1966]) put it, 'No universal history leads from savagery to humanitarianism, but there is one leading from the slingshot to the megaton bomb.' The wars, and the Holocaust which accompanied the Second, were a kind of peak of European achievement, but the Second World War, in particular, also marked an important stage in its decline. Geopolitically, the provincialisation of Europe was marked by the subordination of most of the two halves of the divided continent into the cold war military alliances firmly controlled from Washington and Moscow. Germany, too, was divided, with its former capital, Berlin, officially under the joint control of the Allies. The Europeans withdrew from most of their colonised territories, though leaving settler states in America (where the colonial powers had been expelled earlier), Australasia and southern Africa. An illegal white regime survived in Rhodesia/Zimbabwe from 1965 to 1980 and a white-controlled and explicitly racist state in South Africa till 1989.

Domestically, the three processes identified above modulated into the configuration in which we now live. Democracy was briskly extinguished in the communist bloc in the late 1940s, only to bounce back forty years later. In the rest of Europe, which had been democratic since the end of the war, except for the post-fascist dictatorships in Spain and Portugal and the authoritarian regime in Greece from 1967 to 1974, there was a more diffuse democratisation of social relations, particularly in the wake of the 1968 movements which, though politically unsuccessful, had an important effect on political culture and mores – notably in the rise of 'new' social movements (Touraine 1981). Welfare states were further developed in both parts of Europe, though more slowly after the capitalist economic crisis of the mid-1970s. In the richer parts of the West rights of abode and citizenship were more or less grudgingly accorded to the short- or long-term immigrants recruited to help out with the post-war boom of the thirty glorious years. In another major social change, with the transformation of agriculture after the Second World War the peasants who had been 'nationalised' in Eugen Weber's sense in the late nineteenth-century (Weber 1976) or collectivised in most of the Soviet bloc in the 1950s were increasingly displaced into manufacturing or service occupations (Mendras 1997), leaving agricultural policy, one of the key domains of the European Communities, looking more like a disguised social policy to support the vestiges of rural life. (For excellent overviews of social change in Europe in the second half of the twentieth-century, see Therborn (1995), Mendras (1997) and, more briefly, Outhwaite 2005.)

If 1789 was, as I suggested earlier, the defining event of the modern political imagination, it remains to be seen what place will be given to the anti-communist revolutions of 1989. On the one hand, the 'long' 1989 running from Gorbachev's rise to power in 1985, or the reforms which he initiated soon afterwards, to the end of the USSR in 1991 marks the end of the Cold War which, we should never forget, could easily have killed us all. As events in global risk management go, it doesn't get much bigger than this. On the other hand, a number of commentators have stressed the absence of really new ideas in the 1989 revolutions, especially after the rapid eclipse of civil society movements like Solidarity in Poland or Civic Form in Czechoslovakia; Habermas, for example, has called it the 'catching-up' or 'rectifying' revolution; a return to democracy (and capitalism), and to the 'normal' path of post-Second World War European development. Similarly, the 'new world order' proclaimed by President Bush I was already looking threadbare long before the terrorist attack of September 2001, when the US suffered, in a particularly dramatic form, from a new form of terrorism distinct from that familiar in parts of Europe such as Italy, Spain, Russia and the UK.

The year 1989 also put the seal on what had come, only really in that decade, to be called globalization. Although much of the world, including substantial parts of post-communist Europe, remained relatively untouched by globalizing processes, it was clear that the world had become more of a single space, with the old imagery of First, Second and Third World falling out of use. The nation-state, which had already been somewhat put in question in the European integration process discussed below, was now further problematized. As Martin Albrow (1996: 65), one of the earliest theorists of globalization put it, some of the key elements of the 'Modern Project' became 'forces for fragmentation: the corporate organization, the market, science, culture and the social' (in the sense of social movements). All of these came to transcend the boundaries of the nation-state even more radically than they had previously done, and to undermine it from within and without.

In Europe, what had begun as a reaction to the consequences of nationalism in the two world wars had been developing gradually and haltingly into a new political model: an 'ever closer union' of more and more European states. The ultimate destination or *finalité* of what has become the European Union remains more or less as unclear as when Andrew Shonfield examined it in 1973. Briefly, however, the EU is incipiently post-national, despite or because of its continuing symbiotic relationship with its member-states. It is post-imperial, in that however much it might superficially come to resemble the Austro-Hungarian Empire it will surely retain principles of democracy more characteristic of the national state (Beck and Grande 2004). And it is perhaps (and this is part at least of its appeal), the beginning of a form of post-European cosmopolitan democracy attractive not just to Europe but to many other parts of the world. Jürgen Habermas (1991) has aptly described this as 'Europe's second chance'. The continent or subcontinent exported not just political and cultural modernity, which on the whole people want, and capitalism, which they either want or see as inescapable, but also a nation-state structure which, whatever may be said in its favour (see e.g. Mauss 1969 [1920]) was clearly also responsible for war and genocide. Wherever we might want to locate Europe on the spectrum between 'top of the world class' and the disruptive world bully deserving exclusion, its balance sheet in the second half of what we eurocentrically call the second millennium is at least ambiguous. A federal or semi-federal Europe which was not just a 'fortress Europe' but a Europe for others as well as for itself might be a happier transformation with which to round off the European half-millennium.

I began by asking at what stage in history we might want to say that things become European, and we should also ask when they might cease to be. However strong the historical association between Europe and, say, individualism, democracy or modernity these have long since lost their labels of origin. Modernity, in particular, has a universalising thrust. As Gerard Delanty (2004: 176) puts it, 'Modernity ... is necessarily global in outlook; while it first emerged in western Europe, it is not Western, American, or European, but is an expression of world culture, which increasingly frames the local.' What, then, if anything, is distinctive about European modernity or Europe as a region of global modernity in the early twenty-first-century? Diversity might be a candidate. Not only does Europe have a lot of states and a lot of languages in a fairly small territory, these have a remarkably complex history of shifting positions and alliances. Europeans now tend to be fairly secular by world standards, having earlier displayed considerable enthusiasm for religious warfare and aggressive proselytism. Social democracy, though not of course confined to Europe and now somewhat in eclipse, survives in the form of the 'European social model' which is perhaps less easily found elsewhere. Finally, there is now a new European political model, post-national if not unequivocally federal, ambiguously poised between high ideals and self-interested deals, both internally and in its relation to the rest of the world.

Cosmopolitanism is perhaps the most tempting label to aspire to. Ulrich Beck and Edgar Grande lay down the challenge on the back cover of their recent book (2004): 'Cosmopolitan Europe is in Europe the last really effective utopia. It is about something completely new in the history of humanity, namely the projected image of a state structure which makes its foundation the recognition of cultural otherness.' This is indeed a powerful image, engagingly presented. It is paralleled in the cultural sphere by Gerard Delanty's image of Europe as a site of intercultural translation. Against these, of course, one must set the counter-image of a Europe with a dubious past, egocentric and self-obsessed, traditionally ignorant of cultural otherness outside its borders except as something exotic. But it is at least true, I think, that to conceptualise Europe, or to pursue the project of European integration, requires a degree of cosmopolitan imagination and will which might at least anticipate a more cosmopolitan future.

Social theory in Europe

I shall end with some remarks about European social theory as it reflects and reflects upon these transformations. Clearly, the conceptual categories of social theory as it has existed up to now (state, society, civil society, nation-state, progress, etc.) are European through and through; even if I was writing this chapter in a non-European language I would inevitably be using these categories. There is a clear danger of narcissistic circularity in using concepts derived from a particularistic European self-conception to reinforce a sense of European exceptionalism (Bhambra 2004). On the other hand, to the extent that the things themselves are of European origin or at least most prominent in their European forms, the use of a European vocabulary seems unexceptionable.

Social theory has historically been deep in these conflicts. The Valladolid conference referred to earlier is a striking example from the beginning of the period. A good deal later, Enlightenment thought was not only Eurocentric but often shockingly racist. Evolutionary theory is clearly dangerously close to European self-celebration in its language of higher and lower (Lévy-Bruhl, 1918), even if the implication is that the more 'backward' will eventually catch up. Elsewhere, of course, the inferences drawn may be even more disappointing, that some peoples or societies may never advance ('Völker ewiger Urzeit', in the terms of Kurt Breysig (1907)). It is of course in anthropology, often distinguished from sociology according to the divide between metropolitan and colonial societies, that these issues have been most fully discussed. On the one hand there is the undeniable complicity of anthropology with colonialism; on the other, this is the discipline where an open-minded celebration of other cultures and beliefs is strongest, to the point of annoying anti-relativists in related disciplines.

More generally, to the extent that social theory is focused on the distinctiveness of one aspect or another of European modernity (capitalism for Marx, *Gesellschaft* for Tönnies, capitalism and rationalization for Max Weber, organic solidarity for Durkheim) its angle of approach is inevitably structured by the dualistic contrast between these phenomena and those which preceded them. Marx had little doubt that the world's future was to be capitalist and then, hopefully, communist; the more developed world shows to the less developed the image of its own future. (Later, he prophetically speculated that Russia might skip the capitalist stage, though still within an evolutionary framework.) Durkheim thought in similarly evolutionary terms, believing, for example, that Australian totemic religion was a simple cell-form of the more complex religions prevalent in Europe. Max Weber knew more about the major world religions than most of their believers, yet his focus remained directed by a classically European preoccupation about how far their 'economic ethic' contributed to, or impeded, capitalist development. More broadly:

> Any child of modern European culture will, unavoidably and justifiably, address universal-historical themes with a particular question in mind: What combination of circumstances called forth the

broad range of ideas and cultural forces that on the one hand arose in the West, and only in the West, and on the other hand stood – at least as we like to imagine – in a line of historical development endowed in *all* civilizations with significance and validity?

Weber (2002 [1920])

Before addressing capitalism, his main focus in this text, Weber mentions science, law and jurisprudence, music, architecture, printing, universities, and the state and its administrative staff as characteristically Western phenomena. In a final example, the great historical sociologist Norbert Elias, whose life spanned the twentieth-century, developed a grand theory of what he called the civilising process encompassing European manners and state-formation.

If something like this is the deep structure of European or 'Western' social theory, what Gurminder Bhambra (2004) has called its 'default modernist sensibility', we need to ask how far this limits its explanatory power. Some theorists, whether coming out of postcolonial theory or social anthropology, would say it fundamentally vitiates it. My inclination would be towards a more optimistic view that one can distinguish contingent European or national limitations of focus or vision from the basic categories of reflection which we can derive from the tradition of social theory.

Sudipta Kaviraj (2001) has suggested that we cannot understand non-Western politics only in the categories of Western thought but nor can we do without them. And the same must surely be true of Western contexts. Martin Albrow (Albrow and King 1990) has traced the emergence of a concern with globalisation from earlier phases of sociology; Albrow characterises these as universalism (in classical sociology), the national sociologies of the early twentieth-century, internationalisation (after the Second World War) and indigenisation (a response from the 'Third World' to the dominance of 'Western' categories of theorising). Under conditions of globality, the distinctiveness of the national traditions is weakening and what we are confronting may be essentially a process in which similar work is being done worldwide, with only differences in resources and language operating as barriers to communication.

Conclusion

It is misleading to think of transformations of or in Europe in isolation from 'its' interaction with other parts of the world. This is not a peculiarity of Europe; it is only the pervasive European myth of demiurgal endogenous development which makes it necessary to stress it in a European context. Europe has now been put in its place, its share of world population having declined from 20–25 per cent in the nineteenth-century to 12 per cent in 2000 and an estimated 7 per cent by 2050 (Population Reference Bureau 2004). And yet the EU has a population and GNP greater than the two superpowers of the twentieth-century, the USA and Russia, and retains a kind of cultural dominance out of proportion to its size.

Europe continues to be a major world force, though partly only in virtue of its impressive achievement of integration. Alan Milward (1992) described the development of the European Community as the 'European Rescue of the Nation-State'; it was possibly also the European rescue of Europe from what would otherwise have been an arguably overdue decline.

Note

1 As Beck and Grande (2004) have noted, the contrast between Francis Fukuyama's peaceful vision of the end of history in a convergence towards European- and US-style liberal democracy and Samuel

Huntington's alarming fantasy of a 'clash of civilizations' in many ways replays the Valladolid conference of 1550, between universalistic inclusionism (they too can become Christians) and particularistic rejection of the 'savages'.

References

Adorno, T. W. (1973 [1966]) *Negative Dialectics*, trans. E. B. Ashton, New York: Seabury Press.

Albrow, M. (1996) *The Global Age*, Cambridge: Polity.

Albrow, M. and King, E. (1990) *Globalization, Knowledge and Society*, London: Sage.

Aust, S. and Schmidt-Klingenberg, M. (eds) (2003) *Experiment Europa: Ein Kontinent macht Geschichte*, Stuttgart: Deutsche Verlags-Anstalt.

Beck, U. and Grande, E. (2004) *Das kosmopolitische Europa*, Frankfurt: Suhrkamp.

Bernal, M. (1987, 1991) *Black Athena: The Afro-Asiatic Roots of Classical Civilization*, 2 vols, London: Free Association Books.

Best, G. (ed.) (1988) *The Permanent Revolution: The French Revolution and its Legacy 1789–1989*, Glasgow: Fontana.

Bhambra, G. K. (2004) 'Contesting Modernity', PhD Thesis, University of Sussex.

Breysig, C. (1907) *Die Geschichte der Menschheit (Bd. 1. Die Völker ewiger Urzeit. Erster Band. Die Amerikaner des Nordwestens und des Nordens)*, Berlin: Walter de Gruyter.

Delanty, G. (1995) *Inventing Europe: Idea, Identity, Reality*, Basingstoke: Macmillan.

Delanty, G. (2004) 'Multiple Modernities and Globalization', *Protosociology*, 20, 165–185.

Donzelot, J. (1980 [1977]) *The Policing of Families*, London: Hutchinson.

Donzelot, J. (1984) *L'invention du social*, Paris: Fayard.

Furet, F. (ed.) (1989) *L'héritage de la Revolution française*, Paris: Hachette.

Giddens, Anthony (1994) *Beyond Left and Right: The Future of Radical Politics*, Cambridge: Polity.

Habermas, J. (1991) 'Europe's Second Chance', trans. in J. Habermas, *The Past as Future*, Cambridge: Polity (1994): 73–97.

Kaviraj, S. (2001) 'In Search of Civil Society', in S. Kaviraj and S. Khilnani (eds) *Civil Society: History and Possibilities*, Cambridge: Cambridge University Press.

Lenin, V. I. (1964 [1916]) *Imperialism: The Highest Stage of Capitalism*, Moscow: Progress.

Lévy-Bruhl, L. (1918) *Les fonctions mentales dans les societes inférieures*, Paris: Alcan.

Lipset, S. M. (1964) *The First New Nation: The United States in Historical and Comparative Perspective*, London: Heinemann..

Mann, M. (1986) *The Sources of Social Power, Vol. 1.: A History of Power from the Beginnings to AD 1760*, Cambridge: Cambridge University Press.

Mann, M. (1993) *The Sources of Social Power, Vol. 2.: The Rise of Classes and Nation-States, 1760–1914*, Cambridge: Cambridge University Press.

Mann, M. (1998) 'Is There a Society Called Euro?', in R. Axtmann (ed.) *Globalization and Europe*, London: Pinter.

Mannheim, Karl (1986 [1925]) *Conservatism: A Contribution to the Sociology of Knowledge* (D. Kettler, V. Meja, and N. Stehr (eds)), London: Routledge.

Marshall, T. H. (1950) *Citizenship and Social Class*, London: Cambridge University Press.

Marx, K. (1975 [1844]) 'Zur Kritik der Hegelschen Rechtsphilosophie. Einleitung', in K. Marx, *Early Writings*, Harmondsworth: Penguin, p. 251.

Mauss, M. (1969 [1920]) 'Le nation et l'internationalisme' in M. Mausse, *Ouvres, Vol. 3. Cohésion sociale et division de la sociologie*, Paris: Les éditions de Minuet, pp. 626–634.

Mendras, H. (1970) *La fin des paysans*, Paris: Colin.

Mendras, H. (1997) *L'Europe des Européens*, Paris: Gallimard.

Milward, A. (1992) *The European Rescue of the Nation-State*, London: Routledge.

Needham, J. (1969) *The Grand Titration: Science and Society in China and the West*, London: George, Allen and Unwin.

Outhwaite, W. (2005) 'Social Structure', in R. Sakwa and A. Stevens (eds), *Contemporary Europe*, 2nd edn, London: Palgrave.

Pohoryles, R., Giorgi, L., Schlesinger, P., Rex, J. and Kreutz, H. (eds) (1994) *European Transformations: Five Decisive Years at the Turn of the Century*, Aldershot: Avebury.

Population Reference Bureau (2004) 'Human Population: Fundamentals of Growth Population Growth and Distribution', at http://www.prb.org/Content/NavigationMenu/PRB/Educators/Human_Population/Human_Population__Fundamentals_of_Growth_and_Change.htm

Shonfield, A. (1973) *Europe: Journey to an Unknown Destination*, Reith lectures, 1972, Harmondsworth: Allen Lane.

Sombart, W. (1976 [1906]) *Why is there no Socialism in the United States?*, C. T. Husbands (ed.), London: Macmillan.

Therborn, G. (1995) *European Modernity and Beyond. The Trajectory of European Societies 1945–2000*, London: Sage.

Touraine, A. (1981). *The Voice and the Eye: An Analysis of Social Movements* (trans. A. Duff), Cambridge: Cambridge University Press.

Weber, E. (1976) *Peasants into Frenchmen: The Modernization of Rural France 1870–1914*, Palo Alto, CA: Stanford University Press.

Weber, M. (2002 [1920] 'Collected Essays in the Sociology of Religion', (trans. Stephen Kalberg) in *The Protestant Ethic and the Spirit of Capitalism*, Los Angeles: Roxbury, p. 149.

22

The politics of commemoration

The Holocaust, memory and trauma

Daniel Levy and Natan Sznaider

Assuming that the consequences of devastating events for individuals and collectivities run different courses, why do we use the word 'trauma' to explain a wide array of social and cultural phenomenon? Trauma has traveled far to become a key not only to explain, as originally conceived wounds to the body, but also injuries to spirit, culture, society and politics. Trauma has proliferated into a metaphor deployed to explain almost everything unpleasant that happens to us as individuals and as members of political communities. How do we conceptualize the transition from the trauma of the individual to the traumatized community? What does trauma mean for a theoretical formulation of collective memory? What are the social, legal and political dimensions that inform representations of collective traumata? Wulf Kansteiner (2004) provides an insightful history of the metaphoric diffusion of trauma, criticizing its loose deployment as inadequate. He points out that it is misleading to compare the trauma of an individual survivor to a broader public that has not experienced any comparable violence.

However, for the sociological significance of this transposition, the actually experienced pain, or rather the impossibility of its transference is less significant. What matters for the theoretical vantage point we are exploring here, is how these metaphors of trauma facilitate the appropriation of a culturally celebrated status of victimhood. More specifically, we examine how changing representations of trauma and memory of the Holocaust, and by extension reference to mass atrocities in general, emerge as a constitutive feature of a European identity project.[1] Changing memories of the Holocaust and its function as the paradigmatic trauma of the twentieth-century, serve as an illustration for the contentious nature of cultural representations. We address how 'traumatic' metaphors, addressing acts of extreme violence and innocence, exemplified through representations of the Holocaust, have become a key mechanism to address the precarious balance of universal and particular modes of identification (and theoretical interpretations). The particular experience of the Holocaust has become dislodged from its historical context and been inscribed as a universal code of suffering. By emphasizing the traumatic and subsequent therapeutic dimensions of this process, the dividing line between perpetrators and victims as well as the distinction between historical specificity and universal applicability, is frequently blurred. On this view, representations of Holocaust memories at the end of the twentieth- and the beginning of the twenty-first-century, we suggest, carry implications for both theories of collective memory and ongoing attempts to search for a common European founding moment. In contrast to early nation building efforts that relied on mythological inventions of political communities, nascent European identity seems to revolve around a negative foundational moment through commemorating universal lessons of the Holocaust.

The psychology of trauma

But before 'trauma' turned political, it was institutionalized in other professional discourses. A central feature of trauma theories addressing injuries, usually involves a clear-cut perception of who the victim and who the perpetrator is. Paralleling developments in other fields, we observe a shift from a moral to a medicalized discourse. This view has a long pre-history starting with the psychological conceptualization of trauma in the nineteenth-century. There, the stance toward perpetrators changed from a moral to a therapeutic one, characterized by rational and abstract language. Freud himself triggered a discussion of sexual child abuse within the family in an early article 'The Aetiology of Hysteria' (1896) which argued its prevalence, but soon afterwards reversed himself emphasizing instead 'infantile sexuality' and the role of sexual fantasies. What he had believed to be the actual sexual experiences of children were relegated to the world of childhood fantasies. Many psychoanalysts claim that this retraction, coupled with the discovery of the 'Oedipus complex' was the actual beginning of psychoanalysis as a scientific enterprise.

What matters for our interpretative purposes, is that trauma entered the collective lexicon around the time that many societies were beginning to reevaluate memories of their national past. This was preceded already in the nineteenth-century, by French scientists like Charcot and Janet who discovered mental trauma as the source of people's misery. They perceived of these memories like parasites of the mind. It was around that time that the experience of war was conceptualized as trauma. On the psychological level, the right treatment was supposed to overcome trauma. On the collective level, the 1864 Geneva Convention laid the foundations for contemporary humanitarian law, as a remedy to the atrocities of modern warfare.

Later in the twentieth-century, post-Vietnam reactions in the USA, but also in Europe, had a lasting impact on psychiatry, psychoanalysis and sociology. The American Psychiatric Association acknowledged in 1980 a phenomenon called 'Post-Traumatic Stress Disorder' (PTSD) referring to how people respond to human and natural catastrophes.[2] What is called 'the radical disruption and gaps of traumatic experience' (Caruth 1991: 2) is the source for a 'crisis of truth' that needs to be restored through memory work. The diagnosis calls for a need to uncover previously hidden memories. Restoring psychological health becomes the paramount goal, and recovering memory the means to it. It takes for granted that we are held hostage to earlier trauma. This presupposition applies not only to personal therapy but also to the contemporary culture of therapeutic politics.

The sociology of trauma

Focusing on a shift from psychological to social/political/cultural manifestations, the central theoretical question remains: How can trauma provide the social theorist with a toolbox with which to understand the horrors of the twentieth-century and ours? One of the first sociologists to use trauma as a sociological concept was Kai Erikson (1994).[3] He shifted the notion from an individualized context toward the analysis of 'traumatized communities.' He went as far as to suggest, that 'trauma can create community' (Erikson 1994: 231). Erikson brings trauma not only to sociology but one that focuses on group interest.

This Durkheimian concern also informs Jeffrey Alexander's contribution to shift our attention from psychological assumptions to sociological processes. The specific content of the trauma or how trauma operates collectively is not fully addressed in Erikson's approach. Alexander offers an important corrective to this theoretical gap. He too recognizes the fallacies of psychological trauma theories that remain centered on the individual. In an attempt to link trauma theory to broader issues of collective (rather than individual) identity, he proposes the concept of 'cultural trauma'. It 'occurs when members of a collectivity feel they have been subjected to a horrendous event that leaves indelible marks upon their group consciousness, marking their memories forever and changing their future identity in fundamental and irrevocable ways' (Alexander 2004: 1).

Referring to trauma as a cultural phenomenon implies two significant departures from the psychological literature. For one, choices are made and 'trauma is not something naturally existing; it is something constructed by society' (ibid. 2). Reflexivity is perceived as the prerequisite to shift the language of trauma away from its essentialist and pathological connotations toward a symbolic and institutional context that is constitutive for collective and moral identifications. However, this is a highly contested process and as Alexander points out, 'events are not inherently traumatic. Trauma is a socially mediated attribution' (Alexander 2004: 8). This raises questions about both the agents and the mechanisms of mediation. The attribution of traumatic suffering is frequently organized along two representational dimensions: one revolves around the difference between universal values and particular experiences; the other is related and involves the changing nature of the victim-perpetrator relationship. The respective balance between these elements informs the extent to which memories and representations of trauma are politically and culturally consequential.

These themes are also at the core of Dominique LaCapra's distinction between structural and historical trauma, which he perceives as central for coming to terms with the Holocaust.[4] Structural trauma in his language is related to 'trans-historical absence and appears in all societies and lives' (LaCapra 2001: 76). On this view, everyone is potentially a victim or a survivor. Historical trauma, on the other hand, refers to particular experiences, not to surrogate victims. According to LaCapra, everybody can be subject to structural trauma. However, with respect to historical trauma and its representation, the distinction between victims, perpetrators, and bystanders is crucial. 'Victim' is not a psychological category, but rather a political (social/ethical) one (ibid. 79). Here, we move from psychology to history, from psychoanalysis to politics, from the individual to the collective level.

Sociological investigations of trauma thus focus on how political communities deal with the construction and representation of trauma in collective rather than individual terms. Communities do not remember; they commemorate. Trauma becomes 'collective consciousness' and shared. To ensure that an event is perceived as a trauma it requires a degree of institutionalization and routinization. The proliferation of museal exhibits and memorial sites representing not heroic narrations of nationhood, but traumatic events, indicates the centrality of negative foundational moments. Trauma also becomes inscribed in rituals and law. The latter is particularly salient in societies that have just emerged from ongoing internal strifes, where the dividing lines between perpetrators and victims remain subject to interpretations of the past. Frequently the creation and resolution of collective traumata are addressed in terms of justice, what can be referred to as 'traumatic transition.'[5] 'The cultural construction of trauma begins with . . . a claim to some fundamental injury, an exclamation of the terrifying profanation of some sacred value, a narrative about a horribly destructive social process, and a demand for emotional, institutional, and symbolic reparation and reconstitution' (Alexander 2004: 11). Accordingly, political trials, war crime tribunals, truth and reconciliation commissions all become trauma laboratories.

Traumatic memories: the Holocaust

It is our contention that it was the Holocaust that carried trauma from the personal to the collective level and became synonymous with political evil itself.[6] The Holocaust has become the iconic trauma. It is now a concept that has been dislocated from space and time resulting in its inscription into other acts of injustice and traumatic national memories across the globe. Put differently, it is now perceived as a structural rather than a historical trauma. The boundaries between personal and collective traumata, real and imagined memories, are increasingly blurred.

The controversy surrounding the publication of Binjamin Wilkomirski's *Fragments* in 1995 and the subsequent discovery that his childhood memories from the camps were fabricated, illustrates the conflation of personal and historical memory. It reveals a process fraught with tensions, where the history of trauma (i.e. the career of a theoretical concept) and traumatic histories (i.e. the social construction of Holocaust memories) are mutually reinforcing. Wilkomirski's book is a childhood memoir set in a concentration camp. It became at once a paradigmatic case for Holocaust trauma. Wilkomirski became the living example of what trauma was all about: Childhood survival, years of therapy, an uncanny and a discontinuous story and the experience of the camps. The discovery of his fabrication raised broader questions about the nexus of trauma, memory and representation. Traumatic memories from early childhood cannot stand up to a factual – or even physical, in the sense of a connection to a particular place – account of reality. This lend further credence to the so-called distinction between the 'mythological memories of the victims' and professional historiography. The relationship of history and memory has long been a central feature of Holocaust historiography (Friedlander 1992). 'Trauma' attempts to bridge the memories of the survivors to the scientific tools of the historian and social scientist. Wilkomirski exemplifies how one can claim the emotional traumas that lie at the heart of the trauma mode, namely emotional dissociation. But there is a twist, as he substituted the events of his sheltered childhood with the history of the Jews in the Holocaust. Years of trauma discourse prepared Wilkomirski and his audience for this move. Accordingly, it is not entirely implausible that Wilkomirski actually believed his own fabrication. Structurally, we can all be survivors. Personal trauma has moved via historical trauma to structural trauma. There seems to be a longing for identification with those who suffered.[7] Like 'child abuse,' 'spousal abuse,' and other campaigns for the recognition of victims, the campaign to recognize the 'Holocaust' has a visible history. All these histories are vitally connected to the changing status of victimhood – to its transformation from something to be ashamed of to a sign of grace and moral righteousness.

From traumatic memory to the politics of memory

Prior to the 1960s, there was no 'Holocaust.' There was simply a small 'h' holocaust, which encompassed the killings of World War II, including the mass murder of the Jews. Nazi atrocities were originally interpreted in a universalistic fashion. Jews were considered one of the many victims of Nazism. The first victim was civilization which needed to be restored, as is evidenced in the post-war declarations against genocide and the Declaration on Human Rights. Genocide *is* the universalization of the Holocaust. It is essential to the concept that the

Holocaust is but one instance of a class of (by definition comparable) phenomena. And human rights are genocide taken to one more degree of universalization. The idea of genocide contains the admonition that a moral world cannot merely stand by. Human rights, which have their modern legal origins in the same set of 1948 UN declarations, are tied up in practice with the even stronger assertion that the Holocaust is a slippery slope – that every act of ethnic repression, if not checked, might prepare the way for the next holocaust. As the Declaration put it clearly without any doubt about the connotation: 'Whereas disregard and contempt for human rights have resulted in barbarous acts which have outraged the conscience of mankind, and the advent of a world in which human beings shall enjoy freedom of speech and belief and freedom from fear and want has been proclaimed as the highest aspiration of the common people' (Preamble Universal Declaration of Human Rights, UN 1948). The ultimate justification for Human Rights, thus, is neither human nature, nor some Enlightenment optimism in the rationality of mankind, but memories of catastrophe and trauma. Modern wars created traumas and traumas created means to reckon with them. However, the balance between universalism and particu-larism is not a matter of theoretical preference, but one shaped by historical contingencies.

With the emergence of 'identity politics' in the United States, we observe a shift in rhetoric, from universal concerns to particularistic claims of groups and subcultures. Peter Novick (1999) has demonstrated how a growing focus on the Holocaust coincides with the articulation of new Jewish identities. It was during these decades, when the 'voicing of pain' replaced the voicing of interests in American politics, that World War II made the transition from a holocaust to 'The Holocaust' (Novick 1999). Structural trauma was complemented by the public voices of survivor's historical trauma.

Paradoxically, it was precisely the Americanization of the Holocaust, which despite its origins as a form of Jewish identity politics, contributed to the emergence of a new episte-mological vantage point. With the world-wide success of Steven Spielberg's 'Schindler's List' and the opening of the United States Holocaust Museum in Washington in the early 1990s, the trauma-centric focus on victims and perpetrators, gave way to a witness perspective. Thus the mnemonic significance of the Holocaust was re-defined in the post-Cold War era. The new meaning was shaped in the context of globality marked by an awareness of an inter-connected world, where the role of the bystander shifted public attention to a non-traumatic political discourse. Massive reactions to ethnic cleansing in the Balkans, during the 1990s, renewed legal and ethical attention to the notion of war crimes and genocide. The Holocaust was no longer merely a source of personal and cultural trauma, but assumed an iconic status, that became the source for self-conscious political action (or admittance of failure when mass atrocities were committed under global watch). Since this 'symbolic turn' it has frequently been deployed as a metaphor for mass atrocities and general considerations for human rights. Memories of the Holocaust have become a moral touchstone, a call to action. People are not supposed to suffer. This is true on the personal level and it becomes true on the political level as well. Now, the vulnerability of the body (and mind), as in the original formulation of trauma as blow to the body, and political institutions which try to prevent this kind of vul-nerability, are going hand in hand.

The political institutionalization of Holocaust memory: towards a cosmopolitan Europe and beyond

This vulnerability needs to be communicated which in turn problematizes testimony and evidence. Historical records are turned into trial records, survivor narratives into evidence.

The juridification of Holocaust memories and by extension genocide has its origin in the Nuremberg Trials in the immediate post-war period. These trials were the beginning of historical knowledge about the Holocaust even though the extermination of European Jewry was not at its center. Presiding over the trial Justice Jackson declared:

> The privilege of opening the first trial in history for crimes against the peace of the world imposes a grave responsibility. The wrongs which we seek to condemn and punish have been so calculated, so malignant, and so devastating, that civilization cannot tolerate their being ignored, because it cannot survive their being repeated. That four great nations, flushed with victory and stung with injury stay the hand of vengeance and voluntarily submit their captive enemies to the judgment of the law is one of the most significant tributes that Power has ever paid to Reason.[8]

More is at stake than the operation of justice. Trials are also moments where issues of guilt, sacrifice and renewal are being played out. We treat juridification not merely as a legal judgment, but a socially embedded, meaning-producing act. They are transformative opportunities, where memories of grave injustices are addressed in rituals of restitution and renewal (Osiel 1997). The Nuremberg trial, appealing to a universal language of human rights, was a bridge between historical and structural trauma. It relied mainly on German documents, and, admitted the by now iconic documentary movie 'The Nazi Concentration Camps' as evidence. Voices of survivors as witnesses were almost not heard at Nuremberg, in contradistinction to the Eichmann trial in Jerusalem in 1961, which relied heavily on victims' testimonies. Both trials are paradigmatic expressions of perpetrator and victim centered historiography, respectively. This connects back to the above mentioned distinction between the 'mythological memories of the victims' and professional historiography.

Memories of the Holocaust did not directly cause the emergence of a global legal culture. Rather, they have produced a continued negotiation process between 'international law' (i.e., finding the criteria for degrees of wrongdoing) and 'normative ethics' (based on questions of reason and morality). The moral and juridical reactions to the Holocaust are drawn together by witnesses. This is also displayed in organizations like Amnesty International and Human Rights Watch who base their campaigns on eyewitness accounts of atrocities. Witnessing trauma becomes the modern means against the old fear of suppression or forgetting.[9]

The question remains how this witness perspective has been institutionalized and become politically consequential? As traumatic memories move between the historical and the structural, the psychologization of trauma has eventually given way to its politicization.[10] One, among many examples, for how historical representations of the Holocaust have been translated into a legal codex are the statutes of the recently installed International Criminal Court (ICC), which is a belated implementation of the Nuremberg principles. At the Nuremberg trials the real plaintiff was civilization, as is evidenced in the aforementioned opening remarks by Judge Jackson. Civilization and reason are combined to overcome historical and structural trauma. Structural trauma in the political sphere begins with the idea that modern warfare made everyone victims, so you could not save yourself by being a victor. Therefore to overcome this you need to wipe out or at least to civilize warfare, which was always a possibility. This was the general idea after the trauma of the world wars in the twentieth-century and was reflected in the Nuremberg Trials and the current International Criminal Court. In structural trauma, there is no ultimate difference between victors and vanquished. Whereas in historical trauma, there is an essential divide between victims and perpetrators. And this may also be reflected in trials dealing with specific victim groups (like the Eichmann Trial in Jerusalem in 1961). The notion that everyone is a potential victim of modern warfare became a dominant post-traumatic idea in the 1950s when people were terrified of what is now called 'atomic holocaust'. There is a parallel – and somewhat incompatible – conception of victim consciousness, one universal and one particular, corresponding to the distinction of structural and historical trauma. The particular one highlights the crimes of the aggressor; the universalist one downplays them through the very idea that we are all victims. Both imply a conversion experience as the exposure to trauma involves a redemptive departure from the original traumatic experience. The particular form of victim consciousness depends on its distinction between perpetrator and victim. Under the particular (and historical trauma) system, there can be no victim without a perpetrator – and conversely, to call someone a victim is to instantly accuse someone else of being a perpetrator. For the universal (and structural trauma) conception, the concentration on perpetrators undercuts the whole idea of victim consciousness.

Conclusion: from history to structure and back

Collective consciousness and the expansion of solidarity remain contentious processes that involve ongoing tensions between universal and particularistic visions, of which shifting perceptions of victimhood and perpetrators are prominent aspects. The dissolution of this relationship and the emergence of non-specific actors (i.e. the witness perspective) explain the transition from historical to structural trauma. Structural trauma is based on a history without subjects. Abstract structures (like modernity) are its main components.[11] This comes at the expense of historical trauma, i.e. the specifics and particularities of the event itself. To view the Holocaust in terms of 'structural trauma' removes it from the particular German-Jewish relationship, and resets it into the context of modernity. Accordingly, Germany can cease to be perceived as the exception to the standard path of European national development, instead becoming the exemplification of a common modernity. The Holocaust and World War II are turned into a universal trauma, which can be seen as either the death of the Enlightenment project, or the birth of a new regime of universalized sympathy with the suffering of others as expressed in the formation of a Human Rights regime and the general condemnation of genocide.

Personal and collective trauma have merged. We have entered the world of 'cultural trauma',[12] where humanity as such is taken on a destructive path. One would have thought that the Holocaust be a subject resistant to the cultural or linguistic turn and that it would more than anything else emphasize 'historical realism'. It seems that Social and Cultural Theory has been moving in the opposite direction. The cultural and linguistic turn has introduced the notion of trans-historical trauma into the study of the Holocaust and its subsequent representations. But what is the theoretical mileage gained from this move? Most historians and social scientists are not trained in psychoanalytical language in order to analyze the working through of trauma in personal terms. Conversely, most psychoanalysts are not trained to transfer their trauma terminology to examine history and society.

Let us end with an early European social theorist trying to come to terms with these dilemmata through a language of politics and not psychology. Hannah Arendt (1951) did not need any psychological criteria in order to understand that modern totalitarianism, and especially the concentration camps, constitute a radical break from tradition. This break leads to a crisis in understanding, which demands new political concepts and ways of thinking, including the reassessment of causality in historical thought and the unprecedented nature of the destruction of 'superfluous' people. In her eyes, totalitarian politics canceled the anthropological law of human self-preservation and with it destroyed one of the pillars of civilization. Indeed traumatic, but without the language of trauma. Arendt may have shown us already more than fifty years ago, that when speaking of the unprecedented in politics, the toolbox of your analysis can be political as well. In many ways, this kind of thinking was picked up again in the 1980s in a different mode and without any reference to Arendt. Postmodern thinkers like Lyotard (1988) took the Holocaust as an opportunity to criticize the limitations of conventional scientific procedures to come to terms with it. His by now famous example is the comparison of the Holocaust with an earthquake destroying also the instruments of measuring earthquakes. Decontextualization has reached its outer limits. As much as we are tempted to use 'trauma' as a key concept in contemporary politics, we should be aware of its limits. We are still dealing with people who were killed by other people and people who in the words of Arendt were deprived of their 'rights to have rights.' The Holocaust and other man-made catastrophes were real and it is this reality which defines political responsibility in our age. This is true for social theorists as well. If we think trauma to be a useful concept, we should always keep its human and historical dimension in mind while keeping its structural elements at bay. If not we might as well do without it.

Notes

1 Elsewhere we have looked at the historical and conceptual significance of Holocaust memories for the dissolution of nation-centered memories. See Levy and Sznaider (2002).
2 See American Psychiatric Association, Diagnostic and Statistical Manual of Mental Disorders (1980), Washington, DC: APA. For histories of the concept in clinical and historical terms see Cathy Caruth (1991). See also van der Kolk *et al.* (1996). For a radical constructionist approach to the psychiatric concept of trauma see Ian Hacking (1995: 183–197).
3 For a critique of Erikson's approach from a cultural constructionist perspective see Alexander (2004: 4–5).
4 In addition to LaCapra, Saul Friedlander (1993) is one of the leading scholars of the Holocaust trying to bring trauma to historical analysis.
5 For an overview of such traumatic transitions in terms of justice and memory see W. James Booth (2001)
6 For a detailed comparison of how memories of the Holocaust have converged into a generalized symbol see Daniel Levy and Natan Sznaider (2005).
7 In a review essay Ruth Franklin (2004) writes about a new trend she calls 'Neo-Wilkomirskiism'. Franklin takes issue with the Holocaust writing of the so-called 'Second Generation' (children of Holocaust survivors who have apparently inherited some of the trauma of their parents). They try to identify with their parents and envy them for their traumatic memories. However, the memories are false. What happened here on the personal level can be projected into the collective level as well: Identification with victimization without having actually experienced it.
8 Trial of the Major War Criminals before the International Military Tribunal (1947), Volume II, Proceedings: 11/14/1945–11/30/1945, Nuremberg: IMT, p. 98
9 For a problematization of witnessing see Felman and Laub (1992).
10 A by now classical statement of the interplay between personal and political trauma is Judith Herman (1992). She analyzes traumata like shell shock and sexual abuse in terms of social movements (like the anti-war and feminist movements).
11 See for instance Bauman's (1989) way of dealing with the Holocaust, which is based on the Foucaultian tradition to look at modernity as trauma.
12 See Alexander (2004) for the genealogy of cultural trauma. See Kansteiner, Wulf (2004) for a critique of the concept. Kansteiner points out, that projections of cultural trauma often conflate the distinctions between real victims and what could be called imagined victims. The comparison might be ethically problematic, but remains sociologically relevant.

References

Alexander, J. C. (2002) 'On the Social Construction of Moral Universals: The "Holocaust" from War Crime to Trauma Drama', in *European Journal of Social Theory*, 5(1), 5–85.

Alexander, J. C. (2004) 'Toward a Theory of Cultural Trauma,' in J. Alexander, R. Everman, B. Giesen, N. J. Smelser and P. Sztompka (eds) *Cultural Trauma and Collective Identity*, Berkeley: University of California Press, pp. 1-30.

American Psychiatric Association. (1980) *Diagnostic and Statistical Manual of Mental Disorders*, Washington, DC: APA..

Arendt, H. (1951) *The Origins of Totalitarianism*, New York: Harcourt, Brace, Jovanovich.

Bauman, Z. (1989) *Holocaust and Modernity*, Cambridge: Polity Press.

Booth, W. J. (2001) 'The Unforgotten: Memories of Justice', *American Political Science Review*, 95 (4), 777–791.

Buruma, I. (1995) *Wages of Guilt: Memories of War in Germany and Japan*, New York: Farrar, Straus and Giroux.

Caruth, C. (1991) 'Introduction', *American Imago: Studies in Psychoanalysis and Culture*, 48, 1–12.

Dower, J. (1999) *Embracing Defeat: Japan in the Wake of World War II*, New York: Norton.

Erikson, K. (1994) *A New Species of Trouble: Explorations in Disaster, Trauma, and Community*, New York: Norton.

Felman, S. and Laub, D. (1992) *Testimony: Crises of Witnessing in Literature, Psychoanalysis, and History*, New York: Routledge.

Förster, A. and Beck, B. (2003) 'Post-Traumatic Stress Disorder and World War II: Can a Psychiatric Concept Help us Understand Postwar Society?', in R. Bessel and D. Schumann (eds) *Life after Death: Approaches to a Cultural and Social History of Europe during the 1940s and 1950s*, Cambridge: Cambridge University Press, pp.15–35.

Franklin, R. (2004) 'True Memory, false memory and the Holocaust', *New Republic*, vol. 230 (31 May), 31–38.

Freud, S. (1896) 'The Aetiology of Hysteria', in J. Strachey (ed.) *The Standard Edition of the Complete Psychological Works of Sigmund Freud*, vol 3, London: The Hogarth Press, pp. 189–221.

Friedlander, S. (1992) *Probing the Limits of Representation: Nazism and the Final Solution*, Cambridge: Harvard University Press.

Friedlander, S. (1993) 'Trauma and Transference', in S. Friedlander, *Memory, History and the Extermination of the Jews of Europe*, Indiana: Indiana University Press.

Giesen, B. (2004) 'The Trauma of Perpetrators: The Holocaust as the Traumatic Reference of German National Identity' in J. Alexander, R. Everman, B. Giesen, N. J. Smelser and P. Sztompka (eds) *Cultural Trauma and Collective Identity*, Berkeley: University of California Press: 112–154.

Hacking, I. (1995) *Rewriting the Soul: Multiple Personality and the Sciences of Memory*, Princeton: Princeton University Press.

Herman, J. (1992) *Trauma and Recovery*, New York: Basic Books.

Kansteiner, W. (2004) 'Genealogy of a Categorical Mistake: A Critical Intellectual History of the Cultural Trauma Metaphor', *Rethinking History*, 8(2), 193–221.

Kolk, B. A. van der, L. Weisaeth, and O. van der Hart. (1996) 'History of Trauma in Psychiatry' in B. A. van der Kolk, A. C. McFarlane, and L. Weissaeth (eds) *Traumatic Stress: The Effects of Overwhelming Experience on Mind, Body, and Society*, New York: The Guilford Press: 47–74.

LaCapra, D. (2001) *Writing History, Writing Trauma*, Baltimore: Johns Hopkins University Press.

Levy, D. and N. Sznaider. (2005) *Memory in a Global Age: The Holocaust*, Philadelphia: Temple University Press.

Levy, D. and N. Sznaider. (2002) 'Memory Unbound: The Holocaust and the Formation of Cosmopolitan Memory', *European Journal of Social Theory* 5(1), 87–106.

Leys, R. (2000) *Trauma: A Genealogy*, Baltimore: Johns Hopkins University Press.

Lyotard, J.-F. (1988) *The Differend: Phrases in Dispute*, Minneapolis: University of Minnesota Press.

Novick, P. (1999) *The Holocaust in American Life*, New York: Houghton Mifflin.

Osiel, M. (1997) *Mass Atrocity, Collective Memory, and the Law*, New Brunswick: Transaction Publishers.

United Nations, *Universal Declaration of Human Rights*, http://www.un.org/Overview/rights.html.

Wilkomirski, B. (1995) *Fragments*, New York: Random House: Schoken.

23

Cultural identities

Heidrun Friese

The contemporary condition and current debates are characterised by (renewed) forms of identity politics, be it based on gender, ethnicity, race, religion or the nation.[1] The pluralisation of the public domain, the separation of public spaces along multicultural lines, plural political deliberation with no central, single source of authority or political agency challenge concepts of one common republican public sphere. Renascent particularisms, resurgent ethnicities and proclamations of 'one's own alterity' seeking for recognition and political representation complicate the various tensions inherent in modern social and political thought, trouble proponents of thin liberal democratic and procedural criteria and institutions, and those of thick and substantive cultural identities. The tensions between ascriptive and voluntary identities, the contingency of agency and fixed cultural life scripts, the dilemma between (Kantinan) universalism and (ethical) particularity, universally applicable norms, particular values and cultural differences, disputes between egalitarians and multiculturalists are challenging and limiting the basic assumptions and concerns of liberalism and have led to the reinterpretation of notions such as freedom and equality.

The highly problematic notion 'identity' thus, points towards a variety of questions and tensions. In the first instance, the term refers to the structure of things that are to remain the same, to that which is seen to constitute their unchangeable 'essence' or 'nature' across time and historical transformations. It refers second, to the relation of the singular human being to him- or herself, to intentions, actions, experiences, dreams and memories, and thus to the various instances of the 'self' – however 'selfhood' might have been cast throughout history. Third, it entails references to the historically shifting relations of singular human beings to others, to concepts of belonging and a common and shared (symbolic) world, its intrinsic values and languages, an inclusive 'We' that differs from those of an exclusive 'Them'. The notion thus, contains concepts of the Self and subjectivity, of socio-cultural life and its boundaries, and of time and temporality (Friese 2002: 1).

Accordingly, in 'classical' sociological and philosophical reasoning identity has been related to the 'self-identical, persisting through time as the same, as unified and internally coherent' (Butler 1990: 16), it has been related to modern and enlightened notions of the individual, and thus to reason and self-consciousness, to autonomy and self-determination, the capacity for judgement and moral deliberation and to agency, i.e. the ability to act according to reasonable and ethical criteria. Further to ideas of the individual, what is addressed as well are theories which regard the foundation of the political order (be it a community or the nation), its continuity, cohesion and borders. Within the realm of the political, what comes into sight are questions of political representation, the tensions between liberal designs of universality and a 'neutral', procedural political order and the communitarian version of a 'thick' order of moral(s) and values and most recently, the various concepts of (liberal) multiculturalism. Furthermore, the notion 'identity' contains assumptions about the nature of the economic order, as for instance the idea that human behaviour is guided by interest and thereby serves the common welfare or the concept of organised solidarity, the notion is contained in legal theories, namely that the individual is responsible for past and present actions (Wagner 2002: 32) and last but not least ethical concepts with regard to difference and the Other.

In recent times, the 'modern' version of the notion – and its reference both to the individual and the political order – and versions of 'classical' liberalism have increasingly been challenged by what Jean-Francois Lyotard (1988) called 'a re-writing of modernity'. Together with the 'metaphysics of substance', the notion of identity and its naturalising and essentialist effects have been criticised and the primacy of the subject has been deconstructed (Parker 1990; Sampson 1990). Once the notion of the unitary self is 'de-centred', the various fragments of subjectivity in different contradictory and power-infused discourses come into view. On one hand, coherence and continuity are no longer seen as logical features of the Self or personhood, but are considered as embodied, discontinuous, as socially constructed and as culturally 'instituted and maintained norms of intelligibility' (Butler 1990: 17), on the other hand practices have emerged which – in accordance with the culturalist turn, articulate cultural particularity and – against the pretence of a universalistic order – demand recognition and the representation of difference.

If (the question of) representation is one feature of the liberal democratic political order, one of the foremost questions to be asked is: What kind of political practices could be enacted if the familiar characteristics of identity – unity, continuity and coherence – were no longer its foundation? How can the notion of a 'we' be subverted in a way that nevertheless allows for political action? Does the political – and the very possibility for political action and solidarity – necessarily have to be founded in a commonality of a 'we' or in common interests? Given that the ground for political deliberation is no longer seen in shared interests struggling against antagonistic interests as the Marxist version holds – but becomes increasingly 'culturalised' and enshrined in commonalities based on gender, race, culture or ethnic belonging, what kind of politics thus, could emerge if a 'We' is no longer the all-encompassing and unifying subject for political representation? These questions gain relevance in the postcolonial context as well and can be transposed to questions like: How can the Other be represented without assuming an identity – paradoxically – founded in 'common alterity'? Ultimately, the question is: can we think of possible political practices without assuming some sort of collective identity?(Nancy 1991, 1996) Given recurrent politics of identities and difference – be they based on ethnical or religious grounds – this is a most crucial and urgent question (it has been argued that 'terror' ultimately supports such a politics of identity – the deed is to produce identity and *communitas*, its targets become a *pars pro toto* enclosed in a fixed identity and are to represent a general 'them' as opposed to a 'we' – subsequently the deed is to generate a political subject that it supposes to represent).

The semantic field of the term, its foundations and range encompass both epistemological and – given the various contexts of recurrent politics of identity – the most urgent political questions of our time and harbours a variety of tensions. With the view of the constitution of the Self and personal identity, it allows for the tensions between ascription, determination and choice, between autonomy and belonging, coherence and diffusion. With regard to the political dimension, it entails tensions between inclusion and exclusion, between universalism and particularity, the (moral) requirements of citizenship and the obligations of a community, impartial principles of right and procedures and particularist, 'substantial' policies, between classical liberalism and (multi)culturalism. With regard to ethics, what is involved are the quest for recognition of alterity and otherness.

In the following, elements which are to make up the notion of identity – such as political representation, socio-cultural context, agency, time and temporality – will be looked at as they traverse concepts such as gender, the nation and the community, alterity and the Other.

Gendered identities

Gender establishes a need for rethinking the concept 'identity'. Thus, it is certainly not a coincidence that all too familiar notions of identity came under critical scrutiny by various strands of feminist thought and its inherent tensions have been re-elaborated: the tension between determinism and freedom, between stasis and change, continuity and rupture, the particular and the universal and especially the tensions between body and mind, emotion and reason, the unintelligible and the intelligible and their inscription into the dualistic framework and the binary opposition which is to demarcate the female/male. Whereas settled author-itative accounts conceptualised man as universal, woman was the (negative) other, marked as particular or unrepresentable within a 'phallocentric' economy of signification.

Recent feminist thought endeavours at subverting these established dualisms and the inherent discursive components, the deeply rooted symbolical references and normative nar-ratives that sustain and perpetuate them, it aims at undermining an essentialist view of sex as natural, biological-anatomical determined as well as reifications and determinations of gender. The (symbolic) gendering is seen as a powerful socio-cultural construction which secures the concept of the (male) subject and the marginalisation and subordination of women.

However, what does the notion 'women' designate? A common identity, common inter-ests or the commonalty of subordination? What has to be addressed thus, is the question of representation, the question of the constitution of the political subject 'women' which does not stabilize an – assumed – gender identity, a homogeneous, unifying commonalty and a identifiable 'We' that merely repeats foundational determinations of well-known identity politics. According to Judith Butler (and drawing on Michel Foucault), the (juridical) 'systems of power *produce* the subjects they subsequently come to represent' (Butler 1990: 2, emphasis mine). The notion 'women' thus, can hardly indicate a common identity, a coherence or stability of a given political subject. 'Gender' cannot be conclusively determined because it is not constructed coherently and consistently in different historical, social, cultural contexts and the assumption that there be an all-encompassing, universal root for a feminist political prac-tice *sui generis* is deceptive (Butler 1990: 3). Such an assumption – that there be a universal subject 'woman' that feminism constructs and aims at representing – undermines its own argument and thus, its very practices because it is itself an effect of specific discursive forma-tions. At the same time, it is vital to understand that the construction of the subject to be (politically) represented is always already based on practices of exclusion and inclusion or in other words: on the very practices of domination which are sought to be subverted. Accordingly, what is needed is not trying to find a position 'outside' these powerful structures of language and politics – can there ever be a transcending of these structures? – but a critical working within that matrix and a 'critical genealogy of its own legitimating practices' (Butler,

1990: 5). The double gesture therefore is 'to trace the political operations that produce and conceal what qualifies as the juridical subject of feminism' (Butler 1990: 5), furthermore, what is at stake is the rethinking of the ontological constructions of identity and a critique of the reifications of gender. The task is as well to undermine the notion of unity and the 'globalizing gesture' that constantly neglects multiplicities and shifting subjectivities by assuming 'stable, unified, and agreed upon identity' (Butler 1990: 15). What is aimed at, is thus an 'antifoundational approach' that seeks to overcome concepts and strategies of dialogue that assume clearly definable identities to encounter each other while avoiding the question of the inherent relations of power. Gender becomes a notion that is always already deferred, displaced, out of its position, never fulfilled in a given point of time. As a consequence, Butler opts for opening a political space that allows for open and shifting coalitions, an undisclosed 'assemblage' that 'permits of multiple convergences and divergences without obedience to a normative telos or a definitional closure' (Butler 1990: 16).

Within a complex and powerful network of significant differences, deferences and dislocations, and subjected to a multitude of systems of signs, the subject is seen as the locus of (symbolic) discourses and representations of its cultural context. Such concepts radically question humanist notions of the individual's free will to form and shape her self and the world. What comes into play here, is obviously the agent and the question of *agency*. 'There is no gender identity behind the expression of gender', identity 'is *performatively* constituted by the very "expressions" that are said to be its results' (Butler 1990: 25). In this sense (and in contrast to Monique Wittig's perspective), gender is freed from a reference to any stable, fixed or definable gender identity but is seen as an ongoing performance, a staging in time. It is considered as an acting, gendering is a doing, though not a doing by a free subject, an agent, a doer, an intelligible 'I' which might be said to somehow 'preexist' (its) action, an actor prior to action. Accordingly, 'if identity is asserted through a process of signification, identity is always already signified, and yet continues to signify ... the question of agency is not to be answered through recourse to an I that preexists signification' (Butler 1990: 143). The 'subject is *not determined* by the rules' through which it emerges, 'signification is not a *founding act but rather a regulated process of repetition*' that produces the effects that there be a substance (Butler 1990: 145 original emphasis). Any attempt to subvert identity is possible only within that repetitive process, within repetition. Once identity is conceptualised as a created, generated effect of repetitive signification, inadequate binary constructs, such as free will versus determination can be avoided.

With agency, *time and temporality* come into play and any firm notion of identity or stable telos is inevitably shaken. Simone de Beauvoir already emphasised that one *is* not born as a woman, but one *becomes* one. With the emphasis on becoming, the dimension of time is introduced and gender, its ongoing constructions, productions and repetitions can be seen as a multifarious, incessant 'process ... that cannot rightfully be said to originate or to end' (Butler 1990: 33). At the same time, it is time that allows for repetition, re-shaping and re-signification.

The human self as a coherent unit and its persistence as the 'same' self over time has been considered as being one attribute of identity. According to the seminal work of Erik Erikson which influenced not just social psychology, identity can be understood as 'a subjective sense of *continuous* existence and a coherent memory' (Erikson 1968: 7, emphasis added).[2] It was widely taken for granted that any relation that specifies 'continuing personhood would have to share some key features of the identity relation, such as transitivity and being one-one' (James 2000: 31). Coherence and continuity as the founding criteria for personal identity however, have been questioned by feminist thought as well. First, because, as we have already seen, both are not logical features but socio-cultural norms. Second, because such a view reinforces and sustains the opposition between psychological continuity and bodily continuity and ultimately, the well-known dualism body and mind which again, tacitly marginalises and devalues the feminine (James 2000: 32). Within the tradition of (analytical) philosophy the search was for valid criteria that constitutes both the psychological and the bodily continuity of a person. The body however, was conceptualised as uniform or as a mere container of mind and memory. Memories that are to provide a sense of continuity though, are embodied and thus inevitably pertain to concepts of sex, gender and sexuality. Furthermore, memory as one source for this continuity is not delimited to recollections of the past, continuity has to include aspirations, desire, hope, i.e. the dimension of the future as well, and trauma, an incisive event that disables the inflicted individual to establish a coherent and uninterrupted narrative and a life-story, complicates the well-established relations of psychological and bodily continuity and (personal) identity.

Feminist discourse aims at destabilizing familiar dualisms, such as mind and body, the universal and the particular, ascription and choice, determination and free will and foundationalist frameworks of identity and identity politics. At the same time and not surprisingly, by emphasising the power-laden, yet arbitrariness of the attributes of gender and gender differences feminism re-articulates the familiar ambiguities and tensions between universalist and egalitarian approaches in modern social and philosophical thought on one hand and perspectives that emphasise gender difference and the particularity of experiences that demand particular attention and special provisions on the other. Such re-elaborations of these tensions become relevant as well with regard to questions that concern the political community and the nation and the recent challenges of multiculturalism (Okin et al. 1999).

The nation, the (political) community

Concepts of 'nation' or 'community' – as well as those of gender – centre around highly problematic notions of identity that emphasise coherence, unity and continuity. If the notion identity refers to (idea of) substance, to the relation of the singular human being to others and to time and temporality, the same can be said for these notions (despite the interpretative fluidity of the term 'community', Amit and Rapport 2002: 13–25). And again we encounter specific ambivalences and tensions, which irremediably trouble these concepts. On one hand, the concept is historically 'new', however nationalists vividly claim its antiquity, the universality of the concept stands against its particular articulation and the enormous 'political power' has to be seen vs. the 'philosophical poorness' and the lack of a coherent and systematic theoretical foundation (Anderson 1991: 5). The tensions enclose both 'progression and regression, political rationality and irrationality' (Bhabha 1990: 2), the Janus-faced character of the modern nation and furthermore, those between similarity and difference, inclusion and exclusion, social boundary and identity (Barth 1969; Cohen 1985; Gupta and Ferguson 1997), the universal and the particular, equality and difference (Benhabib 2002).

As Homi Bhabha points out, the nation is a 'cultural representation' of the 'ambivalence of modern society', of 'language itself in the construction . . . of the nation' (Bhabha 1990: 2, 3). The nation thus is not a political configuration meaning 'progress, homogeneity, cultural organicism, the deep nation, the long past' (Bhabha 1990: 4), i.e. identity, unity and continuity. Rather, a nation comes into being through fragmented, contested cultural productions, various narrations, and therefore becomes a precarious threshold of 'meaning that must be crossed, erased, and translated in the process of cultural production' (Bhaba 1990: 4).

Ernest Renan already noted that a nation is not merely based on common religion, language, race, ethnos, interest, language, natural boundaries or a legacy of memories that connect to its present, but is sustained by will and consent, 'the clearly expressed desire to continue a common life', a nation is not an empty container, but an active 'daily plebiscite' (Renan 1990 [1882]: 19). And Benedict Anderson's seminal *Imagined Communities* (1991) aims at an understanding of the nation, its coming into being, its transformations and the profound emotional resonance, identification and legitimacy which are a integral part of the (symbolic) social and cultural productions and 'artefacts' (Anderson 1991: 4) that constitute and generate a nation. The nation and the modern nation-state however are decoupled from an actual base of interaction. It is a laboriously construed invention, 'an imagined political community – and imagined as both inherently limited and sovereign' (ibid. 6). It is imagined insofar as its members will never know all other members of the community, and yet an image of communion, fraternity and comradeship is promoted. The nation is imagined as being limited and its territory confined by boundaries. It is imagined as sovereign both within its borders and in relation to other nations.

The cultural roots of the nation which is able to generate unimaginable sacrifices have been traced to a decline of religious imaginings. Anderson however, does not suggest that secularisation straightforwardly was setting in motion the machine of nationalism, but he aligns the raising of nationalism to proceeding cultural systems, such as the religious community and its sacred languages, the dynastic realm and its centre, the king and its 'divine' authority. Additionally, the 'apprehensions of time' which (early) Christianity conceptualised not as a linear and endless chain of causality as modern historical time is perceived, but as a 'messianic time', a present, in which the Messiah could enter at any moment and in which the present was ready for the 'end of times' in the very present, a certain simultanity 'of past and future in an instantaneous present' (Anderson 1991: 24). From the eighteenth-century onwards, simultaneity is increasingly assured by 'print capitalism', newspapers and the novel. What connects people is the idea of an social 'organism moving . . . through homogeneous, empty time' (ibid. 26) and the simultaneousness of action and disparate events is assured by reading and a collective body of readers which makes up and prefigures the imagined community. Again, time and temporality becomes crucial in the construction of a – alleged – identity of a community (and today, 'electronic capitalism' and its virtual spaces certainly contributes to create simultaneous and imagined communities on a global scale).

Anderson's text is written in the face of growing new identity politics, nationalisms, 'subnationalisms' and the establishment of new nation-states which show the agonistic side of the (unaccomplished) project of inventing a national identity. Paradoxically though, what is increasingly emphasised as well, is the transgression of borders, both within and between nation-states, transnational connections and diasporic communities in the era of post-colonialism and globalisation (Appadurai 1990, 1996; Clifford 1992, 1994, 1999; Bhabha 1994; Friedman 1994; Guarnizo and Smith 1998; Berezin and Schain 2003, to name just a few).

With increasing mobility, capitalist transnationality and forced or voluntary displacement of people and cultural traits in postnational formations in a 'globalizing world', the familiar congruence of time and space has been replaced by a reasoning that emphasises blurred borders, intersections, 'contact zones' (Clifford 1999). Concepts such as 'transnationalism', 'traveling cultures', 'diasporas', 'dislocation' or 'ethnoscapes' indicate 'the loss of place as a dominant metaphor for culture' (Amit and Rapport 2002: 3). Postcolonial perspectives aim at undermining primordialist versions of identity and the articulations of identities are reformulated by diasporic perspectives of dispossession, displacement and adaptation (Gilroy 1993) advocating uncertain and 'hybrid' identities as well as political contestation and empowerment against 'hegemonic' cultures and claims on universally valid norms and values that hold a normative, socio-cultural bias of western liberal and egalitarian ideas.

It has been argued that such perspectives which foster emancipatory ideals by challenging the conventional order of political representation and by rupturing oppressive political practices, social injustice and humiliation are immediately interwoven with a powerful politics of identity that – with nostalgic sorrow – either mourns the irretrievable loss of authenticity, 'difference' and 'Otherness' or, as new nationalisms, communitarianisms and ethnicity movements, fervidly seeks to safeguard one's own and distinct cultural 'authenticity' by mystifying 'difference'. As the 'moralizing revenge of the powerless' (Brown 1995: 23) manifest ressentiment (Brown 1996: 157–164), frustration and the the evocation of guilt are expressions of unredeemed modern promises of social equality and individual freedom. In redress of a closed – alleged – homogeneous and monolithic identity of 'logocentric and Eurocentric thought', so the argument runs, a concept of identity is promoted which – against the liberal democratic achievements of modernity – reasserts irrational forms of cultural traditions and primordial cultural dispositions that are a matter of fate and not of choice. Such a version of identity politics pictures tranquil and idyllic still lives of unchangeable traditions and affirms framed units and unequivocally definable identity – be it the dominant, hegemonic nation or one's own (counter-)community – and inevitably confines the single individual in an unquestionable belonging to such a community and its distinct identity. However, 'insofar as they are premised on exclusion from a universal idea, politicised identities require that ideal, as well as their exclusion from it, for their own perpetuity as identities' (Brown 1996: 155). Given the 'increasingly political manifest failure of liberal universalism to be universal – the transparent fiction of state universality' (ibid. 154), given the marginalization and the increasing individuation in capitalist society and its 'disciplinary productions', identity politics is a form of protest.

Modern liberals – be they advocates of group pluralism (Kymlicka 1995) or 'egalitarians' (Barry 2001) – and multicultural nation-states and its policies however, have to deal with these dilemmas. Not surprisingly, current approaches to politicised identity concern questions of political membership, the compatibility of democratic citizenship and practices that insist on distinct cultural identity, they include debates about the legitimacy of allocating rights to specific disadvantaged groups (such as affirmative action), the equality of opportunity (Miller 2002) and the exemption from universalistic laws. Proponents of thin liberal democratic and procedural criteria and institutions and those of thick and substantive cultural identities debate whether such groups are responsible for the results that cultural practices produce and ask whether specific cultural traditions have a worth of their own which deserve to be fostered and promoted (Kenny 2004: xii; see Taylor 1992; Honig 1993; Gildberg 1994; Kymlicka 1995; Gordon and Newfield 1996; Hall 2000; Barry 2001; Kelly 2002; Haddock and Sutch 2003; Benhabib 2004). In the wake of new nationalisms, social and political thought elaborates on new forms of patriotism (Cohen 1996) and non-foundational approaches of cosmopolitism and (Kantian) cosmopolitan law. With the resistance against social relations based on humiliation (Margalit 1996), the notion that stereotypes about minorities and social practices of stigmatisation, humiliation and degradation (Fraser 1997) injure the self and 'diminish the capacities for self-development' (Nussbaum 2000: 205), subjectivity and agency comes into view.

Re-elaborations of the notion agency and 'radical revision of the social temporality' (Bhabha 1994: 171), the formulation of issues such as cultural difference, political representation, therefore, reveal the ambivalences and tensions of modernity and the modern nation-state. According to Homi Bhabha, the ambivalent 'nation-space becomes the crossroads to a new transnational culture. The "other" is never outside or beyond us, it emerges forcefully, within cultural discourse, when we think we speak most intimately and indigenously "between ourselves"' (Bhabha 1990: 4). At the same time, this gesture erases the distinction between inside and outside, the nation is no longer a unity – based on race, common language, religion, tradition – but an 'articulation of cultural difference' (Bhabha 1990: 5) and thus 'reveals the margins of modernity' (Bhabha 1990: 6). Against (ideological) strategies of containment and closure of the modern national space, the nation comes into being in the nation's liminal spaces, its articulations and productions of difference.

The Other

The impulses of identity politics as well as politics of difference, so it seems, repeat practices that claim ethnic, cultural or religious identity and homogeneity and immutable boundaries are constructed between 'us' and 'them', 'inside' and 'outside'. Ironically, obsessions of exclusion and inclusion are consolidated at a point in time in which 'Western' social and political thought questions petrified collective identities and essentialising naturalistic-identitarian representations, a critique which in the meantime has been adjoined to various 'postmodern ethics' (Benhabib 1992; Bauman 1993; Irigaray 1999; Appiah 2005) of difference and alterity that take account of the irreducible singularity of the Other (Emmanuel Lévinas) and focus on friendship, hospitality and responsibility (Jacques Derrida).

The emerging vital questions thus, are how can modern, plural and pluralistic democracies assure both the equality and particularities without corroding one principle? How to recognise differences without falling into the trap of homogenisation? And again, how to avoid the essentialisation of identities and a strong politics of identity which does not recognise the individual, but enshrines irreducible singularity in a supposed and imaginary community of a 'we'. How to allow for choices? How to allow for the choice not to be 'the woman', 'the gay', 'the black'? How to avoid multicultural essentialism that prescribes social and cultural 'life scripts' (Appiah 1994)? And how can the claim for recognition of differences, of assuring a specific way of life be guaranteed without compromising the universalistic grounds to which equal recognition is inevitably tied?

The emphasis on recognition and responsibility has been one way to engage with these questions. Axel Honneth (1995) distinguishes three modes of intersubjective recognition, ways of relating to oneself and of the practical development of identity, namely love (as recognition of personal independence, self-assertion and the ability to being alone), law (a form of recognition that others are – as oneself is – bearers of rights) and solidarity (an intersubjectivly shared horizon of values which involves reciprocal interest and esteem) which are associated with the social spheres of the family, civil/bourgeois society and the state. Social integration thus, is featured through recognition of emotional relations, the recognition of rights and the orientation of values.[3]

Identity is shaped by self-respect, recognition or mis-recognition. Whereas recognition and identity have historically been related to social hierarchy and honour (and to distinctions 'préferences', inequalities and fixed social position) as Charles Taylor (1992) states, in a modern democratic social configuration it is related to human dignity and thus, conceptualised in an egalitarian way. With the emergence of the modern ideal of self-realisation and a individualised identity, the self's authenticity, the inner voice, self-realisation of one's own qualities and moral perfection,[4] the importance of recognition has been intensified. The 'modern' self is expressed in the assertion of irreducible (group) differences and subsequently, the tension between particular demands for recognition and equal dignity is advanced. On one hand, the historical shift from honour to dignity implies a shift from particularism to universalism. On the other hand, a shift that gave rise to a politics of difference occurred. The idea that 'everyone should be recognized for her unique identity' (Taylor 1992: 38) entails a notion of universalism, because everyone should be recognised as 'having' a particular identity and such a 'universal demand powers an acknowledgement of specificity' (ibid. 39). The principle of equal respect requires to treat people in a way that is blind to differences and to substantial matters, specific ideas and goals (Michael Walzer's Liberalism 1). Whereas such a view requires a neutral public space, the second position demands the recognition and the promotion of particularity and the fostering of substantial issues in order to allow for a good life (Liberalism 2). With regard to proponents of Liberalism 1 it has been argued however, that the claim of neutrality of procedures is itself a reflection of hegemonic culture, a 'particularism masquerading as the universal' (ibid. 44). The question for theories of justice thus is, how to secure equality and respect for everyone in a non-homogenizing way.

The tension between particularism and universalism is taken up by a renewed political theology and a politico-ethical thought which centres around the notion of responsibility. Responsibility on the one hand and duty on the other are tied to reason and to ethical instructions and prescriptions of action which are to be effective with regard to the past, the present and the future. (The amazing shift of central notions of political philosophy from 'fraternity', to 'duty' and from, 'solidarity' to 'responsibility' would merit a critical analysis which cannot be pursued here.) The notion responsibility entails different meanings. It refers to the juridical sphere, in the Judeo-Christian tradition to the responsibility before God and an Other, it refers to evaluation and to the (existentialist's) choice to choose oneself (Taylor 1976).[5]

According to Emmanuel Lévinas (1971) responsibility is not simply an attribute of identity and subjectivity but pertains to the basic structure of subjectivity and is directed towards an Other, for-an-Other. Identity thus, has to be conceptualised from the subject's responsibility. Whereas recognition is conceptualised as an intersubjective (Honneth) or dialogical process (Taylor), responsibility in Lévinas' sense is a non-symmetrical relation. I am responsible for the Other without though expecting reciprocity, the disinterested subject therefore, is subjected to an Other and host of an Other. Accordingly, hospitality, as Jacques Derrida describes it, requires the commitment to unconditional accommodation of the 'absolute, unknown, anonymous' Other, it requires to accept the Other 'at home', to donate, to 'give him a place', without enquiring as to 'identity, name passport, capabilities or origins' (Derrida and Dufourmantelle 1997: 29). This unconditionally, unquestioned acceptance requires neither reciprocity nor identification in name, it ruptures law and its rules which bestow hospitality with conditions and limits (Friese 2004: 72). With reference to Lévinas, for Jacques Derrida – who uses both concepts in a fluid way – the concept duty is the obligation, the virtue asking for a twofold gesture that criticises totalitarian dogmatism as well as the religion of capital. He calls for the duty to accept democracy as a democracy always to come, the duty of hospitality, of respect, esteem of difference, esteem of minorities and the Other's singularity, and the duty to resist xenophobia and nationalism (Derrida 1991). These debates take place in the context of pressing questions related to how contemporary democratic and pluralistic nation-states – unable to dictate commonly shared moral and ethical precepts – should interpret and implement hospitality. The question posed here is how – given the crisis of the modern systems of organised solidarity and in an atmosphere of growing nationalisms, resentment and animosity, general indifference and increasing xenophobia – to hospitably welcome the exiled, the deported, refugees, migrants and those who long for a better life? How to respond to these demands? The question that the arrival of the Other raises is thus that of responsibility – the response to a request posed by an Other – and how to do justice to its unmistakable, irreducible singularity and subjectivity.

Despite the notable differences, these perspectives advance a re-writing of the prominent tensions between universalism and (ethical) particularity, universally applicable norms, particular values and cultural differences. 'The politics of recognition needs to be inflected away from the image of the cultural enclave and deployed as the basis for a political culture in which identity figures as the source and object of dissent, debate and contestation' (Kenny 2004: 162–163). To conclude with a non-conclusion: the notion identity points towards an ambivalent, conflictual, yet productive space. As a site of articulation, a site of the production of signification and meaning, it stages the ambiguities and tensions of modernity. Additionally, once agency and temporality is taken seriously, the concept of identity loses its problematic connotations of homogeneity and totality, of stable substance and timeless essence. Thus understood, identity is no longer opposed to alterity, but a persistent practice of difference which is temporal. Against any attempts of categorical and practical closure, the task is a constant re-opening and re-elaboration, the task is to allow for a keeping open of the rifts and discontinuities the notion entails.

Notes

1 I would like to express my gratitude to Adi Barzilay, Aliza Corb, Deby Babis, Elaine Varady, Emmanuel Witzthum, Gal Engelhard, Joanna Steinhardt, Keren Cohen, Noam Gal, Rachel Brezir, Roberta Markus, Yonatan Livneh, Yuval Katz, participants of the seminar 'Cultural Identities' at the Hebrew University, Jerusalem for vivid, controversial and most inspiring discussions.
2 For a critique of Erikson's concept of and 'ego-identity', see Harré (1990).
3 One may add that 'for a large and rapidly growing part of humankind "recognition" is a nebulous idea and will be nebulous as long as money is shunned as a topic of conversation . . .' (Bauman 2004: 37).
4 Self-realization however, cannot be thought of as a monological process, it is intrinsically tied to dialogue, interaction with 'significant others' (George H. Mead). Identity is not inbuilt in social hierarchy, but has to be dialogically negotiated. For a critical reading of Taylor and an emphasis of re-distribution, see Fraser (1997); for an engagement with Honneth, see Fraser and Honneth (2003).
5 In the first instance, it refers to Roman law, the *jus te voco* and the ability to respond to a juridical instance and entails to being answerable to someone. In the Judeo-Christian tradition, it refers to the accountability before God (and Cain's reply to God's question 'Where is your brother, what have you done? 'I know not, am I my brother's keeper?' implies a double responsibility, namely before God and an Other). In contrast, Immanuel Kant does not refer to responsibility, but the categorical imperative calls for the duty, ie. an autonomous *Pflichtbewußtsein* that expresses an inevitable must and shapes the form and principles of action. Phenomenologically, responsibility refers to the process in which a text 'speaks' and the reader is appealed. The vocative dimension (from *vocare*, to call, voice) of a text appeals to us without being cognitively graspable and thus, it resembles the Heideggerian notion of *Befindlichkeit* as a pathetic understanding of a situation. The call implies as well the request to open towards the one who calls. The convocation refers to a common space of encounter and finally provocation is a call for action. Finally, the vocation implies someone being called.

References

Amit, V. and Rapport, N. (2002) *The Trouble with Community: Anthropological Reflections on Movement, Identity and Collectivity,* London: Pluto Press.
Anderson, B. (1991) *Imagined Communities: Reflections on the Origin and Spread of Nationalism,* London: Routledge.

Appadurai, A. (1990) 'Disjuncture and Difference in the Global Cultural Economy', in M. Featherstone (ed.) *Global Culture: Nationalism, Globalization and Modernity*, London: Sage.

Appadurai, A. (1996) *Modernity at Large: Cultural Dimensions of Globalization*, Minneapolis and London: University of Minnesota Press.

Appiah, K. A. (1994) 'Identity, Authenticity, Survival: Multicultural Societies and Social Reproduction', in A. Gutmann (ed.) *Multiculturalism: Examining the Politics of Recognition*, Princeton: Princeton University Press.

Appiah, K. A. (2005) *The Ethics of Identity*, Princeton: Princeton University Press.

Barry, B. M. (2001) *Culture and Equality: An Egalitarian Critique of Multiculturalism*, Cambridge, MA: Harvard University Press.

Barth, F. (1969) *Ethnic Groups and Boundaries*, London: Allen & Unwin.

Bauman, Z. (1993) *Postmodern Ethics*, Oxford, Blackwell.

Bauman, Z. (2004) *Identity: Conversations with Benedetto Vecchi*, Cambridge: Polity.

Benhabib, S. (1992) *Situating the Self: Gender, Community and Postmodernism in Contemporary Ethics*, London and New York: Routledge.

Benhabib, S. (2002) *The Claims of Culture: Equality and Diversity in the Global Era*, Princeton: Princeton University Press.

Benhabib, S. (2004) *The Rights of Others: Aliens, Residents and Citizens*, Cambridge: Cambridge University Press.

Berezin, M. and M, Schain (eds) (2003) *Europe Without Borders: Remapping Territory, Citizenship, and Identity in a Transnational Age*, Baltimore and London: The John Hopkins University Press.

Bhabha, H. K. (1990) *Nation and Narration*, London, Routledge.

Bhabha, H. K. (1994) *The Locations of Culture*, London/New York: Routledge.

Brown, W. (1995) *States of Injury: Power and Freedom in Late Modernity*, Princeton: Princeton University Press.

Brown, W. (1996) 'Injury, Identity, Politics', in A. F. Gordon and C. Newfield (eds) *Mapping Multiculturalism*, Minneapolis, University of Minnesota Press: 149–66.

Butler, J. (1990) *Gender Trouble: Feminism and the Subversion of Identity*, London: Routledge.

Clifford, J. (1992) 'Travelling Cultures', in L. Grossberg, C. Nelson, and P. A. Treichler (eds) *Cultural Studies*, New York and London: Routledge.

Clifford, J. (1994) 'Diasporas', *Cultural Anthropology*, 9(3), 302–338.

Clifford, J. (1999) *Routes: Travel and Translation in the Late Twentieth Century*, Cambridge, MA and London: Harvard University Press.

Cohen, A. (1985) *The Symbolic Construction of Community*, London and New York: Tavistock.

Cohen, J. (ed.) (1996) *For Love of Country: Debating the Limits of Patriotism*, Boston: Beacon Press.

Derrida, J. (1991) *L'autre cap suivi de La démocratie ajournée*, Paris: Minuit.

Derrida, J. and Dufourmantelle, A. (1997) *De l'hospitalité*, Paris: Calmann-Lévy.

Eisenstadt, S. N. (1998) 'The Construction of Collective Identities: Some Analytical and Comparative Indications', *European Journal of Social Theory*, 1(2), 229–254.

Erikson, E. H. (1968) 'Identity, psychosocial', in *International Encyclopedia of the Social Sciences*, vol. 7, London and New York: Macmillan/Free Press.

Fraser, N. (1997) *Justice Interruptus: Critical Reflections on the 'Postsocialist' Condition*, London and New York: Routledge.

Fraser, N. and Honneth, A. (2003) *Redistribution or Recognition? A Political-Philosophical Exchange* (trans. J. Golb and C. Wilke), London: Verso.

Friedman, J. (1994) *Cultural Identity and Global Process*, London: Sage.

Friese, H. (ed.) (2002) *Identities: Time, Difference and Boundaries*, New York and Oxford: Berghahn.

Friese, H. (2004) 'Spaces of Hospitality', in A. Benjamin and D. Vardoulakis (eds) *Politics of Place: Angelaki, Journal of the Theoretical Humanities*, 9(2), 67–79.

Gildberg, D. T. (1994) *Multiculturalism: A Critical Reader*, Oxford: Blackwell.

Gilroy, P. (1993) *The Black Atlantic: Modernity and Double Consciousness*, Cambridge, MA.: Harvard University Press.

Gordon, A. F. and Newfield, C. (eds) (1996) *Mapping Multiculturalism*, Minneapolis, University of Minnesota Press.

Guarnizo, L. E. and Smith, M. P. (eds) (1998) *Transnationalism from Below*, New Brunswick and London: Transaction Publishers.

Gupta, A. and Ferguson, J. (eds) (1997) *Culture, Power, Place: Explorations in Critical Anthropology*, Durham: Duke University Press.

Haddock, B. and Sutch, P. (eds) (2003) *Multiculturalism, Identity, and Rights*, London: Routledge.

Hall, S. (2000) 'Old and New Identities: Old and New Ethnicities', in L. Back and J. Solomos (eds) *Theories of Race and Racism: A Reader*, London and New York: Routledge.

Hall, S. and du Gay, P. (eds) (1996) *Questions of Cultural Identity*, London: Sage.

Harré, R. (1990) 'Language Games and the Texts of Identity', in J. Shotter and K. J. Gergen (eds) *Texts of Identity*, London: Sage, 20–35.

Honig, B. (1993) *Political Theory and the Displacement of Politics*, Ithaca: Cornell University Press.

Honneth, A. (1995) *The Struggle for Recognition: The Moral Grammar of Social Conflicts*, Cambridge, MA: MIT Press.

Irigaray, L. (1999) *Entre Orient et Occident: De la singularité à la communauté*, Paris: Grasset.

James, S. (2000) 'Feminism and the Philosophy of Mind: the Question of Personal Identity', in M. Fricka and J. Hornsby (eds) *The Cambridge Companion to Feminism in Philosophy*, Cambridge: Cambridge University Press: 29–48.

Kelly, P. (ed.) (2002) *Multiculturalism Reconsidered: Culture and Equality and its Critics*, Cambridge: Polity.

Kenny, M. (2004) *The Politics of Identity: Liberal Political Theory and the Dilemmas of Difference*, Cambridge: Polity.

Kymlicka, W. (1995) *Multicultural Citizenship*, Oxford: Oxford University Press.

Lévinas, E. (1971) *Totalité et infini*, Paris: Biblio.

Lyotard, J-F. (1988) 'Réécrire la modernité', in *L'inhumain. Causeries sur le temps*, Paris: Galilée: 33–44.

Margalit, A. (1996) *The Decent Society*, Cambridge, MA: Harvard University Press.

Miller, D. (2002) 'Liberalism, Equal Opportunities and Cultural Commitments', in P. Kelly (ed.) *Multiculturalism Reconsidered: Culture and Equality and its Critics*, Cambridge: Polity: 45–61.

Nancy, J.-L. (1996) *Être singulier pluriel*, Paris: Galilée.

Nancy, J.-L. (1991) *The Inoperative Community*, Minneapolis and London: University of Minnesota Press (orig. (1990) *La communauté désoeuvrée*, Paris: Christian Bourgeois Ed.)

Nussbaum, M. (2000) *Women and Human Development: The Capabilities Approach*, Cambridge: Cambridge University Press.

Okin, S. M., Cohen, J., Howard, M. and Nussbaum, M. (1999) *Is Multiculturalism Bad for Women?* Princeton: Princeton University Press.

Parker, I. (1990) 'Discourse and Power', in J. Shotter and K. J. Gergen (eds) *Texts of Identity*, London: Sage: 56–69.

Renan, E. (1990 [1882]) 'What is a Nation?', in H. Bhabha (ed.) *Nation and Narration*, London: Routledge.

Sampson, E. E. (1990) 'The Deconstruction of the Self', in J. Shotter and K. J. Gergen (eds) *Texts of Identity*, London: Sage: 1–19.

Taylor, C. (1976) 'Responsibility for Self', in A. O. Rorty (ed.) *The Identities of Persons*, Berkeley: University of California Press: 281–299.

Taylor, C. (1992) *Multiculturalism and 'the Politics of Recognition': An Essay*, Princeton: Princeton University Press.

Wagner, P. (2002) 'Identity and Selfhood as a Problématique', in H. Friese (ed.) *Identities: Time, Difference and Boundaries*, New York and Oxford: Berghahn: 32–55.

24

Nations, belonging and community

Ulf Hedetoft

This chapter will review and discuss some of the principal ways in which the idea of nation has been theoretically activated to explain, construct and contextualize political and cultural community as well as sentiments of belonging and identity. While aiming to examine changing nexuses between the three central notions contained in the title, the analytical optic will be historical, conceptual and cross-disciplinary – as befits an object of study that has engaged prominent scholars in a variety of different disciplines (notably sociology, political science, anthropology, history and psychology) throughout European modernity. Apart from identifying a number of core concepts, *topoi* and interconnections, a further objective will be to indicate not just the theoretical import of different 'schools of thought', but also the societal grounding and historical implications underpinning historical classifications and periodizations. In other words, why do certain explanatory schemes and theoretical templates seem to have more purchase in some periods than others; can we identify any kind of historical 'logic' that ties epistemological progress to the ontology of real-life diachronic processes in the evolution of national communities; and, not least, how have scholars conceptualized new configurations between 'nation-states', 'nations as transborder communities' and 'nations in the global age'?

Foundations and connections

In a well-known statement, Eric Hobsbawm once asserted that no serious scholar of nationalism could possibly be a 'committed political nationalist' (1990: 12), since 'nationalism requires too much belief in what is patently not so'. Partly for this reason and partly because the heyday of nation-states and national communities, *pace* Hobsbawm at least, should be located between 1918 and 1950, he thought that 'very little other than nationalist and racist rhetoric was being written' during the 'classic period of nineteenth-century liberalism', except for the occasional piece by John Stuart Mill (1958 [1861]) and Ernest Renan (1990 [1882]) (ibid.: 2). He could, and should probably, have added Herder and certainly Tönnies' classic piece on *Gesellschaft und Gemeinschaft* (1957 [1887]) to this select list of works trying to apply 'dispassionate analysis' (p. 2) to questions of nations, communities and belonging.

Nevertheless, most scholars of nationalism and nation states would probably agree that the eighteenth- and nineteenth-centuries are not fruitful periods in which to locate a rich volume of scholarly literature shedding light on the nature of 'national communities'. They might also concede that Hobsbawm, in 1990, got it right by arguing that 'the number of works genuinely illuminating the question of what nations and national movements are and what role in historical development they play is larger in the period 1968–1988 than for any earlier period of twice that length' (ibid.: 4).

The implication – that even the period which Hobsbawm identifies as the 'apogee of nationalism' (1918–1950) was theoretically barren – might come as a surprise for some, but is nevertheless not without merits, though the case is made too crudely by the old historian. He gives Hans Kohn (1931, 1967 [1944]) and Carlton Hayes (1931) their due, but neglects not only Tönnies, but also Durkheim, Marcel Mauss and, most remarkably, Max Weber – one of the first to point out that the nation should be 'located in the field of politics' and be appropriately understood as 'a community of sentiment which would adequately manifest itself in a state of its own' (Weber 1994 [1948]: 179).

This definition accords well with not just Renan's volitionist specification of nations as 'a daily plebiscite' (Renan 1990 [1882]), but also with Hobsbawm's four key features: that nationalism, *pace* Ernest Gellner (with whom he here agrees), is a principle holding that the political and national unit should be congruent; that nations and nationalism are inherently modern phenomena, though certain embryonic ('proto-nationalist') dimensions can be found in earlier periods; that the 'national question' is a product of social, economic, political and technological transformations; and that nations are 'dual phenomena', constructed 'from above' but appropriated and reconfigured 'from below', by the 'assumptions, hope, needs, longings and interests of ordinary people' (ibid.: 10). Hence, the content of what constitutes 'a nation' can and will shift over time, and we should not, *a priori*, confuse official pronouncements about the national community with more affective and often anti-establishment popular views.

Hobsbawm thus overlooked some, though not many important contributions to the historical study of national communities – primarily from the fields of sociology and anthropology. But these are excusable slips. On the basis of current knowledge and with the benefit of hindsight, it is easier to gain a full view of continuities and fractures, strong contributions and conspicuous blind spots.

On balance, it is more significant that Hobsbawm was able to identify three nagging problem areas within the theorization of nations, communities and belonging: first, that the knowledge base has multiplied and deepened in untold ways since (approximately) 1970; second, that there is a close correlation between cognitive insight and historical phase – in other words, between the historical 'epistemology' and 'ontology' of nationalism; and third, that the 'nation' looks very different from the 'external scholarly' and the 'internal experienced', the dispassionate and the identifying perspective. The second and third of these problems deserve a few additional comments.

Hobsbawm refers to the Hegelian aphorism that the owl of Minerva flies out at dusk – when phenomena to be explained are past their peak – for a generic explanation of why the scholarship on nation states and nationalism has experienced a boost since 1970 (ibid.: 192; see also Smith 2001: 21). Another way to formulate a similar explanation would be to refer to phases of social transformation as periods in which new and deeper insights tend to surface, because transformations, shocks or revolutions challenge existing assumptions and paradigms (Kuhn 1962). Both ways theorize a particular pattern of interaction between social reality and epistemological progress. The problem lies not in the validity of the approach – i.e. that it explains some, though not all advances in the social sciences – but, first, whether it is the only possible explanatory framework and, second, if it adequately accounts, specifically, for recent advances in the theorization of national communities.

The first of these problems need not concern us much in this context. The second is more crucial. Hobsbawm is only right if:

(a) the period after 1970 can in fact be categorized as the 'dusk' of nationalism and the advent of a new era; and
(b) other factors other than 'distance' and 'less need for practical identification with the national community' cannot reasonably be activated.

On both counts the outcome is less than crystal clear. While it is true that the period after 1970 ushers in some serious challengers to national communities and national identification – in the form of transnational, interdependence-related and global developments – national identity and the nation-state are patently far from moribund, even if from a rational perspective it makes sense to cast them as somewhat anachronistic, paradoxical and even 'tribal'.

This means that other factors must also be activated to explain the interest and insights in the field. Apart from the persistence of and continued fascination with nationalism, with its dualisms and its powerful impact (among people at large as well as intellectuals and political actors, and both as a political and cultural phenomenon), theories of communities and belonging organized around 'the nation' have also increasingly profited from the scholarly realization that this is a genuinely trans-disciplinary object of study which can only be fully understood if concepts and theories from a variety of disciplines are activated simultaneously and in concert. As for explanatory factors, this points us inward towards the structure of academia and the dynamics of epistemology itself rather than outward towards the relevance and topicality of the nation-state and its attendant community feelings.

Finally, the international *system* – though undoubtedly being fast overlaid by a global, *supra*national one – is nevertheless still very much alive, new states (routinely conceiving of themselves as nation-states) being created and seeing their legitimacy in the recognition by, and participation in, the system and its institutions. This is a fact that still adds to the continued relevance of national communities, which continue to engage a multitude of academics – many of whom do, as Hobsbawm concedes, fortunately manage to distance themselves sufficiently from their object of study: 'To be Irish and proudly attached to Ireland ... is not in itself incompatible with the serious study of Irish history' (Hobsbawm 1990: 13). The question is if the 'primordialist' school to be discussed now can be seen to conform to the criteria of 'compatibility' with 'serious' research thus introduced by the radical historian of 'the invention of traditions' (Hobsbawm and Ranger 1983).

Theories of 'dawn': primordialism

In this essay, the notion of 'primordialism' is not employed to refer to a single, theoretically consistent conceptualization of national communities, but as a heuristic designation of different sub-strands held together, positively, by a more or less powerful element of essentialism and presumptions of historical 'rootedness' and continuity, and, negatively, by a marked normative difference from modernist and constructivist frameworks. They are thus theorizations that tend to emphasize the *Gemeinschaft* elements of national belonging and not infrequently to conceive of nations, ethnic groups and forms of communal solidarity as strongly linked (if not coterminous). Further, they will tend to highlight – albeit in varying configurations and with varying degrees of insistence – the historical continuity, anthropological 'constancy', cultural grounding and innate natural properties of 'nationness' as invariables of human bonding, affective belonging and solidary behaviour.

Primordialism comes in three different sub-strands: ethnic perennialism, ethno-symbolism and cultural communitarianism. They are united by their organicist focus and essentialist assumptions, but differ in their view of human volition, social relationism and political contingency as components of communal solidarity and ethno-historical continuity. They further differ on another significant point: whereas it is possible to identify self-admitted representatives of ethno-symbolism (mainly in Europe, e.g. John Armstrong and Anthony Smith) and cultural communitarianism (mainly in North America, e.g. Michael Sandel and Charles Taylor, though the communitarian label has not always been enthusiastically embraced), it is very hard to find scholars who would willingly accept being categorized as 'perennialists'. In fact, 'perennialism' is a rather ghostly presence in studies of nations and nationalism – an epithet that seems to adhere to and characterize the work of others, but never one's own. Perennialism has almost turned into a term of abuse, a derogatory label, an academic stereotype. Walker Connor, whom one might have seen as a relatively thoroughbred exemplar of perennialism (1978, 1993) – due to his emphasis on the psychological continuity of 'shadowy' and 'elusive' ethno-national bonding throughout the history of mankind – nevertheless stresses that nations and ethnic groups are not completely coterminous ('nations are self-aware ethnic groups') and that civic elements and transformations of nationhood play a significant role. And Anthony Smith, whose work in the 1970s and 1980s has often been perceived as perennialist, has, at least since the early 1990s, been intent on distancing himself from the perennialist label while stressing that his own 'ethno-symbolist' approach is qualitatively different and makes allowance for the modernity of nation-states and nationalism (see further below). In brief, no one (except self-proclaimed political or cultural ideologues, like Haider, Powell and LePen) is a perennialist in their own view, while many are seen to be so by others.

This is no doubt a consequence of the increasingly defensive and marginalized position which primordialist approaches have been forced into by the advances of modernist, constructivist and globalist theories of national communities and national belonging. Perennialism pure and simple has become too hard to argue without a strong admixture of modernity and plurality. Nevertheless, whether or not it is seen as an approach in its own right or rather as a name indicating a pronounced normative *tendency*, perennialism is a useful concept. It denotes a view of community, identity and nationhood as immersed in, conditioned through and centrally determined by continuous historical ethnicity, which is seen to be both 'eternal' and the 'independent variable' of collective bonding. Perennialism does not necessarily deny that historical processes and political contexts play a role, but *Gesellschaft* (civic values and citizenship) is always secondary to *Gemeinschaft* (ethnicity, consanguity and kinship). Or in synchronic terms: even though national communities contain both ethnic and civic elements, the latter are subordinated to the former, which enjoy unquestioned *primacy*. Furthermore, in such 'pure' form, perennialism is deterministic, collectivistic and 'objective', i.e. posits ethnic identity and group solidarity as located *beyond* social voluntarism, psychological individuation and republican values, in basic human-needs structures which defy contingent manipulation.

Nevertheless, it is precisely on these counts that both *ethno-symbolism* and *cultural communitarianism* depart from such axiomatic presumptions. In Anthony Smith's words, ethno-symbolism sees 'national identities' as being continually reconstituted through processes of selection of symbolic elements from that ethno-heritage and re-identifications with the reconstituted ethno-heritage. On this view, nations and national identities are 'rooted' in cultural traditions and continuities, which need to be analysed 'in the *longue durée*' (Smith 2001: 31), and which are subject to changes and gradual modifications based on the specifics of different historical contexts and their configurations of actors involved in the processes of identity reconstruction and community formation – but only as long as 'these changes remain within the parameters of an ethno-heritage, or of a historic confluence of such heritages. ... Elites will therefore operate within the limits of the popular resonance of traditional identifications, current historical knowledge and shared historical traditions' (ibid.).

While thus allowing both for the active role of individuals and groups in the continuous process of re-interpreting collective symbols and myths, the limits of identity construction are nevertheless seen to be narrowly constrained by 'objective' constituents of 'the ethnic past' (ibid.: 38). On the other hand, although these components are no doubt 'authentic', they are so only within inverted commas, and should not be 'regarded as perennial' (ibid. 32). Ethno-symbolism gives the devil his due, but when push comes to shove, ethnicity has an essential life of its own, in which 'symbols are the medium and means' (ibid. 32), but where core meanings and memories remain relatively unchanged over long time stretches, buttressing the cultural and territorial stability of communal belonging on the soil of a given *ethnie*'s 'historic homeland' (see Smith 1991: ch. 4).

The explicit product of a latter-day politics of identity and recognition, *communitarianism* is more cognizant of modern developments. The core of communitarian thinking (which comes in two variants, a 'thick' and a 'thin' – cf. Delanty (2002) – and has been developed by prominent political philosophers since the 1970s) is a set of normative and ontological claims about the value of community, the social nature of the Self and the significance of tradition. Particularly, communitarianism focuses on the right of *survival* (due to the intrinsic *worth*) of vulnerable collectivities in the face of increasing external pressures emanating from globalization, pluralization or just the imposition of neutral justice by liberal polities (Taylor 1994). Thus, communitarians, more than ethno-symbolists, recognize that cultural communities are contingent entities, which can both be fundamentally altered and even extinguished by the political conditions determining what Charles Taylor calls the 'age of authenticity'. Where Smith emphasizes the resilience of national communities, Taylor foregrounds their vulnerability. Where Smith points to the significance of long historical continuities, Taylor underscores the specifics of the modern condition. And where Smith, eventually, comes down on the side of objectivist factors of identity determination, Taylor invariably stays with the importance of the dialogic human element, enlightenment ideals of mutual recognition and political voluntarism as salient constituents in the processes that ultimately decide whether cultural communities like the Quebecois are going to survive and thrive – or not.

Nevertheless, in spite of this synchronic focus, communitarianism too builds its case on historical assumptions of the deep rootedness and basic need for collective identities and affective communal belonging. As Taylor puts it, 'what has come about with the modern age is not the need for recognition but the conditions in which the attempt to be recognized can fail' (Taylor 1994: 35). In this sense, communitarianism is a narrative of (real or potential) cultural decline, where immanent, *an sich* authentic identities – now regarded as aboriginal, native, small-state or historical minorities – become conscious of themselves *für sich,* and of the questionable conditions in which they must safeguard their survival. It is modernity which is responsible for their quest for the maintenance and recognition of their autonomy, but the quest is compensatory, reflecting a deeper historical essence beyond retrieval.

Theories of 'high noon': modernism and constructivism

The modernist disagreement with communitarians and other essentialists does not reside in the recognition accorded to cultural belonging and community feeling, as the following statement by Ernest Gellner, written during the last phase of his life, indicates:

> Cultures freeze associations, and endow them with a feel of necessity. They turn mere worlds into *homes*, where men can feel comfortable, where they belong rather than explore, where things have their allocated places and form a system. That is what a culture is. . . . Atomistic individualism is custom-corrosive and culture-corrosive. It facilitates the growth of knowledge . . . but it weakens the authority of cultures and makes the world less habitable, more cold and alien.
>
> (Gellner 1998: 5)

Quite a lyrical, and yet precise description of the (national) cultures that Gellner, in his best-known work (1983), dissected and diagnosed as 'fabrications' resulting from the imperatives of industrialization and its division of labour, and leading to 'exo-socialization', 'high cultures' and linguistic homogenization, because 'nationalism is a theory of political legitimacy, which requires that ethnic boundaries should not cut across political ones' (p. 1). This is where Gellner, and modernists more widely, part ways with the 'primordialists': these specific cultures and this particular theory of legitimate authority are constructions of the modern age, *causally determined* by processes of economic rationalization, secularization and homogenization, proceeding according to a functionalist logic of state/nation congruity, underpinned by enlightenment ideas and conceivable within a general evolutionary history of progress.

With so much emphasis on functionalist causal connections, it is no surprise that Gellner's (anthropologically informed) cultural sensitivity should have been widely overlooked, and his 'fabrication' interpreted as implying 'falsehood' and 'lack of authenticity'. No doubt Gellner was not always totally consistent on these counts, and may also have mellowed somewhat with age. But it should not be forgotten that already the second paragraph of *Nations and Nationalism* speaks to the affective component of national cultures, in terms of the 'anger' aroused when the nationalist principle is violated, and the 'satisfaction' when it is fulfilled. He succinctly points out that '*nations maketh man*; nations are the artefacts of men's convictions and loyalties and solidarities' (p. 7; original emphasis). He also foreshadows Benedict Anderson's 'imagined communities' theory of nationalism (1991 [1983]) and even theories of identity politics and symbolic interactionism when, in the same paragraph, he insists that 'two men are of the same nation if and only if they *recognize* each other as belonging to the same nation' (ibid.; original emphasis; see also Hall 1998).

What unites modernists and constructivists are at least three common presumptions: first, that nation-states, nationalism and national identity are distinctly modern phenomena, and that we must accept the rupture, or at least the dissimilarity, between the modern, industrial, bourgeois age and the various pre-modern (agrarian, archaic, medieval, late-feudal, etc.) historical phases and socio-economic formations in order to explain these facts and processes adequately; this does not mean that pre-modern conditioning features of group solidarity cannot be identified, but they are no more than that: preconditions, pieces in the puzzle, 'proto-national' elements, in Hobsbawm's terminology.

Second, that nationalism – often by way of states and state elites – produces nations, not the other way around. This is the crucial difference between primordialists and modernists. The former root nations in the invariable ethnic propensity of *homo sapiens*, as a supra-historical, anthropomorphic 'fact' and no more than one variant – though a pretty significant one – of ethnic bonding. The latter see nations as products of specific socio-economic, cultural and political developments, as ideational and reflexive artefacts shaped in the image of a specific political ideology, a specific structuration of needs and interests, and a specific 'model' of group solidarity and mutual interaction.

Third, that – ideally at least – states and nations tend to conflate into a single symbiotic nexus within an often implicit and tacit contractual agreement on mutual rights and duties between citizens and rulers, masses and elites, electorates and governments. The civic-republican order, democratically maintained, finds its correlate of cultural belonging in Renan's famous 'daily plebiscite' of nationhood (Renan 1990 [1882]). Modernists and constructivists argue that this intimate coupling of 'nation' and 'state' within the dual perimeters of 'civic' and 'ethnic' dimensions is both a necessary condition for a well-functioning state system and a carefully forged myth of co-extensiveness between culture, politics and territory (Yack 1999), which is rarely, if ever, fulfilled in practice, but precisely as a future goal, a 'subjunctive' ambition more than an 'indicative fact' (Hedetoft 1995), has worked as a powerful engine of (national) progress and dynamism.

How this came to be, has been studied with admirable accuracy by Miroslav Hroch (1985), who exposed the three salient formative phases of nation-building in Europe: that of narrow intellectual elites; that of wider sections of the bourgeois classes; and that of mass popular mobilization. On the other hand, the nexus between states and nations can only be regarded as enduring in a future-oriented perspective if the modern order is seen to be the 'end of history'. And among modernist and constructivist scholars of nationalism, these are hard to find. Nevertheless, regarding the specifics of this question, assessments are divided.

We have already seen that Marxist-inspired historians like Eric Hobsbawm (seconded by many world-systems theorists) see the nation-state as moribund, past its prime: there are period-specific limits to the successful, top-down 'invention of traditions' for the sake of maintaining national loyalties (Hobsbawm and Ranger 1983). Modernists are rarely very explicit about the future of national belonging, and can be said to fall into two sub-compartments, which could be dubbed 'Hegelian optimists' and 'Weberian rationalists'. The former tend to view the modern order as the best of all possible worlds and the community of nations as durable, possibly in new configurations (here they approximate to the ethno-symbolist interpretation, with the exception that modernists are more concerned about the future than the past); whereas the latter, true to the period-specific argumentation of the Gellnerian school, at least intimate that the nation/state nexus is contingent, though hard-and-fast predictions are rare. Interestingly, constructivist modernists like Benedict Anderson (1991 [1983]) and Stuart Hall (e.g. 1996) – more open to the power of imagination, discursive reconstructions of cultural identities and more liminal negotiations of belonging – are often more 'Hegelian' than 'Weberian'. Finally, scholars of democracy, communicative rationality and public space, notably Jürgen Habermas (e.g. 1994, 1997; see also Maier 1988), tend to sit on the fence between a pessimist narrative of the 'decline' of democratic dialogue and the optimism of a 'constitutional patriotism' or of 'nested identities' that might rescue national cultures and belonging, both from the snares of ethnic atavism and the diminishing political legitimacy which might follow from impending disjunctures of 'nations' from 'states'. This is one of the themes that occupy postmodern theories of globalist challenges to national belonging.

Theories of 'dusk': nations in postmodernity

The intimate connection between belonging and community, nationally interpreted – bounded, homogeneous, organic and unitary – has never been more than an ideal, often practically contradicted by messy borders, migratory movements, ethnic minorities, multiple citizenships and multi-ethnic (often imperial) polities. Economic and technological globalization as well as cultural and political transnationalism have multiplied and strengthened such tendencies (Rosenau 1990). They have weakened the sovereign nation-state by means of trans-state 'flows', which create or facilitate 'open' borders, multiple and hybrid forms of identity (Bhabha 1990; Said 2000), or even 'supraterritorial', postnational or cosmopolitan forms of belonging and non-belonging (Basch *et al.* 1994; Appadurai 1996; Castles and Davidson 2000; Hedetoft and Hjort 2002). Territoriality is becoming 'de-territorialized' – concrete 'place' transmuting into abstract 'space' (Carter *et al.* 1993; Massey 1994; Frykman 2004). Entrenched national identity patterns, whether conceived as essential or constructed, are being contested, *inter alia* through qualitatively different forms of migratory processes on a global scale, which give rise to new claims-making and rights-based collectivities, networks and actions (Soysal 1994; Smith and Guarnizo 1998; Vertovec 1999; Christiansen and Hedetoft 2004). In the process, a new kind of homogeneity, and attendant forms of consciousness and allegiance – monstrous to some, utopian to others – are coming into being: belonging to the globe, the region, the corporation or the 'cause', rather than (or in addition to) the nation. Ultimately, this is the contemporary cosmopolitan dream, whose flipside is the globally imposed homogeneity of American cultural hegemony and western supremacy – and possible resultant civilizational confrontations (Barber 1995; Huntington 1996).

In this welter of postmodern challenges to national community and belonging, three discreet modalities can be identified, reflecting different theoretical conceptualizations – in the following order of 'gravity', when measured in terms of the extent to which they seem to contest the nation/state nexus: *multiculturalism* (including theories of hybridization); *transnationalism* (including epistemic communities and diasporic networks); and *cosmopolitanism* (including regional configurations like 'European identity').

In *Rethinking Multiculturalism*, Bhiku Parekh succinctly argues that 'a multicultural society faces two conflicting demands and needs to devise a political structure that enables it to reconcile them in a just and collectively acceptable manner. … Paradoxical as it may seem, the greater and deeper the diversity in a society, the greater the unity and cohesion it requires to hold itself together and nurture its diversity' (2000: 196).

Conceived thus, multiculturalism does not stand in a relationship of opposition to homogeneous nationalism, but is a reformulation of communitarian nationalist identity politics in light of the pressures this traditional model of identity construction has experienced because of global migration or the increasing assertiveness of historical minorities – and ensuing cultural–political diversity (Bauböck 1994; Kymlicka 1995, 2001; Benhabib 1999, 2000). Hence, it is a political response to new conditions for the creation of close linkages of identity, culture or loyalty between states and their popular base, an attempt to domesticate global pressures, modify and diversify the conditions on which citizenship and nationality can be attained and practised.

In functional terms, multiculturalism can hence be seen as an attempt to rescue national communities by forging a sustainable condominium between homogeneity and diversity within the continued framework of the nation-state. Conceived as a political solution to a number of social, ethnic and political *problems*, multiculturalism is an experiment of sorts – one that is increasingly seen to have failed (e.g. Berger 1998; Ascherson 2004; Delanty 2004; Goodhart 2004; Lentin 2004), either because it has proved difficult to define the limits to difference that will ensure continued solidarity and cohesion; because the top-down intention of depoliticizing, domesticating and functionalizing cultural differences through strategies of cooptation, socialization, tolerance and 'positive discrimination' has run into intractable problems; or because nationalist and popularist backlashes against this kind of public diversity management – not least after 11 September 2001 – have made the multicultural matrix difficult to defend and apply.

The other two types, *transnationalism* and *cosmopolitanism*, share a number of features and overlapping boundaries, but should nonetheless be kept distinct. Transnationalism represents the 'logical' (albeit often affectively based) transgression of national attempts at pluricultural diversity management, whether as multiculturalism, hyphenization of identities or cultural hybridization. Transnationalism retains the 'national' foundation of identity formation, but disconnects it from the state as its 'political roof', as Gellner labelled it. In Arjun Appadurai's pithy formulation, 'even as the legitimacy of nation-states in their own territorial context is increasingly under threat, the idea of the nation flourishes transnationally' (1996: 172).

Such 'transnations', the result of increasing global population flows combined with modern communication technologies and diasporic images of 'home' (Rapport and Dawson 1998), in many ways reverse the assumptions on which traditional national communities secure their survival. Not by entering into close identity relations with specific polities, but by transcending, criticizing, sidestepping and evading them, overriding the geopolitical boundaries that divide them while thus forging an entirely cultural conception of nationalism, which can accommodate fluidity and geographical dispersion and do without standard paraphernalia such as sovereignty and territory, but not without a historical and ethnic imaginary bolstered by perpetual high-speed interaction. In this sense, transnational communities are a practical, and sometimes theoretical, critique of the nation in its more traditional form, but it draws its inspiration and sap from it nevertheless. Thus, cleavages between and reimaginings of the nation-state co-exist in a state of continuous and liminal interaction within the parameters of transnationalisms.

For its part, cosmopolitanism – be it as imagined world citizenship (e.g. Beck 2000), as global imaginings, virtual networks or culture (Featherstone 1990; Bauman 1998; Castells 2001) or as global environmental consciousness (Keck and Sikkink 1998) – is less tied to the nation-state framework, but precisely for that reason is also more philosophical, ideological and utopian, and, in practice, is mostly to be found either among global business and academic elites or among certain NGOs working to implement a humanitarian-universalistic rather than a western-pragmatic form of globalization (see different contributions to Lechner and Boli 2004). Martha Nussbaum's edited volume from 1996, *For Love of Country*, is representative of the debates surrounding cosmopolitanism,[1] displaying as it does both the necessary abstractness of cosmopolitan claims to a new identity, which fully transcends the nation-state, and the overwhelming presence of this nation-state nevertheless, even in theorizations of such new forms of consciousness and allegiance. In fact, the argument forwarded by Nussbaum takes its cue from the specific American context, arguing that laudable moral and patriotic values with a US origin should be extended beyond the American border – cosmopolitanism, thus conceived, being hard to distinguish from a particular nationalism writ large, and in turn laying itself open to charges of cultural imperialism in moral garb (Tomlinson 1991).

Unfair as such objections may be, they are evidence that most conceptions of cosmopolitan identity and belonging are still deeply saturated by and rooted in the nation-state as a basic referent and source of values and inspiration. Even if cosmopolitanism is seen to translate into either 'civilizational' security communities or, regionally, into 'European identity' constructs (Weidenfeld 1985; Schlesinger 1992; Delanty 1995; Medrano 2003), such (top-down) imaginings have not yet managed to effect a divorce between themselves as autonomous, let alone primary shapers of identity and belonging, and the nation-state as the core imagined community of both cognitive and affective attachment. In this sense, Alexander Motyl (1999: 113) may have a point: 'if only because the field is bereft of conceptual contenders, modernity can only continue to breed nationalism'. How does this relate to Eric Hobsbawm's predictions about the demise of nationalism? Have we come full circle – does nationalism have 'a navel' after all, as Anthony Smith asserted in a well-known debate with Gellner (see Smith 1996)?

Old problems – new syntheses

This is not the place to try to resolve these sticky questions. It is possible, however, to identify at least three salient points around which there is now a reasonable measure of theoretical consensus.

The first is that the modernity of national communities and the 'postmodern' phenomenon of globalization need not be mutually exclusive. No doubt globalization demands that nation-states and national identities adapt to new circumstances and reinvent themselves, but it does not necessitate their disappearance. In fact, the adaptability (including both ability and will-ingness to adapt) of national belonging is manifested in all the forms discussed so far. So, although the age of American globalization compels us to 'think ourselves beyond the nation' (Appadurai 1996: 158), globality does not *supplant* the nation-state and its forms of homeness. It changes their contexts, situates national identity and belonging differently, and super-imposes itself on nationality as a supplementary frame of reference and value orientation, but 'allows' the nation as a prime referent of communality and belonging to persist.

The second area of consensus is that in a sense 'we are all constructivists now', since at least the overwhelming majority of scholars of nationalism agree that nationalism *is* a construct (imagined, invented or discursively imposed) and *is* a historically rather recent phenomenon. On the other hand, this does not imply waving goodbye to primordialism altogether, since the strength of what could be called 'lived primordialism in practice' is beyond question and needs to be explained. In this regard, there is an incipient realization that the organic attrac-tiveness of national identities does not preclude their 'objective constructedness'. In other words, primordially experienced ties and feelings of 'essential' belonging, given the appro-priate circumstances, can very well be the result of historical invention (Croucher 2004). There is a problem of course: where ideal-type nationalism presupposes that the political and the pre-political community, citizenship and ethnicity, be imagined and socially 'enacted' as one – and in the cultural imaginary be divested of all political or constructed elements – there the global era threatens to disaggregate the two, by making the constructedness of 'authenti-city' explicit and the decoupling not just possible, but evident. On the other hand, reactions by 'nationalists' (ordinary citizens as well as ideologues) to this quandary can be, and often have been, to reject all attempts at de-essentializing national belonging and so much more forcefully to abide by or even re-invent its magnetic qualities.

This finally raises the question of whether Hobsbawm was mistaken about the anachronistic qualities of nationalism. The answer must be 'not entirely'. It is not contradictory to argue that although certain necessary conditions for the persistence of nationalism are still with us and modernity has not vanished (but been equipped with a globally superimposed layer), these conditions do not constitute the most propitious underpinning of national belonging-ness. Nationalism has indeed lost a large share of its forward-looking, progressive potential. The preoccupation of communitarians with the survival of national belonging is as much a reflection of nationalism's loss of cultural power as are multiculturalist attempts to effect a harmonious combination of homogeneity and diversity. Anachronism presupposes a temporal and functional dislocation between 'period' and 'phenomenon'. In the sense that the Janus-faced nature of nationalism is predicated as much on pointing the way forward as on main-taining intimate links with the past, contemporary nationalism in many of its manifestations is no doubt a truncated phenomenenon and in that sense a partial anachronism. But in the sense that as a cultural container of communal belonging it is still (in some domains increasingly) powerful, it is obviously far too early to write it off. Even anachronisms can have a con-temporary function, and if this is nationalism's time of dusk, night seems frightfully long in coming on.

Notes

1   But see also Hannerz (1996); Croucher (2004: ch. 8); Gilroy (2004); various contributions to Hedetoft and Hjort (2002); and Michael Billig on Richard Rorty's nationalism in Billig (1995: ch. 7).

References

Anderson, B. (1991 [1983]) *Imagined Communities*, London: Verso.

Appadurai, A. (1996) *Modernity at Large: Culturalæ Dimensions of Globalization*, Minneapolis: University of Minnesota Press.

Armstrong, J. (1982) *Nations before Nationalism*, Chapel Hill: University of North Carolina Press.

Ascherson, N. (2004) *From multiculturalism to where?*, London: Open Democracy, www.openDemocracy .net, accessed 19 August 2004.

Barber, B. (1995) *Jihad vs McWorld*. New York: Random House.

Basch, L., Glick-Schiller, N. and Blanc, C. S. (1994) *Nations Unbound: Transnational Projects, Postcolonial Predicaments, and Deterritorialized Nation-States*, Basel: Gordon and Breach.

Bauböck, R. (ed.) (1994) *From Aliens to Citizens: Redefining the Status of Immigrants in Europe*, Aldershot: Avebury.

Bauman, Z. (1998) *Globalization: The Human Consequences*, Cambridge: Polity.

Beck, U. (2000) *What is Globalization?*, Cambridge: Polity.

Benhabib, S. (1999) *Kulturelle Vielfalt und demokratische Gleichheit*, Frankfurt am Main: Fischer.

Benhabib, S. (2000) *The Claims of Culture*, Princeton: Princeton University Press.

Berger, P. (ed.) (1998) *The Limits of Social Cohesion: Conflict and Mediation in Pluralist Societies*, Boulder: Westview.

Bhabha, H. (ed.) (1990) *Nation and Narration*, London: Routledge.

Billig, M. (1995) *Banal Nationalism*, London: Sage.

Carter, E., Donald, J. and Squires, J. (eds) (1993) *Space and Place: Theories of Identity and Location*, London: Lawrence & Wishart.

Castells, M. (2001) *The Internet Galaxy*, Oxford: Oxford University Press.

Castles, S. and A. Davidson (2000) *Citizenship and Migration: Globalization and the Politics of Belonging*, Houndmills: Macmillan.

Christiansen, F. and Hedetoft, U. (eds) (2004) *The Politics of Multiple Belonging*, Aldershot: Ashgate.

Connor, W. (1978) 'A nation is a nation, is a state, is an ethnic group, is a . . .', in *Ethnic and Racial Studies*, 1(4): 377–400.

Connor, W. (1993) 'Beyond reason: the nature of the ethno-national bond', in *Ethnic and Racial Studies*, 16(3): 373–389.

Croucher, S. (2004) *Globalization and Belonging*, Lanham and Boulder: Rowman & Littlefield.

Delanty, G. (1995) *Inventing Europe*, Houndmills: Macmillan.

Delanty, G. (2002) 'Communitarianism and Citizenship', in E. F. Isin and B. Turner (eds) *Handbook of Citizenship Studies*, London: Sage.

Delanty, G. (2004) 'The Limits of Diversity: Community Beyond Unity and Difference', in F. Chris-tiansen and U. Hedetoft (eds) *The Politics of Multiple Belonging*, Aldershot: Ashgate.

Featherstone, M. (1990) *Global Culture*, London: Sage.

Frykman, M. P. (ed.) (2004) *Transnational Spaces: Disciplinary Perspectives*, Malmö: IMER/Malmö University.

Gellner, E. (1983) *Nations and Nationalism*, Oxford: Blackwell.

Gellner, E. (1998) *Language and Solitude*, Cambridge: Cambridge University Press.

Gilroy, P. (2004) 'Cosmopolitanism contested', paper given to 22nd Nordic Sociological Conference, August 2004, Malmö University.

Goodhart, D. (2004) 'Discomfort of Strangers', *The Guardian*, 24 February.

Habermas, J. (1994) *The Past as Future*, Lincoln: University of Nebraska Press.

Habermas, J. (1997) *A Berlin Republic: Writings on Germany*, Cambridge: Polity.

Hall, J. (ed.) (1998) *The State of the Nation*, Cambridge: Cambridge University Press

Hall, S. (1996) 'Who Needs Identity?', in S. Hall and P. du Gay (eds), *Questions of Cultural Identity*. London: Sage.

Hannerz, U. (1996) *Transnational Connections*, London: Routledge.

Hayes, C. (1931) *The Historical Evolution of Modern Nationalism*, New York: R. R. Smith.

Hedetoft, U. (1995) *Signs of Nations*, Aldershot: Dartmouth.

Hedetoft, U. (2002) 'Discourses and Images of Belonging: Migrants Between "New Racism", Liberal Nationalism and Globalization', *AMID Working Paper Series* no. 5, Aalborg University.

Hedetoft, U. and Hjort, M. (eds) (2002) *The Postnational Self: Belonging and Identity*, Minneapolis: University of Minnesota Press.

Hobsbawm, E. (1990) *Nations and Nationalism Since 1780*, Cambridge: Cambridge University Press.

Hobsbawm, E. and T. Ranger (eds) (1983) *The Invention of Tradition*, Cambridge: Cambridge University Press.

Hroch, M. (1985) *Social Preconditions of National Survival in Europe*, Cambridge: Cambridge University Press.

Huntington, S. P. (1996) *The Clash of Civilizations and the Remaking of World Order*, New York: Simon & Schuster.

Keck, M. E. and K. Sikkink (eds) (1998) *Activists Beyond Borders*, Ithaca: Cornell University Press.

Kohn, H. (1931) *Nationalism: Its Meaning and History*, Florida: Malabar.

Kohn, H. (1967 [1944]) *The Idea of Nationalism: A Study in Its Origin and Background*, New York: Collier-Macmillan.

Kuhn, T. S. (1962) *The Structure of Scientific Revolutions*, Chicago: Chicago University Press.

Kymlicka, W. (1995) *Multicultural Citizenship: A Liberal Theory of Minority Rights*, Oxford: Clarendon.

Kymlicka, W. (2001) *Politics in the Vernacular: Nationalism, Multiculturalism and Citizenship*, Oxford: Oxford University Press.

Lechner, F. J. and J. Boli (eds) (2004) *The Globalization Reader*, Oxford: Blackwell.

Lentin, A. (2004) *Multiculturalism or anti-racism?*, London: Open Democracy www.openDemocracy.net, accessed 2 September 2004.

Maier, C. (1988) *The Unmasterable Past*, Cambridge, MA: Harvard University Press.

Massey, D. (1994) *Space, Place and Gender*, Minneapolis: University of Minnesota Press.

Medrano, D. (2003) *Framing Europe*, Princeton: Princeton University Press.

Mill, J. S. (1958 [1861]) *Considerations on Representative Government*, in C.V. Shields (ed.), New York: Bobbs-Merrill.

Motyl, A. (1999) *Revolutions, Nations, Empires: Conceptual Limits and Theoretical Possibilities*, New York: Columbia University Press.

Nussbaum, M. (1996) *For Love of Country: Debating the Limits of Patriotism*, Boston: Beacon Press.

Parekh, B. (2000) *Rethinking Multiculturalism*, Houndmills: Macmillan.

Rapport, N. and Dawson, A. (eds) (1998) *Migrants of Identity: Perceptions of Home in a World of Movement*, Oxford and New York: Berg.

Renan, E. (1990 [1882]) 'What is a nation?' [original title 'Qu'est-ce qu'une nation?'], in H. Bhabha (ed.) *Nation and Narration*, London: Routledge.

Rosenau, J. (1990) *Turbulence in World Politics*, Princeton: Princeton University Press.

Said, E. (2000) *Reflections on Exile and Other Essays*, Cambridge, MA: Harvard University Press.

Schlesinger, P. (1992) 'Europeanness: A New Cultural Battlefield', in *Innovation*, 5(1): 11-23.

Smith, A. D. (1991) *National Identity*, London: Penguin.

Smith, A. D. (1996) 'Memory and modernity: Reflections on Ernest Gellner's theory of nationalism', *Nations and Nationalism*, 2(3), 371–388 [The Warwick Debate].

Smith, A. D. (2001) 'Interpretations of National Identity', in A. Dieckhoff and N. Gutierrez (eds) *Modern Roots*, Aldershot: Ashgate.

Smith, M. P. and L. E. Guarnizo (eds) (1998) *Transnationalism From Below*, New Brunswick, NJ: Transaction Publishers.

Soysal, Y. (1994) *Limits of Citizenship: Migrants and Postnational Membership in Europe*, Chicago: Chicago University Press.

Taylor, C. (1994) 'The Politics of Recognition', in A. Gutmann (ed.) *Multiculturalism*, Princeton: Princeton University Press: 25–74.

Tomlinson, J. (1991) *Cultural Imperialism: A Critical Introduction*, London: Pinter.

Tönnies, F. (1957 [1887]) *Community and Society* [original title *Gemeinschaft und Gesellschaft*], East Lansing: Michigan State University Press.

Vertovec, S. (1999) 'Conceiving and Researching Transnationalism', in *Ethnic and Racial Studies*, 22(2), 447–462.

Weber, M. (1994 [1948]). 'The Nation', in H. H. Gerth and C. W. Mills (eds) *From Max Weber: Essays in Sociology*, London: Routledge & Kegan Paul.

Weidenfeld, W. (ed.) (1985) *Die Identität Europas*, Bonn: Bundeszentrale für politische Bildung.

Yack, B. (1999) 'The Myth of the Civic Nation', in R. Beiner (ed.) *Theorizing Nationalism*, New York: State University of New York Press.

25

Theorizing the European city

Engin F. Isin

Theorizing the modern European city has gone through waves of change. Whether as an object of destruction, desire, fear, amazement, fascination, hatred, struggle, and admiration or a subject of government, administration, regulation, control, competition and accumulation, the city looms large in contemporary societies and polities. Throughout the twentieth-century social and political thought developed certain concepts to interpret and transform the modern city. But these concepts have increasingly come up against the complexities of the city in our own epoch. This chapter reviews the European city in modern social and political thought and provides a glimpse of the direction in which it is heading. I organized it around four themes, which are roughly temporal but overlapping and recurring themes in social and political thought and the city. These themes are autonomy, accumulation, difference and security. I suggest that these themes provided the drive and the background against which the essential concepts for interpreting and transforming the modern city were developed.

Before I proceed, however, I would like to discuss three important issues concerning 'theorizing the city'. First, I would like to insist on a difference between the city and cities as objects of analysis. What I mean by this difference can be articulated in the following way. Whatever happens in those 'places' which we end up calling cities, whether defined by this or that criterion, should be distinguished from the city as such, which is not reducible to, but certainly related to, the specific properties of cities. I am convinced that we cannot arrive at an adequate understanding of the city as such by collecting and collating comparative information on cities with their historical and geographical variations. The city as such cannot be an ideal type or universal concept derived from vicissitudes of cities. This ontological difference between the city and cities is akin to the difference Heidegger insisted upon between being and beings (Heidegger 1996 [1927], 2000 [1953]). I have discussed the importance of this difference elsewhere but here I want to emphasize that the proper object of social and political thought is the city not cities, however defined (Isin 2003, 2005). I maintain that the most influential social and political thinkers have recognized this difference and made the city rather than cities as the object of their thought, although, to my knowledge, none expressed this question in terms I am using here (Weber 1958 [1921]; Mumford 1961; Harvey 1973; Castells 1977; Fustel de Coulanges 1978 [1864]). What is at stake with this difference? It is true that despite enormous varieties of cities across times, spaces and polities and differences and similarities they display, it is still possible to maintain an understanding of the city *as such* across these differences. But the city as such is not an ideal type or universal that can be filled with particular properties of cities in different times, spaces and polities. We maintain an understanding of the city as such regardless of these properties and this understanding cannot be reduced to them. Aristotle may well have expressed this understanding when he insisted that the kind of beings we are, are constituted through the city, and are thus of the city (*Politics* (1995): 1253a1, 1253a6). Or, in Heidegger's words, for Greek thought 'The *polis* is the site of history, the Here, *in* which, *out of* which and *for* which history happens' (Heidegger 2000 [1953]: 117/162). As historical beings our understanding of ourselves is of and through the city. This recognition requires that we approach the city differently than an empirical object constituted by facts. The city requires thinking through its unfolding in our *longue durée* experience and understanding of it as such. That understanding unfolds itself only through our work upon ourselves as beings of the city.

The second issue concerns my usage of 'social and political thought on the city'. By that phrase, I do not mean that thought is only produced by 'thinkers' and their practices. Rather, social and political thought on the city includes what Foucault (1972 [1969]) called discursive practices: edicts, directives, proclamations, laws, minor treatises, theories and spatial practices involving thought that constitute the city as its object. Those thinkers with whom I illustrate the main themes of this chapter belong to an order of discourse that is related to, if not embedded in, that order of discourse that takes the city as its object. Yet, theorizing the city is nonetheless irreducible to and distinct from the discourse on the city. While discursive practices aim to produce a practicable knowledge of the city, theorizing the city focuses upon unfolding its essence, which includes an understanding of and orientation towards the practicable knowledge produced by discursive practices but is not reducible to it. Theorizing the city means focusing on the essence of the city, which requires making the distinction between the city and cities as I maintained earlier. Social and political thought on the city therefore includes at least two related but irreducible orders of discourse that have different modalities and functions but are related to each other. While the focus of this chapter is the latter – theorizing the city – its relation to the discourse on the city always constitutes its background and material.

The following themes, autonomy, accumulation, difference and security, are then suggested as ways of understanding the essence of the city in modern European thought, roughly from the end of the eighteenth- to the end of the twentieth-centuries. Within that span I briefly highlight only those thinkers whose thought, mostly implicitly, focused on theorizing the city as such.

The third issue is about the scope of the chapter. While it is modern European thought and the city, as we shall see modern thought is unable to reflect on the city without historical allusions and, if I may say so, illusions. Heidegger may well have expressed the reason for this already when he described polis as the site of history. The city as the site of history always already constitutes the unconscious of our being as historical beings and our thought cannot reflect on the city without its unconscious that emerged and evolved historically over a long span of time. That is why, despite our focus on modern thought on the city, other forms of the city (e.g. polis, civitas, occidental, oriental) constantly provide a background, through allusions and illusions, against which the city forms itself in modern thought.

Autonomy

Modern social and political thought placed its greatest emphasis on the autonomous character of the city. Weber's (1958 [1921]) emphasis, for example, on the importance of autonomous law-making and administration as the distinct hallmarks of the occidental city is well known. Weber thought that the ancient polis and the medieval city were prototypical forms of the autonomous city that provided models for *modern* occidental democracy and citizenship. But this emphasis inherits a paradox: the autonomy of the modern city is inconceivable without the *sovereignty* of the state. While polis and the medieval city evolved as autonomous polities, the modern city is firmly located within the sovereign state. That sovereignty dictates the limits of the possible and impossible in and of the city. In what sense then has the modern city been autonomous? In what sense do the polis and the medieval city provide models of democracy and citizenship for the modern city? This question has been one of the riddles of social and political thought. When one compares the autonomous law making and adminis-tration of the Greek polis or the medieval city, the modern city is not autonomous at all. In fact, the fundamental hallmark of the modern city is that it lacks such autonomy under the auspices of the sovereign state (Frug 1980; Isin 1992). But when compared with the age of the absolutist state, the modern city is only 'relatively autonomous' (Friedrichs 1995). Therein lies the riddle. By describing the modern city as 'relatively autonomous', modern social and political thought both inherits and legitimizes the sovereign state as the supreme authority in and through which the city becomes a 'level' of government, an extension of the state.

From the 1780s onward, this riddle – in what sense the city can be thought to be autono-mous when one recognizes the sovereignty of the state – has bedevilled social and political thought. Liberal thought in the nineteenth-century addresses this riddle by considering the city as a space of democracy, a space without which the state would be impossible. That is to say, the city is the space through which subjects become citizens. For modern social and political thought loyalty, virtue, civics, discipline and subsidiarity become the determining elements of the autonomy of the city (Isin 2000). The work of nations unfolds in the city through which subjects become democratic citizens. Yet, this can still not be called auton-omy. Eventually, modern social and political thought solves this riddle by interpreting the state as the ancient and medieval city writ large. In other words, the difference between the ancient polis and the modern state becomes not one of kind but of degree, more specifically, of scale. This has two far-reaching consequences. First, all ancient and medieval social and political thought begins to speak the modern language: Aristotle (384–322 BCE) begins to speak about the state, Plato (427–347 BCE) about republic, Augustine (354-430 CE) and Dante (1265–1321 CE) also about the state. All modern transpositions consistently assume the city about which these thinkers speak as synonymous with the state and translate it as the state or city-state (Springborg 1992). Second, the European city becomes a species of the occidental city ostensibly because the oriental city never invented autonomy and thus the state. 'Orien-tal' thinkers such as Ibn Sina (980–1037 CE), al-Farabi (*c.* 870–950 CE) and Ibn Rushd (1126–98 CE) are said to be learning about the republic and the state from the occidental thought. As a result, the state for modern social and political thought becomes an innate and teleological end towards which occidental thinkers move even when they may have no conception of it while the oriental thinkers are considered as lacking the conception and learning from the occidental thought. Thus, this peculiar autonomy claims something *sui generis* about the European city as a prototype of the occidental city.

The theme of autonomy that runs through the nineteenth- and early twentieth-centuries becomes not only a perspective from which to see the city at present but also to interpret the city in history. As I said, when compared with its Greek or medieval 'counterparts' the modern city appears anything but autonomous and yet when compared to its absolutist, early modern counterpart, the modern city indeed resembles the cradle of democracy as that which is declared. But it becomes the task of modern social and political thought to render

325

these differences palatable and claim the Greek polis as its progenitor as an act of inheritance. Theorizing the European city becomes impossible without seeing it somehow as part of a great series that originates with the Greeks, runs through the Romans, gets reinvented through Renaissance and climaxes in modern Europe. That is to say, a chain that has been constituted through polis, civitas, Christianopolis and metropolis (Isin 2002). What is astonishing about this chain is that while it presents itself as forward, that is to say it begins with origins and evolves, it is actually backward, that is to say, it begins with the state and traces itself back to its origins. The modern city forms itself in thought as teleological rather than genealogical. It is remarkable to see this chain in Fustel, Weber and Mumford with a relentless focus on the ostensible autonomy of the city. The essence of the occidental city becomes its autonomous character and is written back into its historical forms to differentiate it from the oriental city. Fernand Braudel, for example, thought that history always featured a struggle between the city and the state and that during the medieval period the city was triumphant while it was the reverse in the early modern period (Braudel 1988: 511). This is the same teleological instinct mentioned earlier where even when the concept or reality of the state does not exist, it is said to be defeated and incipient (see also Hansen 2000). Yet, ostensibly the modern period reverses this epic relationship and the city becomes, if not triumphant, that is to say, sovereign, then autonomous. Thus, the sovereignty of the state and its problem of government always call into question this fantasy of autonomy of the modern city.

The question of autonomy of the city then gets incorporated into the question of its government, that is to say, 'local' government. The modern city primarily becomes a question of government of the state and its citizens. Throughout the twentieth-century the government of the city – its powers, administration, jurisdiction, resources – becomes the problem of the government of the state and its ability and capacity for legitimate domination, so much so that the city gets even renamed as 'the local state' (Loughlin 1996).

It is significant to see how this riddle plays itself out in the formation of new Europe in the twentieth-century. The project of Europe, as a project of states and their negotiated 'federation' has been unable to propose or generate an alternative image of the city and its autonomy. Being unable to imagine the city as such, it replicated the image of the city as 'government franchise', an image that represented the city as the cradle of a new Europe. By doing so, all it could do was to reinforce the image of the city as a space of accumulation to which we now turn.

Accumulation

The accumulation of different forms of capital in and through the city or, rather, the city as a space of accumulation is also a strong theme of modern social and political thought on the city. In the nineteenth-century, interpretations of the city already become aware of the distinct role that the city plays either hindering or accelerating accumulation of capital. Already in the 1840s, Engels and Marx recognize the city as both a space of struggle against and liberation of capital (Marx and Engels 1967 [1848], Marx 1976 [1853]; Engels 1993 [1844]). Marx and Engels see a division of labour between the city and its countryside, which is also the source of an antagonism. In fact, the essence of the modern city is its triumph over the countryside (Saunders 1981: 19–20). How does the essence of the city become expressed as accumulation of capital? Marx sees the city as a space of capital where its concentration or deconcentration determines the modes of its accumulation (Katznelson 1992). The city is therefore crucial for accumulation of capital not only because it concentrates means of production but also it concentrates relations for production. Again, this becomes the essence of the occidental city and the European city as its prototype. By contrast, the oriental city lacks spaces of accumulation either for the underdevelopment of its productive forces or inability of its artisans and merchants to free themselves from landowners and clergy. This concentration of means and relations of production sharpen certain inherent contradictions in the occidental city. Thus the city as a space of accumulation is undergirded by these contradictions, which continuously fissures interests and stakes in its investments (Harvey 1985a, 1985b).

The laws of accumulation of capital recognize the importance of the city also in terms of production and reproduction of labour. The concentration of both the means and relations of production in the city bring the two antagonistic classes together and apart. The city is thus also a space of struggle and this struggle and accumulation cannot be conceived independently of each other (Harvey 1985b: 25–27). This is one of the reasons why Marx's expectation that those very laws would engender the demise of accumulation and the hegemony of bourgeoisie would not materialize. At least this appears as one of the conclusions when the urban becomes a question in the middle of the twentieth-century (Castells 1977). The city is then considered a space of collective consumption precisely because it makes possible the reproduction of labour power to accumulate capital. Thus the city is not only a space of production but also of consumption. That is to say, the state is not merely an executive for the bourgeoisie but a broker, though a biased one, between the bourgeoisie and the working class. As such the city as a space of accumulation that not only liberates accumulation but also blocks its possibilities.

The modern city as a space of accumulation is therefore also a *sui generis* aspect of the occidental city and the European city is its prototype. The contradictions the city as a space of accumulation embodies, struggles it engenders, exploitative dangers it contains and emancipating possibilities it affords become aspects of the European city and its modernity. Throughout the nineteenth- and twentieth-centuries this interpretation of the European city holds sway as its claim to being uniquely occidental, that is to say, European. The oriental city is that which cannot become a space of accumulation. More precisely, the oriental city becomes that city which cannot become autonomous because it cannot become a space of accumulation and it cannot become a space of accumulation because it cannot become autonomous. Modernity of the occidental city not only as a corporation with its autonomy but also with its operation as a space of accumulation define its uniqueness and sets itself against the background of the oriental city with its lack of autonomy and absence of accumulation.

Yet, the contradictions of capital accumulation, the struggles it engendered and spaces it created in the city would take an entirely different interpretive inflection towards the end of the twentieth-century. While Marx always insisted on the international circulation of capital and its accumulation, it was the emergence of the modern city as a 'global city' that prompted a new inflection on that old insight. The city then appears as a space of concentration of means and relations of production and consumption on a global scale. The city does not only concentrate regional and national but also international circuits of capital and becomes the space of concentration of command and control of the operations of accumulation processes and, in turn, such command and control means dominating ever broadening circuits of capital with globalization. Hence a new image of the city as a global city emerges where its role is increasingly defined as a node of accumulation through these international circuits of capital (Sassen 1991). Accumulation of capital and production and reproduction of labour means that the state not only brokers between the bourgeoisie and working class and their various factions, but also between national and international circuits of capital, and the city, perhaps the global city, becomes a strategic space for this negotiation and struggle.

327

The internationalization of the circuits of capital that were always inherent in modern accumulation thus becomes unbound and its concentration or deconcentration makes and unmakes spaces of the modern, global, city. The global city becomes a space of accumulation of new kinds of capital and labour (Sassen 1999). The concept embodies a possibility of interpreting the city beyond occidental or oriental claims to uniqueness. If indeed the global city is defined by the concentration and deconcentration of various forms of capital and their trajectories, what differentiates various different cities and their claims of being global cannot depend upon their oriental or occidental histories. The ground therefore on which theorizing the European city imperceptibly shifts towards its specificities rather than universal characteristics. There is nothing universal about the European global city that would make it inherently different than a non-European global city. Rather, the differences would lie in specific trajectories of various forms of capital that concentrates or deconcentrates. A genuine opportunity presents itself perhaps for the first time in modern social political thought to articulate the essence of the city without setting it against the oriental city that ostensibly lacks its qualities. Whether this opportunity fulfils its promise is yet an open question and theorizing the city is not much aided by taxonomic studies of global cities, focusing on variations, vicissitudes and permutations rather than the essence of the global city. Theorizing the global city also presents an opportunity to understand the inherent character of struggles that define the city. If early in the century the focus of struggles that defined the city revolved around political and social rights of working classes, with the accumulation of new forms of capital (social, cultural, symbolic) and labour, struggles increasingly take on recognition of difference as well as struggles of redistribution.

Difference

That the city, especially the modern city, was the gathering together of different social groups and the successful, that is to say, democratic, negotiation of their differences is amongst the most enduring but also recent themes of theorizing the city (Kahn 1987; Fincher and Jacobs 1998). But modern social and political thought on the city did not always work through the issues of domination, heterogeneity, assimilation, integration and cohesion in the same way or manner. Whether these social differences are conceived along class, ethnic, gender, or more broadly cultural terms, difference has been a dominant concern for thought in quite different ways.

Yet, historical differences through which difference itself has been constituted in theorizing the European city is important. The manner in which the difference is constituted, understood and expressed show remarkable historical discontinuities. It is noteworthy to observe, for example, how, within a few decades, understanding of difference in the city shifts quite radically from the manners and habits of the working classes in the 1840s to the manners and habits of immigrants in the 1920s. It is not that the categories 'immigrants' and 'working classes' are mutually exclusive or interchangeable but discourse in the 1920s decisively shifts to racializing and ethnicizing those who arrive in the city in a manner that was inconceivable in the 1840s. As is well known, the concern with dangerous classes in the nineteenth-century is inflected through a bourgeois morality that enacted itself through the morals of the working classes. Yet, by the 1920s, while concern with the dangerous classes is still present, the focus decisively shifts towards the compatibility of new immigrants into the morals of the working classes thus constituted. What partly accounts for this is the arrival of different 'religious', 'ethnic' and 'racial' groups in the city and the problematization of their fit, that is to say, assimilation into the host, that is to say, dominant bourgeois, cultures of the city. Perhaps Louis Wirth's theorization of the city not only as a relatively dense and large settlement but also a heterogeneous settlement signals as much as accelerates this shift in thought (Wirth 1938). Wirth was almost alone in imagining that group differences could exist without being assimilated into the dominant bourgeois culture (Wirth 1964 [1945]). But most of his contemporaries thought otherwise. Thus, throughout the twentieth-century the question of difference remains as the question of the city but mostly articulated as the assimilation of the other. The problem of the government of the city as the problem of the government of the state transforms itself into essentially the question of the assimilation of the other into the city. Both the European city and American city become prototypes of the occidental city where oriental subjects are acculturated and assimilated into bourgeois morality and they become citizens only insofar as they succeed in this assimilation. In other words, the city becomes the essential space and mechanism through which nationalism enacts itself. Throughout the nineteenth- and much of the twentieth-centuries the work of nationalism gets done in and through the city: imagining the nation ethnically, racially, and linguistically, cultivating subjects to imagine their selves as members of that imagined nation, coercing subjects into transforming their ways of being and disposition to conform with that imaginary, creating symbols, practices, icons, ideas and routines that participate in the creation of an imagined nation was all done in and through the city. The nation is not only imagined but also assembled and held together in and through the city. (An important issue amazingly overlooked in studies of nationalism.)

Towards the end of the twentieth-century, however, imagining and urging nationalist assimilation become ever more difficult, if not impossible, and posing the question of the government of the city in terms of assimilation ever more problematic. That is to say, difference increasingly transforms itself from a pathos signifying afflictions of the city to an ethos underlying the promises of the city. As differences pluralize and proliferate, difference becomes a profound question as to how the city is to understand, accommodate and, depending on perspective, recognize it (Young 1990; Fincher and Jacobs 1998; Sandercock 1998). Within a few decades the city is no longer theorized with assimilation as its civilizing mission, but with hospitality as its refuge (Derrida 2000 [1997], 2001). More remarkably, this ethos of pluralization also becomes the quintessential character of the European city and its history is written as a history of its cosmopolitan ethos. It is almost as if the modern city recovers or discovers its cosmopolitical essence as cosmopolis; xenophobia that mobilizes assimilation transforms itself into xenophilia that mobilizes difference. An ironic consequence of this is that while the oriental city was charged with absence of coherence and unity in the early twentieth-century, especially by Weber, now thought constitutes the European city as that space which always cultivated diversity and difference and the oriental city as that space which lacked diversity and imposed sameness and unity (Hourani 1970; Stern 1970; Abu-Lughod 1987). Be that as it may, that very process that mobilizes xenophilia carries within it a number of aporias that lead back to xenophobia. Theorizing the modern city with its cosmopolitan ethos cannot manage to forget its history of nationalist assimilation and xenophobia, and with the increasing appearance of oriental or Islamic others within the city, shows its strength and persistence often enough and remains always within view and reach.

Security

The kind of risk that autonomy, accumulation and difference imply for security, which was symbolized by the dangerous classes, is fundamentally different than the kind of security that becomes a concern in the twenty-first century. The dangerous classes of the modern city were those who could not be disciplined for temporal, spatial and health habits that were conducive to productivity and prosperity of the state. But those who could not conduct themselves properly, who slip in and out not only of different identities but also of abode and jobs, constituted dangerous classes precisely because they were inassimilable but not unreformable. These dangers were internal to and inherent in the city. Thus discourse on dangerous classes thoroughly believed in its capacity to reform the dangerous classes and transform them into appropriate (acquiescent, amiable, productive) working classes.

In the twenty-first-century the danger comes from elsewhere. This elsewhereness of the danger embodies at least two meanings. Those who now constitute a danger are clearly from elsewhere. They are from elsewhere not because they are not from here (which would have been the case around the turn of the twentieth-century) but because they are from those spaces that have been constituted as its oriental other. The anxiety about the danger constituted by those who had been arriving from elsewhere was accumulating throughout the latter part of the twentieth-century but the early twenty-first century becomes a turning point. The city becomes gripped by its anxiety of the radical other who arrives from elsewhere. The second meaning of elsewhere concerns those who are not only inassimilable but also unreformable. The discourse on the city then turns on the question of not assimilation or reform but security and safety against the danger posed by those who are from elsewhere. Combined together, these two meanings constitute the precise meaning of security of the modern city. The discourse that securitizes the city focuses on elimination, defence, eradication, dissolution, suppression and obliteration of the danger and purification and sterilization of the city.

Thus, the securitization of the city encounters the ethos of pluralization and valorization of difference. A significant part of anxiety, hence insecurity, of the city owes to the fact that precisely its securitization has yet to find an ethical way to deal with difference. The discourse on security presses the European city to define itself by fundamental values of Europeanness. The more the city is pressed into its civilizing mission by asserting fundamental values; it generates fundamental values that counter it. Thus, security produces insecurity; the city oscillates between hospitality and hostility. While on the one hand it embraces the other, on the other hand, it repels it. While the city attempts to allay its insecurities from without, it fails to recognize its sources within. The securitization of the city no longer involves building encircling walls but labyrinths of distrust, suspicion and doubt of the other because the other is deemed as a threat to its fundamental values. As mentioned earlier, towards the end of the twentieth-century, it becomes obvious that the city itself is increasingly securitized: fences, gated communities, surveillance cameras, tracking systems, security guards, risk zones assemble together to create defensible spaces and zones ostensibly deterring crime. But this fortress mentality that thrives under an illusory and unattainable will to absolute security is itself a symbol of absolute insecurity brought on by the inability and unwillingness of the dominant groups in the city to recognize their others as others (Davis 1990). It is almost as if the dream of the city as a cosmopolitical space of strangers, of *hostipitality*, as Derrida would imagine it, comes to an end (Simmel 1971 [1903]).

The course of events that the early twenty-first century inaugurates seem to confirm the inner insecurities of dominant groups in the city, which increasingly recognize difference as a problem to be eliminated rather than seeing it either as a pathos that needs a cure as in the early twentieth-century, let alone an ethos that defines the city as in the late twentieth-century. How is, then, social and political thought to theorize the city?

Conclusion

The four themes I have outlined are neither mutually exclusive nor chronologically sequential aspects of theorizing the European city. These four themes dominated social and political thought on the European city precisely because they constitute elements of its modernity so much so that modernity of the city even interprets its own history through those elements. Autonomy, accumulation, difference and security remain aporias of the modern city. The autonomy of the city comes up against its accumulation drives; its valorization of difference comes up against its drive for security; its accumulation drive engenders difference; its difference desires autonomy; its autonomy engenders indifference; its indifference produces dependence; its dependence generates sameness; its sameness desires security. Out of these tensions that the aporias of the city generates, the city is made and remade, in its own image and of the other. If it appears to thought that these four themes have always been dominant elements of the city in history it is because that thought belongs to an epoch, which has understood the city that way. That is to say, it belongs to an epoch, which understood the city in its own image. But that does not mean that theorizing the city cannot question that image and see these themes as much a diagnosis of the essence of the city as an assemblage of images that organizes our understanding of the city. In fact, theorizing the city must mean just that, if anything. Otherwise, thought remains hopelessly within the shadow cast by its understanding of the city and its possibilities, without being able to think differently about its autonomy, accumulation, difference and security.

Acknowledgements

I would like to sincerely thank Gerard Delanty, Bora Isyar and Ebru Üstündag for reading and providing comments and criticisms on an earlier draft of this chapter.

References

Abu-Lughod, J. L. (1987) 'The Islamic City: Historic Myth, Islamic Essence, and Contemporary Relevance', *International Journal of Middle East Studies*, 19: 155–176.

Aristotle (1995) *Politics*, ed. R. F. Stalley, trans. E. Baker, Oxford: Oxford University Press.

Braudel, F. (1988) *The Structures of Everyday Life*, vol. 1, *Civilization and Capitalism 15th – 18th Century*, New York: Harper and Row Publishers.

Castells, M. (1977) *The Urban Question: A Marxist Approach*, London: Edward Arnold.

Davis, M. (1990) *City of Quartz: Excavating the Future in Los Angeles*, London: Verso.

Derrida, J. (2000 [1997]) *Of Hospitality* (trans. A. Dufourmantelle), Stanford, CA: Stanford University Press.

Derrida, J. (2001) *On Cosmopolitanism and Forgiveness* (trans. M. Dooley and M. Hughes), *Thinking in Action*, London: Routledge.

Engels, F. (1993 [1844]) *The Condition of the Working Class in England* (D. McLellan ed.), Oxford: Oxford University Press.

Fincher, R. and Jacobs, J. M. (1998) *Cities of Difference*, New York: Guilford.

Foucault, M. (1972 [1969]) *The Archaeology of Knowledge and the Discourse on Language*, (trans. A. M. S. Smith), New York: Pantheon.

Friedrichs, C. R. (1995) *The Early Modern City, 1450–1750, History of Urban Society in Europe*, London: Longman.

Frug, G. E. (1980) 'The City as a Legal Concept', *Harvard Law Review* 43 (April): 1057, 1105–1108.

Fustel de Coulanges, N. D. (1978 [1864]) *The Ancient City: A Study on the Religion, Laws, and Institutions of Greece and Rome* (trans. W. Small), New York: Doubleday Anchor Books.

Hansen, M. H. (2000) 'The Concepts of City-State and City-State Culture', in M. H. Hansen (ed.) *A Comparative Study of Thirty City-State Cultures: An Investigation*, Copenhagen: Kongelige Danske Videnskabernes Selskab: 11–34.

Harvey, D. (1973) *Social Justice and the City*, London: Edward Arnold.

Harvey, D. (1985a) *Consciousness and the Urban Experience*, Baltimore, MD: The Johns Hopkins University Press.

Harvey, D. (1985b) *The Urbanization of Capital*, Baltimore, MD: The Johns Hopkins University Press.

Heidegger, M. (1996 [1927]) *Being and Time* (trans. J. Stambaugh), *Suny Series in Contemporary Continental Philosophy*, Albany, NY: State University of New York Press.

Heidegger, M. (2000 [1953]) *Introduction to Metaphysics* (trans. G. Fried and R. Polt), New Haven, CT: Yale University Press.

Hourani, A. H. (1970) 'The Islamic City in the Light of Recent Research', in A. H. Hourani and S. M. Stern (eds) *The Islamic City*, Oxford: B. Cassirer: 9–24.

Isin, E. F. (1992) *Cities without Citizens: Modernity of the City as a Corporation*, Montreal: Black Rose Books.

Isin, E. F. (2000) 'Introduction: Democracy, Citizenship and the City', in E. F. Isin (ed.) *Democracy, Citizenship and the Global City*, London: Routledge: 1–21.

Isin, E. F. (2002) *Being Political: Genealogies of Citizenship*, Minneapolis: University of Minnesota Press.

Isin, E. F. (2003) 'Historical Sociology of the City', in G. Delanty and E. F. Isin (eds) *Handbook of Historical Sociology*, London: Sage: 312–325.

Isin, E. F. (2005) 'Engaging, Being, Political', *Political Geography* 24, 373–387.

Kahn, B. M. (1987) *Cosmopolitan Culture: The Gilt-Edged Dream of a Tolerant City*, New York: Macmillan.

Katznelson, I. (1992) *Marxism and the City*, Oxford: Oxford University Press.

Loughlin, M. (1996) *Legality and Locality: The Role of Law in Central-Local Government Relations*, Oxford: Clarendon Press.

Marx, K. (1976 [1853]) *The German Ideology* (ed. C. J. Arthur), New York: International Publishers.

Marx, K. and F. Engels (1967 [1848]) *The Communist Manifesto*, London: Penguin.

Mumford, L. (1961) *The City in History: Its Origins, Its Transformations, and Its Prospects*, London: Harcourt Brace Jovanovich.

Sandercock, L. (1998) *Towards Cosmopolis: Planning for Multicultural Cities*, New York: Wiley.

Sassen, S. (1991) *The Global City: New York, London, Tokyo*, Princeton, NJ: Princeton University Press.

Sassen, S. (1999) 'Whose City Is It? Globalization and the Formation of New Claims', in *Cities and Citizenship* (ed. J. Holston), Durham, NC: Duke University Press: 177–194.

Saunders, P. (1981) *Social Theory and the Urban Question* 2nd edn, New York: Holmes and Meier.

Simmel, G. (1971 [1903]) 'Metropolis and Mental Life', in D. N. Levine (ed.) *On Individuality and Social Forms*, Chicago: University of Chicago Press: 324–339.

Springborg, P. (1992) *Western Republicanism and the Oriental Prince*, Cambridge: Polity Press.

Stern, S. M. (1970) 'The Constitution of the Islamic City', in A. H. Hourani and S. M. Stern (eds) *The Islamic City*, Oxford: B. Cassirer: 25–50.

Weber, M. (1958 [1921]) *The City*, New York: Free Press.

Wirth, L. (1938) 'Urbanism as a Way of Life', *American Journal of Sociology* 44(1): 1–24.

Wirth, L. (1964 [1945]) 'The Problem of Minority Groups', in L. Wirth *On Cities and Social Life: Selected Papers*, Chicago: University of Chicago Press: 244–269.

Young, I. M. (1990) *Justice and the Politics of Difference*, Princeton, NJ: Princeton University Press.

26

Making sense of the public sphere

Klaus Eder

The public sphere[1] is a space between state and society. It is neither a political institution nor a social institution, but an instance from which these institutions are observed and their meaning (especially their legitimacy) is communicated in either an affirmative or a critical way. The public space can thus be described as a third space between the state and society (Somers 1993, 1995, 2001). In this space some speakers turn to a public; media allow that these speakers are heard even beyond the presence of a public. The mass-media turn the public space into functionally specific system of public communication which guarantees that communication in public will go on and address any issues that may be raised (Ferree *et al.* 2002). This idea contains two analytically separate elements: actions of a specific type which is public speaking, and a space where such talking is possible and communicable to other actors. These two elements provide the key for understanding the variation of empirical and theoretical notions of a public sphere.

The theories making sense of the system of public communication vary according to action theoretical assumptions. Theories of rational action conceive this system as a mechanism of coordination of single opinions which works in a way analogous to the market mechanism.[2] This mechanism transforms private opinions into a public opinion. Theories of dramaturgical action emphasize the function of staging, the use of the public stage as a means to create collectivities that share a life-world and a collective consciousness.[3] The theory of communicative action finally makes the strongest assumption: that the public sphere offers a mechanism of generating through public debate a rational discursive universe (Habermas 1989 [1962]). It creates (under certain conditions) 'reason'. This does not imply that public debate creates automatically a rational order which is in the interest of all. But it is a necessary condition for arriving at such a order. Common to all these different approaches is the idea that the public space is the space where 'society' can have a voice which constrains power and profit, i.e. systems of power and markets.

The second aspect regards the space within which public communication takes place. The basic distinction here is the size of the public space. It can vary from interaction-based public spaces where people meet as persons to organized spaces such as party congresses which differentiate between speakers and a public which is restricted in its mode of communication (such as clapping). The most extended form of a public space is the mass-mediated public space where people meet that do not interact at all (such as reading the newspaper every morning during breakfast). These spaces provide the elementary spatial forms which then are combined to form particular public spaces such as a scientific public sphere, an intellectual public sphere, an entertaining public sphere or a political public sphere, the latter bringing together people as participants in the process of collective will formation.

The combination of action and space, of political communication and public space leads us to the idea of a public sphere which relates the public sphere of political communication to public spheres of non-political communication. The political public sphere is distinct from other public spheres by its particular code which is the code of equal access of anybody interested taking part in political will formation. A political public sphere is therefore from an analytical point of view a phenomenon which varies substantially (political or non-political), spatially (small or large), and in time (public opinion as a volatile phenomenon).

Constructing the object of a theory of the public sphere in this way still does not answer the question of why such a theory has gained such momentum in the post-war era in the Western world and recently also in the non-Western world.[4] This is due to a specific Western tradition, the enlightenment, and second, to the experience of Fascism in Western Europe, which shaped the political thinking of post-war intellectuals.

The tradition and the renaissance of the concept of the public space in the German postwar era

The theory of the public sphere is linked to the emergence of enlightenment in Europe, which emphasized in the Kantian tradition the capacity of human beings to make use of their capacity of being reasonable beings. Such reasonableness allowed man (and finally woman) to become autonomous in the sense of following rules of acting in this world as grounded in themselves and no longer derived from some external authority. Such rules are those that everybody would equally accept as a reasonable being. Thus there is an implicit 'publicness' of the rules which autonomous human beings will accept as orienting their action toward the world, including other human beings. Moral rules, the special case of rules toward others, particularly require the public recognition of the rules that are constitutive for autonomous moral persons. A public opinion taken as the voice of such morally competent human beings would thus constrain forces that are imposed on people, such as inequalities resulting from political power and markets.

This idea laid the ground for claiming a sphere of moral action that was free from state control and subject to nothing but the use of moral reasoning, the 'public sphere'. In this public sphere human beings are able to express and to modify if necessary their claims on good reasons for rules of action. When the idea of a public sphere came up it was confronted with enlightened absolutism, a situation which by necessity gave to that idea a critical function. Enlightened absolutism to a certain extent was able to tame this critical function by using the emerging public sphere for staging traditional authority and its symbols of power and deference. Yet, the emerging class of entrepreneurs, petty and capitalist, together with the growing educated strata provided a critical mass of people which took the idea of public debate over norms, whether they are in line with reason or not, seriously. This is the beginning of a society beyond the household, providing a public space in which a public sphere could emerge. This public space consisted of associations, based on the idea of equal and free people reading and debating anything they were concerned about.[5]

In old Europe such a space had to be struggled for against the institutions of traditional political power which reacted with censoring and policing against those questioning the traditional holy order. Thus the history of the making of a public sphere in Western Europe is a history of permanent struggle with authorities.[6] This is different in the United States where the making of the Union was directly linked to the making of a public sphere of autonomous citizens debating among each other to define their collective will. This is what Tocqueville, the first empirical researcher of the public sphere has taken as a key to explaining democracy in America. His explanation has been simple and straightforward: it is the quantity of associational life allowing citizens to debate their will and thus making everybody responsible for the political decisions taken, which are the structural prerequisites of democracy. Such associational life did not exist to that extent in Europe and the lack of democratic forms is thus to be explained by this lack of associational life (what we call today social capital).

Habermas' theory of the public sphere reacts in a similar way to the American experience. It is driven by the post-war situation in Germany, the total failure of democratic reform in the 1930s and the triumph of fascism. This did not happen in the States, where democratic forms seem to have a stronger grounding in the practices of citizens. In this sense Habermas rediscovers what for Americans is self-evident: the role of public debate of all concerned citizens for democratic forms of government. While equipped with the tradition of political philosophy from Kant on, Habermas succeeded in joining the empirical observations of Tocqueville with the Kantian idea of autonomous humans beings. This idea, first fleshed out in 1962 (Habermas 1989), combined a normative reconstruction of the inevitability of rational arguments among autonomous human beings with the participatory nature of political citizenship.

This first work, however, had some empirical drawbacks: it continued the tradition of cultural critique through sociological means by showing that the idea of a public sphere degenerated in the course of capitalist cum statist development, dissolving the once ideal situation of debating citizens into a mass of state clients and mass culture subjects. The mass media supported such development – the end result is the decline of the public sphere.[7]

The second attempt to get to grips with this phenomenon is found in the late work *Between Facts and Norms* (Habermas 1996). Here the idea of a decline is reinterpreted in the light of further empirical evidence which led to reconceiving the link between the normative level of analysis and the empirical forms through which ideas are enacted and communicated. Here the public sphere is taken as the social form which has evolved as a result of the modern differentiation of validity claims as universalistic claims which require public discourse as their constitutive element.

Debates on the public sphere

This model of a public sphere has raised a number of critiques, initially from historians. The main issue has been the comparative differences regarding the emergence of a public sphere in the different European countries. The French case, especially characterized by the suppression of intermediate social groups and associations as a result of the French revolution did not fit into the scenario of bourgeois groups generating through public debate democratic institutions. Moreover, much of what Habermas attributed to civil society took place within political institutions such as utilitarian programs of bettering society. As they were dominating England in the eighteenth and nineteenth centuries, they seem to provide counter cases to the historical claims of Habermas.

Historically oriented sociologists (Zaret 1992; Brewer 1995, Breuilly 1996) and Marxist sociologists (Negt and Kluge 1972; Tucker 1996) criticized the focus on the bourgeois classes in Habermas' account of the formation of a public sphere. The working classes did not figure as relevant actors in this account. Yet, there has been, the counterclaim says, a proletarian public sphere, with its own narratives, making sense of the upcoming industrial-capitalist world in its own terms which differed from the terms in which the elites and bourgeois classes narrated this experience. As later research has shown, a public sphere with its own language and style has developed in parallel and often antagonistically to the public sphere on the bourgeois classes.[8] This critique pointing to another 'forgotten' public sphere has been radicalized by the first-generation students of Habermas, Oskar Negt and Alexander Kluge, who forcefully stated a critique from within the Habermasian paradigm by pointing out that the bourgeois public sphere was far away from the real basis of social life, i.e. from the factories and working places where the mass of people lived and made their experiences. When these masses fight against the dominant class who had appropriated the public sphere as a means of its power, these masses would fight against themselves, since it is they who constitute the public sphere (Negt and Kluge 1972: 13). In this sense the public sphere is conceived as the 'dictatorship of the bourgeoisie'. The idea of the revolutionary bourgeoisie representing society is thus denounced as an illusion which is accompanied in the long run by effects of depoliticizing the masses.

Finally the issue of 'where are the woman?' was raised in spite of the fact that bourgeois women figured prominently in the Habermasian account, at least in the early phase of the making of a public sphere, as those providing the public space within the protected private space of the household (Landes 1988, 1992). The salon has given to women a particular role which they lost as soon as the public sphere moved to the coffeehouses and the political clubs. Women returned later in what Habermas called the decline of the public sphere, namely as icons and as objects of projection in mass media communication such as advertisements.

Such critiques were however minor (and conceded by taking the stand of a philosopher (Habermas 1992)) compared to the theoretical issues that were raised against the idealizing assumptions of this theory of the public sphere (Benhabib 1992; Fraser 1995; Ferree et al. 2002). The alternative model proposed is the 'liberal model' which provided a more pragmatic account of the logic of public communication in terms of collective agreement on what to include and what to exclude from the public realm. Also in empirical research the latter model covered much better what was really going on than the Habermasian one. Another alternative is the elitist model that exists in a competitive version (public accountability as a mechanism for rotating elite personnel) or in a deliberative version (proxy deliberation by un-interested experts).

All these alternative models account well for some of the features of modern public spheres, yet they fail to undermine the Habermasian construction which in its essence is a counter-factual construction: if people were really able to communicate freely with each other, then the ideal of the persuasive strength of good arguments would be the result. In terms of empirical evidence this does not imply that we look for instances for this as opposed to instances of its opposite. It requires nothing but the account of highly particular and decisive events in which this counterfactual force really entered historical processes: i.e. crises which mobilize the public sphere as a mechanism which produces path dependencies for further social change. In normal times such rational force will remain latent.[9]

In this counterfactual sense there exists a way of reconciling these different models. This however presupposes that the assumptions of a theory of communicative action, underlying the Habermasian counterfactualism, are shared. The theory of rational action (in the widest sense) certainly does not share such an assumption of a basic counterfactual world of communicative understanding which cannot be repaired directly by empirical evidence. Such theoretical assumptions are beyond empirical evidence and either justified by a normative position or by an analytical position based on the criterion of the internal consistency of theory construction. Yet there is an empirical aspect to such assumptions: they can be seen as models that fare better or less better while making sense of the empirical indicators of the dynamic process in which the modern public sphere reproduces itself.[10] This leads to the question of how the public sphere 'survives' the changing institutional environments, changing carriers and changing technological and organizational innovations which can be subsumed under the notion of transnationalization and globalization.

Particularistic public spheres and the problem of recognition

With the growing pluralization and heterogenization of modern societies, the requirement of a defined set of people as the carriers of a public sphere is no longer met by constructing a 'nation'. Transnational and subnational publics are expected to emerge that no longer coincide with the nation as the community constituting a nation-state.

Such group-specific public spheres define the range of their commonness through some form of recognition that separates any 'we' from the others. Such a particularistic 'we' meets the requirement of a modern collectivity to the extent that this 'we' is the carrier of a public sphere in itself. In this sense a public sphere comes into being in which women meet and communicate given a particular set of shared understandings of the world that they share among themselves, but do not share with men (Landes 1988, 1992; Villa 1992). Such claims for particular public spheres can be extended to ethnic groups which claim an ethnic identity for themselves that is irreducible to the identity of the nation on whose territory they happen to live. The claim for ethnicity presupposes a substantive claim of difference which collides with the principle of equality of persons (Offe 2001).

Thus the pluralization of public spheres raises a similar problem as the emergence of national public spheres raised with the rise of the nation-state: the mode of relation of a national public to another national public while all claim the universality of their claims of particularity. Since a particular 'we' cannot fully recognize the particularity of the other 'we', it cannot fully communicate with the other 'we'. Thus the basic operator of constituting a public sphere only applies in particular situations. Any conflict between these public spheres therefore raises the delicate problem of how to provide a public sphere for solving the conflicts between particular spheres.

The liberal solution to that problem (Ferree *et al.* 2002) is the exclusion of topics and issues from the agenda to be treated within the public sphere. Particular groups agree on reducing their common ground of communication, i.e. the public sphere that provides the space for communication between these groups to what is communicable. This could lead in the extreme case to a public sphere in which any communication will no longer occur, thus leaving the space for non-communicative action, i.e. power and violence.

This situation raises the problem of the applicability of the assumptions of what constitutes a modern public sphere in particular situations. Such a situationalism still requires some minimal condition for communication[11] as a means for civilizing the force of clashing collective identities.

Understanding other cultures in public discourse

The most serious argument against the theory of the public sphere in its modern normative understanding since Locke is the problem of cultural incommensurability. The criteria through which people evaluate the actions or speech acts of the others, are seen as not holding beyond the confines of a particular speech world ('Sprachspiel'). Cultural divides between civilization lead to public spheres which follow their own and incommensurable cultural logic. People might be able to speak and form correct sentences and even translate, yet they cannot take the perspective of the cultural Other in the way that the cultural compatriots do. This is not Babel where everybody speaks with different tongues, that are united finally by a universal spirit, the Holy Spirit (the first form of occidental cultural imperialism), but a Babel where this spirit turns out to be an illusion since different people make different sense of it.

The thesis of multiple modernities has reacted upon this relativistic position not in a simple universalistic manner, but in a kind of 'anti-anti-relativism' by arguing that the construction of public spheres is a universal phenomenon, yet tied to particular traditions that shape their logic and dynamic (Eisenstadt et al. 2001; Wakeman 2001). In a comparative perspective such traditions provide different paths for the formation of a public sphere, emerging in different socio-cultural environments, which make them distinct regarding the discourses that accompany the formation of these public spheres and distinct in terms of social relations that bind actors together in these public spheres. Yet there is a common dynamic built into this formation process: a logic of inclusion making people equal participants, together with a logic of exclusion defining this same people as 'we' sharing a particular way of life. Given such a conception any public sphere will run into the same problem: how to resolve the paradox of increasing inclusion and increasing exclusion. The solutions then will vary again, depending on the tradition on which it is built.

A particularly interesting phenomenon is the emergence and development of Islamic public spheres (Stauth 1989; Göle 2000; Eickelmann and Salvatore 2002; Salvatore 2005) which shares with Western forms of public spheres a common religious tradition. This common tradition does not in itself guarantee a similar conception of a public sphere. Here the additional intervening variable is the institutional separation of religion and politics, which Islamic countries share with the Christian orthodox tradition. On the intellectual level, the public sphere was reflected upon theoretically in all these traditions, yet the effects of this intellectual work did not produce similar outcomes in terms of institutionalized public spheres. Even when theoretical reflections intersect in both cultures, the concrete forms of public spheres, the actors interacting in it and the mode of communication they use differ. Religious traditions, even from common religious ancestry, produce divergent forms of public spheres in which religious tradition acts as primary organizer of the thinking of a public sphere and the political use of religion as the factors producing a path-dependency in the further evolution of the public sphere (Salvatore 2005).

Western public spheres appear as spatially particular manifestations of a universal phenomenon, that evolves through particular (historical) sequences that are intertwined with the sequencing of this process in other cultures. There is unity and diversity of public spheres which still needs disentangling. The debate on multiple modernities (Eisenstadt et al. 2001) has opened such a perspective. The debate on cultural clashes among these civilizations initiated by Huntington (1996) tends again to close off such a debate of deciding and finding out, when, where and how cultural incommensurability is itself the product of a specific staging of a public sphere.

This debate finally leads to the contested issue of the claim of universality of Western public spheres and the reproach of its Eurocentrism. The theoretical answer to this critique is given by the very construction of the Habermasian theory of the public sphere: public spheres are based on counterfactual assumptions that are at work in human society as such, with the strongest effects so far in those societies entering the path of nation-building and capitalist market economies. The really existing public sphere is the result of counterfactual forces that have to pass the factual power of states and markets. This 'passing test' determines the historically concrete simultaneity of power (the real) and communication (the counterfactual). The ideal-typical result is a model in which states and markets are bound by a 'modern tradition', the will of the people. The historical analysis of this ideal type then shows how real public spheres produce different and often contradictory traditions, thus manifesting different trajectories of the evolution of a 'modern' public sphere. So we are left with identifying in a comparative way 'traditions' which indicate where the counterfactual forces of communicative understanding and the real forces of states and markets 'really' meet.

Civil society: for the good or for bad?

The theory of the public sphere carries even within its own Western tradition a theoretically and normatively critical problem, namely the issue of how to relate interest-oriented action to a rationally conceived public sphere. To follow one's interest is one of the constitutive ideas of constructing a public sphere. People incapable of following their interests remain in social spheres of dependence (as Kant already forcefully argued). Yet, interests freed from such bonds need to be tamed. The public sphere as a result of freeing interests from traditional bonds must act at the same time as the taming force for those interests from which it emerged.

Whether the public sphere as such will succeed in doing so, is contested. The critique of 'public opinion' is a strong argument against it. The way out is a narrower conception of the public sphere as a 'civil society'. Civil society appears as the organized wing of the public sphere, the self-controlling voice of a public that cannot control itself. Thus civil society actors act on the presumption that they 'represent' the interests of the people and that they speak in their name. This is the less problematic the more such civil society actors claim to represent collective interests. Yet, even such collective interests might collide. Then they have to be compared in terms of which one to prefer in a situation of conflicting collective interests. Collective interests will always collide with interests defined as 'private interests', a definition that might again be contested. Thus the public sphere appears as an arena where different actors succeed in imposing preferences for topics and issues or for silencing other topics or issues. Observations on the 'real' functioning of public sphere has given numerous empirical arguments regarding such processes (Ferree *et al.* 2002).

The self-control of the public sphere raises the question of regulating the market character of the public sphere. This culminates in the issue of how the public sphere is able to provide a controlling instance regarding its own 'representatives'.[12] Reconceptualizing the public sphere as a civil society (which logically is a specification of 'society') does not offer an escape from the problem of how the self-control of the public sphere has to be understood within the theory of the public sphere.

Such arguments have led to varying theories based on identifying the 'real' processes governing political communication in a public sphere. The result is – paradoxically – that such theories reproduce old narratives of normative political theories: liberal theories are contrasted with discourse theories, elite theories with discourse theories. With regard to such theories we can however state the varying distance of reality from the varying model. Such models orient us to produce counterfactual statements of how a public sphere would work given certain conditions. Thus we can ask how it would work if we assume a liberal model or another one. Regarding the issue of counterfactuality the discourse theory of Habermas seems to be the most radical one since this theory is constructed as a counterfactual theory which provides a mechanism for explaining which conditions are necessary for making counter-factuals work in the factual worlds of public spheres. Civil society then is an instance, an event that indicates an effect of such counterfactuals in the real world. But we still lack a mechanism explaining why such counterfactuals do not work.

Here a theoretical alternative has its place which has not yet entered this analysis of civil society as an event in the evolution of public spheres: Foucaultian theorizing. This theorizing takes the other extreme of Habermasian counterfactualism: namely power as inherent in the public sphere. The counterfactual is replaced by a radical factual assumption: power per-meating by necessity discourse. This theory provides a way to describe the social closure of discourses, and thus provide a mechanism for explaining why the mechanism of the coun-terfactual force of public debate does not work, why discourses are closed. But it does not provide a mechanism explaining why such closures at times might fail.

Avoiding normative euphemizing of real public spheres, we are left with counterfactual thought experiments. They are methodological devices to identify the processual character of the idea of a public sphere which at times is closing and at other times is opening itself toward public communication. The idea of civil societies might appear as an event in this process where public spheres become more open.

The empirical task then is to identify the mechanisms that keep civil society open (dis-course) or that close it (power). Thus we can identify variation without claiming the nor-mative primacy of one event in the evolution of public spheres over other events. Civil societies, as well as non-civil societies, are mere events in the evolution and reproduction of a public sphere which determine its further path.

The public sphere beyond the cultural container or the nation

The making of supranational institutional arrangements and the concomitant process of the transnationalization of society represent a major break in the evolution of a public sphere. Supranational institutions problematize the national closure of public spheres. The national people and the national public space no longer suffice to control those institutions. The latter expand a social space where we still find national public spheres which are however only partially networked among each other. National public spheres turn into provinces of supra-nationally organized political communities. They continue to exist, yet no longer control what is going on beyond their confines. National publics turn into local publics.

The key case is the case of the European Union. This case has provoked a debate on whether Europe lacks a public space or whether the European Union represents a further step in the process of linking public spaces to changing social and political contexts. That there is a public sphere in Europe seems to be out of question.[13] It has become increasingly well defined as the space in which citizens of European Union can utter their voice freely. There are events that regularly make Europe the object of critical public debate. Politics in Europe is ritualized according to the calendar which guarantees that we are regularly confronted with events that provoke comment. The real problem is that of the democratic coding of this space. The people within this space do not unite 'quasi-naturally' into a coherent body which is conscious of itself as one people. Transnational public spheres have to create out of a diversity of people a 'European demos' capable of constituting a political community.

Instead of concluding that there cannot be a European demos because there is no European public sphere or of concluding that there is no European public sphere because there is no European demos, the making of such a demos could be conceived as the co-evolution of a

European demos and a European public sphere. In this sense Habermas has emphasized the role of constitutional debates in the public sphere as constituting such a space and constituting a European demos. Thus the public sphere becomes the key to democracy in the 'postnational constellation'.[14]

Historically, such a European people constituting a public sphere has already existed: the traditional European elite and popular groups that made themselves heard as voices in Europe. From the renaissance to the period of national liberation and unification a discursive network of elite people (academics, philosophers, musicians, literary figures and artists) had constituted a public sphere in which a European aesthetic and intellectual tradition was created and reproduced. This elite public existed alongside a public sphere in the cities, cross-cutting territorial forms of political domination and creating particular legal and political traditions (Breuilly 1996). This public space provided the ground for the making of middle class 'citizens', the carriers of an autonomous public sphere.

Alongside these elite and city-bound public spheres in Europe a popular public sphere made itself heard at times. The concept as such assumes a homogeneity which it rarely had. Such homogeneity emerged only when revolution or revolts called forth a unifying theme of popular resonance, i.e. suppression and injustice.[15] The normal state of a popular public sphere is to act locally, bound to the communal space of collective experience. The exceptional state is when the many voices of a 'contentious popular Europe' (Tilly *et al.* 1975; Tilly 1986) coalesced and produced rebellion and at times even revolutions.

Present-day Europe continues both modes of existence of a public sphere: an elite public, a middle class public of mobilized citizens and a popular public. These socially embedded publics are constituted and reconstituted as precarious, temporary and fluid issue-specific publics. They turn into consumer publics, lorry driver publics, into human rights publics and environmentally concerned publics.

These issue-specific publics can be conceived as networks, mobilized ad hoc through common preoccupations. The model of a society in Europe consisting of a series of demoi constituted in the course of their mobilization comes close to describing succinctly this phenomenon. Such mobilization has often been contained by national references which produced a conflicting public, a people against other people which worked though the nationalist century in Europe.

A transnational public then exists in Europe as a cross-cutting of elite publics, citizens' publics and popular publics, related to each other by some supranational institutional environment. Movements cultures, youth cultures, tourist cultures and even new religious movement cultures mixed with remnants of old elite cultures, provide a tradition within which the making of a European public as a carrier of a European public sphere produces real events for the continuity of a public sphere in Europe. This turns on a spiral of reciprocal observation of this people and supranational political actors. The consequence is rising protest, the increase in Euroskepticism, a public sphere in which much noise is created thus continuing the tradition of being 'a contentious continent' (Tilly 1986). This mechanism produces a public sphere that transcends the national public spheres in Europe while instrumentalizing the means of public communication offered on the national level.

A parallel process is the emergence (and the making) of a European public opinion, produced by surveys (Eurobarometer) and made public by political institutions (Reif and Inglehart 1991; Niedermayer and Sinnott 1998). The permanent observation of this public opinion is extended by special observatories which look, for example, into the dangers of rising racism and xenophobia in Europe. Thus a mass public in Europe is created, to a large extent produced from above (Trenz 2004). A people is made, not in the direct mode of making a national people, but in the fluid form of a public existing in a latency and becoming manifest in an unforeseeable way. This public is mostly silent, while mass media give it a voice to make sure that what is there is not forgotten, a lesson that is at times hard to take by the dominant political supranational and national actors.

This latent and basically silent public sphere talks indirectly. It is spoken by representatives, by media actors (journalists), NGOs (Statewatch), and other self-declared civil society activists. A European public sphere is not a chimera but a thing that already turns up in critical times. Habermas has interpreted the European protest in the course of the third Iraq war as a sign of an emerging public sphere in Europe. What counts as an event indicating a European public sphere, is the emergence of a debating, conflictual, but open space of political communication.

This does not mean to claim any continuity, stability over time, or normative rightness. It is only the claim that there is a path dependency in the making of a European public sphere that explains why in times of crisis a public sphere becomes visible, transcending the national borders of political communication and producing a political voice in Europe. A transnational public sphere is therefore one which is no longer tied to a reified body of people such as the nation, but to a latent demos that can be there when time requires it. Thus the public sphere can be conceptualized as a mechanism that allows voices to come up, whether in Europe or in other transnational settings (Guidry et al. 2001). Whether this voice has then really been there, when it was timely to do so, is an empirical question and to be answered by the historian.

Conclusion: post-Habermasian theorizing on the public sphere

The theory of the public sphere is a central element in the theory of modern society. It points to the reflexive element accompanying the unfolding of modernity in nationally or imperially bounded societies and to the process of further modernization beyond these boundaries. The plurality of modernities and the plurality of public spheres is due to the highly diverse conditions under which public resonance and public debate is produced given the diversity of the paths of the evolution of present-day societies. In these societies the public sphere can be seen as a mechanism of transforming these societies by the counterfactual reference to the collective will of the people. This mechanism worked at the beginning of democratizing societies as well as in their further course. The explanation for this mechanism is found in the particular structure of public communication unveiled by Habermas' theory of the public sphere, i.e. the counterfactual construction of a world in which free and equal people enter the inescapable logic of public argument. This mechanism can be blocked, undermined, instrumentalized, yet all these practical uses (and misuses) of this mechanism have to reckon with the logic constituting this mechanism: the logic of discursive rationality inherent in human beings endowed with reason and inherent in their mode of relating to the other in a communicative mode.

To describe the failure or fall down of silencing of public spheres as a consequence of the increasing power of state apparatuses and market forces has been a fashionable element in crisis scenarios of modern societies. Two scenarios have dominated the sociological debate: the 'colonization of the life world' through the instrumentalization of mass media by states and markets (Habermas 1987), and the 'tyranny of intimacy' with the effect of destroying the autonomy of the public sphere (Sennett 1977). The first thesis joins the theory of the 'culture industry', the second thesis defends a privileged sphere for social action in public which requires in opposition to social action in private particular competences.

Such critiques however do not do away with the mechanism built into the existence of a public sphere as distorted as it may be. This is what can be called the post-Habermasian solution to the problem of relating the factual and the counterfactual, between the factual paths of evolution and the counterfactual forces working through the mechanism of public communication which provides permanent input into these processes. Deciphering this mechanism in a comparative and processual way is what theorizing the public sphere can contribute to the explanation of modernity in the making.

Notes

1 The term 'public sphere' has differing connotations not only within European languages, but also between European languages and non-European ones. The German term is 'Öffentlichkeit' (an established term) as opposed to 'öffentliche Meinung'; the French distinguish the terms 'l'espace public' (an artificial term) and 'l'opinion publique' (an established term) and the English between public sphere and public opinion (where the latter is the more usual one). In Italian the same distinction between 'la sfera pubblica' (artificial as in French) and 'l'opinione pubblica' is usually made. The term 'public space' offers a further option of naming this 'thing', but will be used in the following as denoting the social space where public communication takes place. The 'ulama' in the Islamic context describes cultural elites specialized for the exchange of arguments, yet remains tied closer to religious traditions than its European counterpart Öffentlichkeit (Salvatore 2005: 226f; Eisenstadt 2002).
2 This is the traditional approach using survey data for constructing a 'political culture' or a 'public opinion'. For the state of the art see Gunn (1995) and Glynn et al. (1999).
3 Such approaches emphasize the rhetorical dynamics involved in creating a public opinion on issues (Page et al. 1987). For the life world embeddedness of public debate see especially Gamson (1999). The processual character of the link of the media to public opinion is emphasized by McCombs (2001).
4 The interest in the idea of a public sphere in the non-Western world is documented in Eisenstadt et al. (2001).
5 This is at least the generally accepted 'story line' of the emergence of the public sphere out of enlightenment. The foremost protagonist of this 'story' has been Habermas (1989 [1962]).
6 England is a special case since it relied on a different social structure in which a society of associations could evolve under the umbrella of kingship on a local level (Somers 1993).
7 Evidence for this is found in Habermas (1992: 430ff) where he states three revisions of his original idea: a different conception of the public-private relationship, the role of media power, and the reconceptualization of the bourgeois public sphere in terms of a communicative rationalization of the life-world.
8 Habermas recognizes this lack of sensitivity pointing out that reading Bahktin's *Rabelais and His World* (1984) had opened his eyes to the cultural differences at stake (Habermas 1992: 427). The 'Cultural Studies' tradition has taken up this topic most forcefully.
9 For the argument of crisis versus normality as provoking different kinds social action see Swidler (1986).
10 This process has an epistemological aspect which is the role of the concept of a public sphere in the course of the historical making of a public sphere. Regarding the role of concept formation as a dimension of the making of a public sphere see Somers (1995, 2001).
11 Such an argument has been proposed forcefully by Kantner (2004).
12 Habermas has seen this problem and given to it a rather pessimistic interpretation in his book on the public sphere. State capitalism will finally engender the decline of the public sphere, a diagnosis that he later recalled (Habermas 1992).
13 Also empirical research corroborates this in its findings. Yet, there is still no consensus on the 'meaning' of a transnational or postnational public sphere. See Eder and Trenz (2003) and Trenz and Eder (2004) as opposed to Gerhards (2001). See also Pérez-Díaz (1998) who links this debate to the problem of a European civil society.
14 See Habermas (2001) who speaks rather of a postnational and not of a transnational situation. A good discussion of how the Habermasian model might work on the European level is found in Kleinsteuber (2001).

15 Here the research of Barrington Moore on injustice is a good yet underrated piece of work (Moore 1978). Movement research has corroborated such findings (Tilly 1985).

References

Bahktin, M. (1984) *Rabelais and His World*, Bloomington, IN: Indiana University Press.

Benhabib, S. (1992) 'Models of public space: Hannah Arendt, the liberal tradition and Jürgen Habermas', in C. Calhoun (ed.) *Habermas and the Public Sphere*, Cambridge, MA: MIT Press: 73–98.

Breuilly, J. (1996) 'Civil society and the public sphere in Hamburg, Lyon and Manchester, 1815–1850', in H. Koopman and M. Lausler (eds) *Vormärzliteratur in europäischer Perspektive I: öffentlichkeit und nationale Identität*, Bielefeld: Aisthesis Verlag: 15–39.

Brewer, J. (1995) 'This, that and the other: Public, social and private in the seventeenth and eighteenth centuries', in D. Castiglione and L. Sharpe (eds) *Shifting the Boundaries: Transformation of the Languages of Public and Private in the Eighteenth Century*, Exeter: University of Exeter Press: 1–21.

Calhoun, C. J. (ed.) (1992) *Habermas and the Public Sphere*, Cambridge, MA: MIT Press.

Carr, S., Francis M., Rivlin, L. G. and Stone, A. M. (1994) *Public Space*, New York: Cambridge University Press.

Eder, K. and Trenz, H. J. (2003) 'The making of a European public space: The case of Justice and Home Affairs', in B. Kohler-Koch (ed.) *Linking EU and National Governance*, Oxford: Oxford University Press: 111–134.

Eickelmann, D. F., and Salvatore, A. (2002) 'The public sphere and Muslim identities', *European Journal of Sociology*, 43: 92–115.

Eisenstadt, S. N. (2002) 'Concluding remarks: Public sphere, civil society, and political dynamics in Islamic societies', in M. Hoexter, S. N. Eisenstadt and N. Levtzion (eds) *The Public Sphere in Muslim Societies*, Albany, NY: SUNY Press: 139–161.

Eisenstadt, S. N., Schluchter, W. and Wittrock, B. (eds) (2001) *Public Spheres and Collective Identities*, New Brunswick, NJ: Transaction Publishers.

Ferree, M. M., Gamson, W. A., Gerhards, J. and Rucht, D. (2002) 'Four models of the public sphere in modern democracies', *Theory and Society*, 31: 289–324.

Fraser, N. (1995) 'Politics, culture, and the public sphere: toward a postmodern conception', in L. Nicholson and S. Seidman (eds) *Social Postmodernism: Beyond Identity Politics*, Cambridge: Cambridge University Press: 287–312

Gamson, W. A. (1999) 'Policy discourse and the language of the life-world', in J. Gerhards and R. Hitzler (eds) *Eigenwilligkeit und Rationalität sozialer Prozesse: Festschrift zum 65 - Geburtstag von Friedhelm Neidhardt*, Opladen: Westdeutscher Verlag: 127–144

Gerhards, J. (2001) 'Missing a European public sphere', in M. Kohli and M. Novak (eds) *Will Europe Work? Integration, Employment and the Social Order*, London: Routledge: 145–158.

Glynn, C. J., Herbst, S., O'Keefe, G. J. and Shapiro, R. Y. (1999) *Public Opinion*, Boulder, CO: Westview Press.

Göle, N. (2000) 'Snapshots of Islamic modernities', *Daedalus*, 129: 91–118.

Guidry, J., Kennedy, M. and Zald, M. (eds) (2001) *Globalization and Social Movements: Culture, Power and the Transnational Public Sphere*, Ann Arbor, MI: University of Michigan Press.

Gunn, J. A. W. (1995) '"Public opinion" in modern political science', in J. Farr, J. S. Dryzek and S. T. Leonard (eds) *Political Science in History: Research Programs and Political Traditions*, Cambridge, MA: Cambridge University Press: 99–122

Habermas, J. (1987) *The Theory of Communicative Action. Lifeworld and System: A Critique of Functionalist Reason*, Volume II, Boston, MA: Beacon Press.

Habermas, J. (1989 [1962]) *The Structural Transformation of the Public Sphere: An Inquiry into a Category of Bourgeois Society*, Cambridge, MA: MIT Press.

Habermas, J. (1992) 'Further reflections on the public sphere', in C. Calhoun (ed.) *Habermas and the Public Sphere*, Cambridge, MA: MIT Press: 421–461.

Habermas, J. (1996) *Between Facts and Norms: Contributions to a Discourse Theory of Law and Democracy*, Oxford: Polity Press.

Habermas, J. (2001) *The Postnational Constellation: Political Essays* (translated, edited, and with an introduction by Max Pensky), Cambridge, MA: MIT Press.

Huntington, S. P. (1996) *The Clash of Civilizations and the Remaking of World Order*, New York: Simon & Schuster.

Kantner, C. (2004) *Kein modernes Babel: kommunikative Voraussetzungen europäischer öffentlichkeit*, Wiesbaden: VS Verlag für Sozialwissenschaften.

Kleinsteuber, H. J. (2001) 'Habermas and the Public Sphere: From a German to a European Perspective', *The Public*, 8: 95–108.

Landes, J. B. (1988) *Women and the Public Sphere in the Age of the French Revolution*, Ithaca, NY: Cornell University Press.

Landes, J. B. (1992) 'Jürgen Habermas, The Structural Transformation of the Public Sphere: A feminist inquiry', *Praxis International*, 12: 106–127.

McCombs, M. E. (2001) *Setting the Agenda: The News Media and Public Opinion*, Cambridge: Polity Press.

Moore, B. (1978) *Injustice: The Social Bases of Obedience and Revolt*, White Plains, NY: M. E. Sharpe.

Negt, O. and A. Kluge (1972) *Öffentlichkeit und Erfahrung: Zur Organisationsanalyse von bürgerlicher und proletarischer öffentlichkeit*, Frankfurt am Main: Suhrkamp.

Niedermayer, O. and R. Sinnott (eds) (1998) *Public Opinion and Internationalized Governance*, Oxford: Oxford University Press.

Offe, C. (2001) 'Political liberalism, group rights and the politics of fear and trust', *Studies in East European Thought*, 53: 167–182.

Page, B. I., Shapiro, R. Y. and Dempsey, G. R. (1987) 'What moves public opinion?', *American Political Science Review*, 81: 23–43.

Pérez-Díaz, V. M. (1998) 'The public sphere and a European civil society', in J. C. Alexander (ed.) *Real Civil Societies: Dilemmas of Institutionalization*, London: Sage: 211–238.

Reif, K-H and R. Inglehart (eds) (1991) *Eurobarometer: The Dynamics of European Public Opinion*, London: Macmillan Press.

Rokkan, S. (1999) *State Formation, Nation Building, and Mass Politics in Europe: The Theory of Stein Rokkan*, Oxford: Oxford University Press.

Salvatore, A. (2005) *The 'Public Sphere': An Axial Genalogy*, Habilitationsschrift: Humboldt-Universität zu Berlin.

Schlesinger, P. R. (2002) 'The Babel of Europe?: An Essay on Networks and Communicative Spaces' (Arena Working Paper 03/22), Oslo: Arena.

Sennet, R. (1977) *The Fall of Public Man*, New York: Knopf.

Somers, M. R. (1993) 'Citizenship and the place of the public sphere: Law, community, and political culture in the transition to democracy', *American Sociological Review*, 58: 587–620.

Somers, M. R. (1995) 'What's political or cultural about political culture and the public sphere?: Toward an historical sociology of concept formation', *Sociological Theory*, 13: 113–144.

Somers, M. R. (2001) 'Romancing the market, reviling the state: Historizing liberalism, privatization, and the competing claims to civil society', in C. Crouch, K. Eder and D. Tambini (eds) *Citizenship, Markets, and the State*, Oxford: Oxford University Press: 23–48.

Soysal, Y. N. (2001) 'Changing boundaries of participation in European public spheres: Reflections on citizenship and civil society', in K. Eder and B. Giesen (eds) *European Citizenship: National Legacies and Postnational Projects*, Oxford: Oxford University Press: 159–179.

Stauth, G. (1989) 'Occidental reason, orientalism, Islamic fundamentalism: A critique', *International Sociology*, 4: 343–364.

Swidler, A. (1986) 'Culture in action: Symbols and strategies', *American Sociological Review*, 51: 273–286.

Tambini, D. (2001) 'The civic networking movement: The internet as a new democratic public sphere?', in C. Crouch, K. Eder and D. Tambini (eds) *Citizenship, Markets, and the State*, Oxford: Oxford University Press: 238–260

Tilly, C. (1985) 'Models and realities of popular collective action', *Social Research*, 52: 717–748.

Tilly, C. (1986) 'European violence and collective action since 1700', *Social Research*, 53: 158–184.

Tilly, C., Tilly, L. A. and Tilly, R. (1975) *The Rebellious Century,* Cambridge, MA: Harvard University Press.

Trenz, H-J. (2004) *Europäische Integration und Öffentlichkeit. Institutionelle Selbstdarstellung und mediale Repräsentation der politischen Gesellschaft Europas*, Habilitationsschrift: Humboldt Universität zu Berlin.

Trenz, H-J. and Eder, K. (2004) 'The democratising dynamics of a European public sphere: Towards a theory of democratic functionalism', *European Journal of Social Theory*, 6: 5–25.

345

Tucker Jr., K. H. (1996) *French Revolutionary Syndicalism and the Public Sphere*, Cambridge: Cambridge University Press.

Villa, D. R. (1992) 'Postmodernism and the public sphere', *American Political Science Review*, 86: 712–721.

Wakeman Jr., F. (2001) 'Boundaries of the Public Sphere in Ming and Qing China', in S. Eisenstadt, W. Schluchter and B.Wittrock (eds) *Public Spheres and Collective Identities*, New Brunswick, NJ: Transaction Publishers: 167–189

Zaret, D. (1992) 'Religion, Science, and Printing in the Public Sphere in Seventeenth Century England', in C. Calhoun (ed.) *Habermas and the Public Sphere*, Cambridge, MA: MIT Press: 212–235.

27

Nature, embodiment and social theory

Phil Macnaghten

It is commonly asserted that the boundaries between culture and nature are in the process of dissolving. The idea of an autonomous nature, separated and divorced from culture, is no longer tenable. Or at least, this is how the argument runs. A number of variants are available.

One variant can be seen in the kind of millennial arguments proposed by Bill McKibben and his claims that we have now reached 'the end of nature' (1988). McKibben claims that human activity, driven by the technological-industrial complex, has now altered whatever we once thought nature was. Wilderness no longer exists in a pristine state, anywhere; forests and farmland has become thoroughly domesticated; even the climate appears to be altered, possibly irrevocably, as we face the threats of climate change. Nature is here confronted by an array of human-imposed threats, from acid rain to global warming, from the extinction of species to the destruction of the rainforest. A new variant emerges with the advent of new genetic and nanotechnologies, with the ability to alter and re-work DNA into new forms of life, evoking images of the 'post-natural' and indeed, the 'post-human' (Hayles 1999, McKibben 2003). Denuded of any external referent nature becomes merely a sign, commodified and preserved by consumer culture, often Disneyfied, devoid of any legitimacy (Wilson 1992).

This kind of argument appeals to a discourse of nature as origins, and of human activity as intrinsically separate from, and antithetical to, a state of nature. Most commonly this discourse is to be found in the writings of environmentalists and conservationists, as well as in environmental studies, environmental ethics, and environmental philosophy. According to this discourse, Kay Milton suggests, 'nature should be conserved in a pristine state, unaffected, as far as possible, by human activity' (1999: 438).

On the other hand, and currently in vogue in some popular science writing, is the proposition that nature refers to a chain of being to which human beings and everything else belongs. Current changes to the environment represent simply a new advance of an ongoing process that has been unfolding since the beginning of life some 4 billion or so years ago. Humans are here seen as animals, as part of nature, and while they may possess unique qualities of language, written culture and opposable thumbs, all animal species are unique in their own way. This critique of 'human exceptionalism' is supported by strands of intellectual thought informed by evolutionary theory, not least in socio-biology (Ridley 2001).

A third variant, common among those influenced by European social theory, is that ideas of nature are, and always have been, informed, shaped and even constituted by culture and history. Raymond Williams, in a seminal essay on the subject, undertook a socio-historical analysis of some of the key transformations of people's understandings of and relationships with nature in the west (1980). Numerous other writers have written about changing attitudes towards and relationships with nature from the time of the Greeks to the present. But it is Williams who most provocatively examines the proposition that ideas of nature contain 'an enormous amount of human history'. Informed by such an approach are various social constructivist studies on environmental issues and controversies, aimed at identifying the ways in which what is taken as 'natural', is in fact shaped by social and historical forces (see Tester 1991; Yearley 1991; Burningham 1998; Burningham and Cooper 1999 amongst others).

A variation of the above is the argument that the dominant enlightenment 'culture of nature' appears to have stopped working so well. Premised on a misguided metaphysics in which the work of facts (i.e. the domain of science) could be separated from the world of values (i.e the domain of values and politics), nature has been dislocated from due political process with all sorts of unforeseen political consequences ranging from BSE to nuclear waste to genetically modified foods (Latour 2004). Arguing that political ecology has to let go of nature, Latour develops the proposition of rekindling a new politics of nature, involving a constitutional agreement in which all kinds of actors are involved, both human and non-human.

Such arguments all tend to support the proposition that the idea of nature as a unit of analysis − and indeed, of politics − is diminishing in potency. Yet, if this is indeed the case, how can such analytical frameworks help explain the apparently continuing and possibly increasing appeal of 'nature' and 'the natural' in everyday life? It is instructive to ask how the popular appeal of 'nature' and 'the natural' is configured within each of the broad discourses highlighted above. In the first and second variants it would appear that people have been duped, in that either nothing is natural or everything is natural. In both cases people are clearly deluded; in both cases the perceptual category of 'the natural' is of little utility, at least in terms of how it is used in common discourse. In more socially constructive accounts it would appear also that people are being tricked in that they are mistaking nature for what is in reality shaped by culture. Indeed, this is the putative power of the natural, to naturalise, and hence to hide from view, its effects in terms of reproducing, legitimating, classifying, excluding and validating certain dominant ideas in society (see Berger 1972; Williams 1980; Bermingham 1996; McClintock 1995; Franklin et al. 2000).

Of course the project of developing a way of talking about nature which both respects its cultural dimensions *and* which embraces its extra-discursive reality is not new (see Benton 1993; Harvey and Haraway 1995; Soper 1995; Gerber 1997; Murdoch 2001). But little research has taken as its starting point how people themselves understand and relate to nature, and of the enduring and transformative context that nature plays in everyday life.

How might one develop alternative, and possibly more culturally-resonant, frameworks to help account for the potency and enduring qualities of the idea of nature − and its sister category, the environment − in everyday life? I will address this through three sections: first through a consideration of how the language of 'the environment' entered into public discourse; second through addressing how such a language may be shifting in relation to dynamics of cultural change in late modernity; and third through setting out empirical research carried out at Lancaster University on the multiple ways in which shifting notions of the environment and nature are shaping novel spaces for political engagement.

The language of the environment

The contemporary configuration of 'the environment' in political and civic life is of relatively recent origin. The environment, as a set of diverse problems, had to be gathered up and presented as all symptomatic of a wider overarching 'global' environmental crisis (Szerszynski 1993; Wynne 1994). Beginning around 1962 with Rachel Carson's *Silent Spring*, the so-called 'prophets of doom' helped formulate a language of 'the environment' radically different from previous concerns over nature, where the environmental threat came to be regarded as of global proportions and as linked to dominant values of modernisation and technological progress (McCormick 1995).

Through the 1970s and early 1980s there was a general broadening of the environmental agenda, guided by resourceful, radicalised and effective NGO activity seeking to demonstrate that there was more or less a single 'global' environment that needed protection. In the UK a succession of 'issues' was put on to the political agenda, including the proliferation of chemicals in the 1960s, resource and energy scarcity in the early 1970s, nuclear power and motorways in the late 1970s, agriculture and countryside issues in the early 1980s, and more recently acid rain, ozone depletion, biodiversity and global warming (Grove-White 1991; Hajer 1995). Chris Rose describes the environment movement in this period as involved in a 'struggle for proof', progressively raising the stakes of diagnosis to show critical damage not just locally, but nationally, internationally, and finally 'globally' (Rose 1993: 287).

What emerged from such processes was a dominant storyline of the 'fragile earth' under stress from human action and in need of care and protection from an imagined global community. Wolfgang Sachs (1999) calls this discourse of the global environment as environmentalism framed through the 'astronaut's perspective'; of the environment perceived as a physical body maintained by a variety of biogeochemical processes rather than as a collection of states and cultures. What remains central to this perspective is the belief that we share the same global environment, that it comprises a set stock of issues, and that these are all symptoms of the same malaise, namely human society's over-exploitation and abuse of the natural world. The storyline of the fragile and vulnerable one earth has remained dominant in contemporary institutional framings of environmental policy and can be identified across a huge array of sustainable development discourses emanating from the mass media, environmental organisations, government bodies and corporations.

In the next section I question the enduring robustness of the storyline of 'the environment' in the light of recent theoretical debates on contemporary social and cultural transformation. Might such debates provide fresh insight on the ways in which people are likely to identify with environmental issues in the context of changing patterns of social life in late modernity?

Social theory and the environment

In an influential Fabian Society pamphlet Michael Jacobs (1999) argues that in crucial ways, the desires and values associated with contemporary environmentalism pay little regard to dynamic and on-going processes of societal and economic transformation. Following the political project articulated in *The Third Way* (Giddens 1998) and subsequently adopted by Tony Blair (1999), he argues that a closer understanding of key dynamics of social change provide a more appropriate contemporary framework in which to reformulate the political project of the environment. He explains:

One of the striking features of environmentalism – and this is true as much of the discourse of sustainable development as of its utopian forebears – is its value-driven nature. Environmental literature tends to start with an analysis of present and predicted environmental degradation; but the next move is nearly always to a normative – that is to say, value-based – description of what the world should instead be like. We should care more about future generations; we should live in harmony with other species; we should consume less; we should share resources more fairly with other nations; we should produce more efficiently. There is of course nothing wrong with such expressions of idealism; but what frequently seems to be missing is the sense of *movement* which might take us from the present world to the desired better one. This is not because environmentalists have no policies to get us from here to there. The sustainable development literature is full of them. But they do not seem very closely connected to what is happening in the world. Modern societies are going through a period of rapid social and economic change – through globalisation, the growth of information technologies, increasing individualism in society, rising inequalities and so on. Much of the time governments and individual businesses are rather desperately trying to cope in the face of these trends. But the environment movement's prescriptions rarely seem to recognise them at all.

(Jacobs 1999: 14, original emphases)

This analysis suggests that 'the environment' has developed as a set of ideals that are largely exclusive and independent from wider influences in society. Thus, environmental organisations appear to have felt little need to be explicit about their underlying beliefs, to relate environmental priorities to wider collective hopes and aspirations, or indeed, to become involved in genuine dialogue with the wider public. This is not to say that environmental organisations have not been hugely successful as a social movement in terms of mobilising people, ideas, values and practices. Rather, this suggests that such organisations have tended to remain somewhat *unreflexive* as to the conditions necessary for advancing mobilisation in the light of recent and ongoing economic, social and cultural change. While Jacobs uses his analysis to set out a prescriptive new policy agenda, the interest of this chapter concerns how such contemporary debates on globalisation and individualisation can provide a framework in which to rethink the relationship between environmental concerns and everyday life.

Globalisation has been usefully defined as the 'intensification of worldwide social relations which link distant localities in such a way that local happenings are shaped by events occurring many miles away and visa versa' (Giddens 1990: 64). As this process has intensified in late modernity, questions of personal agency, and of trust between publics and a wide variety of institutions, become of growing significance. This dynamic is illustrated in the enhanced role played by both the mass media and expert systems in people's perceptions of environmental risks.

In particular, the global media are of major importance to how people understand and make sense of environmental issues. This role has been one not only of communicating and disseminating environmental information to the public, but also of actively constructing and even constituting the contemporary environmental agenda, partly in conjunction with environmental NGOs. This includes the complex interplay of narratives, storylines, images, icons and metaphors through which environmental issues and events gain meaning. Recent research suggests that the media are now an integral part of the cultural process by which environmental meanings are created, circulated and consumed (see Burgess 1990; Yearley 1991; Wilson 1992; Hansen 1993; Anderson 1997).

Indeed, throughout especially the 1980s and 1990s environmental NGOs became increasingly adept at packaging powerful images for the national and international media. Reflexive to media requirement for novelty, drama and human interest, pressure groups and *par excellence* Greenpeace, brought the 'global' environment 'up close'. Specifically, Ross describes a dominant 'genre of meaning' in which the media have tended to frame environmental issues:

> In recent years we have become accustomed to seeing images of a dying planet, variously exhibited in grisly poses of ecological depletion and circulated by all sectors of genocidal atrocities. The clichés of the standard environmental movement are well known to all of us: on the one hand, belching smokestacks, seabirds mired in petrochemical sludge, fish floating belly up, traffic jams in Los Angeles and Mexico City, and clear-cut forests; on the other hand, the redeeming repertoire of pastoral imagery, pristine, green, and unspoiled by human habitation, crowned by the ultimate global spectacle, the fragile, vulnerable ball of spaceship earth.
>
> (Ross 1994: 171)

Ross argues that current media forms reinforce a popular understanding of a particular culture of nature, that of nature as non-human. However, research shows that people are becoming familiar with such media forms, and that in response they are developing a more reflexive relationship to the media and institutional framings of environmental stories (Myers and Macnaghten 1998; Szerszynski and Toogood 1999). Indeed, often the meaning of an environmental story is itself a matter of controversy with different actors seeking to promote opposing framings of a proposed development, a protest, an action and so on. A crucial question then concerns the texture of people's relationships with, and dependency on, those expert institutions that are constructing, framing, disseminating, contesting and responding to environmental risks but to which most people have only mediated access. Hence, a neglected dimension of research on public perceptions concerns the very basis of trust: 'Who to believe?' and 'How to decide who to believe?' (Wynne 1996).

So far I have argued that public trust and confidence in the media and in official institutions is a central ingredient in understanding how people make sense of environmental issues. But across many western democracies the relationship between institutions and their publics has become increasingly fraught because of the apparent growing sense of public disaffection with, and mistrust in, formal politics and mainstream institutions. Clearly tied to such a dynamic is the alleged erosion of tradition and custom in everyday life and the pursuit of more individualised lifestyles (Giddens 1994). The rise of an ethic of individual self-fulfilment has emerged in an age in which the social order of the nation-state, class, ethnicity and the traditional family is thought to be in decline (Beck and Beck-Gernstein 2002).

Theories of individualisation and globalisation pose considerable challenges for policy and politics. Above all, they point to the need to engage more closely with everyday life struggles and realities as the starting point for any future collective action. Yet, the question as to how environmental concerns are tied up with the emergence of this apparently more individualised and globalised society has received little attention. Jacobs (1999) makes a convincing argument that in an individualised society environmental concerns are likely to felt most acutely when they impinge on the body, typically in relation to questions of food and health. He argues that powerful institutional discourses on 'choice' and 'personal autonomy' have led people to take more interest in their own health and well-being. As globalisation makes an almost infinite variety of foods, therapies, medicines, lifestyles, diets and so on available, people feel compulsion to make choices about what they eat and how they live. The spectre of a new and apparently expanding array of 'invisible' environmental risks, out there, impinging more on more directly on the body, engenders additional forms of insecurity and anxiety (Beck 1992; Dunant and Porter 1996; Franklin 1998; Adam 1998).

This raises the possibility that life in the 'risk society' may itself be transforming how people are experiencing nature and the environment. In a more individualised society, the experience of environmental risk may be becoming less about 'saving the planet' and the plight of distant others such as the rainforest, the whale, the tiger. Rather, the environment becomes acutely significant in terms of how it confronts the individual, when it meets 'me', 'head on', 'in here'.

Yet, if the encounter with the environment is becoming more personalised, another set of representations of 'what nature is' may be becoming more significant. The storyline of a 'global nature under threat from humanity' is radically distinct from how nature is encountered 'as an expressive realm of purity and moral power' (Szerszynski 1993). An emergent sociology of the environment has begun to provide insight on the embodied character of human experience of the environment especially when located within the context of specific bodily practices (Bhatti and Church 2001; Cloke and Jones 2001; Franklin 2001; Macnaghten and Urry 2001a). This research suggests that people tend to value their personal environments, not as part of universal and generalised abstractions, but when connected to particular everyday practices and leisure pursuits such as gardening, therapy, walking, fishing, climbing, boating, even motoring.

Towards a new politics of nature

So far I have suggested that wider societal trends – especially those arising from processes of globalisation and individualisation – are impacting on people's identities as political subjects. People's experience of globalisation is simultaneously making people feel more interconnected with the world *and* more vulnerable to global forces increasingly perceived as beyond their control. Individualisation is increasing personal choice and autonomy *while at same time* contributing to new levels of insecurity and anxiety. These transformations raise provocative questions on the changing structure of environmental concerns, values and political beliefs – a point which will be discussed in this section using empirical examples taken from research conducted at Lancaster University over the past decade.

First, it provides theoretical weight to contemporary research findings indicating that public engagement with environmental problems may be shifting from distant threats 'out there' to more proximate threats 'in here' (Jacobs 1999; Macnaghten 2003). Issues such as whales, the Amazon and acid rain, that were prevalent in the 1970s and 1980s, now appear to be migrating towards issues which impinge more directly and more immediately on 'me', my body, my family and my future – such as allergies, traffic, BSE and genetically modified foods.

The sharp expression of public unease in Europe around biotechnology in the late 1990s, in particular relating to GM foods, represents a highly poignant example of a contemporary individualized risk issue. It reflects *par excellence* a risk, largely invisible to our senses, whose future trajectory is highly complex, largely unknown, perhaps incalculable, and where the long-term impacts on the environment and human health may be serious or even irreversible. The encroachment of gene technology into the sinews of everyday life is symbolic of the mounting reliance that we all have on the judgements of 'experts' in conditions of perpetual technological innovation and change. Trust in public institutions, in the regulatory apparatus, in the science underpinning such developments, and in the corporations promoting them, becomes a critical factor in public acceptability (see Grove-White *et al.* 1997, 2000; Marris *et al.* 2001).

Yet it is important to remember that the controversy surrounding GM foods played out differently in particular countries. In the UK, it polarised opinion and gave rise to tabloid headlines about 'Frankenstein foods'; in Germany, it was less openly political, but posed a challenge to the existing regulatory system; and in the US, it was largely ignored by consumers, most of whom seemed relaxed or unaware about the entry of GM into the food chain. As Sheila Jasanoff points out, these different geographies of concern highlight the importance of political culture in the reception of new technologies. Despite the levelling effects of globalisation – mediated through global networks of ideas, images, campaigns, NGO activity and so on – there remain 'persistent differences in national ways of meeting common economic and social challenges' (Jasanoff 2005).

Second, such theoretical resources highlight 'trust' and 'agency' as key organising concepts in understanding contemporary environmental concerns. Indeed, even though a body of public perception research points to the reality of global environmental issues as having become almost a commonplace in everyday life, it indicates too that a perceived lack of 'felt' agency mitigates against collective action. In a recent UK research project, for example, across a variety of group settings, people expressed little sense that much could be achieved – either at the level of the individual or through existing avenues for collective action – to mitigate against global environmental threats (Macnaghten 2003). Individual action tended to be seen as largely ineffective, due to the global scale of the problems and the perception of powerful commercial interests intractably embedded in systems of self-interest antithetical to global sustainability. Indeed, this whole domain of thinking about the environment tended to be clouded in gloom and despondency, a finding that parallels previous public perceptions research on the environment (see Macnaghten *et al.* 1995; Macnaghten and Jacobs 1997).

However, what appeared distinctive in more contemporary discussions were the strategies adopted. In different ways people were now *choosing not to choose* to dwell on global environmental threats, as a pragmatic response to apparently intractable problems, and in order to maintain a positive outlook on life. Reflexive strategies of non-engagement with 'the big picture' – a term which embraced global environmental issues alongside other global issues such as poverty, AIDS, debt, 'the future', and so on – were adopted reflecting how such issues tended to be grouped together as 'negative issues' where personal engagement is felt as likely to be both inconsequential and personally damaging. Such a perceived lack of agency is exacerbated by a collective lack of faith in the effectiveness of those institutions regarded as theoretically responsible for such issues, and hence the apparent intractability of such issues in the face of what Giddens (1990) aptly calls the 'juggernaut of modernity'.

Furthermore, the acknowledged complexity of solving environmental problems in an apparently unsympathetic institutional climate appeared to be connected to the scepticism many people expressed towards those who advocate simple solutions, including certain environmental NGOs. For our participants, the portrayal of environmental problems in simple black and white terms lacked credibility and contradicted their own acknowledged ambivalent responses. Indeed, many felt both implicated in global environmental problems and constrained by competing and more immediate demands. For many people there were no easy answers; there was no longer a clear 'good guy' and 'bad guy', nobody to blame and no one beyond blame. Bound by everyday pressures of work and parenting, people accepted their own partial guilt as consumers, as motorists, as employees of business, as travellers, as outdoor enthusiasts, and so on.

Third, there appears to be a shift in emphasis from a concern with the environment as needing to be 'saved' towards an embracing of an environment that 'saves us' from the pressures and insecurities of modern living. Indeed, a body of literature points to the dangers of assuming that there exists 'one big environment' that is the same for everyone (Cooper 1992; Macnaghten and Urry 1998). In the empirical research highlighted above, we found there were *many different 'environments'*, each connected to people's particular concerns, priorities, social relationships and responsibilities. Three different kinds of encounter were expressed in group discussions.

For many people 'the environment' was perceived as a source of pleasure and transcendence from the burdens and stresses of everyday life. Activities of walking in the countryside, outdoor swimming, mountain biking, rock climbing, gardening, bee-keeping and fishing were discussed as ways of 'being in the environment', in proximity to nature, removed from modernity (see also Edensor 2001; Lewis 2001). In these situations, the expressive purity and moral power of nature arises from a practice in which one can experience a nature that is fundamentally 'other' to that familiar in industrial modernity. Such an experience can be seen as emblematic of what Nigel Thrift (2001) terms 'immersive' practices, often encountered in contemplative and mystical developments, which constitute a 'background' within which nature is encountered as a means of gathering stillness, both inside and outside the body.

Conclusion

The above findings are indicative of a wider body of research which point to ways in which the idea of nature and the environment is being reconfigured in Britain, and possibly more widely, and how such framings have been informed through developments in European social theory.

Why is the idea of nature as a set of 'environmental issues' apparently failing to mobilise large swathes of the public in government-sanctioned environmentally responsible behaviour? And, if this is indeed the case, why does the idea of nature remain potent and enduring in everyday life? Following Goodin's green theory of value we can concur that people want to see some sense and pattern to their lives, that this requires their lives to be set in a wider context, and that nature provides that context (Goodin 1992; see also Adams 1996; Milton 1999). This theory helps to explain the appeal of nature when it becomes embodied in particular localised practices, whether this is walking, gardening, fishing, even hunting. In all such activities we are striving towards a relationship in which we can interact with a nature in a way in which we are only a part of nature, and where nature goes on, more or less, regardless of our own actions.

The depiction of 'the environment' as a set of issues, global in scope and physical in origin, is a configuration that remains universal and abstracted from life. Ingold (1993) usefully critiques the conception of the 'global environment' as one that separates the human from their environment, positioning the subject as if he/she was looking at the globe, detached and outside. By contrast, the nature of the 'lived-in' world, is active and changing, and experienced through practices that actively connect to 'life'. Perhaps this is one explanation for the above.

The temporal aspects are further highlighted by Barbara Adam who distinguishes between nature as a thing (*natura naturans*) and as a process (*natura naturata*) (see also Sheldrake 1990; Williams 1976). Adam argues that:

> we need to reconnect the externalised phenomena to their generative processes, the countryside to its re/production, the forests to its formation. We need to bring into conceptual unity natura naturata and natura naturans ... We need to see the 'product' produced, nature natured, life lived.
>
> (Adam 1998: 33)

Take the tree as an example. Trees live a long time, ranging from hundreds, even thousands of years. The life of a tree commonly exceeds that of humans. Trees change both seasonally and annually, at a pace that unfolds often in symmetry with the unfolding relationships of people, families and communities. Trees are regularly central features in people's sense of place; they are alive yet also fixed in the landscape. Trees mark history in 'lived' terms. As Ingold points out, 'people . . . are as much bound up in the life of the tree as is the tree in the life of the person' (2000: 204). Trees thus exhibit a rhythmic pattern of persistence and change, from the swaying, bending and twisting of branches, to the growth of leafs and ripening of fruit, to eventual death and decay. Like humans, each tree is unique, exhibiting an underlying form or character that transcends the vagaries of illness, the weather and the seasons. In this sense the popular appeal towards trees noted above, and the common symbolism of trees as nature, can be seen as a prime site where people can connect with nature as a living process (Macnaghten and Urry 2001b).

This type of analysis of emerging nature-culture relations is at odds with many of the arguments outlined in the introduction. Goodwin's theory does not require any fundamental divide (or convergence) between a state of nature and one of humanity; nor does it seek to focus on how we commonly confuse nature for what is shaped by culture.

However, perhaps there is a wider societal context in which to situate the current appeal to nature. Environmentalism emerged in the 1970s and 1980s as part of a cultural response to unease with industrial modernity (Grove-White 1991). The urgency of the appeal to nature today is largely a reflection of new forms of technological advance. For example, the promise of new genetic technologies lies in the introduction of new crops, new landscapes, new habitats, new animals, even new humans. In this sense we could say that Goodwin's theory of green value is conditional, the key condition being a profound and enduring sense of unease that industrial modernity is contributing towards 'the death of what [people] are part of, a natural rhythm that operates beyond human control' (Milton 1999: 444). In such conditions the wildness of 'nature', as non-human nature, becomes the needed 'other'. In less pressing times, and in more benign contexts, the 'other' of nature may be less wild and more harmonious, with promises of practices that restore constitutive harmony. We navigate, one might say, between the metaphor of the garden and the wilderness. And when the garden becomes transgenic we flee for the wild woods.

References

Adam, B. (1998) *Timescapes of Modernity: the Environment and Invisible Hazards*, London: Routledge.
Adams, W. (1996) *Future Nature: a Vision for Conservation*, London: Earthscan.
Anderson, A. (1997) *Media, Culture and the Environment*, London: UCL Press.
Beck, U. (1992) *Risk Society: Towards a New Modernity*, London: Sage.
Beck, U. and Beck-Gernstein, E. (2002) *Individualization: Institutionalised Individualism and its Social and Political Consequences*, London: Sage.
Benton, T. (1993) *Natural Relations: Ecology, Animal Rights and Social Justice*, London: Verso.
Berger, J. (1972) *Ways of Seeing*, Harmondsworth: Penguin.
Bermingham, A. (1996) *Landscape and Ideology*, London: Thames and Hudson.
Bhatti, M. and Church, A. (2001) 'Cultivating natures: homes and gardens in late modernity', *Sociology*, 25(2): 365–383.
Blair, T. (1999) *The Third Way*, London: Fabian Society.
Burgess, J. (1990) 'The production and consumption of environmental meanings in the mass media: a research agenda for the 1990s', *Transactions of the Institute of British Geographers*, 15: 139–162
Burningham, K. (1998) 'A noisy road or noisy resident? A demonstration of the utility of social constructionism for analysing environmental problems', *The Sociological Review*, 46: 536–563.
Burningham, K. and Cooper, G. (1999) 'Being constructive: social constructionism and the environment', *Sociology*, 33: 297–316.

Carson, R. (1962) *Silent Spring*, New York: Houghton Mifflin.

Cloke, P. and Jones, O. (2001) 'Dwelling, plane and landscape: an orchard in Somerset', *Environment and Planning A*, 33: 649–666.

Cooper, D. (1992) 'The idea of environment', in D. Cooper and R. Walford (eds) *Horizons in Human Geography*, London: Routledge.

Dunant, S. and Porter, R. (1996) *The Age of Anxiety*, London: Virago.

Edensor, T. (2001) 'Walking in the British countryside: reflexivity, embodied practices and ways to escape', in P. Macnaghten and J. Urry (eds) *Bodies of Nature*, London: Sage.

Franklin, A. (2001) 'Neo-Darwinian leisures, the body and nature: hunting and angling in modernity', *Body and Society*, 7(4): 57–76.

Franklin, J. (ed.) (1998) *The Politics of the Risk Society*, Cambridge: Polity.

Franklin, S., Lury, C. and Stacey, J. (2000) *Global Nature, Global Culture*, London: Sage.

Gerber, J. (1997) 'Beyond dualism – the social construction of nature and the natural and social construction of human beings', *Progress in Human Geography*, 21: 1–17.

Giddens, A. (1990) *The Consequences of Modernity*, Cambridge: Polity.

Giddens, A (1994) *Beyond Left and Right*, Cambridge: Polity.

Giddens, A. (1998) *The Third Way*, Cambridge: Polity.

Goodin, R. (1992) *Green Political Theory*, Cambridge: Polity Press.

Grove-White, R. (1991) 'The emerging shape of environmental conflict in the 1990s', *Royal Society of Arts Journal*, 139: 437–447.

Grove-White, R., Macnaghten, P., Mayer, S. and Wynne, B. (1997) *Uncertain World: Genetically Modified Organisms, Food and Public Attitudes in Britain*, Lancaster: CSEC.

Grove-White, R., Macnaghten, P. and Wynne, B. (2000) *Wising Up: The Public and New Technology*, Lancaster: CSEC.

Hajer, M. (1995) *The Politics of Environmental Discourse: Ecological Modernization and the Policy Process*, Oxford: Clarendon.

Hansen, A. (ed.) (1993) *The Mass Media and Environmental Issues*, Leicester: Leicester University Press.

Harvey, D. and Haraway, D. (1995) 'Nature, politics, and possibilities: a debate and discussion with David Harvey and Donna Haraway', *Environment and Planning D: Society and Space*, 13: 507–527.

Hayles, K. (1999) *How we became Posthuman: Virtual Bodies in Cybernetics, Literature, and Informatics*, Chicago: University of Chicago Press.

Ingold, T. (1993) 'Globes and spheres: the topology of environmentalism', in K. Milton (ed.) *Environmentalism: the View from Anthropology*, London: Routledge.

Ingold, T. (2000) *The Perception of the Environment: Essays in Livelihood, Dwelling and Skill*, London: Routledge.

Jacobs, M. (1999) *Environmental Modernisation: The New Labour Agenda*, London: The Fabian Society.

Jasanoff, S., (2005) *Designs on Nature*, Princeton, NJ: Princeton University Press.

Latour, B. (2004) *The Politics of Nature*, Cambridge, MA: Harvard University Press.

Lewis, N. (2001) 'The climbing body, nature and the experience of modernity', in P. Macnaghten and J. Urry (eds) *Bodies of Nature*, London: Sage.

Macnaghten, P. (2003) 'Embodying the environment in everyday life practices', *Sociological Review*, 51(1): 63–84.

Macnaghten, P., Grove-White, R., Jacobs, M. and Wynne, B. (1995) *Public Perceptions and Sustainability: Indicators, Institutions, Participation*, Preston: Lancashire County Council.

Macnaghten, P. and Jacobs, M. (1997) 'Public identification with sustainable development: investigating public barriers to participation', *Global Environmental Change*, 7(1): 5–24.

Macnaghten, P. and Urry, J. (1998) *Contested Natures*, London: Sage.

Macnaghten, P. and Urry, J. (eds) (2001a) *Bodies of Nature*, London: Sage.

Macnaghten, P. and Urry, J. (2001b) 'Bodies in the woods', in P. Macnaghten and J. Urry (eds) *Bodies of Nature*, London: Sage.

Marris, C., Wynne, B., Simmons, P. and Weldon, S. (2001) 'Public perceptions of agricultural biotechnologies in Europe', Final Report of the PABE research project funded by the Commission of European Communities, Lancaster University: CSEC.

McClintock, A. (1995) *Imperial Leather*, New York: Routledge.

McCormick, J. (1995) *The Global Environmental Movement*, Chichester: Wiley.

McKibben, W. (1988) *The End of Nature*, New York: Viking.

McKibben, W. (2003) *Enough: Genetic Engineering and the End of Human Nature*, London: Bloomsbury.

Milton, K. (1999) 'Nature is already sacred', *Environmental Values*, 8: 437–449.

Murdoch, J. (2001) 'Ecologising sociology: actor-network theory, co-construction and the problem of human exceptionalism', *Sociology*, 35: 111–133.

Myers, G. and Macnaghten, P. (1998) 'Rhetorics of environmental sustainability: commonplaces and places', *Environment and Planning A*, 30: 333–353.

Ridley, M. (2001) 'Re-reading Darwin', *Prospect*, 66: 74–76.

Rose, C. (1993) 'Beyond the struggle for proof: Factors changing the environmental movement', *Environmental Values*, 4: 286–298.

Ross, A. (1994) *The Chicago Gangster Theory of Life: Nature's Debt to Society*, London: Verso.

Sachs, W. (1999) 'Sustainable development and the crisis of nature: on the political anatomy of an oxymoron', in M. Hajer and F. Fischer (eds) *Living with Nature*, Oxford: Oxford University Press.

Sheldrake, R. (1990) *The Rebirth of Nature: the Greening of Science and God*, London: Century.

Soper, K. (1995) *What is Nature?* Oxford: Blackwell.

Szerszynski, B. (1993) 'Uncommon Ground: Moral Discourse, Foundationalism and the Environmental Movement', PhD, Dept of Sociology, Lancaster University.

Szerszynski, B. and M. Toogood (1999) 'Global citizenship, the environment and the mass media', in S. Allen, B. Adam and C. Carter (eds) *The Media Politics of Environmental Risks*, London: UCL Press.

Tester, K. (1991) *Animals and Society: the Humanity of Animal Rights*, London: Routledge.

Thrift, N. (2001) 'Still life in nearly present time: the object of nature', in P. Macnaghten and J. Urry (eds) *Bodies of Nature*, London: Sage.

Williams, R. (1976) *Keywords: a Vocabulary of Culture and Society*, London: Fontana.

Williams, R. (1980) 'Ideas of nature', in R. Williams, *Problems in Materialism and Culture*, London: Verso.

Wilson, A. (1992) *The Culture of Nature: North American Landscape from Disney to the Exxon Valdez*, Cambridge, MA: Blackwell.

Wynne, B. (1994) 'Scientific knowledge and the global environment', in T. Benton and M. Redclift (eds) *Social Theory and the Global Environment*, London: Routledge.

Wynne, B. (1996) 'May the sheep safely graze: a reflexive view of the expert-lay knowledge divide', in S. Lash, B. Szerszynski, and B. Wynne (eds) *Risk, Environment and Modernity: Towards a New Ecology*, London: Sage.

Yearley, S. (1991) *The Green Case: a Sociology of Environmental Issues, Arguments and Politics*, London: Harper Collins Academic.

Part 5

Global perspectives

28

Euros to America

The disciplining, deconstruction and diaspora of American social theory

Ben Agger

In this chapter, I explore the varying influences of European intellectual life on US sociology and social theory. I contend that American sociologists such as Parsons and scholars in other disciplines have imported European theoretical ideas and research agendas to the United States in two distinct waves. The second wave undid the first wave, which entrenched a positivist sociology in the US. But, as I argue, the second wave – mainly German and French social and cultural theory – which was borne of New Left politics, caused 'theory' in the United States to migrate from an increasingly mathematical sociology to other social science and even humanities disciplines. This is why we have the confusing appearance today of an American sociology bereft of theoretical grand narratives, but we find lively theoretically-oriented proto-sociologies in departments and programs of English, cultural studies, women's studies, comparative literature, queer theory and media studies. Some of these issues are explored in H. Stuart Hughes' (1975) *The Sea Change* and in other intellectual histories such as Martin Jay's (1973) *The Dialectical Imagination*, Huyssen's (1986) *After the Great Divide* and Eagleton's (1983) *Literary Theory: An Introduction*. This is autobiography, too: I went to college and graduate school during what I am calling the second wave, beginning in the late 1960s, when Americans were starting to read European intellectual sources for critiques both of disciplinary sociology and of the tumultuous society at large. My mentor in all this was a sociologist from the UK, John O'Neill, whose classes I took at York University in Canada. Already the American literary and cultural worlds were decentering under the press of world and domestic events and of the European writings that helped us understand this tumult.

Parsons reads the classics

Talcott Parsons, a main figure in twentieth-century American sociological theory and the founder of the Social Relations Department at Harvard, introduced the classics of European social theory to an American audience in his 1937 *The Structure of Social Action* and in his various translations of Weber. Parsons tried to make sense of the legacies of Comte, Durkheim, Weber and others such as Pareto who were attempting to build the discipline of sociology and put it on a scientific footing. Later, Parsons used these theoretical syntheses in the 1937 book to prepare the way for his subsequent functionalist theory, unfolded in *The Social System* (1951).

Parsons read Durkheim and Weber as apologists for a world-historical capitalism, epitomized by America in the Eisenhower era. He offered an ontological view of American progress: the nuclear family, nation-state with inviolable borders, civil religion, a consumer-oriented leisure time and of course a market economy. He derived this ahistorical framework from the European founders of sociology, who, on the surface at least – for example, Durkheim's strictures on positivist method and Weber's on objectivity – could be assimilated to Parsons' functionalist, anti-Marxist project. However, Parsons, along with many subsequent American commentators on the European founders, suppressed the ample social, economic and cultural criticism found in books such as Durkheim's (1947) *The Division of Labor in Society* and Weber's (1956) *Economy and Society*.

Parsons purposely suppressed the social and cultural criticisms of Durkheim and especially Weber, who were, like other *fin de siècle* thinkers such as Freud, Simmel, Wittgenstein and Heidegger, increasingly pessimistic about the 'iron cage' of bureaucratic capitalism. As the Frankfurt theorists noted, much of the suspicion of the unalloyed virtues of the Enlightenment derived from Nietzsche, who was born in the year that the young Marx finished the *Economic and Philosophical Manuscripts*. Durkheim felt that anomie (nearly synonymous with alienation in Marx's sense), a byproduct of a society no longer moored to the intimacies of Catholic community, would lead people to commit suicide. Weber lamented the 'loss of meaning' in a rationalized society that substitutes means-ends rationality and a task orientation for more substantive goal setting. Sections in Durkheim and Weber read almost like Marcuse's (1964) *One-Dimensional Man*, with the prominent difference being that Marcuse, always Hegelian Marxist (see Marcuse 1960), remained hopeful about a dialectical resolution of social contradictions.

Parsons produced a sunny Weber (but see Mitzman 1970) who was read as an antagonist of Marx. Although Marcuse's (1968) critique of Weber, 'Rationalization and Capitalism in the Work of Max Weber,' emphasizes the ideological components of Weber's perspectives on rationality and bureaucracy, Weber's critical perspective on the iron cage clearly influenced the Frankfurt School's emerging theory and critique of domination. Parsons' Weber, by contrast, was suited to the emerging bureaucratic capitalism of post-WWII America, stressing not the iron cage and disenchantment of the world but obedience to bureaucratic rules and roles as well as to other aspects of the division of labor such as the differentiation between wage-earning men and women restricted to domesticity.

This is the received Weber of 'conflict theory,' which is positioned (Collins 1974) against Marxism as a perspective on social stratification and inequality that drops out of Marx's utopian dimension. Parsons translated the European classics of social theory in two senses of the term – explained their meaning for Americans and actually translated German into English. Thus he fatefully rendered *Herrschaft* as imperative coordination and not domination, which would have brought his Weber close to the Frankfurt School, which insisted that post-WWII domination is actually deeper than Marx's alienation (seizing hold of people's consciousness and needs).

Marcuse and most Marxists view Weber as conflating capitalist bureaucratic rationality and all possible industrial-age rationalities, thus disqualifying non-imperatively coordinated and even dedifferentiated modes of production and work organization. So for Parsons to use Weber as a buttress for his own functionalism is not entirely untoward, at least inasmuch as he and Weber freeze contemporary capitalist business rationality into ontological cement. But Weber did not soft-pedal his criticisms of this bureaucratized, routinized, disenchanted world. He worried that the 'loss of meaning' would be the price paid for industrial-age progress.

Freud in his later work had much the same view of the trade-off of progress and happiness, advances in the former costing people their tranquility and filling Freud's clinical office with hand-wringing patients.

At issue, then, is whether one uses Weber's, Durkheim's, Simmel's, Freud's and especially Nietzsche's dismal portrayals of the human cost of capitalist rationality and modernization as support for an Eisenhower-era or subsequent neo-liberal portrayal of blissful societal harmony or whether these evaluations of the jagged edge of modernity form the basis of a critical theory that frames their author's insights in a different, more utopian world-historical framework — what Horkheimer in 1937 first called critical theory. Parsons' problem, then, is that his founding authors of European social theory lose a great deal in translation as they cross the Atlantic and have their critical edge blunted in the complacency of Eisenhower's America.

Mills, Gouldner and the 1960s

Parsons' hegemony began to dissolve during the 1960s under pressure of events. His optimistic view of 'pattern maintenance' in the 'social system' simply did not stand the test of time. Monopoly capitalism, racism, sexism, poverty and imperialism dissolved Eisenhower-era hegemony and thus required new theoretical explanations. By 1959, C. Wright Mills in *The Sociological Imagination* criticized Parsons' functionalism and, for the first time in the English language, used the term 'postmodern.' In 1962 Mills published *The Marxists* in which he proclaimed his 'plain Marxism'. Both books inspired the New Left, especially the 1962 Port Huron Statement (Port Huron Statement 1962) of the SDS (Students for a Democratic Society), which stressed participatory democracy and distanced itself from the 'old' left of authoritarian bureaucratic socialism tied to blue-collar labor. By the end of the 1960s, Alvin Gouldner (1970) in *The Coming Crisis of Western Sociology* prepared the way for an integration of sociology and Marxism, drawing from the Hegelianized Marxism of the Frankfurt School. He rejected Weber's and other positivists' pretended objectivity, agreeing with Marx and Engels' 11th Thesis on Feuerbach that ideas must not only understand the world but change it (Marx and Engels 1969).

Other sociological currents during and after the 1960s drew upon non-positivist European intellectual currents, especially phenomenology and existentialism, and argued for a re-orientation of American sociology around themes of action and everyday life. Garfinkel's (1967) ethnomethodology, like Berger and Luckmann's (1967) social phenomenology, drew from Alfred Schutz and his sociological rendering of Edmund Husserl's phenomenology. Garfinkel argued that Parsons' unit actors were cultural dopes where, in fact, people are capable of 'practical reasoning' in the natural attitude, in effect creating social structures and social institutions from the ground up.

During the energized era of the 1960s, extending at least into the early 1970s, American sociology was torn between traditionally positivist and non-positivist versions as debate over the war and civil rights took the mediated academic form of debate over epistemology and methodology. Mills preached relevance, and the dialectic of public and private life. His 'plain Marxism' was actually a Great Plains Marxism, bridging a Texas radical populism and a Marxist take on monopoly capitalism (Baran and Sweezy 1966) and the permanent war economy (Melman 1974). And in *The Sociological Imagination*, a crucial book for the New Left, Mills disputed not only Parsons' functionalism but an emerging overemphasis on method ('Method') that had begun to divert sociologists from asking and answering big questions. This is precisely the compulsive quantitative methodology of what I have called Midwestern empiricism that builds careers instead of theory and thus reinforces Comte's original notion of social physics, not as doctrine but as journal discourse. Unfortunately, Mills died in his early 40s, the New Left lost its grounding in early Marx and Mills, and, as the 1960s wore on, culture triumphed over politics. The debacle of the Chicago Democratic Convention was followed by the stoned bliss and political disengagement of Woodstock Nation. In that context, American sociology took a sharp right turn toward what I have called journal science, for which method is the royal road to truth and theorizing a threat to disciplinary legitimacy in the university and in the corridors of power.

Mills and Gouldner shattered Parsons' hegemony through Marx, even if their counter-hegemony lasted only into the 1970s and not beyond (at least in sociology proper, a story told below). Theirs were mediated Marxisms, situated in America which never had much of a left other than the early-twentieth-century socialist movement of Norman Thomas, Eugene Debs, Upton Sinclair and Jack London (see Jacoby 1981 and Kann 1982). Mills confessed his Marxism in *The Marxists*, whereas Gouldner's (1970) *The Coming Crisis of Western Sociology* was more muted in this respect. It was not until his later *The Dialectic of Ideology and Technology* (1976), composed after he had done more reading in the German, Italian and French Marxisms translated and promulgated by Gouldner's own Washington University colleague Paul Piccone in *Telos* (1971), that Gouldner situated himself clearly within critical theory.

These were 'new' left versions of participatory democracy and various lifeworld-grounded strategies all the way from radical ecology to feminism. Theory met practice during the 1960s as young Midwestern college students like Tom Hayden and eastern 'red diaper' babies like Dick Flacks formulated their own version of leftism appropriate to the anti-authoritarian political structures of SNCC (Student Non-Violent Coordinating Committee) that provided a template for SDS, which played a large role in the movement to end the Vietnam war, southern and northern civil rights and the effort to organize the poor in rust-belt cities such as Newark and Cleveland (under the auspices of an SDS spin-off called ERAP, Economic Research and Action Project).

Parsons represented the tired consensus of the 1950s that was shattering politically with Kennedy's New Frontier, SNCC, the anti-war movement and then the women's movement. This eroding hegemony was expedited by young students and their faculty mentors who were reading and writing about flexible, existentially relevant, humanist Marxisms that sprang from the Hegelian-Marxist traditions of early Lukács (1971) and the Frankfurt School (see Wiggershaus 1994) and from leftist French existentialism (see Poster 1975). These young scholars, some at the doctoral level and others junior faculty, decamped from the 1960s, which ended in political counterrevolution and existential despair (see Marcuse 1972), became tenured radicals and experienced the decline of discourse (see Jacoby 1987 and Agger 1990) as they abandoned a more public vernacular and instead wrote professional treatises and articles for hundreds, not hundreds of thousands, of readers.

After the 1960s: mathematized sociology and the diaspora of theory

By the mid-1970s, as the United States and other western capitalist economies experienced a serious economic downturn, inflation, energy crises and falling real incomes (for the first time since the Depression), the Sputnik-era growth of universities slowed and even began to reverse itself. Sociology, which was on the front lines during the social movements of the 1960s, experienced institutional contraction and falling public legitimacy as faculty openings dried up, student enrollments fell and grants became scarcer. As I document in my *Public*

Sociology (Agger 2000), American sociology responded to this by eliminating essayistic, speculative sociology that characterized the discipline during the late nineteenth-century and the early twentieth-century (Chicago School and the early years of the *American Sociological Review*), becoming instead a mathematics field.

In my 2000 study, I documented the rhetorical displacement of prose and perspective – theorizing – on the journal page by quantitative method and compulsive figural displays. I call this discursive, not doctrinal, positivism because it leaves behind epistemological questioning about the relationship between subject and object (Newton, Locke, Kant, Einstein) and instead purges authorial presence from science in order to recoup the lost legitimacy and credibility of a discipline widely blamed (and blaming itself) for its temporary politicization during the 1960s, with Mills, Gouldner and the New Left.

In this context, social theory – grand narratives that grasp the social totality – was replaced by what Merton (1958) called middle-range theories or 'theories of' – theories of crime, family, migration, suicide, social movements. Theory was reduced to the opening literature-review section of articles and to middle-range perspectives such as social exchange theory and rational-choice theory, both of which have the patina of science and can be modeled mathematically. Indeed, by the neo-conservative 1980s, even Parsons made a brief comeback in the neo-functionalism of Jeffrey Alexander, although this cut against the grain of mathematized journal discourse and was quickly absorbed by the discipline.

All of this was especially ironic because post-1970s sociological positivists, in returning to Comte's promise of a social physics, were drawing on a Newtonian and Lockean philosophy of science by then totally discredited in the physics of relativity theory. Einstein and Heisenberg well understood that the role of the scientist in measurement and analysis is paramount, rejecting the image of the scientific mind as a blank slate. Phenomenology, existentialism, critical theory, postmodernism and feminist theory all rejected the notion of a positivist epistemological subject who can stand outside the world in order to know it. American sociology in seeking to restore its legitimacy by shedding the skin of its 1960s engagements returned to a model of subject–object relations that has virtually no credibility in any other discipline.

Since the 1970s, not only has prose been replaced by figure and number in mainstream American sociology. So have theorists, theory courses in the curriculum, hirings in theory. Theory is widely presented as the discipline's history, not as an enlivening engagement with current issues. Most departments do not integrate theory (of the grand kind) into every course but require it for majors at the very end of their undergraduate curriculum. On the graduate level, seriously quantitative departments may require four methods and statistics courses and at most one theory course. This course is frequently taught by someone who has 'substantive interests' outside of theory, in an empirical domain, and who does not publish in theory.

But because American sociologists are territorial, especially with the discipline's declining institutional prestige which they blame on sociology's engagements during the 1960s, they are reluctant to allow their students to take theory elsewhere, especially in the humanities. This is partly out of defensiveness about non-sociologists pretending to do proto-sociology and partly because they lay claim to Comte, Durkheim and Weber as disciplinary founders in order to give latter-day mathematized empiricism the patina of originary credibility.

Frankfurt, Paris, Birmingham: the new sociologies (outside of sociology)

But theory, in the sense of passionate, broad-gauged engagement with social structure and social action, will not disappear. It has undergone a dispersion or diaspora to disciplines outside of sociology proper, which has continued to become a computer-driven, mathematically modeling, grant-seeking quasi-science discipline. In spite of Burawoy's (2004) recent pronouncements about a mainstream sociology that suddenly embraces what I have called 'public sociology' (the 2004 national American Sociological Association annual meetings presided over by Burawoy had that theme), sociology has abandoned both grand theorizing and an engagement with social problems and social movements. The new sociologies, as I am calling them, are being practiced in departments and programs of English, comparative literature, cultural studies, media studies, women's studies, queer studies, even sometimes in history and anthropology. These new sociologies are indebted to intellectual developments in German and French social and cultural theory and to the Birmingham School of cultural studies.

Peculiarly, sociology in countries such as England, Canada, Australia, New Zealand and both western and eastern Europe has not for the most part emulated the post-1960s mathematization of American sociology but has found ways to integrate German and French theory and cultural studies. This is largely because academic disciplines in those countries were not scandalized by their engagements during the 1960s. They were not scandalized because a 1980s and post-1980s neoconservatism did not succeed in assailing universities ideologically and further linking universities to corporate and state agendas, as occurred in the United States. For example, Derrida died a celebrity in France, and Habermas writes on issues of broad public concern in Germany.

The European authors of critical theory, postmodernism and cultural studies participated in the student movements and social movements of the 1960s. These intellectuals were not stigmatized, and led to recant their youthful enthusiasms, both because Europe has always had a left and because the anti-Vietnam war movement was quite mainstream in Europe, just as the anti-Iraq war movement is today. The New Left did not scandalize British and European intellectuals who recognized that American imperialism lay in scientism as well as in military might but served as a point of departure for their post-1960s writings about everyday life, politics and culture. These European left intellectuals were always, in Jacoby's terms, public intellectuals, not only writing for Gallimard and Suhrkamp but also for *Le Monde* and *Spiegel*. Europe has a much more vital public sphere (see Habermas 1989) in which intellectuals engage with political issues, blending theoretical criticism and practical politics, than has the United States, in which professional academia, with its restricted linguistic codes, has been tightly integrated with corporate and state agendas of applied research.

European intellectuals did not turn their back on the 1960s but developed their theoretical systems and oeuvres out of their New Left engagements, which sometimes took them far afield of traditional Marxism. How else to read the politics imbedded in Foucault, Derrida and Baudrillard?

The new sociologies emerged in American humanities and culturally-oriented departments and programs as the 1960s generation of college and graduate students became members of the professoriate and were frustrated with traditional literary and cultural analysis (see Fekete 1978 on the new criticism). These young scholars read Derrida, Foucault, Baudrillard, Beauvoir, Adorno, Marcuse, Habermas in order to understand the politics of culture as well as the culture of politics. They overcame the aversion to theory (see de Man 1986) of their elders and they came to prominence, and in some cases even dominance, in their disciplines, which welcomed them. Unlike American academic sociology, English, comparative literature, women's and black studies did not repent for their 1960s engagements and become positivist (again), but they transformed themselves into culturally and critically oriented disciplines that, with Derrida, acknowledged that all knowledge is political, perspectival, passionate, gendered, colored, sexual.

Derrida is a major figure in the development of these new proto-sociologies as he added to the momentum already begun by Nietzsche, Wittgenstein and the Frankfurt School in the direction of a non-positivist epistemology (see Antonio 2005). His strictures on the self-deconstructing tendencies of all texts and languages – their tendencies to unravel when probed deeply enough – have had huge impact on the interpretive programs of politicized scholars no longer content to read and teach the great books. Derrida shows that there is no Ur-text, no meta-language, from which one can cleanse the muddying ('undecidable') effects of authorial presence and of language itself ('language games' for Wittgenstein [1953]).

After theory? or, Is there a class in this text?

Terry Eagleton, in his *After Theory* (2003), laments the eclipse of grand-narrative-like social and cultural theory in favor of unfocused, untheorized cultural readings – of videos, television, tattoos. I take this to be the long-term effect of the displacement of Marxist frameworks by postmodernism, which, like mathematical positivism albeit for different reasons, trumps the global with the local – 'readings' replacing theory. And so I do not want to conclude with abundant optimism about the proto-sociologies, the new sociologies, that have blossomed outside of sociology, especially where these are found in literary disciplines averse to large-scale social theorizing and instead are devoted to the close examination of particular texts and discourses. On the one hand, I am concerned that sociology is everywhere, claimed by all, and on the other nowhere, neither in the interpretive disciplines nor in mainstream sociology.

People in the humanities tend to view all the world as a text, ignoring material issues and structures. Perhaps they take too seriously, or simply misunderstand, Derrida's comment that there is nothing outside the text. Derrida was not uttering a solipsist or idealist tenet but noting – the foundation of deconstruction – that one cannot stand outside the text, or the world for that matter, and see it without presupposition, perspective, politics, platform. He was denying the critic an Archimedean vantage outside time and place, much as existentialists, critical theorists and feminists do.

Cultural studies will never be a suitable proto-sociology or social theory if it remains fixated on interpretive issues, 'readings'. Although such acts of critical intervention and interpretation can suit the ideology-critical agenda of Marxists – for example decoding advertising for its hidden assumptions about the 'goods' life – these readings do not substitute for the structural analyses of the nineteenth- and twentieth-century grand narrativists of social theory. The strength of cultural studies is that it recognizes that aesthetic and cultural 'language games' involve, and transact, power.

On the other hand, the problem with anti-interpretive sociology seeking to become again a high science is that it does not put enough weight on texts, failing to recognize that texts are nucleic societies through which power is transacted. This insight into cultural discourses joins the Frankfurt School and postmodernism, which together trace the tendency of texts and discourses in fast capitalism to ooze out of their covers and become lives (see Agger 1989, 2004). They become lives because they are read and enacted quickly, without mediation, as Hegelians term it. Marx's ideology was surpassed by Frankfurt's domination (and Gramsci's hegemony). By now, in the early twenty-first century and our post-Fordist Internetworked capitalism, we have entered yet another stage of ideology, which is characterized by the dispersion of ideology into the world itself. Ideology is now encoded in advertising, brands, slogans, headlines, titles, jargon, lyrics as a veritable celebration of the present as a plenitude of social being (see www.fastcapitalism.com). This dispersion of texts into the world assumes a more permeable boundary than we have ever known between writings and the world, or private and public. The decline of discourse follows from the dispersion of discourse into everyday life, provoking thoughtless, hasty writings and readings that do not gain enough distance from the world in order to understand and oppose it.

But I just criticized the Archimedean distance of positivism, which positions the knower outside of the world. As Adorno knew, without distance one cannot grasp the social totality, which, inverting Hegel, risks being false. I am suggesting, then, that there is a dialectic of closeness (readings that risk immersion) and distance (critique which risks abandoning the world) that needs to command our attention. This is what I take to be the theme of Eagleton's recent book on theory. This dialectic of closeness and distance could be called sociology, which is our practical effort to understand and change our lives, sometimes in concert with others. This is sociology not as positivists intend it but as an immersion in everyday life that does not rule out theorizing but indeed requires it.

I learned sociology in the natural attitude from my mentor John O'Neill, who, when I studied with him, was busily writings books on Merleau-Ponty, Marxism and 'wild sociology' (see O'Neill 1972, 1974). O'Neill embraced the phenomenological and ethnomethodological programs, but, as a Marxist, he rejected Husserl's sharp bifurcation of natural and theoretical attitudes as ahistorical. Everyday life is stupefied, manipulated, 'dominated' in Frankfurt parlance because of the power of ideology, hegemony, media culture. But it doesn't have to be. O'Neill bridged the Husserlian and Schutzian programs, on the one hand, and the eleventh thesis, on the other, producing an engaged sociology that resembles Piccone's (1971) and Paci's (1972) phenomenological Marxism. I studied with O'Neill at a time when Piccone's journal *Telos* was rapidly gathering momentum as the radical intellectual journal of record in the United States. We pored through the articles, both translations and explanations of translations, in order to understand the relevance of European critical theories for our own lives, particularly as we tried to make sense of the 1960s, which began with such hope, but ended dismally in the late 1960s and 1970s with the Weather Underground, Nixon's COINTELPRO and then Watergate.

It is ironic that 1968 was a year of such intellectual exuberance and political transformation in western and eastern Europe, from Paris to Prague. 1968 was a different kind of bellwether in the United States, where 'the whole world was watching' (Gitlin 1980) the beginning of the end of the New Left in the streets of Chicago at the Democratic National Convention. Although that is another story (see Gitlin 1987; Miller 1987; Hayden 1988; Agger forthcoming), what Eagleton terms the end of theory – and with it, both as cause and effect, the end of hope – began in the United States in 1968 and accelerated after Nixon took office. It is notable that sociology, which was pulsating with passion during the 1960s, turned back to science during the retrenching period of the 1970s. As I argued in *Public Sociology*, this was largely because US sociology was embarrassed by its partisanship during the previous decade and wanted to extirpate European theory in favor of mathematical method, hoping to win converts among deans and foundation directors along the way.

This has proven to have been the wrong choice, given the subsequent history of mainstream US sociology. No one reads the leading journals except to scan the article abstracts and literature reviews in order to build career capital. People interested in social issues read the new sociologies found in cultural studies, interdisciplinary studies and the humanities. The problem is that, as Eagleton notes, many of these studies are theoretically impoverished, content to be 'readings' and not full-blown theoretical narratives. Theory needs to belong to sociology because sociology, since Durkheim, Weber and Marx, was *the* discipline to address modernity and now postmodernity. It painted with a broad brush, essayed, speculated, formed concepts, theorized. When these approaches were drummed out of sociology by compulsive, mathematically-oriented methodologists, who identify truth and method, they sought refuge in the proto-sociologies, but were vanquished by those heavily influenced by the French theories of Derrida, Foucault and Baudrillard, who mistrust modernist narrativity.

For its part, the Frankfurt School never made much headway into mainstream sociology. The Columbia Sociology Department, which harbored the Frankfurt scholars during WWII, did not really integrate the members of the Institute for Social Research but used them as pawns in their own empire building. Adorno's (Adorno *et al.* 1950) California study, which emerged in *The Authoritarian Personality*, was read as an empirical contribution to the growing literature on prejudice but not as a theoretical contribution stemming from his and Horkheimer's oeuvre, especially their (1972) *Dialectic of Enlightenment*. In spite of the Frankfurt School's frequent forays into empirical sociology – see, for example, their collective (Frankfurt Institute for Social Research 1972) *Aspects of Sociology* and Adorno's (2000) *Introduction to Sociology* – they have been largely received in America (see Jay's (1985) 'Adorno in America') as anti-empiricists who disdain any engagement with the contemporary moment in favor of an elitist and irrelevant high theorizing. As the mainstream discipline became even more mathematically oriented during and after the 1970s, critical theory was either ignored by American sociologists or, like French postmodern theory, labeled as a Nietzschean project inimical to scientific method.

Indeed, the very term 'critical theory' has a double meaning in the United States. On the one hand, it refers to a body of social theory associated with the Frankfurt School. But more widely it is taken to be an approach to literary and cultural interpretation, critical theory standing for an interpretive approach all the way from semiotics and reader-response theory to feminist and cultural studies. Ironically, the flourishing of what I am calling proto-sociology in humanities disciplines such as English, frequently carried out under the banner of 'theory,' that avoids its demonization in those disciplines and interdisciplinary sites, has not been grounded in the critical sociology of the Frankfurt School, which is nearly as invisible in English and literature programs as in mainstream positivist sociology. This problem is confounded by the prevalence and influence of French postmodern theory in these interpretive disciplines. French theorists' critique of grand narratives like Marxism has tended to displace the critical social theories associated with the Frankfurt School. This is bizarre because the proto-sociologists in humanities and culturally-oriented disciplines have tended to produce their sociological 'readings' through the prism of the anti-totality postures of Lyotard and Baudrillard, where it would have made more sense for them to derive their approach to cultural studies from the critical cultural theories of the Frankfurt School, as Kellner (1995), Gunster (2004) and I (Agger 1992) have argued.

Reprise and prognosis: vulnerable positivism?

Sociology began in Europe and then migrated to the United States. Parsons introduced European themes to the Americas, canonizing Comte, Durkheim and Weber as disciplinary icons. He opposed Marx by dismissing him as a non-sociologist. But then the 1960s saw Parsons overturned by Mills, Gouldner and Garfinkel. Once the 1960s were over, having succumbed to Nixon's counterrevolution and the end of activism, American sociologists turned away from Europe and toward a mathematical version of their discipline. Scandalized by the passions and polemics of anti-war, civil rights and reflexive sociology, they embraced a methods-driven sociology, driving out theory. Theory – postmodernism, cultural studies, feminist thought, queer studies – settled in the humanities, which was transformed unapologetically by the 1960s and never turned to science as an antidote. But the humanities versions of theory tend to reduce society to text and deny materialisms. They also tend to shun grand narratives and, as such, Hegel, Marx, the Frankfurt School. Their sociologies are not structural but cultural. Although, as Horkheimer and Adorno pointed out in the 1940s, the culture industries are well worth examining, they intended cultural studies to be an arm of political economy and not its subordination.

The re-election of Bush Jr. may return us to the conflicts and dialectical opportunities of the 1960s as the United States once again embraces isolation combined with unilateral adventurism and becomes (again) globally reviled, especially in Europe. It will be difficult for American sociologists to remain on the political sidelines given the power of the religious right and the pressing issues of war, peace, poverty, environmental crisis, overpopulation and nuclear proliferation. The US has become polarized into red and blue states and across races and generations, much as it was during the late 1960s, when sociologists embraced activism. It will be interesting to see if sociologists who embrace scientism, which supposedly rescued sociology from the 1960s, can withstand the growing pressure to focus their intellectual work on the urgent political projects of the moment (see Agger 2005).

References

Adorno, T. W. (2000) *Introduction to Sociology*, Palo Alto: Stanford University Press.

Adorno, T. W., Frenkel-Brunswik, E., Levinson, D. J. and Sanford, R. N. (1950) *The Authoritarian Personality*, New York: Harper.

Agger, B. (1989) *Fast Capitalism: A Critical Theory of Significance*, Urbana, IL: University of Illinois Press.

Agger, B. (1990) *The Decline of Discourse: Reading, Writing and Resistance in Postmodern Capitalism*, London: Falmer.

Agger, B. (1992) *Cultural Studies as Critical Theory*, London: Falmer.

Agger, B. (2000) *Public Sociology: From Social Facts to Literary Acts*, Boulder: Rowman & Littlefield.

Agger, B. (2004) *Speeding Up Fast Capitalism: Cultures, Jobs, Families, Schools, Bodies*, Boulder: Paradigm.

Agger, B. (2005) 'Beyond Beltway and Bible Belt: Re-Imagining the Democratic Party and the American Left', in *Fast Capitalism* 1.1. www.fastcapitalism.com.

Agger, B. (forthcoming) *The Sixties at Forty: Generation and Identity among Sixties People*, Boulder: Paradigm.

Antonio, R. (2005) 'Remembering Derrida', in *Fast Capitalism*, 1.1. www.fastcapitalism.com.

Baran, P. and Sweezy, P. (1966) *Labor and Monopoly Capital*, New York: Monthly Review Press.

Berger, P. and Luckmann, T. (1967) *The Social Construction of Reality*, Garden City, NY: Anchor Books.

Burawoy, M. (2004) 'Public Sociologies: A Symposium from Boston College', in *Social Problems*, 51(1): 103–130.

Collins, R. (1974) *Conflict Sociology*, New York: Academic.

Dahrendorf, R. (1968) *Essays in the Theory of Society*, Palo Alto: Stanford University Press.

De Man, P. (1986) *The Resistance to Theory*, Minneapolis: University of Minnesota Press.

Durkheim, E. (1947) *The Division of Labor in Society*, Glencoe, IL: Free Press.

Eagleton, T. (1983) *Literary Theory: An Introduction*, Minneapolis: University of Minnesota Press.

Eagleton, T. (2003) *After Theory*, London: Allen Lane.

Fekete, J. (1978) *The Critical Twilight: Explorations in the Ideology of Anglo-American Literary Theory from Eliot to McLuhan*, London: Routledge and Kegan Paul.

Frankfurt Institute for Social Research (1972) *Aspects of Sociology*, Boston: Beacon.

Garfinkel, H. (1967) *Studies in Ethnomethodology*, Englewood Cliffs, NJ: Prentice-Hall.

Gitlin, T. (1980) *The Whole World is Watching: Mass Media in the Making and Unmaking of the New Left*, Berkeley: University of California Press.

Gitlin, T. (1987) *The Sixties: Years of Hope, Days of Rage*, New York: Bantam.

Gouldner A. W. (1970) *The Coming Crisis of Western Sociology*, New York: Avon.

Gouldner A. W. (1976) *The Dialectic of Ideology and Technology*, New York: Seabury.

Gunster, S. (2004) *Capitalizing on Culture: Critical Theory for Cultural Studies*, Toronto: University of Toronto Press.

Habermas, J. (1989) *The Structural Transformation of the Public Sphere*, Cambridge, Mass: MIT Press.

Hayden, T. (1988) *Reunion: A Memoir*, New York: Random House.

Horkheimer, M. and T. W. Adorno (1972) *Dialectic of Enlightenment*, New York: Herder and Herder.

Hughes, H. S. (1975) *The Sea Change: The Migration of Social Thought*, New York: Harper and Row.

Huyssen, A. (1986) *After the Great Divide: Modernism, Mass Culture, Postmodernism*, Bloomington: Indiana University Press.

Jacoby, R. (1981) *Dialectic of Defeat: Contours of Western Marxism*, New York: Cambridge University Press.

Jacoby, R. (1987) *The Last Intellectuals: American Culture in the Age of Academe*, New York: Basic.

Jay, M. (1973) *The Dialectical Imagination: A History of the Frankfurt School and the Institute for Social Research, 1923–1950*, Boston: Little, Brown.

Jay, M. (1985) 'Adorno in America', in his *Permanent Exiles: Essays on the Intellectual Migration from Germany to America*, New York: Columbia University Press.

Kann, M. (1982) *The American Left*, New York: Praeger.

Kellner, D. (1995) *Media Culture: Cultural Studies, Identity and Politics between Modern and Postmodern*, New York: Routledge.

Lukács, G. (1971) *History and Class Consciousness*, London: Merlin.

Marcuse, H. (1960) *Reason and Revolution: Hegel and the Rise of Social Theory*, Boston: Beacon.

Marcuse, H. (1964) *One-Dimensional Man*, Boston: Beacon.

Marcuse, H. (1968) *Negations: Essays in Critical Theory*, Boston: Beacon.

Marcuse, H. (1972) *Counterrevolution and Revolt*, Boston: Beacon.

Marx, K. and Engels, F. (1969) *Marx/Engels Selected Works*, Moscow: Progress.

Melman, S. (1974) *The Permanent War Economy: American Capitalism in Decline*, New York: Simon and Schuster.

Merton, R. (1958) *Social Theory and Social Structure*, New York: Free Press.

Miller, J. (1987) *'Democracy is in the Streets': From Port Huron to the Siege of Chicago*, New York: Simon and Schuster.

Mills, C. W. (1959) *The Sociological Imagination*, New York: Oxford University Press.

Mills, C. W. (1962) *The Marxists*, New York: Dell.

Mitzman, A. (1970) *The Iron Cage: An Historical Interpretation of Max Weber*, New York: Knopf.

O'Neill, J. (1972) *Sociology as a Skin Trade*, London: Heinemann.

O'Neill, J. (1974) *Making Sense Together: An Introduction to Wild Sociology*, New York: Harper and Row.

Paci, E. (1972) *The Function of the Sciences and the Meaning of Man*, Evanston, IL: Northwestern University Press.

Parsons, T. (1937) *The Structure of Social Action*, New York: McGraw-Hill.

Parsons, T. (1951) *The Social System*, Glencoe, IL: Free Press.

Piccone, P. (1971) 'Phenomenological Marxism', in *Telos* 9: 3-31.

Port Huron Statement of the Students for a Democratic Society (1962) http://coursesa.matrix.msu.edu/~hst306/documents/huron.html, accessed 14 December 2004.

Poster, M. (1975) *Existential Marxism in Postwar France*, Princeton: Princeton University Press.

Weber, M. (1956) *Economy and Society*, Glencoe, IL: Free Press.

Wiggershaus, R. (1994) *The Frankfurt School: History, Theories and Political Significance*, Cambridge: Polity Press.

Wittgenstein, L. (1953) *Philosophical Investigations*, Oxford: Basil Blackwell.

29

Encounters between European and Asian social theory

Fred Dallmayr

So long as it remains true to itself, theorizing partakes in the lived experience of its time, including its traumas and agonies. Among the most prominent features of our age is the process of globalization, that is, the perceived shrinkage of the globe into a commonly shared space. Although acutely felt in the domains of economics and information technology, the significance of this process is not always sufficiently acknowledged by philosophers and social theorists. Sometimes geographical labels are attached to perspectives or schools of thought, like 'Continental philosophy', 'Frankfurt School' and so on – labels whose meaning is often belied by what is happening on the ground. Thus, travelers in distant lands may find there more vibrant resonances of 'Continental' thought than can be found in Europe today, just as seminal ideas of the early 'Frankfurt School' are sometimes more intensely discussed in Asia or Latin America than in their native city. This does not mean that European perspectives are simply disseminated across the world without reciprocity or reciprocal learning. Nor does it mean that local origins are simply erased in favor of a bland universalism (since local origins are often inscribed with concrete and singular sufferings). What it does mean is that landscapes and localities undergo symbolic metamorphoses, and that experiences once localized at a given place increasingly find echoes or resonance chambers among distant societies and peoples.

Symbolic migration today is characteristic of several intellectual or theoretical perspectives – including, perhaps most prominently, the perspective of 'analytical' or 'Anglo-American' philosophy (whose teachings sometimes exert hegemonic claims around the world). However, a similar outreach also marks Continental-European thought and social theory. No doubt, the latter perspective exhibits a great variety of distinct orientations and emphases. Yet, for purposes of the present discussion, I want to highlight what I consider the chief common traits of Continental-European thought as it developed (roughly) during the past century. As it seems to me, the central common trait of this thought – especially when compared with the 'analytical' perspective – is its close attention to the theory-praxis connection, that is, the connection of thinking and doing. This entails an opposition to 'pure' theory or a purely spectatorial theorizing which, aiming at objective knowledge, distances the spectator or analyst rigidly from the targets of his/her analysis. The basic underpinnings of this spectatorial approach can be found in the modern Cartesian worldview which, in separating subject and object (*cogito* and extended matter), provided the engine for the rise of modern science and technology (and generally the replacement of quality by quantity). The difference of outlooks has social implications: while spectatorial theory is congenial to, and favored by, people satisfied on the whole with 'the way things are' and 'the powers that be,' practical theorizing appeals mainly to people alienated from the way of the world and bent on some kind of transformation. Seen in this light, Continental-European thought (in its different versions) has tended to be mostly critical and self-critical – by mounting a sustained critique of the modern cult of science, technology, and the market and, more broadly, of the 'underside of modernity'.

In the present context I include under the label 'Continental-European thought' three main perspectives or schools: critical theory (Frankfurt School); phenomenology and herme-neutics (Freiburg School); and post-structuralism and deconstruction (French School). My contention here is that all three perspectives stand opposed to a purely theoretical (or meta-physical) outlook and are anxious to maintain the theory-praxis connection. This stance is clearly evident in the case of critical theory as articulated in Max Horkheimer's programmatic essay on 'Traditional and Critical Theory' (1972 [1937]), where 'traditional' theory corre-sponds largely to what I have called a purely spectatorial mode of theorizing in opposition to a critical outlook steeped in practical social engagement. Despite a diversity of philosophical and political premises, many of the basic points of Horkheimer's essay find a parallel in both Continental phenomenology and deconstruction. A major affinity resides in the effort to overcome traditional 'metaphysics' (or pure theory) and the predominance of the Cartesian egocentric worldview. In the latter respect, Edmund Husserl's life-work constitutes a crucial waystation, captured in his motto 'to the things themselves' (*zu den Sachen*) and his later turn to the 'life-world' – a turn further radicalized in Heidegger's 'hermeneutical phenomenology' with its stress on 'being-in-the-world' and engaged 'care'. Critical praxis-orientation seems more elusive in the case of post-structuralism, and especially Jacques Derrida whose work is often associated with radical rupture and a complete dismissal of social agency. What is correct about this reputation is Derrida's undeniable radicalization of the critique of the Cartesian *cogito* and his dismantling of human self-identity in favor of a resolute openness to the 'Other's' initiative. Yet, precisely in light of this dismantling, a transformed kind of agency comes into view bent no longer on predatory mastery but on a generous hospitality toward others (akin to Heidegger's 'letting be'). For Derrida, the same openness or generosity is also the hallmark of philosophical thinking or theorizing as such. As he stated at one point (Derrida 2002: 15): 'The right to philosophize becomes increasingly urgent', as does the call for philosophers to evaluate and critique perspectives that 'in the name of a technical-economic-military positi-vism', tend to reduce the field and the chances of an 'open and unrestricted philosophizing' both in colleges and in international life.

Asian critical thought

Derrida's call for a critical kind of theorizing or philosophizing – one opposed to the hege-monic 'positivism' (in technological, military, and economic domains) – obviously resonates with other European perspectives, including Horkheimer's programmatic essay. But it is definitely not restricted to the confines of Europe, and instead has a 'cosmopolitan intent'. As it happens, his summons today finds echoes or resonances in many parts of the world, from Asia to Africa and Latin America. In the following, I shall be able to give only a very limited sample of Asian critical intellectuals voicing their opposition to mainstream positivism as well as to a purely spectatorial (and ethically irresponsible) mode of theorizing. In view of my own frequent and extended visits to India, I shall concentrate my discussion first on theoretical initiatives on the Indian subcontinent, before extending my review to other parts of Asia.

In post-independence India, the closest parallel to the outlook of the early Frankfurt School – as articulated in Horkheimer's essay – can be found in the Centre for the Study of Developing Societies (CSDS) operating in Delhi since 1963. In its structure and design, the Delhi Centre from the beginning resembled its German counterpart: particularly in its emphasis on interdisciplinary cooperation (comprising scholars from the humanities, the social sciences, and psychology) and its concerted effort to bridge the theory-praxis divide. As a result of its interdisciplinary character, studies sponsored or published by the Centre have dealt with a broad spectrum of topics: ranging from the ethnic and social-psychological components of social change to problems of rural development and ethno-agriculture to the role of science and technology in the modern world. In terms of theoretical orientation, a primary role has always been played by Rajni Kothari, the initial founder and longtime director of the Centre. Trained both in India and the West, Kothari has distinguished himself (like Horkheimer) as a scholar and institution builder; in addition he has been an activist on all levels (local, national, and international) of politics. About ten years after founding the Centre, he was instrumental in launching the quarterly *Alternatives*, a journal that soon emerged as a leading forum in India for the discussion of issues relating to social change and global transformation. Both his scholarly and his practical-political talents coalesced in 1980 when, together with other Centre colleagues, he inaugurated the movement '*Lokayan*' (meaning 'dialogue among people'), designed as an arena for the meeting of academics, policy-makers, and activists concerned with grassroots initiatives. His moment of greatest public visibility came in 1989 when, following the defeat of Rajiv Gandhi, he joined the National Front government as a member of the national Planning Commission.

Among Kothari's prolific writings, I want to single out for present purposes these four: *State Against Democracy* (1988a), *Transformation and Survival* (1988b), *Rethinking Development* (1989), and *Growing Amnesia* (1993). Subtitled 'In Search of Humane Governance,' the first volume was written mainly in protest against the policies of Indira and Rajiv Gandhi whose regimes were denounced for their attempt to marshal state power – what Derrida might have called state positivism – against the democratic aspirations of the people. In large measure, the book was meant as a challenge to the relentless process of centralization that, during the post-independence period, was steadily molding India into a uniform 'nation-state' along Western lines. Buttressed by the resources of modern technology and corporate business, this nation-state – in Kothari's view – was re-erecting or deepening the structure of social inequality which the struggle against colonialism had aimed to erase. The situation was further aggravated by the progressive militarization of the state promoted in the name of 'national security'. These and related factors conspired to produce a socio-political crisis which, according to Kothari, was changing or perverting the character of the state: namely, from 'being an instrument of liberation of the masses to being a source of so much oppression for them' (Kothari 1988a: 60). The critique of state-centered accumulation of power was extended into the global arena in the second book, *Transformation and Survival*. Paralleling the growing stratification of domestic society, the operation of the international state system – in Kothari's account – promoted and reinforced a global structure of asymmetry between North and South, 'developed' and 'developing' societies, and center and periphery. As on the national level, this global asymmetry was compounded by the concentration of technological, economic, and military resources in the hands of hegemonic (developed) states or superpowers. In combination, these forces posed a threat to the natural environment, international peace, and ultimately the survival of humankind itself.

As an antidote to these dangers, the two cited volumes formulated an alternative vision of human existence and socio-political life that was not beholden to any of the reigning ideologies of the time. In fact, as Kothari insisted, it was necessary to move beyond both the liberal-capitalist and the orthodox Marxist paradigms, since both derived from the same Cartesian worldview (Kothari 1988a: 2–3): they were both 'offshoots of the same philosophic pedigree of the Enlightenment and nineteenth-century (mechanistic) humanism' with their unlimited faith in progress fueled by technological mastery over nature. In lieu of this 'modernist' and positivist pedigree, the books invoked the legacy of the Mahatma Gandhi whose life-work had challenged Western imperialism while at the same time enlisting popular grassroots beliefs and traditions for democratic purposes. In both his writings and his actions, Gandhi had thus honored 'the moral imperative of treating [ordinary] people as a source in the recovery of a humane order' (Kothari 1988b: 170). In addition to Gandhian teachings, the texts also drew inspiration from various left-leaning modes of political radicalism wedded to the promotion of human freedom and social justice. As used by Kothari, 'freedom' was not a synonym for the pursuit of libertarian self-interest nor for a retreat into public abstinence, but rather denoted the capacity (or capability) for public participation and the promotion of social well-being. To this extent, the notion of 'human rights' signaled not only private entitlements or privileges as rather basic constituents of a good and 'humane' social order.

Kothari's *Rethinking Development* sought to expose both the pitfalls and the muddle-headedness of much of the dominant literature and planning in this field. Both in mainstream writings and mainline policy-making, he noted, 'development' has tended to be equated with unfettered economic and industrial expansion propelled by advances in modern science and technology. As was to be expected, this approach has engendered not only a deadly arms race and a wasteful, consumption-driven economy, but also a pernicious class structure on both the national and the global levels. As a consequence, democracy was under siege both at home and in the world at large. For Kothari, the trouble with the dominant approach was that it was not only difficult to implement but inherently flawed and misguided. Echoing again Horkheimer, his text located the root-problem of the 'developmental' ideology in its attachment to a dominant worldview or philosophical doctrine which, although originating in Europe, was now encircling the globe (Kothari 1989: 48–49): the 'doctrine of modernity' according to which 'the end of life is narrowly defined as to be within the grasp of all – progress based on economic prosperity'. Fueled by Enlightenment teachings, this doctrine presented social advancement entirely as a matter of social engineering, backed up by 'science-based technology'; all that human beings and societies had to do according to this model was to 'discard tradition and superstition and become rational and "modern"'. In language reminiscent (but also sharpening the edge) of the 'dialectic of Enlightenment' articulated by Horkheimer and Theodor Adorno, *Rethinking Development* asked these questions:

> Isn't the theory of progress, as developed in the West, based on an anthropocentric view of nature and a positivist conception of knowledge and science, which are responsible for a model of development spelling domination and exploitation? And if these be the essence of Occidental culture and its contribution to human thought and values shouldn't we discard large parts of it, and look for alternative modes of thought and values embedded in some other cultures?
>
> (Kothari 1989: 51)

Growing Amnesia was published four years later, in the wake of the dismantling of the Soviet Union and the vanishing of the so-called 'nonalignment' policy (sponsored by India and other 'developing' countries). Although widely hailed in the West as the dawn of a new 'world order,' the emerging global situation raised serious worries and apprehensions for Kothari. In his view, the turn of events signaled basically the triumph of corporate capitalism, a triumph that augured ill for the cause of social justice and participatory or grassroots democracy. Given the concentration of power and wealth in developed countries and multinational conglomerates, the existing gulf between North and South, center and periphery was prone to be further deepened, while the fate of underprivileged masses around the world was bound to be abandoned to apathy or else consigned to 'growing amnesia'. Above all, the priority granted to policies of 'deregulation' and 'liberalization' of the market was bought at a steep price (Kothari 1993: 8–9): its overall effect was to 'destabilize the democratic polity, put the masses under severe strain, turn against labor and further marginalize the poor'. To be sure, the remedy for deregulation could not reside in a centralized state bureaucracy controlling and planning every facet of social life in a top-down fashion. In opposition to the dystopias of both the Leviathan-state and unchecked market forces, *Growing Amnesia* sponsored a social-democratic alternative where the apparatus of the modern state was retained but sharply refocused in the direction of democratic participation and self-rule. Embracing again aspects of the Gandhian legacy, the alternative placed a strong accent on political and economic decentralization as an antidote to technocratic or corporate elitism. Such a shift of accent, Kothari argued (Kothari 1993: 123, 134), was guided and inspired by a commitment to 'take people seriously,' by 'respecting their thinking and wisdom' and by fostering institutions that would 'respond to their needs'. Only by following these guideposts was it possible to avoid both plutocracy and rampant consumerism and to establish an economic system that, in Gandhi's words, 'not only produces for the mass of the people but in which the mass of the people are also the producers'.

Next to Kothari, the most prominent member of the Delhi Centre is Ashis Nandy, a senior fellow and sometime director of the institute. In its basic thrust, Nandy shares Kothari's political orientation: the commitment to democratic transformative change – but a change popularly or locally legitimated rather than imposed by hegemonic (colonial or neocolonial) forces. A main difference between the two thinkers has to do with disciplinary focus: whereas Kothari has tended to centerstage issues of political economy and sociology, Nandy – a trained psychologist and psychoanalyst – has been more concerned with psychic or psychocultural sources of popular resistance as well as the inner traumas of colonial oppression. One of his early publications, *At the Edge of Psychology* (1980), traced the intersections linking politics, culture, and psychology, especially as experienced in non-Western societies. His next book, *The Intimate Enemy* (1983), probed these linkages more concretely by focusing on the introjection or internalization of the colonizer's worldview, which, among the colonized, can led to self-hatred and 'loss of self'. Nandy's own alternative vision was outlined in *Traditions, Tyranny, and Utopia* (1987a), especially in the chapter 'Toward a Third World Utopia'. The chapter deliberately took its stand at the grassroots level by viewing the world 'from the bottom up'. As Nandy emphasized (Nandy 1987a: 21, 31–35), the notion 'Third World' was not a timeless, metaphysical idea but rather a political and economic category 'born of poverty, exploitation, indignity and self-contempt'. Given this stark historical background, the formulation of an alternative future for non-Western societies had to start from the experience of 'man-made suffering' – not for the sake of inducing self-pity, but in order to permit a therapeutic 'working through' of the traumas of oppression. As helpmates in this process of coping and working through, the text invoked the healing powers latent in indigenous traditions, especially powers like those tapped in the Gandhian struggle for independence. An additional helpmate was the relative distance of non-Western cultures from the modern

Cartesian paradigm with its dualisms and dichotomics – between subject and object, humans and nature, and colonizers and colonized.

In still more forceful terms, Nandy's alternative vision for the future was spelled out in his essay 'Cultural Frames for Social Transformation: A Credo,' published in the Centre's journal *Alternatives* (1987b). The essay took its point of departure from the anti-colonial struggle in Africa, especially from Amilcar Cabral's stress on popular or indigenous culture as a counterpoint to hegemonic oppression. In Nandy's view, this outlook could be extended to other colonial or postcolonial societies. Basically, the stress on indigenous legacies signaled a defiance of the modern (Western) idea of intellectual and scientific 'expertise' uncontaminated by popular customs or beliefs; it gave voice to societies and peoples 'which have been the victims of history and are now trying to rediscover their own visions of a desirable society' (Nandy 1987b: 113–114). In our time of relentless globalization and Western-style standardization, this kind of self-assertion and defiance gained global significance. To this extent, the stress on 'cultural frames of social transformation' constitutes in our time 'a plea for a minimum cultural plurality in an increasingly uniformized world'. One of the prominent features of global standardization was for Nandy the imposition of the model of the 'nation-state' and Western-style nationalism in all parts of the world, including the Indian subcontinent. This topic was pursued further in his subsequent study, *The Illegitimacy of Nationalism* (1994), which launched a blistering attack on the rise of centralization and nationalist standardization which have become dominant traits of post-independence India. In Nandy's portrayal, nationalism and nation-state structures are basically Western imports foisted indiscriminately on non-Western societies and cultures. Indigenous cultural resources are again marshaled as antidotes to this imposition. Following the lead of Gandhi and Rabindranath Tagore, Nandy stressed the highly ambivalent role of nation-states as agents of both liberation and oppression; as an alternative he postulated a global perspective rooted in 'the tolerance encoded in various traditional ways of life in a highly diverse, plural society' (Nandy 1994: x–xi).

In his critique of nationalism and the nation-state, Nandy comes close to the position of another major intellectual school in post-independence India: the so-called 'Subaltern Studies' project launched by the historian Ranajit Guha around 1982. By comparison with the Delhi Centre, the Subaltern Studies movement (in its early phase) was more directly inspired by the teaching of Antonio Gramsci and humanist Marxism. For members of the movement, the gaining of independence and the erection of the Indian nation-state were only very superficial and ambivalent accomplishments, involving basically the transfer of power from Britain to post-colonial bourgeois and capitalist elites. A major articulation of this outlook was provided by Partha Chatterjee, a prominent social scientist working and teaching in Calcutta. In his *Nationalist Thought and the Colonial World* (1986), Chatterjee denounced nationalist independence as a borrowed ideology and purely 'derivative discourse': concealing and legitimating a mere shift in the agents of domination. His subsequent book, *The Nation and Its Fragments* (1993), offered a more nuanced and differentiated assessment, attentive to recent post-Marxist and post-structuralist tendencies. In this respect, Chatterjee's work is representative of a broader intellectual realignment characterizing the Subaltern Studies movement as a whole. In writing a preface to a volume seeking to provide an overview of the movement, Edward Said perceptively registered a certain shift away from the school's earlier Marxist and Gramscian moorings. As he observed (Guha and Spivak 1988: viii): 'None of the Subaltern Scholars is anything less than a critical student of Karl Marx'; moreover, today 'the influence of structuralist and post-structuralist thinkers like Derrida, Foucault, Roland Barthes and Louis Althusser is evident, along with the influence of British and American thinkers, like E. P. Thompson, Eric Hobsbawm, and others.'

Apart from multi-member institutes and research agendas India is, of course, replete with talented and innovative individual thinkers. For present purposes (given limitations of space), I want to single out three prominent recent philosophers: Daya Krishna, Sundara Rajan, and J. L. Mehta. Trained both in India and the West, Daya Krishna has been keenly attentive to, and critical of, dominant paradigms promulgated by Western social scientists during the Cold War era. Foremost among these were the formulas of 'development' and 'modernization' postulating the progressive assimilation of non-Western societies to Western yardsticks. For Krishna, these formulas were both theoretically confused and socio-politically obnoxious. As he queried in his book *Political Development* (Krishna 1979), how could one speak of linear development in the case of cultural frameworks, more specifically when comparing artworks of modernity with those of Greek antiquity or else with the masterpieces of India and China? Socio-politically, he added (Krishna 1979: 190), the relevant distinction should not be between 'developed' and 'undeveloped,' but between 'good' and 'bad' or legitimate and illegitimate political regimes. His compatriot Sundara Rajan has been similarly critical of linear or one-dimensional schemes of social advancement, relying for his purposes on a combination social phenomenology and Frankfurt School critical theory. As he wrote in his book *Innovative Competence and Social Change* (Rajan 1986: 87–88): 'If the alignment of [Frankfurt-style] communicative competence and [phenomenological] social theory could be defended, then I suggest we have a possibility of carrying over a "transcendental" point of view into the domain of social theory'. In Rajan's later writings, the influence of Continental hermeneutics – especially Paul Riceour's version – became steadily more decisive, leading him to differentiate between contextual 'signification' and a more de-contextualized critical-emancipatory 'symbolization.' In J. L. Mehta's case, finally, the most striking feature of his work are the resonances he developed between Indian classical thought and aspects of Heideggerian ontology and Gadamerian hermeneutics (see, e.g. Mehta, 1976, 1985).

Turning to East Asia, one finds again a plethora of innovative and critical perspectives, developed by both Buddhist and Confucian intellectuals and scholars. In the Buddhist camp, one must mention first of all the renowned Kyoto School of philosophy in Japan, inaugurated by Kitaro Nishida and further developed by such thinkers as Keiji Nishitani, Hajime Tanabe, Hisamatsu Shin'ihi and Masao Abe. In the case of all these thinkers the resonances with Continental thought are pronounced: while Nishida's work makes frequent appeal to Kierkegaard, Bergson and Husserl, the writings of Nishitani and others reveal a more distinct Heideggerian slant. Given the heavy emphasis of the entire school on such key Zen notions of 'nothingness' and 'emptiness' (*sunyata*), one may wonder about the practical implications of their perspective. However, as soon as the affinity of '*sunyata*' with Heidegger's 'nihilating nothingness' is taken into account, the practical and critical impulses spring instantly into view. For clearly, from the angle of nihilation, Buddhist thought can have no truck with totalizing modes of domination (with Derrida's 'technical-economic-military positivism'). The only proper and legitimate form of action or agency, under Zen Buddhist auspices, is a non-possessive and non-domineering kind of action – traditionally called '*wu-wei*,' again akin to Heidegger's 'letting be' (see, e.g. Nishitani 1982; Abe 1985; Dallmayr 1992, 1996). Outside the confines of Kyoto, more resolutely praxis-oriented forms of Buddhist thought have emerged in recent decades in many parts of Asia and South Asia. Sometimes labeled 'Buddhist liberation movement' or movement of 'engaged Buddhism,' this outlook – often aiming at radical social transformation – is represented by such figures as Thich Nhat Hanh (from Vietnam), the Dalai Lama (from Tibet), Sulak Sivaraksa (Thailand), A. T. Ariyaratne (Sri Lanka), and the late Dr Ambedkar (India) (see, e.g. Nhat Hanh 1967; Ambedkar 1984; Sivaraksa 1994; Queen and King 1996). Despite limitations imposed by the regime in mainland China, Confucianism has also experienced a remarkable revival in East and South East Asia, often with a critical edge against centralizing or totalizing types of government (see, e.g. Wei-ming 1985; Bell and Hahm 2003).

Given its far-flung extension from East and South Asia to 'West Asia' and Africa, a few words are also in order on theorizing in the Islamic world. Contrary to simplistic assumptions much in vogue in the West, Islamic societies today are not uniformly dominated by dogmatic-clerical or 'fundamentalist' doctrines, but display a rich welter of intellectual orientations – some of them with clearly practical-critical overtones. In Southeast Asia, the prototype of a critical Muslim intellectual is Chandra Muzaffer, head of an NGO called 'Just World Trust', whose publications and public statements have been exemplary in denouncing both Western aggressive or imperialist policies and unjust or corrupt practices in the Islamic world (see, e.g. Muzaffer 2002, 1993). Some of the liveliest intellectual debates in that part of the world are carried on today in Iran, with 'reformers' and 'conservatives' engaging each other in sustained exchanges on philosophical and political issues – often with a high degree of erudition and sophistication. As in India and East Asia, European resonances can readily be detected in these exchanges, particularly in the arguments of reformers whose writings frequently appeal to Continental perspectives, ranging from the Vienna School to Husserlian phenomenology, Heideggerian ontology, Gadamerian hermeneutics, and French-style postmodernism (see, e.g. Boroujerdi 1996; Mirsepassi, 2000; Jahanbaksh 2001; Jahanbegloo 2004). The influence of phenomenology and hermeneutics can also be found in the works of other Muslim thinkers in West Asia, such as the Egyptian philosopher Hassan Hanafi, while aspects of Frankfurt School critical theory surface in the publications of the Moroccan Mohammed al-Jabiri (see, e.g. Hanafi 1965; al-Jabiri 1999).

Toward a global critical theory?

The preceding discussion was meant to provide a glimpse into arenas of critical-practical theorizing in many Asian counties, and thus to counteract parochial assumptions of a European (or Western) monopoly in the domain of critical philosophy and social thought. As has been shown, resonances of Continental-European thought can be found in the writings and arguments of many Asian thinkers, both in East and South Asia and in the Middle East (or West Asia). In all instances, what is involved is not a one-sided transmission of European ideas to Asia, but rather a dialogical exchange or interaction. In our age of globalization, these interactions are bound to multiply and to deepen, leading to the emergence of a global community of critically engaged intellectuals – an updated and cosmopolitan version of the traditional 'republic of letters'. This development is crucially important in our time of immense superpower predominance, a domination which – following the model of earlier imperial systems – is hostile to the cultivation of critical scrutiny and contestation. To speak with Jacques Derrida, it is imperative in our time to defend the 'right to philosophy', that is, the right to critical theorizing among ordinary people around the world, as an antidote and response to the dictates of a coercive 'technical-economic-military positivism'. In Derrida's sense, this defense is necessary in order to preserve the open spaces needed for unregimented and 'unrestricted' inquiry and questioning – open spaces which, in turn, serve as heralds or anticipations of a 'democracy to come' (Derrida 1992: 77). To express the point in somewhat different language: the emerging global networks of critical thinking can be seen as waystations to the formation of a global public sphere – a sphere indispensable for anything like a democratically constituted cosmopolis.

References

Abe, M. (1985) *Zen and Western Thought*, (ed.) W. R. LaFleur, Honolulu: University of Hawaii Press.

al-Jabiri, M. A. (1999) *Arab-Islamic Philosophy: A Contemporary Critique* (trans. A. Abassi), Austin: Texas University Press.

Ambedkar, B. R. (1984) *The Buddha and His Dharma*, Bombay: Siddharth Publications.

Bell, D. and C. Hahm (eds) (2003) *Confucianism for the Modern World*, Cambridge: Cambridge University Press.

Boroujerdi, M. (1996) *Iranian Intellectuals and the West*, Syracuse, NY: Syracuse University Press.

Chatterjee, P. (1986) *Nationalist Thought and the Colonial World: A Derivative Discourse*, Tokyo: Zed Books.

Chatterjee, P. (1993) *The Nation and Its Fragments: Colonial and Postcolonial Histories*, Princeton: Princeton University Press.

Dallmayr, F. (1992) 'Nothingness and *Sunyata*: A Comparison of Heidegger and Nishitani,' *Philosophy East and West*, 42: 37–48.

Dallmayr, F. (1996) '*Sunyata* East and West: Emptiness and Global Democracy,' in F. Dallmayr, *Beyond Orientalism*, Albany, NY: State University of New York Press.

Derrida, J. (1992) *The Other Heading: Reflections on Today's Europe* (trans. P.-A. Brault and M. B. Naas), Bloomington: Indiana University Press.

Derrida, J. (2002) 'The Right to Philosophy from the Cosmopolitical Point of View,' in J. Derrida, *Ethics, Institutions, and the Right to Philosophy* (trans. Peter P. Trifonas), Lanham, MD: Rowman & Littlefield.

Guha, R. and Spivak, G. C. (eds) (1988) *Selected Subaltern Studies*, New York: Oxford University Press.

Hanafi, H. (1965) *Les méthodes d'exégèse*, Cairo: Conseil des Arts.

Horkheimer, M. (1972 [1937]) 'Traditional and Critical Theory,' in M. Horkheimer, *Critical Theory: Selected Essays* (trans. M. J. O'Connell and others), New York: Herder and Herder.

Jahanbaksh, F. (2001) *Islam, Democracy, and Religious Modernism in Iran, 1953–2000*, Boston: Brill.

Jahanbegloo, R. (ed.) (2004) *Iran: Between Tradition and Modernity*, Lanham, MD: Lexington Books.

Kothari, R. (1988a) *State against Democracy: In Search of Humane Governance*, Delhi: Ajanta.

Kothari, R. (1988b) *Transformation and Survival: In Search of a Humane World Order*, Delhi: Ajanta.

Kothari, R. (1989) *Rethinking Development: In Search for Humane Alternatives*, New York: New Horizons Press.

Kothari, R. (1993) *Growing Amnesia: An Essay on Poverty and the Human Condition*, New Delhi: Viking.

Krishna, D. (1979) *Political Development: A Critical Perspective*, Delhi: Oxford University Press.

Mehta, J. L. (1976) *Martin Heidegger: The Way and the Vision*, Honolulu: Hawaii University Press.

Mehta, J. L. (1985) *India and the West: The Problem of Understanding*, Chico, CA: Scholars Press.

Mirsepassi, A. (2000) *Intellectual Discourse and the Politics of Modernization: Negotiating Modernity in Iran*, Cambridge: Cambridge University Press.

Muzaffer, C. (1993) *Human Rights and the New World Order*, Penang, Malaysia: Just World Trust.

Muzaffer, C. (2002) *Rights, Religion and Reform*, London: Routledge Curzon.

Nandy, A. (1980) *At the Edge of Psychology: Essays in Politics and Culture*, Delhi: Oxford University Press.

Nandy, A. (1983) *The Intimate Enemy: Loss and Recovery of Self under Colonialism*, Delhi: Oxford University Press.

Nandy, A. (1987a) *Tradition, Tyranny and Utopias: Essays in the Politics of Awareness*, Delhi: Oxford University Press.

Nandy, A. (1987b) 'Cultural Frames for Social Transformation: A Credo', *Alternatives*, 12: 113–116.

Nandy, A. (1994) *The Illegitimacy of Nationalism: Rabindranath Tagore and the Politics of Self*, Delhi: Oxford University Press.

Nhat Hanh, T. (1967) *Vietnam: Lotus in a Sea of Fire*, New York: Hill and Wang.

Nishitani, K. (1982) *Religion and Nothingness* (trans. Jan Van Bragt), Berkeley: University of California Press.

Queen, C. S. and King, S. B. (eds) (1996) *Engaged Buddhism: Buddhist Liberation Movements in Asia*, Albany, NY: State University of New York Press.

Rajan, R. S. (1986) *Innovative Competence and Social Change*, Ganeshkind: Poona University Press.

Rajan, R. S. (1987) *Toward a Critique of Cultural Reason*, Delhi: Oxford University Press.

Sivaraksa, S. (1994) *A Buddhist Vision for Renewing Society*, Bangkok: Thai Interreligious Commission for Development.

Wei-ming, T. (1985) *Confucian Thought: Selfhood as Creative Transformation*, Albany, NY: State University of New York Press.

30

Social theory, 'Latin' America and modernity

José Maurício Domingues

Identities, culture and institutions

Two questions are usually at stake when we think about modernity: a quest for identity as well as an attempt to understand in a scientific way the world in which we live. This was the double query Weber (1930 [1905]: 1) raised when he asked about the implications rationalizing processes had for a son of the West as regards their specificity and universal validity of the particular configuration that emerged in that area.

Named as such or not – and usually being interchangeable with the vaguer cultural-geographic notion of the 'West' – global modernity has indeed worked as a backdrop and a crucial element for identity building in the last centuries. Take for instance the debate that ranged over 'Latin' America in the nineteenth- and the twentieth-centuries. Were the people living in that area members of the 'West'? Should they aim at that? Would that be possible? Answers abound, and the positive valuation of the West, and the manner in which this was carried out, had in some part to do with how local populations were esteemed by the political 'elites' and the intellectuals (Domingues 1992). Let me just quote a few examples. Sarmiento (1962 [1845]) – a founding father of Argentina – was adamant on the path to take: we had to choose between 'civilization and barbarism', and waged several wars against anything (including the Iberian heritage) that might resemble the rejection of the West. Some decades afterwards, Rodó (1982 [1900]) saw the supposedly materialist Western immigrants as Shakespeare's *The Tempest* character Caliban and as bringing precisely barbarism to his country Uruguay, against the cultivated and ethereal Ariel, with whom the intellectuals, that is, Prospero, should side. In the aftermath of the Cuban revolution Retamar (1982 [1971]) resumed this debate and claimed that the people was exactly Caliban, exploited by colonialism and imperialism, and that Prospero, a representation of the intellectuals, should side with Caliban against its explorers. This sort of debate has not been especially strong in the subcontinent more recently, but impulses in this direction certainly hide in the apparently taken for granted modernity of these diverse countries in the aftermath of democratization and in the face of recently heightened processes of globalization and perhaps a postmodernist feeling which has cast doubt on the usefulness of such characterizations (Canclini 1990). In any case the subcontinent ended up known as 'Latin' America, a definition that has little to do with any actual cultural background, stemming from Napoleon's III expansionist project to the region (Morse 1982: especially ch. 8) – the reason why it appears here always between quotation marks.

In parallel to this longstanding debate in the area of Spanish colonization, similar discussions took place in Brazil. In one way or another, our specificity, our relationship with the West, what we should take from it, were the central issues. It is worth pointing out that this took on a particularly dramatic tone due to the fact that, differently from areas such as India, China or the Islamic world, where people are fully aware that they were not either modern or westerners, the America that emerged from the Iberian colonization had a *perpendicular* relationship with modernity while at the same it *did not* exist before the European expansion. A deep and still unresolved problem of identity ensued from this uneasy situation. In this regard national and/or subcontinental projects were disputed in the space of what Rama (1985 [1984]) characterized as a Platonist 'city of letters', which had as a starting point not only social development but also an explicit identity problem.

As the social sciences further developed, while identity remained crucial, this discussion assumed however a more consistent and sociological countenance, especially in Brazil, where the problem of the relationship between modernity – or capitalism *tout court*, as Marxists would rather put it – and the country's past became an absolute obsession for social thinking. At this stage suffice it to note that cultural problems as well as institutional questions became central to this debate. The moment and the peculiar features of capitalist development, the specificities of the state, the capitalist, feudal, patrimonial or whatever basic configuration of these societies, the holistic or individualistic thrust of its forms of consciousness, among other traits, were energetically disputed henceforth. That means that modernity has been the central subject of sociological analysis and theory in the subcontinent.

Once again an example may help here. Three books are usually seen as having been particularly powerful influences over the young generation in the 1930s (cf. Cândido 1967): Freyre's (1987 [1933]) cultural anthropologically oriented and celebratory study of the mixture of races; Holanda's (1983 [1936]) Weberian understanding of the impasses of democracy; and Prado Júnior's (1980 [1934]) Marxist outline of the peculiar capitalist development of the colonial period. Although at least the first two of those books had obvious literary, modernist ambitions, they were not part of such a dominating genre, nor did they partake in the strong rhetoric or immediately practical aims of the works typical of a former period. They had, however, strong consequences with regard to the questions that should be envisaged for the development of the country – in terms of race, democracy and socialist revolution. Thus if it was clear that there was a normative, in these cases underlying, aspect to the discussion, that is, a question about what should be done, and why it should, to modernize those societies, a social-scientific approach to the culture and institutions of modernity had to be brought to the fore too, especially since the social sciences were slowly and unevenly introduced in those several 'Latin' American countries, establishing what Fernandes (1977) – Brazil's greatest sociologist to date – saw as a rationalized (that is, westernized) manner to make sense of the social world. That identity questions, however, loom large relentlessly and may become the unrecognized centre of sociologically oriented works is something that is shown in recent attempts at interpretation of the country's modernizing process (cf. Souza 2000).

In a classical piece of work, Zéa (1965) argued that 'Latin' Americans have asked who they are in particular terms, rather than in directly universalistic ones: they could tell that they were not 'men' in general – they were thrown into particular conditions and knew they were not westerners, an angle which the latter in fact usually miss, for they take their condition as universal for the human species. Thus 'Latin' Americans had to understand particularity in order to grasp the human condition in general. Has this changed with the development of an ever more explicit global modernity? This does not seem to be the case. The entire region has 'westernized' – that is, modernized to a great extent; and, although it will never simply become western, these countries are clearly modern now. This does not mean that the problem of identity has disappeared into thin air: it may be dormant at times, but surely it either is openly discussed or remains latent, since we cannot avoid the question of what it is to be modern in the periphery of global modernity, even if the question and the answer must be phrased in quite different terms in relation to how they were phrased before. Other regions have to come to grips with the same sort of problematic – as Africa, for instance, especially after the failure of African Marxism to modernize and democratize those emerging countries (cf. Mbembe 2002).

This is so not only because these are unavoidable human problems, but also because the global unification of modernity, which has proceeded at a fast pace in the last two decades, is pushed through an affirmation of generality and universality, but through a proliferation of more specific and concrete identities as well (see Robertson 1992; Robertson *et al.* 1995). The hybridity of contemporary modernity did not do away with a proliferation of particularities and the continuous production of new and refashioned identities, which are never wholly integrated within a universalist overarching mould. Whence the compulsion to discuss modernity and the relation of the 'rest' of the world to it, conforming a problem which is at once theoretical and closely linked to identity building, in the cognitive, normative and expressive dimensions. While essays of interpretation with a very literary flavour predominated during the nineteenth- and the first half of the twentieth-century, social scientific enterprises have come to the fore with the large processes of social change undergone by the diverse countries of the subcontinent. Social theory finds its bases of support therein.

What do these preliminary remarks press home? In my view, two points. First, that the discussion about modernity always implies an identity problem, and as such it involves cognitive, normative and expressive issues. It is never only a conceptual endeavour. Second, that while cultural questions inevitably come up in the discussion, institutional developments are crucial for a more consistent, social sciences oriented debate, something that is not always, or even often, clear in the 'post-colonial' criticism and the cultural theory that has been highly visible in recent times. Even cultural issues should not be confined to identity matters as they more recently often tend to be. Initially I shall situate how so-called 'Latin' American social theory has dealt with modernity. Then the position of the subcontinent *vis-à-vis* recent 'civilizational theory' will be tackled and a proposal to resume an encompassing theorization about the region within the contemporary, third phase of global modernity will be put forward. In the conclusion, I shall briefly resume the question of identity.

'Latin' American social theory and modernity

In a book intended as both a polemic work and a methodological approach based on phenomenology, Guerreiro Ramos (1965), a Brazilian author, proposed that sociologists should allow their consciousness to be immersed in empirical reality in order that they could 'reduce' their former theoretical notions and thus grasp the concrete reality of the country. Although his strategy was less than appropriate, he was actually trying – in a not so frequently systematic way – to tackle a dramatic problem for social scientists in Iberian colonized America. More radically, Fernandes (1977: 51–68) rejected, in the 1950s, the construction of theories, since there would be no resources available for that, while others still believed that the consolidation of a community of researchers in those countries would eventually and naturally allow for a reworking of Western concepts and theories (Germani 1964: 4–5, 136). From this brief analysis we may perceive what has been a central problem in the region: how to apply the concepts of Western social sciences to countries where they might not properly fit? Was that related to an essentially distinct form of social life or due merely to a time lag in the development of the subcontinent? A number of answers were given to these questions. Rather than providing a methodological discussion, which is rarely effective, or trying the impossible task, within the limits of this article, of reconstructing the whole history of the social sciences in the region, I will follow the issue in a few key theoretical debates that bore it, implicitly or explicitly, in their background.

The first may be furnished by the Marxist dispute over the character of the social formation of the colonial – and post-colonial – regions of south and central America, which had direct political implications for the revolutionary strategy of communists and socialists (see for instance Mariátegui 1968 [1928]; Prado Jr. 1972 [1967]; Sempat Assadourian 1973; Amaral Lapa 1980). While for some these were feudal societies, due especially to the dominance of the great agrarian property as well as legal codes of servitude and nobility, including therein the control of the soil and the labour force, for others capitalism was from the very beginning the mode of production that articulated these societies, since they emerged linked directly to the world market. Both explanations made recourse to Marx's own texts, but do not look very satisfying if closely examined today. Others had a different solution: they tried to define specific modes of production – a colonial mode of production or a slave colonial mode of production. At some point the debate was abandoned, since its political implications dwindled, due to Marxist intellectuals having become less numerous and influential as well as because capitalism became so overwhelming that the historical roots of these societies mattered less for their future. But the fact is that Marxist analysis has never in my view been able to offer a really good answer to the sort of problem it was forced to confront in this regard.

Weberian approaches had also to deal with this adaptation to the peculiarities of the subcontinent. Although they tended to overlook Weber's own warning that ideal types had to be crafted according to one's own view and specific problems of analysis, they applied concepts such as traditional patrimonialism versus rational-legal domination. Again, the more orthodox the form in which the concept was proposed the less it seemed to be able to grasp the reality of the subcontinent (see Werneck Vianna 1999, for a balance). Its dislocation from a concentration on state bureaucracies (Faoro 1958) towards societal patrimonialism (Carvalho Franco 1983), as well as innovations such as the concept of 'neopatrimonialism' (Schwartzman 1982, based on Eisenstadt), which combined the private use of the state with the modernizing features it frankly evinces in those countries, seemed to do the job much more adequately. The same is true as to the (implicitly Weberian) idea that the power of the modern imaginary underpinned a protracted revolution, which in any case has led the subcontinent (e.g. Brazil) to modernity in terms of its main institutions from the nineteenth-century onwards (Fernandes 1975).

The problem is that many of these approaches inadvertently reproduced – even when creative and conceptually sharp – the teleological view of development that especially Weber strongly rejected. Modernization – indeed 'Westernization' *tout court* – was assumed as a goal and/or a tendency in the development of the American societies. Although it was therefore not alone in this enterprise, modernization theory expressed this more strongly than any other sociological framework. Often drawing upon Parsons (especially his pattern variables), such authors produced heavily biased analyses of these countries, stressing their traditional – particularistic, affective, diffuse – action patterns, which were deemed the cause of their backwardness. Simply leaving behind their traditional culture would allow for a thorough modernization of these societies towards universalism, affective neutrality in public life, focused behaviour, etc., hence to economic development (Lipset and Solari 1967). Even authors who had deep theoretical insights and a more complex view of the interplay between Western values and concrete social conditions in 'Latin' America, such as Germani (1969) and Cardoso (1971), *vis-à-vis* businessmen, adopted perspectives often very close to modernization theory – in principle a North American construct, which, despite its totally discredited intellectual bias, still dominates much of 'Latin American studies' in that country (Feres Jr. 2003).

Originally influenced by Durkheim's functionalism and full-blown modernity as a desired *telos* for Argentina, Germani's interpretation of modernizing social process and of Peronism was capable of perceiving how in particular *freedom* mattered for the movement's followers. He also proposed a theory of action that departed very much from Weber's and Parsons' views by introducing 'elective action' (based on freedom thus) as crucial for the institutionalization of modernity (Germani 1965 – see also Domingues and Maneiro 2004). Cardoso in turn was the main – and more moderate – proponent, along with Faletto, of the theory of dependency, the first and so far the only conceptual perspective crafted in the subcontinent to assume planetary prominence (Cardoso and Faletto 1969). While modernization theory put emphasis on the shortcomings of culture for the 'Latin' American institutions and development, Cardoso and Faletto, from a neo-Marxist and neo-Cepalian[1] point of view, brought out the distinct alliances between global capital – imperialism – internal 'elites' and the masses as the key factors for the development of these countries. However, against many other 'dependentists', they stated the possibility of development under conditions of dependency (see Valdés 2003). While Germani's writings clearly advance a theoretical perspective, some timidity – though Cardoso tends to speak of a structural-historical analysis as his methodology – may be grasped through the ambiguous state of the dependency approach: this seeps through Cardoso's (1975) disclaimer that it should not be conceived as a theory, opting instead for a proposal for the analysis of 'concrete situations of dependency' within a more universal theory of capitalist global development.

All these theories dealt with institutions as well as the 'hermeneutic' fabric of 'Latin' America, very much according to the Marxist as well as the mainstream sociological tradition. They all evince the tension between universal concepts and specific realities, which demand the reworking in some measure of pristine theories. However, apart from a few efforts, no general theory has been produced by social scientists in these countries more recently. The particularity of each country has dominated intellectual efforts, as much as did the transition to democracy, for instance in Brazil (Pecaut 1989), Mexico (Zabludovsky and Girola 1995) and Argentina (Rubinich *et al.* 2004). In fact, the role of the state, of electoral politics, of party pluralism, of civil society and related themes has come to the fore in this period, without, however, a proper theory of democracy being proposed. Another element that must be taken into account is that Political Science as a specific field of specialization appeared for the first time independently from sociology in this process. This happened very much under the influence of North American approaches, including rational choice theory and institutionalism, in some part through the return of academics in exile who took their PhDs in the United States (Domingues 2005b). This is true even though a political sociology of democracy has also been developing in the region, based on Habermas, probably the most influential European author in the subcontinent taken as a whole today (see for example, Avritzer *et al.* 1997; Costa 1997; Avritzer 2002).

Contemporarily only a few exceptions may be spotted in terms of general theories. Canclini's (1990) cultural view of subcontinental fragmented 'post-modernity' is perhaps the best example in this regard, being more widely known outside the subcontinent, expressing moreover the force of anthropological perspectives and the importance of cultural and communicational studies (Martín-Barbero 2001: especially ch. 3). Also at a cultural level we find attempts at problematizing America's role in the emergence of modernity (Quijano 1993). Tackling different issues, in a more economic and 'structural' dimension, the same happens with a renewed strand of the 'theory of marginalization', which, rejected by many in the 1970s, has returned with a vengeance, claiming even that tendencies in terms of a superfluous sector of the labour force in the subcontinent's twentieth-century capitalism basically foretold tendencies at work in central capitalist societies today (Nun 2001; Quijano 2004). I have myself tried to work on a general theoretical programme based on the concept of 'collective subjectivity' and the interpretation of contemporary modernity (Domingues 1995a, 2000, 2005a). But this is too little for the maturity, despite many shortcomings, social science disciplines have acquired in the subcontinent, in spite of the false opposition crafted by some authors (Portes 2001) between a vaguely defined 'grand theory' and (supposedly Mertonian) more verifiable 'middle range', empirically based efforts.

All in all, we can actually speak, during a certain period, of a typical 'Latin' American sociological theory, especially insofar as development, modernization and dependency furnished the key areas tackled by the researchers in the subcontinent, although producing diverse answers. Moreover, it has developed precisely from the 1950s to the 1970s, with a close relationship between the diverse academic communities of these countries. This was interrupted by the establishment of violent military dictatorships and was not actually hitherto resumed (Valdés 2003; Domingues 2005b). It is about time that we made efforts in this direction. Of course this must not detract by any means from a close contact with what has been produced in the social sciences elsewhere in the world – indeed the aforementioned period of development of a 'Latin' American sociological theory was one during which the links between the subcontinent and the rest of the world were especially strong. There is no reason for that to change now, although theories crafted in the region must of course be sensitive to its particularities and specific problems. Conversely, we must not forget these debates and traditions, simply adopting the fads of international sociology as though no social theoretical issues had been discussed in 'Latin' America. We must avoid the amnesia that too often besets researchers in the subcontinent. Subtle engagement with specific problems and theories, on the one side, and theoretical advances produced elsewhere, on the other, must be our goal.[2] If the timidity of social theorization precludes a more direct use of that production, it is in any case worth our while trying to connect their sporadic theoretical insights with new theories endogenously developed or imported from elsewhere.

I think that in particular a twofold general theoretical issue demands attention in the subcontinent as well as elsewhere at present, in order that we approach it with greater precision: modernity as a global civilization and its present, third phase. That is what I shall now try to substantiate. Thereby we may be able to provide a conceptually sharp, regionally based, theoretical perspective of contemporary global modernity, which can also work as a contribution to the more general debate that has mobilized the social sciences, especially sociology, across the globe. Moreover, I think also that thereby we can resume, in a different key to be sure, those former concerns with modernization, development and democracy. It goes without saying too that by no means this theoretical approach has any pretension of exclusivity, a silly claim at this stage of development of social theory.

Contemporary global modernity and 'Latin' America

Civilization is a big and hard word, of which the West was usually too fond, especially in order to assert its hegemony ideologically. From barbarism to civilization – Sarmiento's project – plus from primitive to higher cultures, this was the unilinear path envisaged – and recommended – by the West and those who thought, albeit peripherally, they belonged there.[3] However, a number of authors have interestingly tried to develop an approach based on a much more neutral and flexible view of civilization, which I think is useful to start off with a conceptualization of global modernity.

Coming from a functionalist background, although never entirely committed to its tenets, Eisenstadt became increasingly aware of the contingent character of historical developments and of the role collectivities – 'elites', or what he termed 'institutional entrepreneurs'– play in it (Eisenstadt 1990). Creativity was also vital for him, exercised as it were by charismatic leadership. After studying the outbreak of what he called, resuming Jasper, the 'axial civilizations', when a division between sacred and mundane was introduced and a highly productive tension came about with a demand for transcendence and the realization of unearthly values in this life, the manifold *projects* of modernity became the centre of his inquiry (Eisenstadt 1982), along with the resulting 'multiple modernities' (Eisenstadt 2000, 2001 – although he had previously spoken of modernity in the singular, cf. Eisenstadt 1987). It is moreover an outspoken contention of his work that such historical developments stem from the pressure values exert, which eventually results in their being institutionalized – a position which owes a lot to Parsonian sociology (though certainly not to Weber). Several problems can be spotted in Eisenstadt's important contributions, which span more than half a century. Let me point to only three. His conception of collective agency is too reductive – indeed he deals exclusively with what I consider as *highly centred collective subjectivities*, whose projects are clear and whose action is organized in very distinctive and coordinated ways. But we cannot by any means always, and perhaps not even often, explain historical developments in such a manner. His view of modernity as composed by multiple modernities has in addition the liability of apparently considering each country as possessing its own, circumscribed model of modernity. Whether it would be therefore really a civilization, spilling over – and in fact constituting itself – across borders becomes doubtful. Finally it seems clear that such simple and idealistic manner of reckoning with the relationship between values and institutions is untenable, since a two way movement should instead be discerned. Curiously enough, although much more keen on the role of power in historical developments, Arnason (1997: especially 48ff) too sees the manifold process of modernity as closely linked to projects and counter-projects. Unlike Eisenstadt, however, he makes much more room for intercivilizational influences, which are deemed decisive for the present configuration of the world through the interplay between modernity and other civilizations (Arnason 2001).

What to make of the concept of civilization? It is not well specified and is beset with all sorts of problems which the concept of 'society' has traditionally had. Does it imply closed boundaries, basically endogenous dynamics and relative internal homogeneity? Or should we on the contrary see civilizations as open universes, for which exogenous developments are of crucial importance and which are internally often highly heterogeneous? The Marxist concept of 'social formation' (cf. Luporini and Sereni 1973; Anderson 1976) can provide some sort of inspiration here to advance in the direction of this second possibility. Referring to something broader than the concept of 'mode of production' it may be read in two ways: as encompassing a mode of production and its corresponding superstructures or as pointing concretely to a combination of modes of production and their corresponding manifestations at the superstructural level in a concrete space-time configuration. Often one element is dominant and lends shape to the others that are present in concrete social formations.

Bearing this in mind, civilizations can thus be seen as very broad social systems, large 'collective subjectivities' with a low level of centring, where some principles however prevail. They develop in a dilated span and other civilizational patterns can be therein combined with the centrality of some principles of organization. The configuration of such a heterogeneous social system can include in some areas the dominance of certain principles which, although subordinate in the overall framework, have the upper hand in that specific region. These other principles are most likely, however, to have been widely altered by the dominant elements in the overall social formation, while their dynamic is also subordinated to them. Civilizations have causal impact upon one another, since they never develop in total isolation.

We can therefore speak of modernity as *a* civilization, which is not homogeneous or closed, though; in fact it has been combined with elements of other civilizations and has produced a hybrid form, in the global space-time coordinates it has definitely assumed at this stage, in which the forms of consciousness and the institutions of modernity prevail, without detriment to other civilizational influences, which may be dominant in other areas of the modern space-time configuration, although already very much altered by their interplay with modernity. Surely it develops according to some clear projects and counter-projects, but much more decentred and loose historical developments are probably more important, since the very early hours of modernity. It is correct to postulate some sort of ultimate resultant of history and it may be said to have some sort of *telos*; nevertheless these are not the outcome of projects and the movement of centred collective subjectivities (especially of ruling classes and social movements), although they do contribute to them. More disperse and powerful forces push modernity ahead and weave a web of intended and unintended consequences of action which yields in the end the contingent direction of history.

Can thus the view of 'multiple modernities' be sustained, as if the several nation-states or 'societies' which compose the contemporary landscape were discrete units which develop basically according to processes internal to them, with the addition of external influence and borrowings? I do not think so. Instead we must speak of *a* 'multiple modernity'. Nor can we, in view of that, simply speak of the coexistence of several civilizations in the globe today, a situation that still obtained in the nineteenth-century, which does not mean that intercivilizational encounters no longer carry on *within* global modernity. To be sure, we can reject the concept of civilization, due to its historical resonance or to theoretical reasons. In any event, we must nevertheless come up with some sort of general concept of what modernity is, otherwise we proceed just like Molière's M. Jourdain, who talked prose without knowing he was doing so. In more technical terms we must go beyond the use of modernity as an unspecified notion, which remains as cloudy as what Parsons called a 'residual category' – that is, one we must employ to deal with unavoidable research problems but is never actually defined (see Domingues 2000: ch. 3). Although contemporary civilizational theory still needs to be refined, it appears to me as the best solution available, whether we refer to 'modern civilization' or prefer some more neutral term. For the reasons and in the format adduced above, I propose that we use this concept in order to understand the world in which we live.

Modernity is no essence, a set of abstract principles that are realized in specific space-time coordinates. Instead it develops from the actions and movements of individuals and collective subjectivities. In a large measure modern institutions and forms of consciousness are the unintended consequence of desires and concrete options people make in daily life, although more general projects, defined by political and cultural collectivities – for change or conservation of modernity or pre-modern relationships – must also be taken into account. However, although it is no essence, modernity has had at its core the West, where it has first arisen, and then spilt over the whole world. Its 'core' was originally very clearly the West, in terms both of general dynamic and especially of power. The main institutions of modernity first emerged there, in a specific form, and only then were they absorbed and partly autonomously developed in other areas of the globe (see Eisenstadt 1987: 6–9). Surely western

388

modernity has always been entangled with and depended on the whole world to develop, as world systems theory has shown; this does not mean that we should suppose a flat picture of its development, without regard to specific origins and power relations (cf. Wallerstein 1984). It is true too that when it moved further on, modernity combined with other civilizational sources and also the relation between periphery and centre greatly changed, especially through the emergence of other, non-western centres (Japan is the most conspicuous example of this so far). The periphery has moved through migrations and cultural imports and the media into the centre as well. But we are far from a situation in which power has become so dispersed as to allow for a complete dilution of the very notions of core and periphery, contrary to what some are prone to think (for instance Appadurai 1990, and even Hardt and Negri 2000).

It is within this global modern civilization that we must therefore locate 'Latin' America, in its periphery and with its own civilizational combination of elements as well as its own peculiar history. The colonization by the Iberian monarchies and their particular brand of modern forms of consciousness and institutions implied a large scale civilizational encounter in the geographical area, since other civilizations were spread across the subcontinent, to which we must add the forced emigration of many other African civilizational groups in the aftermath of the conquest (see Morse 1982, 1990; Domingues 1995b).[4] The following centuries were witness also to a confrontation of the newly formed societies with civilizational patterns that emerged in northern Europe and the United States, which contributed to the already deep hybridity of these social formations. Modernity eventually set in and now, with its particularities, 'Latin' America shares with the rest of the world what may be called the third phase of modernity. We arrive thus at the second issue I had pointed out above.

An interesting literature about the crisis of 'organized capitalism', as some have defined it, was produced when the limits of Keynesian policies as well as the Welfare State problems became clear in the 1980s. Wagner (1994) lent this body of work an inventive interpretation, emphasizing the discursive aspect of that faltering social formation, and proposed the idea that modernity had traversed two phases – one 'liberal restrict', the other 'organized', which had the state at its core – both followed by crises. The second was moreover interpreted as post-modernity (a step in 'Latin' America taken for instance by Canclini), a definition which Wagner saw as merely a diagnosis of the crisis. In the same vein, Boltanski and Chiapello (1999) put forward the idea, very close to Wagner, who they read with a Weberian bias, of a third phase of capitalism, characterized by the 'world of projects' and the expansion of social 'networks', accompanied by its lay theories of justice.

To deal exactly with such transformations I proposed the thesis of a third phase of modernity that really includes networks (and its mechanism of articulation, 'voluntary collabora-tion') with centrality, but in a broader or less reductionist manner I have called it 'mixed articulated' with the intent of underscoring, in any case at an *analytical* level, the continuing role of hierarchical (articulated by 'command') and market (articulated by 'voluntary inter-change') mechanisms, side by side with networks. The heightened role of the latter stems from an increase of social complexity that demands greater flexibility of the mechanisms of coordination of social action – which hierarchies cannot supply – but at the same time the possibility of solidarity between agents – in which the market is too weak (although often the outcome of selective voluntary collaboration is the exclusion of other individuals and col-lectivities). Therefore neither should we get to conclusions that imply the emergence of social formations which would mean a total rupture with the past, nor should ongoing transfor-mations be overlooked. Besides, the concept of 'uneven and combined' development, at a global, regional and local level as well as in what regards distinct social dimensions within countries and internal regions, must be taken into account in order that we grasp the dynamic of expansion of the third phase of modernity (Domingues 2002, 2005a). That is also how, I think, we must understand contemporary 'Latin' America within modern global civilization.[5]

In 'Latin' America liberal restrict modernity was still more restricted, but its dynamic implied also the dominance of the modern imaginary, the development of modern institutions and the greater or lesser incorporation of the masses to that universe. The second phase, based in general on the corporatist model and a mix of cooptation and repression of the working masses, sometimes including more or less advanced elements of the Welfare State, and having at its kernel the developmentalist state, implied a deepening, in a particular way, of modernity in the subcontinent. The crisis that set in the 1970s has as its counterpart, also in the periphery and especially in this area, the crisis of the model of state intervention that was unevenly implemented between the 1930s and the 1970s. The crisis lasted up to the following decade, but neoliberalism, pushed through by international financial organizations and the powers that won the Cold War, was also really incapable to solve the region's problems – in fact by and large has aggravated them. However, internal processes due to social complexification and the crisis of that model, as well as the impact of the same sort of phenomena at a global level, have landed 'Latin' American modernity in its third phase, although we still grapple, as all other regions, with the initial stages of development of this social formation and have just started to look for solutions for the problems it generates. In some aspects, due to uneven and combined development, the third phase of modernity has evolved more quickly in the subcontinent; in other aspects, and in connection sometimes with greater advances elsewhere, it has in a sense lagged behind. The future is in any case open and the specific conformation it will take in the following years will depend on social struggles and political decisions as much as on the spontaneous evolution of social life in the region and at a global level. Intended and unintended processes, played off by more or less (de)centred collective subjectivities, with their more or less clearly crafted projects, have been operating and will further unfold, as has been the case with all civilizational developments.

It is with this sort of issue in mind that modernization, development and democracy must be rethought in 'Latin' America, hence shedding once again evolutionism, the idea of total planning by the state (without losing sight of its crucial importance) and searching for new mechanisms of social and political, democratic, integration of much more plural and independent masses. What to do is still an open question; social experimentation thus appears as a necessity. On the other hand, the problems identified by recent sociological theory, from the definition of 'risk society' to cosmopolitan democracy will have to be dealt with both at a societal and a social science level, since the subcontinent has its specificities but is indeed part of contemporary global modern civilization. A large field of inquiry, at a theoretical level, is open for 'Latin' American social and sociological theory. It is about time it made a full comeback. To be sure, anthropology, political science, communication studies and jurisprudence will propose key contributions to the debate. Interdisciplinary efforts and the conformation of a general social theory will inevitably and positively find their way. That notwithstanding, sociology will remain a central discipline for the interpretation of modernity, in 'Latin' America as elsewhere today, likewise it originally did in the West and did too in this peripheral region in a more recent past.

Final words

I tried above to situate the twofold character of discussions about modernity and concentrated in the body of the article on the proper theoretical aspect of the debate in 'Latin' America.

Through reviewing some of the main discussions enacted therein, I have argued that a key problem is the adaptation of general theories to the specific realities of the subcontinent. The production of a new sociological, or more broadly, social theory in this area was also identified as a crucial issue and a proposal in this direction introduced in order to theorize contemporary modernity, in the subcontinent and elsewhere. A few final words may be said now as to the other aspect of the debate about modernity, that is, that which refers to identity questions.

As already suggested above, the concern with the 'West' fascinated 'Latin' American intellectuals for a long time. Only slowly did modernity become the focus of inquiry and a key to interpreting such social formations and their unfolding. A dovetailed problem, however, remained in those efforts, often sociologically oriented. In general, the identification of modernity as a set of abstract, rather than historical, principles had the upper hand in those debates. Conversely, and almost paradoxically, the identification of 'Latin' American countries as absolute specificities was very common. Two possibilities responded to this. First, say, a positive view, which implied that they had a specific 'essence', different from that of the West, something that might lead to claims to the existence of specific 'Latin' American civilizations; second, a negative one, which stated that they lacked the modern properties they supposedly should have, which made them therefore backward, or even civilizational aberrations (Domingues 1992).

The understanding of the subcontinent as being part, with its peculiarities and own pathways, of a global modern civilization may help us break free from this rigid dichotomy, which is not very often phrased now but remains unspoken in the background of much of social thought in the region, with the negative view having subtly gained more influence these days. We have for a long time been modern, although we are not, and cannot be, western. This apparent contradiction has largely contributed to constitute our identity. Perhaps a renewed sociological and, more broadly conceived, social theory can help us move beyond this almost necessary misunderstanding. This way the issue raised by Weber and reproduced at the beginning of this essay may be faced up to by our social scientists beyond, but without total detriment of, the issues formerly brought up by the important tradition of essayists which originally tried to offer an interpretation and a programme for our countries. We can thereby both betray and be faithful to our own modern heritage, while at same time drawing upon anything we may find of interest in European social theory as well as in approaches that may develop anywhere across the world.

Notes

1   It is worth noting that although the Economic Commission for Latin America (CEPAL) had economics as its object, it supposed and produced also a sociological perspective, close to what may be called 'historical structuralism', aiming also at planning as the solution for the problems of the region. This bias was shared with most sociologists of the subcontinent, maybe especially but not only in Brazil (Germani, Fernandes, Costa Pinto, Cardoso), who were under the strong influence of Mannheim's rationalizing programme. See Faletto (1996); Domingues (1999).

2   That is for instance Reigadas' (2000) contention in relation to post-colonial theory. Currents such as the 'philosophy of liberation' in 'Latin' America since the 1970s, she argues, had offered numerous insights that are now repeated by post-colonial scholars, although contemporary issues demand a less homogenizing view of the subcontinent than was previously the case.

3   I cannot attempt a detailed analysis of the idea of civilization or of the work of the authors reviewed below – something masterfully carried out by Knöbl (2001: chs 5, 7). My own view can be found in Domingues (2003).

4 In this connection it may be worth mentioning Dussel's (1998) standpoint. For him modernity emerged not due to processes developing within Europe, but due to the discovery of 'Amerindia', for whose management only then certain elements, above all instrumental reason, had to be developed. Indeed intercivilizational encounters have been neglected for too long in the social sciences; the opposite mistake must not be committed, though. We must not lose sight of the particular processes that unfolded within Europe, otherwise we cannot even start to understand – the crux of an extremely large body of historical literature which is not possible to review here – why Portugal and especially Spain were not capable of taking off in the direction of modernity and got stuck half-way in the transition, whereas Britain and North Western Europe more generally managed to achieve such a breakthrough and became the centre and first expression of modern civilization. Forms of consciousness – rationalized individualism above all, as pointed out by Nelson (1969, 1977), who was the main author until recently to stress the importance of intercivilizational encounters – and institutions were fundamental in this regard.

5 For a preliminary theoretical and empirically informed discussion, see Domingues (2005a).

References

Amaral Lapa, J. R. (ed.) (1980) *Modos de produção e realidade brasileira*, Petrópolis: Vozes.

Anderson, P. (1976) *Passages from Antiquity to Feudalism*, London: New Left Books.

Appadurai, A. (1990) 'Disjuncture and Difference in the World Global Economy', in M. Featherstone (ed.), *Global Culture*, London: Sage.

Arnason, J. P. (1997) *Social Theory and Japanese Experience: The Dual Civilization*, London and New York: Kegan Paul International.

Arnason, J. P. (2001) 'Civilizational Patterns and Civilizing Processes', *International Sociology*, 16(3): 387–405.

Avritzer, L. (2002) *Democracy and the Public Space in Latin America*, Princeton: Princeton University Press.

Avritzer, L., Olvera, A. and Peruzzoti, H. (1997) 'Special section about civil society in Latin America', *Constellations*, vol. 4 (1): 88–93.

Boltanski, L. and Chiapello, E. (1999) *Le Nouvel sprit du capitalisme*, Paris: Gallimard.

Canclini, N. G. (1990) *Culturas híbridas: Estratégias para entrar y salir de la modernidad*, Mexico: Grijalbo.

Cândido, A. (1967) 'O significado de Raízes do Brasil', in S. B. de Holanda, *Raízes do Brasil*, Rio de Janeiro: José Olympio, 1983.

Cardoso, F. H. (1971) *Política e desenvolvimento em sociedades dependentes: Ideologia do empresariado industrial argentino e brasileiro*, Rio de Janeiro: Zahar.

Cardoso, F. H. (1975) '"Teoria da dependência" ou análise concreta de situações de dependência?', *O modelo político brasileiro*, São Paulo: Difel, 1977.

Cardoso, F. H. and Faletto, E. (1969) *Dependência e desenvolvimento na América Latina*, Rio de Janeiro: Zahar, 1970.

Carvalho Franco, M. S. (1983) *Homens livres na ordem escravocrata*, São Paulo: Kairós.

Costa, S. (1997) *Dimensionen der Demokratisierung*, Frankfurt am Main: Vervuert.

Domingues, J. M. (1992) 'A América. Intelectuais, interpretações e identidades', in *Do ocidente à modernidade: Intelectuais e mudança social*, Rio de Janeiro: Civilização Brasileira, 2003.

Domingues, J. M. (1995a) *Sociological Theory and Collective Subjectivity*, London and Basingstoke: Macmillan; New York: Saint Martin's Press.

Domingues, J. M. (1995b) 'Richard Morse and the "Iberian-American Path"', *Revista interamericana de bibliografia*, 45(3): 161–169.

Domingues, J. M. (1999) 'Desenvolvimento, modernidade e subjetividade', in *Do ocidente à modernidade. Intelectuais e mudança social*, Rio de Janeiro: Civilização Brasileira, 2003.

Domingues, J. M. (2000) *Social Creativity, Collective Subjectivity and Contemporary Modernity*, London and Basingstoke: Macmillan; New York: Saint Martin's Press.

Domingues, J. M. (2002) 'Modernity, Complexity and Mixed Articulation', *Social Science Information*, 41(3): 383–404.

Domingues, J. M. (2003) 'Modernidade global e análise civilizacional', in *Do ocidente à modernidade: Intelectuais e mudança social*, Rio de Janeiro: Civilização Brasileira.

Domingues, J. M. (2005a) *Modernity Reconstructed*, Cardiff: Wales University Press.

Domingues, J. M. (2005b) 'Sociología brasileña, Latinoamérica y la tercera fase de la modernidad', *Estudios sociológicos*, 66: 591–610.

Domingues, J. M. and M. Maneiro (2004) 'Revisitando Germani: la interpretación de la modernidad y la teoría de la acción', *Desarrollo económico*, 44(175): 397–414.

Dussel, E. (1998) 'Beyond Eurocentrism: the World-System and the Limits of Modernity', in F. Jameson and M. Miyoshi (eds), *The Cultures of Globalization*, Durham: Duke University Press.

Eisenstadt, S. (1982) 'The Axial Age: the Emergence of Transcendental Visions and the Rise of the Clerics', *European Journal of Sociology*, 23(2): 294–314.

Eisenstadt, S. (1987) 'Introduction: Historical Traditions, Modernization and Development', in S. Eisenstadt (ed.), *Patterns of Modernity*, vol. 2, *Beyond the West*, London: Francis Pinter.

Eisenstadt, S. (1990) 'Modes of Structural Differentiation, Elite Structure and Cultural Vision', in J. C. Alexander and P. Colomy (eds), *Differentiation Theory and Social Change*, New York: Columbia University Press.

Eisenstadt, S. (2000) 'Multiple Modernities', *Daedalus (Multiple Modernities)*, 129(1): 1–29.

Eisenstadt, S. (2001) 'The Civilizational Dynamic of Modernity: Modernity as a Distinct Civilization', *International Sociology*, 16(3): 320–340.

Faletto, E. (1996) 'La Cepal y la sociología del desarrollo', *Revista de la Cepal*, 58: 191–204.

Faoro, R. (1958) *Os donos do poder*, Porto Alegre: Globo.

Feres, J. Jnr (2003) 'The History of Counterconcepts: "Latin America" as an Example', *History of Concepts Bulletin*, 6: 14–19.

Fernandes, F. (1975) *A revolução burguesa no Brasil*, Rio de Janeiro: Zahar.

Fernandes, F. (1977) *A sociologia no Brasil*, Petrópolis: Vozes.

Freyre, G. (1987 [1933]) *Casa Grande & Senzala*, Rio de Janeiro: José Olympio.

Germani, G. (1964) *La sociologia en América Latina*, Buenos Aires: Eudeba.

Germani, G. (1965) *Política y sociedad en una época de transición*, Buenos Aires: Paidós.

Germani, G. (1969) *Sociología de la modernización*, Buenos Aires: Paidós.

Hardt, M. and A. Negri (2000) *Empire*, Cambridge, MA: Harvard University Press.

Holanda, S. B. de (1983 [1936]) *Raízes do Brasil*, Rio de Janeiro: José Olympio.

Knöbl, W. (2001) *Spielräume der Modernisierung: Das Ende der Eindeutigkeit*, Weilerwist: Velbrück.

Lipset, M. S. and A. Solari (1967) *Elites in Latin America*, New York: Oxford University Press.

Luporini, C. and E. Sereni (eds) (1973) *El concepto de 'formación económico-social'*: Cuadernos de pasado y presente, *No. 39, Córdoba: Siglo XXI*.

Mariátegui, J. C. (1968 [1928]) *7 Ensayos de interpretación de la realidad peruana*, Lima: Amauta.

Martín-Barbero, J. (2001) *Al sur de la modernidad*, Pittsburgh: Universidad de Pittsburgh – Instituto Internacional de Literatura Iberoamericana.

Mbembe, A. (2002) 'As formas africanas de auto-inscrição', *Estudos Afro-Asiáticos*, 23(1): 171–209.

Morse, R. (1982) *El espejo de Próspero*, Mexico: Siglo XXI.

Morse, R. (1990) *A volta de Machulanaíma: Cinco estudos solenes e uma brincadeira séria*, São Paulo: Companhia das Letras.

Nelson, B. (1969) 'Conscience and the Making of Early Modern Cultures: *The Protestant Ethic* beyond Max Weber', *Social Research*, 39: 4–21.

Nelson, B. (1977) *Der Ursprung der Moderne: Vergleichende Studien zum Zivilizationsprozess*, Frankfurt am Main: Suhrkamp.

Nun, J. (2001) *Marginalidad y exclusión social*, Buenos Aires: Fondo de Cultura Económica.

Pecaut, D. (1989) *Entre le Peuple et la nacion: Les Intellectuels et la politique au Brasil*, Paris: Maison des Sciences de l'Homme.

Prado Jr., C. (1972 [1967]) *A revolução brasileira*, São Paulo: Brasiliense.

Prado Jr, C. (1980 [1934]) *Evolução política do Brasil*, São Paulo: Brasiliense.

Portes, A. (2001) 'Sociology in the Hemisphere: Past Convergencies and a New Conceptual Agenda', in *Working Paper*, No. 6, Program in Latin American Studies, Princeton University.

Quijáno, A. (1993) 'Colonialid del poder, eurocentrismo y América Latina', in E. Lander (ed.) *La colonialid del saber – eurocentrismo y ciencias sociales: Perspectivas latinoamericanas*, Buenos Aires: CLACSO.

Quijano, A. (2004) '"Marginalidad" e "Informalidad" en debate', *Memoria*, 131, www.memoria.com. mx.131.

Rama, A. (1985 [1984]) *A cidade das letras*, São Paulo: Brasiliense.

Ramos, G. (1965) *A redução sociológica*, Rio de Janeiro: Tempo Brasileiro.

Reigadas, C. (2000) 'Modernización e identidad en el pensamiento argentino contemporáneo: Revisando el argumento de la inferioridad', *Revista de filosofía latinoamericana y ciencias sociales*, segunda época, año XXV, No. 22: 47–63.

Retamar, R. F. (1982 [1971]) *Calibán*, in J. H. Rodó and R. F. Retamar, *Ariel/Calibán*, Mexico: SEP/UNAM.

Robertson, R. (1992) *Globalization: Social Theory and Global Culture*, London: Sage.

Robertson, R., S. Lash and M. Featherstone (eds) (1995) *Global Modernities*, London: Sage.

Rodó, J. H. (1982 [1900]) *Ariel*, in J. H. Rodó and R. F. Retamar, *Ariel/Calibán*, Mexico: SEP/UNAM.

Rubinich, L., Moscona, G., Argumendo, A., González, H., De Ipola, E., Rinesi, E., Dri, R., Pía López, M. and Marín, J.C. (2004) *Sociología y política*. Buenos Aires: El Mate.

Sarmiento, D. F. (1962 [1845]) *Civilización y barbarie: Vida de Juan Facundo Quiroga. Aspecto físico, costumbres y hábitos de la República Argentina*, Buenos Aires: Sun.

Schwartzman, S. (1982) *Bases do autoritarismo brasileiro*, Rio de Janeiro: Campus.

Sempat Assadourian, C. (1973) *Modos de producción en América Latina: Cuadernos de pasado y presente*, No. 40, Mexico: Siglo XXI.

Souza, J. (2000) *A modernização seletiva: Uma reinterpretação do dilema brasileiro*, Brasília: Editora UnB.

Valdés, E. D. (2003) *El pensamiento latinoamericano en el siglo XX*, tomo II, Buenos Aires: Biblos.

Wagner, P. (1994) *A Sociology of Modernity*, London: Routledge.

Wallerstein, I. (1984) *The Politics of World-Economy*, Cambridge: Cambridge University Press.

Weber, M. (1930 [1905]) *The Protestant Ethic and the Spirit of Capitalism*, London and Boston: Unwin Hyman.

Werneck Vianna, L. (1999) 'Weber e a interpretação do Brasil', in J. Souza (ed.) *O malandro e o protestante: a tese weberiana e a singularidade cultural brasileira*, Brasília: Editora UnB.

Zabludovsky, G. and L. Girola (1995) 'La teoría sociológica en México en la década de los ochenta', in G. Zabludovsky, *Sociología y política, el debate clásico y contemporáneo*, Mexico: Miguel Angel Porrua.

Zéa, L. (1965) *El pensamiento latinoamericano*, Barcelona: Ariel, 1976.

Epilogue

Asia in European sociology

Bryan S. Turner

In a *Handbook of Contemporary European Social Theory*, it is perhaps appropriate to have an epilogue that considers European social theory in terms of its 'other', namely to consider the importance of the Orient, or more specifically Asia, in the development of European social and sociological theory. I shall in fact be primarily concerned with sociological theory, since it is not my intention to consider the full range of philosophical, literary and artistic reflections on the Orient. Many of these issues have of course been explored in the literature on Orientalism and it would be pointless to reproduce here the well known story about the Orientalist presuppositions of western theory (Said 1978; Turner 1978; Spence 1998; Kurasawa 2004). My task here is partly to document the centrality of 'Asia', specifically India and China, to the analysis of modernity – an umbrella term for democracy, development, industrialisation, progress and revolution – in the evolution of European sociology. Second, I briefly examine how Japan for very obvious reasons became central to much American rather than European sociology after the Second World War. Third, with the death of Mao Zedong in 1976 Chinese intellectuals began a debate about the nature of citizenship in post-Mao China, drawing often enough on the legacy of T. H. Marshall (Goldman and Perry 2002). With the end of the Cultural Revolution and the collapse of European communism (1989–1992), there is the intriguing prospect that the two most dynamic economies of the twenty-first century will be India and China. This transformation of the world economy will mean that Asian intellectuals will, once more, play a major role in shaping the agenda of social theory. This new situation will most likely produce a powerful nationalist statement of social theory in India and China, but the question that we must consider somewhat urgently is: can cosmopolitanism also play a part in the future development of social and sociological theory, or will both be overwhelmed by the nationalist agenda?

The Enlightenment was obviously crucial to the evolution of European social theory. The emphasis on science, universalism and reason established a set of criteria for evaluating enlightened societies that continues to influence critical theory. In the twentieth-century, the Enlightenment became, especially after the critical analyses of Theodor Adorno and Max Horkheimer, a target of sustained intellectual attack, precisely because its version of universal reason was claimed to be blind to cultural differences. Of course, the legacy of the Enlightenment has also had formidable champions, including Jürgen Habermas, for whom the project of (enlightenment) modernity is incomplete. This debate about the negative consequences of the Enlightenment has often focused on Immanuel Kant, but this interpretation seriously neglects the contribution of Gottfried Leibniz to the contemporary debate about cosmopolitanism.

The Enlightenment project of modernity can be dated from the publication of Kant's essay on 'What is Enlightenment?' in November 1784 in the *Berlinische Monatschrift*. Kant defined the Enlightenment as the principle of moral autonomy for the individual; it requires the release of people from their own 'self-incurred tutelage'. Tutelage is the inability to make use of human understanding without direction from another person. This notion of self-incurred tutelage ('selbstverschuldeten ünmuendigkeit') can be translated as 'self-imposed minority', that is a self-imposed childhood. Because Christianity is based on the idea of a loving father, the Enlightenment was a distinctively secular perspective, specifically hostile to the authority of the Catholic Church. Kant's essay thereby expressed the core of western moral philosophy in terms of the conscious, rational, self-directed subject.

Leibniz can be regarded as the German precursor of the French Enlightenment (Perkins 2004). He is probably known primarily as a mathematician, who, independently of Newton, developed the calculus, and for his complex theory of entities (monads), but there is an equally important side to Leibniz's philosophy, which appears remarkably relevant to contemporary social theory. He lived in a period when European trade with the outside world, including Asia, was expanding rapidly. It was a time of intense commerce of commodities, and, alongside this emerging capitalist world economy, Leibniz advocated a 'commerce of light', that is an exchange of mutual enlightenment. Against Spinoza's view that there is only one substance, Leibniz argued that the world is characterised by its infinite diversity, complexity and richness. The world is teeming with entities that exist in their fullest capacity and in a state of harmony. According to Leibniz in the *Discourse on Metaphysics*, God has created the best of all possible worlds (a theodicy) which is 'the simplest in hypotheses and the richest in phenomena'.

What is the significance of this theory of monads for relations with China? Recognition of the diversity of cultures and civilisations leads us to recognise the inherent value of difference. Leibniz, like Spinoza, advocated a tolerance of diverse views, but went beyond the philosophers of his day to establish an ethical imperative to learn from cultural completeness and diversity. He applied this ethic to himself, committing much of his life to studying China from the reports of missionaries and merchants. Differences between monads require exchange, but it also establishes a commonality of culture. Leibniz was not, in modern terms, a cultural relativist. For Leibniz, if all cultures are equal in value, why bother to learn from anyone of them? While all knowledge of the outside world is relativistic, Leibniz argued that, because we are embodied, there are enough innate ideas to make an exchange of enlightenment possible and desirable. Leibniz wrote to Peter the Great, who was at the time engaged in a struggle to protect Muscovy from being overwhelmed by Crimean Tartars, to say that he was not one of those 'impassioned patriots of one country alone' but a person who works for 'the well-being of the whole of mankind, for I consider heaven as my country and cultivated men as my compatriots'. From the doctrine of blind monads, Leibniz developed a hermeneutics of care and generosity that regarded inter-cultural understanding as, not merely a useful anthropological field method, but as an overriding ethical imperative. Leibniz developed a cosmopolitan virtue in his attempt to establish an exchange with China that offers us a guideline for understanding our own times, especially a cosmopolitan exchange with Islam. Leibniz is a sort of rational and moral antidote to the clash of civilizations (Huntington 1993, 2003).

Enlightenment and Encyclopaedia

China and India were important themes of the Enlightenment primarily because they represented despotic government and the absence of rational systems of thought. This idea that, whereas Europe had been shaken by revolutionary struggles, the Orient was stagnant and stationary was established by Hegel, and runs as a continuous theme through Karl Marx and Friedrich Engels, and through Alexis de Tocqueville and J. S. Mill, and found its culmination in Max Weber's comparative sociology of the economic ethics of the world religions.

We might argue therefore that 'Asia' was a creation of the Enlightenment rather than an indigenous concept. The idea of Asia allowed the creation of a notion of world history in which the multi-ethnic Asian empires were contrasted with the Westphalian pattern of sovereign European states. The urban industrial civilisations of Europe were thought to be advanced by comparison with the agrarian empires of the East. Asia was incapable of knowing itself, and would be dependent on European social theory to achieve any critical reflexivity.

The Enlightenment project involved the quest for comprehensive and independent knowledge of the world and was anticipated by the publication of the *Encyclopaedia* (1747–1773) of Denis Diderot. The aim of the *Encyclopaedia* was to produce a comprehensive assembly of the existing scientific knowledge of the world and in this sense the *Encyclopaedia* was a celebration of the scope of secular knowledge against revealed theology. Independence from the Church was an important political underpinning of the Enlightenment project and the ambition of the Enlightenment was to create a new world order grounded in sceptical scientific reasoning. Kant imagined a 'perfect state' in which freedom would be unhindered; hence, global modernity required a cosmopolitan government and perpetual peace. Citizen rights in the late nineteenth- and early twentieth-century were enshrined in the nation-state and national constitutions. These exclusionary rights of the nation-state and the national citizen are not wholly compatible with Kantian cosmopolitanism. The paradox of social change after Kant has been that national differences and cultural particularity appear to have been amplified during the imperialist and colonial expansion of the European states in the nineteenth-century rather than constrained by a normative international order. Indeed, cultural relativism rather than cultural universalism became dominant theme of the emerging social sciences and humanities.

In retrospect we can therefore see the historical origins of sociology in the 1830s as an aspect of the Enlightenment ambition to create a secular science of society that might guide the actions of states. Both Claude Saint Simon and August Comte shared the common view that sociology could lay the foundations of an alternative socialist society that would obey the positivistic laws of development of social science. While positivist sociology was hostile to the political dominance of the Roman Catholic Church, sociology was to be instrumental in establishing a 'religion of humanity' that would replace the religion of the *ancien regime*. This ambiguous view of religion became part of the legacy of classical sociology. In many respects, the legacy of the positivism as method was expressed in Emile Durkheim's epistemological theories and in his sociology of religion, where he also anticipated the possibility of a new universal religion to replace the 'old gods'.

The sociology of despotism: China and India

While Enlightenment philosophy was overtly hostile to religious institutions, the Enlightenment itself had an important impact on religious thought. The Jewish Enlightenment or

Haskalah stressed the importance of the rational individual, natural law, natural rights and religious tolerance. The Jewish Enlightenment sought to make Jews equal citizens with their Christian and secular counterparts in Europe. Moses Mendelssohn for example played an important part in presenting Judaism as a rational religion and these European developments partly paved the way towards Zionism. The problem of religion as a form of rational knowledge also preoccupied the young Marx who in 'the Jewish Question' argued that the 'solution' to the Jewish problem was their movement into the urban proletariat and adoption of secular socialism, but the final emancipation of the Jewish worker could not be achieved by political emancipation alone without a total transformation of capitalism. The point of Marx's argument was that the final demise of religion as a form of consciousness could only be achieved through a transformation of the actual structure of society. It is well known that Marx followed Mill in arguing that India and China had no history, because, in the absence of private property, they had no class structure and hence class struggle could not function as a mechanism of social change. Paradoxically the introduction of property by the British was the catalyst that would drive India into a process of historical change.

The principal contours of the modern debate about western views of the Orient were set by Edward Said's *Orientalism* (1978) and, although Orientalism can be traced back through the encounter between Christian theology and its antagonists, Said's interpretation established the idea of modern Orientalism as a distinctive and pervasive ideology of the Orient as Otherness. While the Occident moves through history in terms of a series of modernising revolutions, the unhistorical Orient is frozen in time and space. Religion played an important role in differentiating between East and West. While different cultures give religion a different content, Christianity was essentially a world religion. For G. W. F. Hegel, religion and philosophy were both modes of access to understanding the Absolute (or God), and the philosophy of religion (*Religionsphilosophie*) differed from theology in that it was the study of religion as such. In Hegel's dialectical scheme, the increasing historical self-awareness of the Spirit was a consequence of the development of Christianity. The philosophical study of religion was an important stage in the historical development of human understanding.

In *Culture and Imperialism*, Said (1993) claimed that the modern identity of the West has been defined by its colonies. These colonies are not merely physical places in a political geography; they also marshal the boundaries and borders of our consciousness by defining our attitudes towards, for example, sexuality and race. Within the paradigm of Weber's Protestant Ethic, the native is defined as somebody who is, not only poor and traditional, but licentious and lazy. In the evolution of English Orientalism, the plays of Shakespeare present an insight into the characterology of Oriental figures. In *The Tempest*, Caliban, who is probably modelled on early encounters with the indigenous peoples of North America, is treacherous and dangerous, contrasting a negative mirror image of Miranda, who is perfect, naive and beautiful. Caliban's lust for 'Admir'd Miranda' forms part of the moral struggle of the play under the watchful eye of the patriarchal fatherly Prospero, whose rational interventions master both storms and characters. It is in some respects the origin of the modern analysis of colonialism, because the magical island offered Shakespeare an ideal context for playing out the struggle between (Christian) reason and its irrational colonial subjects.

In this commentary on Orientalism, I have so far concentrated on the legacy of German sociology, but equally important was the work of Alexis de Tocqueville and J. S. Mill in shaping the sociological study of Asia. Both men shared a view history in which the rise of individualism and democracy was closely associated with the idea of a dynamic Christian civilization, and by contrast the dangers of uniformity in belief that would lead to 'Chinese stationariness'. In *Democracy in America*, which was published as separate volumes in 1835 and

1840, Tocqueville (1945) had seen that the great danger of democracy was that, with the growth of equality, there would emerge a tyranny of opinion over the individual. Voluntary associations were a partial solution to this danger. Mill adopted this view of democracy, arguing that the enfranchisement of the English working class was premature, given their modest state of education and literacy. Mill believed that the lack of progress in Asia was also a product of the absence of this form of individualism. While Tocqueville's views on American democracy are well known, his study *De la colonie en Algerie* (1988) and his occasional remarks on India and China have been neglected.

Tocqueville expressed an enthusiastic support for the civilising mission of the European powers, and again examined China within the framework of a contrast between dynamic and stationary civilizations. Writing to Henry Reeve, the translator of *Democracy in America*, on 12 April 1840, he exclaimed 'In my capacity as a beneficent but disinterested spectator, I can only rejoice in the thought of an invasion of the Celestial Empire by a European army. So at last the mobility of Europe has come to grips with Chinese immobility! It is a great event' (Boesche 1985: 141). Tocqueville adopted the same attitude towards India. Writing to Lord Hatherton on 27 November 1857, he argued that the suppression of the Sepoy Mutiny (1857–1858) was a triumph for Christianity and England's task is 'not only to dominate India, but to civilize it' (Boesche 1985: 360). England can only achieve this larger purpose by abolishing the East India Company and bringing India under the rule of Parliament.

What emerges from this nineteenth-century discussion was a contrast between empire and nation-states as frameworks for social change. Multi-ethnic empires were seen to be bureaucratic and despotic; they suppressed individualism and required cultural uniformity. Turkey – the sick man of Europe – was one illustration; the other was China. By contrast, nation-states were seen to be energetic and dynamic political forms – harbingers of modernity – within which citizenship and the rule of law could protect the individual and individual conscience.

Kant, Weber and the 'Reflecting faith'

The term 'religion' has two etymological roots (Benveniste 1973). First, *relegere* from *legere* means to bring together, to harvest or to gather (in). Second, *religare* from *ligare* means to tie or to bind together. *Relegare* indicates the role of the cult in forming human membership, while *Religare* points to the regulatory practices of religion in the discipline of passions. This distinction formed the basis of Kant's philosophical analysis of religion and morality in *Religion within the Limits of Pure Reason* (Kant 1960) where he distinguished between religion as cult (*des blossen Cultus*) which seeks favours from God through prayer and offerings to bring healing and material wealth to its followers, and religion as moral action (*die Religion des guten Lebenswandels*) that commands human beings to change their behaviour in order to lead a better life. Kant further elaborated this point by an examination of 'reflecting faith' that compels humans to strive for salvation through faith rather than the possession of religious knowledge. Kant's distinction implied that (Protestant) Christianity was the only true 'reflecting faith', and in a sense therefore the model of all authentic religious intentions. The implication of the distinction is that 'Asian religions' are essentially about ritual comforts such as honouring the dead and bringing good luck; only the Abrahamic religions in general and Lutheranism in particular are reflecting faiths.

These Kantian principles were embraced by Weber, who in the *Sociology of Religion* (1966) contrasted the religion of the masses and the religion of the virtuosi. While masses seek earthly comforts from religion, especially healing, the virtuosi fulfil the ethical demands of religion in search of spiritual salvation or inner enlightenment. The religion of the masses requires saints and holy men to satisfy human needs, and hence charisma is corrupted by the demand for miracles and spectacles. More importantly, Weber distinguished between those religions that reject the world by challenging its cultural traditions and religions that seek to escape from the world through mystical flight. The ascetic religions (primarily the Calvinistic radical sects) have had revolutionary consequences for human society, while mysticism is merely passive. The implication of this intellectual tradition is paradoxical (Lehmann and Ouedraogo 2004). First, Christianity (or at least Puritanism) is the only true religion (as a reflecting faith) and second Christianity creates a process of secularisation that spells out its own self-overcoming. The ritualistic nature of 'Asian religions' and the absence of a reflecting faith (asceticism) were brilliantly if prejudicially illustrated in Weber's *The Religion of India* (1958) and *The Religion of China* (1951).

Japan and American sociology

Asian ideas about Asia first emerged with nationalism in the twentieth-century. The nation-state is originally a European concept, as we have already indicated. In the Meiji Restoration, Japan transformed every institution and its national culture from its Chinese legacy to western institutions and culture. While the Tenno regime in the Taika Reform achieved the sinici-sation of the Japanese state, westernisation rather than sinicisation became the national goal in Meiji Japan, not only at the level of the state but also in the economy, society, and culture. This process was famously summarised by Yukichi Fukuzawa (1835–1901) in his nationalist slogan that Japan was 'departing from Asia and joining Europe'. Fukuzawa's slogan was intended to cut ties with China and Confucianism and to establish Japan as a European-style nation-state. While the typical model of westernisation was European, including the United Kingdom, before the Second World War, the model was replaced by the United States after the Second World War. Perhaps the real intention of Japanese nationalism as promoted by Fukuzawa was in fact to enter Asia and to challenge Europe. Similar ideas were afloat in China where the revolutionaries advocated pan-Asianism and sought to break with the legacy of stagnant empires. However, Chinese intellectuals began to reject this Japanese version of modernisation when Japan's colonial intentions became evident in the strategy of the great east-Asian co-prosperity sphere.

In Meiji Japan, the sociology of Herbert Spencer had become known among both senior government officials and intellectuals associated with the movement of the Liberal Democratic Right. Indeed Arinori Mori and Kentaro Kaneko, both of whom participated in developing the draft of the Meiji Constitution, and Taisuke Itagaki, who was the most influential leader of the Liberal Democratic Right movement, visited Spencer and sought his sociological advice on the characteristics of 'industrial society'. Spencer's conception of 'military society' was seen to be relevant to the Tokagawa period, and hence Spencer's peculiar combination of individu-alism and evolutionary thought appeared to resonate with Japanese social theory in this period.

Spencer was therefore the first sociologist whose works came to be translated into Japanese in Meiji and Taisho Japan from 1877 to the early twentieth-century. Japanese academics and civil servants were especially interested in his combination of theory of evolution, utilitarian individualism and laissez-faire economics. Spencer's *Social Statics* (1850), which was translated into Japanese as the *Theory of Equal Right*, was a bestseller as the intellectual framework of the Liberal Democratic Right. *The Man versus the State* was published twice in Japanese translation. His central proposition was the state must not interfere with the individual's freedoms.

Similarly in *Essays on Education and Kindred Subjects* (1963) Spencer had argued that in a society in which industrialism is already well established, free trade is indispensable for maintaining industrial capitalism. This social theory had a strong appeal for Meiji intellectuals, and his sociological perspective on individualism and free trade can be regarded as a pioneer of globalization theory in post-World-War Japan. It is perhaps ironic that Talcott Parsons, who asked provocatively in *The Structure of Social Action* (1937) who reads Spencer any more, should become fascinated by and influential in modern Japan. Parsons had argued in his early articles on Germany that the hierarchical and military values of Nazi Germany, which were promoted within the masculine virtues of student culture, had been responsible for a collective ideology of racism and ant-Semitism. Parsons saw imperial Japan as having a similar pattern of hierarchy and obedience to leadership (Parsons 1971).

It was however Parsons's graduate student Robert Bellah in *Tokugawa Religion* (1957) who demonstrated the relevance of Weber's Protestant Ethic thesis for Japanese modernisation. This was one one of the most influential sociological studies of Japan in contemporary scholarship. It was also a book that, as it were, vindicated Parsons's emphasis on cultural factors in socio-economic change. The book has obviously had its critics (Amstutz 1997), but it has also proved an enduring sociological insight. After completing his doctoral thesis, the oddity of Bellah's academic development was that he spent most of his academic career in American studies and hence his recent *Imagining Japan* (2003), a collection of essays, is interesting in illustrating his dialogue with Japanese intellectual history. The most important chapter is probably the one devoted to Masao Maruyama's *Studies in the Intellectual History of Tokugawa Japan* (1974), whose work first appeared as essays between 1940 and 1944. Maruyama, who was influenced by the Marxism of Franz Borkenau, was keenly aware of the contradictions between Japan's technological development and the cult of the Emperor. Writing in the 1940s, he rejected the slogan that Japan's problems could only be solved by 'overcoming the modern'. Japan's problems arose not because it was too modern, but because it was not modern enough. Maruyama was a powerful early critic of Bellah's *Tokugawa Religion*, which was, according to Maruyama, too generous towards the internal capacity of traditional Japanese culture to generate an authentic independence of spirit. Maruyama complained that Bellah was insufficiently aware of the negative dimensions of Japanese tradition, particularly of the negative aspects of Tokugawa society.

Although American professional sociology has dominated much post-war Japanese social theory, the legacy of Weber remains important. While Japanese sociologists originally explained Japanese success in terms of Weberian arguments derived from the Protestant Ethic thesis, contemporary Japanese scholars have also examined various aspects of 'Asian values' as clues to Japan's economic success. One particularly important work was by Michio Morishima (1982) who in *Why Has Japan 'Succeeded'?* tried to establish a particular Japanese ethos of work as a cultural explanation. More recent scholarship has emphasised the importance of Japanese civil religion which has significant elements of nationalism and imperialism (Schwentker 2005).

Conclusion: nationalism or cosmopolitanism?

The rise of globalisation has meant that European sociologists, such as Ulrich Beck, have paid considerable attention to the possibility and importance of cosmopolitanism. I have argued that this cosmopolitan attitude could be traced back to the early Enlightenment philosophy of Leibniz, who placed so much hope on intellectual openness to China. Optimism about the opportunities for cosmopolitanism is, however, difficult to sustain. China, Japan and Korea are currently in the grip of powerful nationalist ideologies that are likely to have an important impact on the development of social science in those countries. China's attempts to block Japan's quest to become a permanent member of the UN Security Council are associated with criticism of Japanese history textbooks that fail to deal adequately with Japanese atrocities in the World War. The Korean government has taken a similar view of Japanese avoidance of war guilt. These cultural conflicts have been further inflamed by territorial disputes over control of islands in the China Sea. The effervescence of social science in China will most probably be part of a nationalist resurgence associated with the growing economic power of China.

These developments are ironic. In this epilogue I have argued that one criticism of Asia by classical sociology was based on a distinction between empire and nation. Imperial structures were old, decaying and unresponsive; nations were the harbingers of modernisation. In the modern world, this contrast between Asian empires and western nations has been somewhat reversed. While the Asian tigers are becoming nations, western scientists are increasingly preoccupied with the question: is the United States an empire? Studies of empire are typically about the erosion and possible collapse of imperial strategies.

Three publications have been influential in this debate about the possible collapse of the American imperial system. Ferguson (2004) in *Colossus* notes that American imperialism has a long history, but there is a persistent sense that imperialism and democracy do not go together; America is an empire in denial. The United States is confronted by three deficits – economic, manpower and attention. It has become a debt-ridden system, partly propped up by Japanese investment and purchasing powers. The manpower deficit is illustrated by lack of available troops to undertake wars and the attention deficit is illustrated by the denial of empire. Ferguson while critical of American foreign policy, nevertheless believes that an imperial policeman is necessary in order to regulate local conflicts and regional wars. An empire with some claims to democratic transparency is better than an authoritarian policeman.

Michael Hardt and Antonio Negri developed a vitalist view of imperial global power where countervailing forces will eventually threaten empire with decay. In their *Empire* (2000) they argue that the decline of national state sovereignty does not mean the decline of sovereignty but rather its decentralisation and deterritorialisation. The new empire is based on a policeman role, a consensus to intervene, and an appeal to justice, but the success of the new empire will be limited by the fact that it necessarily creates it own opposition which they call 'The Multitude'. Anti-globalisation movements are precursors of a more generalised opposition to imperial power. With this new global empire, there is a new bio-economy requiring surveillance and discipline.

Michael Mann's *Incoherent Empire* (2003) is perhaps the more interesting contribution to the sociology of empire rather than a social theory of imperial institutions. Mann argues that America has become an imperial power, possibly the only viable global power. Mann's problem is not exactly the same as Edward Gibbon's inquiry into the demise of the British Empire through the lens of the rise and fall of the Roman Empire. The American empire is not threatened by the rise of another political force or by the standard problem of over-stretched and over-extended resources. The new empire is challenged by uneven, ineffective and inappropriate power resources resulting in imperial incoherence and failure of foreign policy.

Mann's analysis is couched within a Weberian theory of power. There are three sources of power: military, economic, ideological. In military terms, no power has the capacity to challenge effectively or forcefully American superiority. After Vietnam, there was an acceptance of the Powell doctrine that said America should intervene overseas with overwhelming military force and with minimal American casualties. The Iraq invasion was based on this doctrine, but Mann goes on to note that rogue states, terrorist attacks and guerrilla wars pose military problems for which American technical superiority has few appropriate answers.

Paradoxically America does not have an enemy that is sufficiently technologically sophisticated with which it could appropriately engage. America has smart bombs but not enough well trained foot soldiers. In economic terms, the neo-liberal revolution to free global trade has worked in favour of US interests. While America has championed free trade as the mechanism for economic and political change, no society has ever achieved economic success on the basis of today's liberal strategies. From the perspective of economic history, liberal strategies only work after a country has already gone through protectionism by successfully taxing imports and subsidising exports – Germany and Japan being the primary examples. In Asia, China is also a society that has not followed liberal doctrine – for example in terms of liberalisation of currencies and interest rates. While America has reaped rewards from these global neo-liberal policies in the past, it cannot directly or easily regulate the competing economies of the European Union, Japan, Korea or China. The current trade imbalance is one example. In any case, the poverty and economic inequality produced by neo-liberalism create social conditions in which political oppression, resistance and terrorism flourish. Violent 'new wars' appear to be the most significant negative consequences of these unregulated global changes in the economy (Münkler 2005). In terms of political power, America has failed in foreign policy terms, because it cannot easily or effectively secure the loyalty of its client states. Israel is one example and the failure to bring the political leaders of 'old Europe' into line is another. Finally, it is difficult for America to win an ideological war, because modern forms of global communication, such as the global Net, are deregulated and devolved. While the American liberal press may well have been unable to sustain any critique of the war, various newspapers in the Middle East such as *al-Jazeera* and *al-Quds* ensured the negative effects of American policy have been well publicised.

American economic power remains precarious, given the recent history of the dollar, America's external debt, and the general weakness of the global economy. Critics of the war on terrorism assumed that America would be able to finance the war by taking over Iraq's oil reserves and by allocating reconstruction contracts to American corporations, but the American dollar has been falling on world money markets as investors become increasingly nervous about American indebtedness. In response, oil production is being cut in order to sustain profit levels by exporting countries. Rising oil prices will deflate or delay the global economic recovery, making the management of American indebtedness more problematic. It is inconceivable that further interest rate cuts are possible given the historical low level of rates in America and, although President Bush's strategy of cutting taxes is popular with middle-class voters, it is not realistically a long-term economic solution. The long-term strategy must be to reduce dependency on Middle East oil supplies and expand oil production in Africa and Alaska, but these strategies are also problematic.

The classical debate about empires and their rise and fall remains ironically an important feature of European sociology. While western sociology has been, particularly since 9/11, preoccupied by the question of America's imperial status, contemporary interest in cosmopolitanism as a precondition for an adequate sociology of globalisation will transform European social thought. How nationalism will impinge on the development of Asian social theory remains an open question.

References

Amstutz, G. (1997) *Interpreting Amida: History and Orientalism in the Study of Pure Land Buddhism*, Albany: State University of New York Press.

Benveniste, E. (1973) *Indo-European Language and Society*, London: Faber and Faber.

Bellah, R. N. (1957) *Tokugawa Religion*, Glencoe, IL: Free Press.

Bellah, R. N. (2003) *Imagining Japan: The Japanese Tradition and its Modern Interpretation*, Berkeley: University of California Press.

Boesche, R. (ed.) (1985) *Alexis de Tocqueville: Selected Letters on Politics and Society*, Berkeley: University of California Press.

Ferguson, N. (2004) *Colossus: The Rise and Fall of the American Empire*, London: Allen Lane.

Goldman, M. and Perry, E. J. (eds) (2002) *Changing Meanings of Citizenship in Modern China*, Cambridge, MA: Harvard University Press.

Hardt, M. and Negri, A. (2000) *Empire*, Cambridge: Harvard University Press.

Huntington, S. P. (1993) 'The Clash of Civilizations', *Foreign Affairs* 72(3): 22–48.

Huntington, S.P. (2003) 'America in the World', *The Hedgehog Review* 5(1): 7–18.

Kant, I. (1960) *Religion within the Limits of Pure Reason*, New York: Harper & Row.

Kurasawa, F. (2004) *The Ethnological Imagination: A Cross-cultural Critique of Modernity*, Minneapolis: University of Minnesota Press.

Lehmann, H. and Ouedraogo, J. M. (eds) (2004) *Max Weber's Religionssoziologie in interkultureller Perspektive*, Gottingen: Vandenhoeck & Ruprecht.

Mann, M. (2003) *Incoherent Empire*, London: Verso.

Maruyama, M. (1974) *Studies in the Intellectual History of Tokugawa Japan*, Tokyo: University of Tokyo Press.

Morishima, M. (1982) *Why Has Japan 'Succeeded'?: Western Technology and the Japanese Ethos*, Cambridge: Cambridge University Press.

Münkler, H. (2005) *The New Wars*, Cambridge: Polity Press.

Parsons, T. (1937) *The Structure of Social Action*, New York: McGraw Hill

Parsons, T. (1971) *The System of Modern Societies*, Englewood Cliffs, NJ: Prentice-Hall.

Perkins, F. (2004) *Leibniz and China: A Commerce of Light*, Cambridge: Cambridge University Press.

Said, E. W. (1978) *Orientalism*, New York: Pantheon.

Said, E.W (1993) *Culture and Imperialism*, New York: Knopf.

Schwentker, W. (2005) 'Max Weber's Protestant Ethic and Japanese Social Studies', *Journal of Classical Sociology*, 5(1): 73–92.

Spence, J. (1998) *The Chan's Great Continent: China in Western Minds*, London: Penguin.

Spencer, H. (1850) *Social Statics*, London: Appleton.

Spencer, H.(1876) *Principles of Sociology*, London: Appleton.

Spencer, H. (1963) *Essays on Education and Kindred Subjects*, London: Everyman's Library, 1911

Spencer, H. (1981 [1884]) *The Man Versus the State*, Indianapolis: Liberty Classics.

Tocqueville, A. de. (1945) *Democracy in America*, 2 vols, New York: Vintage Books.

Tocqueville, A. de (1988) *De la colonie en Algerie*, Paris: Complexe.

Turner, B. S. (1978) *Marx and the End of Orientalism*, London: George Allen & Unwin.

Weber, M. (1951) *The Religion of China*, New York: Macmillan.

Weber, M. (1958) *The Religion of India*, Glencoe: Free Press.

Weber, M. (1966) *The Sociology of Religion*, London: Methuen.

Index

academic Marxism 159
action research 127, 128, 130
actor–network theory (ANT) xxiv, 15, 73, 74–5
Aczél, György 139
Adam, Barbara 354
Adorno, Theodor W.: American social theory 366, 368, 369; critical theory xxii, 172–6, 178–82; on Enlightenment 395; German social theory 55, 56, 60; post-Marxism 197; theology 37, 41, 45; on warfare 282
aesthetics 156, 157, 160
Agamben, Giorgio xxi, 104
Age of Revolution (1789–1871) xxi, 4–6
agency: cultural identities 298, 301, 304; Derrida 373; hermeneutic approach xix, xxii, 203–8, 211–14; Italian social theory 100; mediology 76; nature 353; philosophical anthropology 212–15; social sciences xxiv, 17, 18
AIDS 187, 353
Albrow, Martin 284, 286
Alekseyev, Nikolai 157
Alexander, Jeffrey 291, 365
al-Farabi, Abu Nasr 325
al-Jabiri, Mohammed 379
al-Jazeera 403
Allardt, Erik 125
al-Quds 403
Althusser, Louis 5, 60, 70, 92, 160, 192
Altvater, Elmar 194
Ambedkar, B. R. 378
American pragmatism 18, 52, 53, 61, 70, 133
American revolution 27, 29, 281
American social theory: after theory 367–9; Japan 400–1; mathematized sociology 364–5; new sociologies 365–7; the 1960s 363–4;

Parsons 361–3; vulnerable positivism 369–70; *see also* United States
Anderson, Benedict 246, 303, 315, 316
Anderson, Perry 196
anomie 12, 131, 180, 362
anthropology: French social theory 71; German social theory 55, 56; Nordic social theory 129; pragmatism 22; and social theory xix, 285; Spanish social theory 117; theology 39
antinomies 234, 239
Apel, K.-O. 54, 57
Appadurai, Arjun 318
Arboleya, Enrique Gómez 113, 114
Archer, Margaret 17, 90
Arendt, Hannah: cosmopolitanism 246, 247, 251; on freedom 263; Holocaust 295, 296; new German sociology 53; political philosophy 32; theory 37
Argentina 381, 385
Aristotle 52, 185, 261, 324, 325
Ariyaratne, A. T. 378
Arnason, Johann 269, 271, 273, 387
Arnold, Matthew 93
Aron, Raymond 11, 43, 70, 88
artistic critique 73, 74
Asia: China and India 397–9; Enlightenment and Encyclopaedia 397; Japan and American sociology 400–1; nationalism or cosmopolitanism 401–3; overview 395–6; the reflecting faith 399–400
Asian social theory: Asian critical thought 373–9; overview xxv, xxiv, 372–3, 379
Asmus, Valentin 159
Assmann, Jan 38, 237, 238, 260
Aubert, Vilhelm 124, 125, 128, 135
Augustine 325